THE MACMILLAN
OF ENGLISI

D1646496

Edward Leeson has been a professional editor for twenty-five years. He edited the widely acclaimed *New Golden Treasury of English Verse* (published Paperm...

Also by Edward Leeson

The New Golden Treasury of English Verse

THE MACMILLAN ANTHOLOGY
OF

ENGLISH PROSE

Edited by
EDWARD LEESON

PAPERMAC

First published 1994 by Papermac

a division of Pan Macmillan Publishers Limited
Cavaye Place London SW10 9PG
and Basingstoke

Associated companies throughout the world

ISBN 0333 61650 2

1 3 5 7 9 8 6 4 2

A CIP catalogue record for this book is available from
the British Library

Typeset by CentraCet Ltd
Printed and bound in Great Britain by
Mackays of Chatham, Plc, Kent

CONTENTS

ACKNOWLEDGEMENTS

THE editor and publishers are grateful to the following authors, publishers and owners of copyright for giving permission to reproduce some of the poems which appear in this anthology. From *Lucky Jim*, Kingsley Amis, Victor Gollancz; from *Murphy*, Samuel Beckett, Calder Publications Ltd, London. Copyright © The Samuel Beckett Estate 1993. Reprinted by permission of The Samuel Beckett Estate and The Calder Educational Trust, London. From *Zuleika Dobson*, Max Beerbohm, reprinted by permission of Mrs Eva Reichmann; from *Undertones of War*, Edmund Blunden, Penguin Books, reprinted by permission of the Peters Fraser & Dunlop Group Ltd; from *Room at the Top*, John Braine, Methuen; from *Hôtel du Lac*, Anita Brookner, Jonathan Cape Ltd; *Inside Mr Enderby*, Anthony Burgess, William Heinemann Ltd, © Anthony Burgess; *My Early Life*, Sir Winston Churchill, reproduced with permission of Curtis Brown Group Ltd, London, on behalf of the Estate of Sir Winston S. Churchill. Copyright the Estate of Sir Winston S. Churchill. From *Selected Essays*, T. S. Eliot, Faber and Faber Ltd; from *A Passage to India* and *A Room with a View* by E. M. Forster, reprinted by permission of the Provost and Scholars of King's College, Cambridge; from *Cold Comfort Farm*, Stella Gibbons, reprinted by permission of Curtis Brown London on behalf of the Estate of Stella Gibbons; from *Lord of the Flies*, William Golding, Faber and Faber Ltd; from *I, Claudius*, Robert Graves, reprinted by permission of A. P. Watt on behalf of the Trustees of the Robert Graves Copyright Trust; from *Brighton Rock*, Graham Greene, Heinemann, 1938, © Verdant SA 1938; from *Brave New World*, Aldous Huxley, Chatto & Windus, reprinted by permission of Mrs Laura Huxley; from *Goodbye to Berlin*, Christopher Isherwood, Hogarth Press, reprinted by permission of the Estate of Christopher Isherwood; *In Parenthesis*, David Jones, Faber and Faber

Ltd; from *Cider with Rosie*, Laurie Lee, The Hogarth Press; from *Collected Short Stories*, W. Somerset Maugham, William Heinemann Ltd, © Royal Literary Fund; from *The Sea The Sea*, Iris Murdoch, Chatto & Windus; from *Animal Farm* and *Nineteen Eighty-Four*, George Orwell, reprinted by permission of the late Sonia Brownell Orwell and Martin Secker & Warburg Ltd; from *At Lady Molly's*, Anthony Powell, William Heinemann Ltd, © Anthony Powell; from *English Journey*, J. B. Priestley, William Heinemann Ltd, © J. B. Priestley; from *Memoirs of an Infantry Officer*, Siegfried Sassoon, Faber and Faber Ltd; from *Man and Superman*, George Bernard Shaw, reprinted by permission of the Society of Authors on behalf of the Bernard Shaw Estate; from *Saturday Night and Sunday Morning*, Alan Sillitoe, © Alan Sillitoe 1958, 1986; from *The Prime of Miss Jean Brodie*, Muriel Spark, Penguin; from *This Sporting Life*, David Storey, Longmans; from *Brideshead Revisited*, Evelyn Waugh, reprinted by permission of the Peters Fraser & Dunlop Group Ltd; from *The War of the Worlds*, H. G. Wells, reprinted by permission of A. P. Watt Ltd on behalf of The Literary Executors of the Estate of H. G. Wells; from *Pigs Have Wings*, P. G. Wodehouse, Hutchinson, reprinted by permission of The Estate of P. G. Wodehouse.

INTRODUCTION

THE FOUR centuries following the remarkable flowering of creativity during the reign of Elizabeth I have seen the emergence in these islands of a literary tradition of unrivalled richness and variety. The English poetic tradition is already represented in the companion volume, *The New Golden Treasury of English Verse*, and the present anthology endeavours to trace the development of English prose from its hesitant beginnings to the present day.

Other nations have produced fine writers, but surely no other nation has produced so many of them; and, in the face of such abundance, no man can honestly claim to have read everything worth reading. Consequently, no anthology can hope to be in any sense definitive. This selection sets out simply to chart the course of the literary journey from the middle of the sixteenth century to the final quarter of the twentieth, and hopefully to offer at least a taste of the range and versatility of which English prose has proved capable.

The challenge of capturing the essence of four hundred years of English writing in a single manageable volume presents the editor with some difficult decisions if he aspires to offer more than merely a joyless collection of brief specimens of prose style; and since this selection is intended to be read primarily for pleasure, with individual authors represented at length and their work given room to breathe, hard – and sometimes ruthless – choices have had to be made. In many instances only one example of a writer's work is included, and some writers have regrettably had to be omitted altogether.

Lifting passages out of a larger context carries risks of its own, but the extracts included here have been carefully chosen and should require no background explanation. In the early passages the spelling has been modernized and erratic punctuation has been clarified; while occasional problems with obscure vocabulary have been solved by means of discreet glosses in square brackets. The aim throughout has been to make the texts immediately accessible. The arrangement is broadly chronological, with no attempt to classify the extracts. Thus, novelists sit alongside theologians and the philosophical rubs shoulders with the whimsical. The overall effect is hopefully to highlight the wealth and variousness of our literary heritage.

The selection from contemporary authors is necessarily conservative. Faced with the task of choosing work from young writers in mid-career, the editor finds that he has moved from a retrospective survey of four centuries of English prose to the rather different enterprise of 'picking winners' for the future, and the whole character of the anthology changes. The present selection restricts itself to identifying the living tradition of English prose within which contemporary writers work and in which they may eventually take their place.

I wish to thank Ingrid Connell, my editor at Pan Macmillan, for her remarkable patience throughout the long time it has taken for this book to struggle into existence; and I also wish to record my debt to the London Library, whose assistance has once more proved invaluable.

Edward Leeson

SIR THOMAS ELYOT

[The Dance]

IN EVERY dance of a most ancient custom there danceth together a man and a woman, holding each other by the hand or the arm; which betokeneth concord. Now, it behoveth the dancers and also the beholders of them to know all qualities incident to a man and also all qualities to a woman likewise appertaining.

A man in his natural perfection is fierce, hardy, strong in opinion, covetous of glory, desirous of knowledge, appetiting by generation to bring forth his semblable. The good nature of a woman is to be mild, timorous, tractable, benign, of sure remembrance and shamefast. Divers other qualities of each of them might be found out, but these be most apparent and for this time sufficient.

Wherefore when we behold a man and a woman dancing together let us suppose there to be a concord of all the said qualities, being joined together as I have set them in order. And the moving of the man would be more vehement, of the woman more delicate and with less advancing of the body, signifying the courage and strength that ought to be in a man and the pleasant soberness that should be in a woman. And, in this wise, fierceness joined with mildness maketh severity; audacity with timorosity maketh magnanimity; wilful opinion and tractability (which is to be shortly persuaded and moved) maketh constancy a virtue; covetise of glory adorned with benignity causeth honour; desire of knowledge with sure remembrance procureth sapience; shamefastness joined to appetite of generation maketh continence, which is a mean between chastity and inordinate lust. These qualities, in this wise being knit together, and signified in the personages of man and woman dancing, do express or set out the figure of very nobility; which in the higher estate it is contained, the more excellent is the virtue in estimation.

The Book Named the Governor, 1531

ROGER ASCHAM

[The Wind]

To SEE the wind with a man his eyes it is unpossible, the nature of it is so fine and subtle; yet this experience of the wind had I once myself, and that was in the great snow that fell four years ago. I rode in the highway betwixt Topcliffe-upon-Swale and Boroughbridge, the way being somewhat trodden afore by wayfaring men. The fields on both sides were plain and lay almost yard deep with snow. The night afore had been a little frost, so that the snow was hard and crusted above. That morning the sun shone bright and clear. The wind was whistling aloft, and sharp according to the time of the year. The snow in the highway lay loose and trodden with horse feet, so as the wind blew it took the loose snow with it and made it so slide upon the snow in the field, which was hard and crusted by reason of the frost overnight, that thereby I might see very well the whole nature of the wind as it blew that day. And I had a great delight and pleasure to mark it, which maketh me now far better to remember it. Sometime the wind would be not past two yards broad, and so it would carry the snow as far as I could see. Another time the snow would blow over half the field at once. Sometime the snow would tumble softly. By and by it would fly wonderful fast. And this I perceived also: that the wind goeth by streams and not whole together. For I should see one stream within a score on [*twenty paces of*] me, then the space of two score no snow would stir, but after so much quantity of ground another stream of snow at the same very time should be carried likewise but not equally. For the one would stand still when the other flew apace, and so continue sometime swiftlier, sometime slowlier, sometime broader, sometime narrower, as far as I could see. Nor it flew not straight, but sometime it crooked this way, sometime that way, and sometime it ran round about in a compass. And sometime the snow would be lift clean from the ground up into the air, and by and by it would be all clapped to the ground as though there had been no wind at all. Straightway it would rise and fly again. And that which was the most marvel of all: at one time two drifts of snow flew, the one out of the west into the east, the other out of the north into the east; and I saw two winds by reason of the snow, the one cross over the other, as it had been two highways. And again I should hear the wind blow in the air when nothing stirred at the ground. And when all was still where I rode, not very far from me the snow should be lifted wonderfully. This experience made me more marvel at the nature of the wind than it made me cunning in the knowledge of the wind; but yet thereby I learned perfectly that it is no marvel at all though men in a wind lose their length in shooting, seeing so many ways the wind is so variable in blowing.

Toxophilus, 1545

JOHN KNOX

[A Woman's Place]

To PROMOTE a woman to bear rule, superiority, dominion or empire above any realm, nation or city is repugnant to nature, contumely to God, a thing most contrarious to His revealed will and approved ordinance; and finally it is the subversion of good order, of all equity and justice.

In the probation of this proposition, I will not be so curious as to gather whatsoever may amplify, set forth or decore [*illustrate*] the same; but I am purposed, even as I have spoken my conscience in most plain and few words, so to stand content with a simple proof of every member, bringing in for my witness God's ordinance in nature, His plain will revealed in His word, and the minds of such as be most ancient amongst godly writers.

And, first, where that I affirm the empire of a woman to be a thing repugnant to nature, I mean not only that God by the order of His creation hath spoiled woman of authority and dominion, but also that man hath seen, proved and pronounced just causes why that it should be. Man, I say, in many other cases blind, doth in this behalf see very clearly. For the causes be so manifest that they cannot be hid. For who can deny but it repugneth to nature that the blind shall be appointed to lead and conduct such as do see; that the weak, the sick and impotent persons shall nourish and keep the whole and strong; and finally that the foolish, mad and frenetic shall govern the discreet and give counsel to such as be sober of mind? And such be all women, compared unto man in bearing of authority. For their sight in civil regiment is but blindness, their strength weakness, their counsel foolishness, and judgement frenzy, if it be rightly considered.

The First Blast of the Trumpet against
the Monstrous Regiment of Women, 1558

SIR THOMAS HOBY

[Breeding]

I WILL have this our courtier therefore to be a gentleman born and of a good house. For it is a great deal less dispraise for him that is not born a gentleman to fail in the acts of virtue than for a gentleman. If he swerve from the steps of his ancestors, he staineth the name of his family.

And doth not only not get, but loseth that is already gotten. For nobleness of birth is, as it were, a clear lamp that showeth forth and bringeth into light works both good and bad, and inflameth and provoketh unto virtue as well with the fear of slander as also with the hope of praise.

And, whereas this brightness of nobleness doth not discover the works of the unnoble, they have a want of provocation and of fear of slander, and they reckon not themselves bound to wade any further than their ancestors did before them, whereas the noble of birth count it a shame not to arrive at the least at the bounds of their predecessors set forth unto them.

Therefore it chanceth always in a manner, both in arms and in all other virtuous acts, that the most famous men are gentlemen. Because nature in every thing hath deeply sowed that privy seed which giveth a certain force and property of her beginning unto whatsoever springeth of it, and maketh it like unto herself.

As we see by example, not only in the race of horses and other beasts, but also in trees, whose slips [cuttings] and grafts always for the most part are like unto the stock of the tree they came from; and if at any time they grow out of kind [degenerate] the fault is in the husbandman. And the like is in men: if they be trained up in good nurture, most commonly they resemble them from whom they come, and oftentimes pass them; but if they have not one that can well train them up they grow, as it were, wild and never come to their ripeness.

Truth it is, whether it be through the favour of the stars or of nature, some there are born endued with such graces that they seem not to have been born but, rather, fashioned with the very hand of some God, and abound in all goodness both of body and mind. As, again, we see some so unapt and dull that a man will not believe but nature hath brought them into the world for a spite and mockery.

And, like as these with continual diligence and good bringing-up for the most part can bring small fruit, even so the other with little attendance climb to the full perfection of all excellency.

The Book of the Courtier,
Done into English by T. Hoby, 1561

WILLIAM ADLINGTON

[Cupid and Psyche]

WHEN PSYCHE was left alone (saving that she seemed not to be alone, being stirred by so many furies) she was in a tossing mind like the waves of the sea, and although her will was obstinate, and resisted to put into execution the counsel of her sisters, yet she was in doubtful and divers opinions touching her calamity. Sometime she would, sometime she would not; sometime she is bold, sometime she feareth; sometime she mistrusteth, sometime she is moved; sometime she hateth the beast, sometime she loveth her husband – but at length night came, whenas she prepared for her wicked intent.

Soon after her husband came, and when he had kissed and embraced her he fell asleep. Then Psyche (somewhat feeble in body and mind, yet moved by cruelty of fate) received boldness and brought forth the lamp and took the razor, so by her audacity she changed her mind; but when she took the lamp and came to the bedside she saw the most meek and sweetest beast of all beasts, even fair Cupid couched fairly, at whose sight the very lamp increased his light for joy and the razor turned his edge.

But when Psyche saw so glorious a body she greatly feared and, amazed in mind, with a pale countenance all trembling fell on her knees and thought to hide the razor – yea, verily in her own heart, which doubtless she had done, had it not through fear of so great an enterprise fallen out of her hand. And when she saw and beheld the beauty of the divine visage she was well re-created in her mind. She saw his hairs of gold that yielded out a sweet savour; his neck more white than milk; his purple cheeks; his hair hanging comely behind and before, the brightness whereof did darken the light of the lamp; his tender plume feathers, dispersed upon his shoulders like shining flowers, and trembling hither and thither; and his other parts of his body so smooth and so soft that it did not repent Venus to bear such a child. At the bed's feet lay his bow, quiver and arrows that be the weapons of so great a god: which, when Psyche did curiously behold, she marvelling at her husband's weapons took one of the arrows out of the quiver, and pricked herself withal, wherewith she was so grievously wounded that the blood followed, and thereby of her own accord she added love upon love; then, more broiling in the love of Cupid, she embraced him and kissed him and kissed him a thousand times, fearing the measure of his sleep. But, alas, while she was in this great joy, whether it were for envy, for desire to touch this amiable body likewise, there fell out a drop of burning oil from the lamp upon the right shoulder of the god. O rash and bold lamp, the vile ministry of love, how darest thou be so bold as to burn the god of all fire? Whenas he invented thee to the intent that all lovers might with more joy pass the nights in pleasure.

The god being burned in this sort, and perceiving that promise and faith was broken, he fled away, without utterance of any word, from the eyes and hands of his most unhappy wife. But Psyche fortuned to catch him, as he was rising, by the right thigh, and held him fast as he flew above in the air, until such time as constrained by weariness she let go and fell down upon the ground. But Cupid followed her down, and lighted upon the top of a cypress tree, and angerly spake unto her in this manner:

'O simple Psyche, consider with thyself how I, little regarding the commandment of my mother (who willed me that thou shouldst be married to a man of base and miserable condition), did come myself from heaven to love thee, and wounded mine own body with my proper weapons to have thee to my spouse. And did I seem a beast unto thee, that thou shouldst go about to cut off my head with a razor, who loved thee so well? Did not I always give thee a charge? Did not I gently will thee to beware? But those cursed aiders and counsellors of thine shall be worthily rewarded for their pains. As for thee, thou shalt be sufficiently punished by my absence.'

When he had spoken these words he took his flight into the air. Then Psyche fell flat on the ground, and as long as she could see her husband she cast her eyes after him into the air, weeping and lamenting piteously; but when he was gone out of her sight she threw herself into the next running river for the great anguish and dolour that she was in for the lack of her husband; howbeit the water would not suffer her to be drowned, but took pity upon her, in the honour of Cupid which accustomed to broil and burn the river, and threw her upon the bank amongst the herbs.

The XI Books of the Golden Ass, Containing
the Metamorphosis of Lucius Apuleius, 1566

WILLIAM PAINTER

[The Death of Thibault]

Now, as we have before declared, the Capellets and the Montesches were not so well reconciled by the Lord of Verona but that there rested in them such sparks of ancient displeasures as either parties waited for but some light occasion to draw together – which they did in the Easter holy days (as bloody men commonly be most willingly disposed after a good time to commit some nefarious deed) besides the Gate of Bousarie leading to the old castle of Verona. A troop of Capellets rencountered with certain of the Montesches, and without other words began to set upon them. And the Capellets had for chief of their glorious enterprise one called Thibault, cousin-german [*first cousin*] to Julietta, a young man strongly made and of good experience of arms, who exhorted his companions with stout stomachs to repress the boldness of the Montesches, that there might from that time forth no memory of them be left at all.

The rumour of this fray was dispersed throughout all the corners of Verona, that succour might come from all parts of the city to depart [*separate*] the same. Whereof Romeo advertised [*informed*], who walked along the city with certain of his companions, hasted him speedily to the place where the slaughter of his parents and allies were committed; and after he had well advised and beheld many wounded and hurt on both sides he said to his companions: 'My friends, let us part them, for they be so fleshed one upon another as will all be hewed to pieces before the game be done.' And, saying so, he thrust himself amidst the troop, and did no more but part the blows on either side, crying upon them aloud: 'My friends, no more. It is time henceforth that our quarrels cease. For, besides the provocation of God's just wrath, our two families be slanderous to the whole world and are the cause that this commonwealth doth grow unto disorder.'

But they were so eager and furious one against the other, as they gave no heed to Romeo's counsel and bent themselves to kill, dismember, and tear each other in pieces. And the fight was so cruel and outrageous between them as they which looked on were amazed to see them endure those blows, for the ground was all covered with arms, legs, thighs and blood, wherein no sign of cowardice appeared, and maintained their fight so long, that none was able to judge who had the better, until that Thibault, cousin to Julietta, inflamed with ire and rage, turned towards Romeo, thinking with a prick [*thrust*] to run him through. But he was so well armed and defended with a privy coat which he wore ordinarily for the doubt he had of the Capellets as the prick rebounded. Unto whom Romeo made answer: 'Thibault, thou mayest know by the patience which I have had until this present time that I came not hither to fight with thee or thine, but to seek peace and atonement between us, and if thou thinkest that for lack of courage I have failed mine endeavour thou doest great wrong to my reputation. And impute this my sufferance to some other particular respect rather than to want of stomach. Wherefore abuse me not, but be content with this great effusion of blood and murders already committed. And provoke me not, I beseech thee, to pass the bounds of my good will and mine.'

'Ah, traitor,' said Thibault, 'thou thinkest to save thyself by the plot of thy pleasant tongue; but see that thou defend thyself, else presently I will make thee feel that thy tongue shall not guard thy corpse nor yet be the buckler to defend the same from present death.' And, saying so, he gave him a blow with such fury as, had not other warded the same, he had cut off his head from his shoulders. And the one was no readier to lend, but the other incontinently was able to pay again; for he, being not only wrath with the blow that he had received, but offended with the injury which the other had done, began to pursue his enemy with such courage and vivacity as at the third blow with his sword he caused him to fall backward stark dead upon the ground with a prick vehemently thrust into his throat, which he followed till his sword appeared through the hinder part of the same – by reason whereof the conflict ceased. For, besides that Thibault was the chief of his company, he was also born of one of the noblest houses within the city, which caused the potestate [chief magistrate] to assemble his soldiers with diligence for the apprehension and imprisonment of Romeo, who, seeing ill fortune at hand, in secret wise conveyed himself to Friar Lawrence at the Friars Franciscans. And the friar understanding of his fact [deed] kept him in a certain secret place of his convent until fortune did otherwise provide for his safe going abroad.

The bruit [rumour] spread throughout the city of this chance done upon the Lord Thibault. The Capellets in mourning weeds caused the dead body to be carried before the seigniory of Verona, so well to move them to pity as to demand justice for the murder; before whom came also the Montesches declaring the innocency of Romeo and the wilful assault of the other.

The council assembled and witnesses heard on both parts, a strait commandment was given by the lord of the city to give over their weapons; and, touching the offence of Romeo, because he had killed the other in his own defence he was banished Verona for ever.

The Palace of Pleasure, 1566

RAPHAEL HOLINSHED

[Macbeth and the Weird Sisters]

S HORTLY AFTER happened a strange and uncouth wonder, which afterward was the cause of much trouble in the realm of Scotland, as ye shall after hear. It fortuned as Macbeth and Banquo journeyed towards Forres, where the King then lay, they went sporting by the way together without other company save only themselves, passing through the woods and fields; when suddenly in the midst of a land there met them three women in strange and wild apparel, resembling creatures of elder world, whom when they attentively beheld, wondering much at the sight, the first of them spake and said: 'All hail, Macbeth, Thane of Glamis' – for he had lately entered into that dignity and office by the death of his father, Sinel.

The second of them said: 'Hail, Macbeth, Thane of Cawdor.'

But the third said: 'All hail, Macbeth, that hereafter shalt be king of Scotland.'

Then Banquo: 'What manner of women', saith he, 'are you, that seem so little favourable unto me, whereas to my fellow here, besides high offices, ye assign also the kingdom, appointing forth nothing for me at all?'

'Yes,' saith the first of them, 'we promise greater benefits unto thee than unto him, for he shall reign indeed, but with an unlucky end; neither shall he leave any issue behind him to succeed in his place, where contrarily thou indeed shalt not reign at all, but of thee those shall be born which shall govern the Scottish kingdom by long order of continual descent.'

Herewith the foresaid women vanished immediately out of their sight.

This was reputed at the first but some vain fantastical illusion by Macbeth and Banquo, insomuch that Banquo would call Macbeth in jest 'King of Scotland' and Macbeth again would call him in sport likewise 'the father of many kings'. But afterwards the common opinion was that these women were either the weird sisters – that is, as ye would say, the goddesses of destiny – or else some nymphs or fairies endued with knowledge of prophecy by their necromantical science, because everything came to pass as they had spoken. For shortly after, the Thane of Cawdor being condemned at Forres of treason against the King committed, his lands, livings and offices were given of the King's liberality to Macbeth.

The same night after, at supper, Banquo jested with him and said: 'Now, Macbeth, thou hast obtained those things which the two former sisters prophesied, there remaineth only for thee to purchase that which the third said should come to pass.'

Whereupon Macbeth, revolving the thing in his mind, began even then to devise how he might attain to the kingdom; but yet he thought with himself that he must tarry a time, which should advance him thereto by the divine providence as it had come to pass in his former preferment.

But shortly after it chanced that King Duncan, having two sons by his wife which was the daughter of Siward, Earl of Northumberland, he made the elder of them, called Malcolm, Prince of Cumberland, as it were thereby to appoint him his successor in the kingdom immediately after his decease. Macbeth, sore troubled herewith, for that he saw by this means his hope sore hindered – where, by the old laws of the realm, the ordinance was that if he that should succeed were not of able age to take charge upon himself he that was next of blood unto him should be admitted – he began to take counsel how he might usurp the kingdom by force. . . .

The Chronicles of England, Scotland
and Ireland, 1577

WILLIAM HARRISON

[Foppery]

How curious, how nice also, are a number of men and women, and how hardly can the tailor please them in making it fit for their bodies! How many times must it be sent back again to him that made it! What chafing, what fretting, what reproachful language doth the poor workman bear away! And many times when he doth nothing to it at all, yet when it is brought home again it is very fit and handsome. Then must we put it on, then must the long seams of our hose be set by a plumbline; then we puff, then we blow, and finally sweat till we drop, that our clothes may stand well upon us. I will say nothing of our heads, which sometimes are polled, sometimes curled, or suffered to grow at length like woman's locks, many times cut off above or under the ears, round as by a wooden dish. Neither will I meddle with our variety of beards, of which some are shaven from the chin like those of Turks, not a few cut short like to the beard of Marquess Otto, some made round like a rubbing brush, others with a *pique devant* (O fine fashion!) or now and then suffered to grow long, the barbers being grown to be so cunning in this behalf as the tailors. And therefore, if a man have a lean and straight face, a Marquess Otto's cut will make it broad and large; if it be platter-like, a long slender beard will make it seem the narrower; if he be weasel-beaked, then much hair left on the cheeks will make the owner look big like a bowdled [*puffed-up*] hen and so grim as a goose. Some lusty courtiers also and gentlemen of courage do wear either rings of gold, stones or pearl in their ears, whereby they imagine the workmanship of God not to be a little amended. But herein they rather disgrace than adorn their persons, as by their niceness in apparel; for which, I say, most nations do not unjustly deride us, as also for that we do seem to imitate all nations round about us, wherein we be like to the polypus or chameleon, and thereunto bestow most cost upon our arses,

and much more than upon all the rest of our bodies, as
women do likewise upon their heads and shoulders.

The Description of England, 1577

JOHN LYLY

[Euphues]

THIS YOUNG gallant, of more wit than wealth, and yet of
more wealth than wisdom, seeing himself inferior to
none in pleasant conceits, thought himself superior to all in
honest conditions, insomuch that he deemed himself so apt
to all things that he gave himself almost to nothing but
practising of those things commonly which are incident to
these sharp wits – fine phrases, smooth quipping, merry
taunting, using jesting without mean, and abusing mirth
without measure. As therefore the sweetest rose hath his
prickle, the finest velvet his brack [*flaw*], the fairest flour his
bran, so the sharpest wit hath his wanton will and the holiest
head his wicked way. And true it is that some men write,
and most men believe, that in all perfect shapes a blemish
bringeth rather a liking every way to the eyes than a loathing
any way to the mind. Venus had her mole in her cheek
which made her more amiable; Helen her scar on her chin
which Paris called *Cos amaris*, the whetstone of love;
Aristippus his wart; Lycurgus his wen. So likewise, in the
disposition of the mind, either virtue is overshadowed with
some vice or vice overcast with some virtue. Alexander
valiant in war yet given to wine. Tully eloquent in his gloses
[*smooth speeches*] yet vainglorious. Solomon wise yet too
too wanton. David holy but yet an homicide. None more
witty than Euphues, yet at the first none more wicked. The
freshest colours soon fade, the teenest [*sharpest*] razor
soonest turneth his edge, the finest cloth is soonest eaten
with moths, and the cambric sooner stained than the coarse
canvas; which appeareth well in this Euphues, whose wit

being like wax apt to receive any impression, and having the bridle in his own hands either to use the rein or the spur, disdaining counsel, leaving his country, loathing his old acquaintance, thought either by wit to obtain some conquest or by shame to abide some conflict, and leaving the rule of reason rashly ran unto destruction.

Euphues: The Anatomy of Wit, 1578

SIR THOMAS NORTH

[Antony and Cleopatra]

THE MANNER how he fell in love with her was this. Antonius, going to make war with the Parthians, sent to command Cleopatra to appear personally before him when he came into Cilicia, to answer unto such accusations as were laid against her, being this: that she had aided Cassius and Brutus in their war against him. The messenger sent unto Cleopatra to make this summons unto her was called Dellius; who when he had thoroughly considered her beauty, the excellent grace and sweetness of her tongue, he nothing mistrusted that Antonius would do any hurt to so noble a lady, but rather assured himself that within few days she should be in great favour with him. Thereupon he did her great honour, and persuaded her to come into Cilicia as honourably furnished as she could possible; and bade her not to be afraid at all of Antonius, for he was a more courteous lord than any that she had ever seen. Cleopatra on the other side, believing Dellius' words, and guessing by the former access and credit she had with Julius Caesar and Gnaeus Pompey (the son of Pompey the Great) only for her beauty, she began to have good hope that she might more easily win Antonius. For Caesar and Pompey knew her when she was but a young thing, and knew not then what the world meant; but now she went to Antonius at the age when a woman's beauty is at the prime, and she also of best judgement. So she furnished herself with a world of gifts, store of gold and silver, and of riches and other sumptuous ornaments, as is credible enough she might bring from so great a house and from so wealthy and rich a realm as Egypt was. But yet she carried nothing with her wherein she trusted more than in herself, and in the charms and enchantment of her passing beauty and grace.

Therefore, when she was sent unto by divers letters both from Antonius himself and also from his friends, she made so light of it, and mocked Antonius so much, that she disdained to set forward otherwise but to take her barge in the river of Cydnus; the poop whereof was of gold, sails of purple, and the oars of silver, which kept stroke in rowing after the sound of the music of flutes, hautboys, citherns, viols and such other instruments as they played upon in the barge.

And now for the person of herself, she was laid under a pavilion of cloth of gold of tissue, apparelled and attired like the goddess Venus commonly drawn in picture; and hard by her, on either hand of her, pretty fair boys apparelled as painters do set forth god Cupid, with little fans in their hands, with the which they fanned wind upon her. Her ladies and gentlewomen also, the fairest of them, were apparelled like the nymphs Nereides (which are the mermaids of the waters) and like the Graces; some steering the helm, others tending to the tackle and ropes of the barge, out of the which there came a wonderful passing sweet savour of perfumes that perfumed the wharf's side, pestered with innumerable multitudes of people. Some of them followed the barge all along the riverside; others also ran out of the city to see her coming in. So that in the end there ran such multitudes of people one after another to see her that Antonius was left post [*entirely*] alone in the marketplace in his imperial seat to give audience; and there went a rumour in the people's mouths that the goddess Venus was come to play with the god Bacchus for the general good of all Asia.

When Cleopatra landed, Antonius sent to invite her to supper to him; but she sent him word again he should do better rather to come and sup with her. Antonius, therefore, to show himself courteous unto her at her arrival, was contented to obey her, and went to supper to her; where he found such passing sumptuous fare that no tongue can express it. But amongst all other things he most wondered at the infinite number of lights and torches hanged on the top of the house, giving light in every place, so artificially set and ordered by devices, some round, some square, that it was the rarest thing to behold that eye could discern or that ever books could mention.

The next night Antonius, feasting her, contended to pass her in magnificence and fineness; but she overcame him in both.

The Lives of the Noble Grecians and Romans,
Compared Together by . . . Plutarch of Chaeronea, 1579

REGINALD SCOT

[A Remarkable Cure]

B UT THE notablest example hereof is of one that was in great perplexity, imagining that his nose was as big as a house; insomuch that no friend nor physician could deliver him from his conceit, nor yet either ease his grief or satisfy his fancy in that behalf. Till at the last a physician more expert in this humour than the rest used this device following.

First, when he was come in at the chamber door, being wide open, he suddenly stayed and withdrew himself; so as he would not in any wise approach nearer than the door. The melancholic person, musing hereat, asked him the cause why he so demeaned himself. Who answered him in this manner.

'Sir, your nose is so great that I can hardly enter into your chamber but I shall touch it and consequently hurt it.'

'Lo,' quoth he, 'this is the man that must do me good. The residue of my friends flatter me and would hide mine infirmity from me.'

'Well,' said the physician, 'I will cure you, but you must be content to endure a little pain in the dressing'; which he promised patiently to sustain, and conceived certain hope of his recovery.

Then entered the physician into the chamber, creeping close by the walls, seeming to fear the touching and hurting of his nose. Then did he blindfold him; which being done, he caught him by the nose with a pair of pincers and threw down into a tub which he had placed before his patient a great quantity of blood, with many pieces of bullocks' livers, which he had conveyed into the chamber whilst the other's eyes were bound up, and then gave him liberty to see and behold the same. He having done thus again two or three times, the melancholic humour was so qualified that, the man's mind being satisfied, his grief was eased and his disease cured.

The Discovery of Witchcraft, 1584

RICHARD HAKLUYT

[Sir Richard Chancellor at the Court of Ivan the Terrible, 1553]

THE EMPIRE and government of the king is very large, and his wealth at this time exceeding great. And because the city of Moscow is the chiefest of all the rest it seemeth of itself to challenge the first place in this discourse. Our men say that in bigness it is as great as the city of London, with the suburbs thereof. There are many and great buildings in it, but for beauty and fairness nothing comparable to ours. There are many towns and villages also, but built out of order and with no handsomeness. Their streets and ways are not paved with stone as ours are; the walls of their houses are of wood; the roofs for the most part are covered with shingle boards. There is hard by the city a very fair castle, strong and furnished with artillery, whereunto the city is joined directly towards the north with a brick wall. The walls also of the castle are built with brick, and are in breadth and thickness eighteen foot. This castle hath on the one side a dry ditch, on the other side the River Moskva, whereby it is made almost inexpugnable. The same Moskva trending towards the east doth admit into it the company of the River Oka.

In the castle aforesaid there are in number nine churches or chapels, not altogether unhandsome, which are used and kept by certain religious men, over whom there is after a sort of patriarch or governor, and with him other reverend fathers, all which for the greater part dwell within the castle. As for the king's court and palace, it is not of the neatest, only in form it is four-square and of low building, much surpassed and excelled by the beauty and elegancy of the houses of the kings of England. The windows are very narrowly built, and some of them by glass and some others by lattices admit the light; and whereas the palaces of our princes are decked and adorned with hangings of cloth of gold there is none such there. They build and join to all their walls benches; and that not only in the court of the emperor, but in all private men's houses.

Now, after that they had remained about twelve days in the city, there was then a messenger sent unto them to bring them to the king's house; and they being after a sort wearied with their long stay were very ready and willing so to do. And being entered within the gates of the court there sat a very honourable company of courtiers, to the number of one hundred, all apparelled in cloth of gold down to their ankles; and therehence being conducted into the chamber of presence our men began to wonder at the majesty of the emperor. His seat was aloft in a very royal throne, having on his head a diadem or crown of gold, apparelled with a robe all of goldsmiths' work, and in his hand he held a sceptre garnished and beset with precious stones; and besides all other notes and appearances of honour there was a majesty in his countenance proportionable with the excellency of his estate. On the one side of him stood his chief secretary, on the other side the great commander of silence, both of them arrayed also in cloth of gold; and then there sat the council of one hundred and fifty in number, all in like sort arrayed and of great state.

This so honourable an assembly, so great a majesty of the emperor and of the place might very well have amazed our men, and have dashed them out of countenance; but notwithstanding Master Chancellor, being therewithal nothing dismayed, saluted and did his duty to the emperor after the manner of England, and withal delivered unto him the letters of our king, Edward VI. The emperor, having taken and read the letters, began a little to question with them and to ask them of the welfare of our king; whereunto our men answered him directly and in few words. Hereupon our men presented something to the emperor by the chief secretary; which, at the delivery of it, put off his hat, being before all the time covered.

And so the emperor, having invited them to dinner, dismissed them from his presence. And going into the chamber of him that was Master of the Requests to the emperor, and having stayed there the space of two hours, at the last the messenger cometh and calleth them to dinner. They go, and being conducted into the golden court – for so they call it, although not very fair – they find the emperor sitting upon an high and stately seat, apparelled with a robe of silver, and with another diadem on his head. Our men, being placed over against him, sit down.

In the midst of the room stood a mighty cupboard upon a square foot, whereupon stood also a round board in manner of a diamond, broad beneath and towards the top narrow, and every step rose up more narrow than another. Upon this cupboard was placed the emperor's plate, which was so much that the very cupboard itself was scant able to sustain the weight of it. The better part of all the vessels and goblets was made of very fine gold; and amongst the rest there were four pots of very large bigness, which did adorn the rest of the plate in great measure, for they were so high that they thought them at the least five foot long. There were also upon this cupboard certain silver casks, not much differing from the quantity of our firkins, wherein was reserved the emperor's drink. On each side of the hall stood four tables, each of them laid and covered with very clean tablecloths, whereunto the company ascended by three steps or degrees; all which were filled with the assembly present. The guests were all apparelled with linen without and with rich skins within, and so did notably set this royal feast.

The emperor, when he takes any bread or knife in his hand, doth first of all cross himself upon his forehead. They that are in special favour with the emperor sit upon the same bench with him, but somewhat far from him; and before the coming in of the meat the emperor himself, according to an ancient custom of the kings of Muscovy, doth first bestow a piece of bread upon every one of his guests with a loud pronunciation of his title and honour in this manner: 'The great Duke of Muscovy and chief emperor of Russia, John Vasilievich' – and then the officer nameth the guest – 'doth give thee bread.' Whereupon all the guests rise up, and by and by sit down again. This done, the gentleman usher of the hall comes in with a notable company of servants carrying the dishes, and having done his reverence to the emperor puts a young swan in a golden platter upon the table and immediately takes it thence again, delivering it to the carver and seven other of his fellows to be cut up; which being performed, the meat is then distributed to the guests with the like pomp and ceremonies. In the mean time the gentleman usher receives his bread and tasteth to the emperor; and afterward, having done his reverence, he departeth.

Touching the rest of the dishes, because they were brought in out of order, our men can report no certainty; but this is true, that all the furniture of dishes and drinking vessels which were then for the use of a hundred guests was all of pure gold, and the tables were so laden with vessels of gold that there was no room for some to stand upon them.

We may not forget that there were 140 servitors arrayed in cloth of gold that in the dinner-time changed thrice their habit and apparel, which servitors are in like sort served with bread from the emperor as the rest of the guests. Last of all, dinner being ended, and candles brought in – for by this time night was come – the emperor calleth all his guests and noblemen by their names, in such sort that it seems miraculous that a prince, otherwise occupied in great matters of state, should so well remember so many and sundry particular names. The Russians told our men that the reason thereof, as also of the bestowing of bread in that manner, was to the end that the emperor might keep the knowledge of his own household; and withal that such as are under his displeasure might by this means be known.

The Principal Navigations, Voyages, Traffics and Discoveries of the English Nation, 1589–1600

THOMAS LODGE

[A Wrestling Match]

A T LAST, when the tournament ceased, the wrestling began, and the Norman presented himself as a challenger against all comers; but he looked like Hercules when he advanced himself against Achelous, so that the fury of his countenance amazed all that durst attempt to encounter with him in any deed of activity till at last a lusty franklin of the country came with two tall men that were his sons, of good lineaments and comely personage. The eldest of these, doing his obeisance to the king, entered the list and presented himself to the Norman, who straight coped with him and, as a man that would triumph in the glory of his strength, roused himself with such fury that not only he gave him the fall but killed him with the weight of his corpulent personage; which the younger brother seeing, leaped presently into the place and, thirsty after the revenge, assailed the Norman with such valour that at the first encounter he brought him to his knees, which repulsed so the Norman that, recovering himself, fear of disgrace doubling his strength, he stepped so sternly to the young franklin that, taking him up in his arms, he threw him against the ground so violently that he broke his neck and so ended his days with his brother. At this unlooked-for massacre the people murmured and were all in a deep passion of pity; but the franklin, father unto these, never changed his countenance, but as a man of courageous resolution took up the bodies of his sons without show of outward discontent.

All this while stood Rosader and saw this tragedy; who, noting the undoubted virtue of the franklin's mind, alighted off from his horse and presently sat down on the grass and commanded his boy to pull off his boots, making him ready to try the strength of this champion. Being furnished as he would, he clapped the franklin on the shoulder and said thus:

'Bold yeoman, whose sons have ended the term of their years with honour, for that I see thou scornest fortune with patience, and thwartest the injury of fate with content in brooking the death of thy sons, stand awhile, and either see me make a third in their tragedy or else revenge their fall with an honourable triumph.'

The franklin, seeing so goodly a gentleman to give him such courteous comfort, gave him hearty thanks, with promise to pray for his happy success. With that Rosader vailed bonnet [doffed his cap] to the king, and lightly leaped within the lists, where noting more the company than the combatant he cast his eye upon the troop of ladies that glistered there like the stars of heaven. But at last Love, willing to make him as amorous as he was valiant, presented him with the sight of Rosalind, whose admirable beauty so inveigled the eye of Rosader that, forgetting himself, he stood and fed his looks on the favour of Rosalind's face; which she perceiving blushed, which was such a doubling of her beauteous excellence that the bashful red of Aurora at the sight of unacquainted Phaethon was not half so glorious.

The Norman, seeing this young gentleman fettered in the looks of the ladies, drave him out of his memento [reverie] with a shake by the shoulder. Rosader, looking back with an angry frown as if he had been wakened from some pleasant dream, discovered to all by the fury of his countenance that he was a man of some high thoughts. But when they all noted his youth and the sweetness of his visage, with a general applause of favours, they grieved that so goodly a young man should venture in so base an action; but, seeing it were to his dishonour to hinder him from his enterprise, they wished him to be graced with the palm of victory. After Rosader was thus called out of his *memento* by the Norman, he roughly clapped to him with so fierce an encounter that they both fell to the ground and with the violence of the fall were forced to breathe. In which space the Norman called to mind by all tokens that this was he whom Saladin had appointed him to kill; which conjecture made him stretch every limb and try every sinew, that working his death he might recover the gold which so bountifully was promised him. On the contrary part, Rosader while he breathed was not idle, but still cast his eye upon Rosalind, who to encourage him with a favour lent him such an amorous look as might have made the most coward desperate: which glance of Rosalind so fired the passionate desires of Rosader that, turning to the Norman, he ran upon him and braved him with a strong encounter. The Norman received him as valiantly, that there was a sore combat, hard to judge on whose side fortune would be prodigal. At last Rosader, calling to mind the beauty of his new mistress, the fame of his father's honours, and the disgrace that should fall to his house by his misfortune, roused himself and threw the Norman against the ground, falling upon his chest with so willing a weight that the Norman yielded nature her due and Rosader the victory.

The death of this champion, as it highly contented the franklin as a man satisfied with revenge, so it drew the king and all the peers into a great admiration that so young years and so beautiful a personage should contain such martial excellence; but when they knew him to be the youngest son of Sir John of Bordeaux the king rose from his seat and embraced him, and the peers entreated him with all favourable courtesy, commending both his valour and his virtues, wishing him to go forward in such haughty deeds that he might attain to the glory of his father's honourable fortunes.

As the king and lords graced him with embracing, so the ladies favoured him with their looks, especially Rosalind, whom the beauty and valour of Rosader had already touched. But she accounted love a toy, and fancy a momentary passion, that as it was taken in with a gaze might be shaken off with a wink, and therefore feared not to dally in the flame; and, to make Rosader know she affected him, took from her neck a jewel and sent it by a page to the young gentleman.

Rosalind, 1590

SIR PHILIP SIDNEY

[The Art of Horsemanship]

HE STAYED till I caused Mopsa bid him do something upon his horse; which no sooner said than with a kind rather of quick gesture than show of violence you might see him come towards me, beating the ground in so due time as no dancer can observe better measure. If you remember the ship we saw once when the sea went high upon the coast of Argos, so went the beast. But he, as if centaur-like he had been one piece with the horse, was no more moved than one with the going of his own legs; and in effect so did he command him as his own limbs: for, though he had both spurs and wand, they seemed rather marks of sovereignty than instruments of punishment, his hand and leg, with most pleasing grace, commanding without threatening, and rather remembering than chastising; at least, if sometimes he did, it was so stolen as neither our eyes could discern it nor the horse with any change did complain of it – he ever going so just with the horse, either forthright or turning, that it seemed as he borrowed the horse's body, so he lent the horse his mind. In the turning one might perceive the bridle hand somewhat gently stir; but indeed so gently as it did rather distil virtue than use violence. Himself, which methinks is strange, showing at one instant both steadiness and nimbleness; sometimes making him turn close to the ground like a cat, when scratchingly she wheels about after a mouse; sometimes with a little move rising before; now like a raven leaping from ridge to ridge, then like one of Dametas' kids bound over the hillocks; and all so done as neither the lusty kind showed any roughness nor the easier any idleness, but still like a well-obeyed master, whose beck is enough for a discipline, ever concluding each thing he did with his face to me-wards, as if thence came not only the beginning but the ending of his motions.

The Countess of Pembroke's Arcadia, 1590

[The New Drama]

OUR TRAGEDIES and comedies, not without cause cried out against, observing rules neither of honest civility nor skilful poetry, excepting *Gorboduc* – again, I say, of those that I have seen – which notwithstanding, as it is full of stately speeches and well-sounding phrases, climbing to the height of Seneca his style, and as full of notable morality, which it doth most delightfully teach, and so obtain the very end of poesy, yet in truth it is very defectious in the circumstances, which grieves me, because it might not remain as an exact model of all tragedies. For it is faulty both in place and time, the two necessary companions of all corporal actions. For where the stage should always represent but one place, and the uttermost time presupposed in it should be, both by Aristotle's precept and common reason, but one day, there is both many days and many places inartificially imagined. But if it be so in *Gorboduc*, how much more in all the rest? where you shall have Asia of the one side and Afric of the other, and so many other under-kingdoms, that the player, when he cometh in, must ever begin with telling where he is, or else the tale will not be conceived. Now you shall have three ladies walk to gather flowers, and then we must believe the stage to be a garden. By and by, we hear news of shipwreck in the same place, and then we are to blame if we accept it not for a rock. Upon the back of that, comes out a hideous monster with fire and smoke, and then the miserable beholders are bound to take it for a cave. While in the mean time two armies fly in, represented with four swords and bucklers, and then what hard heart will not receive it for a pitched field? Now, of time they are much more liberal, for ordinary it is that two young princes fall in love; after many traverses, she is got with child, delivered of a fair boy; he is lost, groweth a man, falleth in love, and is ready to get another child; and all this in two hours' space – which how absurd it is in sense even sense may imagine, and Art hath taught, and all ancient examples justified, and, at this day, the ordinary players in Italy will not err in.

The Defence of Poesy, 1595

[Poetry]

N ow, THEREIN of all sciences – I speak still of humane, and according to the human conceit – is our poet the monarch. For he doth not only show the way, but giveth so sweet a prospect into the way as will entice any man to enter into it. Nay, he doth, as if your journey should lie through a fair vineyard, at the very first give you a cluster of grapes, that, full of that taste, you may long to pass further. He beginneth not with obscure definitions, which must blur the margent with interpretations, and load the memory with doubtfulness; but he cometh to you with words set in delightful proportion, either accompanied with, or prepared for, the well enchanting skill of music; and with a tale forsooth he cometh unto you, with a tale which holdeth

children from play and old men from the chimney-corner.
And, pretending no more, doth intend the winning of the
mind from wickedness to virtue, even as the child is often
brought to take most wholesome things by hiding them in
such other as have a pleasant taste; which, if one should
begin to tell them the nature of aloes or rhubarb they should
receive, would sooner take their physic at their ears than at
their mouth. So is it in men, most of which are childish in
the best things till they be cradled in their graves. Glad they
will be to hear the tales of Hercules, Achilles, Cyrus,
Aeneas; and, hearing them, must needs hear the right
description of wisdom, valour and justice; which, if they had
been barely, that is to say philosophically, set out, they
would swear they be brought to school again.

The Defence of Poesy, 1595

ROBERT GREENE

[The Art of Horse-Stealing]

To THE effecting of this base villainy of prigging, or
horse-stealing, there must of necessity be two at the
least, and that is the prigger and the marter. The prigger is
he that steals the horse, and the marter is he that receives
him, and chops and changeth him away in any fair, mart or
other place where any good rent for horses is. And their
method is thus: the prigger, if he be a lance-man, that is,
one that is already horsed, then he hath more followers with
him, and they ride like gentlemen, and commonly in the
form of drovers; and so, coming into pasture grounds or
enclosures, as if they meant to survey for cattle, do take an
especial and perfect view where prancers or horses be that
are of worth, and whether they have horse-locks or no.
Then lie they hovering about till fit opportunity serve, and
in the night they take him or them away; and are skilful in
the black art for picking open the trammels or locks, and so

make haste till they be out of those quarters. Now, if the priggers steal a horse in Yorkshire, commonly they have vent [*sale*] for him in Surrey, Kent or Sussex, and their marters that receive them at his hand chops them away in some blind [*out-of-the-way*] fairs after they have kept them a month or two till the hue and cry be ceased and passed over. Now, if their horses be of any great value, and sore sought after, and so branded or ear-marked that they can hardly sell him without extreme danger, either they brand him with a cross-brand upon the former, or take away his ear-mark, and so keep him at hard meat [*dry fodder*] till he be whole, or else sell him in Cornwall or Wales, if he be in Cumberland, Lincolnshire, Norfolk or Suffolk. But this is if the horse be of great value and worthy the keeping. Marry, if he be only coloured and without brands, they will straight spot him by sundry policies, and in a black horse mark saddle-spots or star him in the forehead and change his tail; which secrets I omit, lest I should give too great a light to others to practise such lewd villainies.

But again to our lance-men priggers, who, as before I said, cry with the lapwing farthest from their nest and from their place of residence where their most abode is; furthest from thence they steal their horses, and then in another quarter as far off they make sale of them by the marter's means, without it be some base prigger that steals of mere necessity and, beside, is a trailer. The trailer is one that goeth on foot, but meanly attired like some plain gran [*old man*] of the country, walking in a pair of boots without spurs, or else without boots, having a long staff on his neck and a black buckram bag at his back, like some poor client that had some writing in it; and there he hath his saddle, bridle and spurs, stirrups and stirrup-leathers, so quaintly and artificially made that it may be put in the slop [*baggy part*] of a man's hose. For his saddle is made without any tree, yet hath it cantle and bolsters, only wrought artificially of cloth and bombast, with folds to wrap up in a short room; his stirrups are made with vices and gins that one may put them in a pair of gloves, and so are his spurs, and then a little white leather headstall and reins, with a small Scottish brake or snaffle, all so featly formed that, as I said before, they may be put in a buckram bag. Now, this trailer he bestrides the horse which he priggeth, and saddles and bridles him as orderly as if he were his own, and then carrieth him far from the place of his breed, and there sells him.

The Second Part of Cony-Catching, 1591

GABRIEL HARVEY

[The Character of Robert Greene]

I WAS altogether unacquainted with the man, and never once saluted him by name, but who in London hath not heard of his dissolute and licentious living; his fond disguising of a Master of Arts with ruffianly hair, unseemly apparel and more unseemly company; his vainglorious and thrasonical braving [*boastful swaggering*]; his piperly extemporizing and Tarletonizing [*clowning*]; his apish counterfeiting of every ridiculous and absurd toy; his fine cozening of jugglers and finer juggling with cozeners; his villainous cogging and foisting [*cheating and roguery*]; his monstrous swearing and horrible forswearing; his impious profaning of sacred texts; his other scandalous and blasphemous raving; his riotous and outrageous surfeiting; his continual shifting of lodgings; his plausible mustering and banqueting of roisterly acquaintance at his first coming; his beggarly departing in every hostess' debt; his infamous resorting to the Bankside, Shoreditch, Southwark and other filthy haunts; his obscure lurking in basest corners; his pawning of his sword, cloak and what not, when money came short; his impudent pamphleting, fantastical interluding [*acting*] and desperate libelling when other cozening shifts failed; his employing of Ball (surnamed Cutting Ball) till he was intercepted at Tyburn, to levy a crew of his trustiest companions to guard him in danger of arrests; his keeping of the foresaid Ball's sister, a sorry ragged quean, of whom he had his base son, Infortunatus

Greene; his forsaking of his own wife, too honest for such a husband? Particulars are infinite. His contemning of superiors, deriding of other, and defying of all good order?

Four Letters . . ., 1592

RICHARD HOOKER

[Order]

M OSES IN describing the work of Creation attributeth speech unto God: 'God said, Let there be light; let there be a firmament; let the waters under the heaven be gathered together into one place; let the earth bring forth; let there be lights in the firmament of heaven.' Was this only the intent of Moses, to signify the infinite greatness of God's power by the easiness of his accomplishing such effects, without travail, pain or labour? Surely it seemeth that Moses had herein besides this a further purpose: namely, first, to teach that God did not work as a necessary but a voluntary agent, intending beforehand and decreeing with Himself that which did outwardly proceed from Him; secondly, to show that God did then institute a law general to be observed by creatures, and therefore, according to the manner of laws, the institution thereof is described as being established by solemn injunction. His commanding those things to be which are, and to be in such sort as they are, to keep that tenor and course which they do, importeth the establishment of nature's law. This world's first creation, and the preservation since of things created, what is it but only so far forth a manifestation by execution what the eternal law of God is concerning things natural? And as it cometh to pass in a kingdom rightly ordered that after a law is once published it presently takes effect far and wide, all states framing themselves thereunto, even so let us think it fareth in the natural course of the world; since the time that God did first proclaim the edicts of his law upon it, heaven

and earth have hearkened unto His voice, and their labour
hath been to do His will. He made a law for the rain, He
gave His decree unto the sea that the waters should not pass
His commandment. Now, if Nature should intermit her
course, and leave altogether, though it were but for a while,
the observation of her own laws; if those principal and
mother elements of the world, whereof all things in this
lower world are made, should lose the qualities which they
now have; if the frame of that heavenly arch erected over
our heads should loosen and dissolve itself; if celestial
spheres should forget their wonted motions, and by irregular
volubility turn themselves any way as it might happen; if the
prince of the lights of heaven, which now as a giant doth
run his unwearied course, should, as it were through a
languishing faintness, begin to stand and rest himself; if the
moon should wander from her beaten way; the times and
seasons of the year blend themselves by disordered and
confused mixture; the winds breathe out their last gasp, the
clouds yield no rain, the earth be defeated of heavenly
influence, the fruits of the earth pine away as children at the
withered breasts of their mothers, no longer able to yield
them relief; what would become of man himself, whom
these things now do all serve? See we not plainly that
obedience of creatures unto the law of nature is the stay of
the whole world?

Of the Laws of Ecclesiastical Polity, 1593

THOMAS NASHE

[An Englishman Abroad]

A T MY first coming to Rome, I, being a youth of the
English cut, wore my hair long, went apparelled in
light colours, and imitated four or five sundry nations in my
attire at once; which no sooner was noted, but I had all the
boys of the city in a swarm wondering about me.

I had not gone a little farther, but certain officers crossed
the way of me and demanded to see my rapier; which when
they found – as also my dagger – with his point unblunted
they would have haled me headlong to the strappado, but
that with money I appeased them, and my fault was more
pardonable in that I was a stranger, altogether ignorant of
their customs.

Note, by the way, that it is the use in Rome for all men
whatsoever to wear their hair short; which they do not so
much for conscience' sake, or any religion they place in it,
but because the extremity of the heat is such there that, if
they should not do so, they should not have a hair left on
their heads to stand upright when they were scared with
sprites. And he is counted no gentleman amongst them that
goes not in black; they dress their jesters and fools only in
fresh colours and say variable garments do argue unsteadi-
ness and unconstancy of affections.

The reason of their strait ordinance for carrying weapons
without points is this: the bandittos, which are certain
outlaws that lie betwixt Rome and Naples, and besiege the
passage, that none can travel that way without robbing.
Now and then, hired for some few crowns, they will steal to
Rome and do a murther, and betake them to their heels
again. Disguised as they go, they are not known from
strangers; sometimes they will shroud themselves under the
habit of grave citizens. In this consideration, neither citizen
or stranger, gentleman, knight, marquis, or any, may wear
any weapon endamageable, upon pain of the strappado. I
bought it out; let others buy experience of me better cheap.

The Unfortunate Traveller; or,
The Life of Jack Wilton, 1594

SIR WALTER RALEGH

[The Orinoco]

WHEN THREE days more were overgone, our companies began to despair, the weather being extreme hot, the river bordered with very high trees that kept away the air, and the current against us every day stronger than other; but we evermore commanded our pilots to promise an end the next day, and used it so long as we were driven to assure them from four reaches of the river to three, and so to two, and so to the next reach. But so long we laboured as many days were spent, and so driven to draw ourselves to harder allowance – our bread even at the last and no drink at all – and our men and ourselves so wearied and scorched, and doubtful withal whether we should ever perform it or no, the heat increasing as we drew towards the line, for we were now in five degrees.

The farther we went on, our victual decreasing and the air breeding great faintness, we grew weaker and weaker when we had most need of strength and ability; for hourly the river ran more violently than other against us, and the barge, wherries and ship's boat of Captain Gifford and Captain Calfield had spent all their provisions, so as we were brought into despair and discomfort, had we not persuaded all the company that it was but only one day's work more to attain the land where we should be relieved of all we wanted and, if we returned, that we were sure to starve by the way, and that the world would also laugh us to scorn.

On the banks of these rivers were divers sorts of fruits good to eat, flowers and trees of that variety as were sufficient to make ten volumes of herbals. We relieved ourselves many times with the fruits of the country, and sometimes with fowl and fish. We saw birds of all colours, some carnation, some crimson, orange tawny, purple, green, watchet [*light blue*], and of all other sorts, both simple and mixed; as it was unto us a great good passing of the time to behold them, besides the relief we found by killing some store of them with our fowling-pieces – without which, having little or no bread, and less drink, but only the thick and troubled water of the river, we had been in a very hard case.

Our old pilot of the Ciawani – whom, as I said before, we took to redeem Ferdinando – told us that if we would enter a branch of the river on the right hand with our barge and wherries, and leave the galley at anchor the while in the great river, he would bring us to a town of the Arwacas where we should find store of bread, hens, fish, and of the country wine, and persuaded us that departing from the galley at noon we might return ere night. I was very glad to hear this speech, and presently took my barge with eight musketeers, Captain Gifford's wherry with himself and four musketeers, and Captain Calfield with his wherry and as many, and so we entered the mouth of this river; and because we were persuaded that it was so near we took no victual with us at all. When we had rowed three hours, we marvelled we saw no sign of any dwelling, and asked the pilot where the town was. He told us a little farther. After three hours more, the sun being almost set, we began to suspect that he led us that way to betray us, for he confessed that those Spaniards which fled from Trinidado, and also those that remained with Carapana in Emeria, were joined together in some village upon that river. But when it grew towards night, and we demanding where the place was, he told us but four reaches more. When we had rowed four and four we saw no sign; and our poor watermen, even heartbroken and tired, were ready to give up the ghost, for we had now come from the galley near forty miles.

At the last we determined to hang the pilot and, if we had well known the way back again by night, he had surely gone. But our own necessities pleaded sufficiently for his safety: for it was as dark as pitch, and the river began so to narrow itself, and the trees to hang over from side to side, as we were driven with arming swords to cut a passage through those branches that covered the water. We were very desirous to find this town, hoping of a feast because we made but a short breakfast aboard the galley in the morning and it was now eight o'clock at night and our stomachs began to gnaw apace; but whether it was best to return or go on we began to doubt, suspecting treason in the pilot more and more. But the poor old Indian ever assured us that it was but a little farther, and but this one turning and that turning; and at last, about one o'clock after midnight, we saw a light, and rowing towards it we heard the dogs of the village.

When we landed, we found few people; for the lord of that place was gone with divers canoes above four hundred miles off upon a journey towards the head of Oroonoko to trade for gold and to buy women of the cannibals, who afterward unfortunately passed by us as we rode at an anchor in the port of Morequito in the dark of night, and yet came so near us as his canoes grated against our barges. He left one of his company at the port of Morequito, by whom we understood that he had brought thirty young women, divers plates of gold, and had great store of fine pieces of cotton cloth and cotton beds. In his house we had good store of bread, fish, hens and Indian drink, and so rested that night; and in the morning, after we had traded with such of his people as came down, we returned towards our galley and brought with us some quantity of bread, fish and hens.

The Discovery of Guiana, 1596

[Tyranny]

THAT WHICH we properly call tyranny is a violent form of government, not respecting the good of the subject, but only the pleasure of the commander. I purposely forbear to say that it is the unjust rule of one over many; for very truly doth Cleon in Thucydides tell the Athenians that their dominion over their subjects was none other than a mere tyranny, though it were so that they themselves were a great city and a popular estate. Neither is it peradventure greatly needful that I should call this form of commanding violent, since it may well and easily be conceived that no man willingly performs obedience to one regardless of his life and welfare unless himself be either a madman or – which is little better – wholly possessed with some extreme passion of love. The practice of tyranny is not always of a like extremity; for some lords are more gentle than others to their very slaves and he that is most cruel to some is mild enough towards others, though it be but for his own advantage. Nevertheless, in large dominions wherein the ruler's discretion cannot extend itself unto notice of the difference which might be found between the worth of several men, it is commonly seen that the taste of sweetness drawn out of oppression hath so good a relish as continually inflames the tyrant's appetite and will not suffer it to be restrained with any limits of respect. Why should he seek out bounds to prescribe unto his desires, who cannot endure the face of one so honest as may put him in remembrance of any moderation? It is much that he hath gotten by extorting from some few; by sparing none he should have riches in goodly abundance. He hath taken a great deal from everyone: but everyone could have spared more. He hath wrung all their purses, and now he hath enough; but, as covetousness is never satisfied, he thinks that all this is too little for a stock, though it were indeed a good yearly income. Therefore he deviseth new tricks of robbery, and is not better pleased with the gains than with the art of getting. He is hated for this, and he knows it well; but he thinks by cruelty to change hatred into fear. So he makes it his exercise to torment and murder all whom he suspecteth: in which course, if he suspect none unjustly, he may be said to deal craftily; but, if innocency be not safe, how can all this make any conspirator to stand in fear, since the traitor is no worse rewarded than the quiet man? Wherefore he can think upon none other security than to disarm all his subjects; to fortify himself within some strong place; and for defence of his person and state to hire as many lusty soldiers as shall be thought sufficient. These must not be of his own country; for, if not every one, yet some one or other might chance to have a feeling of the public misery. This considered, he allures unto him a desperate rabble of strangers, the most unhonest that can be found; such as have neither wealth nor credit at home, and will therefore be careful to support him by whose only favour they are maintained. Now, lest any of these, either by detestation of his wickedness or – which in wicked men is most likely – by promise of greater reward than he doth give, should be drawn to turn his sword against the tyrant himself, they shall all be permitted to do as he doth; to rob, to ravish, to murder and to satisfy their own appetites in most outrageous manner; being thought so much the more assured to their master by how much the more he sees them grow hateful to all men else. Considering in what age and in what language I write, I must be fain to say that these are not dreams – though some Englishmen perhaps, that were unacquainted with history, lighting upon this leaf, might suppose this discourse to be little better.

This is to show both how tyranny grows to stand in need of mercenary soldiers, and how those mercenaries are, by mutual obligation, firmly assured unto the tyrant.

The History of the World, 1614

FRANCIS BACON

Of Truth

'WHAT IS truth?' said jesting Pilate, and would not stay for an answer. Certainly there be that delight in giddiness, and count it a bondage to fix a belief, affecting free will in thinking as well as in acting. And though the sects of philosophers of that kind be gone, yet there remain certain discoursing wits which are of the same veins, though there be not so much blood in them as was in those of the ancients. But it is not only the difficulty and labour which men take in finding out of truth, nor again that when it is found it imposeth upon men's thoughts, that doth bring lies in favour, but a natural though corrupt love of the lie itself. One of the later schools of the Grecians examineth the matter, and is at a stand to think what should be in it, that men should love lies, where neither they make for pleasure, as with poets, nor for advantage, as with the merchant, but for the lie's sake. But I cannot tell. This same truth is a naked and open daylight that doth not show the masques and mummeries and triumphs of the world half so stately and daintily as candle-lights. Truth may perhaps come to the price of a pearl, that showeth best by day, but it will not rise to the price of a diamond or carbuncle, that showeth best in varied lights. A mixture of a lie doth ever add pleasure. Doth any man doubt that if there were taken out of men's minds vain opinions, flattering hopes, false valuations, imaginations as one would, and the like, but it would leave the minds of a number of men poor shrunken things, full of melancholy and indisposition, and unpleasing to themselves? One of the fathers, in great severity, called poesy 'vinum daemonum' [*the wine of devils*], because it filleth the imagination, and yet it is but with the shadow of a lie. But it is not the lie that passeth through the mind, but the lie that sinketh in and settleth in it, that doth the hurt, such as we spake of before. But howsoever these things are thus in men's depraved judgements and affections, yet truth, which only doth judge itself, teacheth that the inquiry of truth, which is the love-making or wooing of it, the knowledge of truth, which is the presence of it, and the belief of truth, which is the enjoying of it, is the sovereign good of human nature. The first creature of God in the works of the days was the light of the sense; the last was the light of reason; and His sabbath work ever since, is the illumination of His spirit. First, He breathed light upon the face of the matter or chaos; then He breathed light into the face of man; and still He breatheth and inspireth light into the face of His chosen. The poet that beautified the sect that was otherwise inferior to the rest saith yet excellently well: 'It is a pleasure to stand upon the shore and to see ships tossed upon the sea; a pleasure to stand in the window of a castle and to see a battle and the adventures thereof below; but no pleasure is comparable to the standing upon the vantage ground of truth' – a hill not to be commanded [*looked down on by others*], and where the air is always clear and serene – 'and to see the errors and wanderings and mists and tempests in the vale below'; so always that this prospect be with pity, and not with swelling or pride. Certainly it is heaven upon earth to have man's mind move in charity, rest in providence, and turn upon the poles of truth.

To pass from theological and philosophical truth to the truth of civil business: it will be acknowledged even by those that practise it not that clear and round dealing is the honour of man's nature, and that mixture of falsehood is like alloy in coin of gold and silver, which may make the metal work the better, but it embaseth it. For these winding and crooked courses are the goings of the serpent, which goeth basely upon the belly and not upon the feet. There is no vice that doth so cover a man with shame as to be found false and perfidious; and therefore Montaigne saith prettily when he inquired the reason why the word of the lie should be such a disgrace and such an odious charge. Saith he: 'If it be well weighed, to say that a man lieth is as much as to say that he is brave towards God and a coward towards men.' For a lie faces God, and shrinks from man. Surely the wickedness of falsehood and breach of faith cannot possibly be so highly expressed as in that it shall be the last peal to call the judgements of God upon the generations of men; it being foretold that when Christ cometh, 'He shall not find faith upon the earth'.

Of Studies

STUDIES SERVE for delight, for ornament and for ability. Their chief use for delight is in privateness and retiring; for ornament is in discourse; and for ability is in the judgement and disposition of business. For expert men can execute, and perhaps judge of particulars, one by one; but the general counsels, and the plots and marshalling of affairs come best from those that are learned. To spend too much time in studies is sloth; to use them too much for ornament is affectation; to make judgement wholly by their rules is the humour of a scholar. They perfect nature and are perfected by experience, for natural abilities are like natural plants that need pruning by study; and studies themselves do give forth directions too much at large, except they be bounded in by experience. Crafty men contemn studies, simple men admire them, and wise men use them; for they teach not their own use; but that is a wisdom without them and above them, won by observation. Read not to contradict and confute; nor to believe and take for granted; nor to find talk and discourse; but to weigh and consider. Some books are to be tasted, others to be swallowed, and some few to be chewed and digested: that is, some books are to be read only in parts; others to be read, but not curiously; and some few to be read wholly, and with diligence and attention. Some books also may be read by deputy, and extracts made of them by others, but that would be only in the less important arguments and the meaner sort of books; else distilled books are like common distilled waters, flashy [*insipid*] things. Reading maketh a full man, conference a ready man, and writing an exact man; and, therefore, if a man write little, he had need have a great memory; if he confer little, he had need have a present wit; and if he read little, he had need have much cunning, to seem to know that he doth not. Histories make men wise, poets witty, the mathematics subtle, natural philosophy deep, moral grave, logic and rhetoric able to contend. 'Abeunt studia in mores' [*Studies go to make up a man's character*]. Nay, there is no stand or impediment in the wit, but may be wrought out by fit studies, like as diseases of the body may have appropriate exercises. Bowling is good for the stone and reins [*bladder and kidneys*], shooting for the lungs and breast; gentle walking for the stomach; riding for the head; and the like. So, if a man's wit be wandering, let him study the mathematics; for in demonstrations, if his wit be called away never so little, he must begin again. If his wit be not apt to distinguish or find difference, let him study the schoolmen; for they are 'Cymini sectores' [*splitters of hairs*]. If he be not apt to beat over matters [*cover the ground thoroughly*], and to call up one thing to prove and illustrate another, let him study the lawyers' cases. So every defect of the mind may have a special receipt [*prescription*].

Essays, 1597

THOMAS DELONEY

[Simon Eyre Honours a Promise]

A T THIS time it came into his mind what a promise once he made to the prentices, being at breakfast with them at their going to the conduit – speaking to his lady in this wise:

'Good Lord,' quoth he, 'what a change have we had within these thirty years, and how greatly hath the Lord blessed us since that! Blessed be His name for it! I do remember when I was a young prentice what a match I made upon a Shrove Tuesday morning, being at the conduit among other of my companions. Trust me, Wife,' quoth he, ''tis worth the hearing, and I'll tell thee how it fell out. After we had filled our tankards with water, there was some would needs have me set down my tankard and go with them to breakfast, as many times before I had done; to which I consented. And it was a breakfast of pudding-pies. I shall never forget it. But, to make short, when the shot came to be paid, each one drew out his money, but I had not one penny in my purse and credit I had none in the place; which when I beheld, being abashed, I said: "Well, my masters, do you give me my breakfast this time, and in requital thereof, if ever I be Mayor of London, I'll bestow a breakfast on all the prentices of the City." These were the words – little thinking, God wot, that ever it should come to pass. But such was the great goodness of our God, who setteth up the humble and pulleth down the proud, to bring whom He pleaseth to the seat of honour. For, as the Scripture witnesseth, "Promotion cometh neither from the east nor from the west, but from Him that is the giver of all good things, the mighty Lord of heaven and earth." Wherefore, Wife, seeing God hath bestowed that upon me that I never looked for, it is reason that I should perform my promise. And, being able now, I'll pay that which then I was not able to do, for I would not have men say that I am like the ebon-tree, that neither bears leaves nor fruit. Wherefore, Wife, seeing that Shrove Tuesday is so near at hand, I will upon that day fulfil my promise which upon that day I made.'

'Truly, my lord,' quoth she, 'I will be right willing thereunto.'

Then answered my lord: 'As thou dost love me, let them want neither pudding-pies nor pancakes, and look what other good cheer is to be had. I will refer all to your discretion.'

Hereupon great provision was made for the prentices' breakfast. And, Shrove Tuesday being come, the Lord Mayor sent word to the aldermen that in their several wards they should signify his mind to the citizens to crave their favours that their prentices might come to his house to breakfast, and that for his sake they might play all the day after. Hereupon it was ordered that at the ringing of a bell in every parish the prentices should leave work and shut up their shops for that day; which being ever since yearly observed, it is called Pancake Bell.

The prentices being all assembled, my Lord Mayor's house was not able to hold them, they were such a multitude; so that, besides the great hall, all the gardens were set with tables, and in the backside tables were set, and every other spare place was also furnished, so that at length they were all placed. And while meat was bringing in, to delight their ears as well as to feed their bodies, and to drown the noise of their prattlings, drums and trumpets were pleasantly sounded. That being ended, the waits of the city, with divers other sorts of music, played also to beguile the time and to put off all discontent. After the first service were all the tables plentifully furnished with pudding-pies and pancakes in very plentiful manner; and the rest that remained was given to the poor. Wine and ale in very great measure they had given, insomuch that they had no lack, nor excess to cause them to be disordered. And in the midst of this their merriment the Lord Mayor in his scarlet gown, and his lady in like manner, went in amongst them, bidding them all most heartily welcome, saying unto them that his promise so long ago made he hath at length performed. At what time they, in token of thankfulness, flung up their caps, giving a great shout, and incontinently they all quietly departed.

The Gentle Craft, 1597

JOHN CHAMBERLAIN

[An Ambush]

ABOUT NINE o'clock in the morning Sir Charles Cavendish, being at his new building [*in Nottinghamshire*], which is some quarter of a mile from his little house where he and his lady do lie, and going from thence to a brick kiln as far distant from that building as that is from his house, being attended by these three persons only, Henry Ogle, Lancelot Ogle his page, and one horsekeeper, he discerned to the number of about twenty horse on the side of a hill, which he thought to be Sir John Byron with company hunting. But suddenly, they all galloping apace towards him, he perceived he was betrayed; whereupon, being upon a little nag, he put spurs to him, thinking to recover the new building, but the tit [*horse*] fell with him, and before he could recover out of the stirrup he was overtaken; and before he could draw his sword two pistols were discharged upon him, and one of them with a round bullet hit him in the inner side of the thigh but missed the bone, and lies yet in the flesh near the point of his buttock. He hath also divers small shot in several parts of his thigh and body thereabouts, which are thought came out of the same pistol.

Notwithstanding, so strong was the hand of God with him as, after this wound received, he and his two poor men and boy unhorsed six of them and killed two in the place. A third fell down in the forest and is thought dead also, and the fourth was left behind in the same place so sore hurt as it is not thought he can recover, and lieth in the village adjoining. Upon this some of the workmen came towards them, being without weapons. John Stanhope, who was the hindmost during all the fight, was now the foremost in running away, carrying all the rest of his hirelings with him.

Sir Charles is hurt also in the head and in the hand, but these two are but small hurts, and the surgeons do assuredly hope that there is no great danger in the other wounds with the pistol, though by incision they intend to take out the bullet, which is within an inch and a half of the skin. Sir Charles and his three had rapiers and daggers only.

They left behind them six good geldings, whereof some are worth twenty pounds apiece, two or three cloaks, two rapiers, two pistols, one sword and dagger, and some of their hats, all which are safely kept by Sir Charles. All this company did all the morning before lie in the forest, seeming as though they had been a-hunting. One of them that were killed was a keeper, whom Stanhope that morning took with him as he found him in his park, without boots or weapon but a pikestaff which he had, and, as the fellow confessed before he died, he know not thither he was carried, or what to do, until he came to the hillside where they stayed so long.

This is the truth of that accident.

Letter to Dudley Carleton, 28 June 1599

JOHN FLORIO

[Animal Intelligence]

W E TEACH blackbirds, starlings, ravens, piots [*magpies*] and parrots to chat; and that facility we perceive in them to lend us their voice so supple and their wind so tractable that so we may frame and bring it to a certain number of letters and syllables witnesseth they have a kind of inward reason which makes them so docile and willing to learn. I think every man is cloyed and wearied with seeing so many apish and mimic tricks that jugglers teach their dogs, as the dances where they miss not one cadence of the sounds or notes they hear. Mark but the divers turnings and several kinds of motions which by the commandment of their bare words they make them perform.

But I wonder not a little at the effect which is ordinary amongst us; and that is the dogs which blind men use, both in city and country. I have observed how suddenly they will stop when they come before some doors where they are wont to receive alms; how carefully they will avoid the shock of carts and coaches, even when they have room enough to pass by themselves. I have seen some going along a town ditch leave a plain and even path and take a worse, that so they might draw their master from the ditch. How could a man make the dog conceive his charge was only to look to his master's safety, and for his service to despise his own commodity and good? And how should he have the knowledge that such a path would be broad enough for him, but not for a blind man? Can all this be conceived without reason?

We must not forget what Plutarch affirmeth to have seen a dog in Rome do before the Emperor Vespasian the father in the Theatre of Marcellus. This dog served a juggler, who was to play a fiction of many faces and sundry countenances, where he also was to act a part. Amongst other things he was for a long while to counterfeit and feign himself dead because he had eaten of a certain drug. Having swallowed a piece of bread, which was supposed to be the drug, he began suddenly to stagger and shake as if he had been giddy; then, stretching and laying himself along as stiff as if he were stark dead, suffered himself to be dragged and haled from one place to another, according to the subject and plot of the play; and, when he knew his time, first he began fair and softly to stir, as if he were roused out of a dead slumber, then lifting up his head he looked and stared so ghastly that all the bystanders were amazed.

The oxen which in the King's gardens of Susa were taught to water them and to draw water out of deep wells turned certain great wheels, to which were fastened great buckets – as in many places of Languedoc is commonly seen – and, being every one appointed to draw just a hundred turns a day, they were so accustomed to that number as it was impossible by any compulsion to make them draw one more; which task ended, they would suddenly stop.

We are grown striplings before we can tell a hundred; and many nations have lately been discovered that never knew what numbers meant. More discourse is required to teach others than to be taught. And omitting what Democritus judged and proved, which is that beasts have instructed us in most of our arts – as the spider to weave and sew, the swallow to build, the swan and the nightingale music, and divers beasts, by imitating them, the art of physic – Aristotle is of opinion that nightingales teach their young ones to sing, wherein they employ both long time and much care; whence it followeth that those which we keep tame in cages and have not had leisure to go to their parents' school lose much grace in their singing. Whereby we may conclude they are much amended by discipline and study. And amongst those that run wild their song is not all one nor alike. Each one hath learned either better or worse, according to his capacity. And so jealous are they in their prenticeship that to excel one another they will so stoutly contend for the mastery that many times such as are vanquished die; their wind and strength sooner failing than their voice. The young ones will very sadly sit recording their lesson, and are often seen labouring how to imitate certain song-notes. The scholar listeneth attentively to his master's lesson, and

carefully yieldeth account of it; now one and then another
shall hold his peace. Mark but how they endeavour to
amend their faults, and how the elder striveth to reprove
the youngest.

Arrius protesteth to have seen an elephant who on every
thigh had a cymbal hanging and one fastened to his trunk,
at the sound of which all other elephants danced in a round,
now rising aloft, then louting [*bowing*] full low at certain
cadences, even as the instrument directed them, and was
much delighted with the harmony. In the great shows of
Rome elephants were ordinarily seen taught to move and
dance at the sound of a voice certain dances, wherein were
many strange shifts, interchanges, caperings and cadences
very hard to be learned. Some have been noted to con and
practise their lessons using much study and care, as being
loth to be chidden and beaten of their masters.

'An Apology of Raymond Sebond', in
The Essays of Michael Lord of Montaigne, 1603

JAMES I

[The Evils of Tobacco]

A ND FOR the vanities committed in this filthy custom, is
it not both great vanity and uncleanness that at the
table, a place of respect, of cleanliness, of modesty, men
should not be ashamed to sit tossing of tobacco-pipes and
puffing of the smoke of tobacco, one to another, making the
filthy smoke and stink thereof to exhale athwart the dishes
and infect the air when very often men that abhor it are at
their repast? Surely smoke becomes a kitchen far better
than a dining-chamber, and yet it makes a kitchen also
oftentimes in the inward parts of men, soiling and infecting
them with an unctuous and oily kind of soot, as hath been
found in some great tobacco-takers that after their death
were opened. And not only meat-time, but no other time

nor action is exempted from the public use of this uncivil trick; so as if the wives of Dieppe list to contest with this nation for good manners their worst manners would in all reason be found at least not so dishonest as ours are in this point. The public use whereof, at all times and in all places, hath now so far prevailed as divers men very sound both in judgement and complexion have been at last forced to take it also without desire: partly because they were ashamed to seem singular – like the two philosophers that were forced to duck themselves in that rainwater, and so become fools as well as the rest of the people; and partly to be as one that was content to eat garlic – which he did not love – that he might not be troubled with the smell of it in the breath of his fellows. And is it not a great vanity that a man cannot heartily welcome his friend now, but straight they must be in hand with tobacco? No, it is become in place of a cure a point of good fellowship, and he that will refuse to take a pipe of tobacco among his fellows, though by his own election he would rather feel the savour of a sink, is accounted peevish and no good company, even as they do with tippling in the cold eastern countries. Yea, the mistress cannot in a more mannerly kind entertain her servant than by giving him out of her fair hand a pipe of tobacco. But herein is not only a great vanity, but a great contempt of God's good gifts, that the sweetness of man's breath, being a good gift of God, should be wilfuly corrupted by this stinking smoke, wherein, I must confess, it hath too strong a virtue: and so that which is an ornament of nature, and can neither by an artifice be at the first acquired nor once lost be recovered again, shall be filthily corrupted with an incurable stink, which vile quality is as directly contrary to that wrong opinion which is holden of the wholesomeness thereof as the venom of putrefaction is contary to the virtue preservative.

Moreover, which is a great iniquity, and against all humanity, the husband shall not be ashamed to reduce thereby his delicate, wholesome and clean-complexioned wife to that extremity that either she must also corrupt her sweet breath therewith or else resolute to live in a perpetual stinking torment.

Have you not reason, then, to be ashamed, and to forbear this filthy novelty, so basely grounded, so foolishly received and so grossly mistaken in the right use thereof? In your abuse thereof sinning against God, harming yourselves both in persons and goods, and taking also thereby the marks and notes of vanity upon you; by the custom thereof making yourselves to be wondered at by all foreign civil nations, and by all strangers that come among you to be scorned and contemned. A custom loathsome to the eye, hateful to the nose, harmful to the brain, dangerous to the lungs, and in the black stinking fume thereof nearest resembling the horrible Stygian smoke of the pit that is bottomless.

A Counterblast to Tobacco, 1604

SIR JOHN HARINGTON

[Christian IV of Denmark Pays a State Visit to the Court of James I]

I CAME here a day or two before the Danish king came, and from the day he did come until this hour I have been well nigh overwhelmed with carousal and sports of all kinds. The sports began each day in such manner and such sort as well nigh persuaded me of Mahomet's paradise. We had women – and indeed wine, too – of such plenty as would have astonished each sober beholder. Our feasts were magnificent, and the two royal guests did most lovingly embrace each other at table. I think the Dane hath strangely wrought on our good English nobles; for those, whom I never could get to taste good liquor, now follow the fashion and wallow in beastly delights. The ladies abandon their sobriety and are seen to roll about in intoxication. In good sooth, the Parliament did kindly to provide his Majesty so seasonably with money, for there hath been no lack of good living – shows, sights and banquetings from morn to eve.

One day a great feast was held, and after dinner the

representation of Solomon his Temple and the coming of
the Queen of Sheba was made – or, as I may better say, was
meant to have been made – before their Majesties, by
device of the Earl of Salisbury and others. But, alas! as all
earthly things do fail to poor mortals in enjoyment, so did
prove our presentment hereof. The lady who did play the
Queen's part did carry most precious gifts to both their
Majesties; but, forgetting the steps arising to the canopy,
overset her caskets into his Danish Majesty's lap, and fell at
his feet, though I rather think it was in his face. Much was
the hurry and confusion; cloths and napkins were at hand to
make all clean. His Majesty then got up and would dance
with the Queen of Sheba; but he fell down and humbled
himself before her, and was carried to an inner chamber and
laid on a bed of state, which was not a little defiled with the
presents of the Queen which had been bestowed on his
garments – such as wine, cream, jelly, beverage, cakes,
spices and other good matters.

The entertainment and show went forward, and most of
the presenters went backward or fell down; wine did so
occupy their upper chambers. Now did appear, in rich dress,
Hope, Faith and Charity. Hope did essay to speak, but wine
rendered her endeavours so feeble that she withdrew and
hoped the King would excuse her brevity. Faith was then all
alone, for I am certain she was not joined with good works,
and left the Court in a staggering condition. Charity came
to the King's feet, and seemed to cover the multitude of sins
her sisters had committed. In some sort she made obeisance
and brought gifts, but said she would return home again as
there was no gift which heaven had not already given his
Majesty. She then returned to Hope and Faith, who were
both sick and spewing in the lower hall. Next came Victory
in bright armour, and presented a rich sword to the King,
who did not accept it but put it by with his hand; and, by a
strange medley of versification, did endeavour to make suit
to the King. But Victory did not triumph long, for after
much lamentable utterance she was led away like a silly
captive and laid to sleep in the outer steps of the ante-
chamber. Now did Peace make entry and strive to get
foremost to the King; but I grieve to tell how great wrath

she did discover unto those of her attendants, and, much
contrary to her own semblance, most rudely made war with
her olive branch, and laid on the pates of those who did
oppose her coming.

I have much marvelled at these strange pageantries, and
they do bring to my remembrance what passed of this sort
in our Queen's days, of which I was sometime an humble
presenter and assistant; but I ne'er did see such lack of good
order, discretion and sobriety as I have now done. I have
passed much time in seeing the royal sports of hunting and
hawking, where the manners were such as made me devise
[conclude] the beasts were pursuing the sober creation, and
not man in quest of exercise or food. I will now, in good
sooth, declare to you, who will not blab, that the Gunpowder fright is got out of all our heads, and we are going
on hereabouts as if the Devil was contriving every man
should blow up himself, by wild riot, excess, and devastation
of time and temperance. The great ladies do go well masked,
and indeed it be the only show of their modesty, to conceal
their countenance; but, alack, they meet with such countenance to uphold their strange doings that I marvel not at
aught that happens.

Letter to Mr Secretary Barlow, July 1606

JOSEPH HALL

The Hypocrite

A HYPOCRITE is the worst kind of player by so much as
he acts the better part; which hath always two faces;
ofttimes, two hearts, that can compose his forehead to
sadness and gravity while he bids his heart be wanton and
careless within and in the mean time laughs within himself
to think how smoothly he hath cozened the beholder; in
whose silent face are written the characters of religion,
which his tongue and gestures pronounce but his hands

recant; that hath a clean face and garment, with a foul soul; whose mouth belies his heart, and his fingers belie his mouth. Walking early up into the city, he turns into the great church and salutes one of the pillars on one knee, worshipping that God which at home he cares not for; while his eye is fixed on some window, on some passenger, and his heart knows not whither his lips go. He rises and, looking about with admiration, complains of our frozen charity; commends the ancient. At church he will ever sit where he may be seen best; and in the midst of the sermon pulls out his tables [*notebook*] in haste as if he feared to lose that note, when he writes either his forgotten errand or nothing; then he turns his Bible with a noise to seek an omitted quotation, and folds the leaf as if he had found it; and asks aloud the name of the preacher and repeats it, whom he publicly salutes, thanks, praises, invites, entertains with tedious good counsel, with good discourse – if it had come from an honester mouth. He can command tears when he speaks of his youth; indeed, because it is past, not because it was sinful: himself is not better, but the times are worse. All other sins he reckons up with detestation, while he loves and hides his darling in his bosom. All his speech returns to himself, and every occurrent draws in a story to his own praise. When he should give, he looks about him and says, 'Who sees me?' No alms, no prayers fall from him without a witness, belike lest God should deny that He hath received them; and when he hath done, lest the world should not know it, his own mouth is his trumpet to proclaim it. With the superfluity of his usury he builds a hospital, and harbours them whom his extortion hath spoiled; so, while he makes many beggars, he keeps some. He turneth all gnats into camels; and cares not to undo the world for a circumstance; flesh on a Friday is more abomination to him than his neighbour's bed; he abhors more not to uncover at the name of Jesus than to swear by the name of God. When a rhymer reads his poem to him, he begs a copy and persuades the press. There is nothing that he dislikes in presence that in absence he censures not. He comes to the sickbed of his stepmother and weeps; when he secretly fears her recovery. He greets his friend in the street with so clear a countenance, so fast a closure [*so warm an embrace*], that the other thinks he reads his heart in his face; and shakes hands, with an indefinite invitation of 'When will you come?' and, when his back is turned, joys that he is so well rid of a guest. Yet if that guest visit him unfeared [*undismayed*] he counterfeits a smiling welcome; and excuses his cheer, when closely he frowns on his wife for too much. He shows well, and says well; and himself is the worst thing he hath. In brief he is the stranger's saint; the neighbour's disease; the blot of goodness; a rotten stick in a dark night; a poppy in a cornfield; an ill-tempered candle with a great snuff that in going out smells ill; an angel abroad, a devil at home; and worse when an angel than when a devil.

Characters of Virtues and Vices, 1608

THOMAS DEKKER

How a Gallant Should Behave Himself in a Playhouse

WHETHER THEREFORE the gatherers of the public or private playhouse stand to receive the afternoon's rent, let our gallant, having paid it, presently advance himself up to the throne of the stage. I mean not into the lords' room, which is now but the stage's suburbs. No, those boxes, by the iniquity of custom, conspiracy of waiting-women and gentlemen ushers, that there sweat together, and the covetousness of sharers [*theatre-owners*], are contemptibly thrust into the rear, and much new satin is there damned by being smothered to death in darkness. But on the very rushes where the comedy is to dance, yea, and under the state [*royal canopy*] of Cambyses himself, must our feathered estridge [*ostrich*], like a piece of ordnance, be planted valiantly – because impudently – beating down the mews and hisses of the opposed rascality.

For do but cast up a reckoning what large comings-in are

pursed up by sitting on the stage. First a conspicuous eminence is gotten; by which means the best and most essential parts of a gallant – good clothes, a proportionable leg, white hand, the Persian lock and a tolerable beard – are perfectly revealed.

By sitting on the stage you have a signed patent to engross the whole commodity of censure, may lawfully presume to be a girder [critic] and stand at the helm to steer the passage of scenes; yet no man shall once offer to hinder you from obtaining the title of an insolent, overweening coxcomb.

By sitting on the stage, you may, without travelling for it, at the very next door ask whose play it is; and by that quest of enquiry the law warrants you to avoid much mistaking. If you know not the author, you may rail against him; and peradventure so behave yourself that you may enforce the author to know you.

By sitting on the stage, if you be a knight you may happily get you a mistress; if a mere Fleet Street gentleman, a wife; but assure yourself, by continual residence you are the first and principal man in election to begin the number of 'We Three'.

By spreading your body on the stage, and by being a justice in examining of plays, you shall put yourself into such true scenical authority that some poet shall not dare to present his Muse rudely upon your eyes, without having first unmasked her, rifled her, and discovered all her bare and most mystical parts before you at a tavern, when you most knightly shall, for his pains, pay for both their suppers.

By sitting on the stage, you may with small cost purchase the dear acquaintance of the boys; have a good stool for sixpence; at any time know what particular part any of the infants [boy actors] present; get your match lighted; examine the play-suits' lace, and perhaps win wagers upon laying 'tis copper, etc. And to conclude: whether you be a fool or a justice of peace, a cuckold or a captain, a Lord Mayor's son or a dawcock [simpleton], a knave or an under-sheriff – of what stamp soever you be, current or counterfeit, the stage like time will bring you to most perfect light and lay you

open. Neither are you to be hunted from thence, though the
scarecrows in the yard hoot at you, hiss at you, spit at you –
yea, throw dirt even in your teeth. 'Tis most gentleman-like
patience to endure all this and to laugh at the silly animals;
but if the rabble, with a full throat, cry, 'Away with the
fool,' you were worse than a madman to tarry by it; for the
gentleman and the fool should never sit on the stage
together.

The Gull's Hornbook, 1609

THOMAS CORYAT

[Table Manners]

I OBSERVED a custom in all those Italian cities and towns
through which I passed that is not used in any other
country that I saw in my travels, neither do I think that any
other nation of Christendom doth use it, but only Italy. The
Italians, and also most strangers that are commorant [*resident*] in Italy, do always at their meals use a little fork when
they cut their meat. For, while with their knife, which they
hold in one hand, they cut the meat out of the dish, they
fasten their fork, which they hold in their other hand, upon
the same dish; so that whatsoever he be that, sitting in the
company of any others at meal, should unadvisedly touch
the dish of meat with his fingers, from which all at the table
do cut, he will give occasion of offence unto the company,
as having transgressed the laws of good manners, insomuch
that for his error he shall be at the least brow-beaten if not
reprehended in words. This form of feeding I understand is
generally used in all places of Italy, their forks being for the
most part made of iron or steel, and some of silver, but
those are used only by gentlemen. The reason of this their
curiosity is because the Italian cannot by any means endure
to have his dish touched with fingers, seeing all men's fingers
are not alike clean. Hereupon I myself thought good to

imitate the Italian fashion by this forked cutting of meat, not only while I was in Italy, but also in Germany, and oftentimes in England since I came home; being once quipped for that frequent using of my fork by a certain learned gentleman, a familiar friend of mine, one Master Laurence Whitaker, who in his merry humour doubted not to call me at table *furcifer* [*fork-bearer*], only for using a fork at feeding, but for no other cause.

Coryat's Crudities, 1611

THE KING JAMES BIBLE
1611

[Abraham and Isaac]

A<small>ND IT</small> came to pass after these things, that God did tempt Abraham, and said unto him, Abraham: and he said, Behold, here I am.

And he said, Take now thy son, thine only son Isaac, whom thou lovest, and get thee into the land of Moriah; and offer him there for a burnt offering upon one of the mountains which I will tell thee of.

And Abraham rose up early in the morning, and saddled his ass, and took two of his young men with him, and Isaac his son, and clave the wood for the burnt offering, and rose up, and went unto the place of which God had told him.

And then on the third day Abraham lifted up his eyes, and saw the place afar off.

And Abraham said unto his young men, Abide ye here with the ass; and I and the lad will go yonder and worship, and come again to you.

And Abraham took the wood of the burnt offering, and laid it upon Isaac his son; and he took the fire in his hand, and a knife; and they went both of them together.

And Isaac spake unto Abraham his father, and said, My

father: and he said, Here am I, my son. And he said, Behold the fire and the wood: but where is the lamb for a burnt offering?

And Abraham said, My son, God will provide himself a lamb for a burnt offering: so they went both of them together.

And they came to the place which God had told him of; and Abraham built an altar there, and laid the wood in order, and bound Isaac his son, and laid him on the altar upon the wood.

And Abraham stretched forth his hand, and took the knife to slay his son.

And the angel of the Lord called unto him out of heaven, and said, Abraham, Abraham: and he said, Here am I.

And he said, Lay not thine hand upon the lad, neither do thou any thing unto him: for now I know that thou fearest God, seeing thou hast not withheld thy son, thine only son from me.

And Abraham lifted up his eyes, and looked, and behold, behind him a ram caught in a thicket by his horns: and Abraham went and took the ram, and offered him up for a burnt offering in the stead of his son.

Genesis, 22.1–13

[The Parable of the Good Samaritan]

AND, BEHOLD, a certain lawyer stood up, and tempted him, saying, Master, what shall I do to inherit eternal life?

He said unto him, What is written in the law? how readest thou?

And he answering said, Thou shalt love the Lord thy God with all thy heart, and with all thy soul, and with all thy strength, and with all thy mind; and thy neighbour as thyself.

And he said unto him, Thou hast answered right: this do, and thou shalt live.

But he, willing to justify himself, said unto Jesus, And who is my neighbour?

And Jesus answering said, A certain man went down from Jerusalem to Jericho, and fell among thieves, which stripped him of his raiment, and wounded him, and departed, leaving him half dead.

And by chance there came down a certain priest that way: and when he saw him, he passed by on the other side.

And likewise a Levite, when he was at the place, came and looked on him, and passed by on the other side.

But a certain Samaritan, as he journeyed, came where he was: and when he saw him, he had compassion on him.

And went to him, and bound up his wounds, pouring in oil and wine, and set him on his own beast, and brought him to an inn, and took care of him.

And on the morrow when he departed, he took out two pence, and gave them to the host, and said unto him, Take care of him; and whatsoever thou spendest more, when I come again, I will repay thee.

Which now of these three, thinkest thou, was neighbour unto him that fell among the thieves?

And he said, He that shewed mercy on him. Then said Jesus unto him, Go and do thou likewise.

The Gospel According to St Luke, 10.25–37

[Jesus before Pilate]

AND JESUS stood before the governor: and the governor asked him, saying, Art thou the King of the Jews? And Jesus said unto him, Thou sayest.

And when he was accused of the chief priests and elders, he answered nothing.

Then said Pilate unto him, Hearest thou not how many things they witness against thee?

And he answered him to never a word; insomuch that the governor marvelled greatly.

Now at that feast the governor was wont to release unto the people a prisoner, whom they would.

And they had then a notable prisoner, called Barabbas.

Therefore when they were gathered together, Pilate said unto them, Whom will ye that I release unto you? Barabbas, or Jesus which is called Christ?

For he knew that for envy they had delivered him.

When he was set down on the judgment seat, his wife sent unto him, saying, Have thou nothing to do with that just man: for I have suffered many things this day in a dream because of him.

But the chief priests and elders persuaded the multitude that they should ask for Barabbas, and destroy Jesus.

The governor answered and said unto them, Whether of the twain will ye that I release unto you? They said, Barabbas. Pilate saith unto them, What shall I do then with Jesus which is called Christ? They all say unto him, Let him be crucified.

And the governor said, Why, what evil hath he done? But they cried out the more, saying, Let him be crucified.

When Pilate saw that he could prevail nothing, but that rather a tumult was made, he took water, and washed his hands before the multitude, saying, I am innocent of the blood of this just person: see ye to it.

Then answered all the people, and said, His blood be on us, and on our children.

Then released he Barabbas unto them: and when he had scourged Jesus, he delivered him to be crucified.

Then the soldiers of the governor took Jesus into the common hall, and gathered unto him the whole band of soldiers.

And they stripped him, and put on him a scarlet robe.

And when they had platted a crown of thorns, they put it upon his head, and a reed in his right hand: and they bowed the knee before him, and mocked him, saying, Hail, King of the Jews!

And they spit upon him, and took the reed, and smote him on the head.

And after that they had mocked him, they took the robe

off from him, and put his own raiment on him, and led him
away to crucify him.

The Gospel According to St Matthew, 27.11–31

SIR THOMAS OVERBURY

A Melancholy Man

Is a strayer from the drove: one that nature made socia-
ble, because she made him man, and a crazed disposition
hath altered. Impleasing to all, as all to him. Straggling
thoughts are his content: they make him dream waking,
there's his pleasure. His imagination is never idle; it keeps
his mind in a continual motion, as the poise [*weight*] the
clock. He winds up his thoughts often, and as often unwinds
them; Penelope's web thrives faster. He'll seldom be found
without the shade of some grove in whose bottom a river
dwells. He carries a cloud in his face, never fair weather;
his outside is framed to his inside, in that he keeps a
decorum, both unseemly. Speak to him: he hears with his
eyes; ears follow his mind, and that's not at leisure. He
thinks business, but never does any; he is all contemplation,
no action. He hews and fashions his thoughts as if he meant
them to some purpose; but they prove unprofitable, as a
piece of wrought timber to no use. His spirits and the sun
are enemies; the sun bright and warm, his humour black
and cold. Variety of foolish apparitions people his head;
they suffer him not to breathe according to the necessities
of nature, which makes him sup up a draught of as much
air at once as would serve at thrice. He denies nature her
due in sleep, and overpays her with watchfulness. Nothing
pleaseth him long but that which pleaseth his own fantasies;
they are the consuming evils and evil consumptions that
consume him alive. Lastly he is a man only in show, but
comes short of the better part: a whole reasonable soul,

which is a man's chief pre-eminence and sole mark from creatures sensible.

Characters, 1614

ROBERT BURTON

[The Dangers of Idleness]

IN A commonwealth where there is no public enemy, there is, likely, civil wars, and they rage upon themselves. This body of ours, when it is idle and knows not how to bestow itself, macerates [*wastes away*] and vexeth itself with cares, griefs, false fears, discontents and suspicions; it tortures and preys upon his own bowels and is never at rest. Thus much I dare boldly say: he or she that is idle, be they of what condition they will, never so rich, so well allied, fortunate, happy, let them have all things in abundance and felicity that heart can wish and desire, all contentment, so long as he or she or they are idle they shall never be pleased, never well in body and mind, but weary still, sickly still, vexed still, loathing still, weeping, sighing, grieving, suspecting, offended with the world, with every object, wishing themselves gone or dead, or else carried away with some foolish fantasy or other. And this is the true cause that so many great men, ladies and gentlewomen labour of this disease in country and city; for idleness is an appendix to nobility, they count it a disgrace to work, and spend all their days in sports, recreations and pastimes, and will therefore take no pains, be of no vocation. They feed liberally, fare well, want exercise, action, employment (for to work, I say, they may not abide), and company to their desires, and thence their bodies become full of gross humours, wind, crudities, their minds disquieted, dull, heavy, etc. Care, jealousy, fear of some diseases, sullen fits, weeping fits seize too familiarly on them. For what will not fear and fantasy work in an idle body? What distempers will they not cause? When the

Children of Israel murmured against Pharaoh in Egypt, he commanded his officers to double their task and let them get straw themselves and yet make their full number of bricks; for the sole cause why they mutiny and are evil at ease is *they are idle.* When you shall hear and see so many discontented persons in all places where you come, so many several [*different*] grievances, unnecessary complaints, fears, suspicions, the best means to redress it is to set them awork, so to busy their minds; for the truth is they are idle. Well they may build castles in the air for a time, and soothe up themselves with fantastical and pleasant humours, but in the end they will prove as bitter as gall; they shall be still, I say, discontent, suspicious, fearful, jealous, sad, fretting and vexing of themselves; so long as they be idle, it is impossible to please them.

[Love's Power]

A YOUNG gentleman of Rome, the same day that he was married, after dinner with the bride and his friends went a-walking into the fields, and towards evening to the tennis-court to recreate himself. Whilst he played, he put his ring upon the finger of Venus' *statua*, which was thereby, made in brass. After he had sufficiently played, and now made an end of his sport, he came to fetch his ring; but Venus had bowed her finger in, and he could not get it off. Whereupon, loath to make his company tarry at present, there he left it, intending to fetch it the next day or at some more convenient time; went thence to supper, and so to bed. In the night, when he should come to perform those nuptial rites, Venus steps between him and his wife (unseen or felt of her) and told him that she was his wife, that he had betrothed himself unto her by that ring which he put upon her finger. She troubled him for some following nights. He, not knowing how to help himself, made his moan to one Palumbus, a learned magician in those days, who gave him a letter and bid him at such a time of the night, in such

a crossway at the town's end where old Saturn would pass
by with his associates in procession, as he commonly did,
deliver that script with his own hands to Saturn himself. The
young man, of a bold spirit, accordingly did it; and when
the old fiend had read it he called Venus to him, who rode
before him, and commanded her to deliver his ring, which
she forthwith did, and so the gentleman was freed.

The Anatomy of Melancholy, What It Is.
With All the Kinds, Causes, Symptoms,
Prognostics, and Several Cures of It . . ., 1621

JOHN DONNE

['No Man is an Island']

Now, this bell tolling softly for another says to me, 'Thou
must die'.

PERCHANCE HE for whom this bell tolls may be so ill as
that he knows not it tolls for him; and perchance I may
think myself so much better than I am, as that they who are
about me, and see my state, may have caused it to toll for
me, and I know not that. The Church is catholic, universal,
and so are all her actions; all that she does belongs to all.
When she baptises a child, that action concerns me; for that
child is thereby connected to that head which is my head,
too, and engrafted into that body whereof I am a member.
And when she buries a man that action concerns me. All
mankind is of one author and is one volume. When one
man dies, one chapter is not torn out of the book, but
translated into a better language; and every chapter must be
so translated. God employs several translators. Some pieces
are translated by age, some by sickness, some by war, some
by justice; but God's hand is in every translation, and His
hand shall bind up all our scattered leaves again for that
library where every book shall lie open to one another. As

therefore the bell that rings to a sermon calls not upon the preacher only, but upon the congregation to come, so this bell calls us all; but how much more me, who am brought so near the door by this sickness. There was a contention as far as a suit (in which both piety and dignity, religion and estimation were mingled) which of the religious orders should ring to prayers first in the morning; and it was determined that they should ring first that rose earliest. If we understand aright the dignity of this bell that tolls for our evening prayer, we would be glad to make it ours by rising early, in that application, that it might be ours as well as his whose indeed it is. The bell doth toll for him that thinks it doth; and though it intermit again, yet from that minute that that occasion wrought upon him he is united to God. Who casts not up his eye to the sun when it rises, but who takes off his eye from a comet when that breaks out? Who bends not his ear to any bell which upon any occasion rings, but who can remove it from that bell which is passing a piece of himself out of this world? No man is an island, entire of itself; every man is a piece of the continent, a part of the main. If a clod be washed away by the sea, Europe is the less, as well as if a promontory were, as well as if a manor of thy friends or of thine own were. Any man's death diminishes me, because I am involved in mankind. And therefore never send to know for whom the bell tolls; it tolls for *thee*.

Devotions upon Emergent Occasions, 1624

JOHN EARLE

A Pretender to Learning

I s one that would make all others more fools than himself, for though he know nothing he would not have the world know so much. He conceits nothing in learning but the opinion, which he seeks to purchase without it, though he might with less labour cure his ignorance than hide it. He is indeed a kind of scholar-mountebank, and his art our delusion. He is tricked out in all the accoutrements of learning, and at the first encounter none passes better. He is oftener in his study than at his book, and you cannot pleasure him better than to deprehend [call unannounced upon] him. Yet he hears you not till the third knock, and then comes out very angry, as interrupted. You find him in his slippers and a pen in his ear, in which formality he was asleep. His table is spread wide with some classic folio, which is as constant to it as the carpet, and hath laid open in the same page this half year. His candle is always a longer sitter-up than himself, and the boast of his window at midnight. He walks much alone in the posture of medi-tation, and has a book still before his face in the fields. His pocket is seldom without a Greek Testament or Hebrew Bible, which he opens only in the church, and that when some stander-by looks over. He has his sentences for company, some scatterings of Seneca and Tacitus, which are good upon all occasions. If he read anything in the morning, it comes up all at dinner; and as long as that lasts the discourse is his. He is a great plagiary of tavern wit, and comes to sermons only that he may talk of Austin [Augus-tine]. His parcels are the mere scrapings from company, yet he complains at parting what time he has lost. He is wondrously capricious to seem a judgement, and listens with a sour attention to what he understands not. He talks much of Scaliger, and Casaubon, and the Jesuits, and prefers some unheard-of Dutch names before them all. He has verses to bring in upon these and these hints, and it shall go hard but he will wind in his opportunity. He is critical in a language he cannot construe, and speaks seldom under Arminius in divinity. His business and retirement and caller-away is his study, and he protests no delight to it compar-able. He is a great nomenclator of authors, which he has read in general in the catalogue, and in particular in the title, and goes seldom so far as the dedication. He never talks of anything but learning, and learns all from talking. Three encounters with the same men pump him, and then he only puts in or gravely says nothing. He has taken pains

to be an ass, though not to be a scholar, and is at length
discovered and laughed at.

Microcosmography; or,
A Piece of the World Discovered, 1628

BEN JONSON

[William Shakespeare]

I REMEMBER, the players have often mentioned it as an
honour to Shakespeare that in his writing, whatsoever he
penned, he never blotted out line. My answer hath been,
would he had blotted a thousand; which they thought a
malevolent speech. I had not told posterity this, but for
their ignorance, who choose that circumstance to commend
their friend by, wherein he most faulted; and to justify mine
own candour (for I loved the man, and do honour his
memory – on this side idolatry – as much as any). He was
indeed honest, and of an open and free nature; had an
excellent fancy, brave notions and gentle expressions –
wherein he flowed with that facility that sometime it was
necessary he should be stopped: *sufflaminandus erat* ['*he
needs to be checked*'], as Augustus said of Haterius. His wit
was in his own power. Would the rule of it had been so,
too. Many times he fell into those things could not escape
laughter – as when he said in the person of Caesar, one
speaking to him: 'Caesar, thou dost me wrong.' He replied,
'Caesar did never wrong, but with just cause,' and such like,
which were ridiculous. But he redeemed his vices with his
virtues. There was ever more in him to be praised than to
be pardoned.

Timber; or, Discoveries, 1640

EDWARD, LORD HERBERT OF CHERBURY

[Fencing]

THE NEXT exercise a young man should learn (but not before he is eleven or twelve years of age) is fencing; for the attaining of which the Frenchman's rule is excellent, *bon pied bon œil*, by which to teach men how far they may stretch out their feet when they would make a thrust against their enemy, lest either should overstride themselves or, not striding far enough, fail to bring the point of their weapon home. The second part of his direction adviseth the scholar to keep a fixed eye upon the point of his enemy's sword, to the intent he may both put by or ward the blows and thrusts made against him, and together direct the point of his sword upon some part of his enemy that lieth naked and open to him.

The good fencing masters, in France especially, when they present a foil, or fleuret, to their scholars, tell him it hath two parts, one of which he calleth the fort or strong, and the other the foible or weak. With the fort or strong, which extends from the part of the hilt next the sword about a third part of the whole length, thereof he teacheth his scholars to defend themselves, and put by and ward the thrusts and blows of his enemy, and with the other two-third parts to strike or thrust as he shall see occasion; which rule also teacheth how to strike or thrust high or low as his enemy doth, and briefly to take his measure and time upon his adversary's motions, whereby he may both defend himself or offend his adversary, of which I have had much experiment and use both in the fleuret, or foil, as also when I fought in earnest with many persons at one and the same time, as will appear in the sequel of my life. And, indeed, I think I shall not speak vaingloriously of myself if I say that no man understood the use of his weapon better than I did, or hath more dexterously prevailed himself thereof on all

occasions; since I found no man could be hurt but through
some error in fencing.

The Life of Lord Herbert of Cherbury,
Written by Himself,
first published 1765, written *c.*1643

SIR THOMAS BROWNE

[Witchcraft]

I HAVE ever believed, and do now know, that there are
witches. They that doubt of these do not only deny them,
but spirits; and they are obliquely and upon consequence a
sort, not of infidels, but atheists. Those that to confute their
incredulity desire to see apparitions shall questionless never
behold any, nor have the power to be so much as witches;
the Devil hath them already in a heresy as capital as
witchcraft, and to appear to them were but to convert them.
Of all the delusions wherewith he deceives mortality, there
is not any that puzzleth me more than the legerdemain of
changelings. I do not credit those transformations of reasonable creatures into beasts, or that the Devil hath a power to
transpeciate a man into a horse, who tempted Christ (as a
trial of His divinity) to convert but stones into bread. I could
believe that spirits use with man the act of carnality, and
that in both sexes; I conceive they may assume, steal or
contrive a body wherein there may be action enough to
content decrepit lust, or passion to satisfy more active
veneries [*sexual desires*], yet in both without a possibility of
generation; and therefore that opinion that Antichrist
should be born of the Tribe of Dan by conjunction with the
Devil is ridiculous, and a conceit fitter for a rabbin than a
Christian. I hold that the Devil doth really possess some
men, the spirit of melancholy others, the spirit of delusion
others; that as the Devil is concealed and denied by some,
so God and good angels are pretended by others, whereof

the late defection of the Maid of Germany [*who claimed to have fasted for thirty years*] hath left a pregnant example.

Again, I believe that all that use sorceries, incantations and spells are not witches or, as we term them, magicians. I conceive there is a traditional magic, not learned immediately from the Devil, but at second hand from his scholars; who, having once the secret betrayed, are able and do empirically practise without his advice, they both proceeding upon the principles of nature: where actives [*heat and cold*] aptly conjoined to disposed passives [*moisture and dryness*], will under any master produce their effects. Thus I think at first a great part of philosophy was witchcraft, which being afterward derived to one another proved but philosophy, and was indeed no more but the honest effects of nature. What invented by us is philosophy, learned from him is magic. We do surely owe the discovery of many secrets to the discovery of good and bad angels.

Religio Medici, 1643

[Immortality]

IN VAIN do individuals hope for immortality, or any patent from oblivion, in preservations below the Moon. Men have been deceived even in their flatteries above the Sun, and studied conceits to perpetuate their names in heaven. The various cosmography of that part hath already varied the names of contrived constellations: Nimrod is lost in Orion, and Osiris in the Dog Star. While we look for incorruption in the heavens, we find they are but like the Earth: durable in their main bodies, alterable in their parts; whereof, beside comets and new stars, perspectives [*telescopes*] begin to tell tales. And the spots that wander about the Sun, with Phaeton's favour, would make clear conviction.

There is nothing strictly immortal but immortality; whatever hath no beginning may be confident of no end. All others have a dependent being, and within the reach of destruction, which is the peculiar of that necessary essence that cannot destroy itself; and the highest strain of omnipotency to be so powerfully constituted as not to suffer even from the power of itself. But the sufficiency of Christian immortality frustrates all earthly glory, and the quality of either state after death makes a folly of posthumous memory. God who can only destroy our souls, and hath assured our resurrection, either of our bodies or names hath directly promised no duration. Wherein there is so much of chance that the boldest expectants have found unhappy frustration; and to hold long subsistence seems but a scape in oblivion. But man is a noble animal, splendid in ashes and pompous in the grave, solemnising nativities and deaths with equal lustre, nor omitting ceremonies of bravery in the infamy of his nature.

Life is a pure flame, and we live by an invisible sun within us. A small fire sufficeth for life, great flames seemed too little after death, while men vainly affected precious pyres and to burn like Sardanapalus, but the wisdom of funeral laws found the folly of prodigal blazes and reduced undoing fires unto the rule of sober obsequies, wherein few could be so mean as not to provide wood, pitch, a mourner and an urn.

Five languages secured not the epitaph of Gordianus; the man of God lives longer without a tomb than any by one, invisibly interred by angels, and adjudged to obscurity, though not without some marks directing human discovery. Enoch and Elias without either tomb or burial, in an anomalous state of being, are the great examples of perpetuity, in their long and living memory, in strict account being still on this side death, and having a late part yet to act upon this stage of Earth. If in the decretory term of the world [the Last Judgement] we shall not all die but be changed, according to received translation, the last day will make but few graves. At least, quick resurrections will anticipate lasting sepultures; some graves will be opened before they be quite closed, and Lazarus be no wonder. When many that feared to die shall groan that they can die but once, the dismal state is the second and living death,

when life puts despair on the damned; when men shall wish
the coverings of mountains, not of monuments, and annihilation shall be courted.

Hydriotaphia: Urn-Burial . . ., 1658

JOHN MILTON

[Shaping the Young Men of England]

THEREFORE, ABOUT an hour and a half ere they eat at
noon should be allowed them for exercise, and due rest
afterwards; but the time for this may be enlarged at
pleasure, according as their rising in the morning shall be
early. The exercise which I command first is the exact use of
their weapon [*sword*], to guard, and to strike safely with
edge or point. This will keep them healthy, nimble, strong,
and well in breath; is also the likeliest means to make them
grow large and tall, and to inspire them with a gallant and
fearless courage; which, being tempered with seasonable
lectures and precepts to make them of true fortitude and
patience, will turn into a native and heroic valour, and make
them hate the cowardice of doing wrong. They must be also
practised in all the locks and grips of wrestling, wherein
Englishmen are wont to excel, as need may often be in fight
to tug, to grapple, and to close. And this, perhaps, will be
enough wherein to prove and heat their single strength.

The interim of unsweating themselves regularly, and
convenient rest before meat, may both with profit and
delight be taken up in recreating and composing their
travailed spirits with the solemn and divine harmonies of
music heard or learned either whilst the skilful organist plies
his grave and fancied [*fanciful*] descant in lofty fugues, or
the whole symphony with artful and unimaginable touches
adorn and grace the well-studied chords of some choice
composer; sometimes the lute or soft organ-stop, waiting on
elegant voices either to religious, martial, or civil ditties,

which, if wise men and prophets be not extremely out, have a great power over dispositions and manners to smooth and make them gentle from rustic harshness and distempered passions. The like would also not be unexpedient after meat, to assist and cherish nature in her first concoction, and send their minds back to study in good tune and satisfaction.

Where having followed it under vigilant eyes until about two hours before supper, they are, by a sudden alarum or watchword, to be called out on their military motions, under sky or covert, according to the season, as was the Roman wont; first on foot, then, as their age permits, on horseback to all the art of cavalry; that having in sport, but with much exactness and daily muster, served out the rudiments of their soldiership in all the skill of embattling, marching, encamping, fortifying, besieging, and battering, with all the helps of ancient and modern stratagems, tactics, and warlike maxims, they may, as it were out of a long war, come forth renowned and perfect commanders in the service of their country.

They would not then, if they were trusted with fair and hopeful armies, suffer them for want of just and wise discipline to shed away from about them like sick feathers, though they be never so oft supplied; they would not suffer their empty and unrecruitable colonels of twenty men in a company to quaff out or convey into secret hoards the wages of a delusive list and miserable remnant; yet in the meanwhile to be overmastered with a score or two of drunkards, the only soldiery left about them, or else to comply with all rapines and violences. No, certainly, if they knew aught of that knowledge which belongs to good men or good governors, they would not suffer these things.

But to return to our own institute. Besides these constant exercises at home, there is another opportunity of gaining experience to be won from pleasure itself abroad: in those vernal seasons of the year, when the air is calm and pleasant, it were an injury and sullenness against nature not to go out and see her riches and partake in her rejoicing with heaven and earth. I should not, therefore, be a persuader of them of studying much then, after two or three years that they have well laid their grounds, but to ride out in companies with prudent and staid guides to all the quarters of the land, learning and observing all places of strength, all commodities of building and of soil for towns and tillage, harbours, and ports for trade. Sometimes taking sea as far as to our navy, to learn there also what they can in the practical knowledge of sailing and sea-fight.

These ways would try all their peculiar gifts of nature, and if there were any secret excellence among them, would fetch it out and give it fair opportunity to advance itself by, which could not but mightily redound to the good of this nation, and bring into fashion again those old admired virtues and excellences, with far more advantage now in this purity of Christian knowledge.

Nor shall we then need the monsieurs of Paris to take our hopeful youth into their slight and prodigal custodies, and send them over back again transformed into mimics, apes, and kickshaws [*comic grotesques*].

Of Education, 1644

[Censorship]

IF WE think to regulate printing, thereby to rectify manners, we must regulate all recreations and pastimes, all that is delightful to man. No music must be heard, no song be set or sung, but what is grave and Doric. There must be licensing dancers, that no gesture, motion, or deportment be taught our youth but what by their allowance shall be thought honest; for such Plato was provided of. It will ask more than the work of twenty licensers to examine all the lutes, the violins, and the guitars in every house; they must not be suffered to prattle as they do, but must be licensed what they may say. And who shall silence all the airs and madrigals that whisper softness in chambers? The windows also, and the balconies, must be thought on; there are shrewd books, with dangerous frontispieces, set to sale: who shall prohibit them, shall twenty licensers? The villages also must have their visitors to inquire what lectures the bagpipe and rebeck reads, even to the balladry and the gamut of every municipal fiddler; for these are the countryman's Arcadias, and his Montemayors. Next, what more national corruption, for which England hears ill abroad, than household gluttony? Who shall be the rectors of our daily rioting? And what shall be done to inhibit the multitudes that frequent those houses where drunkenness is sold and harboured? Our garments also should be referred to the licensing of some more sober work-masters, to see them cut into a less wanton garb. Who shall regulate all the mixed conversation of our youth, male and female together, as is the fashion of this country? Who shall still appoint what shall be discoursed, what presumed, and no further? Lastly, who shall forbid and separate all idle resort, all evil company? These things will be, and must be; but how they shall be least hurtful, how least enticing, herein consists the grave and governing wisdom of a state. To sequester out of the world into Atlantic and Utopian polities, which never can be drawn into use, will not mend our condition; but to ordain wisely as in this world of evil, in the midst whereof God hath placed us unavoidably. Nor is it Plato's licensing of books will do this, which necessarily pulls along with it so many other kinds of licensing, as will make us all both ridiculous and weary, and yet frustrate; but those unwritten, or at least unconstraining, laws of virtuous education, religious and civil nurture, which Plato there mentions as the bonds and ligaments of the commonwealth, the pillars and the sustainers of every written statute; these they be, which will bear chief sway in such matters as these, when all licensing will be easily eluded. Impunity and remissness for certain are the bane of a commonwealth; but here the great art lies, to discern in what the law is to bid restraint and punishment, and in what things persuasion only is to work.

Areopagitica, 1644

THOMAS HOBBES

[The Natural Condition of Mankind]

NATURE HATH made men so equal in the faculties of body and mind as that, though there be found one man sometimes manifestly stronger in body or of quicker mind than another, yet when all is reckoned together the difference between man and man is not so considerable as that one man can thereupon claim to himself any benefit to which another may not pretend as well as he. For, as to the strength of body, the weakest has strength enough to kill the strongest, either by secret machination or by confederacy with others that are in the same danger with himself.

And, as to the faculties of the mind (setting aside the arts grounded upon words, and especially that skill of proceeding upon general and infallible rules, called science, which very few have, and but in few things, as being not a native faculty, born with us, nor attained, as prudence, while we look after somewhat else), I find yet a greater equality amongst men than that of strength. For prudence is but experience, which equal time equally bestows on all men in those things they equally apply themselves unto. That which may perhaps make such equality incredible is but a vain conceit of one's own wisdom, which almost all men think they have in greater degree than the vulgar; that is, than all men but themselves and a few others whom by fame or for concurring with themselves they approve. For such is the nature of men that, howsoever they may acknowledge many others to be more witty, or more eloquent, or more learned, yet they will hardly believe there be many so wise as themselves; for they see their own wit at hand and other men's at a distance. But this proveth rather that men are in that point equal than unequal. For there is not ordinarily a greater sign of the equal distribution of any thing than that every man is contented with his share.

From this equality of ability ariseth equality of hope in the attaining of our ends. And therefore if any two men desire the same thing, which nevertheless they cannot both enjoy, they become enemies; and in the way to their end (which is principally their own conservation, and sometimes their delectation only) endeavour to destroy or subdue one another. And from hence it comes to pass that, where an invader hath no more to fear than another man's single power, if one plant, sow, build or possess a convenient seat others may probably be expected to come prepared with forces united, to dispossess and deprive him not only of the fruit of his labour, but also of his life or liberty. And the invader, again, is in the like danger of another.

And from this diffidence of one another there is no way for any man to secure himself so reasonable as anticipation; that is, by force or wiles to master the persons of all men he can, so long till he see no other power great enough to endanger him – and this is no more than his own conservation requireth, and is generally allowed. And because there be some that, taking pleasure in contemplating their own power in the acts of conquest, which they pursue farther than their security requires; if others, that otherwise would be glad to be at ease within modest bounds, should not by invasion increase their power they would not be able, long time, by standing only on their defence, to subsist. And, by consequence, such augmentation of dominion over men, being necessary to a man's conservation, it ought to be allowed him.

Again, men have no pleasure (but on the contrary a great deal of grief) in keeping company where there is no power able to overawe them all. For every man looketh that his companion should value him at the same rate he sets upon himself; and upon all signs of contempt or undervaluing naturally endeavours, as far as he dares (which amongst them that have no common power to keep them in quiet is far enough to make them destroy each other), to extort a greater value from his contemners by damage and from others by the example.

So that in the nature of man we find three principal causes of quarrel. First, competition; secondly, diffidence; thirdly, glory.

The first maketh man invade for gain; the second for

safety; and the third for reputation. The first use violence to make themselves masters of other men's persons, wives, children and cattle; the second to defend them; the third for trifles, as a word, a smile, a different opinion, and any other sign of undervalue, either direct in their persons or by reflection in their kindred, their friends, their nation, their profession or their name.

Hereby it is manifest that during the time men live without a common power to keep them all in awe they are in that condition which is called war; and such a war as is of every man against every man. For war consisteth not in battle only, or the act of fighting, but in a tract of time wherein the will to contend by battle is sufficiently known; and therefore the notion of *time* is to be considered in the nature of war as it is in the nature of weather. For as the nature of foul weather lieth not in a shower or two of rain, but in an inclination thereto of many days together; so the nature of war consisteth not in actual fighting, but in the known disposition thereto during all the time there is no assurance to the contrary. All other time is peace.

Whatsoever therefore is consequent to a time of war, where every man is enemy to every man, the same is consequent to the time wherein men live without other security than what their own strength and their own invention shall furnish them withal. In such condition, there is no place for industry, because the fruit thereof is uncertain; and consequently no culture of the earth, no navigation nor use of the commodities that may be imported by the sea, no commodious building, no instruments of moving and removing such things as require much force, no knowledge of the face of the earth, no account of time, no arts, no letters, no society – and, which is worst of all, continual fear, and danger of violent death; and the life of man solitary, poor, nasty, brutish and short.

Leviathan; or, The Matter, Form and
Power of a Commonwealth, 1651

GEORGE HERBERT

The Parson's Life

THE COUNTRY parson is exceeding exact in his life, being holy, just, prudent, temperate, bold, grave in all his ways. And because the two highest points of life wherein a Christian is most seen are patience and mortification – patience in regard of afflictions, mortification in regard of lusts and affections, and the stupefying and deading of all the clamorous powers of the soul – therefore he hath thoroughly studied these, that he may be an absolute master and commander of himself for all the purposes which God hath ordained him. Yet in these points he labours most in those things which are most apt to scandalize his parish. And, first, because country people live hardly, and therefore as feeling their own sweat, and consequently knowing the price of money, are offended much with any who by hard usage increase their travail, the country parson is very circumspect in avoiding all covetousness, neither being greedy to get, nor niggardly to keep, nor troubled to lose any worldly worth; but in all his words and actions slighting and disesteeming it, even to a wondering that the world should so much value wealth, which in the day of wrath hath not one dram of comfort for us. Secondly, because luxury is a very visible sin, the parson is very careful to avoid all kinds thereof, but especially that of drinking, because it is the most popular vice; into which if he come, *he prostitutes himself* both to shame and sin, and by having *fellowship with the unfruitful works of darkness* he disableth himself of authority *to reprove them*. For sins make all equal whom they find together; and then they are worst who ought to be best. Neither is it for the servant of Christ to haunt inns and taverns or alehouses *to the dishonour of his person and office*. The parson doth not so, but orders his life in such a fashion that when death takes him, as the Jews and Judas did Christ, he may say as He did, *I sat daily with you teaching in the Temple*. Thirdly, because country people (as

indeed all honest men) do much esteem their word, it being
the life of buying and selling and dealing in the world,
therefore the parson is very strict in keeping his word, though
it be to his own hindrance, as knowing that if he be not so he
will quickly be discovered and disregarded; neither will they
believe him in the pulpit whom they cannot trust in conversation. As for oaths and apparel, the disorders thereof are
also very manifest. The parson's yea is yea, and nay nay;
and his apparel plain but reverend, and clean, without spots
or dust or smell, the purity of his mind breaking out and
dilating itself even to his body, clothes and habitation.

The Priest to His Temple;
or, The Country Parson, 1652

IZAAK WALTON

[Fishing for Eels]

IT IS granted by all or most men that eels, for about six
months, that is to say the six cold months of the year, stir
not up or down, neither in the rivers nor in the pools in
which they usually are, but get into the soft earth or mud;
and there many of them together bed themselves, and live
without feeding upon anything, as I have told you some
swallows have been observed to do in hollow trees, for
those six cold months. And this the eel and swallow do, as
not being able to endure winter weather; for Gesner quotes
Albertus to say that in the year 1125, that year's winter
being more cold than usually, eels did, by nature's instinct,
get out of the water into a stack of hay in a meadow upon
dry ground, and there bedded themselves; but yet, at last, a
frost killed them. And our Camden relates that, in Lancashire, fishes were digged out of the earth with spades where
no water was near to the place. I shall say little more of the
eel but that, as it is observed he is impatient of cold, so it

hath been observed that in warm weather an eel has been known to live five days out of the water.

And lastly let me tell you that some curious searchers into the natures of fish observe that there be several sorts or kinds of eels: as the silver eel, the green or greenish eel, with which the river of Thames abounds, and those are called grigs; and a blackish eel, whose head is more flat and bigger than ordinary eels; and also an eel whose fins are reddish, and but seldom taken in this nation, and yet taken sometimes. These several kind of eels are, some say, diversely bred: as, namely, out of the corruption of the earth, and some by dew, and other ways, as I have said to you; and yet it is affirmed by some for a certain that the silver eel is bred by generation, but not by spawning as other fish do, but that her brood come alive from her, being then little live eels no bigger nor longer than a pin; and I have had too many testimonies of this to doubt the truth of it myself; and if I thought it needful I might prove it, but I think it is needless.

And this eel, of which I have said so much to you, may be caught with divers kinds of baits: as, namely, with powdered beef; with a lob or garden worm; with a minnow; or gut of a hen, chicken, or the guts of any fish; or with almost anything, for he is a greedy fish. But the eel may be caught especially with a little, a very little lamprey, which some call a pride, and may in the hot months be found many of them in the River Thames and in many mud-heaps in other rivers; yea, almost as usually as one finds worms in a dunghill.

Next note that the eel seldom stirs in the day, but then hides himself; and therefore he is usually caught by night, with one of these baits of which I have spoken; and may be then caught by laying hooks, which you are to fasten to the bank or twigs of a tree; or by throwing a string across the stream with many hooks at it, and those baited with the aforesaid baits; and a clod, or plummet, or stone, thrown into the river with this line, that so you may in the morning find it near to some fixed place, and then take it up with a drag-hook or otherwise. But these things are, indeed, too common to be spoken of; and an hour's fishing with any angler will teach you better, both for these and many other common things in the practical art of angling, than a week's discourse. I shall therefore conclude this direction for taking the eel by telling you that in a warm day in summer I have taken many a good eel by sniggling, and have been much pleased with that sport.

And because you, that are but a young angler, know not what sniggling is, I will now teach it to you. You remember I told you that eels do not usually stir in the daytime, for then they hide themselves under some covert, or under boards or planks about flood-gates or weirs or mills, or in holes on the riverbanks; so that you, observing your time in a warm day, when the water is lowest, may take a strong small hook, tied to a strong line or to a string about a yard long; and then into one of these holes, or between any boards about a mill, or under any great stone or plank, or any place where you think an eel may hide or shelter herself, you may, with the help of a short stick, put in your bait, but leisurely, and as far as you may conveniently; and it is scarce to be doubted, but if there be an eel within the sight of it, the eel will bite instantly and as certainly gorge it; and you need not doubt to have him if you pull him not out of the hole too quickly, but pull him out by degrees; for he, lying folded double in his hole, will, with the help of his tail, break all, unless you give him time to be wearied with pulling, and so get him out by degrees, not pulling too hard.

The Compleat Angler, 1653

DOROTHY OSBORNE

['An Inconsiderate Passion']

Sir,
I am extremely sorry that your letter miscarried but I am confident my b[rother] has it not. As cunning as he is, he

could not hide it so from me, but that I should discover it some way or other. No, he was here, and both his men, when this letter should have come, and not one of them stirred out that day; indeed, the next day they went all to London. The note you writ to Jane came in one of Nan's by Collins, but nothing else. It must be lost by the porter that was sent with it, and 'twas very unhappy that there should be anything in it of more consequence than ordinary; it may be numbered amongst the rest of our misfortunes, all which an inconsiderate passion has occasioned. You must pardon me, I cannot be reconciled to it; 't has been the ruin of us both. 'Tis true that nobody must imagine to themselves ever to be absolute masters on't, but there is great difference betwixt that and yielding to it, between striving with it and soothing it up till it grows too strong for one. Can I remember how ignorantly and innocently I suffered it to steal upon me by degrees? How under a mask of friendship I cozened myself into that which, had it appeared to me at first in its true shape, I had feared and shunned? Can I discern that it has made the trouble of your life, and cast a cloud upon mine that will help to cover me in my grave? Can I know that it wrought so upon us both as to make neither of us friends to one another, but agree in running wildly to our own destruction and perhaps of some more innocent persons who might live to curse our folly that gave them so miserable a being? Ah, if you love yourself or me, you must confess that I have reason to condemn this senseless passion that wheresoe'er it comes destroys all that entertain it, nothing of judgement or discretion can live with it, and puts everything else out of order before it can find a place for itself. What has it not brought my poor Lady Anne Blount to? She is the talk of all the footmen and boys in the street, and will be company for them shortly, who yet is so blinded by her passion as not at all to perceive the misery she has brought herself to; and this fond love of hers has so rooted all sense of nature out of her heart that they say she is no more moved than a statue with the affliction of a father and mother that doted on her and had placed the comfort of their lives in her preferment. With all this, is it not manifest to the whole world that Mr Blount could not consider anything in this action but his own interest, and that he makes her a very ill return for all her kindness? If he had loved her truly, he would have died rather than have been the occasion of this misfortune to her.

My cousin [Elizabeth] Fr[anklin] (as you observe very well) may say fine things now she is warm in Moor Park, but she is very much altered in her opinions since her marriage, if these be her own. She left a gentleman that I could name whom she had much more of kindness for than ever she had for Mr Fr[anklin] because his estate was less, and upon the discovery of some letters that her mother intercepted suffered herself to be persuaded that twenty-three hundred pound a year was better than twelve, though with a person she loved, and has recovered it so well that you see she confesses there is nothing in her condition she desires to alter at the charge of a wish. She's happier by much than I shall ever be, but I do not envy her. May she long enjoy it, and I an early and quiet grave, free from the trouble of this busy world, where all with passion pursue their own interests at their neighbours' charges, where nobody is pleased but somebody complains on't, and where 'tis impossible to be without giving and receiving injuries. You would know what I would be at, and how I intend to dispose of myself. Alas, were I in my own disposal, you should come to my grave to be resolved; but grief alone will not kill. All that I can say, then, is that I resolve on nothing but to arm myself with patience, to resist nothing that is laid upon me, nor struggle for what I have no hope to get. I have no ends nor no designs, nor will my heart ever be capable of any; but, like a country wasted by a civil war, where two opposing parties have disputed their right so long till they have made it worth neither of their conquests, 'tis ruined and desolated by the long strife within it to that degree as 'twill be useful to none, nobody that knows the condition 'tis in will think it worth the gaining, and I shall not cozen anybody with it. No, really, if I may be permitted to desire anything, it shall be only that I may injure nobody but myself. I can bear anything that reflects only upon me – or, if I cannot, I can die; but I would fain die innocent that

I might hope to be happy in the next world though never in this.

I take it a little ill that you should conjure me by anything, with a belief that 'tis more powerful with me than your kindness. No, assure yourself what that alone cannot gain will be denied to all the world. You would see me, you say. You may do so if you please, though I know not to what end. You deceive yourself if you think it would prevail upon me to alter my intentions. Besides, I can make no contrivances; all must be here, and I just endure the noise it will make and undergo the censures of a people that choose ever to give the worst interpretation that anything will bear. Yet, if it can be any ease to you to make me more miserable than I am, never spare me. Consider yourself only and not me at all; 'tis no more than I deserve for not accepting what you offered me whilst 'twas in your power to make it good, as you say it then was. You were prepared, it seems; but I was surprised, I confess it. 'Twas a kind fault, though, and you may pardon it with more reason than I have to forgive it myself. And let me tell you this, too: as lost and as wretched as I am, I have still some sense of my reputation left in me. I find that to my last I shall attempt to preserve it as clear as I can; and to do that I must, if you see me thus, make it the last of our interviews. What can excuse me if I should entertain any person that is known to pretend to me, when I can have no hope of ever marrying him, and what hope can I have of that when the fortune that can only make it possible to me depends upon a thousand accidents and contingencies: the uncertainty of the place 'tis in, and the government it may fall under, your father's life, or his success, his disposal of himself and then of his fortune, besides the time that I must necessarily be required to produce all this, and the changes that may proba[bly] bring with it which 'tis impossible for us to foresee. All this considered, what have I to say for myself when people shall ask what 'tis I expect? Can there be anything vainer than such a [hope?] upon such grounds? You must needs see the folly on't yourself, and therefore examine your own heart what 'tis fit for me to do, and what you can do for a person you love and that deserves your compassion if nothing else: a person that will always have an inviolable friendship for you, a friendship that shall take up all the room my passion held in my heart and govern there as master till death come to take possession and turn it out. Why should you make an impossibility where there is none? A thousand accidents might have taken me from you, and you must have borne it. Why should not your own resolution work as much upon you as necessity and time does infallibly upon all people? Your father would take it very ill, I believe, if you should pretend to love me better than he did my Lady; yet she is dead, and he lives and perhaps may do to love again. There is a gentlewoman in this country that loved so passionately for six or seven years that her friends who kept her from marrying, fearing her death, consented to it; and within half a year her husband died, which afflicted her so strongly nobody thought she would have lived. She saw no light but candles in three year nor came abroad in five, and now that 'tis some nine years past she is passionately taken again with another, and how long she has been so nobody knows but herself. This is to let you see 'tis not impossible what I ask, nor unreasonable. Think on't and attempt it at least, but do it sincerely and do not help your passion to master you. As you have ever loved me, do this. The carrier shall bring your letters to Suffolk House to Jones [the saddler]. I shall long to hear from you; but, if you should deny me the only hope that's left me, I must beg you will defer it till Christmas Day be past – for, to deal freely with you, I have some devotions to perform then which must not be disturbed with anything, and nothing is like to do it so much as so sensible an affliction. Adieu.

Letter to Sir William Temple,
17/18 December 1653

JOHN EVELYN

[A Whale]

[*3 June 1658*] A large whale was taken betwixt my land butting on the Thames and Greenwich, which drew an infinite concourse to see it, by water, coach and on foot, from London and all parts. It appeared first below Greenwich at low water, for at high water it would have destroyed all the boats, but lying now in shallow water encompassed with boats after a long conflict it was killed with a harping iron [*harpoon*], struck in the head, out of which spouted blood and water by two tunnels, and after an horrid groan it ran quite on shore and died. Its length was fifty-eight foot, height sixteen; black-skinned like coach leather, very small eyes, great tail, only two small fins, a picked [*tapering*] snout, and a mouth so wide that divers men might have stood upright in it; no teeth, but sucked the slime only as through a grate of that bone which we call whalebone; the throat yet so narrow as would not have admitted the least of fishes. The extremes of the cetaceous bones hang downwards from the upper jaw, and was hairy towards the ends and bottom within side: all of it prodigious, but in nothing more wonderful than that an animal of so great a bulk should be nourished only by slime through those grates.

[The City Ravaged by Fire]

[*7 September 1666*] I went this morning on foot from Whitehall as far as London Bridge, through the late Fleet Street, Ludgate Hill, by St Paul's, Cheapside, Exchange, Bishopsgate, Aldersgate, and out to Moorfields, thence through Cornhill, etc., with extraordinary difficulty, clambering over heaps of yet smoking rubbish and frequently mistaking where I was. The ground under my feet so hot that it even burnt the soles of my shoes. In the mean time his Majesty got to the Tower by water, to demolish the houses about the graff [*moat*], which being built entirely about it, had they taken fire and attacked the White Tower where the magazine of powder lay, would undoubtedly not only have beaten down and destroyed all the bridge, but sunk and torn the vessels in the river, and rendered the demolition beyond all expression for several miles about the country.

At my return I was infinitely concerned to find that goodly church St Paul's now a sad ruin, and that beautiful portico (for structure comparable to any in Europe, as not long before repaired by the late king) now rent in pieces, flakes of vast stone split asunder, and nothing remaining entire but the inscription in the architrave, showing by whom it was built, which had not one letter of it defaced. It was astonishing to see what immense stones the heat had in a manner calcined [*reduced to powder*], so that all the ornaments, columns, friezes, capitals and projectures of massy Portland stone flew off, even to the very roof, where a sheet of lead covering a great space (no less than six acres by measure) was totally melted; the ruins of the vaulted roof falling broke into St Faith's, which being filled with the magazines of books belonging to the Stationers, and carried thither for safety, they were all consumed, burning for a week following. It is also observable that the lead over the altar at the east end was untouched, and among the divers monuments the body of one bishop remained entire. Thus lay in ashes that most venerable church, one of the most ancient pieces of early piety in the Christian world, beside near one hundred more. The lead, ironwork, bells, plate, etc., melted; the exquisitely wrought Mercers' Chapel, the sumptuous Exchange, the august fabric of Christ Church, all the rest of the companies' halls, splendid buildings, arches, entries, all in dust; the fountains dried up and ruined, whilst the very waters remained boiling; the voragos [*chasms*] of subterranean cellars, wells and dungeons, formerly warehouses, still burning in stench and dark clouds of smoke, so that in five or six miles' traversing about I did not see one load of timber unconsumed, nor many stones but what were calcined white as snow. The people who now walked about the ruins appeared like men in some dismal desert or, rather, in some great city laid waste by a cruel enemy; to which was added the stench that came from some poor creatures' bodies, beds and other combustible goods. Sir Thomas Gresham's statue, though fallen from its niche in the Royal Exchange, remained entire, when all those of the kings since the Conquest were broken to pieces; also the standard in Cornhill, and Queen Elizabeth's effigies, with some vast arms on Ludgate, continued with but little detriment, whilst the vast iron chains of the City streets, hinges, bars and gates of prisons were many of them melted and reduced to cinders by the vehement heat. Nor was I yet able to pass through any of the narrower streets, but kept the widest; the ground and air, smoke and fiery vapour continued so intense that my hair was almost singed and my feet unsufferably surbated [*sore*]. The by-lanes and narrower streets were quite filled up with rubbish, nor could one have possibly known where he was but by the ruins of some church or hall that had some remarkable tower or pinnacle remaining. I then went towards Islington and Highgate, where one might have seen 200,000 people of all ranks and degrees dispersed and lying along by their heaps of what they could save from the fire, deploring their loss and, though ready to perish for hunger and destitution, yet not asking one penny for relief, which to me appeared a stranger sight than any I had yet beheld. His Majesty and Council indeed took all imaginable care for their relief by proclamation for the country to come in and refresh them with provisions. In the midst of all this calamity and confusion, there was, I know not how, an alarm begun that the French and Dutch, with whom we were now in hostility, were not only landed, but even entering the City. There was in truth some days before great suspicion of those two nations joining; and now that they had been the occasion of firing the town. This report did so terrify that on a sudden there was such an uproar and tumult that they ran from their goods and, taking what weapons they could come at, they could not be stopped from falling on some of those nations whom they casually met, without sense or reason. The clamour and peril grew so excessive that it made the whole Court amazed, and they did with infinite pains and great difficulty reduce and appease the people, sending troops of soldiers and guards to cause them to retire into the fields again, where they were watched all this night. I left them pretty quiet, and came home sufficiently weary and broken. Their spirits thus a little calmed, and the affright abated, they now began to repair into the suburbs about the City, where such as had friends or opportunity got shelter for the present, to which his Majesty's proclamation also invited them.

From the Diary

ROBERT BOYLE

[Elements]

'I HALF-EXPECTED, Carneades, that after you had so freely declared your doubting whether there be any determinate number of elements you would have proceeded to question whether there be any elements at all. And I confess it will be a trouble to me if you defeat me of my expectation; especially since you see the leisure we have allowed us may probably suffice to examine that paradox, because you have so largely deduced already many things pertinent to it that you need but intimate how you would have them applied and what you would infer from them.'

Carneades having in vain represented that their leisure could be but very short, that he had already prated very long, that he was unprepared to maintain so great and so invidious a paradox, was at length prevailed with to tell his friend: 'Since, Eleutherius, you will have me discourse extempore of the paradox you mention, I am content (though more, perhaps, to express my obedience than my opinion) to tell you that (supposing the truth of Helmont's and Paracelsus's alkahestical experiments [*alkahest: the uni-*

versal solvent supposed to exist by the alchemists], if I may so call them), though it may seem extravagant, yet it is not absurd to doubt whether, for aught has been proved, there be a necessity to admit any elements, or hypostatical principles, at all.

'And, as formerly, so now, to avoid the needless trouble of disputing severally with the Aristotelians and the chemists, I will address myself to oppose them I have last named, because their doctrine about the elements is more applauded by the moderns as pretending highly to be grounded upon experience. And, to deal not only fairly but favourably with them, I will allow them to take in earth and water to their other principles. Which I consent to the rather that my discourse may the better reach the tenents [*opinions*] of the Peripatetics, who cannot plead for any so probably as for those two elements; that of fire above the air being generally by judicious men exploded as an imaginary thing; and the air not concurring to compose mixed bodies as one of their elements, but only lodging in their pores or, rather, replenishing, by reason of its weight and fluidity, all those cavities of bodies here below, whether compounded or not, that are big enough to admit it and are not filled up with any grosser substance.

'And, to prevent mistakes, I must advertise [*inform*] you that I now mean by elements, as those chemists that speak plainest do by their principles, certain primitive and simple, or perfectly unmingled, bodies; which not being made of any other bodies, or of one another, are the ingredients of which all those called perfect mixed bodies are immediately compounded, and into which they are ultimately resolved. Now, whether there be any one such body to be constantly met with in all, and each, of those that are said to be elemented bodies is the thing I now question.

'By this state of the controversy you will, I suppose, guess that I need not be so absurd as to deny that there are such bodies as earth and water and quicksilver and sulphur; but I look upon earth and water as component parts of the universe or, rather, the terrestrial globe, not of all mixed bodies. And, though I will not peremptorily deny that there may sometimes either a running mercury or a combustible

substance be obtained from a mineral, or even a metal, yet
I need not concede either of them to be an element in the
sense above declared – as I shall have occasion to show you
by and by.

'To give you, then, a brief account of the grounds I intend
to proceed upon, I must tell you that in matters of philosophy this seems to me a sufficient reason to doubt of a
known and important proposition: that the truth of it is not
yet by any competent proof made to appear. And, con-
gruously hereunto, if I show that the grounds upon which
men are persuaded that there are elements are unable to
satisfy a considering man, I suppose my doubts will appear
rational.

'Now, the considerations that induce me to think that
there are elements may be conveniently enough referred to
two heads: namely, the one, that it is necessary that Nature
make use of elements to constitute the bodies that are
reputed mixed; and, the other, that the resolution of such
bodies manifests that Nature had compounded them of
elementary ones.'

The Sceptical Chemist, 1661

THOMAS FULLER

Oysters

THE BEST in England, fat, salt, green-finned, are bred
near Colchester, where they have an excellent art to
feed them in pits made for the purpose. King James was
wont to say he was a very valiant man who first adventured
on eating of oysters; most probably mere hunger put men
first on that trial. Thus necessity hath often been the
purveyor to provide diet for delicacy itself, famine making
men to find out those things which afterwards proved not
only wholesome, but delicious. Oysters are the only meat
which men eat alive, and yet account it no cruelty. Some-

times pearls considerable both in bulk and brightness have been found within them.

Pikes

THEY ARE found plentifully in this shire [*Lincolnshire*], being the freshwater wolves, and therefore an old pond-pike is a dish of more state than profit to the owners, seeing a pike's belly is a little fishpond where lesser of all sorts have been contained. Sir Francis Bacon alloweth it (although tyrants generally be short-lived) the survivor of all freshwater fish, attaining to forty years, and some beyond the seas have trebled that term. The flesh thereof must needs be fine and wholesome, if it be true what is affirmed, that in some sort it cheweth the cud, and yet the less and middle size pikes are preferred for sweetness before those that are greater. It breedeth but once (whilst other fishes do often) in a year; such the providence of nature preventing their more multiplying, lest the waters should not afford subjects enough for their tyranny. For want of other fish they will feed on one another; yea, what is four-footed shall be fish with them if it once come into their jaws (biting sometimes for cruelty and revenge, as well as for hunger), and because we have publicly professed that to delight as well as to inform is our aim in this book let the ensuing story (though unwarranted with a cited author) find the reader's acceptance.

A cub fox, drinking out of the River Arnus in Italy, had his head seized on by a mighty pike, so that neither could free themselves, but were engrappled together. In this contest a young man runs into the water, takes them both out alive, and carrieth them to the Duke of Florence, whose palace was hard by. The porter would not admit him without promising of sharing his full half in what the duke should give him. To which he (hopeless otherwise of entrance) condescended. The duke, highly affected with the rarity, was in giving him a good reward, which the other refused, desiring his highness would appoint one of his guard to give him an hundred lashes, that so his porter might have fifty, according to his composition. And here my intelligence leaveth me how much further the jest was followed.

But to return to our English pikes, wherein this county is eminent, especially in that river which runneth by Lincoln, whence this proverb: 'Witham pike England hath none like.'

The History of the Worthies of England, 1662

LUCY HUTCHINSON

[The Courting of Lucy Apsley]

HER MOTHER and friends had a great desire she should marry, and were displeased that she refused many offers which they thought advantageous enough; she was obedient, loth to displease them, but more herself in marrying such as she could find no inclination to. The troublesome pretensions of some of the courtiers had made her willing to try whether she could bring her heart to her mother's desire; but being, by a secret working which she then understood not, averted, she was troubled to return, lest some might believe it was a secret liking for them which had caused her dislike of others; and being a little disturbed with these things and melancholy, Mr Hutchinson, appearing, as he was, a person of virtue and honour, who might be safely and advantageously conversed with, she thought God had sent her a happy relief. Mr Hutchinson, on the other side, having been told and seeing how she shunned all other men, and how civilly she entertained him, believed that a secret power had wrought a mutual inclination between them, and daily frequented her mother's house, and had the opportunity of conversing with her in those pleasant walks which, at that sweet season of the spring, invited all the neighbouring inhabitants to seek their joys; where, though they were never alone, yet they had every day opportunity for converse with each other, which the rest shared not in, while every one minded their own delights.

They had not six weeks enjoyed this peace, but the young men and women, who saw them allow each other that kindness which they did not afford commonly to others, first began to grow jealous and envious at it, and after to use all the malicious practices they could invent to break the friendship. Among the rest, that gentleman who at the first had so highly commended her to Mr Hutchinson now began to caution him against her, and to disparage her with such subtle insinuations as would have ruined any love less constant and honourable than his. The women, with witty spite, represented all her faults to him, which chiefly terminated in the negligence of her dress and habit and all womanish ornaments, giving herself wholly up to study and writing. Mr Hutchinson, who had a very sharp and pleasant wit, retorted all their malice with such just reproofs of their idleness and vanity as made them hate her, who, without affecting it, had so engaged such a person in her protection as they with all their arts could not catch. He, in the meanwhile, prosecuted his love with so much discretion, duty and honour that at the length, through many difficulties, he accomplished his design. I shall pass by all the little amorous relations, which, if I would take the pains to relate, would make a true history of a more handsome management of love than the best possible romances describe; but these are to be forgotten as the vanities of youth, not worthy of mention among the greater transactions of his life. There is this only to be recorded: that never was there a passion more ardent and less idolatrous; he loved her better than his life, with inexpressible tenderness and kindness, had a most high obliging esteem of her, yet still considered honour, religion and duty above her, nor ever suffered the intrusion of such a dotage as should blind him from marking her imperfections; these he looked upon with such an indulgent eye as did not abate his love and esteem of her, while it augmented his care to blot out all those spots which might make her appear less worthy of that respect he paid her; and thus indeed he soon made her more equal to him than he found her; for she was a very faithful mirror, reflecting truly, though but dimly, his own glories upon him so long as he was present; but she, that was nothing before his inspection gave her a fair figure, when he was removed was only filled with a dark mist, and never could again take in any delightful object nor return any shining representation. The greatest excellency she had was the power of apprehending and the virtue of loving his; so as his shadow she waited on him everywhere, till he was taken into that region of light which admits of none, and then she vanished into nothing. It was not her face he loved; her honour and her virtue were his mistresses; and these (like Pygmalion's) images were of his own making, for he polished and gave form to what he found with all the roughness of the quarry about it; but meeting with a compliant subject for his own wise government he found as much satisfaction as he gave, and never had occasion to number his marriage among his infelicities.

*Memoirs of the Life of Colonel Hutchinson, c.*1664–71

ROBERT HOOKE

A Louse

BOTH ITS motion and rest is very strange, and pleasant, and differing from those of most other creatures I have observed; for, where it ceases from moving its body, the tail of it seeming much lighter than the rest of its body, and a little lighter than the water it swims in, presently buoys it up to the top of the water, where it hangs suspended with the head always downward; and like our Antipodes, if they do by a frisk get below that superficies, they presently ascend again into it, if they cease moving, until they tread, as it were, under that superficies with their tails; the hanging of these in this posture put me in mind of a certain creature I have seen in London that was brought out of America, which would very firmly suspend itself by the tail, with the head downwards, and was said to sleep in that posture, with her young ones in her false belly, which is a purse, provided by nature for the production, nutrition and preservation of the young ones, which is described by Piso in the twenty-fourth chapter of the fifth book of his *Natural History of Brazil*.

The motion of it was with the tail forwards, drawing its self backwards, by the striking to and fro of that tuft which grew out of one of the stumps of its tail. It had another motion, which was more suitable to that of other creatures, and that is, with the head forward: for by the moving of his chaps (if I may so call the parts of its mouth) it was able to move itself downwards very gently towards the bottom, and did, as 'twere, eat up its way through the water.

Micrographia; or, Some Physiological
Descriptions of Minute Bodies Made
by Magnifying Glasses, 1665

SAMUEL PEPYS

[The Great Fire]

[*2 September 1666*] Lord's Day. Some of our maids sitting up late last night to get things ready against our feast today, Jane called us up about three in the morning to tell us of a great fire they saw in the City. So I rose and slipped on my nightgown and went to her window, and thought it to be on the back side of Mark Lane at the farthest; but, being unused to such fires as followed, I thought it far enough off, and so went to bed again and to sleep. About seven rose again to dress myself, and there looked out at the window and saw the fire not so much as it was, and farther off. So to my closet [*private room*] to set things to rights after yesterday's cleaning. By and by Jane comes and tells me that she hears that above 300 houses have been burned down tonight by the fire we saw, and that it is now burning down all Fish

Street by London Bridge. So I made myself ready presently
and walked to the Tower, and there got up upon one of the
high places, [*Lieutenant of the Tower*] Sir John Robinson's
little son going up with me; and there I did see the houses
at that end of the bridge all on fire, and an infinite great fire
on this and the other side the end of the bridge; which,
among other people, did trouble me for poor little Mitchell
and our Sarah on the bridge. So down, with my heart full of
trouble, to the Lieutenant of the Tower, who tells me that
it began this morning in the King's baker's house in Pudding
Lane, and that it hath burned down St Magnus' Church and
most part of Fish Street already. So I down to the waterside
and there got a boat, and through bridge, and there saw a
lamentable fire. Poor Mitchell's house, as far as the Old
Swan, already burned that way, and the fire running farther
that in a very little time it got as far as the Steelyard while I
was there. Everybody endeavouring to remove their goods,
and flinging into the river or bringing them into lighters that
lay off. Poor people staying in their houses as long as till the
very fire touched them, and then running into boats or
clambering from one pair of stair by the waterside to
another. And, among other things, the poor pigeons, I
perceive, were loath to leave their houses, but hovered
about the windows and balconies till they burned their wings
and fell down. Having stayed, and in an hour's time seen the
fire rage every way – and nobody, to my sight, endeavouring
to quench it, but to remove their goods and leave all to the
fire – and having seen it get as far as the Steelyard, and the
wind mighty high and driving it into the City, and everything, after so long a drought, proving combustible, even
the very stones of churches and, among other things, the
poor steeple by which pretty Mrs [*Horsley*] lives, and
whereof my old schoolfellow Elborough is parson, taken
fire in the very top and there burned till it fell down, I to
Whitehall with a gentleman with me who desired to go off
from the Tower to see the fire in my boat, and there up to
the King's closet in the chapel, where people came about
me and I did give them an account dismayed them all. And
word was carried in to the King; so I was called for and did
tell the King and Duke of York what I saw, and that unless

his Majesty did command houses to be pulled down nothing could stop the fire. They seemed much troubled, and the King commanded me to go to my Lord Mayor from him and command him to spare no houses but to pull down before the fire every way. The Duke of York bid me tell him that if he would have any more soldiers he shall; and so did my Lord Arlington afterwards, as a great secret. Here meeting with Captain Cocke, I in his coach, which he lent me, and [*John*] Creed with me, to Paul's; and there walked along Watling Street as well as I could, every creature coming away loaden with goods to save, and here and there sick people carried away in beds. Extraordinary good goods carried in carts and on backs. At last met my Lord Mayor in Canning Street, like a man spent, with a handkercher about his neck. To the King's message, he cried like a fainting woman: 'Lord! what can I do? I am spent! People will not obey me. I have been pulling down houses, but the fire overtakes us faster than we can do it.' That he needed no more soldiers; and that, for himself, he must go and refresh himself, having been up all night. So he left me, and I him, and walked home, seeing people all almost distracted and no manner of means used to quench the fire. The houses, too, so very thick thereabouts, and full of matter for burning, as pitch and tar, in Thames Street; and warehouses of oil and wines and brandy and other things. Here I saw Mr Isaac Houblon, the handsome man, prettily dressed and dirty, at his door at Dowgate, receiving some of his brothers' things whose houses were on fire; and, as he says, have been removed twice already, and he doubts (as it soon proved) that they must be in a little time removed from his house also, which was a sad consideration. And to see the churches all filling with goods by people who themselves should have been quietly there at this time. By this time it was about twelve o'clock, and so home. . . .

[*5 September*] . . . to the fire, and there find greater hopes than I expected; for my confidence of finding our office on fire was such that I durst not ask anybody how it was with us till I came and saw it not burned. But going to the fire I find, by the blowing up of houses and the great help given by the workmen out of the King's yards, sent up by Sir William Penn, there is a good stop given to it, as well at Mark Lane end as ours; it having only burned the dial of [*All Hallows*] Barking Church and part of the porch, and was there quenched. Up to the top of Barking steeple, and there saw the saddest sight of desolation that ever I saw. Everywhere great fires. Oil-cellars and brimstone and other things burning. I became afraid to stay there long; and therefore down again as fast as I could, the fire being spread as far as I could see, and to Sir William Penn's. . . .

[*7 September*] Up by five o'clock and, blessed be God, find all well, and by water to Paul's Wharf. Walked thence and saw all the town burned, and a miserable sight of Paul's church, with all the roofs fallen and the body of the choir fallen into St Faith's [*St Paul's crypt*]; Paul's school also; Ludgate and Fleet Street; my father's house, and the church, and a good part of the Temple the like. So to Creed's lodging near the New Exchange, and there find him laid down upon a bed; the house all unfurnished, there being fears of the fire's coming to them. There borrowed a shirt of him and washed. To Sir William Coventry at St James's, who lay without curtains, having removed all his goods; as the King at Whitehall and everybody had done and was doing. He hopes we shall have no public distractions [*unrest*] upon this fire, which is what everybody fears, because of the talk of the French having a hand in it. And it is a proper time for discontents; but all men's minds are full of care to protect themselves and save their goods. The militia is in arms everywhere. Our fleets, he tells me, have been in sight one of another, and most unhappily by foul weather were parted, to our great loss, as in reason they do conclude; the Dutch being come out only to make a show and please their people; but in a very bad condition as to stores, victuals and men. . . .

From the Diary

THOMAS SPRAT

[The English Genius]

THE PLAGUE [*of 1665*] was indeed an irreparable damage
to the whole kingdom; but that which chiefly added to
the misery was the time wherein it happened. For what
could be a more deplorable accident than that so many
brave men should be cut off by the 'arrow that flies in the
dark', when our country was engaged in a foreign war
[*against the Dutch*], and when their lives might have been
honourably ventured on a glorious theatre in its defence?
And we had scarce recovered this first misfortune, when we
received a second, and a deeper, wound [*the Great Fire of
1666*]; which cannot be equalled in all history, if either we
consider the obscurity of its beginning, the irresistible violence of its progress, the horror of its appearance, or the
wideness of the ruin it made in one of the most renowned
cities of the world.

Yet when, on the one side, I remember what desolation
these scourges of mankind have left behind them; and, on
the other, when I reflect on the magnanimity wherewith the
English nation did support the mischiefs: I find that I have
not more reason to bewail the one than to admire the other.

Upon our return after the abating of the plague, what else
could we expect but to see the streets unfrequented, the
river forsaken, the fields deformed with the graves of the
dead, and the terrors of death still abiding on the faces of
the living? But instead of such dismal sights there appeared
almost the same throngs in all public places, the same noise
of business, the same freedom of converse, and with the
return of the King the same cheerfulness returning on the
minds of the people as before.

Nor was their courage less in sustaining the second
calamity, which destroyed their houses and estates. This the
greatest losers endured with such undaunted firmness of
mind that their example may incline us to believe that not
only the best natural but the best moral philosophy, too,

may be learned from the shops of mechanics. It was indeed an admirable thing to behold with what constancy the meanest artificers saw all the labours of their lives and the support of their families devoured in an instant. The affliction, 'tis true, was widely spread over the whole nation: every place was filled with signs of pity and commiseration. But those who had suffered most seemed the least affected with the loss: no unmanly bewailings were heard in the few streets that were preserved; they beheld the ashes of their houses and gates and temples without the least expression of pusillanimity. If philosophers had done this, it had well become their possession of wisdom. If gentlemen, the nobleness of their breeding and blood would have required it. But that such greatness of heart should be found amongst the poor artisans and the obscure multitude is no doubt one of the most honourable events that ever happened. Yet still there is one circumstance behind, which may raise our wonder higher; and that is that amidst such horrible ruins they still prosecuted the war with the same vigour and courage against three of the most powerful states of all Europe. What records of time, or memory of past ages, can show us a greater testimony of an invincible and heroic genius than this of which I now speak? that the sound of the heralds proclaiming new wars should be pleasant to the people, when the sad voice of the bellman was scarce yet gone out of their ears? that the increase of their adversaries' confederates, and of their own calamities, should be so far from affrighting them that they rather seemed to receive from thence a new vigour and resolution? and that they should still be eager upon victories and triumphs, when they were thought almost quite exhausted by so great destructions?

From this observation my mind begins to take comfort, and to presage that as this terrible disease and conflagration were not able to darken the honour of our Prince's arms, so they will not hinder the many noble arts which the English have begun under his reign on the strength of these hopes and encouragements. I will now return to my former thoughts, and to the finishing of my interrupted design. And I come with the more earnestness to perfect it, because it seems to me that from the sad effects of these disasters there may a new and a powerful argument be raised to move us to double our labours about the secrets of nature.

A new city is to be built, on the most advantageous seat of all Europe for trade and command. This therefore is the fittest season for men to apply their thoughts to the improving of the materials of building, and to the inventing of better models for houses, roofs, chimneys, conduits, wharfs and streets – all which have been already under the consideration of the Royal Society, and that, too, before they had such a sad occasion of bringing their observations into practice. The mortality of this pestilence exceeded all others of later ages. But the remembrance of it should rather enliven than damp our industry. When mankind is overrun with such horrible invasions of death, they should from thence be universally alarmed to use more diligence about preventing them for the future.

The History of the Royal Society of London,
for the Improving of Natural Knowledge, 1667

ABRAHAM COWLEY

Of Greatness

THE FIRST ambitious men in the world, the old giants, are said to have made an heroical attempt of scaling Heaven in despite of the gods, and they cast Ossa upon Olympus and Pelion upon Ossa; two or three mountains more they thought would have done their business, but the thunder spoiled all the work when they were come up to the third storey, 'And what a noble plot was crossed, And what a brave design was lost'.

A famous person of their offspring, the late giant of our nation [*Oliver Cromwell*], when, from the condition of a very inconsiderable captain, he had made himself lieutenant general of an army of little Titans, which was his first mountain; and afterwards general, which was his second; and after that absolute tyrant of three kingdoms, which was the third, and almost touched the heaven which he affected; is believed to have died with grief and discontent because he could not attain to the honest name of a king, and the old formality of a crown, though he had before exceeded the power by a wicked usurpation. If he could have compassed that, he would perhaps have wanted something else that is necessary to felicity, and pined away for the want of the title of an emperor or a god. The reason of this is that greatness has no reality in nature, but is a creature of the fancy – a notion that consists only in relation and comparison. It is indeed an idol; but St Paul teaches us that an idol is nothing in the world. There is in truth no rising or meridian of the sun, but only in respect to several places; there is no right or left, no upper hand in nature; everything is little and everything is great according as it is diversely compared. There may be perhaps some villages in Scotland or Ireland where I might be a great man; and in that case I should be like Caesar – you would wonder how Caesar and I should be like one another in anything – and choose rather to be the first man of the village than second at Rome. Our country is called Great Britain in regard only of a lesser of the same name; it would be but a ridiculous epithet for it when we consider it together with the kingdom of China. That, too, is but a pitiful rood of ground in comparison of the whole earth besides; and this whole globe of earth, which we account so immense a body, is but one point or atom in relation to those numberless worlds that are scattered up and down in the infinite space of the sky which we behold.

Works, 1668

JOHN DRYDEN

[Ben Jonson]

A s for Jonson, to whose character I am now arrived, if we look upon him while he was himself (for his last plays were but his dotages), I think him the most learned and judicious writer which any theatre ever had. He was a most severe judge of himself as well as others. One cannot say he wanted wit, but rather that he was frugal of it. In his works you find little to retrench or alter. Wit, and language, and humour also in some measure, we had before him; but something of art was wanting to the drama till he came. He managed his strength to more advantage than any who preceded him. You seldom find him making love in any of his scenes, or endeavouring to move the passions; his genius was too sullen and saturnine to do it gracefully, especially when he knew he came after those who had performed both to such an height. Humour was his proper sphere; and in that he delighted most to represent mechanic people. He was deeply conversant in the ancients, both Greek and Latin, and he borrowed boldly from them: there is scarce a poet or historian among the Roman authors of those times whom he has not translated in *Sejanus* and *Catiline*. But he has done his robberies so openly that one may see he fears not to be taxed by any law. He invades authors like a monarch; and what would be theft in other poets is only victory in him. With the spoils of these writers he so represents old Rome to us, in its rites, ceremonies, and customs, that if one of their poets had written either of his tragedies, we had seen less of it than in him. If there was any fault in his language, 'twas that he weaved it too closely and laboriously, in his comedies especially: perhaps, too, he did a little too much Romanise our tongue, leaving the words which he translated almost as much Latin as he found them: wherein, though he learnedly followed their language, he did not enough comply with the idiom of ours. If I would compare him with Shakespeare, I must acknowledge him the more correct poet, but Shakespeare the greater wit. Shakespeare was the Homer, or father of our dramatic poets; Jonson was the Virgil, the pattern of elaborate writing; I admire him, but I love Shakespeare. To conclude of him; as he has given us the most correct plays, so in the precepts which he has laid down in his *Discoveries*, we have as many and profitable rules for perfecting the stage, as any wherewith the French can furnish us.

An Essay of Dramatic Poesy, 1668

[Chaucer]

H E M U S T have been a man of a most wonderful comprehensive nature, because, as it has been truly observed of him, he has taken into the compass of his *Canterbury Tales* the various manners and humours (as we now call them) of the whole English nation in his age. Not a single character has escaped him. All his pilgrims are severally distinguished from each other; and not only in their inclinations, but in their very physiognomies and persons. Baptista Porta could not have described their natures better than by the marks which the poet gives them. The matter and manner of their tales, and of their telling, are so suited to their different educations, humours and callings that each of them would be improper in any other mouth. Even the grave and serious characters are distinguished by their several sorts of gravity: their discourses are such as belong to their age, their calling and their breeding; such as are becoming of them, and of them only. Some of his persons are vicious, and some virtuous; some are unlearned, or (as Chaucer calls them) lewd, and some are learned. Even the ribaldry of the low characters is different: the Reeve, the Miller and the Cook are several [*different*] men, and distinguished from each other as much as the mincing Lady Prioress and the broad-speaking, gap-toothed Wife of Bath. But enough of this; there is such a variety of game springing up before me that I am distracted in my choice, and know not which to follow. 'Tis sufficient to say, according to the proverb, that *here is God's plenty*. We have our forefathers and great-grandames all before us, as they were in Chaucer's days: their general characters are still remaining in mankind, and even in England, though they are called by other names than those of monks, and friars, and canons, and lady abbesses, and nuns; for mankind is ever the same, and nothing lost out of nature, though everything is altered.

> From preface to *Fables, Ancient and Modern,*
> *Translated into Verse from Homer,*
> *Ovid, Boccace, and Chaucer*, 1700

SIR ISAAC NEWTON
[The 'Crucial Experiment']

[*Early in 1666*] I took two boards, and placed one of them close behind the prism at the window, so that the light might pass through a small hole, made in it for that purpose, and fall on the other board, which I placed at about twelve foot distance, having first made a small hole in it also, for some of that incident light to pass through. Then I placed another prism behind this second board, so that the light trajected through both the boards might pass through that also, and be again refracted before it arrived at the wall. This done, I took the first prism in my hand, and turned it to and fro slowly about its axis, so much as to make the several parts of the image cast on the second board successively pass through the hole in it, that I might observe to what places on the wall the second prism would refract them. And I saw by the variation of those places that the light tending to that end of the image towards which the refraction of the first prism was made did in the second prism suffer a refraction considerably greater than the light tending to the other end. And so the true cause of the length of that image was detected to be no other than that light consists of *rays differently refrangible*, which, without any respect to a difference in their incidence, were, according to their degrees of refrangibility, transmitted towards divers parts of the wall.

When I understood this, I left off my aforesaid glass-works; for I saw that the perfection of telescopes was hitherto limited not so much for want of glasses truly figured according to the prescriptions of optic authors (which all men have hitherto imagined) as because that light itself is a *heterogeneous mixture of differently refrangible rays*. So that, were a glass so exactly figured as to collect any one sort of rays into one point, it could not collect those also into the same point which having the same incidence upon the same medium are apt to suffer a different refraction. Nay, I wondered that, seeing the difference of refrangibility was so great as I found it, telescopes should arrive to that perfection they are now at. For, measuring the refractions in one of my prisms, I found that, supposing the common sine of incidence upon one of its planes was 44 parts, the sine of the refraction of the utmost rays on the red end of the colours, made out of the glass into the air, would be 68 parts, and the sine of refraction of the utmost rays on the other end 69 parts: so that the difference is about a 24th or 25th part of the whole refraction. And consequently the object-glass of any telescope cannot collect all the rays which come from one point of an object so as to make them convene at its focus in less room than in a circular space whose diameter is the 50th part of the diameter of its aperture; which is an irregularity some hundreds of times greater than a circularly figured lens of so small a section as the object-glasses of long telescopes are would cause by the unfitness of its figure, were light uniform.

This made me take reflections into consideration, and finding them regular, so that the angle of reflection of all sorts of rays was equal to their angle of incidence, I understood that by their mediation optic instruments might be brought to any degree of perfection imaginable, provided a reflecting substance could be found which would polish as finely as glass and reflect as much light as glass transmits and the art of communicating to it a parabolic figure be also attained. But these seemed very great difficulties, and I almost thought them insuperable, when I further considered that every irregularity in a reflecting superficies makes the rays stray five or six times more out of their due course than the like irregularities in a refracting one: so that a much greater curiosity would be here requisite than in figuring glasses for refraction.

Amidst these thoughts I was forced from Cambridge by the intervening plague, and it was more than two years before I proceeded further. But then having thought on a tender way of polishing proper for metal, whereby, as I imagined, the figure also would be corrected to the last, I began to try what might be effected in this kind, and by degrees so far perfected an instrument (in the essential parts of it like that I sent to London) by which I could discern Jupiter's four concomitants, and showed them divers times to two others of my acquaintance. I could also discern the Moon-like phase of Venus, but not very distinctly, nor without some niceness in disposing the instrument.

> Letter to Henry Oldenburg, Secretary to
> the Royal Society, 6 February 1672

JOHN BUNYAN

[The Slough of Despond]

Now, I saw in my dream, that, when Obstinate was gone back, Christian and Pliable went talking over the plain; and thus they began their discourse.

CHRISTIAN. Come, neighbour Pliable, how do you do? I am glad you are persuaded to go along with me. Had even Obstinate himself but felt what I have felt of the powers and terrors of what is yet unseen, he would not thus lightly have given us the back.

PLIABLE. Come, neighbour Christian, since there are

none but us two here, tell me now further what the things are, and how to be enjoyed, whither we are going.

CHRISTIAN. I can better conceive of them with my mind, than speak of them with my tongue; but yet, since you are desirous to know, I will read of them in my book.

PLIABLE. And do you think that the words of your book are certainly true?

CHRISTIAN. Yes, verily; for it was made by him that cannot lie.

PLIABLE. Well said; what things are they?

CHRISTIAN. There is an endless kingdom to be inhabited, and everlasting life to be given us, that we may inhabit that kingdom for ever.

PLIABLE. Well said; and what else?

CHRISTIAN. There are crowns of glory to be given us, and garments that will make us shine like the sun in the firmament of heaven!

PLIABLE. This is very pleasant; and what else?

CHRISTIAN. There shall be no more crying, nor sorrow; for He that is owner of the place will wipe all tears from our eyes.

PLIABLE. And what company shall we have there?

CHRISTIAN. There we shall be with seraphims and cherubims, creatures that will dazzle your eyes to look on them. There also you shall meet with thousands and tens of thousands that have gone before us to that place; none of them are hurtful, but loving and holy; every one walking in the sight of God, and standing in his presence with acceptance for ever. In a word, there we shall see the elders with their golden crowns; there we shall see the holy virgins with their golden harps; there we shall see men that by the world were cut in pieces, burnt in flames, eaten of beasts, drowned in the seas, for the love that they bare to the lord of the place, all well, and clothed with immortality as with a garment.

PLIABLE. The hearing of this is enough to ravish one's heart. But are these things to be enjoyed? How shall we get to be sharers thereof?

CHRISTIAN. The Lord, the Governor of the country, hath recorded that in this book; the substance of which is, If we be truly willing to have it, He will bestow it upon us freely.

PLIABLE. Well, my good companion, glad am I to hear of these things: come on, let us mend our pace.

CHRISTIAN. I cannot go so fast as I would, by reason of this burden that is on my back.

Now, I saw in my dream, that just as they had ended this talk they drew near to a very miry slough, that was in the midst of the plain; and they, being heedless, did both fall suddenly into the bog. The name of the slough was Despond. Here, therefore, they wallowed for a time, being grievously bedaubed with the dirt; and Christian, because of the burden that was on his back, began to sink in the mire.

PLIABLE. Then said Pliable, Ah! neighbour Christian, where are you now?

CHRISTIAN. Truly, said Christian, I do not know.

PLIABLE. At this Pliable began to be offended, and angrily said to his fellow, Is this the happiness you have told me all this while of? If we have such ill speed at our first setting out, what may we expect betwixt this and our journey's end? May I get out again with my life, you shall possess the brave country alone for me. And, with that, he gave a desperate struggle or two, and got out of the mire on that side of the slough which was next to his own house; so away he went, and Christian saw him no more.

Wherefore Christian was left to tumble in the Slough of Despond alone; but still he endeavoured to struggle to that side of the slough that was still further from his own house, and next to the wicket-gate; the which he did, but could not get out, because of the burden that was upon his back: but I beheld in my dream, that a man came to him, whose name was Help, and asked him, what he did there?

CHRISTIAN. Sir, said Christian, I was bid go this way by a man called Evangelist, who directed me also to yonder gate, that I might escape the wrath to come; and as I was going thither I fell in here.

HELP. But why did you not look for the steps?

CHRISTIAN. Fear followed me so hard, that I fled the next way, and fell in.

HELP. Then said he, Give me thy hand: so he gave him his hand, and he drew him out, and set him upon sound ground, and bid him go on his way.

Then I stepped to him that plucked him out, and said, Sir, Wherefore, since over this place is the way from the City of Destruction to yonder gate, is it that this plat is not mended, that poor travellers might go thither with more security? And he said unto me, This mire slough is such a place as cannot be mended; it is the descent whither the scum and filth that attends conviction for sin doth continually run, and therefore it is called the Slough of Despond; for still, as the sinner is awakened about his lost condition, there ariseth in his soul many fears, and doubts and discouraging apprehensions, which all of them get together, and settle in this place. And this is the reason for the badness of this ground.

It is not the pleasure of the King that this place should remain so bad. His labourers also have, by the direction of His Majesty's surveyors, been for above these sixteen hundred years employed about this patch of ground, if perhaps it might have been mended: yea, and to my knowledge, said he, here have been swallowed up at least twenty thousand cart-loads, yea, millions of wholesome instructions, that have at all seasons been brought from all places of the King's dominions, and they that can tell say that they are the best materials to make good ground of the place; if so be it might have been mended, but it is the Slough of Despond still, and so will be when they have done what they can.

True, there are, by the direction of the Lawgiver, certain good and substantial steps, placed even through the very midst of this slough; but at such time as this place doth much spew out its filth, as it doth against the change of weather, these steps are hardly seen; or, if they be, men, through the dizziness of their heads, step beside, and then they are bemired to purpose, notwithstanding the steps be there; but the ground is good when they are once got in at the gate.

Now, I saw in my dream, that by this time Pliable was got home to his house again, so that his neighbours came to visit him; and some of them called him wise man for coming back, and some called him fool for hazarding himself with Christian; others again did mock at his cowardliness, saying, Surely, since you began to venture, I would not have been so base as to have given out for a few difficulties. So Pliable sat sneaking among them. But at last he got more confidence, and then they all turned their tales, and began to deride poor Christian behind his back.

The Pilgrim's Progress, 1678

THOMAS TRAHERNE
[The Vision Splendid]

ALL APPEARED new, and strange at first, inexpressibly rare, and delightful, and beautiful. I was a little stranger which at my entrance into the world was saluted and surrounded with innumerable joys. My knowledge was divine. I knew by intuition those things which since my apostasy I collected again by the highest reason. My very ignorance was advantageous. I seemed as one brought into the estate of innocence. All things were spotless and pure and glorious: yea, and infinitely mine, and joyful and precious. I knew not that there were any sins, or complaints, or laws. I dreamed not of poverties, contentions or vices. All tears and quarrels were hidden from mine eyes. Everything was at rest, free, and immortal. I knew nothing of sickness or death, or exaction, in the absence of these I was entertained like an angel with the works of God in their splendour and glory; I saw all in the peace of Eden; heaven and earth did sing my Creator's praises and could not make more melody to Adam than to me. All time was eternity, and a perpetual sabbath. Is it not strange that an infant should be heir of the world, and see those mysteries which the books of the learned never unfold?

*

The corn was orient and immortal wheat, which never should be reaped, nor was ever sown. I thought it had stood from everlasting to everlasting. The dust and stones of the street were as precious as gold. The gates were at first the end of the world, the green trees when I saw them first through one of the gates transported and ravished me; their sweetness and unusual beauty made my heart to leap, and almost mad with ecstasy, they were such strange and wonderful thing. The men! Oh, what venerable and reverend creatures did the aged seem! Immortal cherubims! And young men glittering and sparkling angels, and maids strange seraphic pieces of life and beauty! Boys and girls tumbling in the street, and playing, were moving jewels. I knew not that they were born or should die. But all things abided eternally as they were in their proper places. Eternity was manifest in the light of the day, and something infinite behind everything appeared: which talked with my expectation and moved my desire. The city seemed to stand in Eden, or to be built in heaven. The streets were mine, the temple was mine, the people were mine, their clothes and gold and silver was mine, as much as their sparkling eyes, fair skins and ruddy faces. The skies were mine, and so were the sun and moon and stars, and all the world was mine, and I the only spectator and enjoyer of it. I knew no churlish proprieties, nor bounds nor divisions: but all proprieties and divisions were mine: all treasures and the possessors of them. So that with much ado I was corrupted; and made to learn the dirty devices of this world. Which now I unlearn, and become as it were a little child again, that I may enter into the Kingdom of God.

The Centuries of Meditations, c.1679

JOHN AUBREY

William Shakespeare

M R WILLIAM Shakespeare was born at Stratford-upon-Avon in the county of Warwick. His father was a butcher, and I have been told heretofore by some of the neighbours that when he was a boy he exercised his father's trade, but when he killed a calf he would do it in a high style and make a speech. There was at this time another butcher's son in this town that was held not at all inferior to him for a natural wit, his acquaintance and coetanian, but died young.

This William, being inclined naturally to poetry and acting, came to London, I guess, about eighteen; and was an actor at one of the playhouses, and did act exceedingly well. Now, Ben Jonson was never a good actor, but an excellent instructor.

He began early to make essays at dramatic poetry, which at that time was very low, and his plays took well.

He was a handsome well-shaped man, very good in company, and of a very ready and pleasant smooth wit.

The humour of the constable in *Midsummer Night's Dream* he happened to take at Grendon in Bucks (I think it was Midsummer Night that he happened to lie there) which is the road from London to Stratford, and there was living that constable about 1642 when I first came to Oxon. Ben Jonson and he did gather humours of men daily wherever they came. One time he was at the tavern at Stratford-super-Avon; one Combes, an old rich usurer, was to be buried. He makes there this extempore epitaph:

> Ten in the hundred the devil allows;
> But Combes will have twelve, he swears and avows.
> If anyone asks who lies in this tomb,
> 'Hoh!' quoth the devil. ''Tis my John o' Combe.'

He was wont to go to his native country once a year. I think I have been told that he left two or three hundred pounds there and thereabout to a sister.

I have heard Sir William Davenant and Mr Thomas Shadwell, who is counted the best comedian we have now, say that he had a most prodigious wit, and did admire his natural parts beyond all other dramatical writers.

His comedies will remain wit as long as the English tongue is understood, for that he handles *mores hominum* ['*the ways of man*']. Now, our present writers reflect so much on particular persons and coxcombies that twenty years hence they will not be understood.

Though as Ben Jonson says of him that he had little Latin and less Greek, he understood Latin pretty well, for he had been in his younger years a schoolmaster in the country.

He was wont to say that he never blotted out a line in his life. Said Ben Jonson, 'I wish he had blotted out a thousand.'

Edward de Vere, Earl of Oxford

THIS EARL of Oxford, making of his low obeisance to Queen Elizabeth, happened to let a fart; at which he was so abashed and ashamed that he went to travel, seven years. On his return the Queen welcomed him home, and said, 'My Lord, I had forgot the fart.'

Mr Nicholas Hill was one of the most learned men of his time – a great mathematician and philosopher, and a poet and traveller; but no writer that I ever heard of – or, if he was, his writings had the usual fate of those not printed in the author's lifetime. He was (or leaning) a Roman Catholic. He was so eminent for knowledge that he was the favourite of the great Earl of Oxford, who had him to accompany him in his travels (he was his steward), which were so splendid and sumptuous that he lived at Florence in more grandeur than the Duke of Tuscany. This Earl spent forty thousand pounds per annum in seven years' travel.

In his travels with his lord (I forget whether Italy or

Germany, but I think the former) a poor man begged him to give him a penny. 'A penny!' said Mr Hill. 'What dost say to ten pound?'

'Ah, ten pound!' said the beggar. 'That would make a man happy.'

N. Hill gave him immediately ten pounds and put it down upon account, 'Item. To a beggar ten pounds to make him happy'; which his Lordship allowed and was well pleased at it.

As I have heard, it was that great antiquary King Charles the First his observation that the three ancientest families of Europe for nobility were the Veres in England, Earls of Oxford, and the Fitzgeralds in Ireland, Earls of Kildare, and Montmorency in France.

Surliness and inurbanity too common in England. Chastise these very severely. A better instance of a squeamish and disobliging, slighting, insolent, proud fellow perhaps cannot be found than in Gwynn, the Earl of Oxford's secretary. No reason satisfies him, but he overweens and cuts some sour faces that would turn the milk in a fair lady's breast.

*Brief Lives c.*1679; first published 1813

GEORGE SAVILE, MARQUESS OF HALIFAX

[A Trimmer]

H E PROFESSES solemnly that, were it in his power to choose, he would rather have his ambition bounded by the commands of a great and wise master than let it range with a popular licence, though crowned with success; yet he cannot commit such a sin against the glorious thing called Liberty, nor let his soul stoop so much below itself as to be content without repining to have his reason wholly subdued or the privilege of acting like a sensible creature torn from him by the imperious dictates of unlimited authority, in what hand soever it happens to be placed. What is there in this that is so criminal as to deserve the penalty of that most singular apophthegm, 'A Trimmer is worse than a rebel!' What do angry men ail, to rail so against moderation? Does it not look as if they were going to some very scurvy extreme that is too strong to be digested by the more considering part of mankind? These arbitrary methods, besides the injustice of them, are – God be thanked – very unskilful, too; for they fright the birds, by talking so loud, from coming into the nets that are laid for them; and when men agree to rifle a house they seldom give warning or blow a trumpet; but there are some small statesmen who are so full-charged with their own expectations that they cannot contain.

And kind heaven, by sending such a seasonable curse upon their undertakings, has made their ignorance an antidote against their malice. Some of these cannot treat peaceably; yielding will not satisfy them, they will have men by storm. There are others that must have plots to make their service more necessary, and have an interest to keep them alive, since they are to live upon them; and persuade the king to retrench his own greatness so as to shrink into the head of a party, which is the betraying him into such an unprincely mistake, and to such a wilful diminution of himself, that they are the last enemies he ought to allow himself to forgive. Such men, if they could, would prevail with the sun to shine only upon them and their friends, and to leave all the rest of the world in the dark. This is a very unusual monopoly, and may come within the equity of the law, which makes it treason to imprison the king. When such unfitting bounds are put to his favour, and he confined to the narrow limits of a particular set of men that would enclose him, these honest and loyal gentlemen, if they may be allowed to bear witness for themselves, make a king their engine and degrade him into a property, at the very time that their flattery would make him believe they paid divine worship to him. Besides these, there is a flying squadron on both sides, they are afraid the world should agree; small dabblers in conjuring that raise angry apparitions to keep men from being reconciled, like wasps that fly up and down, buzz and sting men to keep them unquiet; but these insects are commonly short-lived creatures, and no doubt in a little time mankind will be rid of them. They were giants at least who fought once against heaven, but for such pygmies as these to contend against it is such a provoking folly that the insolent bunglers ought to be laughed and hissed out of the world for it. They should consider there is a soul in that great body the people, which may for a time be drowsy and unactive, but when the leviathan is roused it moves like an angry creature, and will neither be convinced nor resisted. The people can never agree to show their united powers till they are extremely tempted and provoked to it; so that to apply cupping-glasses to a great beast naturally disposed to sleep, and to force the tame thing, whether it will or no, to be valiant, must be learnt out of some other book than Machiavel, who would never have prescribed such a pre-posterous method. It is to be remembered that if princes have law and authority on their sides the people on theirs may have Nature, which is a formidable adversary. Duty, Justice, Religion, nay, even human prudence, too, bids the people suffer anything rather than resist; but uncorrected Nature, where'er it feels the smart, will run to the nearest remedy. Men's passions, in this case, are to be considered as well as their duty, let it be never so strongly enforced; for if their passions are provoked, they being as much a part of us as our limbs, they lead men into a short way of arguing that admits no distinction; and from the foundation of self-defence they will draw inferences that will have miserable effects upon the quiet of a government.

Our Trimmer therefore dreads a general discontent, because he thinks it differs from a rebellion only as a spotted fever does from the plague, the same species under a lower degree of malignity; it works several ways, sometimes like a slow poison that has its effects at a great distance from the time it was given; sometimes like dry flag [grass] prepared to catch at the first fire, or like seed in the ground ready to sprout up on the first shower. In every shape 'tis fatal, and our Trimmer thinks no pains can be so great as to prevent it.

The Character of a Trimmer, 1688

JOHN SELDEN

[Pleasure]

PLEASURE IS nothing else but the intermission of pain, the enjoying of something I am in great trouble for till I have it.

'Tis a wrong way to proportion other men's pleasures to ourselves; 'tis like a little child using a little bird, 'O poor bird, thou shalt sleep with me'; so lays it in his bosom, and stifles it with his hot breath: the bird had rather be in the cold air. And yet, too, 'tis the most pleasing flattery to like what other men like.

'Tis most undoubtedly true that all men are equally given to their pleasure; only thus, one man's pleasure lies one way, and another's another. Pleasures are all alike simply considered in themselves: he that hunts or he that governs the Commonwealth, they both please themselves alike, only we commend that whereby we ourselves receive some benefit; as if a man place his delight in things that tend to the common good. He that takes pleasure to hear sermons enjoys himself as much as he that hears plays; and could he that loves plays endeavour to love sermons possibly he might bring himself to it as well as to any other pleasure. At first it may seem harsh and tedious, but afterwards 'twould be pleasing and delightful. So it falls out in that which is the great pleasure of some men, tobacco; at first they could not abide it, and now they cannot be without it.

Whilst you are upon earth, enjoy the good things that are here (to that end were they given), and be not melancholy and wish yourself in heaven. If a king should give you the keeping of a castle, with all things belonging to it, orchards, gardens, &c., and bid you use them; withal promise you that, after twenty years to remove you to the Court, and to make you a Privy Counsellor; if you should neglect your castle, and refuse to eat of those fruits, and sit down, and whine, and wish you were a Privy Counsellor, do you think the King would be pleased with you?

Table-Talk, 1689

JOHN LOCKE

[Liberty]

EVERYONE, I think, finds in himself a *power* to begin or forbear, continue or put an end to several actions in himself. From the consideration of the extent of the power of the mind over the actions of the man, which everyone finds in himself, arise the ideas of *liberty* and *necessity*.

All the actions, that we have any idea of, reducing themselves, as has been said, to these two, viz. thinking and motion, so far as a man has the power to think, or not to think; to move, or not to move, according to the preference or direction of his own mind, so far is a man *free*. Wherever any performance or forbearance are not equally in a man's power; wherever doing or not doing, will not equally follow upon the preference of his mind, there he is not *free*, though perhaps the action may be voluntary. So that the idea of *liberty* is the idea of a power in any agent to do or forbear any action, according to the determination or thought of the mind, whereby either of them is preferred to the other; where either of them is not in the power of the agent to be produced by him according to his volition, there he is not at *liberty*, that agent is under *necessity*. So that liberty cannot be where there is no thought, no volition, no will; but there may be thought, there may be will, there may be volition, where there is no liberty. A little consideration of an obvious instance or two may make this clear.

A tennis-ball, whether in motion, by the stroke of a racket, or lying still at rest, is not by anyone taken to be a free agent. If we inquire into the reason, we shall find it is because we conceive not a tennis-ball to think, and consequently not to have any volition, or preference of motion to rest, or *vice versa*; and therefore has not liberty, is not a free agent; but all its both motion and rest come under our idea of necessary, and are so called. Likewise a man falling into the water (a bridge breaking under him) has not herein liberty, is not a free agent. For, though he has volition, though he prefers his not falling to falling; yet, the forbearance of that motion not being in his power, the stop or cessation of that motion follows not upon his volition; and therefore therein he is not free. So a man striking himself, or his friend, by a convulsive motion of his arm, which it is not in his power, by volition or the direction of his mind, to stop or forbear; nobody thinks he has, in this, liberty; everyone pities him, as acting by necessity and constraint.

Again, suppose a man be carried, whilst fast asleep, into a room where is a person he longs to see and speak with; and be there locked fast in, beyond his power to get out: he awakes, and is glad to find himself in so desirable a company, which he stays willingly in, i.e. prefers his stay to going away. I ask, Is not this stay voluntary? I think nobody will doubt it; and yet, being locked fast in, it is evident he is not at liberty not to stay, he has not freedom to be gone. So that liberty is not an idea belonging to volition or preferring; but to the person having the power of doing, or forbearing to do, according as the mind shall choose or direct. Our idea of liberty reaches as far as that power, and no farther. For wherever restraint comes to check that power, or compulsion takes away that indifference to act or not to act, there liberty, and our notion of it, presently ceases.

An Essay Concerning Human Understanding, 1690

SIR WILLIAM TEMPLE

[Poetry and Music]

WHETHER IT be that the fierceness of the Gothic humours or noise of their perpetual wars frighted it away, or that the unequal mixture of the modern languages would not bear it, certain it is that the great heights and excellency both of poetry and music fell with the Roman learning and empire, and have never since recovered the admiration and applauses that before attended them. Yet, such as they are amongst us, they must be confessed to be the softest and sweetest, the most general and most innocent amusements of common time and life. They still find room in the courts of princes and the cottages of shepherds. They serve to revive and animate the dead calm of poor or idle lives, and to allay or divert the violent passions and perturbations of the greatest and the busiest men. And both these effects are of equal use to human life; for the mind of man is like the sea, which is neither agreeable to the beholder nor the voyager in a calm or in a storm, but is so to both when a little agitated by gentle gales; and so the mind, when moved by soft and easy passions or affections. I know very well that many who pretend to be wise by the forms of being grave are apt to despise both poetry and music as toys and trifles too light for the use or entertainment of serious men. But whoever find themselves wholly insensible to these charms would, I think, do well to keep their own counsel, for fear of reproaching their own temper and bringing the goodness of their natures, if not their understandings, into question. It may be thought at least an ill sign, if not an ill constitution, since some of the Fathers went so far as to esteem the love of music a sign of predestination, as a thing divine and reserved for the felicities of heaven itself. While this world lasts, I doubt not but the pleasure and request of these two entertainments will do so, too, and happy those that content themselves with these or any other so easy and so innocent, and do not trouble the world or other men because they cannot be quiet themselves, though nobody hurts them.

When all is done, human life is at the greatest and the best but like a froward child that must be played with and humoured a little to keep it quiet till it falls asleep, and then the care is over.

'Upon Poetry', *Miscellanea: The Second Part*, 1690

CELIA FIENNES

[Newcastle, c. 1695]

As I drew nearer and nearer to Newcastle I met with and saw abundance of little carriages with a yoke of oxen and a pair of horses together, which is to convey the coals from the pits to the barges on the river. There is little sort of dung-pots. I suppose they hold not above two or three chauldron. This is the sea-coal which is pretty much like small coal, though some is round coals, yet none like the cleft coals, and this is what the smiths use, and it cakes in the fire and makes a great heat, but it burns not up light unless you put most round coals which will burn light, but then it's soon gone and that part of the coal never cakes, therefore the small sort is as good as any – if it's black and shining, that shows its goodness. This country all about is full of this coal, the sulphur of it taints the air and it smells strongly to strangers – upon a high hill two miles from Newcastle I could see all about the country which was full of coalpits.

Newcastle lies in a bottom very low; it appears from this hill a great flat. I saw all by the River Tyne which runs along to Tynemouth five or six miles off, which I could see very plain and the Scheld which is the key or fort at the mouth of the river which disembogues itself into the sea; all this was in view on this high hill which I descended – five mile more, in all nine from that place.

Newcastle is a town and county of itself, standing part in Northumberland, part in the bishopric of Durham, the River

Tyne being the division. It's a noble town though in a bottom; it most resembles London of any place in England, its buildings lofty and large, of brick mostly or stone. The streets are very broad and handsome and very well pitched, and many of them with very fine conduits of water in each always running into a large stone cistern for everybody's use. Their shops are good and are of distinct trades, not selling many things in one shop as is the custom in most country towns and cities; here is one market for corn, another for hay, besides all other things which takes up two or three streets. Saturday was their biggest market-day, which was the day I was there, and by reason of the extreme heat resolved to stay till the sun was low ere I proceeded farther, so had the opportunity of seeing most of the market, which is like a fair for all sorts of provision, and good and very cheap. I saw one buy a quarter of lamb for 3*d* and 2*d* apiece: good large poultry. Here is leather, woollen and linen and all sorts of stands for baubles. They have a very indifferent sort of cheese – little things, looks black on the outside. There is a very pleasant bowling green, a little walk out of the town with two rows of trees on each side making it very shady; there is a fine entertaining house that makes up the fourth side, before which is a paved walk and epiasses of brick.

From the Diary

APHRA BEHN

[The Noble Savage]

B UT BEFORE I give you the story of this gallant slave 'tis fit I tell you the manner of bringing them to these new colonies; for those they make use of there are not natives of the place, for those we live with in perfect amity, without daring to command 'em; but on the contrary caress 'em with all the brotherly and friendly affection in the world; trading with 'em for fish, venison, buffalo skins, and little rarities;

as marmosets, a sort of monkey as big as a rat or weasel, but of a marvellous and delicate shape, and has face and hands like an human creature; and coucheries, a little beast in the form and fashion of a lion, as big as a kitten but so exactly made in all parts like that noble beast that it is it in miniature. Then for little parakeets, great parrots, macaws, and a thousand other birds and beasts of wonderful and surprising forms, shapes and colours. For skins of prodigious snakes, of which there are some threescore yards in length; as is the skin of one that may be seen at his Majesty's antiquaries, where are also some rare flies of amazing forms and colours presented to 'em by myself, some as big as my fist, some less; and all of various excellencies such as art cannot imitate. Then we trade for feathers, which they order into all shapes, make themselves little short habits of 'em, and glorious wreaths for their heads, necks, arms and legs, whose tinctures are unconceivable. I had a set of these presented to me, and gave 'em to the King's Theatre, and it was the dress of the Indian queen, infinitely admired by persons of quality, and were unimitable. Besides these, a thousand little knacks and rarities in nature, and some of art; as their baskets, weapons, aprons, etc. We dealt with 'em with beads of all colours, knives, axes, pins and needles; which they used only as tools to drill holes with in their ears, noses and lips, where they hang a great many little things; as long beads, bits of tin, brass or silver beat thin and any shining trinkets. The beads they weave into aprons about a quarter of an ell long and of the same breadth, working them very prettily in flowers of several colours of beads; which apron they wear just before 'em, as Adam and Eve did the fig-leaves; the men wearing a long stripe of linen, which they deal with us for. They thread these beads also on long cotton-threads, and make girdles to tie their aprons to, which come twenty times or more about the waist; and they cross, like a shoulder-belt, both ways, and round their necks, arms and legs. This adornment, with their long black hair and the face painted in little specks or flowers here and there, makes 'em a wonderful figure to behold. Some of the beauties, which indeed are finely shaped – as almost all are – and who have pretty features, are very charming and novel; for they have all that is called beauty except the colour, which is a reddish yellow or, after a new oiling, which they often use to themselves, they are of the colour of a new brick, but smooth, soft and sleek. They are extreme modest and bashful, very shy, and nice of being touched. And, though they are all thus naked, if one lives for ever among 'em there is not to be seen an indecent action or glance; and being continually used to see one another so unadorned, so like our first parents before the Fall, it seems as if they had no wishes; there being nothing to heighten curiosity, but all you can see you see at once, and every moment see; and where there is no novelty there can be no curiosity. Not but I have seen a handsome young Indian dying for love of a very beautiful young Indian maid; but all his courtship was to fold his arms, pursue her with his eyes, and sighs were all his language: while she, as if no such lover were present – or, rather, as if she desired none such – carefully guarded her eyes from beholding him, and never approached him but she looked down with all the blushing modesty I have seen in the most severe and cautious of our world. And these people represented to me an absolute idea of the first state of innocence before man knew how to sin: and 'tis most evident and plain that simple Nature is the most harmless, inoffensive and virtuous mistress. 'Tis she alone, if she were permitted, that better instructs the world than all the inventions of man: religion would here but destroy that tranquillity they possess by ignorance; and laws would but teach 'em to know offence, of which now they have no notion. They once made mourning and fasting for the death of the English governor, who had given his hand to come on such a day to 'em, and neither came nor sent; believing when once a man's word was passed nothing but death could or should prevent his keeping it. And when they saw he was not dead they asked him what name they had for a man who promised a thing he did not do. The governor told them such a man was a liar, which was a word of infamy to a gentleman. Then one of 'em replied: 'Governor, you are a liar, and guilty of that infamy.' They have a native justice which knows no fraud; and they understand no vice or cunning but when they are taught by the white men. They have plurality of wives, which, when they grow old, they serve those that succeed 'em, who are young; but with a servitude easy and respected; and unless they take slaves in a war they have no other attendants.

Oroonoko; or, The Royal Slave, 1696

ANTHONY ASHLEY COOPER, EARL OF SHAFTESBURY

[Industry and Idleness]

IN BRUTES, and other creatures, who have not the use of reason or reflection (at least not after the manner of mankind) 'tis so ordered in nature, that by their daily search after food, and their application either towards the business of their livelihood, or the affairs of their species or kind, almost their whole time is taken up, and they fail not to find full employment for their passion, according to that degree of agitation to which they are fitted, and which their constitution requires. If any one of these creatures be taken out of his natural laborious state, and placed amidst such a plenty as can profusely administer to all his appetites and wants; it may be observed, that as his circumstances grow thus luxuriant, his temper and passions have the same growth. When he comes, at any time, to have the accommodations of life at a cheaper and easier rate than was at first intended him by nature, he is made to pay dear for 'em in another way; by losing his natural good disposition, and the orderliness of his kind or species.

This needs not to be demonstrated by particular instances. Whoever has the least knowledge of natural history, or has been an observer of the several breeds of creatures, and their ways of life, and propagation, will easily understand this difference of orderliness between the wild and the tame of the same species. The latter acquire new habits; and deviate from their original nature. They lose even the common instinct and ordinary ingenuity of their kind; nor can they ever regain it, whilst they continue in this pampered state: but being turned to shift abroad, they resume the natural affection and sagacity of their species. They learn to unite in stricter fellowship; and grow more concerned for their offspring. They provide against the seasons, and make the most of every advantage given by nature for the support and maintenance of their particular species, against such as are foreign and hostile. And thus as they grow busy and employed, they grow regular and good. Their petulancy and vice forsakes them with their idleness and ease.

It happens with mankind, that whilst some are by necessity confined to labour, others are provided with abundance of all things, by the pains and labour of inferiors. Now, if among the superior and easy sort, there be not something of fit and proper employment raised in the room of what is wanting in common labour and toil; if instead of an application to any sort of work, such as has a good and honest end in society (as letters, sciences, arts, husbandry, public affairs, economy, or the like) there be a thorough neglect of all duty or employment; a settled idleness, supineness, and inactivity; this of necessity must occasion a most relaxed and dissolute state: it must produce a total disorder of the passions, and break out in the strangest irregularities imaginable.

We see the enormous growth of luxury in capital cities, such as have been long the seat of empire. We see what improvements are made in vice of every kind, where numbers of men are maintained in lazy opulence, and wanton plenty. 'Tis otherwise with those who are taken up in honest and due employment, and have been well inured to it from their youth. This we may observe in the hardy remote provincials, the inhabitants of smaller towns, and the industrious sort of common people; where 'tis rare to meet with any instances of those irregularities, which are known in courts and palaces, and in the rich foundations of easy and pampered priests.

'An Inquiry Concerning Virtue, or Merit', 1699

EDWARD HYDE, EARL OF CLARENDON

[The Battle of Naseby]

[*1645*] Upon the 13th of June the King received intelligence that Fairfax was advanced to Northampton with a strong army, much superior to the numbers he had formerly been advertised of. Whereupon he retired next day to Harborough, and meant to have gone back to Leicester, that he might draw more foot out of Newark and stand upon his defence till the other forces, which he expected, could come up to him. But that very night an alarum was brought to Harborough that Fairfax himself was quartered within six miles. A council was presently called, and the former resolution of retiring presently laid aside, and a new one as quickly taken to fight; to which there was always an immoderate appetite when the enemy was within any distance. They would not stay to expect his coming, but would go back to meet him. And so, in the morning early, being Saturday the 14th of June, all the army was drawn up upon a rising ground of very great advantage about a mile south from Harborough (which was at their back) and there put in order to give or receive the charge. The main body of the foot was led by the Lord Ashley (whom the King had lately made a baron), consisting of about two thousand and five hundred foot; the right wing of horse, being about two thousand, was led by Prince Rupert; the left wing of horse, consisting of all the northern horse, with those from Newark, which did not amount to above sixteen hundred, was commanded by Sir Marmaduke Langdale. In the reserve were the King's Life Guard, commanded by the Earl of Lindsey, and Prince Rupert's regiment of foot, both which did make very little above eight hundred; with the King's Horse Guards, commanded by the Lord Bernard Stuart (newly made Earl of Lichfield), which made that day about five hundred horse.

The army thus disposed, in good order, made a stand on that ground to expect the enemy. About eight of the clock in the morning it began to be doubted whether the intelligence they had received of the enemy was true. Upon which the scoutmaster was sent to make farther discovery; who, it seems, went not far enough, but returned and averred that he had been three or four miles forward and could neither discover nor hear any thing of them; and presently a report was raised in the army that the enemy was retired. Prince Rupert thereupon drew out a party of horse and musketeers, both to discover and engage them, the army remaining still in the same place and posture they had been in. And his Highness had not marched above a mile when he received certain intelligence of their advance, and in a short time after he saw the van of their army, but it seems not so distinctly but that he conceived they were retiring. Whereupon he advanced nearer with his horse, and sent back that the army should march up to him; and the messenger who brought the order said that the Prince desired they should make haste. Hereupon the advantage ground was quitted, and the excellent order they were in, and an advance made towards the enemy as well as might be. By that time they had marched about a mile and a half, the horse of the enemy were discerned to stand upon a high ground about Naseby; and, from thence seeing the manner of the King's march in a full *campania*, they had leisure and opportunity to place themselves with all the advantages they could desire. The Prince his natural heat and impatience could never endure an enemy long in his view, nor believe that they had the courage to endure his charge. And so the army was engaged before the cannon was turned, or the ground made choice of upon which they were to fight: so that courage was only to be relied upon, where all conduct failed so much.

It was about ten of the clock when the battle began; and the first charge was given by Prince Rupert, who, with his own and his brother Prince Maurice his troop, performed it with his usual vigour, and was so well seconded that he bore down all before him, and was master of six pieces of the rebels' best cannon. The Lord Ashley, with his foot, though against the hill, advanced upon their foot, who discharged their cannon at them, but overshot them, and so did their musketeers, too. For the foot on either side hardly saw each other until they were within carabine-shot, and so only gave one volley; the King's foot, according to their usual custom, falling in with their swords and the butt-ends of their muskets, with which they did very notable execution, and put the enemy into great disorder and confusion. The right wing of horse and foot being thus fortunately engaged and advanced, the left wing, under Sir Marmaduke Langdale, in five bodies, advanced with equal resolution; and was encountered by Cromwell, who commanded the right wing of the enemy's horse, with seven bodies greater and more numerous than either of the other, and had, besides the odds in number, the advantage of the ground; for the King's horse were obliged to march up the hill before they could charge them; yet they did their duty as well as the place and great inequality of numbers would enable them to do. But being flanked on both sides by the enemy's horse, and pressed hard before they could get to the top of the hill, they gave back, and fled farther and faster than became them. Four of the enemy's bodies, close and in good order, followed them, that they might not rally again; which they never thought of doing; and the rest charged the King's foot, who had so much the advantage over theirs; whilst Prince Rupert, with the right wing, pursued those horse which he had broken and defeated.

The King's reserve of horse, which was his own guards, with himself in the head of them, were even ready to charge those horse who followed those of the left wing, when, on a sudden, such a panic fear seized upon them that they all ran near a quarter of a mile without stopping; which happened upon an extraordinary accident, which hath seldom fallen out, and might well disturb and disorder very resolute troops, as these were the best horse in the army. The King, as was said before, was even upon the point of charging the enemy, in the head of his guards, when the Earl of Cornwall, who rode next to him (a man never suspected for infidelity, nor one from whom the King would have received counsel in such a case), on a sudden laid his hand on the bridle of the King's horse, and swearing two or three full-mouthed Scots oaths (for of that nation he was), said, 'Will you go upon your death in an instant?' and, before his Majesty understood what he would have, turned his horse round; upon which a word ran through the troops that they should march to the right hand; which was both from charging the enemy, or assisting their own men. And upon this they all turned their horses and rode upon the spur, as if they were every man to shift for himself.

It is very true that, upon the more soldierly word *Stand*, which was sent to run after them, many of them returned to the King; though the former unlucky word carried more from him. And by this time Prince Rupert was returned with a good body of those horse which had attended him in his prosperous charge on the right wing; but they having, as they thought, acted their parts, they could never be brought to rally themselves again in order, or to charge the enemy. And that difference was observed shortly from the beginning of the war, in the discipline of the King's troops and of those which marched under the command of Cromwell (for it was only under him, and had never been notorious under Essex or Waller), that though the King's troops prevailed in the charge, and routed those they charged, they never rallied themselves again in order, nor could be brought to make a second charge again the same day: which was the reason that they had not an entire victory at Edgehill; whereas Cromwell's troops, if they prevailed, or though they were beaten and routed, presently rallied again, and stood in good order till they received new orders. All that the King and Prince could do could not rally their broken troops, which stood in sufficient numbers upon the field, though they often endeavoured it with the manifest hazard of their own persons. So that in the end the King was compelled to quit the field, and to leave Fairfax master of all his foot, cannon and baggage; amongst which was his own cabinet, where his most secret papers were, and letters between the Queen and him; of which they shortly after made that barbarous use as was agreeable to their natures, and published them in print, that is, so much of them as they thought would asperse either of their Majesties and improve the prejudice they had raised against them, and concealed other parts which would have vindicated them from many particulars with which they had aspersed them.

It will not be seasonable in this place to mention the names of those noble persons who were lost in this battle, when the King and his kingdom were lost in it; though there were above one hundred and fifty officers, and gentlemen of prime quality, whose memories ought to be preserved, who were dead upon the spot. The enemy left no manner of barbarous cruelty unexercised that day, and in the pursuit killed above one hundred women, whereof some were officers' wives of quality.

The History of the Rebellion and
Civil Wars in England, 1702

GEORGE BERKELEY

[Idea and Reality]

I DO not argue against the existence of any one thing that we can apprehend, either by sense or reflection. That the things I see with my eyes and touch with my hands do exist, really exist, I make not the least question. The only thing whose existence we deny is that which philosophers call matter or corporeal substance. And in doing of this there is no damage done to the rest of mankind, who, I dare say, will never miss it. The atheist indeed will want the colour of an empty name to support his impiety; and the philosophers may possibly find they have lost a great handle for trifling and disputation.

If any man thinks this detracts from the existence or reality of things, he is very far from understanding what has been premised in the plainest terms I could think of. Take here an abstract of what has been said. There are spiritual substances, minds, or human souls, which will or excite ideas in themselves at pleasure; but these are faint, weak, and unsteady in respect of others they perceive by sense, which being impressed upon them according to certain rules or laws of nature, speak themselves the effects of a mind more powerful and wise than human spirits. These latter are said to have more *reality* in them than the former: by which is meant that they are more affecting, orderly, and distinct, and that they are not fictions of the mind perceiving them. And in this sense the sun that I see by day is the real sun, and that which I imagine by night is the idea of the former. In the sense here given of *reality*, it is evident that every vegetable, star, mineral, and in general each part of the mundane system, is as much a *real being* by our principles as by any other. Whether others mean anything by the term *reality* different from what I do, I ask them to look into their own thoughts and see.

It will be urged that thus much at least is true, that is, that we take away all corporeal substances. To this my answer is that, if the word *substance* be taken in the vulgar sense, for a combination of sensible qualities, such as extension, solidity, weight and the like, this we cannot be accused of taking away. But if it be taken in a philosophical sense, for the support of accidents or qualities without the mind, then indeed I acknowledge that we take it away, if one may be said to take away that which never had any existence, not even in the imagination.

But, say you, it sounds very harsh to say we eat and drink ideas, and are clothed with ideas. I acknowledge it does so, the word *idea* not being used in common discourse to signify the several combinations of sensible qualities, which are called *things*: and it is certain that any expression which varies from the familiar use of language will seem harsh and ridiculous. But this does not concern the truth of the proposition, which in other words is no more than to say we are fed and clothed with those things which we perceive immediately by our senses. The hardness or softness, the colour, taste, warmth, figure, and such like qualities, which combined together constitute the several sorts of victuals and apparel, have been shown to exist only in the mind that perceives them; and this is all that is meant by calling them *ideas*; which word, if it was as ordinarily used as *thing*,

would sound no harsher nor more ridiculous than it. I am
not for disputing about the propriety but the truth of the
expression. If therefore you agree with me that we eat and
drink and are clad with the immediate objects of sense
which cannot exist unperceived or without the mind, I shall
readily grant it is more proper or conformable to custom
that they should be called things rather than ideas.

If it be demanded why I make use of the word *idea*, and
do not rather in compliance with custom call them *things*,
answer I do it for two reasons: first, because the term *thing*,
in contradistinction to *idea*, is generally supposed to denote
something existing without the mind; secondly, because
thing has a more comprehensive signification than *idea*,
including spirits or thinking things as well as ideas. Since
therefore the objects of sense exist only in the mind, and
are also thoughtless and inactive, I chose to mark them by
the word *idea*, which implies those properties.

*A Treatise Concerning the Principles
of Human Knowledge*, 1710

SIR RICHARD STEELE

[The Spectator Club]

THE FIRST of our society is a gentleman of Worcester-
shire, of ancient descent, a baronet, his name Sir Roger
de Coverley. His great-grandfather was inventor of that
famous country dance which is called after him. All who
know that shire are very well acquainted with the parts and
merits of Sir Roger. He is a gentleman that is very singular
in his behaviour, but his singularities proceed from his good
sense, and are contradictions to the manners of the world,
only as he thinks the world is in the wrong. However, this
humour creates him no enemies, for he does nothing with
sourness or obstinacy; and his being unconfined to modes
and forms, makes him but the readier and more capable to

please and oblige all who know him. When he is in town he lives in Soho Square: it is said he keeps himself a bachelor by reason he was crossed in love, by a perverse beautiful widow of the next county to him. Before this disappointment, Sir Roger was what you call a fine gentleman, had often supped with my Lord Rochester and Sir George Etherege, fought a duel upon his first coming to town, and kicked Bully Dawson in a public coffee-house for calling him youngster. But being ill-used by the abovementioned widow, he was very serious for a year and a half; and though his temper being very naturally jovial, he at last got over it, he grew careless of himself and never dressed afterwards; he continues to wear a coat and doublet of the same cut that were in fashion at the time of his repulse, which, in his merry humours, he tells us, has been in and out twelve times since he first wore it. 'Tis said Sir Roger grew humble in his desires after he had forgot this cruel beauty, insomuch that it is reported he has frequently offended in point of chastity with beggars and gypsies: but this is looked upon by his friends rather as matter of raillery than truth. He is now in his fifty-sixth year, cheerful, gay, and hearty, keeps a good house both in town and country; a great lover of mankind; but there is such a mirthful cast in his behaviour, that he is rather beloved than esteemed: his tenants grow rich, his servants look satisfied, all the young women profess love to him, and the young men are glad of his company; when he comes into a house he calls the servants by their names, and talks all the way up stairs to a visit. I must not omit that Sir Roger is a Justice of the *Quorum*; that he fills the chair at a quarter session with great abilities, and three months ago gained universal applause by explaining a passage in the Game Act.

The gentleman next in esteem and authority among us, is another bachelor, who is a member of the Inner Temple, a man of great probity, wit, and understanding; but he has chosen his place of residence rather to obey the direction of an old humoursome father than in pursuit of his own inclinations. He was placed there to study the laws of the land, and is the most learned of any of the house in those of the stage. Aristotle and Longinus are much better understood by him than Littleton or Coke. The father sends up every post questions relating to marriage articles, leases, and tenures, in the neighbourhood; all which questions he agrees with an attorney to answer and take care of in the lump: he is studying the passions themselves, when he should be inquiring into the debates among men which arise from them. He knows the argument of each of the Orations of Demosthenes and Tully, but not one case in the reports of our own courts. No one ever took him for a fool, but none, except his intimate friends, know he has a great deal of wit. This turn makes him at once both disinterested and agreeable: as few of his thoughts are drawn from business, they are most of them fit for conversation. His taste of books is a little too just for the age he lives in; he has read all, but approves of very few. His familiarity with the customs, manners, actions, and writings of the ancients, makes him a very delicate observer of what occurs to him in the present world. He is an excellent critic, and the time of the play, is his hour of business; exactly at five he passes through New Inn, crosses through Russell Court, and takes a turn at Will's till the play begins; he has his shoes rubbed and his periwig powdered at the barber's as you go into the Rose. It is for the good of the audience when he is at a play, for the actors have an ambition to please him.

The person of next consideration is Sir Andrew Freeport, a merchant of great eminence in the City of London: a person of indefatigable industry, strong reason, and great experience. His notions of trade are noble and generous, and (as every rich man has usually some sly way of jesting, which would make no great figure were he not a rich man) he calls the sea the British Common. He is acquainted with commerce in all its parts, and will tell you that it is a stupid and barbarous way to extend dominion by arms; for true power is to be got by arts and industry. He will often argue, that if this part of our trade were well cultivated, we should gain from one nation; and if another, from another. I have heard him prove, that diligence makes more lasting acquisitions than valour, and that sloth has ruined more nations than the sword. He abounds in several frugal maxims, among which the greatest favourite is, 'A penny saved is a penny got'. A general trader of good sense is pleasanter company than a general scholar; and Sir Andrew having a natural unaffected eloquence, the perspicuity of his discourse gives the same pleasure that wit would in another man. He has made his fortunes himself; and says that England may be richer than other kingdoms, by as plain methods as he himself is richer than other men; though at the same time I can say this of him, that there is not a point in the compass but blows home a ship in which he is an owner.

Next to Sir Andrew in the club-room sits Captain Sentry, a gentleman of great courage, good understanding, but invincible modesty. He is one of those that deserve very well, but are very awkward at putting their talents within the observation of such as should take notice of them. He was some years a captain, and behaved himself with great gallantry in several engagements and at several sieges; but having a small estate of his own, and being next heir to Sir Roger, he has quitted a way of life in which no man can rise suitably to his merit, who is not something of a courtier as well as a soldier. I have heard him often lament, that in a profession where merit is placed in so conspicuous a view, impudence should get the better of modesty. When he has talked to this purpose I never heard him make a sour expression, but frankly confess that he left the world because he was not fit for it. A strict honesty and an even regular behaviour are in themselves obstacles to him that must press through crowds who endeavour at the same end with himself, the favour of a commander. He will however in this way of talk excuse generals for not disposing according to men's desert, or inquiring into it: for, says he, that great man who has a mind to help me, has as many to break through to come at me, as I have to come at him; therefore he will conclude, that the man who would make a figure, especially in a military way, must get over all false modesty, and assist his patron against the importunity of other pretenders by a proper assurance in his own vindication. He says it is a civil cowardice to be backward in asserting what you ought to expect, as it is a military fear to be slow in attacking when it is your duty. With this candour does the gentleman speak of himself and others. The same frankness runs through all his conversation. The military part of his life has furnished him with many adventures, in the relation of which he is very agreeable to the company; for he is never over-bearing, though accustomed to command men in the utmost degree below him; nor ever too obsequious, from an habit of obeying men highly above him.

But that our society may not appear a set of humourists [*cranks*] unacquainted with all the gallantries and pleasures of the age, we have among us the gallant Will Honeycomb, a gentleman who according to his years should be in the decline of his life, but having ever been very careful of his person, and always had a very easy fortune, time has made but very little impression, either by wrinkles on his forehead, or traces in his brain. His person is well turned, of a good height. He is very ready at that sort of discourse with which men usually entertain women. He has all his life dressed very well, and remembers habits as others do men. He can smile when one speaks to him, and laughs easily. He knows the history of every mode, and can inform you from which of the French King's wenches our wives and daughters had this manner of curling their hair, that way of placing their hoods; whose frailty was covered by such a sort of petticoat, and whose vanity to show her foot made that part of the dress so short in such a year. In a word, all his conversation and knowledge has been in the female world: as other men of his age will take notice to you what such a minister said upon such and such an occasion, he will tell you when the Duke of Monmouth danced at Court such a woman was then smitten, another was taken with him at the head of his troop in the Park. In all these important relations, he has ever about the same time received a kind glance or a blow of a fan from some celebrated beauty, mother of the present Lord such-a-one. If you speak of a young Commoner [*MP*] that said a lively thing in the House, he starts up, 'He has good blood in his veins, Tom Mirabell begot him, the rogue cheated me in that affair; that young fellow's mother used me more like a dog than any woman I ever made advances to.' This way of talking of his very much enlivens the conversation among us of a more sedate turn; and I find there is not one of the company but myself, who rarely speak at all, but speaks of him as of that sort of man who is usually called a well-bred fine gentleman. To conclude his character, where women are not concerned, he is an honest worthy man.

I cannot tell whether I am to account him whom I am next to speak of, as one of our company; for he visits us but seldom, but when he does it adds to every man else a new enjoyment of himself. He is a clergyman, a very philosophic man, of general learning, great sanctity of life, and the most exact good breeding. He has the misfortune to be of a very weak constitution, and consequently cannot accept of such cares and business as preferments in his function would oblige him to: he is therefore among divines what a chamber-counsellor is among lawyers. The probity of his mind, and the integrity of his life, create him followers, as being eloquent or loud advances others. He seldom introduces the subject he speaks upon; but we are so far gone in years that he observes, when he is among us, an earnestness to have him fall on some divine topic, which he always treats with much authority, as one who has no interests in this world, as one who is hastening to the object of all his wishes, and conceives hope from his decays and infirmities. These are my ordinary companions.

The Spectator, no. 2, Friday, 2 March 1711

JOSEPH ADDISON

[Sir Roger at the Assizes]

A MAN'S first care should be to avoid the reproaches of his own heart; his next, to escape the censures of the world; if the last interferes with the former, it ought to be entirely neglected; but otherwise there cannot be a greater satisfaction to an honest mind, than to see those appro-bations which it gives itself seconded by the applauses of the public: a man is more sure of his conduct, when the verdict which he passes upon his own behaviour is thus warranted and confirmed by the opinion of all that know him.

My worthy friend Sir Roger is one of those who is not only at peace within himself, but beloved and esteemed by all about him. He receives a suitable tribute for his universal benevolence to mankind, in the returns of affection and goodwill, which are paid him by every one that lives within his neighbourhood. I lately met with two or three odd instances of that general respect which is shown to the good old knight. He would needs carry Will Wimble and myself with him to the county assizes: as we were upon the road Will Wimble joined a couple of plain men who rode before us, and conversed with them for some time; during which my friend Sir Roger acquainted me with their characters.

'The first of them,' says he, 'that has a spaniel by his side, is a yeoman of about an hundred pounds a year, an honest man: he is just within the Game Act, and qualified to kill an hare or a pheasant; he knocks down a dinner with his gun twice or thrice a week: and by that means lives much cheaper than those who have not so good an estate as himself. He would be a good neighbour if he did not destroy so many partridges: in short he is a very sensible man; shoots flying; and has been several times foreman of the petty jury.

'The other that rides along with him is Tom Touchy, a fellow famous for taking the law of every body. There is not one in the town where he lives that he has not sued at a quarter sessions. The rogue had once the impudence to go to law with the widow. His head is full of costs, damages, and ejectments; he plagued a couple of honest gentlemen so long for a trespass in breaking one of his hedges, till he was forced to sell the ground it enclosed to defray the charges of the prosecution: his father left him fourscore pounds a year; but he has cast and been cast [*won and lost cases*] so often, that he is not now worth thirty. I suppose he is going upon the old business of the willow tree.'

As Sir Roger was giving me this account of Tom Touchy, Will Wimble and his two companions stopped short until we came up to them. After having paid their respects to Sir Roger, Will told him that Mr Touchy and he must appeal to him upon a dispute that arose between them. Will it seems had been giving his fellow-traveller an account of his angling one day in such a hole; when Tom Touchy, instead of hearing out his story, told him, that Mr such an one, if he pleased, might *take the law of him* for fishing in that part of the river. My friend Sir Roger heard them both upon a round trot; and after having paused some time, told them, with the air of a man who would not give his judgement rashly, that *much might be said on both sides.* They were neither of them dissatisfied with the knight's determination, because neither of them found himself in the wrong by it; upon which we made the best of our way to the assizes.

The court was sat before Sir Roger came; but notwithstanding all the justices had taken their places upon the bench, they made room for the old knight at the head of them; who, for his reputation in the country, took occasion to whisper in the judge's ear, *that he was glad his lordship had met with so much good weather in his circuit.* I was listening to the proceedings of the court with much attention, and infinitely pleased with that great appearance and solemnity which so properly accompanies such a public administration of our laws; when, after about an hour's sitting, I observed to my great surprise, in the midst of a trial, that my friend Sir Roger was getting up to speak. I was in some pain for him till I found he had acquitted himself of two or three sentences, with a look of much business and great intrepidity.

Upon his first rising the court was hushed, and a general whisper ran among the country people that Sir Roger *was up.* The speech he made was so little to the purpose, that I shall not trouble my readers with an account of it; and I believe was not so much designed by the knight himself to inform the court, as to give him a figure in the eye, and keep up his credit in the country.

I was highly delighted, when the court rose, to see the gentlemen of the country gathering about my old friend, and striving who should compliment him most; at the same time that the ordinary people gazed upon him at a distance, not a little admiring his courage, that was not afraid to speak to the judge.

In our return home we met with a very odd accident; which I cannot forbear relating, because it shows how desirous all who know Sir Roger are of giving him marks of their esteem. When we were arrived upon the verge of his estate, we stopped at a little inn to rest ourselves and our horses. The man of the house had, it seems, been formerly a servant in the knight's family; and to do honour to his old master, had some time since, unknown to Sir Roger, put him up in a sign-post before the door; so that 'the Knight's Head' had hung out upon the road about a week before he himself knew anything of the matter. As soon as Sir Roger was acquainted with it, finding that his servant's indiscretion proceeded wholly from affection and goodwill, he only told him that he had made him too high a compliment; and when the fellow seemed to think that could hardly be, added with a more decisive look, that it was too great an honour for any man under a duke; but told him at the same time, that it might be altered with a very few touches, and that he himself would be at the charge of it. Accordingly, they got a painter by the knight's directions to add a pair of whiskers to the face, and by a little aggravation of the features to change it into the *Saracen's Head*. I should not have known this story, had not the innkeeper, upon Sir Roger's alighting, told him in my hearing, that his honour's head was brought back last night with the alterations that he had ordered to be made in it. Upon this my friend with his usual cheerfulness related the particulars above mentioned, and ordered the head to be brought into the room. I could not forbear discovering greater expressions of mirth than ordinary upon the appearance of this monstrous face, under which, notwithstanding it was made to frown and stare in a most extraordinary manner, I could still discover a distant resemblance of my old friend. Sir Roger, upon seeing me laugh, desired me to tell him truly if I thought it possible for people to know him in that disguise. I at first kept my usual silence: but upon the knight conjuring me to tell him whether it was not still more like himself than a Saracen, I composed my countenance in the best manner I could, and replied, *That much might be said on both sides.*

These several adventures, with the knight's behaviour in them, gave me as pleasant a day as ever I met with in any of my travels.

The Spectator, no. 122, Friday, 20 July 1711

LADY MARY WORTLEY MONTAGU

[Ingrafting]

Adrianople, 1 April 1717

IN MY opinion, dear S[arah], I ought rather to quarrel with you for not answering my Nijmegen letter of August till December, than to excuse my not writing again till now. I am sure there is on my side a very good excuse for silence, having gone such tiresome land-journeys, though I don't find the conclusion of them so bad as you seem to imagine. I am very easy here, and not in the solitude you fancy me. The great number of Greeks, French, English, and Italians, that are under our protection, make their court to me from morning till night; and, I'll assure you, are many of them fine ladies; for there is no possibility for a Christian to live easily under this government but by the protection of an ambassador – and the richer they are, the greater is their danger.

Those dreadful stories you have heard of the *plague* have very little foundation in truth. I own I have much ado to reconcile myself to the sound of a word which has always given me such terrible ideas, though I am convinced there is little more in it than in a fever. As a proof of this, let me tell you that we passed through two or three towns most violently infected. In the very next house where we lay (in one of those places) two persons died of it. Luckily for me I was so well deceived that I knew nothing of the matter; and I was made believe, that our second cook had only a great cold. However, we left our doctor to take care of him, and yesterday they both arrived here in good health; and I am now let into the secret that he has had the *plague*. There are many that escape it; neither is the air ever infected. I am persuaded that it would be as easy a matter to root it out here as out of Italy and France; but it does so little mischief, they are not very solicitous about it, and are content to suffer this distemper instead of our variety, which they are utterly unacquainted with.

A propos of distempers, I am going to tell you a thing that will make you wish yourself here. The small-pox, so fatal, and so general amongst us, is here entirely harmless by the invention of *ingrafting*, which is the term they give it. There is a set of old women who make it their business to perform the operation every autumn, in the month of September, when the great heat is abated. People send to one another to know if any of their family has a mind to have the small-pox; they make parties for this purpose, and when they are met (commonly fifteen or sixteen together), the old woman comes with a nut-shell full of the matter of the best sort of small-pox, and asks what vein you please to have opened. She immediately rips open that you offer to her with a large needle (which gives you no more pain than a common scratch), and puts into the vein as much matter as can lie upon the head of her needle, and after that binds up the little wound with a hollow bit of shell; and in this manner opens four or five veins. The Grecians have commonly the superstition of opening one in the middle of the forehead, one in each arm, and one on the breast, to mark the sign of the cross; but this has a very ill effect, all these wounds leaving little scars, and is not done by those that are not superstitious, who choose to have them in the legs, or that part of the arm that is concealed. The children or young patients play together all the rest of the day, and are in perfect health to the eighth. Then the fever begins to seize them, and they keep their beds two days, very seldom three. They have very rarely above twenty or thirty in their faces, which never mark; and in eight days' time they are as well as before their illness. Where they are wounded, there remain running sores during the distemper, which I don't doubt is a great relief to it. Every year thousands undergo this operation; and the French ambassador says pleasantly, that they take the small-pox here by way of diversion, as they take the waters in other countries. There is no example of any one that has died in it; and you may believe I am well satisfied of the safety of this experience, since I intend to try it on my dear little son.

I am patriot enough to take pains to bring this useful invention into fashion in England; and I should not fail to write to some of our doctors very particularly about it, if I knew any one of them, that I thought had virtue enough to destroy such a considerable branch of their revenue for the good of mankind. But that distemper is too beneficial to them, not to expose to all their resentment the hardy wight that should undertake to put an end to it. Perhaps, if I live to return, I may, however, have courage to war with them. Upon this occasion admire the heroism in the heart of your friend, etc., etc.

Letter to Sarah Chiswell

DANIEL DEFOE

[A Discovery]

IT HAPPENED one day, about noon, going towards my boat, I was exceedingly surprised with the print of a man's naked foot on the shore, which was very plain to be seen on the sand. I stood like one thunderstruck, or as if I had seen an apparition. I listened, I looked round me, but I could hear nothing, nor see anything; I went up to a rising ground to look farther; I went up the shore, and down the shore, but it was all one: I could see no other impression but that one. I went to it again to see if there were any more, and to observe if it might not be my fancy; but there was no room for that, for there was exactly the print of a foot – toes, heel, and every part of a foot. How it came thither, I knew not, nor could in the least imagine. But after innumerable fluttering thoughts like a man perfectly confused and out of himself, I came home to my fortification, not feeling, as we say, the ground I went on, but terrified to the last degree, looking behind me at every two or three steps, mistaking every bush and tree, and fancying every stump at a distance to be a man. Nor is it possible to describe how many various shapes my affrighted imagination represented things to me in; how many wild ideas were formed every moment in my fancy, and what strange unaccountable whimseys came into my thoughts by the way.

When I came to my castle (for so I think I called it ever after this), I fled into it like one pursued. Whether I went over by the ladder, as first contrived, or went in at the hole in the rock, which I called a door, I cannot remember; for never frighted hare fled to cover, or fox to earth, with more terror of mind than I to this retreat.

I had no sleep that night; the farther I was from the occasion of my fright, the greater my apprehensions were, which is something contrary to the nature of such things, and especially to the usual practice of all creatures in fear; but I was so embarrassed with my own frightful ideas of the thing, that I formed nothing but dismal imaginations to myself, even though I was now a great way off it. Sometimes I fancied it must be the devil; and reason joined in with me upon this supposition; for how should any other thing in human shape come into the place? Where was the vessel that brought them? What marks were there of any other footsteps? And how was it possible a man should come there? But then to think that Satan should take human shape upon him in such a place, where there could be no manner of occasion for it, but to leave the print of his foot behind him, and that even for no purpose too, for he could not be sure I should see it – this was an amazement the other way. I considered that the devil might have found out abundance of other ways to have terrified me than this of the simple print of a foot; that as I lived quite on the other side of the island, he would never have been so simple as to leave a mark in a place where it was ten thousand to one whether I should ever see it or not, and in the sand too, which the first surge of the sea, upon a high wind, would have defaced entirely. All this seemed inconsistent with the thing itself, and with all the notions we usually entertain of the subtlety of the devil.

Abundance of such things as these assisted to argue me out of all apprehensions of its being the devil; and I presently concluded then, that it must be some more dangerous creature; viz., that it must be some of the savages of the mainland over against me, who had wandered out to sea in their canoes, and either driven by the currents or by contrary winds, had made the island, and had been on shore, but were gone away again to sea; being as loath, perhaps, to have stayed in this desolate island as I would have been to have had them.

While these reflections were rolling upon my mind, I was very thankful in my thought, that I was so happy as not to be thereabouts at that time, or that they did not see my boat, by which they would have concluded that some inhabitants had been in the place, and perhaps have searched farther for me. Then terrible thoughts raked my imagination about their having found my boat, and that there were people here; and that, if so, I should certainly have them come again in greater numbers, and devour me; that if it should happen that they should not find me, yet they would find my enclosure, destroy all my corn, and carry away all my flock of tame goats, and I should perish at last for mere want.

Thus my fear banished all my religious hope; all that former confidence in God, which was founded upon such wonderful experience as I had had of His goodness, now vanished; as if He that had fed me by miracle hitherto, could not preserve by His power the provision which He had made for me by His goodness. I reproached myself with my laziness, that would not sow any more corn one year than would just serve me till the next season, as if no accident could intervene to prevent my enjoying the crop that was upon the ground; and this I thought so just a reproof, that I resolved for the future to have two or three years' corn beforehand, so that, whatever might come, I might not perish for want of bread.

How strange a checkerwork of Providence is the life of man! and by what secret differing springs are the affections hurried about, as differing circumstances present! Today we love what tomorrow we hate; today we seek what tomorrow we shun; today we desire what tomorrow we fear, nay, even tremble at the apprehension of. This was exemplified in me at this time in the most lively manner imaginable; for I, whose only affliction was, that I seemed banished from human society, that I was alone, circumscribed by the boundless ocean, cut off from mankind, and condemned to what I call silent life; that I was as one whom Heaven thought not worthy to be numbered among the living, or to appear amongst the rest of his creatures; that to have seen one of my own species would have seemed to me a raising me from death to life, and the greatest blessing that Heaven itself, next to the supreme blessing of salvation, could bestow; I say, that I should now tremble at the very apprehensions of seeing a man, and was ready to sink into the ground at but the shadow or silent appearance of a man having set his foot on the island.

The Life and Adventures of Robinson Crusoe,
Written by Himself, 1719

[Newgate]

I GOT no sleep for several nights or days after I came into that wretched place, and glad I would have been for some time to have died there, though I did not consider dying as it ought to be considered neither; indeed, nothing could be filled with more horror to my imagination than the very place, nothing was more odious to me than the company that was there. Oh! if I had but been sent to any place in the world, and not to Newgate, I should have thought myself happy.

In the next place, how did the hardened wretches that were there before me triumph over me! What! Mrs Flanders come to Newgate at last? What! Mrs Mary, Mrs Molly, and after that plain Moll Flanders! They thought the devil had helped me, they said, that I had reigned so long; they expected me there many years ago, they said, and was I come at last? Then they flouted me with dejections, welcomed me to the place, wished me joy, bid me have a good heart, not be cast down, things might not be so bad as I feared, and the like; then called for brandy, and drank to me, but put it all up to my score, for they told me I was but just come to the college, as they called it, and sure I had money in my pocket, though they had none.

I asked one of this crew how long she had been there. She said four months. I asked her how the place looked to her when she first came into it. Just as it did now to me, says she, dreadful and frightful; that she thought she was in hell; 'and I believe so still,' adds she, 'but it is natural to me now, I don't disturb myself about it.' 'I suppose,' says I, 'you are in no danger of what is to follow?' 'Nay,' says she, 'you are mistaken there, I am sure, for I am under sentence, only I pleaded my belly, but am no more with child than the judge that tried me, and I expect to be called down next session.' This 'calling down' is calling down to their former judgement, when a woman has been respited for her belly, but proves not to be with child, or if she has been with child, and has been brought to bed. 'Well,' says I, 'and are you thus easy?' 'Ay,' says she, 'I can't help myself; what signifies being sad? if I am hanged, there's an end of me.' And away she turned dancing, and sings as she goes, the following piece of Newgate wit:

> If I swing by the string,
> I shall hear the bell ring,
> And then there's an end of poor Jenny.

I mention this because it would be worth the observation of any prisoner, who shall hereafter fall into the same misfortune, and come to that dreadful place of Newgate, how time, necessity, and conversing with the wretches that are there familiarises the place to them; how at last they become reconciled to that which at first was the greatest dread upon their spirits in the world, and are as impudently cheerful and merry in their misery as they were when out of it.

I cannot say, as some do, this devil is not so black as he is painted; for indeed no colours can represent that place to the life, nor any soul conceive aright of it but those who have been sufferers there. But how hell should become by degrees so natural, and not only tolerable, but even agreeable, is a thing unintelligible but by those who have experienced it, as I have.

The Fortunes and Misfortunes of
Moll Flanders, 1722

BERNARD DE MANDEVILLE

[Crime and Punishment]

IN A populous city it is not difficult for a young rascal, that has pushed himself into a crowd, with a small hand and nimble fingers to whip away a handkerchief or snuffbox from a man who is thinking on business and regardless of his pocket. Success in small crimes seldom fails of ushering in greater, and he that picks pockets with impunity at twelve is likely to be a housebreaker at sixteen and a thorough-paced villain long before he is twenty. Those who are cautious as well as bold, and no drunkards, may do a world of mischief before they are discovered; and this is one of the greatest inconveniences of such vast overgrown cities as London or Paris, that they harbour rogues and villains as granaries do vermin: they afford a perpetual shelter to the worst of people, and are places of safety to thousands of criminals who daily commit thefts and burglaries, and yet, by often changing their places of abode, may conceal themselves for many years and will perhaps forever escape the hands of justice unless by chance they are apprehended in a fact. And when they are taken the evidences perhaps want clearness or are otherwise insufficient, the depositions are not strong enough, juries and often judges are touched with compassion. Prosecutors, though vigorous at first, often relent before the time of trial comes on: few men prefer the public safety to their own ease; a man of good nature is not easily reconciled with the taking away of another man's life, though he has deserved the gallows. To be the cause of anyone's death, though justice requires it, is what most people are startled at, especially men of conscience and probity, when they want judgement or resolution. As this is the reason that thousands escape that deserve to be capitally punished, so it is likewise the cause that there are so many offenders who boldly venture in hopes that, if they are taken, they shall have the same good fortune of getting off.

But, if men did imagine and were fully persuaded that, as surely as they committed a fact that deserved hanging, so surely they would be hanged, executions would be very rare, and the most desperate felon would almost as soon hang himself as he would break open a house. To be stupid and ignorant is seldom the character of a thief. Robberies on the highway and other bold crimes are generally perpetrated by rogues of spirit and a genius, and villains of any fame are commonly subtle cunning fellows that are well versed in the methods of trials and acquainted with every quirk in the law that can be of use to them, that overlook not the smallest flaw in an indictment, and know how to make an advantage of the least slip of an evidence and everything else that can serve their turn to bring 'em off.

It is a mighty saying that it is better that five hundred guilty people should escape than that one innocent person should suffer. This maxim is only true as to futurity, and in relation to another world; but it is very false in regard to the temporal welfare of the society. It is a terrible thing a man should be put to death for a crime he is not guilty of; yet so oddly circumstances may meet in the infinite variety of accidents that it is possible it should come to pass, all the wisdom that judges and conscientiousness that juries may be possessed of notwithstanding. But where men endeavour to avoid this with all the care and precaution human prudence is able to take, should such a misfortune happen perhaps once or twice in half a score years, on condition that all that time justice should be administered with all the strictness and severity, and not one guilty person suffered to escape with impunity, it would be a vast advantage to a nation, not only as to the securing of everyone's property and the peace of the society in general, but it would likewise save the lives of hundreds, if not thousands, of necessitous wretches that are daily hanged for trifles and who would never have attempted anything against the law – or, at least, not have ventured on capital crimes – if the hopes of getting off should they be taken had not been one of the motives that animated their resolution. Therefore where the laws are plain and severe all the remissness in the execution of them, lenity of juries and frequency of pardons are in the main a much greater cruelty to a populous state or kingdom than the use of racks and the most exquisite torments.

The Fable of the Bees; or, Private Vices,
Public Benefits, 1723 edition

JONATHAN SWIFT

[A Voyage to Lilliput: Native Hospitality]

I LAY down on the grass, which was very short and soft; where I slept sounder than ever I remember to have done in my life and, as I reckoned, above nine hours; for when I awaked it was just daylight. I attempted to rise, but was not able to stir; for as I happened to lie on my back I found my arms and legs were strongly fastened on each side to the ground; and my hair, which was long and thick, tied down in the same manner. I likewise felt several slender ligatures across my body, from my armpits to my thighs. I could only look upwards: the sun began to grow hot, and the light offended my eyes. I heard a confused noise about me, but in the posture I lay could see nothing except the sky. In a little time I felt something alive moving on my left leg, which advancing gently forward over my breast came almost up to my chin; when, bending my eyes downwards as much as I could, I perceived it to be a human creature not six inches high, with a bow and arrow in his hands, and a quiver at his back. In the mean time, I felt at least forty more of the same kind (as I conjectured) following the first. I was in the utmost astonishment, and roared so loud that they all ran back in a fright; and some of them, as I was afterwards told, were hurt with the falls they got by leaping from my sides upon the ground. However, they soon returned; and one of them, who ventured so far as to get a full sight of my face, lifting up his hands and eyes by way of admiration, cried out in a shrill, but distinct voice, *Hekinah Degul*. The others repeated the same words several times, but I then knew not what they meant. I lay all this while, as the reader may believe, in great uneasiness. At length, struggling to get loose, I had the fortune to break the strings and wrench out the pegs that fastened my left arm to the ground; for, by lifting it up to my face, I discovered the methods they had taken to bind me; and, at the same time, with a violent pull, which gave me excessive pain, I a little loosened the strings that tied down my hair on the left side; so that I was just able to turn my head about two inches. But the creatures ran off a second time, before I could seize them; whereupon there was a great shout in a very shrill accent; and after it ceased I heard one of them cry aloud, *Tolgo Phonac*; when in an instant I felt above an hundred arrows discharged on my left hand, which pricked me like so many needles; and, besides, they shot another flight into the air, as we do bombs in Europe; whereof many, I suppose, fell on my body (though I felt them not), and some on my face, which I immdiately covered with my left hand. When this shower of arrows was over, I fell agroaning with grief and pain; and then, striving again to get loose, they discharged another volley larger than the first; and some of them attempted with spears to stick me in the sides; but, by good luck, I had on me a buff jerkin, which they could not pierce. I thought it the most prudent method to lie still; and my design was to continue so till night, when, my left hand being already loose, I could easily free myself. And as for the inhabitants, I had reason to believe I might be a match for the greatest armies they could bring against me, if they were all of the same size with him that I saw. But fortune disposed otherwise of me. When the people observed I was quiet, they discharged no more arrows. But by the noise increasing I knew their numbers were greater; and about four yards from me, over against my right ear, I heard a knocking for above an hour, like people at work; when turning my head that way, as well as the pegs and strings would permit me, I saw a stage erected about a foot and a half from the ground, capable of holding four of the inhabitants, with two or three ladders to mount it. From whence one of them, who seemed to be a person of quality, made me a long speech, whereof I understood not one syllable. But I should have mentioned that before the principal person began his oration he cried out three times *Langro Dehul san* (these words and the former were afterwards repeated and explained to me). Whereupon immediately about fifty of the inhabitants came and cut the strings that fastened the left side of my head, which gave me the liberty of turning it to the right, and of observing the person and gesture of him who was to speak. He appeared to be of a middle age, and taller than any of the other three who attended him; whereof one was a page, who held up his train, and seemed to be somewhat longer than my middle finger; the other two stood one on each side to support him. He acted every part of an orator; and I could observe many periods of threatenings, and others of promises, pity and kindness. I answered in a few words, but in the most submissive manner, lifting up my left hand and both my eyes to the sun, as calling him for a witness; and being almost famished with hunger, having not eaten a morsel for some hours before I left the ship, I found the demands of nature so strong upon me that I could not forbear showing my impatience (perhaps against the strict rules of decency) by putting my finger frequently in my mouth, to signify that I wanted food. The *Hurgo* (for so they call a great lord, as I afterwards learnt) understood me very well. He descended from the stage, and commanded that several ladders should be applied to my sides, on which above an hundred of the inhabitants mounted and walked towards my mouth, laden with baskets full of meat, which had been provided and sent thither by the King's orders upon the first intelligence he received of me. I observed there was the flesh of several animals, but I could not distinguish them by the taste. There were shoulders, legs and loins shaped like those of mutton, and very well dressed, but smaller than the wings of a lark. I eat them by two or three at a mouthful; and took three loaves at a time, about the bigness of musket bullets. They supplied me as fast as they could, showing a thousand marks of wonder and astonishment at my bulk and appetite. I then made another sign that I wanted drink. They found by my eating that a small quantity would not suffice me; and, being a most ingenious people, they slung up with great dexterity one of their largest hogsheads; then rolled it towards my head, and beat out the top; I drank it off at a draught, which I might well do, for it hardly held half a pint, and tasted like a small wine of Burgundy, but much more delicious. They brought me a second hogshead, which I drank in the same manner, and made signs for more, but they had none to give me. When I had performed these wonders, they shouted for joy, and danced upon my breast, repeating several times as they did at first, *Hekinah Degul*. They made me a sign that I should throw down the two hogsheads, but first warned the people below to stand out of the way, crying aloud, *Borach Mivola*; and when they saw the vessels in the air there was an universal shout of *Hekinah Degul*. I confess I was often tempted, while they were passing backwards and forwards on my body, to seize forty or fifty of the first that came in my reach, and dash them against the ground. But the remembrance of what I had felt, which probably might not be the worst they could do; and the promise of honour I made them, for so I interpreted my submissive behaviour, soon drove out those imaginations. Besides, I now considered myself as bound by the laws of hospitality to a people who had treated me with so much expense and magnificence. However, in my thoughts I could not sufficiently wonder at the intrepidity of these diminutive mortals, who durst venture to mount and walk on my body while one of my hands was at liberty without trembling at the very sight of so prodigious a creature as I must appear to them. After some time, when they observed that I made no more demands for meat, there appeared before me a person of high rank from his Imperial Majesty. His Excellency, having mounted on the small of my right leg, advanced forwards up to my face, with about a dozen of his retinue; and producing his credentials under the signet royal, which he applied close to my eyes, spoke about ten minutes, without any signs of anger, but with a kind of determinate resolution; often pointing forwards, which, as I afterwards found, was towards the capital city, about half a mile distant, whither it was agreed by his Majesty in council that I must be conveyed. I answered in few words, but to no purpose, and made a sign with my hand that was loose, putting it to the other (but over his Excellency's head, for fear of hurting him or his train), and then to my own head and body, to signify that I desired my liberty. It appeared that he understood me well enough; for he shook his head by way of disapprobation, and held his hand in a posture to show that I must be carried as a prisoner. However, he made other signs to let me understand that I should have meat and drink enough, and very good treatment. Whereupon I once more thought of attempting to break my bonds; but again, when I felt the smart of their arrows upon my face and hands, which were all in blisters, and many of the darts still sticking in them; and observing likewise that the number of my enemies increased; I gave tokens to let them know that they might do with me what they pleased.

Travels into Several Remote Nations
of the World . . . by Lemuel Gulliver, 1726

[A Modest Proposal]

I THINK it is agreed by all parties that this prodigious number of children, in the arms, or on the backs, or at the heels of their mothers, and frequently of their fathers, is in the present deplorable state of the kingdom a very great additional grievance; and therefore whoever could find out a fair, cheap and easy method of making these children sound and useful members of the commonwealth would deserve so well of the public as to have his statue set up for a preserver of the nation.

But my intention is very far from being confined to provide only for the children of professed beggars. It is of a much greater extent, and shall take in the whole number of infants at a certain age, who are born of parents in effect as little able to support them as those who demand our charity in the streets.

As to my own part, having turned my thoughts for many years upon this important subject, and maturely weighed the several schemes of other projectors, I have always found them grossly mistaken in their computation. It is true a child just dropped from its dam may be supported by her milk for a solar year with little other nourishment, at most not above the value of two shillings, which the mother may certainly get, or the value in scraps, by her lawful occupation of begging, and it is exactly at one year old that I propose to provide for them, in such a manner as, instead of being a charge upon their parents or the parish, or wanting food for the rest of their lives, they shall, on the contrary, contribute to the feeding and partly to the clothing of many thousands.

There is likewise another great advantage in my scheme: that it will prevent those voluntary abortions and that horrid practice of women murdering their bastard children, alas! too frequent among us, sacrificing the poor innocent babes, I doubt, more to avoid the expense than the shame, which would move tears and pity in the most savage and inhuman breast.

The number of souls in this kingdom being usually reckoned one million and a half, of these I calculate there may be about two hundred thousand couple whose wives are breeders, from which number I substract thirty thousand couples who are able to maintain their own children, although I apprehend there cannot be so many under the present distresses of the kingdom; but, this being granted, there will remain an hundred and seventy thousand breeders. I again substract fifty thousand for those women who miscarry or whose children die by accident or decease within the year. There only remain an hundred and twenty thousand children of poor parents annually born. The question therefore is how this number shall be reared and provided for, which, as I have already said, under the present situation of affairs is utterly impossible by all the methods hitherto proposed, for we can neither employ them in handicraft or agriculture; we neither build houses (I mean in the country) nor cultivate land. They can seldom pick up a livelihood by stealing till they arrive at six years old, except where they are of towardly parts, although I confess they learn the rudiments much earlier, during which time they can, however, be properly looked upon only as probationers, as I have been informed by a principal gentleman in the county of Cavan, who protested to me that he never knew above one or two instances under the age of six, even in a part of the kingdom so renowned for the quickest proficiency in the art.

I am assured by our merchants that a boy or girl before twelve years old is no saleable commodity, and even when they come to this age they will not yield above three pounds, or three pounds and half a crown at most, on the exchange, which cannot turn to account either to the parents or the kingdom, the charge of nutriment and rags having been at least four times that value.

I shall now therefore humbly propose my own thoughts, which I hope will not be liable to the least objection.

I have been assured by a very knowing American of my acquaintance in London that a young healthy child well nursed is at a year old a most delicious, nourishing and wholesome food, whether stewed, roasted, baked or boiled, and I make no doubt that it will equally serve in a fricassee or a ragout.

I do therefore humbly offer it to public consideration that of the hundred and twenty thousand children already computed twenty thousand may be reserved for breed, whereof only one fourth part to be males, which is more than we allow to sheep, black cattle or swine, and my reason is that these children are seldom the fruits of marriage, a circumstance not much regarded by our savages, therefore one male will be sufficient to serve four females. That the remaining hundred thousand may at a year old be offered in sale to the persons of quality and fortune through the kingdom, always advising the mother to let them suck plentifully in the last month, so as to render them plump and fat for a good table. A child will make two dishes at an entertainment for friends, and when the family dines alone the fore or hind quarter will make a reasonable dish, and seasoned with a little pepper or salt will be very good boiled on the fourth day, especially in winter.

I have reckoned upon a medium that a child just born will weigh twelve pounds, and in a solar year if tolerably nursed increaseth to twenty-eight pound.

I grant this food will be somewhat dear, and therefore very proper for landlords, who, as they have already devoured most of the parents, seem to have the best title to the children.

Infant's flesh will be in season throughout the year, but more plentiful in March, and a little before and after, for we are told by a grave author, an eminent French physician, that fish being a prolific diet there are more children born in Roman Catholic countries about nine months after Lent than at any other season. Therefore, reckoning a year after Lent, the markets will be more glutted than usual, because the number of Popish infants is at least three to one in this kingdom, and therefore it will have one other collateral advantage by lessening the number of papists among us.

I have already computed the charge of nursing a beggar's child (in which list I reckon all cottagers, labourers and four-fifths of the farmers) to be about two shillings *per annum*, rags included, and I believe no gentleman would repine to give ten shillings for the carcass of a good fat child, which, as I have said, will make four dishes of excellent nutritive meat, when he hath only some particular friend, or his own family, to dine with him. Thus the squire will learn to be a good landlord, and grow popular among his tenants, the mother will have eight shillings neat profit and be fit for work till she produces another child.

> *A Modest Proposal for Preventing the Children of Poor People from Being a Burthen to Their Parents, or the Country, and for Making Them Beneficial to the Public*, 1729

WILLIAM LAW

Concerning the Nature and Extent of Christian Devotion

DEVOTION IS neither private nor public prayer, but prayers whether private or public are particular parts or instances of devotion. Devotion signifies a life given or devoted to God.

He therefore is the devout man, who lives no longer to his own will, or the way and spirit of the world, but to the sole will of God, who considers God in everything, who serves God in everything, who makes all the parts of his common life parts of piety by doing everything in the name of God and under such rules as are conformable to His glory.

We readily acknowledge that God alone is to be the rule and measure of our prayers; that in them we are to look wholly unto Him, and act wholly for Him; that we are only to pray in such a manner, for such things, and such ends as are suitable to His glory.

Now, let anyone but find out the reason why he is to be thus strictly pious in his prayers and he will find the same as strong a reason to be as strictly pious in all the other parts of his life. For there is not the least shadow of a reason why we should make God the rule and measure of our prayers, why we should then look wholly unto Him and pray according to His will, but what equally proves it necessary for us to look wholly unto God and make Him the rule and measure of all the other actions of our life. For any ways of life, any employment of our talents, whether of our parts, our time or money, that is not strictly according to the will of God, that is not for such ends as are suitable to His glory, are as great absurdities and failings as prayers that are not according to the will of God. For there is no other reason why our prayers should be according to the will of God, why they should have nothing in them but what is wise and holy and heavenly, there is no other reason for this, but that our lives may be of the same nature, full of the same wisdom, holiness and heavenly tempers, that we may live unto God in the same spirit that we pray unto Him. Were it not our strict duty to live by reason, to devote all the actions of our lives to God, were it not absolutely necessary to walk before Him in wisdom and holiness and all heavenly conversation, doing everything in His name, and for His glory, there would be no excellency or wisdom in the most heavenly prayers. Nay, such prayers would be absurdities; they would be like prayers for wings, when it was no part of our duty to fly.

As sure, therefore, as there is any wisdom in praying for the spirit of God, so sure it is that we are to make that spirit the rule of all our actions; as sure as it is our duty to look wholly unto God in our prayers, so sure is it that it is our duty to live wholly unto God in our lives. But we can no more be said to live unto God unless we live unto Him in all the ordinary actions of our life, unless He be the rule and measure of all our ways, than we can be said to pray unto God unless our prayers look wholly unto Him. So that unreasonable and absurd ways of life, whether in labour or diversion, whether they consume our time or our money, are like unreasonable and absurd prayers, and are as truly an offence unto God.

'Tis for want of knowing or at least considering this that we see such a mixture of ridicule in the lives of so many people. You see them strict as to some times and places of devotion, but when the service of the church is over they are but like those who seldom or never come there. In their way of life, their manner of spending their time and money, in their cares and fears, in their pleasures and indulgences, in their labour and diversions, they are like the rest of the world. This makes the loose part of the world generally make a jest of those who are devout, because they see their devotion goes no further than their prayers, and that when they are over they live no more unto God till the time of prayer returns again; but live by the same humour and fancy, and in as full an enjoyment of all the follies of life, as other people. This is the reason why they are the jest and scorn of careless and worldly people; not because they are really devoted to God, but because they appear to have no other devotion but that of occasional prayers.

A Serious Call to a Devout and Holy Life, 1728

DAVID HUME

[Experience]

WE HAVE remarked that the conclusion which we draw from a present object to its absent cause or effect is never founded on any qualities which we observe in that object considered in itself; or, in other words, that 'tis impossible to determine otherwise than by experience what will result from any phenomenon, or what has preceded it. But, though this be so evident in itself that it seemed not to require any proof, yet some philosophers have imagined that there is an apparent cause for the communication of motion, and that a reasonable man might immediately infer the motion of one body from the impulse of another without having recourse to any past observation. That this opinion is false will admit of an easy proof. For, if such an inference may be drawn merely from the ideas of body, of motion and of impulse, it must amount to a demonstration, and must imply the absolute impossibility of any contrary supposition. Every effect, then, beside the communication of motion implies a formal contradiction; and 'tis impossible, not only that it can exist, but also that it can be conceived. But we may soon satisfy ourselves of the contrary by forming a clear and consistent idea of one body's moving upon another, and of its rest immediately upon the contact; or of its returning back in the same line in which it came; or of its annihilation; or circular or elliptical motion: and, in short, of an infinite number of other changes which we may suppose it to undergo. These suppositions are all confident and natural; and the reason why we imagine the communication of motion to be more consistent and natural not only than those suppositions, but also than any other natural effect, is founded on the relation of *resemblance* betwixt the cause and effect, which is here united to experience, and binds the objects in the closest and most intimate manner to each other, so as to make us imagine them to be absolutely inseparable. Resemblance, then, has the same or a parallel influence with experience; and, as the only immediate effect of experience is to associate our ideas together, it follows that all belief arises from the association of ideas, according to my hypothesis.

'Tis universally allowed by the writers on optics that the eye at all times sees an equal number of physical points, and that a man on the top of a mountain has no larger an image presented to his senses than when he is cooped up in the narrowest court or chamber. 'Tis only by experience that he infers the greatness of the object from some peculiar qualities of the image; and this inference of the judgement he confounds with sensation, as is common on other occasions. Now, 'tis evident that the inference of the judgement is here much more lively than what is usual in our common reasonings, and that a man has a more vivid conception of the vast extent of the ocean from the image he receives by the eye when he stands on the top of a high promontory than merely from hearing the roaring of the waters. He feels a more sensible pleasure from its magnificence; which is a proof of a more lively idea. And he confounds his judgement with sensation; which is another proof of it. But, as the inference

is equally certain and immediate in both cases, this superior
vivacity of our conception in one case can proceed from
nothing but this: that in drawing an inference from the sight,
beside the customary conjunction, there is also a resemblance betwixt the image and the object we infer; which
strengthens the relation, and conveys the vivacity of the
impression to the related idea with an easier and more
natural movement.

A Treatise of Human Nature: Being an
Attempt to Introduce the Experimental
Method of Reasoning into Moral Subjects, 1739

HENRY ST JOHN, VISCOUNT BOLINGBROKE

[The Patriot King]

THE SITUATION of Great Britain, the character of her
people, and the nature of her government, fit her for
trade and commerce. Her climate and her soil make them
necessary to her well-being. By trade and commerce we
grew a rich and powerful nation, and by their decay we are
growing poor and impotent. As trade and commerce enrich,
so they fortify, our country. The sea is our barrier, ships are
our fortresses, and the mariners, that trade and commerce
alone can furnish, are the garrisons to defend them. France
lies under great disadvantages in trade and commerce, by
the nature of her government. Her advantages, in situation,
are as great at least as ours. Those that arise, from the
temper and character of her people, are a little different
perhaps, and yet upon the whole equivalent. Those of her
climate and her soil are superior to ours, and indeed to
those of any European nation. The United Provinces have
the same advantages that we have in the nature of their
government, more perhaps in the temper and character of
their people, less to be sure in their situation, climate, and

soil. But, without descending into a longer detail of the advantages and disadvantages attending each of these nations in trade and commerce, it is sufficient for my present purpose to observe, that Great Britain stands in a certain middle between the other two, with regard to wealth and power arising from these springs. A less, and less constant, application to the improvement of these may serve the ends of France; a greater is necessary in this country; and a greater still in Holland. The French may improve their natural wealth and power by the improvement of trade and commerce. We can have no wealth, nor power by consequence, as Europe is now constituted, without the improvement of them, nor in any degree but proportionably to this improvement. The Dutch cannot subsist without them. They bring wealth to other nations, and are necessary to the wellbeing of them; but they supply the Dutch with food and raiment, and are necessary even to their being.

The result of what has been said is, in general, that the wealth and power of all nations depending so much on their trade and commerce, and every nation being, like the three I have mentioned, in such different circumstances of advantage or disadvantage in the pursuit of this common interest; a good government, and therefore the government of a Patriot King, will be directed constantly to make the most of every advantage that nature has given or art can procure, towards the improvement of trade and commerce. And this is one of the principal criterions by which we are to judge, whether governors are in the true interest of the people, or not.

It results, in particular, that Great Britain might improve her wealth and power in a proportion superior to that of any nation who can be deemed her rival, if the advantages she has were as wisely cultivated, as they will be in the reign of a Patriot King. To be convinced more thoroughly of this truth, a very short process of reasoning will suffice. Let any man, who has knowledge enough for it, first compare the natural state of Great Britain, and of the United Provinces, and then their artificial state together; that is, let him consider minutely the advantages we have by the situation, extent, and nature of our island, over the inhabitants of a few salt marshes gained on the sea, and hardly defended from it: and after that, let him consider how nearly these provinces have raised themselves to an equality of wealth and power with the kingdom of Great Britain. From whence arises this difference of improvement? It arises plainly from hence: the Dutch have been from the foundation of their common-wealth, a nation of patriots and merchants. The spirit of that people has not been diverted from these two objects, the defence of their liberty, and the improvement of their trade and commerce; which have been carried on by them with uninterrupted and unslackened application, industry, order, and economy. In Great Britain the case has not been the same, in either respect; but here we confine ourselves to speak of the last alone.

Trade and commerce, such as they were in those days, had been sometimes, and in some instances, before the reign of Queen Elizabeth, encouraged and improved: but the great encouragements were given, the great extensions and improvements were made, by that glorious princess. To her we owe that spirit of domestic and foreign trade which is not quite extinguished. It was she who gave that rapid motion to our whole mercantile system which is not entirely ceased. They both flagged under her successor; were not revived under his son; were checked, diverted, clogged, and interrupted, during our civil wars: and began to exert new vigour after the restoration, in a long course of peace; but met with new difficulties, too, from the confirmed rivalry of the Dutch, and the growing rivalry of the French. To one of these the pusillanimous character of James the first gave many scandalous occasions: and the other was favoured by the conduct of Charles the second, who never was in the true interest of the people he governed. From the revolution to the death of queen Anne, however trade and commerce might be aided and encouraged in other respects, they were necessarily subjected to depredations abroad, and over-loaded by taxes at home, during the course of two great wars. From the accession of the late king to this hour, in the midst of a full peace, the debts of the nation continue much the same, the taxes have been increased, and for eighteen years of this time we have tamely suffered continual depredations from the most contemptible maritime power in Europe, that of Spain.

A Patriot King will neither neglect, nor sacrifice, his country's interest. No other interest, neither a foreign nor a domestic, neither a public nor a private, will influence his conduct in government. He will not multiply taxes wantonly, nor keep up those unnecessarily which necessity has laid, that he may keep up legions of tax-gatherers. He will not continue national debts, by all sorts of political and other profusion; nor, more wickedly still, by a settled purpose of oppressing and impoverishing the people; that he may with greater ease corrupt some, and govern the whole, according to the dictates of his passions and arbitrary will. To give ease and encouragement to manufactory at home, to assist and protect trade abroad, to improve and keep in heart the national colonies, like so many farms of the mother country, will be principal and constant parts of the attention of such a Prince. The wealth of the nation he will most justly esteem to be his wealth, the power his power, the security and the honour, his security and honour: and, by the very means by which he promotes the two first, he will wisely preserve the two last; for by these means, and by these alone, can the great advantage of the situation of this kingdom be taken and improved.

The Idea of a Patriot King, c.1740

JOHN ARBUTHNOT

[The Varnish of Time]

THE DAY of the christening being come, and the house filled with gossips, the levity of whose conversation suited but ill with the gravity of Dr Cornelius, he cast about how to pass this day more agreeably to his character; that is to say, not without some profitable conference, nor wholly without observance of some ancient custom.

He remembered to have read in Theocritus that the cradle
of Hercules was a shield; and being possessed of an ancient
buckler, which he held as a most inestimable relic, he
determined to have the infant laid therein, and in that
manner brought into the study to be shown to certain
learned men of his acquaintance.

The regard he had for this shield had caused him formerly
to compile a dissertation concerning it, proving from the
several properties, and particularly the colour of the rust,
the exact chronology thereof.

With this treatise, and a moderate supper, he proposed to
entertain his guests; though he had also another design: to
have their assistance in the calculation of his son's nativity.

He therefore took the buckler out of a case (in which he
always kept it, lest it might contract any modern rust) and
entrusted it to his house-maid, with orders that, when the
company was come, she should lay the child carefully in it,
covered with a mantle of blue satin.

The guests were no sooner seated but they entered into a
warm debate about the *Triclinium*, and the manner of
Decubitus of the ancients, which Cornelius broke off in this
manner:

'This day, my friends, I purpose to exhibit my son before
you: a child not wholly unworthy of inspection as he is
descended from a race of virtuosi. Let the physiognomists
examine his features; let the chirographists behold his palm;
but, above all, let us consult for the calculation of his
nativity. To this end, as the child is not vulgar, I will not
present him unto you in a vulgar manner. He shall be
cradled in my ancient shield, so famous through the univers-
ities of Europe. You all know how I purchased that invaluable piece of antiquity at the great (though, indeed,
inadequate) expense of all the plate of our family, how
happily I carried it off, and how triumphantly I transported
it hither – to the inexpressible grief of all Germany. Happy
in every circumstance but that it broke the heart of the great
Melchior Insipidus!'

Here he stopped his speech upon sight of the maid, who
entered the room with the child. He took it in his arms and
proceeded.

'Behold, then, my child; but first behold the shield. Behold this rust – or rather let me call it this precious *aerugo*. Behold this beautiful varnish of time – this venerable verdure of so many ages—'

In speaking these words, he slowly lifted up the mantle which covered it, inch by inch; but at every inch he uncovered his cheeks grew paler, his hand trembled, his nerves failed, till on sight of the whole the tremor became universal. The shield and the infant both dropped to the ground, and he had only strength enough to cry out: 'O God! my shield, my shield!'

The truth was, the maid (extremely concerned for the reputation of her own cleanliness and her young master's honour) had scoured it as clean as her andirons.

Cornelius sunk back on a chair, the guests stood astonished, the infant squalled, the maid ran in, snatched it up again in her arms, flew into her mistress's room and told what had happened. Downstairs in an instant hurried all the gossips, where they found the Doctor in a trance.

Memoirs of . . . Martin Scriblerus, first published 1741

HENRY FIELDING

[Joseph and Mrs Slipslop]

SHE WAS a maiden gentlewoman of about forty-five years of age, who having made a small slip in her youth had continued a good maid ever since. She was not at this time remarkably handsome; being very short, and rather too corpulent in body, and somewhat red, with the addition of pimples in the face. Her nose was likewise rather too large, and her eyes too little; nor did she resemble a cow so much in her breath, as in two brown globes which she carried before her; one of her legs was also a little shorter than the other, which occasioned her to limp as she walked. The fair creature had long cast the eyes of affection on Joseph, in which she had not met with quite so good success as she probably wished, though besides the allurements of her native charms, she had given him tea, sweetmeats, wine, and other delicacies, of which, by keeping the keys, she had the absolute command. Joseph, however, had not returned the least gratitude to all these favours, not even so much as a kiss; though I would not insinuate she was so easily to be satisfied: for surely then he would have been highly blameable. The truth is, she was arrived at an age when she thought she might indulge herself in any liberties with a man, without the danger of bringing a third person into the world to betray them. She imagined, that by so long a self-denial, she had not only made amends for the small slip of her youth above hinted at: but had likewise laid up a quantity of merit to excuse any future failings. In a word, she resolved to give a loose to her amorous inclinations, and pay off the debt of pleasure which she found she owed herself, as fast as possible.

With these charms of person, and in this disposition of mind, she encountered poor Joseph at the bottom of the stairs, and asked him if he would drink a glass of something good this morning. Joseph, whose spirits were not a little cast down, very readily and thankfully accepted the offer; and together they went into a closet, where having delivered him a full glass of ratifia, and desired him to sit down, Mrs Slipslop thus began:

'Sure nothing can be a more simple *contract* in a woman, than to place her affections on a boy. If I had ever thought it would have been my fate, I should have wished to die a thousand deaths rather than live to see that day. If we like a man, the lightest hint *sophisticates*. Whereas a boy *proposes* upon us to break through all the *regulations* of modesty, before we can make any *oppression* upon him.' Joseph, who did not understand a word she said, answered, '*Yes, madam*'; – 'Yes, madam!' replied Mrs Slipslop with some warmth. 'Do you intend to *result* my passion? Is it not enough, ungrateful as you are, to make no return to all the favours I have done you: but you must treat me with *ironing*? Barbarous monster! how have I deserved that my passion should be *resulted* and treated with *ironing*?'

'Madam,' answered Joseph, 'I don't understand your hard words: but I am certain, you have no occasion to call me ungrateful: for so far from intending you any wrong, I have always loved you as well as if you had been my own mother.' 'How, sirrah!' says Mrs Slipslop in a rage: 'Your own mother! Do you *assinuate* that I am old enough to be your mother? I don't know what a stripling may think: but I believe a man would *refer* me to any green-sickness silly girl *whatsomdever*: but I ought to despise you rather than be angry with you, for *referring* the conversation of girls to that of a woman of sense.' 'Madam,' says Joseph, 'I am sure I have always valued the honour you did me by your conversation; for I know you are a woman of learning.' 'Yes, but, Joseph,' said she a little softened by the compliment to her learning, 'if you had a value for me, you certainly would have found some method of showing it me; for I am *convicted* you must see the value I have for you. Yes, Joseph, my eyes, whether I would or no, must have declared a passion I cannot conquer. – Oh! Joseph!—'

As when a hungry tigress, who long had traversed the woods in fruitless search, sees within the reach of her claws a lamb, she prepares to leap on her prey; or as a voracious pike, of immense size, surveys through the liquid element a roach or gudgeon which cannot escape her jaws, opens them wide to swallow the little fish: so did Mrs Slipslop prepare to lay her violent amorous hands on the poor Joseph, when luckily her mistress's bell rung, and delivered the intended martyr from her clutches.

The History of the Adventures of
Joseph Andrews, 1742

[The Foundling]

MR ALLWORTHY had been absent a full quarter of a year in London, on some very particular business, though I know not what it was; but judge of its importance,

by its having detained him so long from home, whence he
had not been absent a month at a time during the space of
many years. He came to his house very late in the evening,
and after a short supper with his sister, retired much fatigued
to his chamber. Here, having spent some minutes on his
knees, a custom which he never broke through on any
account, he was preparing to step into bed, when, upon
opening the clothes, to his great surprise, he beheld an
infant, wrapped up in some coarse linen, in a sweet and
profound sleep, between his sheets. He stood some time
lost in astonishment at this sight; but, as good-nature had
always the ascendant in his mind, he soon began to be
touched with sentiments of compassion for the little wretch
before him. He then rang his bell, and ordered an elderly
woman servant to rise immediately and come to him, and in
the mean time was so eager in contemplating the beauty of
innocence, appearing in those lively colours with which
infancy and sleep always display it, that his thoughts were
too much engaged to reflect that he was in his shirt, when
the matron came in. She had indeed given her master
sufficient time to dress himself; for out of respect to him,
and regard to decency, she had spent many minutes in
adjusting her hair at the looking-glass, notwithstanding all
the hurry in which she had been summoned by the servant,
and though her master, for ought she knew, lay expiring in
an apoplexy, or in some other fit.

   It will not be wondered at, that a creature, who had so
strict a regard to decency in her own person, should be
shocked at the least deviation from it in another. She
therefore no sooner opened the door, and saw her master
standing by the bed-side in his shirt, with a candle in his
hand, than she started back in a most terrible fright, and
might perhaps have swooned away, had he not now recollected his being undressed, and put an end to her terrors,
by desiring her to stay without the door till he had thrown
some clothes over his back, and was become incapable of
shocking the pure eyes of Mrs Deborah Wilkins, who,
though in the fifty-second year of her age, vowed she had
never beheld a man without his coat. Sneerers and prophane
wits may perhaps laugh at her first fright, yet my graver

reader, when he considers the time of night, the summons from her bed, and the situation in which she found her master, will highly justify and applaud her conduct; unless the prudence, which must be supposed to attend maidens at that period of life at which Mrs Deborah had arrived, should a little lessen his admiration.

When Mrs Deborah returned into the room, and was acquainted by her master with the finding the little infant, her consternation was rather greater than his had been; nor could she refrain from crying out, with great horror of accent as well as look, 'My good sir! what's to be done?' Mr Allworthy answered, she must take care of the child that evening, and in the morning he would give orders to provide it a nurse. 'Yes, sir,' says she, 'and I hope your worship will send out your warrant to take up the hussy its mother (for she must be one of the neighbourhood) and I should be glad to see her committed to Bridewell; and whipped at the cart's tail. Indeed such wicked sluts cannot be too severely punished. I'll warrant 'tis not her first, by her impudence in laying it to your worship.' 'In laying it to me! Deborah,' answered Allworthy, 'I can't think she hath any such design. I suppose she hath only taken this method to provide for her child; and truly I am glad she hath not done worse.' 'I don't know what is worse,' cries Deborah, 'than for such wicked strumpets to lay their sins at honest men's doors; and though your worship knows your own innocence, yet the world is censorious; and it hath been many an honest man's hap to pass for the father of children he never begot; and if your worship should provide for the child, it may make the people the apter to believe; besides, why should your worship provide for what the parish is obliged to maintain? For my own part, if it was an honest man's child indeed; but for my own part, it goes against me to touch these misbegotten wretches, whom I don't look upon as my fellow creatures. Faugh, how it stinks! It doth not smell like a Christian. If I might be so bold to give my advice, I would have it put in a basket, and sent out and laid at the churchwarden's door. It is a good night, only a little rainy and windy; and if it was well wrapped up, and put in a warm basket, it is two to one but it lives till it is found in the morning. But if it should not, we have discharged our duty in taking proper care of it; and it is, perhaps, better for such creatures to die in a state of innocence, than to grow up and imitate their mothers; for nothing better can be expected of them.'

There were some strokes in this speech which, perhaps, would have offended Mr Allworthy, had he strictly attended to it; but he had now got one of his fingers into the infant's hand, which by its gentle pressure, seeming to implore his assistance, had certainly out-pleaded the eloquence of Mrs Deborah, had it been ten times greater than it was. He now gave Mrs Deborah positive orders to take the child to her own bed, and to call up a maid-servant to provide it pap, and other things against it waked. He likewise ordered that proper clothes should be procured for it early in the morning, and that it should be brought to himself as soon as he was stirring.

Such was the discernment of Mrs Wilkins, and such the respect she bore her master, under whom she enjoyed a most excellent place, that her scruples gave way to his peremptory commands; and she took the child under her arms, without any apparent disgust at the illegality of its birth; and declaring it was a sweet little infant, walked off with it to her own chamber.

Allworthy here betook himself to those pleasing slumbers which a heart that hungers after goodness is apt to enjoy when thoroughly satisfied: as these are possibly sweeter than what are occasioned by any other hearty meal, I should take more pains to display them to the reader, if I knew any air to recommend him to for the procuring such an appetite.

The History of Tom Jones, a Foundling, 1749

SAMUEL JOHNSON

[Richard Savage]

WHOEVER WAS acquainted with him was certain to be solicited for small sums, which the frequency of the request made in time considerable, and he was therefore quickly shunned by those who were become familiar enough to be trusted with his necessities; but his rambling manner of life, and constant appearance at houses of public resort, always procured him a new succession of friends, whose kindness had not been exhausted by repeated requests; so that he was seldom absolutely without resources, but had in his utmost exigencies this comfort, that he always imagined himself sure of speedy relief.

It was observed that he always asked favours of this kind without the least submission or apparent consciousness of dependence, and that he did not seem to look upon a compliance with his request as an obligation that deserved any extraordinary acknowledgements; but a refusal was resented by him as an affront, or complained of as an injury: nor did he readily reconcile himself to those who either denied to lend, or gave him afterwards any intimation that they expected to be repaid.

He was sometimes so far compassionated by those who knew both his merit and distresses that they received him into their families, but they soon discovered him to be a very incommodious inmate; for, being always accustomed to an irregular manner of life, he could not confine himself to any stated hours, or pay any regard to the rules of a family, but would prolong his conversation till midnight, without considering that business might require his friend's application in the morning; and, when he had persuaded himself to retire to bed, was not, without equal difficulty, called up to dinner: it was therefore impossible to pay him any distinction without the entire subversion of all economy, a kind of establishment which, wherever he went, he always appeared ambitious to overthrow.

It must therefore be acknowledged, in justification of mankind, that it was not always by the negligence or coldness of his friends that Savage was distressed, but because it was in reality very difficult to preserve him long in a state of ease. To supply him with money was a hopeless attempt, for no sooner did he see himself master of a sum sufficient to set him free from care for a day, than he became profuse and luxurious. When once he had entered a tavern, or engaged in a scheme of pleasure, he never retired till want of money obliged him to some new expedient. If he was entertained in a family nothing was any longer to be regarded there but amusements and jollity: wherever Savage entered he immediately expected that order and business should fly before him, that all should thenceforward be left to hazard, and that no dull principle of domestic management should be opposed to his inclination, or intrude upon his gaiety.

His distresses, however afflictive, never dejected him; in his lowest state he wanted not spirit to assert the natural dignity of wit, and was always ready to repress that insolence which superiority of fortune incited, and to trample on that reputation which rose upon any other basis than that of merit: he never admitted any gross familiarities, or submitted to be treated otherwise than as an equal. Once, when he was without lodging, meat, or clothes, one of his friends, a man not indeed remarkable for moderation in his prosperity, left a message, that he desired to see him about nine in the morning. Savage knew that his intention was to assist him; but was very much disgusted that he should presume to prescribe the hour of his attendance, and, I believe, refused to visit him, and rejected his kindness.

An Account of the Life of
Mr Richard Savage, 1744

[Literary Fame]

THAT EMINENCE of learning is not to be gained without labour, at least equal to that which any other kind of greatness can require, will be allowed by those who wish to elevate the character of a scholar; since they cannot but know, that every human acquisition is valuable in proportion to the difficulty employed in its attainment. And that those who have gained the esteem and veneration of the world, by their knowledge or their genius, are by no means exempt from the solicitude which any other kind of dignity produces, may be conjectured from the innumerable artifices which they make use of to degrade a superior, to repress a rival, or obstruct a follower; artifice so gross and mean, as to prove evidently how much a man may excel in learning, without being either more wise or more virtuous than those whose ignorance he pities or despises.

Nothing therefore remains, by which the student can gratify his desire of appearing to have built his happiness on a more firm basis than his antagonist, except the certainty with which his honours are enjoyed. The garlands gained by the heroes of literature must be gathered from summits equally difficult to climb with those that bear the civic or triumphal wreaths, they must be worn with equal envy, and guarded with equal care from those hands that are always employed in efforts to tear them away; the only remaining hope is, that their verdure is more lasting, and that they are less likely to fade by time, or less obnoxious to the blasts of accident.

Even this hope will receive very little encouragement from the examination of the history of learning, or observation of the fate of scholars in the present age. If we look back into past times, we find innumerable names of authors once in high reputation, read perhaps by the beautiful, quoted by the witty, and commented upon by the grave; but of whom we now know only that they once existed. If we consider the distribution of literary fame in our own time, we shall find it a possession of very uncertain tenure;

sometimes bestowed by a sudden caprice of the public, and again transferred to a new favourite, for no other reason than that he is new; sometimes refused to long labour and eminent desert, and sometimes granted to very slight pretensions; lost sometimes by security and negligence, and sometimes by too diligent endeavours to retain it.

A successful author is equally in danger of the diminution of his fame, whether he continues or ceases to write. The regard of the public is not to be kept but by tribute, and the remembrance of past service will quickly languish, unless successive performances frequently revive it. Yet in every new attempt there is new hazard, and there are few who do not at some unlucky time, injure their own characters by attempting to enlarge them.

The Rambler, 29 May 1750

[Patronage]

To The Right Honourable the Earl of Chesterfield

My Lord   February 1755
I have been lately informed, by the proprietor of *The World*, that two papers, in which my Dictionary is recommended to the public, were written by your Lordship. To be so distinguished, is an honour, which, being very little accustomed to favours from the great, I know not well how to receive, or in what terms to acknowledge.

When, upon some slight encouragement, I first visited your Lordship, I was overpowered, like the rest of mankind, by the enchantment of your address; and could not forbear to wish that I might boast myself *Le vainqueur du vainqueur de la terre*; – that I might obtain that regard for which I saw the world contending; but I found my attendance so little encouraged, that neither pride nor modesty would suffer me to continue it. When I had once addressed your Lordship in public, I had exhausted all the art of pleasing which a retired and uncourtly scholar can possess. I had done all that I could; and no man is well pleased to have his all neglected, be it ever so little.

Seven years, my Lord, have now passed, since I waited in your outward rooms, or was repulsed from your door; during which time I have been pushing on my work through difficulties, of which it is useless to complain, and have brought it, at last, to the verge of publication, without one act of assistance, one word of encouragement, or one smile of favour. Such treatment I did not expect, for I never had a patron before.

The shepherd in Virgil grew at last acquainted with Love, and found him a native of the rocks.

Is not a patron, my Lord, one who looks with unconcern on a man struggling for life in the water, and, when he has reached ground, encumbers him with help? The notice which you have been pleased to take of my labours, had it been early, had been kind; but it has been delayed till I am indifferent, and cannot enjoy it; till I am solitary, and cannot impart it; till I am known, and do not want it. I hope it is no very cynical asperity not to confess obligations where no benefit has been received, or to be unwilling that the public should consider me as owing that to a patron, which providence has enabled me to do for myself.

Having carried on my work thus far with so little obligation to any favourer of learning, I shall not be disappointed though I should conclude it, if less be possible, with less; for I have been long wakened from that dream of hope, in which I once boasted myself with so much exultation, my Lord, your Lordship's most humble, most obedient servant,

SAM. JOHNSON

Quoted in Boswell's *Life of Samuel Johnson*

['Harmless Drudgery']

T HE CHIEF glory of every people arises from its authors: whether I shall add anything by my own writings to the reputation of English literature, must be left to time: much of my life has been lost under the pressures of disease; much has been trifled away; and much has always been spent in provision for the day that was passing over me; but I shall not think my employment useless or ignoble, if by my assistance foreign nations, and distant ages, gain access to the propagators of knowledge, and understand the teachers of truth; if my labours afford light to the repositories of science, and add celebrity to Bacon, to Hooker, to Milton, and to Boyle.

When I am animated by this wish, I look with pleasure on my book, however defective, and deliver it to the world with the spirit of a man that has endeavoured well. That it will immediately become popular I have not promised to myself: a few wild blunders, and risible absurdities, from which no work of such multiplicity was ever free, may for a time furnish folly with laughter, and harden ignorance in contempt; but useful diligence will at last prevail, and there never can be wanting some who distinguish desert; who will consider that no dictionary of a living tongue can ever be perfect, since while it is hastening to publication, some words are budding, and some falling away; that a whole life cannot be spent upon syntax and etymology, and that even a whole life would not be sufficient; that he, whose design includes whatever language can express, must often speak of what he does not understand; that a writer will sometimes be hurried by eagerness to the end, and sometimes faint with weariness under a task, which Scaliger compares to the labours of the anvil and the mine; that what is obvious is not always known, and what is known is not always present; that sudden fits of inadvertency will surprise vigilance, slight avocations will seduce attention, and casual eclipses of the mind will darken learning; and that the writer shall often in vain trace his memory at the moment of need, for that which yesterday he knew with intuitive readiness, and which will come uncalled into his thoughts tomorrow.

In this work, when it shall be found that much is omitted, let it not be forgotten that much likewise is performed; and though no book was ever spared out of tenderness to the author, and the world is little solicitous to know whence proceeded the faults of that which it condemns; yet it may gratify curiosity to inform it, that the *English Dictionary* was written with little assistance of the learned, and without any patronage of the great; not in the soft obscurities of retirement, or under the shelter of academic bowers, but amidst inconvenience and distraction, in sickness and in sorrow: and it may repress the triumphs of malignant criticism to observe, that if our language is not here fully displayed, I have only failed in an attempt which no human powers have hitherto completed. If the lexicons of ancient tongues, now immutably fixed, and comprised in a few volumes, be yet, after the toil of successive ages, inadequate and delusive; if the aggregate knowledge, and co-operating diligence of the Italian academicians, did not secure them from the censure of Beni; if the embodied critics of France, when fifty years had been spent upon their work, were obliged to change its economy, and give their second edition another form, I may surely be contented without the praise of perfection, which, if I could obtain, in this gloom of solitude, what would it avail me? I have protracted my work till most of those whom I wished to please, have sunk into the grave, and success and miscarriage are empty sounds: I therefore dismiss it with frigid tranquillity, having little to fear or hope from censure or from praise.

Preface to *A Dictionary of the English Language*, 1755

[The Art of Flying]

THE WORKMAN was pleased to find himself so much regarded by the prince, and resolved to gain yet higher honours. 'Sir,' said he, 'you have seen but a small part of what the mechanic sciences can perform. I have been long of opinion, that, instead of the tardy conveyance of ships and chariots, man might use the swifter migration of wings; that the fields of air are open to knowledge, and that only ignorance and idleness need crawl upon the ground.'

This hint rekindled the prince's desire of passing the mountains; having seen what the mechanist had already performed, he was willing to fancy that he could do more; yet resolved to inquire further before he suffered hope to afflict him by disappointment. 'I am afraid,' said he to the artist, 'that your imagination prevails over your skill, and that you now tell me rather what you wish than what you know. Every animal has his element assigned him; the birds have the air, and man and beasts the earth.' 'So,' replied the mechanist, 'fishes have the water, in which yet beasts can swim by nature, and men by art. He that can swim needs not despair to fly: to swim is to fly in a grosser fluid, and to fly is to swim in a subtler. We are only to proportion our power of resistance to the different density of the matter through which we are to pass. You will be necessarily upborn by the air, if you can renew any impulse upon it, faster than the air can recede from the pressure.'

'But the exercise of swimming,' said the prince, 'is very laborious; the strongest limbs are soon wearied; I am afraid the act of flying will be yet more violent, and wings will be of no great use, unless we can fly further than we can swim.'

'The labour of rising from the ground,' said the artist, 'will be great, as we see it in the heavier domestic fowls; but, as we mount higher, the earth's attraction, and the body's gravity, will be gradually diminished, till we shall arrive at a region where the man will float in the air without any tendency to fall: no care will then be necessary, but to move forwards, which the gentlest impulse will effect. You,

Sir, whose curiosity is so extensive, will easily conceive with what pleasure a philosopher, furnished with wings, and hovering in the sky, would see the earth, and all its inhabitants, rolling beneath him, and presenting to him successively, by its diurnal motion, all the countries within the same parallel. How must it amuse the pendent spectator to see the moving scene of land and ocean, cities and deserts! To survey with equal security the marts of trade, and the fields of battle; mountains infested by barbarians, and fruitful regions gladdened by plenty, and lulled by peace! How easily shall we then trace the Nile through all his passage; pass over to distant regions, and examine the face of nature from one extremity of the earth to the other!'

'All this,' said the prince, 'is much to be desired, but I am afraid that no man will be able to breathe in these regions of speculation and tranquillity. I have been told, that respiration is difficult upon lofty mountains, yet from these precipices, though so high as to produce great tenuity of the air, it is very easy to fall: therefore I suspect, that from any height, where life can be supported, there may be danger of too quick descent.'

'Nothing,' replied the artist, 'will ever be attempted, if all possible objections must be first overcome. If you will favour my project I will try the first flight at my own hazard. I have considered the structure of all volant animals, and find the folding continuity of the bat's wings most easily accommodated to the human form. Upon this model I shall begin my task tomorrow, and in a year expect to tower into the air beyond the malice or pursuit of man. But I will work only on this condition, that the art shall not be divulged, and that you shall not require me to make wings for any but ourselves.'

'Why,' said Rasselas, 'should you envy others so great an advantage? All skill ought to be exerted for universal good; every man has owed much to others, and ought to repay the kindness that he has received.'

'If men were all virtuous,' returned the artist, 'I should with great alacrity teach them all to fly. But what would be the security of the good, if the bad could at pleasure invade them from the sky? Against an army sailing through the clouds neither walls, nor mountains, nor seas, could afford any security. A flight of northern savages might hover in the wind, and light at once with irresistible violence upon the capital of a fruitful region that was rolling under them. Even this valley, the retreat of princes, the abode of happiness, might be violated by the sudden descent of some of the naked nations that swarm on the coast of the southern sea.'

The prince promised secrecy, and waited for the performance, not wholly hopeless of success. He visited the work from time to time, observed its progress, and remarked many ingenious contrivances to facilitate motion, and unite levity with strength. The artist was every day more certain that he should leave vultures and eagles behind him, and the contagion of his confidence seized upon the prince.

In a year the wings were finished, and, on a morning appointed, the maker appeared furnished for flight on a little promontory: he waved his pinions a while to gather air, then leaped from his stand, and in an instant dropped into the lake. His wings, which were of no use in the air, sustained him in the water, and the prince drew him to land, half dead with terror and vexation.

The History of Rasselas, Prince of Abyssinia, 1759

[Highland Economy]

NEAR THE way, by the water-side, we espied a cottage. This was the first Highland hut that I had seen; and as our business was with life and manners, we were willing to visit it. To enter a habitation without leave, seems to be not considered here as rudeness or intrusion. The old laws of hospitality still give this licence to a stranger.

A hut is constructed with loose stones, ranged for the most part with some tendency to circularity. It must be placed where the wind cannot act upon it with violence, because it has no cement; and where the water will run easily away, because it has no floor but the naked ground. The wall, which is commonly about six feet high, declines from the perpendicular a little inward. Such rafters as can be procured are then raised for a roof, and covered with heath, which makes a strong and warm thatch, kept from flying off by ropes of twisted heath, of which the ends, reaching from the centre of the thatch to the top of the wall, are held firm by the weight of a large stone. No light is admitted but at the entrance, and through a hole in the thatch, which gives vent to the smoke. This hole is not directly over the fire, lest the rain should extinguish it; and the smoke therefore naturally fills the place before it escapes. Such is the general structure of the houses in which one of the nations of this opulent and powerful island has been hitherto content to live. Huts however are not more uniform than palaces; and this which we were inspecting was very far from one of the meanest, for it was divided into several apartments; and its inhabitants possessed such property as a pastoral poet might exalt into riches.

When we entered, we found an old woman boiling goat's-flesh in a kettle. She spoke little English, but we had interpreters at hand; and she was willing enough to display her whole system of economy. She has five children, of which none are yet gone from her. The eldest, a boy of thirteen, and her husband, who is eighty years old, were at work in the wood. Her next two sons were gone to Inverness to buy meal, by which oatmeal is always meant. Meal she considered as expensive food, and told us, that in Spring, when the goats gave milk, the children could live without it. She is mistress of sixty goats, and I saw many kids in an enclosure at the end of her house. She had also some poultry. By the lake we saw a potato-garden, and a small spot of ground on which stood four shucks [stooks], containing each twelve sheaves of barley. She has all this from the labour of their own hands, and for what is necessary to be bought, her kids and her chickens are sent to market.

With the true pastoral hospitality, she asked us to sit down and drink whisky. She is religious, and though the kirk is four miles off, probably eight English miles, she goes thither every Sunday. We gave her a shilling, and she begged snuff; for snuff is the luxury of a Highland cottage.

A Journey to the Western Islands
of Scotland, 1775

SAMUEL RICHARDSON

[A Woman's Fool]

I WAS there in a moment, and found all owing to the carelessness of Mrs Sinclair's cook-maid, who, having sat up to read the simple history of Dorastus and Faunia when she should have been in bed, had set fire to an old pair of calico window-curtains.

She had had the presence of mind in her fright, to tear down the half-burnt valance as well as curtains, and had got them, though blazing, into the chimney by the time I came up; so that I had the satisfaction to find the danger happily over.

Meantime Dorcas, after she had directed me upstairs, not knowing the worst was over, and expecting every minute the house would be in a blaze, out of tender regard for her lady (I shall for ever love the wench for it) ran to her door, and rapping loudly at it, in a recovered voice, cried out with a shrillness equal to her love, Fire! Fire! – The house is on fire! – Rise, madam! – This instant rise – if you would not be burnt in your bed!

No sooner had she made this dreadful outcry, but I heard her lady's door with hasty violence unbar, unbolt, unlock, and open, and my charmer's voice sounding like that of one going into a fit.

You may believe how much I was affected. I trembled with concern for her, and hastened down faster than the alarm of fire had made me run up, in order to satisfy her that all the danger was over.

When I had *flown down* to her chamber door, there I beheld the charmingest creature in the world, supporting herself on the arm of the gasping Dorcas, sighing, trembling, and ready to faint, with nothing on but an under-petticoat, her lovely bosom half-open, and her feet just slipped into her shoes. As soon as she saw me, she panted, and struggled to speak; but could only say, Oh, Mr Lovelace! and down was ready to sink.

I clasped her in my arms with an ardour she never felt before: My dearest life! fear nothing: I have been up – the danger is over – the fire is got under – And how (foolish devil! to Dorcas) could you thus, by your hideous yell, alarm and frighten my angel!

Oh, Jack! how her sweet bosom, as I clasped her to mine, heaved and panted! I could even distinguish her dear heart flutter, flutter, flutter, against mine; and for a few minutes, I feared she would go into fits.

Lest the half-lifeless charmer should catch cold in this undress, I lifted her to her bed, and sat down by her upon the side of it, endeavouring with the utmost tenderness, as well of action as expression, to dissipate her terrors.

But what did I get by this my generous care of her, and by my *successful* endeavour to bring her to herself? – Nothing, ungrateful as she was! but the most passionate exclamations: for we had both already forgot the occasion, dreadful as it was, which had thrown her into my arms; I, from the joy of encircling the almost disrobed body of the loveliest of her sex; she, from the greater terrors that arose from finding herself in my arms, and both seated on the bed from which she had been so lately frighted.

And now, Belford, reflect upon the distance the watchful charmer had hitherto kept me at. Reflect upon my love, and upon my sufferings for her: reflect upon her vigilance, and how long I had lain in wait to elude it; the awe I had stood in, because of her frozen virtue and overniceness; and that I never before was so happy with her; and then think how ungovernable must be my transports in those happy moments! And yet, in my own account, I was both decent and generous. The following lines, altered to the first person, come nearest of any I can recollect, to the rapturous occasion:

> Bowing, I kneel'd, and her forc'd hand I press'd,
> With sweet compulsion, to my beating breast;
> O'er it, in ecstasy, my lips bent low,
> And tides of sighs 'twixt her grasp'd fingers flow.
> High beat my hurry'd pulse, at each fierce kiss,
> And ev'ry burning sinew ach'd with bliss.

But, far from being affected by an address so fervent (although from a man she had so lately owned a regard for, and with whom, but an hour or two before, she had parted with so much satisfaction), that I never saw a bitterer, or more moving grief, when she came fully to herself.

She appealed to Heaven against my *treachery*, as she called it; while I, by the most solemn vows, pleaded my own equal fright, and the reality of the danger that had alarmed us both.

She conjured me, in the most solemn and affecting manner, by turns threatening and soothing, to quit her apartment, and permit her to hide herself from the light, and from every human eye.

I besought her pardon, yet could not avoid offending; and repeatedly vowed that the next morning's sun should witness our espousals. But taking, I suppose, all my protestations of this kind, as an indication that I intended to proceed to the last extremity, she would hear nothing that I said; but, redoubling her struggles to get from me, in broken accents, and exclamations the most vehement, she protested that she would not survive what she called a treatment so disgraceful and villainous; and, looking all wildly round her as if for some instrument of mischief, she espied a pair of sharp-pointed scissors on a chair by the bedside, and endeavoured to catch them up, with design to make her words good on the spot.

Seeing her desperation, I begged her to be pacified; that she would hear me speak but one word, declaring that I intended no dishonour to her: and having seized the scissors, I threw them into the chimney; and she still insisting vehemently upon my distance, I permitted her to take the chair.

But, oh, the sweet discomposure! – Her bared shoulders and arms, so inimitably fair and lovely: her spread hands crossed over her charming neck; yet not half concealing its glossy beauties: the scanty coat, as she rose from me, giving the whole of her admirable shape and fine-turned limbs: her eyes running over, yet seeming to threaten future vengeance: and at last her lips uttering what every indignant look and glowing feature portended; exclaiming as if I had done the worst I could do, and vowing never to forgive me; wilt thou wonder that I could avoid resuming the incensed, the already too-much-provoked fair one?

I did; and clasped her once more to my bosom: but, considering the delicacy of her frame, her force was amazing, and showed how much in earnest she was in her resentment; for it was with the utmost difficulty that I was able to hold her: nor could I prevent her sliding through my arms, to fall upon her knees: which she did at my feet. And there, in the anguish of her soul, her streaming eyes lifted up to my face with supplicating softness, hands folded, dishevelled hair; for her night head-dress having fallen off in her struggling, her charming tresses fell down in naturally shining ringlets, as if officious to conceal the dazzling beauties of her neck and shoulders; her lovely bosom too heaving with sighs, and broken sobs, as if to aid her quivering lips in pleading for her – in this manner, but when her grief gave way to her speech, in words pronounced with that emphatical propriety which distinguishes this admirable creature in her elocution from all the women I ever heard speak; did she implore my compassion, and my honour.

'Consider me, *dear* Lovelace,' were her charming words!—'on my knees I beg you to consider me, as a poor creature who has no protector but you; who has no defence but your honour: by that honour! by your humanity! by all you have vowed! I conjure you not to make me abhor myself! Not to make me vile in my own eyes!'

I mentioned the morrow as the happiest day of my life.

Tell me not of tomorrow; if indeed you mean me honourably, *now*, this very instant NOW! you must show, and begone! You can never in a whole long life repair the evils you may NOW make me suffer!

Wicked wretch! – insolent villain! – Yes, she called me insolent villain, although so much in my power! And for what? – only for kissing (with passion indeed) her inimitable neck, her lips, her cheeks, her forehead, and her streaming eyes, as this assemblage of beauties offered itself at once to my ravished sight; she continuing kneeling at my feet, as I sat.

If I *am* a villain, madam – And then my grasping but trembling hand – I hope I did not hurt the tenderest and loveliest of all her beauties – If I am a villain, madam—

She tore my ruffle, shrunk from my happy hand, with amazing force and agility, as with my other arm I would have encircled her waist.

Indeed you are! – The worst of villains! – Help! dear blessed people! and screamed – No help for a poor creature!—

Am I then a villain, madam? – *Am* I then a villain, say you? – and clasped both my arms about her, offering to raise her to my bounding heart—

Oh no! – and yet you are! – And again I was her *dear* Lovelace! – Her hands again clasped over her charming bosom – Kill me! kill me! – if I am odious enough in your eyes, to deserve this treatment; and I will thank you! – Too long, much too long, has my life been a burden to me! – or, wildly looking all around her, give me but the means, and I will instantly convince you that my honour is dearer to me than my life!

Then, with still folded hands, and fresh-streaming eyes, I was her *blessed* Lovelace; and she would thank me with her latest breath if I would permit her to make that preference, or free her from farther indignities.

I sat suspended for a moment. By my soul, thought I, thou art upon full proof an angel and no woman! Still, however, close clasping her to my bosom, as I had raised her from her knees, she again slid through my arms, and dropped upon them: – 'See, Mr Lovelace! – Good God!

that I should live to see this hour, and to bear this treatment! – see, at your feet a poor creature, imploring your pity, who for your sake is abandoned of all the world! Let not my father's curse thus dreadfully operate! Be not *you* the inflicter, who have been the *cause* of it! But spare me! I beseech you spare me! – for how have I deserved this treatment from you? – For your own sake, if not for my sake, and as you would that God Almighty, in your last hour, should have mercy upon you, spare me!'—

What heart but must have been penetrated?

I would again have raised the dear suppliant from her knees; but she would not be raised, till my softened mind, she said, had yielded to her prayer, and bid her rise to be innocent.

Rise then, my angel, rise, and be what you are, and all you wish to be! Only pronounce me pardoned for what has passed, and tell me you will continue to look upon me with that eye of favour and serenity, which I have been blessed with for some days past, and I will submit to my beloved conqueress, whose power never was at so great an height with me, as now; and retire to my apartment.

God Almighty, said she, hear your prayers in your most arduous moments, as you have heard mine! And now leave me, this moment leave me, to my own recollection; in *that* you will leave me to misery enough, and more than you ought to wish your bitterest enemy.

Impute not everything, my best beloved, to design; for design it was not—

Oh, Mr Lovelace!—

Upon my soul, madam, the fire was real – (and so it was, Jack!) – The house might have been consumed by it, as you will be convinced in the morning by ocular demonstration.

Oh, Mr Lovelace!—

Let my passion for you, madam, and the unexpected meeting of you at your chamber door, in an attitude so charming—

Leave me, leave me, this moment! – I beseech you, leave me; looking wildly and in confusion, now about her, and now upon herself.

Excuse me, dearest creature, for those liberties which, innocent as they were, your too great delicacy may make you take amiss.

No more! no more! – Leave me, I beseech you! Again looking upon herself, and around her, in a sweet confusion. – Begone! Begone! – Then weeping, she struggled ve-hemently to withdraw her hands, which all the while I held between mine – Her struggles! Oh, what additional charms, as now I reflect, did her struggles give to every feature, every limb, of a person so sweetly elegant and lovely!

Impossible! my dearest life, till you pronounce my pardon! – Say but you forgive me! – Say you do!

I beseech you, begone! Leave me to myself, that I may think what I *can* do, and what I *ought* to do.

That, my dearest creature, is not enough. You must tell me that I am forgiven; that you will see me tomorrow, as if nothing had happened.

And then, clasping her again in my arms, hoping she would not forgive me—

I will – I do forgive you – wretch that you are!

Nay, my Clarissa! And is it such a reluctant pardon, mingled with a word so upbraiding, that I am to be put off with, when you are thus (clasping her close to me) in my power?

I do, I *do* forgive you!

Heartily?

Yes, heartily!

And freely?

Freely!

And will you look upon me tomorrow, as if nothing had passed?

Yes, yes!

I cannot take these peevish affirmatives, so much like intentional negatives! – Say you will, upon your honour!

Upon my honour, then – Oh, now, begone! begone! and never—

What, never, my angel! – Is this forgiveness?

Never, said she, let what has passed be remembered more!

I insisted upon one kiss to seal my pardon – and retired

like a fool, a woman's fool, as I was! – I sneakingly retired!
– Couldst thou have believed it?

*Clarissa; or, The History of
a Young Lady*, 1747–8

LAURENCE STERNE

[Tristram's Conception]

I WISH either my father or my mother, or indeed both of
them, as they were in duty both equally bound to it, had
minded what they were about when they begot me; had
they duly considered how much depended upon what they
were then doing; that not only the production of a rational
Being was concerned in it, but that possibly the happy
formation and temperature of his body, perhaps his genius
and the very cast of his mind; – and, for aught they knew to
the contrary, even the fortunes of his whole house might
take their turn from the humours and dispositions which
were then uppermost; – Had they duly weighed and considered all this, and proceeded accordingly, – I am verily
persuaded I should have made a quite different figure in the
world, from that, in which the reader is likely to see me. –
Believe me, good folks, this is not so inconsiderable a thing
as many of you may think it; – you have all, I dare say,
heard of the animal spirits, as how they are transmuted from
father to son &c. &c. – and a great deal to that purpose: –
Well, you may take my word, that nine parts in ten of a
man's sense or his nonsense, his successes and miscarriages
in this world depend upon their motions and activity, and
the different tracts and trains you put them into, so that
when they are once set a-going, whether right or wrong, 'tis
not a halfpenny matter, – away they go cluttering like hey-
go-mad; and by treading the same steps over and over again,
they presently make a road of it, as plain and as smooth as
a garden-walk, which, when they are once used to, the

Devil himself sometimes shall not be able to drive them off it.

Pray, my dear, quoth my mother, *have you not forgot to wind up the clock? – Good G—!* cried my father, making an exclamation, but taking care to moderate his voice at the same time, – *Did ever woman, since the creation of the world, interrupt a man with such a silly question?* Pray, what was your father saying? – Nothing.

– Then, positively, there is nothing in the question, that I can see, either good or bad. – Then, let me tell you, Sir, it was a very unseasonable question at least, – because it scattered and dispersed the animal spirits, whose business it was to have escorted and gone hand-in-hand with the HOMUNCULUS, and conducted him safe to the place destined for his reception.

The HOMUNCULUS, Sir, in however low and ludicrous a light he may appear, in this age of levity, to the eye of folly or prejudice: – to the eye of reason in scientific research, he stands confessed – a BEING guarded and circumscribed with rights: – The minutest philosophers, who, by the bye, have the most enlarged understandings (their souls being inversely as their enquiries), shew us incontestably. That the HOMUNCULUS is created by the same hand, – engendered in the same course of nature, – endowed with the same locomotive powers and faculties with us: – That he consists as we do, of skin, hair, fat, flesh, veins, arteries, ligaments, nerves, cartilages, bones, marrow, brains, glands, genitals, humours, and articulations; – is a Being of as much activity, – and, in all senses of the word, as much and as truly our fellow-creature as my Lord Chancellor of England. – He may be benefited, – he may be injured, – he may obtain redress; – in a word, he has all the claims and rights of humanity, which Tully, Puffendorff, or the best ethic writers allow to arise out of that state and relation.

Now, dear Sir, what if any accident had befallen him in his way alone? – or that, through terror of it, natural to so young a traveller, my little gentleman had got to his journey's end miserably spent; – his muscular strength and virility worn down to a thread; – his own animal spirits ruffled beyond description, – and that in this sad disordered state of nerves, he had laid down a prey to sudden starts, or a series of melancholy dreams and fancies for nine long, long months together. – I tremble to think what a foundation had been laid for a thousand weaknesses both of body and mind, which no skill of the physician or the philosopher could ever afterwards have set thoroughly to rights.

I was begot in the night, betwixt the first Sunday and the first Monday in the month of March, in the year of our Lord one thousand seven hundred and eighteen. I am positive I was. – But how I came to be so very particular in my account of a thing which happened before I was born, is owing to another small anecdote known only in our own family, but now made public for the better clearing up this point.

My father, you must know, who was originally a Turkey merchant, but had left off business for some years, in order to retire to, and die upon, his paternal estate in the county of——, was, I believe, one of the most regular men in everything he did, whether 'twas matter of business, or matter of amusement, that ever lived. As a small specimen of this extreme exactness of his, to which he was in truth a slave, – he had made it a rule for many years of his life, – on the first Sunday night of every month throughout the whole year, – as certain as ever the Sunday night came, – to wind up a large house-clock, which we had standing upon the backstairs head, with his own hands: – And being somewhere between fifty and sixty years of age, at the time I have been speaking of, – he had likewise gradually brought some other little family concernments to the same period, in order, as he would often say to my uncle Toby, to get them all out of the way at one time, and be no more plagued and pestered with them the rest of the month.

It was attended with but one misfortune, which, in a great measure, fell upon myself, and the effects of which I fear I shall carry with me to my grave; namely, that from an unhappy association of ideas which have no connection in nature, it so fell out at length, that my poor mother could never hear the said clock wound up, – but the thoughts of some other things unavoidably popped into her head – &

vice versa: – which strange combination of ideas, the sagacious Locke, who certainly understood the nature of these things better than most men, affirms to have produced more wry actions than all other sources of prejudice whatsoever.

The Life and Opinions of Tristram Shandy,
Gentleman, Vol. 1, 1759

[The *Fille de Chambre*]

IT WAS a fine still evening in the latter end of the month of May – the crimson window curtains (which were of the same colour as those of the bed) were drawn close – the sun was setting and reflected through them so warm a tint into the fair *fille de chambre*'s face – I thought she blushed – the idea of it made me blush myself – we were quite alone; and that super-induced a second blush before the first could get off.

There is a sort of a pleasing half guilty blush, where the blood is more in fault than the man – 'tis sent impetuous from the heart, and virtue flies after it – not to call back, but to make the sensation of it more delicious to the nerves – 'tis associated.—

But I'll not describe it. – I felt something at first within me which was not in strict unison with the lesson of virtue I had given her the night before – I sought five minutes for a card – I knew I had not one. – I took up a pen – I laid it down again – my hand trembled – the devil was in me.

I know as well as anyone, he is an adversary, whom if we resist, he will fly from us – but I seldom resist him at all; from a terror, that though I may conquer, I may still get a hurt in the combat – so I give up the triumph, for security; and instead of thinking to make him fly, I generally fly myself.

The fair *fille de chambre* came close up to the bureau where I was looking for a card – took up the first pen I cast down, then offered to hold me the ink: she offered it so sweetly, I was going to accept it – but I durst not – I have nothing, my dear, said I, to write upon. – Write it, said she, simply, upon anything.—

I was just going to cry out, Then I will write it, fair girl! upon thy lips.—

If I do, said I, I shall perish – so I took her by the hand, and led her to the door, and begged she would not forget the lesson I had given her – She said, Indeed she would not – and as she uttered it with some earnestness, she turned about, and gave me both her hands, closed together, into mine – it was impossible not to compress them in that situation – I wished to let them go; and all the time I held them, I kept arguing within myself against it – and still I held them on. – In two minutes I found I had all the battle to fight over again – and I felt my legs and every limb about me tremble at the idea.

The foot of the bed was within a yard and a half of the place where we were standing – I had still hold of her hands – and how it happened I can give no account, but I neither asked her – nor drew her – nor did I think of the bed – but so it did happen, we both sat down.

I'll just show you, said the fair *fille de chambre*, the little purse I have been making today to hold your crown. So she put her hand into her right pocket, which was next me, and felt for it for some time – then into the left – 'She had lost it' – I never bore expectation more quietly – it was in her right pocket at last – she pulled it out; it was of green taffeta, lined with a little bit of white quilted satin, and just big enough to hold the crown – she put it into my hand – it was pretty; and I held it ten minutes with the back of my hand resting upon her lap – looking sometimes at the purse, sometimes on one side of it.

A stitch or two had broke out in the gathers of my stock – the fair *fille de chambre*, without saying a word, took out her little hussif, threaded a small needle, and sewed it up – I foresaw it would hazard the glory of the day; and as she passed her hand in silence across and across my neck in the manoeuvre, I felt the laurels shake which fancy had wreathed about my head.

A strap had given way in her walk, and the buckle of her

shoe was just falling off – See, said the *fille de chambre*, holding up her foot – I could not for my soul but fasten the buckle in return, and putting in the strap – and lifting up the other foot with it, when I had done, to see both were right – in doing it too suddenly – it unavoidably threw the fair *fille de chambre* off her centre – and then—

A Sentimental Journey through France and Italy by Mr Yorick, 1768

JAMES BOSWELL

[Amorous Play]

[*Thursday, 19 May 1763*] . . . at seven, being in high glee, I called upon Miss Watts, whom I found by herself, neatly dressed and looking very well. I was free and easy with her, and begged that she would drink a glass of wine with me at the Shakespeare, which she complied with. I told her my name was Macdonald, and that I was a Scotch Highlander. She said she liked them much, as they had always spirit and generosity. We were shown into a handsome room and had a bottle of choice sherry. We sat near two hours and became very cheerful and agreeable to each other. I told her with a polite freedom, 'Madam, I tell you honestly I have no money to give you, but if you allow me favours without it, I shall be much obliged to you.' She smiled and said she would. Her maid then brought her a message that a particular friend from the country was waiting for her; so that I was obliged to give her up this night, as I determined to give her no money. She left me pleased, and said she hoped to have the pleasure of my company at tea when it was convenient. This I faithfully promised and took as a good sign of her willingness to establish a friendly communication with me.

I then sallied forth to the Piazza in rich flow of animal spirits and burning with fierce desire. I met two very pretty little girls who asked me to take them with me. 'My dear girls,' said I, 'I am a poor fellow. I can give you no money. But if you choose to have a glass of wine and my company and let us be gay and obliging to each other without money, I am your man.' They agreed with great good humour. So back to the Shakespeare I went. 'Waiter,' said I, 'I have got here a couple of human beings; I don't know how they'll do.' 'I'll look, your Honour,' cried he, and with inimitable effrontery stared them in the face and then cried, 'They'll do very well.' 'What,' said I, 'are they good fellow-creatures? Bring them up, then.' We were shown into a good room and had a bottle of sherry before us in a minute. I surveyed my seraglio and found them both good subjects for amorous play. I toyed with them and drank about and sung 'Youth's the Season' and thought myself Captain Macheath; and then I solaced my existence with them, one after the other, according to their seniority. I was quite *raised*, as the phrase is: thought I was in a London tavern, the Shakespeare's Head, enjoying high debauchery after my sober winter. I parted with my ladies politely and came home in a glow of spirits.

London Journal

[The Character of Samuel Johnson]

D R SAMUEL Johnson's character, religious, moral, political, and literary, nay his figure and manner, are, I believe, more generally known than those of almost any man; yet it may not be superfluous here to attempt a sketch of him. Let my readers then remember that he was a sincere and zealous Christian, of high church of England and monarchial principles, which he would not tamely suffer to be questioned; steady and inflexible in maintaining the obligations of piety and virtue, both from a regard to the order of society, and from a veneration for the Great Source of all order; correct, nay stern in his taste; hard to please, and easily offended, impetuous and irritable in his temper, but of a most humane and benevolent heart; having a mind stored with a vast and various collection of learning and knowledge, which he communicated with peculiar perspicuity and force, in rich and choice expression. He united a most logical head with a most fertile imagination, which gave him an extraordinary advantage in arguing; for he could reason close or wide, as he saw best for the moment. He could, when he chose it, be the greatest sophist that ever wielded a weapon in the schools of declamation; but he indulged this only in conversation; for he owned he sometimes talked for victory; he was too conscientious to make error permanent and pernicious, by deliberately writing it. He was conscious of his superiority. He loved praise when it was brought to him; but was too proud to seek for it. He was somewhat susceptible of flattery. His mind was so full of imagery, that he might have been perpetually a poet. It has been often remarked, that in his poetical pieces, which it is to be regretted are so few, because, so excellent, his style is easier than in his prose. There is deception in this: it is not easier, but better suited to the dignity of verse; as one may dance with grace, whose motions, in ordinary walking, – in the common step, are awkward. He had a constitutional melancholy, the clouds of which darkened the brightness of his fancy, and gave a gloomy cast to his whole course of thinking: yet, though grave and awful in his deportment, when he thought it necessary or proper, he frequently indulged himself in pleasantry and sportive sallies. He was prone to superstition, but not to credulity. Though his imagination might incline him to a belief of the marvellous, and the mysterious, his vigorous reason examined the evidence with jealousy. He had a loud voice, and a slow deliberate utterance, which no doubt gave some additional weight to the sterling metal of his conversation. His person was large, robust, I may say approaching to the gigantic, and grown unwieldy from corpulency. His countenance was naturally of the cast of an ancient statue, but somewhat disfigured by the scars of that *evil*, which, it was formerly imagined the *royal touch* could cure. He was now in his sixty-fourth year, and was become a little dull of hearing. His sight had always been somewhat weak; yet, so much does mind govern, and even supply the deficiency of organs, that his perceptions were uncommonly quick and accurate. His head, and sometimes also his body, shook with a kind of motion like the effect of a palsy; he appeared to be frequently disturbed by cramps, or convulsive contractions, of the nature of that distemper called *St Vitus's dance*. He wore a full suit of plain brown clothes, with twisted-hair-buttons of the same colour, a large bushy greyish wig, a plain shirt, black worsted stockings, and silver buckles. Upon this tour, when journeying, he wore boots, and a very wide brown cloth great coat, with pockets which might have almost held the two volumes of his folio dictionary; and he carried in his hand a large English oak stick.

[Highland Coquetry]

WHEN WE had advanced a good way by the side of Loch Ness, I perceived a little hut, with an old-looking woman at the door of it. I thought here might be a scene that would amuse Dr Johnson; so I mentioned it to him. 'Let's go in,' said he. We dismounted, and we and our guides entered the hut. It was a wretched little hovel of earth only, I think, and for a window had only a small hole, which was stopped with a piece of turf, that was taken out occasionally to let in light. In the middle of the room or space which we entered, was a fire of peat, the smoke going out at a hole in the roof. She had a pot upon it, with goat's flesh, boiling. There was at one end under the same roof, but divided by a kind of partition made of wattles, a pen or fold in which we saw a good many kids.

Dr Johnson was curious to know where she slept. I asked one of the guides, who questioned her in Erse. She answered with a tone of emotion, saying (as he told us) she was afraid we wanted to go to bed to her. This *coquetry*, or whatever it may be called, of so wretched a being, was truly ludicrous. Dr Johnson and I afterwards were merry upon it. I said, it was he who alarmed the poor woman's virtue. 'No, sir,' said he, 'she'll say, "There came a wicked young fellow, a wild dog, who I believe would have ravished me, had there not been with him a grave old gentleman, who repressed him: but when he gets out of the sight of his tutor, I'll warrant you he'll spare no woman he meets, young or old."' 'No, sir,' I replied, 'she'll say, "There was a terrible ruffian who would have forced me, had it not been for a civil decent young man who, I take it, was an angel sent from heaven to protect me."'

Dr Johnson would not hurt her delicacy, by insisting on 'seeing her bedchamber', like Archer in *The Beaux' Stratagem*. But my curiosity was more ardent; I lighted a piece of paper, and went into the place where the bed was. There was a little partition of wicker, rather more neatly done than that for the fold, and close by the wall was a kind of bedstead of wood with heath upon it by way of bed; at the foot of which I saw some sort of blankets or covering rolled up in a heap. The woman's name was Fraser; so was her husband's. He was a man of eighty. Mr Fraser of Balnain allows him to live in this hut, and keep sixty goats, for taking care of his woods, where he then was. They had five children, the eldest only thirteen. Two were gone to Inverness to buy meal; the rest were looking after the goats. This contented family had four stacks of barley, twenty-four sheaves in each. They had a few fowls. We were informed that they lived all the spring without meal, upon milk and curds and whey alone. What they get for their goats, kids, and fowls, maintains them during the rest of the year.

She asked us to sit down and take a dram. I saw one chair. She said she was as happy as any woman in Scotland. She could hardly speak any English except a few detached words. Dr Johnson was pleased at seeing, for the first time, such a state of human life. She asked for snuff. It is her luxury, and she uses a great deal. We had none; but gave her sixpence apiece. She then brought out her whisky bottle. I tasted it; as did Joseph and our guides: so I gave her sixpence more. She sent us away with many prayers in Erse.

The Journal of a Tour to the Hebrides, 1785

[Johnson's Dictionary]

B UT THE year 1747 is distinguished as the epoch, when
Johnson's arduous and important work, his *Dictionary
of the English Language*, was announced to the world, by
the publication of its Plan or *Prospectus*.

How long this immense undertaking had been the object
of his contemplation, I do not know. I once asked him by
what means he had attained to that astonishing knowledge
of our language, by which he was enabled to realise a design
of such extent, and accumulated difficulty. He told me, that
'it was not the effect of particular study; but that it had
grown up in his mind insensibly.' I have been informed by
Mr James Dodsley, that several years before this period,
when Johnson was one day sitting in his brother Robert's
shop, he heard his brother suggest to him, that a Dictionary
of the English Language would be a work that would be well
received by the public; that Johnson seemed at first to catch
at the proposition, but, after a pause, said, in his abrupt
decisive manner, 'I believe that I shall not undertake it.'
That he, however, had bestowed much thought upon the
subject, before he published his *Plan*, is evident from the
enlarged, clear, and accurate views which it exhibits; and
we find him mentioning in that tract, that many of the
writers whose testimonies were to be produced as authorities, were selected by Pope; which proves that he had
been furnished, probably by Mr Robert Dodsley, with
whatever hints that eminent poet had contributed towards a
great literary project, that had been the subject of important
consideration in a former reign.

The booksellers who contracted with Johnson, single and
unaided, for the execution of a work, which in other
countries has not been effected but by the co-operating
exertions of many, were Mr Robert Dodsley, Mr Charles
Hitch, Mr Andrew Millar, the two Messieurs Longman, and
the two Messieurs Knapton. The price stipulated was fifteen
hundred and seventy-five pounds.

The *Plan* was addressed to Philip Dormer, Earl of Chesterfield, then one of his Majesty's Principal Secretaries of State; a nobleman who was very ambitious of literary distinction, and who, upon being informed of the design, had expressed himself in terms very favourable to its success. There is, perhaps in every thing of any consequence, a secret history which it would be amusing to know, could we have it authentically communicated. Johnson told me, 'Sir, the way in which the *Plan* of my *Dictionary* came to be inscribed to Lord Chesterfield, was this: I had neglected to write it by the time appointed. Dodsley suggested a desire to have it addressed to Lord Chesterfield. I laid hold of this as a pretext for delay, that it might be better done, and let Dodsley have his desire. I said to my friend, Dr Bathurst, "Now if any good comes of my addressing to Lord Chesterfield, it will be ascribed to deep policy, when, in fact, it was only a casual excuse for laziness." '

It is worthy of observation, that the *Plan* has not only the substantial merit of comprehension, perspicuity, and precision, but that the language of it is unexceptionably excellent; it being altogether free from that inflation of style, and those uncommon but apt and energetic words, which in some of his writings have been censured, with more petulance than justice; and never was there a more dignified strain of compliment than that in which he courts the attention of one who, he had been persuaded to believe, would be a respectable patron. . . .

While the *Dictionary* was going forward, Johnson lived part of the time in Holborn, part in Gough-square, Fleet-street; and he had an upper room fitted up like a counting-house for the purpose, in which he gave to the copyists their several tasks. The words, partly taken from other dictionaries, and partly supplied by himself, having been first written down with spaces left between them, he delivered in writing their etymologies, definitions, and various significations. The authorities were copied from the books themselves, in which he had marked the passages with a black-lead pencil, the traces of which could easily be effaced. I have seen several of them, in which that trouble had not been taken; so that they were just as when used by the copyists. It is remarkable, that he was so attentive in the choice of the passages in which words were authorised, that one may read page after page of his *Dictionary* with improvement and pleasure; and it should not pass unobserved, that he has quoted no author whose writings had a tendency to hurt sound religion and morality.

The necessary expence of preparing a work of such magnitude for the press, must have been a considerable deduction from the price stipulated to be paid for the copyright. I understand that nothing was allowed by the booksellers on that account; and I remember his telling me, that a large portion of it having by mistake been written upon both sides of the paper, so as to be inconvenient for the compositor, it cost him twenty pounds to have it transcribed upon one side only.

He is now to be considered as 'tugging at his oar', as engaged in a steady continued course of occupation, sufficient to employ all his time for some years; and which was the best preventive of that constitutional melancholy which was ever lurking about him, ready to trouble his quiet. But his enlarged and lively mind could not be satisfied without more diversity of employment, and the pleasure of animated relaxation. He therefore not only exerted his talents in occasional composition very different from Lexicography, but formed a club in Ivy-lane, Paternoster-row, with a view to enjoy literary discussion, and amuse his evening hours. . . .

Mr Andrew Millar, bookseller in the Strand, took the principal charge of conducting the publication of Johnson's *Dictionary*; and as the patience of the proprietors was repeatedly tried and almost exhausted, by their expecting that the work would be completed within the time which Johnson had sanguinely supposed, the learned author was often goaded to dispatch, more especially as he had received all the copy-money, by different drafts, a considerable time before he had finished his task. When the messenger who carried the last sheet to Millar returned, Johnson asked him, 'Well, what did he say?' – 'Sir, (answered the messenger) he said, thank God I have done with him.' 'I am glad (replied Johnson, with a smile) that he thanks God for anything.'. . .

A few of his definitions must be admitted to be erroneous. Thus, *Windward* and *Leeward*, though directly of opposite meaning, are defined identically the same way; as to which inconsiderable specks it is enough to observe, that his Preface announces that he was aware there might be many such in so immense a work; nor was he at all disconcerted when an instance was pointed out to him. A lady once asked him how he came to define *Pastern* the *knee* of a horse: instead of making an elaborate defence, as she expected, he at once answered, 'Ignorance, Madam, pure ignorance.' His definition of *Network* has been often quoted with sportive malignity, as obscuring a thing in itself very plain, But to these frivolous censures no other answer is necessary than that with which we are furnished by his own Preface.

[A Frisk]

O NE NIGHT when Beauclerk and Langton had supped at a tavern in London, and sat till about three in the morning, it came into their heads to go and knock up Johnson, and see if they could prevail on him to join them in a ramble. They rapped violently at the door of his chambers in the Temple, till at last he appeared in his shirt, with his little black wig on the top of his head, instead of a nightcap, and a poker in his hand, imagining, probably, that some ruffians were coming to attack him. When he discovered who they were, and was told their errand, he smiled, and with great good humour agreed to their proposal: 'What, is it you, you dogs! I'll have a frisk with you.' He was soon drest, and they sallied forth together into Covent-Garden, where the greengrocers and fruiterers were beginning to arrange their hampers, just come in from the country. Johnson made some attempts to help them; but the honest gardeners stared so at his figure and manner, and

odd interference, that he soon saw his services were not
relished. They then repaired to one of the neighbouring
taverns, and made a bowl of that liquor called *Bishop*, which
Johnson had always liked; while in joyous contempt of
sleep, from which he had been roused, he repeated the
festive lines,

> 'Short, O short then be thy reign,
> And give us to the world again!'

They did not stay long, but walked down to the Thames,
took a boat, and rowed to Billingsgate. Beauclerk and
Johnson were so well pleased with their amusement, that
they resolved to persevere in dissipation for the rest of the
day: but Langton deserted them, being engaged to breakfast
with some young Ladies. Johnson scolded him for 'leaving
his social friends, to go and sit with a set of wretched *un-
idea'd* girls'. Garrick being told of this ramble, said to him
smartly, 'I heard of your frolick t'other night. You'll be in
the Chronicle.' Upon which Johnson afterwards observed,
'*He* durst not do such a thing. His *wife* would not *let* him!'

[Boswell's First Meeting with Johnson, 16 May 1763]

M R THOMAS Davies, the actor, who then kept a bookseller's shop in Russell Street, Covent Garden, told
me that Johnson was very much his friend, and came
frequently to his house, where he more than once invited
me to meet him; but by some unlucky accident or other he
was prevented from coming to us.

Mr Thomas Davies was a man of good understanding and
talents, with the advantage of a liberal education. Though
somewhat pompous, he was an entertaining companion; and
his literary performances have no inconsiderable share of
merit. He was a friendly and very hospitable man. Both he
and his wife (who has been celebrated for her beauty),
though upon the stage for many years, maintained an

uniform decency of character; and Johnson esteemed them, and lived in as easy an intimacy with them as with any family which he used to visit. Mr Davies recollected several of Johnson's remarkable sayings, and was one of the best of the many imitators of his voice and manner, while relating them. He increased my impatience more and more to see the extraordinary man whose works I highly valued, and whose conversation was reported to be so peculiarly excellent.

At last, on Monday the 16th of May, when I was sitting in Mr Davies's back-parlour, after having drunk tea with him and Mrs Davies, Johnson unexpectedly came into the shop; and Mr Davies having perceived him through the glass door in the room in which we were sitting, advancing towards us, – he announced his aweful approach to me, somewhat in the manner of an actor in the part of Horatio, when he addresses Hamlet on the appearance of his father's ghost, 'Look, my Lord, it comes'. I found that I had a very perfect idea of Johnson's figure, from the portrait of him painted by Sir Joshua Reynolds soon after he had published his *Dictionary*, in the attitude of sitting in his easy chair in deep meditation, which was the first picture his friend did for him, which Sir Joshua very kindly presented to me, and from which an engraving has been made for this work. Mr Davies mentioned my name, and respectfully introduced me to him. I was much agitated; and recollecting his prejudice against the Scotch, of which I had heard so much, I said to Davies: 'Don't tell him where I come from.' – 'From Scotland,' cried Davies roguishly. 'Mr Johnson, (said I) I do indeed come from Scotland, but I cannot help it.' I am willing to flatter myself that I meant this as a light pleasantry to soothe and conciliate him, and not as an humiliating abasement at the expense of my country. But, however that might be, this speech was somewhat unlucky; for with that quickness of wit for which he was so remarkable, he seized the expression 'come from Scotland', which I used in the sense of being of that country, and, as if I had said that I had come away from it, or left it, retorted: 'That, sir, I find, is what a very great many of your countrymen cannot help.' This stroke stunned me a good deal; and when we had sat down, I felt myself not a little embarrassed, and apprehensive of what might come next. He then addressed himself to Davies: 'What do you think of Garrick? He has refused me an order for the play for Miss Williams, because he knows the house will be full, and that an order would be worth three shillings.' Eager to take any opening to get into conversation with him, I ventured to say, 'O, Sir, I cannot think Mr Garrick would grudge such a trifle to you.' 'Sir,' (said he, with a stern look) 'I have known David Garrick longer than you have done; and I know no right you have to talk to me on the subject.' Perhaps I deserved this check; for it was rather presumptuous in me, an entire stranger, to express any doubt of the justice of his animadversion upon his old acquaintance and pupil. I now felt myself much mortified, and began to think that the hope which I had long indulged of obtaining his acquaintance was blasted. And, in truth, had not my ardour been uncommonly strong, and my resolution uncommonly persevering, so rough a reception might have deterred me for ever from making any further attempts. Fortunately, however, I remained upon the field not wholly discomfited; and was soon rewarded by hearing some of his conversation. . . .

[Hodge]

JOHNSON'S LOVE of little children, which he discovered upon all occasions, calling them 'pretty dears', and giving them sweetmeats, was an undoubted proof of the real humanity and gentleness of his disposition.

His uncommon kindness to his servants, and serious concern, not only for their comfort in this world, but their happiness in the next, was another unquestionable evidence of what all, who were intimately acquainted with him, knew to be true.

Nor would it be just, under this head, to omit the fondness which he shewed for animals which he had taken under his protection. I shall never forget the indulgence with which

he treated Hodge, his cat: for whom he himself used to go
out and buy oysters, lest the servants having that trouble
should take a dislike to the poor creature. I am, unluckily,
one of those who have an antipathy to a cat, so that I am
uneasy when in the room with one; and I own, I frequently
suffered a good deal from the presence of this same Hodge.
I recollect him one day scrambling up Dr Johnson's breast,
apparently with much satisfaction, while my friend smiling
and half-whistling, rubbed down his back, and pulled him
by the tail; and when I observed he was a fine cat, saying,
'Why, yes, Sir, but I have had cats whom I liked better than
this'; and then as if perceiving Hodge to be out of countenance, adding, 'but he is a very fine cat, a very fine cat
indeed.'

This reminds me of the ludicrous account which he gave
Mr Langton, of the despicable state of a young Gentleman
of good family. 'Sir, when I heard of him last, he was
running about town shooting cats.' And then in a sort of
kindly reverie, he bethought himself of his own favourite
cat, and said, 'But Hodge shan't be shot; no, no, Hodge
shall not be shot.'

The Life of Samuel Johnson, LLD, 1791

HORACE WALPOLE

[Flight]

THE LOWER part of the castle was hollowed into several
intricate cloisters; and it was not easy for one under so
much anxiety to find the door that opened into the cavern.
An awful silence reigned throughout those subterranean
regions, except now and then some blasts of wind that shook
the doors she had passed, and which grating on the rusty
hinges were re-echoed through that long labyrinth of darkness. Every murmur struck her with new terror; – yet more
she dreaded to hear the wrathful voice of Manfred urging

his domestics to pursue her. She trod as softly as impatience would give her leave, – yet frequently stopped and listened to hear if she was followed. In one of those moments she thought she heard a sigh. She shuddered, and recoiled a few paces. In a moment she thought she heard the step of some person. Her blood curdled; she concluded it was Manfred. Every suggestion that horror could inspire rushed into her mind. She condemned her rash flight, which had thus exposed her to his rage in a place where her cries were not likely to draw any body to her assistance – Yet the sound seemed not to come from behind; – if Manfred knew where she was, he must have followed her: she was still in one of the cloisters, and the steps she had heard were too distinct to proceed from the way she had come. Cheered with this reflection, and hoping to find a friend in whoever was not the prince; she was going to advance, when a door that stood a-jar, at some distance to the left, was opened gently; but ere her lamp, which she held up, could discover who opened it, the person retreated precipitately on seeing the light.

Isabella, whom every incident was sufficient to dismay, hesitated whether she should proceed. Her dread of Manfred soon outweighed every other terror. The very circumstance of the person avoiding her, gave her a sort of courage. It could only be, she thought, some domestic belonging to the castle. Her gentleness had never raised her an enemy, and conscious innocence made her hope that, unless sent by the prince's order to seek her, his servants would rather assist than prevent her flight. Fortifying herself with these reflections, and believing, by what she could observe, that she was near the mouth of the subterraneous cavern, she approached the door that had been opened; but a sudden gust of wind that met her at the door extinguished her lamp, and left her in total darkness.

Words cannot paint the horror of the princess's situation. Alone in so dismal a place, her mind imprinted with all the terrible events of the day, hopeless of escaping, expecting every moment the arrival of Manfred, and far from tranquil on knowing she was within reach of somebody, she knew not whom, who for some cause seemed concealed thereabouts, all these thoughts crowded on her distracted mind, and she was ready to sink under her apprehensions. She addressed herself to every saint in heaven, and inwardly implored their assistance. For a considerable time she remained in an agony of despair. At last, as softly as was possible, she felt for the door, and, having found it, entered trembling into the vault from whence she had heard the sigh and steps. It gave her a kind of momentary joy to perceive an imperfect ray of clouded moonshine gleam from the roof of the vault, which seemed to be fallen in, and from whence hung a fragment of earth or building, she could not distinguish which, that appeared to have been crushed inwards. She advanced eagerly towards this chasm, when she discerned a human form standing close against the wall.

She shrieked, believing it the ghost of her betrothed Conrad. The figure advancing, said in a submissive voice, Be not alarmed, lady; I will not injure you. Isabella, a little encouraged by the words and tone of voice of the stranger, and recollecting that this must be the person who had opened the door, recovered her spirits enough to reply, Sir, whoever you are, take pity on a wretched princess standing on the brink of destruction: assist me to escape from this fatal castle, or in a few moments I may be made miserable for ever. Alas! said the stranger, what can I do to assist you? I will die in your defence; but I am unacquainted with the castle, and want— Oh! said Isabella, hastily interrupting him, help me but to find a trap-door that must be hereabout, and it is the greatest service you can do me; for I have not a minute to lose. Saying these words she felt about on the pavement, and directed the stranger to search likewise for a smooth piece of brass inclosed in one of the stones. That, said she, is the lock, which opens with a spring, of which I know the secret. If I can find that, I may escape – if not, alas, courteous stranger, I fear I shall have involved you in my misfortunes: Manfred will suspect you for the accomplice of my flight, and you will fall a victim to his resentment. I value not my life, said the stranger; and it will be some comfort to lose it in trying to deliver you from his tyranny. Generous youth, said Isabella, how shall I ever requite— As she uttered those words, a ray of moonshine streaming through a cranny of the ruin above shone directly on the lock they sought – Oh, transport! said Isabella, here is the trap-door! and taking out a key, she touched the spring, which starting aside discovered an iron ring.

The Castle of Otranto, 1765

OLIVER GOLDSMITH

[A Family Portrait]

M Y WIFE and daughters happening to return a visit to neighbour Flamborough's, found that family had lately got their pictures drawn by a limner, who travelled the country, and took likenesses for fifteen shillings a head. As this family and ours had long a sort of rivalry in point of taste, our spirit took the alarm at this stolen march upon us; and, notwithstanding all I could say, and I said much, it was resolved that we should have our pictures done too.

Having, therefore, engaged the limner – for what could I do? – our next deliberation was to show the superiority of our tastes in the attitudes. As for our neighbour's family, there were seven of them, and they were drawn with seven oranges – a thing quite out of taste, no variety in life, no composition in the world. We desired to have something in a brighter style; and, after many debates, at length came to a unanimous resolution of being drawn together, in one large historical family piece. This would be cheaper, since one frame would serve for all, and it would be infinitely more genteel; for all families of any taste were now drawn in the same manner. As we did not immediately recollect an historical subject to hit us, we were contented each with being drawn as independent historical figures. My wife desired to be represented as Venus, and the painter was desired not to be too frugal of his diamonds in her stomacher and hair. Her two little ones were to be as Cupids by her side; while I, in my gown and band, was to present her with my books on the Whistonian controversy. Olivia would be drawn as an Amazon, sitting upon a bank of flowers, dressed in a green joseph [*caped overcoat*], richly laced in gold, and a whip in her hand. Sophia was to be a shepherdess, with as many sheep as the painter could put in for nothing; and Moses was to be dressed out with a hat and white feather. Our taste so much pleased the Squire, that he insisted on being put in as one of the family, in the character of Alexander the Great, at Olivia's feet. This was considered by us all as an indication of his desire to be introduced into the family, nor could we refuse his request. The painter was therefore set to work, and, as he wrought with assiduity and expedition, in less than four days the whole was completed. The piece was large, and, it must be owned, he did not spare his colours; for which my wife gave him great encomiums. We were all perfectly satisfied with his performance; but an unfortunate circumstance had not occurred till the picture was finished, which now struck us with dismay. It was so very large, that we had no place in the house to fix it. How we all came to disregard so material a point is inconceivable; but certain it is, we had been all greatly remiss. The picture, therefore, instead of gratifying our vanity, as we hoped, leaned, in a most mortifying manner, against the kitchen wall, where the canvas was stretched and painted, much too large to be got through any of the doors, and the jest of all our neighbours. One compared it to Robinson Crusoe's long-boat, too large to be removed; another thought it more resembled a reel in a bottle; some wondered how it could be got out, but still more were amazed how it ever got in.

The Vicar of Wakefield, 1766

SIR WILLIAM BLACKSTONE

[Trial by Jury]

THE IMPARTIAL administration of justice, which secures both our persons and our properties, is the great end of civil society. But if that be entirely entrusted to the magistracy, a select body of men, and those generally selected by the prince or such as enjoy the highest offices in the state, their decisions, in spite of their own natural integrity, will have frequently an involuntary bias towards those of their own rank and dignity: it is not to be expected from human nature, that *the few* should be always attentive to the interests and good of *the many*. On the other hand, if the power of judicature were placed at random in the hands of the multitude, their decisions would be wild and capricious, and a new rule of action would be every day established in our courts. It is wisely therefore ordered, that the principles and axioms of law, which are general propositions, flowing from abstracted reason, and not accommodated to times or to men, should be deposited in the breasts of the judges, to be occasionally applied to such facts as come properly ascertained before them. For here partiality can have little scope: the law is well known, and is the same for all ranks and degrees; it follows as a regular conclusion from the premises of fact pre-established. But in settling and adjusting a question of fact, when entrusted to any single magistrate, partiality and injustice have an ample field to range in; either by boldly asserting that to be proved which is not so, or more artfully by suppressing some circumstances, stretching and warping others, and distinguishing away the remainder. Here therefore a competent number of sensible and upright jurymen, chosen by lot from among those of the middle rank, will be found the best investigators of truth, and the surest guardians of public justice. For the most powerful individual in the state will be cautious of committing any flagrant invasion of another's right, when he knows that the fact of his oppression must be examined and decided by twelve indifferent men, not appointed till the hour of trial; and that, when once the fact is ascertained, the law must of course redress it. This therefore preserves in the hands of the people that share which they ought to have in the administration of public justice, and prevents the encroachments of the more powerful and wealthy citizens. Every new tribunal, erected for the decision of facts, without the intervention of a jury (whether composed of justices of the peace, commissioners of the revenue, judges of a court of conscience, or any other standing magistrates) is a step towards establishing aristocracy, the most oppressive of absolute governments. The feudal system, which, for the sake of military subordination, pursued an aristocratical plan in all its arrangements of property, had been intolerable in times of peace, had it not been wisely counterpoised by that privilege, so universally diffused through every part of it, the trial by the feudal peers. And in every country on the Continent, as the trial by the peers has been gradually disused, so the nobles have increased in power, till the state has been torn to pieces by rival factions, and oligarchy in effect has been established, though under the shadow of regal government; unless where the miserable commons have taken shelter under absolute monarchy, as the lighter evil of the two. And, particularly, it is a circumstance well worthy an Englishman's observation, that in Sweden the trial by jury, that bulwark of northern liberty, which continued in its full vigour so lately as the middle of the last century, is now fallen into disuse: and that there, though the regal power is in no country so closely limited, yet the liberties of the commons are extinguished, and the government is degenerated into a mere aristocracy. It is therefore, upon the whole, a duty which every man owes to his country, his friends, his posterity, and himself, to maintain to the utmost of his power this valuable constitution in all its rights; to restore it to its ancient dignity, if at all impaired by the different value of property, or otherwise deviated from its first institution; to amend it, wherever it is defective; and, above all, to guard with the most jealous circumspection against the introduction of new and arbitrary methods of trial, which, under a variety of plausible pretences, may in time imperceptibly undermine this best preservative of English liberty.

Commentaries on the Laws of England, Vol. 3, 1768

TOBIAS SMOLLETT

[The Postilion]

TUESDAY LAST the squire took his place in a hired coach and four, accompanied by his sister and mine, and Mrs Tabby's maid, Winifred Jenkins, whose province it was to support Chowder on a cushion in her lap. I could scarce refrain from laughing when I looked into the vehicle, and saw that animal sitting opposite to my uncle, like any other passenger. The squire, ashamed of his situation, blushed to the eyes: and, calling to the postilions to drive on, pulled the glass up in my face. I, and his servant, John Thomas, attended them on horseback.

Nothing worth mentioning occurred, till we arrived on the edge of Marlborough Downs. There one of the four horses fell, in going down hill at a round trot; and the postilion behind, endeavouring to stop the carriage, pulled it on one side into a deep rut, where it was fairly overturned. I had rode on about two hundred yards before; but, hearing a loud scream, galloped back and dismounted, to give what assistance was in my power. When I looked into the coach, I could see nothing distinctly, but the nether end of Jenkins, who was kicking her heels and squalling with great vociferation. All of a sudden, my uncle thrust up his bare pate, and bolted through the window, as nimble as a grasshopper, having made use of poor Win's posteriors as a step to rise in his ascent – The man (who had likewise quitted his horse) dragged this forlorn damsel, more dead than alive, through the same opening. Then Mr Bramble, pulling the door off its hinges with a jerk, laid hold on Liddy's arm, and brought her to the light; very much frighted, but little hurt. It fell to my share to deliver our aunt Tabitha, who had lost her cap in the struggle, and being rather more than half frantic, with rage and terror, was no bad representation of one of the sister Furies that guard the gates of hell – She expressed no sort of concern for her brother, who ran about in the cold, without his periwig, and worked with the most astonishing agility, in helping to disentangle the horses from the carriage: but she cried, in a tone of distraction, 'Chowder! Chowder! my dear Chowder! my poor Chowder is certainly killed!'

This was not the case – Chowder, after having tore my uncle's leg in the confusion of the fall, had retreated under the seat, and from thence the footman drew him by the neck; for which good office, he bit his fingers to the bone. The fellow, who is naturally surly, was so provoked at this assault, that he saluted his ribs with a hearty kick, exclaiming, 'Damn the nasty son of a bitch, and them he belongs to!' A benediction, which was by no means lost upon the implacable virago his mistress – Her brother, however, prevailed upon her to retire into a peasant's house, near the scene of action, where his head and hers were covered, and poor Jenkins had a fit – Our next care was to apply some sticking plaster to the wound in his leg, which exhibited the impression of Chowder's teeth; but he never opened his lips against the delinquent – Mrs Tabby, alarmed at this scene, 'You say nothing, Matt (cried she); but I know your mind – I know the spite you have to that poor unfortunate animal! I know you intend to take his life away!' 'You are mistaken, upon my honour! (replied the squire, with a sarcastic smile) I should be incapable of harbouring any such cruel design against an object so amiable and inoffensive; even if he had not the happiness to be your favourite.'

John Thomas was not so delicate. The fellow, whether really alarmed for his life, or instigated by the desire of revenge, came in, and bluntly demanded, that the dog should be put to death; on the supposition, that if ever he should run mad hereafter, he, who had been bit by him, would be infected – My uncle calmly argued upon the absurdity of his opinion, observing, that he himself was in the same predicament, and would certainly take the precaution he proposed, if he was not sure he ran no risk of infection. Nevertheless, Thomas continued obstinate; and, at length declared, that if the dog was not shot immediately, he himself would be his executioner – This declaration opened the flood-gates of Tabby's eloquence, which would have shamed the first-rate oratress of Billingsgate. The footman retorted in the same style; and the squire dismissed him from his service, after having prevented me from giving him a good horse-whipping for his insolence.

The coach being adjusted, another difficulty occurred – Mrs Tabitha absolutely refused to enter it again, unless another driver could be found to take the place of the postilion; who, she affirmed, had overturned the carriage from malice aforethought – After much dispute, the man resigned his place to a shabby country fellow, who undertook to go as far as Marlborough, where they could be better provided; and at that place we arrived about one o'clock, without farther impediment. Mrs Bramble, however, found new matter of offence; which, indeed, she has a particular genius for extracting at will from almost every incident in life. We had scarce entered the room at Marlborough, where we stayed to dine, when she exhibited a formal complaint against the poor fellow who had superseded the postilion. She said he was such a beggarly rascal that he had ne'er a shirt to his back, and had the impudence to shock her sight by showing his bare posteriors, for which act of indelicacy he deserved to be set in the stocks. Mrs Winifred Jenkins confirmed the assertion, with respect to his nakedness, observing, at the same time, that he had a skin as fair as alabaster.

'This is a heinous offence, indeed (cried my uncle) let us hear what the fellow has to say in his own vindication.' He was accordingly summoned, and made his appearance, which was equally queer and pathetic. He seemed to be about twenty years of age, of a middling size, with bandy legs, stooping shoulders, high forehead, sandy locks, pinking eyes, flat nose, and long chin – but his complexion was of a sickly yellow; his looks denoted famine, and the rags that he wore could hardly conceal what decency requires to be covered – My uncle, having surveyed him attentively, said, with an ironical expression in his countenance, 'An't you ashamed, fellow, to ride postilion without a shirt to cover your backside from the view of the ladies in the coach?' 'Yes, I am, an please your noble honour (answered the man) but necessity has no law, as the saying is – And more than that, it was an accident – My breeches cracked behind, after I had got into the saddle' – 'You're an impudent varlet (cried Mrs Tabby) for presuming to ride before persons of fashion without a shirt' – 'I am so, an please your worthy ladyship (said he) but I am a poor Wiltshire lad – I ha'n't a shirt in the world, that I can call my own, nor a rag of clothes, and please your ladyship, but what you see – I have no friend nor relation upon earth to help me out – I have had the fever and ague these six months, and spent all I had in the world upon doctors, and to keep soul and body together; and, saving your ladyship's good presence, I ha'n't broke bread these four and twenty hours.'

Mrs Bramble, turning from him, said, she had never seen such a filthy tatterdemalion, and bid him begone; observing, that he would fill the room full of vermin – Her brother darted a significant glance at her, as she retired with Liddy into another apartment, and then asked the man if he was known to any person in Marlborough? – When he answered, that the landlord of the inn had known him from his infancy; mine host was immediately called, and being interrogated on the subject, declared that the young fellow's name was Humphry Clinker. That he had been a love begotten babe, brought up in the work-house, and put out apprentice by the parish to a country black-smith, who died before the boy's time was out: that he had for some time worked under his ostler, as a helper and extra postilion, till he was taken ill of the ague, which disabled him from getting his bread: that, having sold or pawned every thing he had in the world for his cure and subsistence, he became so miserable and shabby, that he disgraced the stable, and was dismissed; but that he never heard any thing to the prejudice of his character in other respects. 'So that the fellow being sick and destitute (said my uncle) you turned him out to die in the streets.' 'I pay the poor's rate (replied the other) and I have no right to maintain idle vagrants, either in sickness or health; besides, such a miserable object would have brought a discredit upon my house.'

'You perceive (said the squire, turning to me) our landlord is a Christian of bowels – Who shall presume to censure the morals of the age, when the very publicans exhibit such examples of humanity? – Heark ye, Clinker, you are a most notorious offender – You stand convicted of sickness, hunger, wretchedness, and want – But, as it does not belong to me to punish criminals, I will only take upon me the task of giving you a word of advice – Get a shirt with all convenient dispatch, that your nakedness may not henceforward give offence to travelling gentlewomen, especially maidens in years.'

So saying, he put a guinea into the hand of the poor fellow, who stood staring at him in silence, with his mouth wide open, till the landlord pushed him out of the room.

The Expedition of Humphry Clinker, 1771

PHILIP DORMER STANHOPE, 4th EARL OF CHESTERFIELD

[The Art of Pleasing]

London, 16 October 1747

Dear Boy,

The art of pleasing is a very necessary one to possess; but a very difficult one to acquire. It can hardly be reduced to rules; and your own good sense and observation will teach you more of it than I can. 'Do as you would be done by,' is the surest method that I know of pleasing. Observe carefully what pleases you in others, and probably the same things in you will please others. If you are pleased with the complaisance and attention of others to your humours, your tastes, or your weaknesses, depend upon it, the same complaisance and attention on your part, to theirs, will equally please them. Take the tone of the company that you are in, and do not pretend to give it; be serious, gay, or even trifling, as you find the present humour of the company: this is an attention due from every individual to the majority. Do not tell stories in company; there is nothing more tedious and disagreeable: if by chance you know a very short story, and exceedingly applicable to the present subject of conversation, tell it in as few words as possible; and even then, throw out that you do not love to tell stories; but that the shortness of it tempted you.

Of all things, banish the egotism out of your conversation, and never think of entertaining people with your own personal concerns or private affairs; though they are interesting to you, they are tedious and impertinent to everybody else: besides that, one cannot keep one's own private affairs too secret. Whatever you think your own excellencies may be, do not affectedly display them in company; nor labour, as many people do, to give that turn to the conversation, which may supply you with an opportunity of exhibiting them. If they are real, they will infallibly be discovered, without your pointing them out yourself, and with much more advantage. Never maintain an argument with heat and clamour, though you think or know yourself to be in the right; but give your opinions modestly and coolly, which is the only way to convince; and, if that does not do, try to change the conversation, by saying, with good-humour, 'We shall hardly convince one another; nor is it necessary that we should, so let us talk of something else.'

Remember that there is a local propriety to be observed in all companies; and that what is extremely proper in one company, may be, and often is, highly improper in another.

The jokes, the *bon mots*, the little adventures, which may do very well in one company, will seem flat and tedious when related in another. The particular characters, the habits, the cant of one company may give merit to a word, or a gesture, which would have none at all if divested of those accidental circumstances. Here people very commonly err; and fond of something that has entertained them in one company, and in certain circumstances, repeat it with emphasis in another, where it is either insipid, or, it may be, offensive, by being ill-timed or misplaced.

Nay, they often do it with this silly preamble, 'I will tell you an excellent thing,' or, 'I will tell you the best thing in the world.' This raises expectations, which when absolutely disappointed, make the relator of this excellent thing look, very deservedly, like a fool.

If you would particularly gain the affection and friendship of particular people, whether men or women, endeavour to find out their predominant excellency, if they have one, and their prevailing weakness, which everybody has; and do justice to the one, and something more than justice to the other. Men have various objects in which they may excel, or at least would be thought to excel; and though they love to hear justice done to them, where they know that they excel, yet they are most and best flattered upon those points where they wish to excel, and yet are doubtful whether they do or not. As for example: Cardinal Richelieu, who was undoubtedly the ablest statesman of his time, or perhaps of any other, had the idle vanity of being thought the best poet too: he envied the great Corneille his reputation, and ordered a criticism to be written upon the *Cid*. Those, therefore, who flattered skilfully, said little to him of his abilities in state affairs, or at least but *en passant*, and as it might naturally occur. But the incense which they gave him – the smoke of which they knew would turn his head and in their favour – was as a *bel esprit* and a poet. Why? – Because he was sure of one excellency, and distrustful as to the other.

You will easily discover every man's prevailing vanity by observing his favourite topic of conversation; for every man talks most of what he has most a mind to be thought to excel in. Touch him but there, and you touch him to the quick. The late Sir Robert Walpole (who was certainly an able man) was little open to flattery upon that head, for he was in no doubt himself about it; but his prevailing weakness was, to be thought to have a polite and happy turn to gallantry – of which he had undoubtedly less than any man living. It was his favourite and frequent subject of conversation, which proved to those who had any penetration that it was his prevailing weakness, and they applied to it with success.

Women have, in general, but one object, which is their beauty; upon which, scarce any flattery is too gross for them to follow. Nature has hardly formed a woman ugly enough to be insensible to flattery upon her person; if her face is so shocking that she must, in some degree, be conscious of it, her figure and air, she trusts, make ample amends for it. If her figure is deformed, her face, she thinks, counterbalances it. If they are both bad, she comforts herself that she has graces; a certain manner; a *je ne sais quoi* still more engaging than beauty. This truth is evident, from the studied and elaborate dress of the ugliest woman in the world. An undoubted, uncontested, conscious beauty is, of all women, the least sensible of flattery upon that head; she knows it is her due, and is therefore obliged to nobody for giving it her. She must be flattered upon her understanding, which, though she may possibly not doubt of herself, yet she suspects that men may distrust.

Do not mistake me, and think that I mean to recommend to you abject and criminal flattery: no; flatter nobody's vices or crimes: on the contrary, abhor and discourage them. But there is no living in the world without a complaisant indulgence for people's weaknesses, and innocent, though ridiculous, vanities. If a man has a mind to be thought wiser, and a woman handsomer, than they really are, their error is a comfortable one to themselves, and an innocent one with regard to other people; and I would rather make them my friends by indulging them in it, than my enemies by endeavouring (and that to no purpose) to undeceive them.

There are little attentions, likewise, which are infinitely engaging, and which sensibly affect that degree of pride and self-love, which is inseparable from human nature; as they are unquestionable proofs of the regard and consideration which we have for the persons to whom we pay them. As for example: to observe the little habits, the likings, the antipathies, and the tastes of those whom we would gain; and then take care to provide them with the one, and to secure them from the other; giving them genteelly to understand, that you had observed they liked such a dish or such a room; for which reason you had prepared it: or, on the contrary, that having observed they had an aversion to such a dish, a dislike to such a person, etc., you had taken care to avoid presenting them. Such attention to such trifles flatters self-love much more than greater things, as it makes people think themselves almost the only objects of your thoughts and care.

These are some of the *arcana* necessary for your initiation in the great society of the world. I wish I had known them better at your age; I have paid the price of three-and-fifty years for them, and shall not grudge it if you reap the advantage. Adieu!

Letters Written by the Earl of Chesterfield to His Son, Philip Stanhope, 1774

EDWARD GIBBON

[The Immortality of the Soul]

THE WRITINGS of Cicero represent in the most lively colours the ignorance, the errors, and the uncertainty of the ancient philosophers with regard to the immortality of the soul. When they are desirous of arming their disciples against the fear of death, they inculcate, as an obvious though melancholy position, that the fatal stroke of our dissolution releases us from the calamities of life; and that those can no longer suffer who no longer exist. Yet there were a few sages of Greece and Rome who had conceived a more exalted, and, in some respects, a juster idea of human nature, though it must be confessed that, in the sublime inquiry, their reason had been often guided by their imagination, and that their imagination had been prompted by their vanity. When they viewed with complacency the extent of their own mental powers, when they exercised the various mental faculties of memory, of fancy, and of judgment, in

the most profound speculations or the most important
labours, and when they reflected on the desire of fame,
which transported them into future ages, far beyond the
bounds of death and of the grave, they were unwilling to
confound themselves with the beasts of the field, or to
suppose that a being, for whose dignity they entertained the
most sincere admiration, could be limited to a spot of earth,
and to a few years of duration. With this favourable pre-
possession they summoned to their aid the science, or rather
the language, of metaphysics. They soon discovered that, as
none of the properties of matter will apply to the operations
of the mind, the human soul must consequently be a
substance distinct from the body, pure, simple, and spiritual,
incapable of dissolution, and susceptible of a much higher
degree of virtue and happiness after the release from its
corporeal prison. From these specious and noble principles
the philosophers who trod in the footsteps of Plato deduced
a very unjustifiable conclusion, since they asserted, not only
the future immortality, but the past eternity of the human
soul, which they were too apt to consider as a portion of the
infinite and self-existing spirit which pervades and sustains
the universe. A doctrine thus removed beyond the senses
and the experience of mankind might serve to amuse the
leisure of a philosophic mind; or, in the silence of solitude,
it might sometimes impart a ray of comfort to desponding
virtue; but the faint impression which had been received in
the schools was soon obliterated by the commerce and
business of active life. We are sufficiently acquainted with
the eminent persons who flourished in the age of Cicero and
of the first Caesars, with their actions, their characters, and
their motives, to be assured that their conduct in this life
was never regulated by any serious conviction of the rewards
or punishments of a future state. At the bar and in the
senate of Rome the ablest orators were not apprehensive
of giving offence to their hearers by exposing that doctrine
as an idle and extravagant opinion, which was rejected
with contempt by every man of a liberal education and
understanding.

Since therefore the most sublime efforts of philosophy
can extend no farther than feebly to point out the desire,

the hope, or, at most, the probability of a future state, there is nothing, except a divine revelation that can ascertain the existence and describe the condition of the invisible country which is destined to receive the souls of men after their separation from the body. But we may perceive several defects inherent to the popular religions of Greece and Rome which rendered them very unequal to so arduous a task. 1. The general system of their mythology was unsupported by any solid proofs; and the wisest among the Pagans had already disclaimed its usurped authority. 2. The description of the infernal regions had been abandoned to the fancy of painters and of poets, who peopled them with so many phantoms and monsters who dispensed their rewards and punishments with so little equity, that a solemn truth, the most congenial to the human heart, was oppressed and disgraced by the absurd mixture of the wildest fictions. 3. The doctrine of a future state was scarcely considered among the devout polytheists of Greece and Rome as a fundamental article of faith. The providence of the gods, as it related to public communities rather than to private individuals, was principally displayed on the visible theatre of the present world. The petitions which were offered on the altars of Jupiter and Apollo expressed the anxiety of their worshippers for temporal happiness, and their ignorance or indifference concerning a future life. The important truth of the immortality of the soul was inculcated with more diligence as well as success in India, in Assyria, in Egypt, and in Gaul; and since we cannot attribute such a difference to the superior knowledge of the barbarians, we must ascribe it to the influence of an established priesthood, which employed the motives of virtue as the instrument of ambition.

We might naturally expect that a principle so essential to religion would have been revealed in the clearest terms to the chosen people of Palestine, and that it might safely have been intrusted to the hereditary priesthood of Aaron. It is incumbent on us to adore the mysterious dispensations of Providence, when we discover that the doctrine of the immortality of the soul is omitted in the law of Moses; it is darkly insinuated by the prophets; and during the long period which elapsed between the Egyptian and the Baby-lonian servitudes, the hopes as well as fears of the Jews appear to have been confined within the narrow compass of the present life. After Cyrus had permitted the exiled nation to return into the promised land, and after Ezra had restored the ancient records of their religion, two celebrated sects, the Sadducees and the Pharisees, insensibly arose at Jerusa-lem. The former, selected from the more opulent and distinguished ranks of society, were strictly attached to the literal sense of the Mosaic law, and they piously rejected the immortality of the soul as an opinion that received no countenance from the divine book, which they revered as the only rule of their faith. To the authority of Scripture the Pharisees added that of tradition, and they accepted, under the name of traditions, several speculative tenets from the philosophy or religion of the eastern nations. The doctrines of fate or pre-destination, of angels and spirits, and of a future state of rewards and punishments, were in the number of these new articles of belief; and as the Pharisees, by the austerity of their manners, had drawn into their party the body of the Jewish people, the immortality of the soul became the prevailing sentiment of the synagogue under the reign of the Asmonaean princes and pontiffs. The temper of the Jews was incapable of contenting itself with such a cold and languid assent as might satisfy the mind of a Polytheist; and as soon as they admitted the idea of a future state, they embraced it with the zeal which has always formed the characteristic of the nation. Their zeal, however, added nothing to its evidence, or even probability; and it was still necessary that the doctrine of life and immortality, which had been dictated by nature, approved by reason, and received by superstition, should obtain the sanction of divine truth from the authority and example of Christ.

When the promise of eternal happiness was proposed to mankind on condition of adopting the faith, and of observ-ing the precepts, of the Gospel, it is no wonder that so advantageous an offer should have been accepted by great numbers of every religion, of every rank, and of every province in the Roman Empire. The ancient Christians were animated by a contempt for their present existence, and by a just confidence of immortality, of which the doubtful and imperfect faith of modern ages cannot give us any adequate notion. In the primitive church the influence of truth was very powerfully strengthened by an opinion which, however it may deserve respect for its usefulness and antiquity, has not been found agreeable to experience. It was universally believed that the end of the world, and the kingdom of heaven, were at hand. The near approach of this wonderful event had been predicted by the apostles; the tradition of it was preserved by their earliest disciples, and those who understood in their literal sense the discourses of Christ himself were obliged to expect the second and glorious coming of the Son of Man in the clouds, before that generation was totally extinguished which had beheld his humble condition upon earth, and which might still be witness of the calamities of the Jews under Vespasian or Hadrian. The revolution of seventeen centuries has instructed us not to press too closely the mysterious language of prophecy and revelation; but as long as, for wise purposes, this error was permitted to subsist in the church, it was productive of the most salutary effects on the faith and practice of Christians, who lived in the awful expectation of that moment when the globe itself, and all the various race of mankind, should tremble at the appearance of their divine Judge.

The History of the Decline and Fall
of the Roman Empire, 1776–88

ADAM SMITH

[The Division of Labour]

THE EFFECTS of the division of labour, in the general business of society, will be more easily understood, by considering in what manner it operates in some particular manufactures. It is commonly supposed to be carried furthest in some very trifling ones; not perhaps that it really is carried further in them than in others of more importance: but in those trifling manufactures which are destined to supply the small wants of but a small number of people, the whole number of workmen must necessarily be small; and those employed in every different branch of the work can often be collected into the same workhouse, and placed at once under the view of the spectator. In those great manufactures, on the contrary, which are destined to supply the great wants of the great body of the people, every different branch of the work employs so great a number of workmen, that it is impossible to collect them all into the same workhouse. We can seldom see more, at one time, than those employed in one single branch. Though in such manufactures, therefore, the work may really be divided into a much greater number of parts, than in those of a more trifling nature, the division is not near so obvious, and has accordingly been much less observed.

To take an example, therefore, from a very trifling manufacture, but one in which the division of labour has been very often taken notice of, the trade of a pin-maker: a workman not educated to this business (which the division of labour has rendered a distinct trade), nor acquainted with the use of the machinery employed in it (to the invention of which the same division of labour has probably given occasion), could scarce, perhaps, with his utmost industry, make one pin in a day, and certainly could not make twenty. But in the way in which this business is now carried on, not only the whole work is a peculiar trade, but it is divided into a number of branches, of which the greater part are likewise peculiar trades. One man draws out the wire; another straights it; a third cuts it; a fourth points it; a fifth grinds it at the top for receiving the head; to make the head requires two or three distinct operations; to put it on is a peculiar business; to whiten the pins is another; it is even a trade by itself to put them into the paper; and the important business of making a pin is, in this manner, divided into about eighteen distinct operations, which, in some manufactories, are all performed by distinct hands, though in others the same man will sometimes perform two or three of them. I have seen a small manufactory of this kind, where ten men only were employed, and where some of them consequently performed two or three distinct operations. But though they were very poor, and therefore but indifferently accommodated with the necessary machinery, they could, when they exerted themselves, make among them about twelve pounds of pins in a day. There are in a pound upwards of four thousand pins of a middling size. Those ten persons, therefore, could make among them upwards of forty-eight thousand pins in a day. Each person, therefore, making a tenth part of forty-eight thousand pins, might be considered as making four thousand eight hundred pins in a day. But if they had all wrought separately and independently, and without any of them having been educated to this peculiar business, they certainly could not each of them have made twenty, perhaps not one pin a day; that is, certainly, not the two hundred and fortieth, perhaps not the four thousand eight hundredth, part of what they are at present capable of performing, in consequence of a proper division and combination of their different operations.

The Wealth of Nations, 1776

FANNY BURNEY

[Prejudice]

WE WENT last night to see the Fantocini [*puppets*], where we had infinite entertainment from the performance of a little comedy, in French and Italian, by puppets, so admirably managed, that they both astonished and diverted us all, except the Captain, who has a fixed and most prejudiced hatred of whatever is not English.

When it was over, while we waited for the coach, a tall elderly woman brushed quickly past us, calling out, 'My God! what shall I do?'

'Why what *would* you do?' cried the Captain.

'*Ma foi, Monsieur*,' answered she, 'I have lost my company, and in this place I don't know nobody.'

There was something foreign in her accent, though it was difficult to discover whether she was an English or a French woman. She was very well dressed, and seemed so entirely at a loss what to do, that Mrs Mirvan proposed to the Captain to assist her.

'Assist her!' cried he, 'ay, with all my heart; – let a link-boy call her a coach.'

There was not one to be had, and it rained very fast.

'*Mon Dieu*,' exclaimed the stranger, 'what shall become of me? *Je suis au désespoir!*'

'Dear Sir,' cried Miss Mirvan, 'pray let us take the poor lady into our coach. She is quite alone, and a foreigner—'

'She's never the better for that,' answered he: 'she may be a woman of the town, for any thing you know.'

'She does not appear such,' said Mrs Mirvan, 'and indeed she seems so much distressed, that we shall but follow the golden rule, if we carry her to her lodgings.'

'You are mighty fond of new acquaintance,' returned he, 'but first let us know if she be going our way.'

Upon enquiry, we found that she lived in Oxford Road, and, after some disputing, the Captain, surlily, and with a very bad grace, consented to admit her into his coach; though he soon convinced us, that he was determined she should not be too much obliged to him, for he seemed absolutely bent upon quarrelling with her: for which strange inhospitality, I can assign no other reason, than that she appeared to be a foreigner.

The conversation began, by her telling us, that she had been in England only two days; that the gentlemen belonging to her were Parisians, and had left her, to see for a hackney-coach, as her own carriage was abroad; and that she had waited for them till she was quite frightened, and concluded that they had lost themselves.

'And pray,' said the Captain, 'why did you go to a public place without an Englishman?'

'*Ma foi*, Sir,' answered she, 'because none of my acquaintance is in town.'

'Why then,' said he, 'I'll tell you what; your best way is to go out of it yourself.'

'*Pardie, Monsieur,*' returned she, 'and so I shall; for, I promise you, I think the English a parcel of brutes; and I'll go back to France as fast as I can, for I would not live among none of you.'

'Who wants you?' cried the Captain; 'do you suppose, Madam French, we have not enough of other nations to pick our pockets already? I'll warrant you, there's no need of you for to put in your oar.'

'Pick your pockets, Sir! I wish nobody wanted to pick your pockets no more than I do; and I'll promise you, you'd be safe enough. But there's no nation under the sun can beat the English for ill-politeness: for my part, I hate the very sight of them, and so I shall only just visit a person of quality or two, of my particular acquaintance, and then I shall go back again to France.'

'Ay, do,' cried he, 'and then go to the devil together, for that's the fittest voyage for the French and the quality.'

'We'll take care, however,' cried the stranger, with great vehemence, 'not to admit none of your vulgar, unmannered English among us.'

'O never fear,' (returned he coolly) 'we shan't dispute the point with you; you and the quality may have the devil all to yourselves.'

Desirous of changing the subject of a conversation which now became very alarming, Miss Mirvan called out, 'Lord, how slow the man drives!'

'Never mind, Moll,' said her father, 'I'll warrant you he'll drive fast enough tomorrow, when you're going to Howard Grove.'

'To Howard Grove!' exclaimed the stranger; 'why, *mon Dieu*, do you know Lady Howard?'

'Why, what if we do?' answered he, 'that's nothing to you; she's none of *your* quality, I'll promise you.'

'Who told you that?' cried she, 'you don't know nothing about the matter; besides, you're the ill-bredest person ever I see; and as to your knowing Lady Howard, I don't believe no such a thing; unless, indeed, you are her steward.'

The Captain, swearing terribly, said, with great fury, '*You* would much sooner be taken for her wash-woman.'

'Her wash-woman, indeed! – Ha, ha, ha! – why you ha'n't no eyes; did you ever see a wash-woman in such a gown as this? – besides, I'm no such mean person, for I'm as good as Lady Howard, and as rich too; and besides, I'm now come to England to visit her.'

'You may spare yourself that there trouble,' said the Captain, 'she has paupers enough about her already.'

'Paupers, Mr! – no more a pauper than yourself, nor so much neither; – but you're a low, dirty fellow, and I shan't stoop to take no more notice of you.'

'Dirty fellow!' (exclaimed the Captain, seizing both her wrists) 'hark you, Mrs Frog, you'd best hold your tongue, for I must make bold to tell you, if you don't, that I shall make no ceremony of tripping you out of the window; and there you may lie in the mud till some of your Monsieurs come to help you out of it.'

Their encreasing passion quite terrified us; and Mrs Mirvan was beginning to remonstrate with the Captain, when we were all silenced by what follows.

'Let me go, villain that you are, let me go, or I'll promise you I'll get you put to prison for this usage; I'm no common person, I assure you, and, *ma foi*, I'll go to Justice Fielding about you; for I'm a person of fashion, and I'll make you know it, or my name i'n't Duval.'

I heard no more: amazed, frightened, and unspeakably shocked, an involuntary exclamation of *Gracious Heaven!* escaped me, and, more dead than alive, I sunk into Mrs Mirvan's arms. But let me draw a veil over a scene too cruel for a heart so compassionately tender as yours; it is sufficient that you know this supposed foreigner proved to be Madam Duval, – the grandmother of your Evelina!

O, Sir, to discover so near a relation in a woman who had thus introduced herself! – what would become of me, were it not for you, my protector, my friend, and my refuge?

My extreme concern, and Mrs Mirvan's surprise, immediately betrayed me. But I will not shock you with the manner of her acknowledging me, or the bitterness, the *grossness* – I cannot otherwise express myself, – with which she spoke of those unhappy past transactions you have so pathetically related to me. All the misery of a much-injured parent, dear, though never seen, regretted, though never known, crowded so forcibly upon my memory, that they rendered this interview – one only excepted – the most afflicting I can ever know.

*Evelina; or, A Young Lady's Entrance
into the World*, 1778

JAMES WOODFORDE

[Election Day]

[*13 April 1784*] Nancy breakfasted, made a running dinner upon a mutton steak about one o'clock, and then set off in Lenewade Bridge chaise with my upper maid with her, as likewise my servant lad, for Norwich, to be at the county election for Members of Parliament, which begins tomorrow at the Shire Hall on Castle Hill. It was talked that there would be a severe contest between Sir John Wodehouse, Sir Edward Astley and Mr Coke, but yesterday it was the common report that Coke had declined the poll. I am – as is Mr Custance – for Sir John Wodehouse only, Sir Edward Astley having made an unlucky junction with Mr Coke, whose parliamentary conduct has been quite opposite of late, Sir Edward Astley having voted for the popular Mr Pitt and Mr Coke for Fox and Lord North. My maid and boy returned from Norwich about five o'clock. They brought me word that Nancy got very well there and is at Mr Priest's, being invited thither by them. Very soon after Nancy went I took a ride to Weston House, but both Mr and Mrs Custance were gone to Norwich. I stayed about an hour with the little folks and returned home to dinner by three o'clock.

[*14 April 1784*] I breakfasted upon some mutton broth about six o'clock and very soon after breakfast I mounted my

mare and went [to] Norwich, and Will went with me, for to
be at the county election for Members of Parliament. We
got to Norwich a little after eight o'clock, put up my horses
at the Woolpack, and then walked to Mr Priest's and there
made a second breakfast on tea and toast. Nancy was not
downstairs. About ten o'clock the Market Place and streets
in Norwich were lined with people, and almost all with
Wodehouse's cockades in their hats. After breakfast I went
to Mr Brewster's and got six cockades, all for Wodehouse –
three of them blue and pink with 'Wodehouse' wrote in
silver on the blue, the other three plain blue and pink for
my servants at home. About eleven o'clock Sir John Wodehouse, preceded with a great many flags and a band of
music, made his public entry on horseback, attended with
between two and three thousand men on horseback. They
came through St Giles's, then through the Market Place,
then marched on to the Shire House on the Castle Hill, and
there Sir John Wodehouse with Sir Edward Astley were
unanimously chosen Members for the county. After that
they had dressed themselves handsomely and were chaired
first round the Castle Hill and then three times round the
Market Place amidst an innumerable number of spectators
and the loudest acclamations of 'Wodehouse for ever'. Sir
Edward Astley met with little applause, having joined Coke
before. I never saw such universal joy all over the city as
was shown in behalf of Sir John Wodehouse. I dined at Mr
Priest's with him, his wife, son John, Mr Priest of Reepham
and daughter Becky and two strange ladies. We had for
dinner some whitings and a fillet of veal. Paid at Studwell's
china shop a small bill of three shillings.

[Mr Decker's Balloon]

[*1 June 1785*] About three o'clock this afternoon a violent
tempest arose at Norwich in the north-east, very loud
thunder with strong white lightning with heavy rain – which

lasted about an hour – immediately after which Mr Decker's balloon with Decker himself in a boat annexed to it ascended from Quantrell's Gardens and very majestically. It was out of sight in about ten minutes, but appeared again on his descent. It went in a south-east direction – I saw it from Brecondale Hill, and it went almost over my head. Mr and Mrs Custance and Nancy were at Mackay's Gardens. They saw it also very plain from thence. A vast concourse of people were assembled to see it. It was rather unfortunate that the weather proved so unfavourable – but added greatly to the courage of Decker that he ascended so very soon after the tempest. It also bursted twice before he ascended in it, upon the filling it; if it had not, a girl about fourteen was to have went with him in it – but after so much gas had been let out it would not carry both.

From the Diary

GILBERT WHITE

[Gossamer]

O N SEPTEMBER the 21st, 1741, being then on a visit, and intent on field-diversions, I rose before daybreak: when I came into the enclosures, I found the stubbles and clover-grounds matted all over with a thick coat of cobweb, in the meshes of which a copious and heavy dew hung so plentifully that the whole face of the country seemed, as it were, covered with two or three setting-nets drawn one over another. When the dogs attempted to hunt, their eyes were so blinded and hoodwinked that they could not proceed, but were obliged to lie down and scrape the incumbrances from their faces with their fore-feet, so that, finding my sport interrupted, I returned home musing in my mind on the oddness of the occurrence.

As the morning advanced the sun became bright and

warm, and the day turned out one of those most lovely ones which no season but the autumn produces: cloudless, calm, serene, and worthy of the South of France itself.

About nine an appearance very unusual began to demand our attention, a shower of cobwebs falling from very elevated regions, and continuing, without any interruption, till the close of the day. These webs were not single filmy threads, floating in the air in all directions, but perfect flakes of rags; some near an inch broad, and five or six long, which fell with a degree of velocity which showed they were considerably heavier than the atmosphere.

On every side as the observer turned his eyes might he behold a continual succession of fresh flakes falling into his sight, and twinkling like stars as they turned their sides towards the sun.

How far this wonderful shower extended would be difficult to say; but we know that it reached Bradley, Selborne, and Alresford, three places which lie in a sort of a triangle, the shortest of whose sides is about eight miles in extent.

At the second of those places there was a gentleman (for whose veracity and intelligent turn we have the greatest veneration) who observed it the moment he got abroad; but concluded that, as soon as he came upon the hill above his house, where he took his morning rides, he should be higher than this meteor, which he imagined might have been blown, like thistle-down, from the common above: but, to his great astonishment, when he rode to the most elevated part of the down, 300 feet above his fields, he found the webs in appearance still as much above him as before; still descending into sight in a constant succession, and twinkling in the sun, so as to draw the attention of the most incurious.

Neither before nor after was any such fall observed; but on this day the flakes hung in the trees and hedges so thick, that a diligent person sent out might have gathered baskets full.

The remark that I shall make on these cobweb-like appearances, called gossamer, is, that, strange and superstitious as the notions about them were formerly, nobody in these days doubts but that they are the real production of small spiders, which swarm in the fields in fine weather in autumn, and have a power of shooting out webs from their tails so as to render themselves buoyant, and lighter than air. But why these apterous insects should that day take such a wonderful aerial excursion, and why their webs should at once become so gross and material as to be considerably more weighty than air, and to descend with precipitation, is a matter beyond my skill. If I might be allowed to hazard a supposition, I should imagine that those filmy threads, when first shot, might be entangled in the rising dew, and so drawn up, spiders and all, by a brisk evaporation into the region where clouds are formed: and if the spiders have a power of coiling and thickening their webs in the air, as Dr Lister says they have, then, when they were become heavier than the air, they must fall.

Every day in fine weather, in autumn chiefly, do I see those spiders shooting out their webs and mounting aloft: they will go off from your finger if you will take them into your hand. Last summer one alighted on my book as I was reading in the parlour; and, running to the top of the page, and shooting out a web, took its departure from thence. But what I most wondered at, was that it went off with considerable velocity in a place where no air was stirring; and I am sure that I did not assist it with my breath. So that these little crawlers seem to have, while mounting, some locomotive power without the use of wings, and to move in the air, faster than the air itself.

The Natural History and Antiquities
of Selborne, 1788

SIR JOSHUA REYNOLDS

[Thomas Gainsborough]

THE FIRST thing required to excel in our art, or I believe in any art, is, not only a love for it, but even an enthusiastic ambition to excel in it. This never fails of success proportioned to the natural abilities with which the artist has been endowed by Providence. Of Gainsborough, we certainly know that his passion was not the acquirement of riches, but excellence in his art; and to enjoy that honourable fame which is sure to attend it. That *he felt this ruling passion strong in death*, I am myself a witness. A few days before he died, he wrote me a letter to express his acknowledgement for the good opinion I entertained of his abilities and the manner in which (he had been informed) I always spoke of him; and desired he might see me once more before he died. I am aware how flattering it is to myself to be thus connected with the dying testimony which this excellent painter bore to his art. But I cannot prevail on myself to suppress that I was not connected with him by any habits of familiarity; if any little jealousies had subsisted between us, they were forgotten in those moments of sincerity; and he turned towards me as one who was engrossed by the same pursuits, and who deserved his good opinion, by being sensible of his excellence. Without entering into a detail of what passed at this last interview, the impression of it upon my mind was that his regret at losing life was principally the regret of leaving his art; and more especially as he now began, he said, to see what his deficiencies were; which, he said, he flattered himself in his last works were in some measure supplied.

When such a man as Gainsborough arrives to great fame without the assistance of an academical education, without travelling to Italy, or any of those preparatory studies which have been so often recommended, he is produced as an instance how little such studies are necessary; since so great excellence may be acquired without them. This is an inference not warranted by the success of any individual; and I trust it will not be thought that I wish to make this use of it.

It must be remembered that the style and department of art which Gainsborough chose, and in which he so much excelled, did not require that he should go out of his own country for the objects of his study; they were everywhere about him; he found them in the streets and in the fields; and from the models thus accidentally found he selected with great judgement such as suited his purpose. As his studies were directed to the living world principally, he did not pay a general attention to the works of the various masters, though they are, in my opinion, always of great use, even when the character of our subject requires us to depart from some of their principles. It cannot be denied that excellence in the department of the art which he professed may exist without them; that in such subjects, and in the manner that belongs to them, the want of them is supplied, and more than supplied, by natural sagacity and a minute observation of particular nature. If Gainsborough did not look at nature with a poet's eye, it must be acknowledged that he saw her with the eye of a painter; and gave a faithful, if not a poetical, representation of what he had before him.

Though he did not much attend to the works of the great historical painters of former ages, yet he was well aware that the language of the art, the art of imitation, must be learned somewhere; and as he knew that he could not learn it in an equal degree from his contemporaries, he very judiciously applied himself to the Flemish School, who are undoubtedly the greatest masters of one necessary branch of art; and he did not need to go out of his own country for examples of that school: from that he learnt the harmony of colouring, the management and disposition of light and shadow, and every means which the masters of it practised, to ornament and give splendour to their works. And to satisfy himself as well as others, how well he knew the mechanism and artifice which they employed to bring out that tone of colour which we so much admire in their works, he occasionally made copies from Rubens, Teniers and Van Dyck, which it would be no disgrace to the most accurate connoisseur to mistake, at the first sight, for the works of those masters. What he thus learned, he applied to the originals of nature, which he saw with his own eyes; and imitated, not in the manner of those masters, but in his own.

Whether he most excelled in portraits, landskips, or fancy-pictures, it is difficult to determine: whether his portraits were most admirable for exact truth of resemblance, or his landskips for a portrait-like representation of nature, such as we see in the works of Rubens, Ruysdael, and others of those schools. In his fancy-pictures, when he had fixed on his object of imitation, whether it was the mean and vulgar form of a wood-cutter, or a child of an interesting character, as he did not attempt to raise the one, so neither did he lose any of the natural grace and elegance of the other; such a grace, and such an elegance, as are more frequently found in cottages than in courts. This excellence was his own, the result of his particular observation and taste; for this he was certainly not indebted to the Flemish School, nor indeed to any school; for his grace was not academical, or antique, but selected by himself from the great school of nature; and there are yet a thousand modes of grace, which are neither theirs, nor his, but lie open in the multiplied scenes and figures of life, to be brought out by skilful and faithful observers.

Upon the whole, we may justly say that whatever he attempted he carried to a high degree of excellence. It is to the credit of his good sense and judgement that he never did attempt that style of historical painting for which his previous studies had made no preparation.

And here it naturally occurs to oppose the sensible conduct of Gainsborough in this respect to that of our late excellent Hogarth, who, with all his extraordinary talents, was not blessed with this knowledge of his own deficiency; or of the bounds which were set to the extent of his own powers. After this admirable artist had spent the greatest part of his life in an active, busy, and we may add successful attention to the ridicule of life; after he had invented a new species of dramatic painting, in which probably he will never be equalled, and had stored his mind with infinite materials to explain and illustrate the domestic and familiar scenes of common life, which were generally, and ought to have been always, the subject of his pencil; he very imprudently, or rather presumptuously, attempted his great historical style, for which his previous habits had by no means prepared him: he was indeed so entirely unacquainted with the principles of this style that he was not even aware that any artificial preparation was at all necessary. It is to be regretted that any part of the life of such a genius should be fruitlessly employed. Let his failure teach us not to indulge ourselves in the vain imagination that by a momentary resolution we can give either dexterity to the hand or a new habit to the mind.

I have, however, little doubt but that the same sagacity which enabled those two extraordinary men to discover their true object, and the peculiar excellence of that branch of art which they cultivated, would have been equally effectual in discovering the principles of the higher style; if they had investigated those principles with the same eager industry which they exerted in their own department. As Gainsborough never attempted the heroic style, so neither did he destroy the character and uniformity of his own style by the idle affectation of introducing mythological learning in any of his pictures. Of this boyish folly we see instances enough, even in the works of great painters. When the Dutch School attempt this poetry of our art in their landskips, their performances are beneath criticism; they become only an object of laughter. This practice is hardly excusable, even in Claude Lorrain, who had shown more discretion if he had never meddled with such subjects.

A Discourse Delivered at the Opening of the
Royal Academy, Dec. 10th, 1788, 1789

EDMUND BURKE

[Marie-Antoinette]

IT IS now sixteen or seventeen years since I saw the queen of France, then the dauphiness, at Versailles; and surely never lighted on this orb, which she hardly seemed to touch, a more delightful vision. I saw her just above the horizon, decorating and cheering the elevated sphere she just began to move in, – glittering like the morning-star, full of life, and splendour, and joy. Oh! What a revolution! and what an heart must I have, to contemplate without emotion that elevation and that fall! Little did I dream when she added titles of veneration to those of enthusiastic, distant, respectful love, that she should ever be obliged to carry the sharp antidote against disgrace concealed in that bosom; little did I dream that I should have lived to see such disasters fallen upon her in a nation of gallant men, in a nation of men of honour and of cavaliers. I thought ten thousand swords must have leaped from their scabbards to avenge even a look that threatened her with insult. – But the age of chivalry is gone. – That of sophisters, economists, and calculators, has succeeded; and the glory of Europe is extinguished for ever. Never, never more, shall we behold that generous loyalty to rank and sex, that proud submission, that dignified obedience, that subordination of the heart, which kept alive, even in servitude itself, the spirit of an exalted freedom. The unbought grace of life, the cheap defence of nations, the nurse of manly sentiment and heroic enterprise is gone! It is gone, that sensibility of principle, that chastity of honour, which felt a stain like a wound, which inspired courage whilst it mitigated ferocity, which ennobled whatever it touched, and under which vice itself lost half its evil, by losing all its grossness.

Reflections on the Revolution in France, 1790

THOMAS PAINE

[Governing beyond the Grave]

THE ENGLISH Parliament of 1688 did a certain thing, which, for themselves and their constituents, they had a right to do, and which it appeared right should be done: But, in addition to this right, which they possessed by delegation, *they set up another right by assumption*, that of binding and controlling posterity to the end of time. The case, therefore, divides itself into two parts; the right which they possessed by delegation, and the right which they set up by assumption. The first is admitted; but, with respect to the second, I reply –

There never did, there never will, and there never can exist a parliament, or any description of men, or any generation of men, in any country, possessed of the right or the power of binding and controlling posterity to the '*end of time*', or of commending for ever how the world shall be governed, or who shall govern it; and therefore, all such clauses, acts or declarations, by which the makers of them attempt to do what they have neither the right nor the power to do, nor the power to execute, are in themselves null and void. – Every age and generation must be as free to act for itself, *in all cases*, as the ages and generations which preceded it. The vanity and presumption of governing beyond the grave, is the most ridiculous and insolent of all tyrannies. Man has no property in man; neither has any generation a property in the generations which are to follow. The parliament or the people of 1688, or of any other period, has no more right to dispose of the people of the present day, or to bind or to control them *in any shape whatever*, than the parliament or the people of the present day have to dispose of, bind or control those who are to live a hundred or a thousand years hence. Every generation is, and must be, competent to all the purposes which its occasions require. It is the living, and not the dead, that are to be accommodated. When man ceases to be, his power and his wants cease with him; and having no longer any participation in the concerns of this world, he has no longer any authority in directing who shall be its governors, or how its government shall be organised, or how administered.

I am not contending for nor against any form of government, nor for nor against any party here or elsewhere. That which a whole nation chooses to do, it has a right to do. Mr Burke says, No. Where then *does* the right exist? I am contending for the rights of the *living*, and against their being willed away, and controlled and contracted for, by the manuscript assumed authority of the dead; and Mr Burke is contending for the authority of the dead over the rights and freedom of the living. There was a time when kings disposed of their crowns by will upon their deathbeds, and consigned the people, like beasts of the field, to whatever successor they appointed. This is now so exploded as scarcely to be remembered, and so monstrous as hardly to be believed: But the parliamentary clauses upon which Mr Burke builds his political church, are of the same nature.

The laws of every country must be analogous to some common principle. In England, no parent or master, nor all the authority of parliament, omnipotent as it has called itself, can bind or control the personal freedom even of an individual beyond the age of twenty-one years: On what ground of right, then, could the parliament of 1688, or any other parliament, bind all posterity for ever?

Those who have quitted the world, and those who are not yet arrived at it, are as remote from each other, as the utmost stretch of mortal imagination can conceive: What possible obligation, then, can exist between them; what rule or principle can be laid down, that of two non-entities, the one out of existence, and the other not in, and who can never meet in this world, the one should control the other to the end of time?

In England, it is said that money cannot be taken out of the pockets of people without their consent: But who authorised, or who could authorise the parliament of 1688 to control and take away the freedom of posterity, (who were not in existence to give or withhold their consent), and limit and confine their right of acting in certain cases for ever?

Rights of Man: Being an Answer to Mr Burke's
Attack on the French Revolution, 1791–2

MARY WOLLSTONECRAFT

[The Weaker Sex]

A KING is always a king, and a woman always a woman. His authority and her sex ever stand between them and rational converse. With a lover, I grant, she should be so, and her sensibility will naturally lead her to endeavour to excite emotion, not to gratify her vanity, but her heart. This I do not allow to be coquetry; it is the artless impulse of nature. I only exclaim against the sexual desire of conquest when the heart is out of the question.

This desire is not confined to women. 'I have endeavoured,' says Lord Chesterfield, 'to gain the hearts of twenty women, whose persons I would not have given a fig for.' The libertine who, in a gust of passion, takes advantage of unsuspecting tenderness, is a saint when compared with this cold-hearted rascal – for I like to use significant words. Yet only taught to please, women are always on the watch to please, and with true heroic ardour endeavour to gain hearts merely to resign or spurn them when the victory is decided and conspicuous.

I must descend to the minutiae of the subject.

I lament that women are systematically degraded by receiving the trivial attentions which men think it manly to pay to the sex, when in fact, they are insultingly supporting their own superiority. It is not condescension to bow to an inferior. So ludicrous, in fact, do these ceremonies appear to me that I scarcely am able to govern my muscles when I see a man start with eager and serious solicitude to lift a handkerchief or shut a door, when the *lady* could have done it herself, had she only moved a pace or two.

A wild wish has just flown from my heart to my head, and I will not stifle it, though it may excite a horse-laugh. I do earnestly wish to see the distinction of sex confounded in society, unless where love animates the behaviour. For this distinction is, I am firmly persuaded, the foundation of the weakness of character ascribed to woman; is the cause why the understanding is neglected, whilst accomplishments are acquired with sedulous care; and the same cause accounts for their preferring the graceful before the heroic virtues.

Mankind, including every description, wish to be loved and respected by *something*, and the common herd will always take the nearest road to the completion of their wishes. The respect paid to wealth and beauty is the most certain and unequivocal, and, of course, will always attract the vulgar eye of common minds. Abilities and virtues are absolutely necessary to raise men from the middle rank of life into notice, and the natural consequence is notorious – the middle rank contains most virtue and abilities. Men have thus, in one station at least, an opportunity of exerting themselves with dignity, and of rising by the exertions which really improve a rational creature; but the whole female sex are, till their character is formed, in the same condition as the rich, for they are born – I now speak of a state of civilization – with certain sexual privileges; and whilst they are gratuitously granted them, few will ever think of works of supererogation to obtain the esteem of a small number of superior people.

A Vindication of the Rights of Women, 1792

ARTHUR YOUNG

[The National Assembly]

[*Versailles, 15 June 1789*] This has been a rich day, and such an one as ten years ago none could believe would ever arrive in France; a very important debate being expected on what in our House of Commons would be termed the state of the nation. My friend Mons. Lazowski and myself were at Versailles by eight in the morning. We went immediately to the hall of the States to secure good seats in the gallery; we found some deputies already there, and a pretty numer-

ous audience collected. The room is too large; none but
stentorian lungs, or the finest clearest voices can be heard;
however the very size of the apartment, which admits 2000
people, gave a dignity to the scene. It was indeed an
interesting one. The spectacle of the representatives of
twenty-five millions of people, just emerging from the evils
of 200 years of arbitrary power, and rising to the blessings
of a freer constitution, assembled with open doors under
the eye of the public, was framed to call into animated
feelings every latent spark, every emotion of a liberal
bosom; to banish whatever ideas might intrude of their
being a people too often hostile to my own country, and to
dwell with pleasure on the glorious idea of happiness to a
great nation; of felicity to millions yet unborn. Mons. l'Abbé
Sieyès opened the debate. He is one of the most zealous
sticklers for the popular cause; carries his ideas not to a
regulation of the present government, which he thinks too
bad to be regulated at all, but wishes to see it absolutely
overturned; being in fact a violent republican. This is the
character he commonly bears, and in his pamphlets he
seems pretty much to justify such an idea. He speaks
ungracefully and uneloquently, but logically, or rather reads
so, for he read his speech, which was prepared. His motion,
or rather string of motions, was to declare themselves the
representatives known and verified of the French nation,
admitting the right of all absent deputies (the nobility and
clergy) to be received among them on the verification of
their powers. Mons. de Mirabeau spoke without notes, for
nearly an hour, with a warmth, animation, and eloquence,
that entitles him to the reputation of an undoubted orator.
He opposed the words *known* and *verified*, in the proposition of Abbé Sieyès, with great force of reasoning; and
proposed, in lieu, that they should declare themselves
simply *représentants du peuple français*; that no *veto* should
exist against their resolves in any other assembly; that all
taxes are illegal, but should be granted during the present
session of the States, and no longer; that the debt of the
King should become the debt of the nation, and be secured
on funds accordingly. Mons. de Mirabeau was well heard,
and his proposition much applauded. Mons. de Mounier, a

deputy from Dauphiné, of great reputation, and who has also published some pamphlets, very well approved by the public, moved a different resolution, to declare themselves the legitimate representatives of the majority of the nation; that they should vote by head and not by order: and that they should never acknowledge any right in the representatives of the clergy or nobility to deliberate separately. Mons. Rabaut-Saint-Étienne, a Protestant from Languedoc, also an author, who has written in the present affairs, and a man of considerable talents, spoke also, and made his proposition, which was to declare themselves the representatives of the people of France; to declare all taxes null; to regrant them during the sitting of the States; to verify and consolidate the debt; and to vote a loan. All which were well approved except the loan, which was not at all to the feeling of the assembly. This gentleman speaks clearly and with precision, and only passages of his speech from notes. Mons. Barnave, a very young man, from Grenoble, spoke without notes with great warmth and animation. Some of his periods were so well rounded, and so eloquently delivered, that he met with much applause, several members crying – *bravo!*

In regard to their general method of proceeding, there are two circumstances in which they are very deficient; the spectators in the galleries are allowed to interfere in the debates by clapping their hands, and other noisy expressions of approbation. This is grossly indecent; it is also dangerous; for, if they are permitted to express approbation, they are, by parity of reason, allowed expressions of dissent; and they may hiss as well as clap; which it is said, they have sometimes done: – this would be, to overrule the debate and influence the deliberations. Another circumstance, is the want of order among themselves; more than once today there were an hundred members on their legs at a time, and Mons. Bailly absolutely without power to keep order. This arises very much from complex motions being admitted; to move a declaration relative to their title, to their powers, to taxes, to a loan, etc. etc. all in one proposition, appears to English ears preposterous, and certainly is so. Specific motions, founded on single and simple propositions, can alone produce order in debate; for it is endless to have five hundred members declaring their reasons of assent to one part of a complex proposition, and their dissent to another part. A debating assembly should not proceed to any business whatever till they have settled the rules and orders of their proceedings, which can only be done by taking those of other experienced assemblies, confirming them as they find useful, and altering such as require to be adapted to different circumstances.

Travels in France during the Years
1787, 1788 and 1789, 1792

WILLIAM GODWIN

[Revolution]

A<small>ND HERE</small> let us consider what is the nature of revolution. Revolution is engendered by an indignation against tyranny, yet is itself ever more pregnant with tyranny. The tyranny which excites its indignation can scarcely be without its partisans; and, the greater is the indignation excited, and the more sudden and vast the fall of the oppressors, the deeper will be the resentment which fills the minds of the losing party. What more unavoidable than that men should entertain some discontent at being violently stripped of their wealth and their privileges? What more venial than that they should feel some attachment to the sentiments in which they were educated, and which, it may be, but a little before, were the sentiments of almost every individual in the community? Are they obliged to change their creed, precisely at the time at which I see reason to alter mine? They have but remained at the point at which we both stood a few years ago. Yet this is the crime which a revolution watches with the greatest jealousy, and punishes with the utmost severity. The crime which is thus marked with the deepest reprobation is not the result of relaxation of principle, of profligate living, or of bitter and inexorable hatred. It is a fault not the least likely to occur in a man of untainted honour, of an upright disposition, and dignified and generous sentiments.

Revolution is instigated by a horror against tyranny, yet its own tyranny is not without peculiar aggravations. There is no period more at war with the existence of liberty. The unrestrained communication of opinions has always been subjected to mischievous counteraction, but upon such occasions it is trebly fettered. At other times men are not so much alarmed for its effects. But in a moment of revolution, when everything is in crisis, the influence even of a word is dreaded, and the consequent slavery is complete. Where was there a revolution in which a strong vindication of what it was intended to abolish was permitted, or indeed almost any species of writing or argument, that was not, for the most part, in harmony with the opinions which happened to prevail? An attempt to scrutinize men's thoughts, and punish their opinions, is of all kinds of despotism the most odious; yet this attempt is peculiarly characteristic of a period of revolution.

The advocates of revolution usually remark 'that there is no way to rid ourselves of our oppressors, and prevent new ones from starting up in their room, but by inflicting on them some severe and memorable retribution'. Upon this statement it is particularly to be observed that there will be oppressors as long as there are individuals inclined, either from perverseness, or rooted and obstinate prejudice, to take party with the oppressor. We have therefore to terrify not only the man of crooked ambition but all those who would support him, either from a corrupt motive, or a well-intentioned error. Thus, we propose to make men free; and the method we adopt is to influence them, more rigorously than ever, by the fear of punishment. We say that government has usurped too much, and we organize a government tenfold more encroaching in its principles and terrible in its proceedings. Is slavery the best project that can be devised for making men free? Is a display of terror the readiest mode for rendering them fearless, independent and enterprising?

During a period of revolution, enquiry, and all those

patient speculations to which mankind are indebted for their greatest improvements, are suspended. Such speculations demand a period of security and permanence; they can scarcely be pursued when men cannot foresee what shall happen tomorrow, and the most astonishing vicissitudes are affairs of perpetual recurrence. Such speculations demand leisure, and a tranquil and dispassionate temper; they can scarcely be pursued when all the passions of man are afloat, and we are hourly under the strongest impressions of fear and hope, apprehension and desire, dejection and triumph. Add to this, what has been already stated, respecting the tendency of revolution, to restrain the declaration of our thoughts, and put fetters upon the licence of investigation.

Another circumstance proper to be mentioned is the inevitable duration of the revolutionary spirit. This may be illustrated from the change of government in England in 1688. If we look at the revolution strictly so called, we are apt to congratulate ourselves that the advantages it procured, to whatever they may amount, were purchased by a cheap and bloodless victory. But, if we would make a solid estimate, we must recollect it as the procuring cause of two general wars, of nine years under King William, and twelve under Queen Anne; and two intestine rebellions (events worthy of execration, if we call to mind the gallant spirit and generous fidelity of the Jacobites, and their miserable end) in 1715 and 1745. Yet this was, upon the whole, a mild and auspicious revolution. Revolutions are a struggle between two parties, each persuaded of the justice of its cause, a struggle not decided by compromise or patient expostulation, but by force only. Such a decision can scarcely be expected to put an end to the mutual animosity and variance.

Enquiry Concerning Political Justice, 1793

ANN RADCLIFFE

[The Dark Veil]

'UP THE staircase the signora lies,' said Barnardine.
    'Lies!' repeated Emily faintly, as she began to ascend.

'She lies in the upper chamber,' said Barnardine.

As they passed up, the wind, which poured through the narrow cavities in the wall, made the torch flare, and it threw a stronger gleam upon the grim and sallow countenance of Barnardine, and discovered more fully the desolation of the place – the rough stone walls, the spiral stairs black with age, and a suit of ancient armour, with an iron visor, that hung upon the walls, and appeared a trophy of some former victory.

Having reached a landing-place, 'You may wait here, lady,' said he, applying a key to the door of the chamber, 'while I go up and tell the signora you are coming.'

'That ceremony is unnecessary,' replied Emily; 'my aunt will rejoice to see me.'

'I am not sure of that,' said Barnardine, pointing to the room he had opened; 'come in here, lady, while I step up.'

Emily, surprised and somewhat shocked, did not dare to oppose him further; but, as he was turning away with the torch, desired he would not leave her in darkness. He looked around, and, observing a tripod lamp that stood on the stairs, lighted and gave it to Emily, who stepped forward into a large old chamber, and he closed the door. As she listened anxiously to his departing steps, she thought he descended, instead of ascended, the stairs: but the gusts of wind that whistled round the portal would not allow her to hear distinctly any other sound. Still, however, she listened, and perceiving no step in the room above, where he had affirmed Madame Montoni to be, her anxiety increased, though she considered that the thickness of the floor in this strong building might prevent any sound reaching her from the upper chamber. The next moment, in a pause of the wind, she distinguished Barnardine's step descending to the court, and then thought she heard his voice; but the rising gust again overcoming other sounds, Emily, to be certain on this point, moved softly to the door, which, on attempting to open it, she discovered was fastened. All the horrid apprehensions that had lately assailed her, returned at this instant with redoubled force; and no longer appeared like the exaggerations of a timid spirit, but seemed to have been sent to warn her of her fate. She now did not doubt that Madame Montoni had been murdered, perhaps in this very chamber; or that she herself was brought hither for the same purpose. The countenance, the manners, and the recollected words of Barnardine when he had spoken of her aunt, confirmed her worst fears. For some moments she was incapable of considering any means by which she might attempt an escape. Still she listened, but heard footsteps neither on the stairs nor in the room above; she thought, however, that she again distinguished Barnardine's voice below, and went to a grated window, that opened upon the court, to inquire further. Here she plainly heard his hoarse accents mingling with the blast that swept by, but they were lost again so quickly that their meaning could not be interpreted; and then the light of a torch, which seemed to issue from the portal below, flashed across the court, and the long shadow of a man, who was under the archway, appeared upon the pavement. Emily, from the hugeness of this sudden portrait, concluded it to be that of Barnardine; but other deep tones which passed in the wind soon convinced her he was not alone, and that his companion was not a person very liable to pity.

When her spirits had overcome the first shock of her situation, she held up the lamp to examine if the chamber afforded a possibility of an escape. It was a spacious room, whose walls, wainscoted with rough oak, showed no casement but the grated one which Emily had left, and no other door than that by which she had entered. The feeble rays of the lamp, however, did not allow her to see at once its full extent; she perceived no furniture, except, indeed, an iron chair fastened in the centre of the chamber, immediately over which, depending on a chain from the ceiling, hung an iron ring. Having gazed upon these for some time with wonder and horror, she next observed iron bars below, made for the purpose of confining the feet, and on the arms of the chair were rings of the same metal. As she continued to survey them, she concluded that they were instruments of torture; and it struck her that some poor wretch had once been fastened in this chair, and had there been starved to death. She was chilled by the thought; but what was her agony when, in the next moment, it occurred to her that her aunt might have been one of these victims, and that she herself might be the next! An acute pain seized her head, she was scarcely able to hold the lamp; and, looking round for support, was seating herself, unconsciously, in the iron chair itself: but suddenly perceiving where she was, she started from it in horror, and sprung towards a remote end of the room. Here again she looked round for a seat to sustain her, and perceived only a dark curtain, which, descending from the ceiling to the floor, was drawn along the whole side of the chamber. Ill as she was, the appearance of this curtain struck her, and she paused to gaze upon it in wonder and apprehension.

It seemed to conceal a recess of the chamber; she wished, yet dreaded, to lift it, and to discover what it veiled; twice she was withheld by a recollection of the terrible spectacle her daring hand had formerly unveiled in an apartment of the castle, till, suddenly conjecturing that it concealed the body of her murdered aunt, she seized it in a fit of desperation, and drew it aside. Beyond appeared a corpse stretched on a kind of low couch, which was crimsoned with human blood, as was the floor beneath. The features, deformed by death, were ghastly and horrible, and more than one livid wound appeared in the face. Emily, bending over the body, gazed, for a moment, with an eager frenzied eye; but, in the next, the lamp dropped from her hand, and she fell senseless at the foot of the couch.

The Mysteries of Udolpho, 1794

MATTHEW LEWIS

[The Ravisher]

GUIDED BY the moonbeams, he proceeded up the stair-case with slow and cautious steps. He looked round him every moment with apprehension and anxiety. He saw a spy in every shadow, and heard a voice in every murmur of the night-breeze. Consciousness of the guilty business on which he was employed appalled his heart, and rendered it more timid than a woman's. Yet still he proceeded. He reached the door of Antonia's chamber. He stopped and listened. All was hushed within. The total silence persuaded him that his intended victim was retired to rest, and he ventured to lift up the latch. The door was fastened, and resisted his efforts. But no sooner was it touched by the talisman, than the bolt flew back. The ravisher stepped on, and found himself in the chamber where slept the innocent girl, unconscious how dangerous a visitor was drawing near her couch. The door closed after him, and the bolt shot again into its fastening.

Ambrosio advanced with precaution. He took care not a board should creak under his foot, and held his breath as he approached the bed. His first attention was to perform the magic ceremony, as Matilda had charged him: he breathed thrice upon the silver myrtle, pronounced over it Antonia's name, and laid it upon her pillow. The effects which it had already produced permitted not his doubting its success in prolonging the slumbers of his devoted mistress, and no sooner was the enchantment performed, than he considered her to be absolutely in his power, and his eyes flashed with lust and impatience. He now ventured to cast a glance upon the sleeping beauty. A single lamp, burning before the statue of St Rosolia, shed a faint light through the room, and permitted him to examine all the charms of the lovely object before him. The heat of the weather had obliged her to throw off part of the bed-clothes. Those which still covered her Ambrosio's insolent hand hastened to remove.

She lay with her cheek reclining upon one ivory arm: the other rested on the side of the bed with graceful indolence. A few tresses of her hair had escaped from beneath the muslin which confined the rest, and fell carelessly over her bosom, as it heaved with slow and regular suspiration. The warm air had spread her cheek with higher colour than usual. A smile inexpressibly sweet played round her ripe and coral lips, from which every now and then escaped a gentle sigh, or an half-pronounced sentence. An air of enchanting innocence and candour pervaded her whole form; and there was a sort of modesty in her very nakedness which added fresh stings to the desires of the lustful monk.

He remained for some moments devouring those charms with his eyes, which soon were to be subjected to his ill-regulated passions. Her mouth half opened seemed to solicit a kiss: he bent over her: he joined his lips to hers, and drew in the fragrance of her breath with rapture. This momentary pleasure increased his longing for still greater. His desires were raised to that frantic height by which brutes are agitated. He resolved not to delay for one instant longer the accomplishment of his wishes, and hastily proceeded to tear off those garments which impeded the gratification of his lust.

'Gracious God!' exclaimed a voice behind him: 'Am I not deceived? Is not this an illusion?'

Terror, confusion, and disappointment accompanied these words, as they struck Ambrosio's hearing. He started, and turned towards the voice. Elvira stood at the door of the chamber, and regarded the monk with looks of surprise and detestation.

A frightful dream had represented to her Antonia on the verge of a precipice. She saw her trembling on the brink; every moment seemed to threaten her fall; and she heard her exclaim with shrieks, 'Save me, mother! save me! – yet a moment, and it will be too late.' Elvira woke in terror. The vision had made too strong an impression upon her mind to permit her resting till assured of her daughter's safety. She hastily started from her bed, threw on a loose night-gown, and, passing through the closet in which slept the waiting-woman, reached Antonia's chamber just in time to rescue her from the grasp of the ravisher.

His shame and her amazement seemed to have petrified into statues both Elvira and the monk. They remained gazing upon each other in silence. The lady was the first to recover herself.

'It is no dream,' she cried: 'it is really Ambrosio, who stands before me. It is the man whom Madrid esteems a saint, that I find at this late hour near the couch of my unhappy child. Monster of hypocrisy! I already suspected your designs, but forbore your accusation in pity to human frailty. Silence would now be criminal. The whole city shall be informed of your incontinence. I will unmask you, villain, and convince the Church what a viper she cherishes in her bosom.'

The Monk: A Romance, 1795

JOSEPH PRIESTLEY

[Experimental Philosophy]

B UT NOTHING of a nature foreign to the duties of my profession [*as a minister*] engaged my attention while I was at Leeds so much as the prosecution of my experiments relating to electricity, and especially to the doctrine of air. The last I was led into in consequence of inhabiting a house adjoining to a public brewery, where I at first amused myself with making experiments on the fixed air [*carbon dioxide*] which I found ready-made in the process of fermentation. When I removed from that house I was under the necessity of making the fixed air for myself; and one experiment leading to another, as I have distinctly and faithfully noted in my various publications on the subject, I by degrees, contrived a convenient apparatus for the purpose, but of the cheapest kind.

When I began these experiments, I knew very little of chemistry, and had in a manner no idea on the subject before I attended a course of chemical lectures, delivered in the academy at Warrington, by Dr Turner, of Liverpool. But I have often thought that upon the whole this circumstance was no disadvantage to me; as in this situation I was led to devise an apparatus, and processes of my own, adapted to my peculiar views. Whereas, if I had been previously accustomed to the usual chemical processes, I should not have so easily thought of any other; and without new modes of operation I should hardly have discovered anything materially new.

My first publication on the subject of air was in 1772. It was a small pamphlet on the method of impregnating water with fixed air; which being immediately translated into French, excited a great degree of attention to the subject, and this was much increased by the publication of my first paper of experiments, in a large article of the *Philosophical Transactions*, the year following, for which I received the gold medal of the [*Royal*] Society. My method of impregnating water with fixed air was considered at a meeting of the College of Physicians, before whom I made the experiments, and by them it was recommended to the Lords of the Admiralty (by whom they had been summoned for the purpose) as likely to be of use in the sea scurvy.

The only person in Leeds who gave much attention to my experiments was Mr Hey, a surgeon. He was a zealous Methodist, and wrote answers to some of my theological tracts; but we always conversed with the greatest freedom on philosophical subjects, without mentioning anything relating to theology. When I left Leeds, he begged of me the earthen trough in which I had made all my experiments on air while I was there. It was such a one as is there commonly used for washing linen.

Having succeeded so well in the *History of Electricity*, I was induced to undertake the history of all the branches of experimental philosophy; and at Leeds I gave out proposals for that purpose, and published the *History of Discoveries Relating to Vision, Light, and Colours*. This work, also, I believe I executed to general satisfaction, and being an undertaking of great expense, I was under the necessity of publishing it by subscription. The sale, however, was not such as to encourage me to proceed with a work of so much labour and expense; so that after purchasing a great number of books, to enable me to finish my undertaking, I was obliged to abandon it, and to apply wholly to original experiments.

In writing the *History of Discoveries Relating to Vision*, I was much assisted by Mr Michell, the discoverer of the method of making artificial magnets. Living at Thornhill, not very far from Leeds, I frequently visited him, and was very happy in his society, as I also was in that of Mr Smeaton, who lived still nearer to me. He made me a present of his excellent air pump, which I constantly use to this day. Having strongly recommended his construction of this instrument, it is now generally used; whereas before that, hardly any had been made during the twenty years which had elapsed after the account that he had given of it in the *Philosophical Transactions*.

I was also instrumental in reviving the use of large electrical machines and batteries in electricity, the generality of electrical machines being little more than playthings at the time that I began my experiments. The first very large electrical machine was made by Mr Nairne, in consequence of a request made to me by the Grand Duke of Tuscany, to get him the best machine that we could make in England. This, and another that he made for Mr Vaughan, were constituted on a plan of my own. But afterwards Mr Nairne made large machines on a more simple and improved construction; and in consideration of the service which I had rendered him, he made me a present of a pretty large machine of the same kind.

Memoirs of the Rev. Dr Joseph Priestley
to the Year 1795. Written by Himself, 1795

THOMAS MALTHUS

[Poor Relief]

THE POOR laws of England tend to depress the general condition of the poor in these two ways. Their first obvious tendency is to increase population without increasing the food for its support. A poor man may marry with little or no prospect of being able to support a family in independence. They may be said therefore in some measure to create the poor which they maintain, and as the provisions of the country must, in consequence of the increased population, be distributed to every man in smaller proportions, it is evident that the labour of those who are not supported by parish assistance will purchase a smaller quantity of provisions than before and consequently more of them must be driven to ask for support.

Secondly, the quantity of provisions consumed in workhouses upon a part of the society that cannot in general be considered as the most valuable part diminishes the shares that would otherwise belong to more industrious and more worthy members, and thus in the same manner forces more to become dependent. If the poor in the workhouses were to live better than they now do, this new distribution of the money of the society would tend more conspicuously to depress the condition of those out of the workhouses by occasioning a rise in the price of provisions.

Fortunately for England, a spirit of independence still remains among the peasantry. The poor laws are strongly calculated to eradicate this spirit. They have succeeded in part, but had they succeeded as completely as might have been expected their pernicious tendency would not have been so long concealed.

Hard as it may appear in individual instances, dependent poverty ought to be held disgraceful. Such a stimulus seems to be absolutely necessary to promote the happiness of the great mass of mankind, and every general attempt to weaken this stimulus, however benevolent its apparent intention, will always defeat its own purpose. If men are induced to marry from a prospect of parish provision, with little or no chance of maintaining their families in independence, they are not only unjustly tempted to bring unhappiness and dependence upon themselves and children, but they are tempted, without knowing it, to injure all in the same class with themselves. A labourer who marries without being able to support a family may in some respects be considered as an enemy to all his fellow-labourers.

I feel no doubt whatever that the parish laws of England have contributed to raise the price of provisions and to lower the real price of labour. They have therefore contributed to impoverish that class of people whose only possession is their labour. It is also difficult to suppose that they have not powerfully contributed to generate that carelessness and want of frugality observable among the poor, so contrary to the disposition frequently to be remarked among petty tradesmen and small farmers. The labouring poor, to use a vulgar expression, seem always to live from hand to mouth. Their present wants employ their whole attention, and they seldom think of the future. Even when they have an opportunity of saving they seldom exercise it, but all that is beyond their present necessities goes, generally speaking, to the ale-house. The poor laws of England may therefore be said to diminish both the power and the will to save among the common people, and thus to weaken one of the strongest incentives to sobriety and industry, and consequently to happiness.

It is a general complaint among master manufacturers that high wages ruin all their workmen, but it is difficult to conceive that these men would not save a part of their high wages for the future support of their families, instead of spending it in drunkenness and dissipation, if they did not rely on parish assistance for support in case of accidents. And that the poor employed in manufactures consider this assistance as a reason why they may spend all the wages they earn and enjoy themselves while they can appears to be evident from the number of families that, upon the failure of any great manufactory, immediately fall upon the parish, when perhaps the wages earned in this manufactory while it flourished were sufficiently above the price of common country labour to have allowed them to save enough for their support till they could find some other channel for their industry.

A man who might not be deterred from going to the ale-house from the consideration that on his death, or sickness, he should leave his wife and family upon the parish might yet hesitate in thus dissipating his earnings if he were assured that, in either of these cases, his family must starve or be left to the support of casual bounty. In China, where the real as well as nominal price of labour is very low, sons are yet obliged by law to support their aged and helpless parents. Whether such a law would be advisable in this country I will not pretend to determine. But it seems at any rate highly improper, by positive institutions, which render dependent poverty so general, to weaken that disgrace, which for the best and most humane reasons ought to attach to it.

An Essay on the Principle of Population, 1798

MUNGO PARK

[Moorish Captivity]

[*March 1796*] The Moors, though very indolent themselves, are rigid taskmasters, and keep every person under them in full employment. My boy Demba was sent to the woods to collect withered grass for Ali's horses; and, after a variety of projects concerning myself, they at last found out an employment for me; this was no other than the respectable office of *barber*. I was to make my first exhibition in this capacity in the royal presence, and to be honoured with the task of shaving the head of the young prince of Ludamar. I accordingly seated myself upon the sand, and the boy, with some hesitation, sat down beside me. A small razor, about three inches long, was put into my hand, and I was ordered to proceed; but whether from my own want of skill, or the improper shape of the instrument, I unfortunately made a slight incision in the boy's head, at the very commencement of the operation; and the king observing the awkward manner in which I held the razor, concluded that his son's head was in very improper hands, and ordered me to resign the razor, and walk out of the tent. This I considered as a very fortunate circumstance; for I had laid it down as a rule, to make myself as useless and insignificant as possible, as the only means of recovering my liberty.

March 18th. – Four Moors arrived from Jarra with Johnson my interpreter, having seized him before he had received any intimation of my confinement: and bringing with them a bundle of clothes that I had left at Daman Jumma's house, for my use, in case I should return by the way of Jarra. Johnson was led into Ali's tent and examined; the bundle was opened, and I was sent for to explain the use of the different articles. I was happy, however, to find that Johnson had committed my papers to the charge of one of Daman's wives. When I had satisfied Ali's curiosity respecting the different articles of apparel, the bundle was again tied up, and put into a large cowskin bag, that stood in a corner of the tent. The same evening Ali sent three of his people to inform me, that there were many thieves in the neighbourhood, and that to prevent the rest of my things from being stolen, it was necessary to convey them all into his tent. My clothes, instruments, and every thing that belonged to me, were accordingly carried away; and though the heat and dust made clean linen very necessary and refreshing, I could not procure a single shirt out of the small stock I had brought along with me. Ali was, however, disappointed, by not finding among my effects the quantity of gold and amber that he expected; but to make sure of every thing, he sent the same people, on the morning following, to examine whether I had any thing concealed about my person. They, with their usual rudeness, searched every part of my apparel, and stripped me of all my gold, amber, my watch, and one of my pocket compasses. I had fortunately, in the night, buried the other compass in the sand; and this, with the clothes I had on, was all that the tyranny of Ali had now left me.

The gold and amber were highly gratifying to Moorish avarice, but the pocket compass soon became an object of superstitious curiosity. Ali was very desirous to be informed why that small piece of iron, the needle, always pointed to the Great Desert; and I found myself somewhat puzzled to answer the question. To have pleaded my ignorance, would have created a suspicion that I wished to conceal the real truth from him; I therefore told him, that my mother resided far beyond the sands of Sahara, and that whilst she was alive the piece of iron would always point that way, and serve as a guide to conduct me to her, and that if she was dead, it would point to her grave. Ali now looked at the compass with redoubled amazement; turned it round and round repeatedly; but observing that it always pointed the same way, he took it up with great caution, and returned it to me, manifesting that he thought there was something of magic in it, and that he was afraid of keeping so dangerous an instrument in his possession.

March 20th. – This morning a council of chief men was held in Ali's tent respecting me; their decisions, though they were all unfavourable to me, were differently related by different persons. Some said that they intended to put me to death; others, that I was only to lose my right hand; but the most probable account was that which I received from Ali's own son, a boy about nine years of age, who came to me in the evening, and, with much concern, informed me that his uncle had persuaded his father to put out my eyes, which they said resembled those of a cat, and that all the Bushreens had approved of this measure. His father, however, he said, would not put the sentence into execution until Fatima the queen, who was at present in the north, had seen me.

Travels in the Interior of Africa, 1799

MARIA EDGEWORTH

[Chairing the Member]

MY MASTER did not relish the thoughts of a troublesome canvass, and all the ill-will he might bring upon himself by disturbing the peace of the county, besides the expense, which was no trifle; but all his friends called upon one another to subscribe, and they formed themselves into a committee, and wrote all his circular letters for him, and engaged all his agents, and did all the business unknown to him; and he was well pleased that it should be so at last, and my lady herself was very sanguine about the election; and there was open house kept night and day at Castle Rackrent, and I thought I never saw my lady look so well in her life as she did at that time. There were grand dinners, and all the gentlemen drinking success to Sir Condy till they were carried off; and then dances and balls, and the ladies all finishing with a raking pot of tea in the morning. Indeed, it was well the company made it their choice to sit up all nights, for there were not half beds enough for the sights of people that were in it, though there were shake-downs in the drawing-room always made up before sunrise for those that liked it. For my part, when I saw the doings that were going on, and the loads of claret that went down the throats of them that had no right to be asking for it, and the sights of meat that went up to table and never came down, besides what was carried off to one or t'other below stair, I couldn't but pity my poor master, who was to pay for all; but I said nothing, for fear of gaining myself ill-will. The day of election will come some time or other, says I to myself, and all will be over; and so it did, and a glorious day it was as any I ever had the happiness to see.

'Huzza! huzza! Sir Condy Rackrent for ever!' was the first thing I hears in the morning, and the same and nothing else all day, and not a soul sober only just when polling, enough to give their votes as became 'em, and to stand the brow-beating of the lawyers, who came tight enough upon us; and many of our freeholders were knocked off, having never a freehold that they could safely swear to, and Sir Condy was not willing to have any man perjure himself for his sake, as was done on the other side, God knows; but no matter for that. Some of our friends were dumbfounded by the lawyers asking them: Had they ever been upon the ground where their freeholds lay? Now, Sir Condy being tender of the consciences of them that had not been on the ground, and so could not swear to a freehold when cross-examined by them lawyers, sent out for a couple of cleavesful of the sods of his farm of Gulteeshinnagh; and as soon as the sods came into town, he set each man upon his sod, and so then, ever after, you know, they could fairly swear they had been upon the ground. We gained the day by this piece of honesty. I thought I should have died in the streets for joy when I seed my poor master chaired, and he bareheaded, and it raining as hard as it could pour; but all the crowds following him up and down, and he bowing and shaking hands with the whole town.

'Is that Sir Condy Rackrent in the chair?' says a stranger man in the crowd.

'The same,' says I. 'Who else should it be? God bless him!'

'And I take it, then, you belong to him?' says he.

'Not at all,' says I; 'but I live under him, and have done so these two hundred years and upwards, me and mine.'

'It's lucky for you, then,' rejoins he, 'that he is where he is; for was he anywhere else but in the chair, this minute he'd be in a worse place; for I was sent down on purpose to put him up [put him in gaol], and here's my order for doing so in my pocket.'

It was a writ that villain the wine merchant had marked against my poor master for some hundreds of an old debt, which it was a shame to be talking of at such a time as this.

'Put it in your pocket again, and think no more of it anyways for seven years to come, my honest friend,' says I; 'he's a member of Parliament now, praised be God, and such as you can't touch him; and if you'll take a fool's advice, I'd have you keep out of the way this day, or you'll run a good chance of getting your deserts amongst my master's friends, unless you choose to drink his health like everybody else.'

Castle Rackrent, 1800

DOROTHY WORDSWORTH

[Beggars]

ON TUESDAY, May 27th [*1800*], a very tall woman, tall much beyond the measure of tall women, called at the door. She had on a very long brown cloak, and a very white cap without bonnet – her face was excessively brown, but it had plainly once been fair. She led a little bare-footed child about two years old by the hand and said her husband who was a tinker was gone before with the other children. I gave her a piece of bread. Afterwards on my road to Ambleside, beside the bridge at Rydale, I saw her husband sitting by the roadside, his two asses feeding beside him and the two young children at play upon the grass. The man did not beg. I passed on and about a quarter of a mile further I saw two boys before me, one about ten, the other about eight years old, at play chasing a butterfly. They were wild figures, not very ragged, but without shoes and stockings; the hat of the elder was wreathed round with yellow flowers; the younger, whose hat was only a rimless crown, had stuck it round with laurel leaves. They continued at play till I drew very near and then they addressed me with the beggars' cant and the whining voice of sorrow. I said: 'I served your mother this morning.' (The boys were so like the woman who had called at the door that I could not be mistaken.) 'Oh,' says the elder, 'you could not serve my mother, for she's dead and my father's on at the next town – he's a potter.' I persisted in my assertion and that I would give them nothing. Says the elder, 'Come, let's away,' and away they flew like lightning. They had, however, sauntered so long in their road that they did not reach Ambleside before me, and I saw them go up to Matthew Harrison's house with their wallet upon the elder's shoulder, and creeping with a beggar's complaining foot. On my return through Ambleside I met in the street the mother driving her asses; in the two panniers of one of which were the two little children, whom she was chiding and threatening with the wand which she used to drive on her asses, while the little things hung in wantonness over the pannier's edge. The woman had told me in the morning that she was of Scotland, which her accent fully proved, but that she had lived, I think, at Wigton, that they could not keep a house and so they travelled.

Saturday morning [*13th March 1802*] It was as cold as ever it has been all winter, very hard frost. I baked pies, bread, and seed-cake for Mr Simpson. William finished 'Alice Fell', and then he wrote the poem of the beggar woman ['Beggars'] taken from a woman whom I had seen in May (now nearly two years ago) when John and he were at Gallow Hill. I sat with him at intervals all the morning, took down his stanzas, etc. After dinner we walked to Rydale, for letters. It was terribly cold; we had two or three brisk hail showers. The hailstones looked clean and pretty upon the dry clean road. Little Peggy Simpson was standing at the door catching the hailstones in her hand. She grows very like her mother. When she is sixteen years old I dare say that to her grandmother's eye she will seem as like to what her mother was as any rose in her garden is like the rose that grew there years before. No letters at Rydale. We drank tea as soon as we reached home. After tea I read to William that account of the little boys belonging to the tall woman; and an unlucky thing it was, for he could not escape from those very words, and so he could not write the poem. He left it unfinished and went tired to bed. In our walk from Rydale he had got warmed with the subject and had half cast the poem.

From the Grasmere Journals

WILLIAM WORDSWORTH

[*Lyrical Ballads*]

THE PRINCIPAL object, then, proposed in these Poems was to choose incidents and situations from common life, and to relate or describe them, throughout, as far as was possible in a selection of language really used by men, and, at the same time, to throw over them a certain colouring of imagination, whereby ordinary things should be presented to the mind in an unusual aspect; and, further, and above all, to make these incidents and situations interesting by tracing in them, truly though not ostentatiously, the primary laws of our nature: chiefly, as far as regards the manner in which we associate ideas in a state of excitement. Humble and rustic life was generally chosen, because, in that condition, the essential passions of the heart find a better soil in which they can attain their maturity, are less under restraint, and speak a plainer and more emphatic language; because in that condition of life our elementary feelings co-exist in a state of greater simplicity, and consequently, may be more accurately contemplated, and more forcibly communicated; because the manners of rural life germinate from those elementary feelings, and, from the necessary character of rural occupations, are more easily comprehended, and are more durable; and, lastly, because in that condition the passions of men are incorporated with the beautiful and permanent forms of nature. The language, too, of these men has been adopted (purified indeed from what appear to be its real defects, from all lasting and rational causes of dislike or disgust) because such men hourly communicate with the best objects from which the best part of language is originally derived; and because, from their rank in society and the sameness and narrow circle of their intercourse, being less under the influence of social vanity, they convey their feelings and notions in simple and unelaborated expressions. Accordingly, such a language, arising out of repeated experience and regular feelings, is a more permanent, and a far more philosophical language, than that which is frequently substituted for it by Poets, who think that they are conferring honour upon themselves and their art, in proportion as they separate themselves from the sympathies of men, and indulge in arbitrary and capricious habits of expression, in order to furnish food for fickle tastes, and fickle appetites, of their own creation. . . .

I have said that poetry is the spontaneous overflow of powerful feelings; it takes its origin from emotion recollected in tranquillity: the emotion is contemplated till, by a species of re-action, the tranquillity gradually disappears, and an emotion, kindred to that which was before the subject of contemplation, is gradually produced, and does itself actually exist in the mind. In this mood successful composition generally begins, and in a mood similar to this it is carried on; but the emotion, of whatever kind, and in whatever degree, from various causes, is qualified by various pleasures, so that in describing any passions whatsoever, which are voluntarily described, the mind will upon the whole, be in a state of enjoyment. If Nature be thus cautious to preserve in a state of enjoyment a being so employed, the Poet ought to profit by the lesson held forth to him, and ought especially to take care, that, whatever passions he communicates to his Reader, those passions, if his Reader's mind be sound and vigorous, should always be accompanied with an overbalance of pleasure. Now the music of harmonious metrical language, the sense of difficulty overcome, and the blind association of pleasure which has been previously received from works of rhyme or metre of the same or similar construction, an indistinct perception perpetually renewed of language closely resembling that of real life, and yet, in the circumstance of metre, differing from it so widely – all these imperceptibly make up a complex feeling of delight, which is of the most important use in tempering the painful feeling always found intermingled with powerful descriptions of the deeper passions. This effect is always produced in pathetic and impassioned poetry; while, in lighter compositions, the ease and gracefulness with which

the Poet manages his numbers are themselves confessedly a
principal source of the gratification of the Reader. All that
it is *necessary* to say, however, upon this subject, may be
effected by affirming, what few persons will deny, that, of
two descriptions, either of passions, manners, or characters,
each of them equally well executed, the one in prose and
the other in verse, the verse will be read a hundred times
where the prose is read once.

Preface to *Lyrical Ballads*, 2nd edn, 1802

SYDNEY SMITH

Female Education

A GREAT deal has been said of the original difference
of capacity between men and women; as if women
were more quick and men more judicious – as if women were
more remarkable for delicacy of association, and men for
stronger powers of attention. All this, we confess, appears
to us very fanciful. That there is a difference in the understandings of the men and the women we every day meet
with, everybody, we suppose, must perceive; but there is
none surely which may not be accounted for by the difference of circumstances in which they have been placed,
without referring to any conjectural difference of original
conformation of mind. As long as boys and girls run about
in the dirt, and trundle hoops together, they are both
precisely alike. If you catch up one half of these creatures,
and train them to a particular set of actions and opinions,
and the other half to a perfectly opposite set, of course their
understandings will differ, as one or the other sort of
occupations has called this or that talent into action. There
is surely no occasion to go into any deeper or more abstruse
reasoning, in order to explain so very simple a phenomenon.
Taking it, then, for granted, that nature has been as
bountiful of understanding to one sex as the other, it is

incumbent on us to consider what are the principal objections commonly made against the communication of a greater share of knowledge to women than commonly falls to their lot at present: for though it may be doubted whether women should learn all that men learn, the immense disparity which now exists between their knowledge we should hardly think could admit of any rational defence. It is not easy to imagine that there can be any just cause why a woman of forty should be more ignorant than a boy of twelve years of age. If there be any good at all in female ignorance, this (to use a very colloquial phrase) is surely too much of a good thing.

Something in this question must depend, no doubt, upon the leisure which either sex enjoys for the cultivation of their understandings: – and we cannot help thinking, that women have fully as much, if not more, idle time upon their hands than men. Women are excluded from all the serious business of the world; men are lawyers, physicians, clergymen, apothecaries, and justices of the peace – sources of exertion which consume a great deal more time than producing and suckling children; so that if the thing is a thing that ought to be done – if the attainments of literature are objects really worthy the attention of females, they cannot plead the want of leisure as an excuse for indolence and neglect. The lawyer who passes his day in exasperating the bickerings of Roe and Doe, is certainly as much engaged as his lady, who has the whole of her morning before her to correct the children and pay the bills. The apothecary, who rushes from an act of phlebotomy in the western parts of the town to insinuate a bolus in the east, is surely as completely absorbed as that fortunate female who is darning the garment or preparing the repast of her Aesculapius at home; and in every degree and situation of life, it seems that men must necessarily be exposed to more serious demands upon their time and attention, than can possibly be the case with respect to the other sex. We are speaking always of the fair demands which ought to be made upon the time and attention of women; for, as the matter now stands, the time of women is considered as worth nothing at all. Daughters are kept to occupation in sewing, patching, mantua-making, and mending, by which it is impossible they can earn tenpence a day. The intellectual improvement of women is considered to be of such subordinate importance, that twenty pounds paid for needle-work would give to a whole family leisure to acquire a fund of real knowledge. They are kept with nimble fingers and vacant understandings, till the season for improvement is utterly past away, and all chance of forming more important habits completely lost. We do not therefore say that women have more leisure than men, if it be necessary they should lead the life of artisans; but we make this assertion only upon the supposition that it is of some importance women should be instructed; and that many ordinary occupations, for which a little money will find a better substitute, should be sacrificed to this consideration.

We bar, in this discussion, any objection which proceeds from the mere novelty of teaching women more than they are already taught. It may be useless that their education should be improved, or it may be pernicious; and these are the fair grounds on which the question may be argued. But those who cannot bring their minds to consider such an unusual extension of knowledge, without connecting with it some sensation of the ludicrous, should remember, that, in the progress from absolute ignorance, there is a period when cultivation of the mind is new to every rank and description of persons. A century ago, who would have believed that country gentlemen could be brought to read and spell with the ease and accuracy which we now so frequently remark, – or supposed that they could be carried up even to the elements of ancient and modern history? Nothing is more common, or more stupid, than to take the actual for the possible – to believe that all which is, is all which can be; first to laugh at every proposed deviation from practice as impossible – then, when it is carried into effect, to be astonished that it did not take place before.

It is said, that the effect of knowledge is to make women pedantic and affected; and that nothing can be more offensive, than to see a woman stepping out of the natural modesty of her sex, to make an ostentatious display of her literary attainments. This may be true enough; but the answer is so trite and obvious, that we are almost ashamed to make it. All affectation and display proceed from the supposition of possessing something better than the rest of the world possesses. Nobody is vain of possessing two legs and two arms; – because that is the precise quantity of either sort of limb which every body possesses. Who ever heard a lady boast that she understood French? – for no other reason, that we know of, but because everybody in these days does understand French; and though there may be some disgrace in being ignorant of that language, there is little or no merit in its acquisition. Diffuse knowledge generally among women, and you will at once cure the conceit which knowledge occasions while it is rare. Vanity and conceit we shall of course witness in men and women as long as the world endures: – but by multiplying the attainments upon which these feelings are founded, you increase the difficulty of indulging them, and render them much more tolerable, by making them the proofs of a much higher merit. When learning ceases to be uncommon among women, learned women will cease to be affected.

Edinburgh Review, 1808

JANE AUSTEN

[Mr Darcy]

IN A few days Mr Bingley returned Mr Bennet's visit, and sat about ten minutes with him in his library. He had entertained hopes of being admitted to a sight of the young ladies, of whose beauty he had heard much; but he saw only the father. The ladies were somewhat more fortunate, for they had the advantage of ascertaining from an upper window, that he wore a blue coat and rode a black horse.

An invitation to dinner was soon afterwards dispatched; and already had Mrs Bennet planned the courses that were to do credit to her housekeeping, when an answer arrived which deferred it all. Mr Bingley was obliged to be in town the following day, and consequently unable to accept the honour of their invitation, &c. Mrs Bennet was quite disconcerted. She could not imagine what business he could have in town so soon after his arrival in Hertfordshire; and she began to fear that he might be always flying about from one place to another, and never settled at Netherfield as he ought to be. Lady Lucas quieted her fears a little by starting the idea of his being gone to London only to get a large party for the ball; and a report soon followed that Mr Bingley was to bring twelve ladies and seven gentlemen with him to the assembly. The girls grieved over such a number of ladies; but were comforted the day before the ball by hearing, that instead of twelve, he had brought only six with him from London, his five sisters and a cousin. And when the party entered the assembly room, it consisted of only five altogether; Mr Bingley, his two sisters, the husband of the eldest, and another young man.

Mr Bingley was good looking and gentlemanlike; he had a pleasant countenance, and easy, unaffected manners. His sisters were fine women, with an air of decided fashion. His brother-in-law, Mr Hurst, merely looked the gentleman; but his friend Mr Darcy soon drew the attention of the room by his fine, tall person, handsome features, noble mien; and the report which was in general circulation within five minutes after his entrance, of his having ten thousand a year. The gentlemen pronounced him to be a fine figure of a man, the ladies declared he was much handsomer than Mr Bingley, and he was looked at with great admiration for about half the evening, till his manners gave a disgust which turned the tide of his popularity; for he was discovered to be proud, to be above his company, and above being pleased; and not all his large estate in Derbyshire could then save him from having a most forbidding, disagreeable countenance, and being unworthy to be compared with his friend.

Mr Bingley had soon made himself acquainted with all the principal people in the room; he was lively and unreserved, danced every dance, was angry that the ball closed so early, and talked of giving one himself at Netherfield.

Such amiable qualities must speak for themselves. What a contrast between him and his friend! Mr Darcy danced only once with Mrs Hurst and once with Miss Bingley, declined being introduced to any other lady, and spent the rest of the evening in walking about the room, speaking occasionally to one of his own party. His character was decided. He was the proudest, most disagreeable man in the world, and every body hoped that he would never come there again. Amongst the most violent against him was Mrs Bennet, whose dislike of his general behaviour, was sharpened into particular resentment, by his having slighted one of her daughters.

Elizabeth Bennet had been obliged, by the scarcity of gentlemen, to sit down for two dances; and during part of that time, Mr Darcy had been standing near enough for her to overhear a conversation between him and Mr Bingley, who came from the dance for a few minutes, to press his friend to join it.

'Come, Darcy,' said he, 'I must have you dance. I hate to see you standing about by yourself in this stupid manner. You had much better dance.'

'I certainly shall not. You know how I detest it, unless I am particularly acquainted with my partner. At such an assembly as this, it would be insupportable. Your sisters are engaged, and there is not another woman in the room, whom it would not be a punishment to me to stand up with.'

'I would not be so fastidious as you are,' cried Bingley, 'for a kingdom! Upon my honour, I never met with so many pleasant girls in my life, as I have this evening; and there are several of them you see uncommonly pretty.'

'*You* are dancing with the only handsome girl in the room,' said Mr Darcy, looking at the eldest Miss Bennet.

'Oh! she is the most beautiful creature I ever beheld! But there is one of her sisters sitting down just behind you, who is very pretty, and I dare say, very agreeable. Do let me ask my partner to introduce you.'

'Which do you mean?' and turning round, he looked for a moment at Elizabeth, till catching her eye, he withdrew his own and coldly said, 'She is tolerable; but not handsome enough to tempt *me*; and I am in no humour at present to give consequence to young ladies who are slighted by other men. You had better return to your partner and enjoy her smiles, for you are wasting your time with me.'

Mr Bingley followed his advice. Mr Darcy walked off; and Elizabeth remained with no very cordial feelings towards him. She told the story however with great spirit among her friends; for she had a lively, playful disposition, which delighted in any thing ridiculous.

The evening altogether passed off pleasantly to the whole family. Mrs Bennet had seen her eldest daughter much admired by the Netherfield party. Mr Bingley had danced with her twice, and she had been distinguished by his sisters. Jane was as much gratified by this, as her mother could be, though in a quieter way. Elizabeth felt Jane's pleasure. Mary had heard herself mentioned to Miss Bingley as the most accomplished girl in the neighbourhood; and Catherine and Lydia had been fortunate enough to be never without partners, which was all that they had yet learnt to care for at a ball. They returned therefore in good spirits to Longbourn, the village where they lived, and of which they were the principal inhabitants. They found Mr Bennet still up. With a book he was regardless of time; and on the present occasion he had a good deal of curiosity as to the event of an evening which had raised such splendid expectations. He had rather hoped that all his wife's views on the stranger would be disappointed; but he soon found that he had a very different story to hear.

'Oh! my dear Mr Bennett,' as she entered the room, 'we have had a most delightful evening, a most excellent ball. I wish you had been there. Jane was so admired, nothing could be like it. Every body said how well she looked; and Mr Bingley thought her quite beautiful, and danced with her twice. Only think of *that* my dear; he actually danced with her twice; and she was the only creature in the room that he asked a second time. First of all, he asked Miss Lucas. I was so vexed to see him stand up with her; but, however, he did not admire her at all: indeed, nobody can, you know; and he seemed quite struck with Jane as she was going down the dance. So, he enquired who she was, and got introduced, and asked her for the two next. Then, the two third he danced with Miss King, and the two fourth with Maria Lucas, and the two fifth with Jane again, and the two sixth with Lizzy, and the Boulanger—'

'If he had had any compassion for *me*,' cried her husband impatiently, 'he would not have danced half so much! For God's sake, say no more of his partners. Oh! that he had sprained his ankle in the first dance!'

'Oh! my dear,' continued Mrs Bennet, 'I am quite delighted with him. He is so excessively handsome! and his sisters are charming women. I never in my life saw any thing more elegant than their dresses. I dare say the lace upon Mrs Hurst's gown—'

Here she was interrupted again. Mr Bennet protested against any description of finery. She was therefore obliged to seek another branch of the subject, and related, with much bitterness of spirit and some exaggeration, the shocking rudeness of Mr Darcy.

'But I can assure you,' she added, 'that Lizzy does not lose much by not suiting *his* fancy; for he is a most disagreeable, horrid man, not at all worth pleasing. So high and so conceited that there was no enduring him! He walked here, and he walked there, fancying himself so very great! Not handsome enough to dance with! I wish you had been there, my dear, to have given him one of your set downs. I quite detest the man.'

Pride and Prejudice, 1813

[Improvements]

H E HAD been visiting a friend in a neighbouring county, and that friend having recently had his grounds laid out by an improver, Mr Rushworth was returned with his head full of the subject, and very eager to be improving his own place in the same way; and though not saying much to the purpose, could talk of nothing else. The subject had been already handled in the drawing-room; it was revived in the dining-parlour. Miss Bertram's attention and opinion was evidently his chief aim; and though her deportment showed rather conscious superiority than any solicitude to oblige him, the mention of Sotherton Court, and the ideas attached to it, gave her a feeling of complacency, which prevented her from being very ungracious.

'I wish you could see Compton,' said he, 'it is the most complete thing! I never saw a place so altered in my life. I told Smith I did not know where I was. The approach *now* is one of the finest things in the country. You see the house in the most surprising manner. I declare when I got back to Sotherton yesterday, it looked like a prison – quite a dismal old prison.'

'Oh! for shame!' cried Mrs Norris. 'A prison, indeed! Sotherton Court is the noblest old place in the world.'

'It wants improvement, ma'am, beyond any thing. I never saw a place that wanted so much improvement in my life; and it is so forlorn, that I do not know what can be done with it.'

'No wonder that Mr Rushworth should think so at present,' said Mrs Grant to Mrs Norris, with a smile; 'but depend upon it, Sotherton will have *every* improvement in time which his heart can desire.'

'I must try to do something with it,' said Mr Rushworth, 'but I do not know what. I hope I shall have some good friend to help me.'

'Your best friend upon such an occasion,' said Miss Bertram, calmly, 'would be Mr Repton, I imagine.'

'That is what I was thinking of. As he has done so well by Smith, I think I had better have him at once. His terms are five guineas a day.'

'Well, and if they were *ten*,' cried Mrs Norris, 'I am sure *you* need not regard it. The expense need not be any impediment. If I were you, I should not think of the expense. I would have every thing done in the best style, and made as nice as possible. Such a place as Sotherton Court deserves every thing that taste and money can do. You have space to work upon there, and grounds that will well reward you. For my own part, if I had any thing within the fiftieth part of the size of Sotherton, I should be always planting and improving, for naturally I am excessively fond of it. It would be too ridiculous of me to attempt any thing where I am now, with my little half acre. It would be quite a burlesque. But if I had more room, I should take a prodigious delight in improving and planting. We did a vast deal in that way at the parsonage; we made it quite a different place from what it was when we first had it. You young ones do not remember much about it, perhaps. But if dear Sir Thomas were here, he could tell you what improvements we made; and a great deal more would have been done, but for poor Mr Norris's sad state of health. He could hardly ever get out, poor man, to enjoy any thing, and *that* disheartened me from doing several things that Sir Thomas and I used to talk of. If it had not been for *that*, we should have carried on the garden wall, and made the plantation to shut out the churchyard, just as Dr Grant has done. We were always doing something, as it was. It was only the spring twelvemonth before Mr Norris's death, that we put in the apricot against the stable wall, which is now grown such a noble tree, and getting to such perfection, sir,' addressing herself then to Dr Grant.

'The tree thrives well beyond a doubt, madam,' replied Dr Grant. 'The soil is good; and I never pass it without regretting, that the fruit should be so little worth the trouble of gathering.'

'Sir, it is a moor park, we bought it as a moor park, and it cost us – that is, it was a present from Sir Thomas, but I saw the bill, and I know it cost seven shillings, and was charged as a moor park.'

'You were imposed on, ma'am,' replied Dr Grant; 'these potatoes have as much the flavour of a moor park apricot, as the fruit from that tree. It is an insipid fruit at the best; but a good apricot is eatable, which none from my garden are.'

'The truth is, ma'am,' said Mrs Grant, pretending to whisper across the table to Mrs Norris, 'that Dr Grant hardly knows what the natural taste of our apricot is; he is scarcely ever indulged with one, for it is so valuable a fruit, with a little assistance, and ours is such a remarkably large, fair sort, that what with early tarts and preserves, my cook contrives to get them all.'

Mrs Norris, who had begun to redden, was appeased, and, for a little while, other subjects took place of the improvements of Sotherton. Dr Grant and Mrs Norris were seldom good friends; their acquaintance had begun in dilapidations, and their habits were totally dissimilar.

After a short interruption, Mr Rushworth began again. 'Smith's place is the admiration of all the country; and it was a mere nothing before Repton took it in hand. I think I shall have Repton.'

'Mr Rushworth,' said Lady Bertram, 'if I were you, I would have a very pretty shrubbery. One likes to get out into a shrubbery in fine weather.'

Mr Rushworth was eager to assure her ladyship of his acquiescence, and tried to make out something complimentary; but between his submission to *her* taste, and his having always intended the same himself, with the super-added objects of professing attention to the comfort of ladies in general, and of insinuating, that there was one only whom he was anxious to please, he grew puzzled; and Edmund was glad to put an end to his speech by a proposal of wine. Mr Rushworth, however, though not usually a great talker, had still more to say on the subject next his heart. 'Smith has not much above a hundred acres altogether in his grounds, which is little enough, and makes it more surprising that the place can have been so improved. Now, at Sotherton, we have a good seven hundred, without reckoning the water meadows; so that I think, if so much could be done at Compton, we need not despair. There have been two or three fine old trees cut down that grew too near the house, and it opens the prospect amazingly, which makes me think that Repton, or any body of that sort, would certainly have the avenue at Sotherton down; the avenue that leads from the west front to the top of the hill you know,' turning to Miss Bertram particularly as he spoke. But Miss Bertram thought it most becoming to reply:

'The avenue! Oh! I do not recollect it. I really know very little of Sotherton.'

Fanny, who was sitting on the other side of Edmund, exactly opposite Miss Crawford, and who had been attentively listening, now looked at him, and said in a low voice,

'Cut down an avenue! What a pity! Does not it make you think of Cowper? "Ye fallen avenues, once more I mourn your fate unmerited."'

He smiled as he answered, 'I am afraid the avenue stands a bad chance, Fanny.'

'I should like to see Sotherton before it is cut down, to see the place as it is now, in its old state; but I do not suppose I shall.'

'Have you never been there? No, you never can; and unluckily it is out of distance for a ride. I wish we could contrive it.'

'Oh! it does not signify. Whenever I do see it, you will tell me how it has been altered.'

'I collect,' said Miss Crawford, 'that Sotherton is an old place, and a place of some grandeur. In any particular style of building?'

'The house was built in Elizabeth's time, and is a large, regular, brick building – heavy, but respectable looking, and has many good rooms. It is ill placed. It stands in one of the lowest spots of the park; in that respect, unfavourable for improvement. But the woods are fine, and there is a stream, which, I dare say, might be made a good deal of. Mr Rushworth is quite right, I think, in meaning to give it a modern dress, and I have no doubt that it will be all done extremely well.'

Miss Crawford listened with submission, and said to herself, 'He is a well bred man; he makes the best of it.'

'I do not wish to influence Mr Rushworth,' he continued, 'but had I a place to new fashion, I should not put myself in the hands of an improver. I would rather have an inferior degree of beauty, of my own choice, and acquired progressively. I would rather abide by my own blunders than by his.'

'*You* would know what you were about of course – but that would not suit *me*. I have no eye or ingenuity for such matters, but as they are before me; and had I a place of my own in the country, I should be most thankful to any Mr Repton who would undertake it, and give me as much beauty as he could for my money; and I should never look at it, till it was complete.'

'It would be delightful to *me* to see the progress of it all,' said Fanny.

Mansfield Park, 1814

[Match-Making]

MR KNIGHTLEY, in fact, was one of the few people who could see faults in Emma Woodhouse, and the only one who ever told her of them: and though this was not particularly agreeable to Emma herself, she knew it would be so much less so to her father, that she would not have him really suspect such a circumstance as her not being thought perfect by every body.

'Emma knows I never flatter her,' said Mr Knightley; 'but I meant no reflection on any body. Miss Taylor has been used to have two persons to please; she will now have but one. The chances are that she must be a gainer.'

'Well,' said Emma, willing to let it pass – 'you want to hear about the wedding, and I shall be happy to tell you, for we all behaved charmingly. Every body was punctual, every body in their best looks. Not a tear, and hardly a long face to be seen. Oh! no, we all felt that we were going to be only half a mile apart, and were sure of meeting every day.'

'Dear Emma bears every thing so well,' said her father. 'But, Mr Knightley, she is really very sorry to lose poor Miss Taylor, and I am sure she *will* miss her more than she thinks for.'

Emma turned away her head, divided between tears and smiles.

'It is impossible that Emma should not miss such a companion,' said Mr Knightley. 'We should not like her so well as we do, sir, if we could suppose it. But she knows how much the marriage is to Miss Taylor's advantage; she knows how very acceptable it must be at Miss Taylor's time of life to be settled in a home of her own, and how important to her to be secure of a comfortable provision, and therefore cannot allow herself to feel so much pain as pleasure. Every friend of Miss Taylor must be glad to have her so happily married.'

'And you have forgotten one matter of joy to me,' said Emma, 'and a very considerable one – that I made the match myself. I made the match, you know, four years ago; and to have it take place, and be proved in the right, when so many people said Mr Weston would never marry again, may comfort me for any thing.'

Mr Knightley shook his head at her. Her father fondly replied, 'Ah! my dear, I wish you would not make matches and foretell things, for whatever you say always comes to pass. Pray do not make any more matches.'

'I promise you to make none for myself, papa; but I must, indeed, for other people. It is the greatest amusement in the world! And after such success you know! – Every body said that Mr Weston would never marry again. Oh dear, no! Mr Weston, who had been a widower so long, and who seemed so perfectly comfortable without a wife, so constantly occupied either in his business in town or among his friends here, always acceptable wherever he went, always cheerful – Mr Weston need not spend a single evening in the year alone if he did not like it. Oh, no! Mr Weston certainly would never marry again. Some people even talked of a promise to his wife on her death-bed, and others of the son and the uncle not letting him. All manner of solemn nonsense was talked on the subject, but I believed none of it. Ever since the day (about four years ago) that Miss Taylor and I met with him in Broadway Lane, when, because it began to mizzle, he darted away with so much gallantry, and borrowed two umbrellas for us from Farmer Mitchell's, I made up my mind on the subject. I planned the match from that hour; and when such success has blessed me in this instance, dear papa, you cannot think that I shall leave off match-making.'

'I do not understand what you mean by "success",' said Mr Knightley. 'Success supposes endeavour. Your time has been properly and delicately spent, if you have been endeavouring for the last four years to bring about this marriage. A worthy employment for a young lady's mind! But if, which I rather imagine, your making the match, as you call it, means only your planning it, your saying to yourself one idle day, "I think it would be a very good thing for Miss Taylor if Mr Weston were to marry her," and saying it again to yourself every now and then afterwards – why do you talk of success? where is your merit? – what are you proud of? – you made a lucky guess; and *that* is all that can be said.'

'And have you never known the pleasure and triumph of a lucky guess? – I pity you. – I thought you cleverer – for depend upon it, a lucky guess is never merely luck. There is always some talent in it. And as to my poor word "success", which you quarrel with, I do not know that I am so entirely without any claim to it. You have drawn two pretty pictures – but I think there may be a third – a something between the do-nothing and the do-all. If I had not promoted Mr Weston's visits here, and given many little encouragements, and smoothed many little matters, it might not have come to any thing after all. I think you must know Hartfield enough to comprehend that.'

'A straight-forward, open-hearted man, like Weston, and a rational unaffected woman, like Miss Taylor, may be safely left to manage their own concerns. You are more likely to have done harm to yourself, than good to them, by interference.'

'Emma never thinks of herself, if she can do good to others,' rejoined Mr Woodhouse, understanding but in part. 'But, my dear, pray do not make any more matches, they are silly things, and break up one's family circle grievously.'

'Only one more, papa; only for Mr Elton. Poor Mr Elton! You like Mr Elton, papa, – I must look about for a wife for him. There is nobody in Highbury who deserves him – and he has been here a whole year, and has fitted up his house so comfortably that it would be a shame to have him single any longer – and I thought when he was joining their hands today, he looked so very much as if he would like to have the same kind office done for him! I think very well of Mr Elton, and this is the only way I have of doing him a service.'

'Mr Elton is a very pretty young man to be sure, and a

very good young man, and I have a great regard for him.
But if you want to show him any attention, my dear, ask
him to come and dine with us some day. That will be a
much better thing. I dare say Mr Knightley will be so kind
as to meet him.'

'With a great deal of pleasure, sir, at any time,' said Mr
Knightley laughing; 'and I agree with you entirely that it
will be a much better thing. Invite him to dinner, Emma,
and help him to the best of the fish and the chicken, but
leave him to choose his own wife. Depend upon it, a man of
six- or seven-and-twenty can take care of himself.'

Emma, 1816

[Romance]

THEY MET by appointment; and as Isabella had arrived
nearly five minutes before her friend, her first address
naturally was – 'My dearest creature, what can have made
you so late? I have been waiting for you at least this age!'

'Have you, indeed! – I am very sorry for it; but really I
thought I was in very good time. It is but just one. I hope
you have not been here long?'

'Oh! these ten ages at least. I am sure I have been here
this half hour. But now, let us go and sit down at the other
end of the room, and enjoy ourselves. I have an hundred
things to say to you. In the first place, I was so afraid it
would rain this morning, just as I wanted to set off; it looked
very showery, and that would have thrown me into agonies!
Do you know, I saw the prettiest hat you can imagine, in a
shop window in Milsom Street just now – very like yours,
only with coquelicot ribbons instead of green; I quite longed
for it. But, my dearest Catherine, what have you been doing
with yourself all this morning? – Have you gone on with
Udolpho?'

'Yes, I have been reading it ever since I woke; and I am
got to the black veil.'

'Are you, indeed? How delightful! Oh! I would not tell you what is behind the black veil for the world! Are you not wild to know?'

'Oh! yes, quite; what can it be? – But do not tell me – I would not be told upon any account. I know it must be a skeleton, I am sure it is Laurentina's skeleton. Oh! I am delighted with the book! I should like to spend my whole life in reading it. I assure you, if it had not been to meet you, I would not have come away from it for all the world.'

'Dear creature! how much I am obliged to you; and when you have finished *Udolpho*, we will read *The Italian* together; and I have made out a list of ten or twelve more of the same kind for you.'

'Have you, indeed! How glad I am! – What are they all?'

'I will read you their names directly; here they are, in my pocket-book. *Castle of Wolfenbach, Clermont, Mysterious Warnings, Necromancer of the Black Forest, Midnight Bell, Orphan of the Rhine,* and *Horrid Mysteries*. Those will last us some time.'

'Yes, pretty well; but are they all horrid, are you sure they are all horrid?'

'Yes, quite sure; for a particular friend of mine, a Miss Andrews, a sweet girl, one of the sweetest creatures in the world, has read every one of them. I wish you knew Miss Andrews, you would be delighted with her. She is netting herself the sweetest cloak you can conceive. I think her as beautiful as an angel, and I am so vexed with the men for not admiring her! – I scold them all amazingly about it.'

'Scold them! Do you scold them for not admiring her?'

'Yes, that I do. There is nothing I would not do for those who are really my friends. I have no notion of loving people by halves, it is not my nature. My attachments are always excessively strong. I told Captain Hunt at one of our assemblies this winter, that if he was to tease me all night, I would not dance with him, unless he would allow Miss Andrews to be as beautiful as an angel. The men think us incapable of real friendship you know, and I am determined to shew them the difference. Now, if I were to hear any body speak slightingly of you, I should fire up in a moment:

– but that is not at all likely, for *you* are just the kind of girl to be a great favourite with the men.'

'Oh! dear,' cried Catherine, colouring, 'how can you say so?'

'I know you very well; you have so much animation, which is exactly what Miss Andrews wants, for I must confess there is something amazingly insipid about her. Oh! I must tell you, that just after we parted yesterday, I saw a young man looking at you so earnestly – I am sure he is in love with you.' Catherine coloured, and disclaimed again. Isabella laughed. 'It is very true, upon my honour, but I see how it is; you are indifferent to every body's admiration, except that of one gentleman, who shall be nameless. Nay, I cannot blame you – (speaking more seriously) – your feelings are easily understood. Where the heart is really attached, I know very well how little one can be pleased with the attention of any body else. Every thing is so insipid, so uninteresting, that does not relate to the beloved object! I can perfectly comprehend your feelings.'

'But you should not persuade me that I think so very much about Mr Tilney, for perhaps I may never see him again.'

'Not see him again! My dearest creature, do not talk of it. I am sure you would be miserable if you thought so.'

'No, indeed, I should not. I do not pretend to say that I was not very much pleased with him; but while I have *Udolpho* to read, I feel as if nobody could make me miserable. Oh! the dreadful black veil! My dear Isabella, I am sure there must be Laurentina's skeleton behind it.'

'It is so odd to me, that you should never have read *Udolpho* before; but I suppose Mrs Morland objects to novels.'

'No, she does not. She very often reads *Sir Charles Grandison* herself; but new books do not fall in our way.'

'*Sir Charles Grandison*! That is an amazing horrid book, is it not? – I remember Miss Andrews could not get through the first volume.'

'It is not like *Udolpho* at all; but yet I think it is very entertaining.'

'Do you indeed! – you surprise me; I thought it had not been readable. But, my dearest Catherine, have you settled what to wear on your head tonight? I am determined at all events to be dressed exactly like you. The men take notice of *that* sometimes you know.'

'But it does not signify if they do,' said Catherine, very innocently.

'Signify! Oh, heavens! I make it a rule never to mind what they say. They are very often amazingly impertinent if you do not treat them with spirit, and make them keep their distance.'

'Are they? – Well, I never observed *that*. They always behave very well to me.'

'Oh! they give themselves such airs. They are the most conceited creatures in the world, and think themselves of so much importance! – By the bye, though I have thought of it a hundred times, I have always forgot to ask you what is your favourite complexion in a man. Do you like them best dark or fair?'

'I hardly know. I never much thought about it. Something between both, I think. Brown – not fair, and not very dark.'

'Very well, Catherine. That is exactly he. I have not forgot your description of Mr Tilney; – "a brown skin, with dark eyes, and rather dark hair". – Well, my taste is different. I prefer light eyes, and as to complexion – do you know – I like a sallow better than any other. You must not betray me, if you should ever meet with one of your acquaintance answering that description.'

'Betray you! – What do you mean?'

'Nay, do not distress me. I believe I have said too much. Let us drop the subject.'

Catherine, in some amazement, complied; and after remaining a few moments silent, was on the point of reverting to what interested her at that time rather more than any thing else in the world, Laurentina's skeleton; when her friend prevented her, by saying, – 'For Heaven's sake! let us move away from this end of the room. Do you know, there are two odious young men who have been

staring at me this half hour. They really put me quite out of
countenance. Let us go and look at the arrivals. They will
hardly follow us there.'

Northanger Abbey, 1818

ROBERT OWEN

[The Formation of Character]

[*Hitherto the community of New Lanark*] had not been
taught the most valuable domestic and social habits: such as
the most economical method of preparing food; how to
arrange their dwellings with neatness, and to keep them
always clean and in order; but, what was of infinitely more
importance, they had not been instructed how to train their
children to form them into valuable members of the community, or to know what principles existed, which, when
properly applied to practice from infancy, would ensure
from man to man, without chance of failure, a just, open,
sincere, and benevolent conduct.

It was in this stage of the progress of improvement, that
it became necessary to form arrangements for surrounding
them with circumstances which should gradually prepare the
individuals to receive and firmly retain those domestic and
social acquirements and habits. For this purpose a building,
which may be termed the 'new institution', was erected in
the centre of the establishment, with an enclosed area before
it. The area is intended for a playground for the children of
the villagers, from the time they can walk alone until they
enter the school.

It must be evident to those who have been in the practice
of observing children with attention, that much of good or
evil is taught to or acquired by a child at a very early period
of its life; that much of temper or disposition is correctly or
incorrectly formed before he attains his second year; and
that many durable impressions are made at the termination

of the first twelve or even six months of his existence. The children, therefore, of the uninstructed and ill-instructed, suffer material injury in the formation of their characters during these and the subsequent years of childhood and youth.

It was to prevent, or as much as possible to counteract, these primary evils, to which the poor and working classes are exposed when infants, that the area became part of the New Institution.

Into this playground the children are to be received as soon as they can freely walk alone; to be superintended by persons instructed to take charge of them.

As the happiness of man chiefly, if not altogether, depends on his own sentiments and habits, as well as those of the individuals around him; and as any sentiments and habits may be given to all infants, it becomes of primary importance that those alone should be given to them which can contribute to their happiness. Each child, therefore, on his entrance into the playground, is to be told in language which he can understand, that 'he is never to injure his playfellows; but that, on the contrary, he is to contribute all in his power to make them happy'. This simple precept, when comprehended in all its bearings, and the habits which will arise from its early adoption into practice, *if no counteracting principle be forced upon the young mind*, will effectually supersede all the errors which have hitherto kept the world in ignorance and misery. So simple a precept, too, will be easily taught, and as easily acquired; for the chief employment of the superintendents will be to prevent any deviation from it in practice. The older children, when they shall have experienced the endless advantages from acting on this principle, will, by their example, soon enforce the practice of it on the young strangers: and the happiness, which the little groups will enjoy from this rational conduct, will ensure its speedy and general and willing adoption. The habit also which they will acquire at this early period of life by continually acting on the principle, will fix it firmly; it will become easy and familiar to them, or, as it is often termed, natural.

Thus, by merely attending to the evidence of our senses

respecting human nature, and disregarding the wild, inconsistent, and absurd theories in which man has been hitherto trained in all parts of the earth, we shall accomplish with ease and certainty the supposed Herculean labour of forming a rational character in man, and that, too, chiefly before the child commences the ordinary course of education.

The character thus early formed will be as durable as it will be advantageous to the individual and to the community; for by the constitution of our nature, when once the mind fully understands that which is true, the impression of that truth cannot be erased except by mental disease or death; while error must be relinquished at every period of life, whenever it can be made manifest to the mind in which it has been received. This part of the arrangement, therefore, will effect the following purposes:

The child will be removed, so far as is at present practicable, from the erroneous treatment of the yet untrained and untaught parents.

The parents will be relieved from the loss of time and from the care and anxiety which are now occasioned by attendance on their children from the period when they can go alone to that at which they enter the school.

The child will be placed in a situation of safety, where, with its future schoolfellows and companions, it will acquire the best habits and principles, while at mealtimes and at night it will return to the caresses of its parents; and the affections of each are likely to be increased by the separation.

A New View of Society, 2nd edn, 1816

DAVID RICARDO

On Machinery

EVER SINCE I first turned my attention to questions of political economy, I have been of opinion that such an application of machinery to any branch of production as should have the effect of saving labour was a general good, accompanied only with that portion of inconvenience which in most cases attends the removal of capital and labour from one employment to another. It appeared to me that, provided the landlords had the same money rents, they would be benefited by the reduction in the prices of some of the commodities on which those rents were expended, and which reduction of price could not fail to be the consequence of the employment of machinery. The capitalist, I thought, was eventually benefited precisely in the same manner. He, indeed, who made the discovery of the machine, or who first usefully applied it, would enjoy an additional advantage by making great profits for a time; but, in proportion as the machine came into general use, the price of the commodity produced would, from the effects of competition, sink to its cost of production, when the capitalist would get the same money profits as before, and he would only participate in the general advantage as a consumer, by being enabled, with the same money revenue, to command an additional quantity of comforts and enjoyments. The class of labourers also, I thought, was equally benefited by the use of machinery, as they would have the means of buying more commodities with the same money wages, and I thought that no reduction of wages would take place because the capitalist would have the power of demanding and employing the same quantity of labour as before, although he might be under the necessity of employing it in the production of a new or, at any rate, of a different commodity. If, by improved machinery, with the employment of the same quantity of labour, the quantity of stockings could be quadrupled, and the demand for stockings were only doubled, some labourers would necessarily be discharged from the stocking trade; but as the capital which employed them was still in being, and as it was the interest of those who had it to employ it productively, it appeared to me that it would be employed on the production of some other commodity useful to the society, for which there could not fail to be a demand; for I was, and am, deeply impressed with the truth of the observation of Adam Smith, that 'the desire for food is limited in every man by the narrow capacity of the human stomach, but the desire of the conveniences and ornaments of building, dress, equipage, and household furniture, seems to have no limit or certain boundary'. As, then, it appeared to me that there would be the same demand for labour as before, and that wages would be no lower, I thought that the labouring class would, equally with the other classes, participate in the advantage, from the general cheapness of commodities arising from the use of machinery.

These were my opinions, and they continue unaltered, as far as regards the landlord and the capitalist; but I am convinced that the substitution of machinery for human labour is often very injurious to the interests of the class of labourers.

My mistake arose from the supposition that whenever the net income of a society increased, its gross income would also increase; I now, however, see reason to be satisfied that the one fund, from which landlords and capitalists derive their revenue, may increase, while the other, that upon which the labouring class mainly depend, may diminish, and therefore it follows, if I am right, that the same cause which may increase the net revenue of the country may at the same time render the population redundant, and deteriorate the condition of the labourer.

The Principles of Political Economy
and Taxation, 1817

MARY SHELLEY

[The Monster]

IT WAS on a dreary night of November that I beheld the accomplishment of my toils. With an anxiety that almost amounted to agony, I collected the instruments of life around me, that I might infuse a spark of being into the lifeless thing that lay at my feet. It was already one in the morning; the rain pattered dismally against the panes, and my candle was nearly burnt out, when, by the glimmer of the half-extinguished light, I saw the dull yellow eye of the creature open; it breathed hard, and a convulsive motion agitated its limbs.

How can I describe my emotions at this catastrophe, or how delineate the wretch whom with such infinite pains and care I had endeavoured to form? His limbs were in proportion, and I had selected his features as beautiful. Beautiful! – Great God! His yellow skin scarcely covered the work of muscles and arteries beneath; his hair was of a lustrous black, and flowing; his teeth of a pearly whiteness; but these luxuriances only formed a more horrid contrast with his watery eyes, that seemed almost of the same colour as the dun white sockets in which they were set, his shrivelled complexion and straight black lips.

The different accidents of life are not so changeable as the feelings of human nature. I had worked hard for nearly two years, for the sole purpose of infusing life into an inanimate body. For this I had deprived myself of rest and health. I had desired it with an ardour that far exceeded moderation; but now that I had finished, the beauty of the dream vanished, and breathless horror and disgust filled my heart. Unable to endure the aspect of the being I had created, I rushed out of the room, and continued a long time traversing my bedchamber, unable to compose my mind to sleep. At length lassitude succeeded to the tumult I had before endured; and I threw myself on the bed in my clothes, endeavouring to seek a few moments of forgetfulness. But it was in vain: I slept, indeed, but I was disturbed by the wildest dreams. I thought I saw Elizabeth, in the bloom of health, walking in the streets of Ingolstadt. Delighted and surprised, I embraced her; but as I imprinted the first kiss on her lips, they became livid with the hue of death; her features appeared to change, and I thought that I held the corpse of my dead mother in my arms; a shroud enveloped her form, and I saw the grave-worms crawling in the folds of the flannel. I started from my sleep with horror;

a cold dew covered my forehead, my teeth chattered, and every limb became convulsed: when, by the dim and yellow light of the moon, as it forced its way through the window shutters, I beheld the wretch – the miserable monster whom I had created. He held up the curtain of the bed; and his eyes, if eyes they may be called, were fixed on me. His jaws opened, and he muttered some inarticulate sounds, while a grin wrinkled his cheeks. He might have spoken, but I did not hear; one hand was stretched out, seemingly to detain me, but I escaped, and rushed down stairs. I took refuge in the courtyard belonging to the house which I inhabited; where I remained during the rest of the night, walking up and down in the greatest agitation, listening attentively, catching and fearing each sound as if it were to announce the approach of the demoniacal corpse to which I had so miserably given life.

Oh! no mortal could support the horror of that counten-ance. A mummy again endued with animation could not be so hideous as that wretch. I had gazed on him while unfinished; he was ugly then; but when those muscles and joints were rendered capable of motion, it became a thing such as even Dante could not have conceived.

I passed the night wretchedly. Sometimes my pulse beat so quickly and hardly that I felt the palpitation of every artery; at others, I nearly sank to the ground through languor and extreme weakness. Mingled with this horror, I felt the bitterness of disappointment; dreams that had been my food and pleasant rest for so long a space were now become a hell to me; and the change was so rapid, the overthrow so complete!

Morning, dismal and wet, at length dawned, and dis-covered to my sleepless and aching eyes the church of Ingolstadt, its white steeple and clock, which indicated the sixth hour. The porter opened the gates of the court, which had that night been my asylum, and I issued into the streets, pacing them with quick steps, as if I sought to avoid the wretch whom I feared every turning of the street would present to my view. I did not dare return to the apartment which I inhabited, but felt impelled to hurry on, although drenched by the rain which poured from a black and comfortless sky.

Frankenstein; or, The Modern Prometheus, 1818

THOMAS LOVE PEACOCK
[Table-Talk]

SCYTHROP, ATTENDING one day the summons to dinner, found in the drawing-room his friend Mr Cypress the poet, whom he had known at college, and who was a great favourite of Mr Glowry. Mr Cypress said, he was on the point of leaving England, but could not think of doing so without a farewell-look at Nightmare Abbey and his respected friends, the moody Mr Glowry and the mysterious Mr Scythrop, the sublime Mr Flosky and the pathetic Mr Listless; to all of whom, and the morbid hospitality of the melancholy dwelling in which they were then assembled, he assured them he should always look back with as much affection as his lacerated spirit could feel for anything. The sympathetic condolence of their respective replies was cut short by Raven's announcement of 'dinner on table'.

The conversation that took place when the wine was in circulation, and the ladies were withdrawn, we shall report with our usual scrupulous fidelity.

MR GLOWRY. You are leaving England, Mr Cypress. There is a delightful melancholy in saying farewell to an old acquaintance, when the chances are twenty to one against ever meeting again. A smiling bumper to a sad parting, and let us all be unhappy together.

MR CYPRESS (*filling a bumper*). This is the only social habit that the disappointed spirit never unlearns.

THE REVEREND MR LARYNX (*filling*). It is the only piece of academical learning that the finished educatee retains.

MR FLOSKY (*filling*). It is the only objective fact which the sceptic can realize.

SCYTHROP (*filling*). It is the only styptic for a bleeding heart.

THE HONOURABLE MR LISTLESS (*filling*). It is the only trouble that is very well worth taking.

MR ASTERIAS (*filling*). It is the only key of conversational truth.

MR TOOBAD (*filling*). It is the only antidote to the great wrath of the devil.

MR HILARY (*filling*). It is the only symbol of perfect life. The inscription 'HIC NON BIBITUR' ['*Here you will not drink*'] will suit nothing but a tombstone.

MR GLOWRY. You will see many fine old ruins, Mr Cypress; crumbling pillars, and mossy walls – many a one-legged Venus and headless Minerva – many a Neptune buried in sand – many a Jupiter turned topsy-turvy – many a perforated Bacchus doing duty as a water-pipe – many reminiscences of the ancient world, which I hope was better worth living in than the modern; though, for myself, I care not a straw more for one than the other, and would not go twenty miles to see anything that either could show.

MR CYPRESS. It is something to seek, Mr Glowry. The mind is restless, and must persist in seeking, though to find is to be disappointed. Do you feel no aspirations towards the countries of Socrates and Cicero? No wish to wander among the venerable remains of the greatness that has passed for ever?

MR GLOWRY. Not a grain.

SCYTHROP. It is, indeed, much the same as if a lover should dig up the buried form of his mistress, and gaze upon relics which are anything but herself, to wander among a few mouldy ruins, that are only imperfect indexes to lost volumes of glory, and meet at every step the more melancholy ruins of human nature – a degenerate race of stupid and shrivelled slaves, grovelling in the lowest depths of servility and superstition.

THE HONOURABLE MR LISTLESS. It is the fashion to go abroad. I have thought of it myself, but am hardly equal to the exertion. To be sure, a little eccentricity and originality are allowable in some cases; and the most eccentric and original of all characters is an Englishman who stays at home.

SCYTHROP. I should have no pleasure in visiting countries that are past all hope of regeneration. There is great hope of our own; and it seems to me that an Englishman, who, either by his station in society, or by his genius, or (as in your instance, Mr Cypress) by both, has the power of essentially serving his country in its arduous struggle with its domestic enemies, yet forsakes his country, which is still so rich in hope, to dwell in others which are only fertile in the ruins of memory, does what none of those ancients, whose fragmentary memorials you venerate, would have done in similar circumstances.

MR CYPRESS. Sir, I have quarrelled with my wife; and a man who has quarrelled with his wife is absolved from all duty to his country. I have written an ode to tell the people as much, and they may take it as they list.

SCYTHROP. Do you suppose, if Brutus had quarrelled with his wife, he would have given it as a reason to Cassius for having nothing to do with his enterprise? Or would Cassius have been satisfied with such an excuse?

MR FLOSKY. Brutus was a senator; so is our dear friend: but the cases are different. Brutus had some hope of political good: Mr Cypress has none. How should he, after what we have seen in France?

SCYTHROP. A Frenchman is born in harness, ready saddled, bitted, and bridled, for any tyrant to ride. He will fawn under his rider one moment, and throw him and kick him to death the next; but another adventurer springs on his back, and by dint of whip and spur on he goes as before. We may, without much vanity, hope better of ourselves.

MR CYPRESS. I have no hope for myself or for others. Our life is a false nature; it is not in the harmony of things; it is an all-blasting upas, whose root is earth, and whose leaves are the skies which rain their poison-dews upon mankind. We wither from our youth; we gasp with unslaked thirst for unattainable good; lured from the first to the last by phantoms – love, fame, ambition, avarice – all idle, and all ill – one meteor of many names, that vanishes in the smoke of death.

MR FLOSKY. A most delightful speech, Mr Cypress. A most amiable and instructive philosophy. You have only to impress its truth on the minds of all living men, and life will then, indeed, be the desert and the solitude; and I must do you, myself, and our mutual friends, the justice to observe, that let society only give fair play at one and the same time, as I flatter myself it is inclined to do, to your system of morals, and my system of metaphysics, and Scythrop's system of politics, and Mr Listless's system of manners, and Mr Toobad's system of religion, and the result will be as fine a mental chaos as even the immortal Kant himself could ever have hoped to see; in the prospect of which I rejoice.

Nightmare Abbey, 1818

MARY RUSSELL MITFORD
[Conjugal Discipline]

WE ARE not yet arrived within sight of Master Weston's cottage, snugly hidden behind a clump of elms; but we are in full hearing of Dame Weston's tongue, raised as usual to scolding pitch. The Westons are new arrivals in our neighbourhood, and the first thing heard of them was a complaint from the wife to our magistrate of her husband's beating her: it was a regular charge of assault – an information in full form. A most piteous case did Dame Weston make of it, softening her voice for the nonce into a shrill tremulous whine, and exciting the mingled pity and anger – pity towards herself, anger towards her husband – of the whole female world, pitiful and indignant as the female world is wont to be on such occasions. Every woman in the parish railed at Master Weston; and poor Master Weston was summoned to attend the bench on the ensuing Saturday, and answer the charge; and such was the clamour abroad and at home, that the unlucky culprit, terrified at the sound of a warrant and a constable, ran away, and was not heard of for a fortnight.

At the end of that time he was discovered, and brought to the bench; and Dame Weston again told her story, and, as before, on the full cry. She had no witnesses, and the bruises of which she made complaint had disappeared, and there were no women present to make common cause with the sex. Still, however, the general feeling was against Master Weston; and it would have gone hard with him when he was called in, if a most unexpected witness had not risen up in his favour. His wife had brought in her arms a little girl about eighteen months old, partly perhaps to move compassion in her favour; for a woman with a child in her arms is always an object that excites kind feelings. The little girl had looked shy and frightened, and had been as quiet as a lamb during her mother's examination; but she no sooner saw her father, from whom she had been a fortnight separated, than she clapped her hands, and laughed, and cried, 'Daddy! daddy!' and sprang into his arms, and hung round his neck, and covered him with kisses – again shouting, 'Daddy, come home! daddy! daddy!' – and finally nestled her little head in his bosom, with a fulness of contentment, an assurance of tenderness and protection such as no wife-beating tyrant ever did inspire, or ever could inspire, since the days of King Solomon. Our magistrates acted in the very spirit of the Jewish monarch: they accepted the evidence of nature, and dismissed the complaint. And subsequent events have fully justified their decision; Mistress Weston proving not only renowned for the feminine accomplishment of scolding (tongue-banging, it is called in our parts, a compound word which deserves to be Greek), but is actually herself addicted to administering the conjugal discipline, the infliction of which she was pleased to impute to her luckless husband.

Our Village, 1819

CHARLES MATURIN

[Amateurs in Suffering]

IT IS actually possible to become *amateurs in suffering.* I
have heard of men who have travelled into countries
where horrible executions were to be daily witnessed, for
the sake of that excitement which the sight of suffering
never fails to give, from the spectacle of a tragedy, or an
auto da fe, down to the writhings of the meanest reptile on
whom you can inflict torture, and feel that torture is the
result of your own power. It is a species of feeling of which
we never can divest ourselves, – a triumph over those whose
sufferings have placed them below us, and no wonder, –
suffering is always an indication of weakness, – we glory in
our impenetrability. *I* did, as we burst into the cell. The
wretched husband and wife were locked in each other's
arms. You may imagine the scene that followed. Here I
must do the Superior reluctant justice. He was a man (of
course from his conventual feelings) who had no more idea
of the intercourse between the sexes, than between two
beings of a different species. The scene that he beheld could
not have revolted him more, than if he had seen the horrible
loves of the baboons and the Hottentot women, at the Cape
of Good Hope; or those still more loathsome unions
between the serpents of South America and their human
victims, when they can catch them, and twine round them
in folds of unnatural and ineffable union. He really stood as
much astonished and appalled, to see two human beings of
different sexes, who dared to love each other in spite of
monastic ties, as if he had witnessed the horrible conjunctions
I have alluded to. Had he seen vipers engendering in that
frightful knot which seems the pledge of mortal hostility,
instead of love, he could not have testified more horror, –
and I do him the justice to believe he felt all he testified.
Whatever affectation he might employ on points of conventual austerity, there was none here. Love was a thing he
always believed connected with sin, even though conse-

crated by the name of a sacrament, and called marriage, as it is in our church. But, love in a convent! – Oh, there is no conceiving his rage; still less is it possible to conceive the majestic and overwhelming extent of that rage, when strengthened by principle, and sanctified by religion. I enjoyed the scene beyond all power of description. I saw those wretches, who had triumphed over me, reduced to my level in a moment, – their passions all displayed, and the display placing me a hero triumphant above all. I had crawled to the shelter of their walls, a wretched degraded outcast, and what was my crime? Well, – you shudder, I have done with that. I can only say what drove me to it. And here were beings whom, a few months before, I would have knelt to as to the images round the shrine, – to whom, in the moments of my desperate penitence, I would have clung as to the 'horns of the altar', all brought as low, and lower than myself. 'Sons of the morning', as I deemed them in the agonies of my humiliation, 'how were they fallen!' I feasted on the degradation of the apostate monk and novice, – I enjoyed, to the core of my ulcerated heart, the passion of the Superior, – I felt that they were all men like myself. Angels, as I had thought them, they had all proved themselves mortal; and, by watching their motions, and flattering their passions, and promoting their interest, or setting up my own in opposition to them all, while I made them believe it was only theirs I was intent on, I might make shift to contrive as much misery to others, and to carve out as much occupation to myself, as if I were actually living in the world. Cutting my father's throat was a noble feat certainly, (I ask your pardon, I did not mean to extort that groan from you), but here were hearts to be cut, – and to the core every day, and all day long, so I never could want employment.

Melmoth the Wanderer, 1820

JAMES HENRY LEIGH HUNT

[Getting Up on Cold Mornings]

S OME PEOPLE say it is a very easy thing to get up of a cold morning. You have only, they tell you, to take the resolution; and the thing is done. This may be very true; just as a boy at school has only to take a flogging, and the thing is over. But we have not at all made up our minds upon it; and we find it a very pleasant exercise to discuss the matter, candidly, before we get up. This at least is not idling, though it may be lying. It affords an excellent answer to those, who ask how lying in bed can be indulged in by a reasoning being – a rational creature. How? Why, with the argument calmly at work in one's head, and the clothes over one's shoulder. Oh – it is a fine way of spending a sensible, impartial half-hour.

If these people would be more charitable, they would get on with their argument better. But they are apt to reason so ill, and to assert so dogmatically, that one could wish to have them stand round one's bed of a bitter morning, and lie before their faces. They ought to hear both sides of the bed, the inside and out. If they cannot entertain themselves with their own thoughts for half an hour or so, it is not the fault of those who can. If their will is never pulled aside by the enticing arms of imagination, so much the luckier for the stage-coachman.

Candid inquiries into one's decumbency, besides the greater or less privileges to be allowed a man in proportion to his ability of keeping early hours, the work given his faculties, etc., will at least concede their due merits to such representations as the following. In the first place, says the injured but calm appealer, I have been warm all night, and find my system in a state perfectly suitable to a warm-blooded animal. To get out of this state into the cold, besides the inharmonious and uncritical abruptness of the transition, is so unnatural to such a creature, that the poets, refining upon the tortures of the damned, make one of their greatest agonies consist in being suddenly transported from heat to cold – from fire to ice. They are 'haled' out of their 'beds', says Milton, by 'harpy-footed furies' – fellows who come to call them. On my first movement towards the anticipation of getting up, I find that such parts of the sheets and bolster, as are exposed to the air of the room, are stone-cold. On opening my eyes, the first thing that meets them is my own breath rolling forth, as if in the open air, like smoke out of a cottage chimney. Think of this symptom. Then I turn my eyes sideways and see the window all frozen over. Think of that. Then the servant comes in. 'It is very cold this morning, is it not?' – 'Very cold, sir.' – 'Very cold indeed, isn't it?' – 'Very cold indeed, sir.' – 'More than usually so, isn't it, even for this weather?' (Here the servant's wit and good-nature are put to a considerable test, and the inquirer lies on thorns for the answer.) 'Why, sir . . . I think it *is*.' (Good creature! There is not a better, or more truth-telling servant going.) 'I must rise, however – get me some warm water.' – Here comes a fine interval between the departure of the servant and the arrival of the hot water; during which, of course, it is of 'no use' to get up. The hot water comes. 'Is it quite hot?' – 'Yes, sir.' – 'Perhaps too hot for shaving: I must wait a little?' – 'No, sir; it will just do.' (There is an over-nice propriety sometimes, an officious zeal of virtue, a little troublesome.) 'Oh – the shirt – you must air my clean shirt; – linen gets very damp this weather.' – 'Yes, sir.' Here another delicious five minutes. A knock at the door. 'Oh, the shirt – very well. My stockings – I think the stockings had better be aired too.' – 'Very well, sir.' – Here another interval. At length everything is ready, except myself. I now, continues our incumbent (a happy word, by the bye, for a country vicar) – I now cannot help thinking a good deal – who can? – upon the unnecessary and villainous custom of shaving: it is a thing so unmanly (here I nestle closer) – so effeminate (here I recoil from an unlucky step into the colder part of the bed). – No wonder that the Queen of France took part with the rebels against the degenerate King, her husband, who first affronted her smooth visage with a face like her own. The Emperor Julian never showed the luxuriancy of his genius to better advantage than in reviving the flowing beard. Look at Cardinal Bembo's picture – at Michael Angelo's – at Titian's – at Shakespeare's – at Fletcher's – at Spenser's – at Chaucer's – at Alfred's – at Plato's – I could name a great man for every tick of my watch. – Look at the Turks, a grave and otiose people. – Think of Haroun Al Raschid and Bed-ridden Hassan. – Think of Wortley Montagu, the worthy son of his mother, a man above the prejudice of his time. – Look at the Persian gentlemen, whom one is ashamed of meeting about the suburbs, their dress and appearance are so much finer than our own. – Lastly, think of the razor itself – how totally opposed to every sensation of bed – how cold, how edgy, how hard! how utterly different from anything like the warm and circling amplitude, which 'Sweetly recommends itself Unto our gentle senses'. Add to this, benumbed fingers, which may help you to cut yourself, a quivering body, a frozen towel, and a ewer full of ice; and he that says there is nothing to oppose in all this, only shows, at any rate, that he has no merit in opposing it.

Thomson the poet, who exclaims in his Seasons – 'Falsely luxurious! Will not man awake?' used to lie in bed till noon, because he said he had no motive in getting up. He could imagine the good of rising; but then he could also imagine the good of lying still; and his exclamation, it must be allowed, was made upon summer-time, not winter. We must proportion the argument to the individual character. A money-getter may be drawn out of his bed by three and fourpence; but this will not suffice for a student. A proud man may say, 'What shall I think of myself, if I don't get up?' but the more humble one will be content to waive his prodigious notion of himself, out of respect to his kindly bed. The mechanical man shall get up without any ado at all; and so shall the barometer. An ingenious lier in bed will find hard matter of discussion even on the score of health and longevity. He will ask us for our proofs and precedents of the ill effects of lying later in cold weather; and sophisticate much on the advantages of an even temperature of body; of the natural propensity (pretty universal) to have one's way; and of the animals that roll themselves up, and sleep all the winter. As to longevity, he will ask whether the longest life is of necessity the best; and whether Holborn is the handsomest street in London.

The Indicator, 1820

THOMAS DE QUINCEY

[Ann]

BEING MYSELF at that time of necessity a peripatetic, or a walker of the streets, I naturally fell in more frequently with those female peripatetics who are technically called street-walkers. Many of these women had occasionally taken my part against watchmen who wished to drive me off the steps of houses where I was sitting. But one amongst them, the one on whose account I have at all introduced this subject – yet no! let me not class thee, oh noble-minded Ann, with that order of women; let me find, if it be possible, some gentler name to designate the condition of her to whose bounty and compassion, ministering to my necessities when all the world had forsaken me, I owe it that I am at this time alive. – For many weeks I had walked at nights with this poor friendless girl up and down Oxford-street, or had rested with her on steps and under the shelter of porticos. She could not be so old as myself; she told me, indeed, that she had not completed her sixteenth year. By such questions as my interest about her prompted, I had gradually drawn forth her simple history. Hers was a case of ordinary occurrence (as I have since had reason to think), and one which, if London beneficence had better adapted its arrangements to meet it, the power of the law might oftener be interposed to protect, and to avenge. But the stream of London charity flows in a channel which, though deep and mighty, is yet noiseless and underground; not obvious or readily accessible to poor houseless wanderers: and it cannot be denied that the outside air and framework of London society is harsh, cruel, and repulsive. In any case, however, I saw that part of her injuries might easily have been redressed; and I urged her often and earnestly to lay her complaint before a magistrate: friendless as she was, I assured her that she would meet with immediate attention; and that English justice, which was no respecter of persons, would speedily and amply avenge her on the brutal ruffian who had plundered her little property. She promised me often that she would; but she delayed taking the steps I pointed out from time to time; for she was timid and dejected to a degree which showed how deeply sorrow had taken hold of her young heart: and perhaps she thought justly that the most upright judge, and the most righteous tribunals, could do nothing to repair her heaviest wrongs. Something, however, would perhaps have been done: for it had been settled between us at length, but unhappily on the very last time but one that I was ever to see her, that in a day or two we should go together before a magistrate, and that I should speak on her behalf. This little service it was destined, however, that I should never realize. Meantime, that which she rendered to me, and which was greater than I could ever have repaid her, was this: – One night, when we were pacing slowly along Oxford-street, and after a day when I had felt more than usually ill and faint, I requested her to turn off with me into Soho-square: thither we went; and we sat down on the steps of a house, which, to this hour, I never pass without a pang of grief, and an inner act of homage to the spirit of that unhappy girl, in memory of the noble action which she there performed. Suddenly, as we sat, I grew much worse: I had been leaning my head against her bosom; and all at once I sank from her arms and fell backwards on the steps. From the sensations I then had, I felt an inner conviction of the liveliest kind that without some powerful and reviving stimulus, I should either have died on the spot – or should at least have sunk to a point of exhaustion from which all re-ascent under my friendless circumstances would soon have become hopeless. Then it was, at this crisis of my fate, that my poor orphan companion – who had herself met with little but injuries in the world – stretched out a saving hand to me. Uttering a cry of terror, but without a moment's delay, she ran off into

Oxford-street, and in less time than could be imagined, returned to me with a glass of port wine and spices, that acted upon my empty stomach, (which at that time would have rejected all solid food) with an instantaneous power of restoration: and for this glass the generous girl without a murmur paid out of her own humble purse at a time – be it remembered! – when she had scarcely wherewithal to purchase the bare necessaries of life, and when she could have no reason to expect that I should ever be able to reimburse her. – Oh! youthful benefactress! how often in succeeding years, standing in solitary places, and thinking of thee with grief of heart and perfect love, how often have I wished that, as in ancient times the curse of a father was believed to have a supernatural power, and to pursue its object with a fatal necessity of self-fulfilment, – even so the benediction of a heart oppressed with gratitude, might have a like prerogative; might have power given to it from above to chase – to haunt – to way-lay – to overtake – to pursue thee into the central darkness of a London brothel, or (if it were possible) into the darkness of the grave – there to awaken thee with an authentic message of peace and forgiveness, and of final reconciliation!

I do not often weep: for not only do my thoughts on subjects connected with the chief interests of man daily, nay hourly, descend a thousand fathoms 'too deep for tears'; not only does the sternness of my habits of thought present an antagonism to the feelings which prompt tears – wanting of necessity to those who, being protected usually by their levity from any tendency to meditative sorrow, would by that same levity be made incapable of resisting it on any casual access of such feelings: – but also, I believe that all minds which have contemplated such objects as deeply as I have done, must, for their own protection from utter despondency, have early encouraged and cherished some tranquillizing belief as to the future balances and the hieroglyphic meanings of human sufferings. On these accounts, I am cheerful to this hour; and, as I have said, I do not often weep. Yet some feelings, though not deeper or more passionate, are more tender than others; and often, when I walk at this time in Oxford-street by dreamy lamp-light, and

hear those airs played on a barrel-organ which years ago
solaced me and my dear companion (as I must always call
her), I shed tears. . . .

Confessions of an English Opium-Eater, 1821

SIR WALTER SCOTT

[The Murder of Amy Dudley]

O N THE next day, when evening approached, Varney
summoned Foster to the execution of their plan. Tider
and Foster's old man-servant were sent on a feigned errand
down to the village, and Anthony himself, as if anxious to
see that the Countess suffered no want of accommodation,
visited her place of confinement. He was so much staggered
at the mildness and patience with which she seemed to
endure her confinement, that he could not help earnestly
recommending to her not to cross the threshold of her room
on any account whatever, until Lord Leicester should come,
'Which,' he added, 'I trust in God, will be very soon.' Amy
patiently promised that she would resign herself to her fate,
and Foster returned to his hardened companion with his
conscience half-eased of the perilous load that weighed on
it. 'I have warned her,' he said; 'surely in vain is the snare
set in sight of any bird!'

He left, therefore, the Countess's door unsecured on the
outside, and, under the eye of Varney, withdrew the supports which sustained the falling trap, which, therefore, kept
its level position merely by a slight adhesion. They withdrew
to wait the issue on the ground-floor adjoining, but they
waited long in vain. At length Varney, after walking long to
and fro, with his face muffled in his cloak, threw it suddenly
back, and exclaimed, 'Surely never was a woman fool
enough to neglect so fair an opportunity of escape!'

'Perhaps she is resolved,' said Foster, 'to await her
husband's return.'

'True! – most true,' said Varney, rushing out, 'I had not thought of that before.'

In less than two minutes, Foster, who remained behind, heard the tread of a horse in the court-yard, and then a whistle similar to that which was the Earl's usual signal; – the instant after the door of the Countess's chamber opened, and in the same moment the trap-door gave way. There was a rushing sound – a heavy fall – a faint groan – and all was over.

At the same instant, Varney called in at the window, in an accent and tone which was an indescribable mixture betwixt horror and raillery, 'Is the bird caught? – is the deed done?'

'O God, forgive us!' replied Anthony Foster.

'Why, thou fool,' said Varney, 'thy toil is ended, and thy reward secure. Look down into the vault – what seest thou?'

'I see only a heap of white clothes, like a snow-drift,' said Foster. 'O God, she moves her arm!'

'Hurl something down on her. – Thy gold chest, Tony – it is an heavy one.'

'Varney, thou art an incarnate fiend!' replied Foster; – 'There needs nothing more – she is gone!'

'So pass our troubles,' said Varney, entering the room; 'I dreamed not I could have mimicked the Earl's call so well.'

'Oh, if there be judgement in Heaven, thou hast deserved it,' said Foster, 'and wilt meet it! – Thou hast destroyed her by means of her best affections – It is a seething of the kid in the mother's milk!'

'Thou art a fanatical ass,' replied Varney; 'let us now think how the alarm should be given, – the body is to remain where it is.'

But their wickedness was to be permitted no longer; – for, even while they were at this consultation, Tressilian and Raleigh broke in upon them, having obtained admittance by means of Tider and Foster's servant, whom they had secured at the village.

Anthony Foster fled on their entrance; and, knowing each corner and pass of the intricate old house, escaped all search. But Varney was taken on the spot; and, instead of expressing compunction for what he had done, seemed to take a fiendish pleasure in pointing out to them the remains of the murdered Countess, while at the same time he defied them to show that he had any share in her death. The despairing grief of Tressilian, on viewing the mangled and yet warm remains of what had lately been so lovely and so beloved, was such, that Raleigh was compelled to have him removed from the place by force, while he himself assumed the direction of what was to be done.

Varney, upon a second examination, made very little mystery either of the crime or of its motives; alleging, as a reason for his frankness, that though much of what he confessed could only have attached to him by suspicion, yet such suspicion would have been sufficient to deprive him of Leicester's confidence, and to destroy all his towering plans of ambition. 'I was not born,' he said, 'to drag on the remainder of life a degraded outcast, – nor will I so die, that my fate shall make a holiday to the vulgar herd.'

From these words it was apprehended he had some design upon himself, and he was carefully deprived of all means by which such could be carried into execution. But like some of the heroes of antiquity, he carried about his person a small quantity of strong poison, prepared probably by the celebrated Demetrius Alasco. Having swallowed this potion over-night, he was found next morning dead in his cell; nor did he appear to have suffered much agony, his countenance presenting, even in death, the habitual expression of sneering sarcasm, which was predominant while he lived. 'The wicked man,' saith Scripture, 'hath no bonds in his death.'

The fate of his colleague in wickedness was long unknown. Cumnor Place was deserted immediately after the murder; for, in the vicinity of what was called the Lady Dudley's Chamber, the domestics pretended to hear groans, and screams, and other supernatural noises. After a certain length of time, Janet, hearing no tidings of her father, became the uncontrolled mistress of his property, and conferred it with her hand upon Wayland, now a man of settled character, and holding a place in Elizabeth's household. But it was after they had been both dead for some years, that their eldest son and heir, in making some researches about Cumnor Hall, discovered a secret passage, closed by an iron door, which, opening from behind the bed in the Lady Dudley's Chamber, descended to a sort of cell, in which they found an iron chest containing a quantity of gold, and a human skeleton stretched above it. The fate of Anthony Foster was now manifest. He had fled to this place of concealment, forgetting the key of the spring-lock; and being barred from escape, by the means he had used for preservation of that gold, for which he had sold his salvation, he had there perished miserably. Unquestionably the groans and screams heard by the domestics were not entirely imaginary, but were those of this wretch, who, in his agony, was crying for relief and succour.

Kenilworth, 1821

CHARLES LAMB

[The Demon Drink]

DEHORTATIONS FROM the use of strong liquors have been the favourite topic of sober declaimers in all ages, and have been received with abundance of applause by water-drinking critics. But with the patient himself, the man that is to be cured, unfortunately their sound has seldom prevailed. Yet the evil is acknowledged, the remedy simple. Abstain. No force can oblige a man to raise the glass to his head against his will. 'Tis as easy as not to steal, not to tell lies.

Alas! the hand to pilfer, and the tongue to bear false witness, have no constitutional tendency. These are actions indifferent to them. At the first instance of the reformed will, they can be brought off without a murmur. The itching finger is but a figure in speech, and the tongue of the liar can with the same natural delight give forth useful truths, with which it has been accustomed to scatter their pernicious contraries. But when a man has commenced sot—

O pause, thou sturdy moralist, thou person of stout nerves and a strong head, whose liver is happily untouched, and ere thy gorge riseth at the *name* I have written, first learn what the *thing* is; how much of compassion, how much of human allowance, thou mayst virtuously mingle with thy disapprobation. Trample not on the ruins of a man. Exact not, under so terrible a penalty as infamy, a resuscitation from a state of death almost as real as that from which Lazarus rose not but by a miracle.

Begin a reformation, and custom will make it easy. But what if the beginning be dreadful, the first steps not like climbing a mountain but going through fire? what if the whole system must undergo a change violent as that which we conceive of the mutation of form in some insects? what if a process comparable to flaying alive be to be gone through? is the weakness that sinks under such struggles to be confounded with the pertinacity which clings to other vices, which have induced no constitutional necessity, no engagement of the whole victim, body and soul?

I have known one in that state, when he has tried to abstain but for one evening, – though the poisonous potion had long ceased to bring back its first enchantments, though he was sure it would rather deepen his gloom than brighten it, – in the violence of the struggle, and the necessity he has felt of getting rid of the present sensation at any rate, I have known him to scream out, to cry aloud, for the anguish and pain of the strife within him.

Why should I hesitate to declare, that the man of whom I speak is myself? I have no puling apology to make to mankind. I see them all in one way or another deviating from the pure reason. It is to my own nature alone I am accountable for the woe that I have brought upon it.

I believe that there are constitutions, robust heads and iron insides, whom scarce any excesses can hurt; whom brandy (I have seen them drink it like wine), at all events whom wine, taken in ever so plentiful measure, can do no worse injury to than just to muddle their faculties, perhaps never very pellucid. On them this discourse is wasted. They would but laugh at a weak brother, who, trying his strength with them, and coming off foiled from the contest, would fain persuade them that such agonistic exercises are dangerous. It is to a very different description of persons I speak.

It is to the weak, the nervous; to those who feel the want of some artificial aid to raise their spirits in society to what is no more than the ordinary pitch of all around them without it. This is the secret of our drinking. Such must fly the convivial board in the first instance, if they do not mean to sell themselves for term of life.

Twelve years ago I had completed my six-and-twentieth year. I had lived from the period of leaving school to that time pretty much in solitude. My companions were chiefly books, or at most one or two living ones of my own book-loving and sober stamp. I rose early, went to bed betimes, and the faculties which God had given me, I have reason to think, did not rust in me unused.

About that time I fell in with some companions of a different order. They were men of boisterous spirits, sitters up a-nights, disputants, drunken; yet seemed to have something noble about them. We dealt about the wit, or what passes for it after midnight, jovially. Of the quality called fancy I certainly possessed a larger share than my companions. Encouraged by their applause, I set up for a professed joker! I, who of all men am least fitted for such an occupation, having, in addition to the greatest difficulty which I experience at all times of finding words to express my meaning, a natural nervous impediment in my speech!

Reader, if you are gifted with nerves like mine, aspire to any character but that of a wit. When you find a tickling relish upon your tongue disposing you to that sort of conversation, especially if you find a preternatural flow of ideas setting in upon you at the sight of a bottle and fresh glasses, avoid giving way to it as you would fly your greatest destruction. If you cannot crush the power of fancy, or that within you which you mistake for such, divert it, give it some other play. Write an essay, pen a character or description, – but not as I do now, with tears trickling down your cheeks.

To be an object of compassion to friends, of derision to foes; to be suspected by strangers, stared at by fools; to be esteemed dull when you cannot be witty, to be applauded for witty when you know that you have been dull; to be called upon for the extemporaneous exercise of that faculty which no premeditation can give; to be spurred on to efforts which end in contempt; to be set on to provoke mirth which procures the procurer hatred; to give pleasure and be paid with squinting malice; to swallow draughts of life-destroying wine which are to be distilled into airy breath to tickle vain auditors; to mortgage miserable morrows for nights of madness; to waste whole seas of time upon those who pay it back in little inconsiderable drops of grudging applause, – are the wages of buffoonery and death.

Time, which has a sure stroke at dissolving all connections which have no solider fastening than this liquid cement, more kind to me than my own taste or penetration, at length opened my eyes to the supposed qualities of my first friends. No trace of them is left but in the vices which they introduced, and the habits they infixed. In them my friends survive still, and exercise ample retribution for any supposed infidelity that I may have been guilty of towards them.

'Confessions of a Drunkard', 1822

WILLIAM HAZLITT

[Bill Neate v. The Gas-Man]

THE *swells* were parading in their white box-coats, the outer ring was cleared with some bruises on the heads and shins of the rustic assembly (for the *cockneys* had been distanced by the sixty-six miles); the time drew near; I had got a good stand; a bustle, a buzz, ran through the crowd; and from the opposite side entered Neate, between his second and bottle-holder. He rolled along, swathed in his loose great coat, his knock-knees bending under his huge bulk; and, with a modest cheerful air, threw his hat into the ring. He then just looked round, and began quietly to undress; when from the other side there was a similar rush and an opening made, and the Gas-man [*Thomas Hickman*] came forward with a conscious air of anticipated triumph,

too much like the cock-of-the-walk. He strutted about more
than became a hero, sucked oranges with a supercilious air,
and threw away the skin with a toss of his head, and went
up and looked at Neate, which was an act of supererogation.
The only sensible thing he did was, as he strode away from
the modern Ajax, to fling out his arms, as if he wanted to
try whether they would do their work that day. By this time
they had stripped, and presented a strong contrast in appearance. If Neate was like Ajax, 'with Atlantean shoulders, fit
to bear' the pugilistic reputation of all Bristol, Hickman
might be compared to Diomed, light, vigorous, elastic, and
his back glistened in the sun, as he moved about, like a
panther's hide. There was now a dead pause – attention was
awe-struck. Who at that moment, big with a great event,
did not draw his breath short – did not feel his heart throb?
All was ready. They tossed up for the sun, and the Gas-man
won. They were led up to the *scratch* – shook hands, and
went at it.

In the first round everyone thought it was all over. After
making play a short time, the Gas-man flew at his adversary
like a tiger, struck five blows in as many seconds, three first,
and then following him as he staggered back, two more,
right and left, and down he fell, a mighty ruin. There was a
shout, and I said, 'There is no standing this.' Neate seemed
like a lifeless lump of flesh and bone, round which the Gas-
man's blows played with the rapidity of electricity or lightning, and you imagined he would only be lifted up to be
knocked down again. It was as if Hickman held a sword or
a fire in that right hand of his, and directed it against an
unarmed body. They met again, and Neate seemed, not
cowed, but particularly cautious. I saw his teeth clenched
together and his brows knit close against the sun. He held
out both his arms at full length straight before him, like two
sledge-hammers, and raised his left an inch or two higher.
The Gas-man could not get over this guard – they struck
mutually and fell, but without advantage on either side. It
was the same in the next round; but the balance of power
was thus restored – the fate of the battle was suspended. No
one could tell how it would end. This was the only moment
in which opinion was divided; for, in the next, the Gas-man

aiming a mortal blow at his adversary's neck, with his right hand, and failing from the length he had to reach, the other returned it with his left at full swing, planted a tremendous blow on his cheek-bone and eye-brow, and made a red ruin of that side of his face. The Gas-man went down, and there was another shout – a roar of triumph as the waves of fortune rolled tumultuously from side to side. This was a settler. Hickman got up, and 'grinned horrible a ghastly smile', yet he was evidently dashed in his opinion of himself; it was the first time he had ever been so punished; all one side of his face was perfect scarlet, and his right eye was closed in dingy blackness, as he advanced to the fight, less confident, but still determined. After one or two rounds, not receiving another such remembrancer, he rallied and went at it with his former impetuosity. But in vain. His strength had been weakened, – his blows could not tell at such a distance, – he was obliged to fling himself at his adversary, and could not strike from his feet; and almost as regularly as he flew at him with his right hand, Neate warded the blow, or drew back out of its reach, and felled him with the return of his left. There was little cautious sparring – no half-hits – no tapping and trifling, none of the *petit-maitre-ship* of the art – they were almost all knock-down blows: – the fight was a good stand-up fight. The wonder was the half-minute time. If there had been a minute or more allowed between each round, it would have been intelligible how they should by degrees recover strength and resolution; but to see two men smashed to the ground, smeared with gore, stunned, senseless, the breath beaten out of their bodies; and then, before you recover from the shock, to see them rise up with new strength and courage, stand ready to inflict or receive mortal offence, and rush upon each other 'like two clouds over the Caspian' – this is the most astonishing thing of all: – this is the high and heroic state of man! From this time forward the event became more certain every round; and about the twelfth it seemed as if it must have been over. Hickman generally stood with his back to me; but in the scuffle, he had changed positions, and Neate just then made a tremendous lunge at him, and hit him full in the face. It was doubtful whether he would fall backwards or forwards; he hung suspended for a second or two, and then fell back, throwing his hands in the air, and with his face lifted up to the sky. I never saw any thing more terrific than his aspect just before he fell. All traces of life, of natural expression, were gone from him. His face was like a human skull, a death's head, spouting blood. The eyes were filled with blood, the nose streamed with blood, the mouth gaped blood. He was not like an actual man, but like a preternatural, spectral appearance, or like one of the figures in Dante's *Inferno*. Yet he fought on after this for several rounds, still striking the first desperate blow, and Neate standing on the defensive, and using the same cautious guard to the last, as if he had still all his work to do; and it was not till the Gas-man was so stunned in the seventeenth or eighteenth round, that his senses forsook him, and he could not come to time, that the battle was declared over. Ye who despise the FANCY, do something to shew as much *pluck*, or as much self-possession as this, before you assume a superiority which you have never given a single proof of by any one action in the whole course of your lives! – When the Gas-man came to himself, the first words he uttered were, 'Where am I? What is the matter?' – 'Nothing is the matter, Tom, – you have lost the battle, but you are the bravest man alive.' And Jackson whispered to him, 'I am collecting a purse for you, Tom.' Vain sounds, and unheard at that moment! Neate instantly went up and shook him cordially by the hand, and seeing some old acquaintance, began to flourish with his fists, calling out, 'Ah! you always said I couldn't fight – What do you think now?' But all in good humour, and without any appearance of arrogance; only it was evident Bill Neate was pleased that he had won the fight. When it was over, I asked Cribb if he did not think it was a good one. He said, '*Pretty well!*' The carrier-pigeons now mounted into the air, and one of them flew with the news of her husband's victory to the bosom of Mrs Neate. Alas, for Mrs Hickman!

'The Fight', 1822

WILLIAM COBBETT

[The Isle of Thanet]

Thursday Afternoon, 4th September 1823

IN QUITTING Sandwich, you immediately cross a river up which vessels bring coals from the sea. This marsh is about a couple of miles wide. It begins at the sea-beach, opposite the Downs, to my right hand, coming from Sandwich, and it wheels round to my left and ends at the sea-beach, opposite Margate roads. This marsh was formerly covered with the sea, very likely; and hence the land within this sort of semicircle, the name of which is Thanet, was called an *Isle*. It is, in fact, an island now, for the same reason that Portsea is an island, and that New York is an island; for there certainly is the water in this river that goes round and connects one part of the sea with the other. I had to cross this river, and to cross the marsh, before I got into the famous Isle of Thanet, which it was my intention to cross. Soon after crossing the river, I passed by a place for making salt, and could not help recollecting that there are no excisemen in these salt-making places in France, that, before the Revolution, the French were most cruelly oppressed by the duties on salt, that they had to endure, on that account, the most horrid tyranny that ever was known, except, perhaps, that practised in an Exchequer that shall here be nameless; that thousands and thousands of men and women were every year sent to the galleys for what was called smuggling salt; that the fathers and even the mothers were imprisoned or whipped if the children were detected in smuggling salt: I could not help reflecting, with delight, as I looked at these salt-pans in the Isle of Thanet; I could not help reflecting, that in spite of Pitt, Dundas, Perceval, and the rest of the crew, in spite of the caverns of Dover and the Martello Towers in Romney Marsh: in spite of all the spies and all the bayonets, and the six hundred millions of Debt and the hundred and fifty millions of dead-weight, and the two hundred millions of poor-rates that are now squeezing the borough-mongers, squeezing the farmers, puzzling the fellows at Whitehall and making Mark Lane a scene of greater interest than the Chamber of the Privy Council; with delight as I jogged along under the first beams of the sun, I reflected, that, in spite of all the malignant measures that had brought so much misery upon England, the gallant French people had ridded themselves of the tyranny which sent them to the galleys for endeavouring to use without tax the salt which God sent upon their shores. Can any man tell why we should still be paying five, or six, or seven shillings a bushel for salt, instead of one? We did pay fifteen shillings a bushel, tax. And why is two shillings a bushel kept on? Because, if they were taken off, the salt-tax-gathering crew must be discharged! This tax of two shillings a bushel, causes the consumer to pay five, at the least, more than he would if there were no tax at all! When, great God! when shall we be allowed to enjoy God's gifts, in freedom, as the people of France enjoy them? On the marsh I found the same sort of sheep as on Romney Marsh; but the cattle here are chiefly Welsh; black, and called runts. They are nice hardy cattle; and, I am told, that this is the description of cattle that they fat all the way up on this north side of Kent. When I got upon the corn land in the Isle of Thanet, I got into a garden indeed. There is hardly any fallow; comparatively few turnips. It is a country of corn. Most of the harvest is in; but there are some fields of wheat and of barley not yet housed. A great many pieces of lucerne, and all of them very fine. I left Ramsgate to my right about three miles, and went right across the island to Margate; but that place is so thickly settled with stock-jobbing cuckolds, at this time of the year, that, having no fancy to get their horns stuck into me, I turned away to my left when I got within about half a mile of the town. I got to a little hamlet, where I breakfasted; but could get no corn for my horse, and no bacon for myself! All was corn around me. Barns, I should think, two hundred feet long; ricks of enormous size and most numerous; crops of wheat, five quarters to an acre, on the average; and a public-house without either bacon or corn! The labourers' houses, all along through this island, beggarly in the extreme. The people dirty, poor-looking; ragged, but particularly *dirty*. The men and boys with dirty faces, and dirty smock-frocks, and dirty shirts; and, good God! what a difference between the wife of a labouring man here, and the wife of a labouring man in the forests and woodlands of Hampshire and Sussex! Invariably have I observed, that the richer the soil, and the more destitute of woods; that is to say, the more purely a corn country, the more miserable the labourers. The cause is this, the great, the big bull frog grasps all. In this beautiful island every inch of land is appropriated by the rich. No hedges, no ditches, no commons, no grassy lanes: a country divided into great farms; a few trees surround the great farmhouse. All the rest is bare of trees; and the wretched labourer has not a stick of wood, and has no place for a pig or cow to graze, or even to lie down upon. The rabbit countries are the countries for labouring men. There the ground is not so valuable. There it is not so easily appropriated by the few. Here, in this island, the work is almost all done by the horses. The horses plough the ground; they sow the ground; they hoe the ground; they carry the corn home; they thresh it out; and they carry it to market: nay, in this island, they *rake* the ground; they rake up the straggling straws and ears; so that they do the whole, except the reaping and the mowing. It is impossible to have an idea of any thing more miserable than the state of the labourers in this part of the country.

Rural Rides, 1830

THOMAS CARLYLE

[The Storming of the Bastille, 14 July 1789]

ALL MORNING, since nine, there has been a cry every-where: To the Bastille! Repeated 'deputations of citizens' have been here, passionate for arms; whom De Launay has got dismissed by soft speeches through portholes. Towards noon, Elector Thuriot de la Rosière gains admittance; finds De Launay indisposed for surrender; nay disposed for blowing up the place rather. Thuriot mounts with him to the battlements: heaps of paving stones, old iron and missiles lie piled; cannon all duly levelled; in every embrasure a cannon, – only drawn back a little! But outwards, behold, O Thuriot, how the multitude flows on, welling through every street: tocsin furiously pealing, all drums beating the *générale*: the Suburb Saint-Antoine rolling hitherward wholly, as one man! Such vision (spectral yet real) thou, O Thuriot, as from thy Mount of Vision, beholdest in this moment: prophetic of what other Phantasmagories, and loud-gibbering Spectral Realities, which thou yet beholdest not, but shalt! '*Que voulez-vous?*' said De Launay, turning pale at the sight, with an air of reproach, almost of menace. 'Monsieur', said Thuriot, rising into the moral-sublime, 'what mean *you*? Consider if I could not precipitate *both* of us from this height', – say only a hundred feet, exclusive of the walled ditch! Whereupon De Launay fell silent. Thuriot shows himself from some pinnacle, to comfort the multitude becoming suspicious, fremescent: then descends; departs with protest; with warning addressed also to the Invalides, – on whom, however, it produces but a mixed indistinct impression. The old heads are none of the clearest; besides, it is said, De Launay has been profuse of beverages (*prodigua des buissons*). They think, they will not fire, – if not fired on, if they can help it; but must, on the whole, be ruled considerably by circumstances.

Woe to thee, De Launay, in such an hour, if thou canst not, taking some one firm decision, *rule* circumstances! Soft speeches will not serve; hard grapeshot is questionable; but hovering between the two is *un*questionable. Ever wilder swells the tide of men; their infinite hum waxing ever louder, into imprecations, perhaps into crackle of stray musketry, – which latter, on walls nine feet thick, cannot do execution. The Outer Drawbridge has been lowered for Thuriot; new *deputation of citizens* (it is the third, and noisiest of all) penetrates that way into the Outer Court: soft speeches producing no clearance of these, De Launay gives fire; pulls up his Drawbridge. A slight sputter; – which has *kindled* the too combustible chaos; made it a roaring fire-chaos! Bursts forth Insurrection, at sight of its own blood (for there were deaths by that sputter of fire), into endless rolling explosion of musketry, distraction, execration; – and over head, from the Fortress, let one great gun, with its grapeshot, go booming, to show what we *could* do. The Bastille is besieged!

On, then, all Frenchmen, that have hearts in your bodies! Roar with all your throats, of cartilage and metal, ye Sons of Liberty; stir spasmodically whatsoever of utmost faculty is in you, soul, body, or spirit; for it is the hour! Smite, thou Louis Tournay, cartwright of the Marais, old-soldier of the Regiment Dauphiné; smite at that Outer Drawbridge chain, though the fiery hail whistles round thee! Never, over nave or felloe, did thy axe strike such a stroke. Down with it, man; down with it to Orcus: let the whole accursed Edifice sink thither, and Tyranny be swallowed up for ever! Mounted, some say, on the roof of the guard-room, some 'on bayonets stuck into joints of the wall', Louis Tournay smites, brave Aubin Bonnemère (also an old soldier) seconding him: the chain yields, breaks; the huge Drawbridge slams down, thundering (*avec fracas*). Glorious: and yet, alas, it is still but the outworks. The Eight grim Towers, with their Invalide musketry, their paving stones and cannon-mouths, still soar aloft intact; – Ditch yawning impassable, stone-faced; the inner Drawbridge with its *back* towards us: the Bastille is still to take!

To describe this Siege of the Bastille (thought to be one of the most important in History) perhaps transcends the talent of mortals. Could one but, after infinite reading, get to understand so much as the plan of the building! But there is open Esplanade, at the end of the Rue Saint-Antoine; there are such Forecourts, *Cour Avancé, Cour de l'Orme*, arched Gateway (where Louis Tournay now fights); then new drawbridges, dormant-bridges, rampart-bastions, and the grim Eight Towers: a labyrinthic Mass, high-frowning there, of all ages from twenty years to four hundred and twenty; – beleaguered, in this its last hour, as we said, by mere Chaos come again! Ordnance of all calibres; throats of all capacities; men of all plans, every man his own engineer: seldom since the war of Pygmies and Cranes was there seen so anomalous a thing. Half-pay Elie is home for a suit of regimentals; no one would heed him in coloured clothes: half-pay Hulin is haranguing Gardes Françaises in the Place de Grève. Frantic Patriots pick up the grapeshots; bear them, still hot (or seemingly so), to the Hôtel-de-Ville: – Paris, you perceive, is to be burnt! Flesselles is 'pale to the very lips', for the roar of the multitude grows deep. Paris wholly has got to the acme of its frenzy; whirled, all ways, by panic madness. At every street-barricade, there whirls simmering a minor whirlpool, – strengthening the barricade, since God knows what is coming; and all minor whirlpools play distractedly into that grand Fire-Mahlstrom which is lashing round the Bastille.

And so it lashes and it roars. Cholat the wine-merchant has become an impromptu cannoneer. See Georget, of the Marine Service, fresh from Brest, ply the King of Siam's cannon. Singular (if we were not used to the like): Georget lay, last night, taking his ease at an inn; the King of Siam's cannon also lay, knowing nothing of *him*, for a hundred years. Yet now, at the right instant, they have got together, and discourse eloquent music. For, hearing what was toward, Georget sprang from the Brest Diligence, and ran. Gardes Françaises also will be here, with real artillery: were not the walls so thick! – Upwards from the Esplanade, horizontally from all neighbouring roofs and windows, flashes one irregular deluge of musketry, without effect. The Invalides lie flat, firing comparatively at their ease from behind stone; hardly through portholes, show the tip of a nose. We fall, shot; and make no impression!

Let conflagration rage; of whatsoever is combustible! Guard-rooms are burnt, Invalides mess-rooms. A distracted 'Perukemaker with two fiery torches' is for burning 'the saltpetres of the Arsenal'; – had not a woman run screaming; had not a Patriot, with some tincture of Natural Philosophy, instantly struck the wind out of him (butt of musket on pit of stomach), overturned barrels, and stayed the devouring element. A young beautiful lady, seized escaping in these Outer Courts, and thought falsely to be De Launay's daughter, shall be burnt in De Launay's sight; she lies swooned on a paillasse: but again a Patriot, it is brave Aubin Bonnemère the old soldier, dashes in, and rescues her. Straw is burnt; three cartloads of it, hauled thither, go up in white smoke: almost to the choking of Patriotism itself; so that Elie had, with singed brows, to drag back one cart; and Réole the 'gigantic haberdasher' another. Smoke as of Tophet; confusion as of Babel; noise as of the Crack of Doom!

Blood flows; the aliment of new madness. The wounded are carried into houses of the Rue Cerisaie; the dying leave their last mandate not to yield till the accursed Stronghold fall. And yet, alas, how fall? The walls are so thick! Deputations, three in number, arrive from the Hôtel-de-Ville; Abbé Fauchet (who was of one) can say, with what almost superhuman courage of benevolence. These wave their Town-flag in the arched Gateway; and stand, rolling their drum; but to no purpose. In such Crack of Doom, De Launay cannot hear them, dare not believe them: they return, with justified rage, the whew of lead still singing in their ears. What to do? The Firemen are here, squirting with their fire-pumps on the Invalides cannon, to wet the touchholes; they unfortunately cannot squirt so high; but produce only clouds of spray. Individuals of classical knowledge propose *catapults*. Santerre, the sonorous Brewer of the Suburb Saint-Antoine, advises rather that the place be fired, by a 'mixture of phosphorus and oil-of-turpentine spouted up through forcing pumps': O Spinola-Santerre, hast thou the mixture *ready*? Every man his own engineer! And still the fire-deluge abates not: even women are firing, and Turks; at least one woman (with her sweetheart), and one Turk. Gardes Françaises have come: real cannon, real cannoneers. Usher Maillard is busy; half-pay Elie, half-pay Hulin rage in the midst of thousands.

How the great Bastille Clock ticks (inaudible) in its Inner Court there, at its ease, hour after hour; as if nothing special, for it or the world, were passing! It tolled One when the firing began; and is now pointing towards Five, and still the firing slakes not. – Far down, in their vaults, the seven

Prisoners hear muffled din as of earthquakes; their Turnkeys answer vaguely.

Woe to thee, De Launay, with thy poor hundred Invalides! Broglie is distant, and his ears heavy: Besenval hears, but can send no help. One poor troop of Hussars has crept, reconnoitring, cautiously along the Quais, as far as the Pont Neuf. 'We are come to join you,' said the Captain; for the crowd seems shoreless. A large-headed dwarfish individual, of smoke-bleared aspect, shambles forward, opening his blue lips, for there is sense in him; and croaks: 'Alight then, and give up your arms!' The Hussar-Captain is too happy to be escorted to the Barriers, and dismissed on parole. Who the squat individual was? Men answer, It is M. Marat, author of the excellent pacific *Avis au Peuple*! Great truly, O thou remarkable Dogleech, is this thy day of emergence and new-birth: and yet this same day come four years—! – But let the curtains of the Future hang.

What shall De Launay do? One thing only De Launay could have done: what he said he would do. Fancy him sitting, from the first, with lighted taper, within arm's length of the Powder-Magazine; motionless, like old Roman Senator, or Bronze Lamp-holder; coldly apprising Thuriot, and all men, by a slight motion of his eye, what his resolution was: – Harmless he sat there, while unharmed; but the King's Fortress, meanwhile, could, might, would, or should, in nowise be surrendered, save to the King's Messenger: one old man's life is worthless, so it be lost with honour; but think, ye brawling *canaille*, how will it be when a whole Bastille springs skyward! – In such statuesque, taper-holding attitude, one fancies De Launay might have left Thuriot, the red Clerks of the Basoche, Curé of Saint-Stephen and all the tag-rag-and-bobtail of the world, to work their will.

And yet, withal, he could not do it. Hast thou considered how each man's heart is so tremulously responsive to the hearts of men; hast thou noted how omnipotent is the very sound of many men? How their shriek of indignation palsies the strong soul; their howl of contumely withers with unfelt pangs? The Ritter Glück confessed that the ground-tone of the noblest passage, in one of his noblest Operas, was the voice of the Populace he had heard at Vienna, crying to their Kaiser: Bread! Bread! Great is the combined voice of men; the utterance of their *instincts*, which are truer than their *thoughts*: it is the greatest a man encounters, among the sounds and shadows which make up this World of Time. He who can resist that, has his footing somewhere *beyond* Time. De Launay could not do it. Distracted, he hovers between two; hopes in the middle of despair; surrenders not his Fortress; declares that he will blow it up, seizes torches to blow it up, and does not blow it. Unhappy old De Launay, it is the death-agony of thy Bastille and thee! Jail, Jailoring and Jailor, all three, such as they may have been, must finish.

For four hours now has the World-Bedlam roared: call it the World-Chimera, blowing fire! The poor Invalides have sunk under their battlements, or rise only with reversed muskets: they have made a white flag of napkins: go beating the *chamade*, or seeming to beat, for one can hear nothing. The very Swiss at the Portcullis look weary of firing; disheartened in the fire-deluge: a porthole at the drawbridge is opened, as by one that would speak. See Huissier Maillard, the shifty man! On his plank, swinging over the abyss of that stone Ditch; plank resting on parapet, balanced by weight of Patriots, – he hovers perilous: such a Dove towards such an Ark! Deftly, thou shifty Usher: one man already fell; and lies smashed, far down there, against the masonry! Usher Maillard falls not: deftly, unerring he walks, with outspread palm. The Swiss holds a paper through his porthole; the shifty Usher snatches it, and returns. Terms of surrender: Pardon, immunity to all! Are they accepted? – '*Foi d'officier*, On the word of an officer', answers half-pay Hulin, – or half-pay Elie, for men do not agree on it, 'they are!' Sinks the drawbridge, – Usher Maillard bolting it when down; rushes-in the living deluge: the Bastille is fallen! *Victoire! La Bastille est prise!*

The French Revolution, 1837

ROBERT SMITH SURTEES

[The Festive Season]

IT WAS a most tempestersome night, and, having eaten and drank to completion, I determined to go and see if my aunt, in Cavendish Street, was alive; and after having been nearly blown out to France several times, I succeeded in making my point and running to ground. The storm grew worser and worser, and when I came to open the door to go away, I found it blocked with snow, and the drifts whirling about in all directions. My aunt, who is a werry feeling woman, insisted on my staying all night, which only made the matter worse, for when I came to look out in the morning I found the drift as high as the first floor winder, and the street completely buried in snow. Having breakfasted, and seeing no hopes of emancipation, I hangs out a flag of distress – a red wipe – which, after flapping about for some time, drew three or four sailors and a fly-man or two. I explained from the winder how dreadfully I was situated, prayed of them to release me, but the wretches did nothing but laugh, and ax wot I would give to be out. At last one of them, who acted as spokesman, proposed that I should put an armchair out of the winder, and pay them five shillings each for carrying me home on their shoulders. It seemed a vast of money, but the storm continuing, the crowd increasing, and I not wishing to kick up a row at my aunt's, after offering four and sixpence, agreed to their terms, and throwing out a chair, plumped up to the middle in a drift. Three cheers followed the feat, which drew all the neighbours to the winders, when about half a dozen fellows, some drunk, some sober, and some half-and-half, pulled me into the chair, hoisted me on to their shoulders, and proceeded into St James's Street, bellowing out, 'Here's the new member for Brighton! Here's the boy wot sleeps in Cavendish Street! Huzzah, the old 'un for ever! There's an elegant man for a small tea-party! Who wants a fat chap to send to their friends for Christmas?' The noise they made was quite tremendious, and the snow in many places being up to their middles, we made werry slow progress, but still they would keep me in the chair, and before we got to the end of the street the crowd had increased to some hundreds. Here they began snow-balling, and my hat and wig soon went flying, and then there was a fresh holloa. 'Here's Mr Wigney, the member for Brighton,' they cried out; 'I say, old boy, are you for the ballot? You must call on the King this morning; he wants to give you a Christmas-box.' Just then one of the front bearers tumbled, and down we all rolled into a drift, just opposite Daly's backey shop. There were about twenty of us in together, but being pretty near the top, I was soon on my legs, and seeing an opening, I bolted right forward – sent three or four fellows flying – dashed down the passage behind Saxby's wine vaults, across the Steyne, floundering into the drifts, followed by the mob, shouting and pelting me all the way. This double made some of the beggars over-shoot the mark, and run past the statue of George the Fourth, but, seeing their mistake, or hearing the other portion of the pack running in the contrary direction, they speedily joined heads and tails, and gave me a devil of a burst up the narrow lane by the Wite 'Orse 'Otel. Fortunately Jonathan Boxall's door was open, and Jonathan himself in the passage bar, washing some decanters. 'Look sharp, Jonathan!' said I, dashing past him as wite as a miller, 'look sharp! come out of that, and be after clapping your great carcase against the door to keep the Philistines out, or they'll be the death of us both.' Quick as thought the door was closed and bolted before ever the leaders had got up, but, finding this the case, the mob halted and proceeded to make a deuce of a kick-up before the house, bellowing and shouting like mad fellows, and threatening to pull it down if I did not show. Jonathan got narvous, and begged and intreated me to address them. I recommended him to do it himself, but he said he was quite unaccustomed to public speaking, and he would stand two glasses of 'cold without' if I would. 'Hot with,' said I, 'and I'll do it.' 'Done,' said he, and he knocked the snow off my coat, pulled my wig straight, and made me look decent, and took me to a bow-winder'd room on the first floor, threw up the sash, and exhibited me to the company outside. I bowed and kissed my hand like a candidate. They cheered and shouted, and then called for silence whilst I addressed them. 'Gentlemen,' said I, 'Who are you?' 'Why, we be the men wot carried your honour's glory from Cavendish Street, and wants to be paid for it.' 'Gentlemen,' said I, 'I'm no orator, but I'm a honest man; I pays everybody twenty shillings in the pound, and no mistake (cheers). If you had done your part of the bargain, I would have done mine, but 'ow can you expect to be paid after spilling me? This is a most inclement day, and, whatever you may say to the contrary, I'm not Mr Clement Wigney.' – 'No, nor Mr Faithful neither,' bellowed one of the bearers. – 'Gentlemen,' said I, 'you'll get the complaints of the season, chilblains and influhensa, if you stand dribbling there in the snow. Let me advise you to mizzle, for, if you don't, I'm blowed if I don't divide a whole jug of cold water equally amongst you. Go home to your wives and children, and don't be after annoying an honest, independent, amiable publican, like Jonathan Boxall. That's all I've got to say, and if I was to talk till I'm black in the face, I couldn't say nothing more to the purpose; so, I wishes you all "A Merry Christmas and an 'Appy New Year".'

'On "The Age"'; reprinted in *Jorrocks's Jaunts and Jollities*, 1838

BENJAMIN DISRAELI

[The Two Nations]

'IT IS a community of purpose that constitutes society,' continued the younger stranger; 'without that, men may be drawn into contiguity, but they still continue virtually isolated.'

'And is that their condition in cities?'

'It is their condition everywhere; but in cities that condition is aggravated. A density of population implies a severer struggle for existence, and a consequent repulsion of elements brought into too close contact. In great cities men are brought together by the desire of gain. They are not in a state of co-operation, but of isolation, as to the making of fortunes; and for all the rest they are careless of neighbours. Christianity teaches us to love our neighbour as ourself; modern society acknowledges no neighbour.'

'Well, we live in strange times,' said Egremont, struck by the observation of his companion, and relieving a perplexed spirit by an ordinary exclamation, which often denotes that the mind is more stirred than it cares to acknowledge, or at the moment is able to express.

'When the infant begins to walk, it also thinks that it lives in strange times,' said his companion.

'Your inference?' asked Egremont.

'That society, still in its infancy, is beginning to feel its way.'

'This is a new reign,' said Egremont, 'perhaps it is a new era.'

'I think so,' said the younger stranger.

'I hope so,' said the elder one.

'Well, society may be in its infancy,' said Egremont, slightly smiling; 'but, say what you like, our Queen reigns over the greatest nation that ever existed.'

'Which nation?' asked the younger stranger, 'for she reigns over two.'

The stranger paused; Egremont was silent, but looked inquiringly.

'Yes,' resumed the younger stranger after a moment's interval. 'Two nations; between whom there is no inter-course and no sympathy; who are as ignorant of each other's habits, thoughts, and feelings, as if they were dwellers in different zones, or inhabitants of different planets; who are formed by a different breeding, are fed by a different food, are ordered by different manners, and are not governed by the same laws.'

'You speak of—' said Egremont, hesitatingly.

'THE RICH AND THE POOR.'

Sybil; or, The Two Nations, 1845

CHARLOTTE BRONTË

[An Impediment]

W E ENTERED the quiet and humble temple; the priest waited in his white surplice at the lowly altar, the clerk beside him. All was still: two shadows only moved in a remote corner. My conjecture had been correct: the strangers had slipped in before us, and they now stood by the vault of the Rochesters, their backs towards us, viewing through the rails the old time-stained marble tomb, where a kneeling angel guarded the remains of Damer de Rochester, slain at Marston Moor in the time of the civil wars; and of Elizabeth, his wife.

Our place was taken at the communion rails. Hearing a cautious step behind me, I glanced over my shoulder: one of the strangers – a gentleman, evidently – was advancing up the chancel. The service began. The explanation of the intent of matrimony was gone through; and then the clergyman came a step further forward, and, bending slightly towards Mr Rochester, went on.

'I require and charge you both (as ye will answer at the dreadful day of judgement, when the secrets of all hearts shall be disclosed), that if either of you know any impediment why ye may not lawfully be joined together in matrimony, ye do now confess it; for be ye well assured that so many as are coupled together otherwise than God's word doth allow, are not joined together by God, neither is their matrimony lawful.'

He paused, as the custom is. When is the pause after that sentence ever broken by reply? Not, perhaps, once in a hundred years. And the clergyman, who had not lifted his eyes from his book, and had held his breath but for a moment, was proceeding: his hand was already stretched towards Mr Rochester, as his lips unclosed to ask, 'Wilt thou have this woman for thy wedded wife?' – when a distinct and near voice said: – 'The marriage cannot go on: I declare the existence of an impediment.'

The clergyman looked up at the speaker, and stood mute; the clerk did the same; Mr Rochester moved slightly, as if an earthquake had rolled under his feet: taking a firmer footing, and not turning his head or eyes, he said, 'Proceed.'

Profound silence fell when he had uttered that word, with deep but low intonation. Presently Mr Wood said: – 'I cannot proceed without some investigation into what has been asserted, and evidence of its truth or falsehood.'

'The ceremony is quite broken off,' subjoined the voice behind us. 'I am in a condition to prove my allegation: an insuperable impediment to this marriage exists.'

Mr Rochester heard, but heeded not: he stood stubborn and rigid: making no movement, but to possess himself of my hand. What a hot and strong grasp he had! – and how like quarried marble was his pale, firm, massive front at this moment! How his eye shone, still, watchful, and yet wild beneath!

Mr Wood seemed at a loss. 'What is the nature of the impediment?' he asked. 'Perhaps it may be got over – explained away?'

'Hardly,' was the answer: 'I have called it insuperable, and I speak advisedly.'

The speaker came forwards, and leaned on the rails. He continued, uttering each word distinctly, calmly, steadily, but not loudly.

'It simply consists in the existence of a previous marriage. Mr Rochester has a wife now living.'

My nerves vibrated to those low-spoken words as they had never vibrated to thunder – my blood felt their subtle violence as it had never felt frost or fire: but I was collected, and in no danger of swooning. I looked at Mr Rochester: I made him look at me. His whole face was colourless rock: his eye was both spark and flint. He disavowed nothing: he seemed as if he would defy all things. Without speaking; without smiling; without seeming to recognize in me a human being, he only twined my waist with his arm, and riveted me to his side.

'Who are you?' he asked of the intruder.

'My name is Briggs – a solicitor of —— Street, London.'

'And you would thrust on me a wife?'

'I would remind you of your lady's existence, sir; which the law recognizes, if you do not.'

'Favour me with an account of her – with her name, her parentage, her place of abode.'

'Certainly.' Mr Briggs calmly took a paper from his pocket, and read out in a sort of official, nasal voice:—

'"I affirm and can prove that on the 20th October, AD— (a date of fifteen years back) Edward Fairfax Rochester, of Thornfield Hall, in the county of ——, and of Ferndean Manor, in ——shire, England, was married to my sister, Bertha Antoinetta Mason, daughter of Jonas Mason, merchant, and of Antoinetta his wife, a Creole – at —— church, Spanish Town, Jamaica. The record of the marriage will be found in the register of that church – a copy of it is now in my possession. Signed, Richard Mason."'

'That – if a genuine document – may prove I have been married, but it does not prove that the woman mentioned therein as my wife is still living.'

'She was living three months ago,' returned the lawyer.

'How do you know?'

'I have a witness to the fact; whose testimony even you, sir, will scarcely controvert.'

'Produce him – or go to hell.'

'I will produce him first – he is on the spot: Mr Mason, have the goodness to step forward.'

Mr Rochester, on hearing the name, set his teeth; he experienced, too, a sort of strong convulsive quiver; near to him as I was, I felt the spasmodic movement of fury or despair run through his frame. The second stranger, who had hitherto lingered in the background, now drew near; a pale face looked over the solicitor's shoulder – yes, it was Mason himself. Mr Rochester turned and glared at him. His eye, as I have often said, was a black eye: it had now a tawny, nay a bloody light in its gloom; and his face flushed – olive cheek, and hueless forehead received a glow, as from spreading, ascending heart-fire: and he stirred, lifted his strong arm – he could have struck Mason – dashed him on the church-floor – shocked by ruthless blow the breath from his body – but Mason shrank away, and cried faintly, 'Good God!' Contempt fell cool on Mr Rochester – his passion died as if a blight had shrivelled it up: he only asked, 'What have *you* to say?'

An inaudible reply escaped Mason's white lips.

'The devil is in it if you cannot answer distinctly. I again demand, what have *you* to say?'

'Sir – sir' – interrupted the clergyman, 'do not forget you are in a sacred place.' Then addressing Mason, he inquired gently, 'Are you aware, sir, whether or not this gentleman's wife is still living?'

'Courage,' urged the lawyer, – 'speak out.'

'She is now living at Thornfield Hall,' said Mason, in more articulate tones: 'I saw her there last April. I am her brother.'

'At Thornfield Hall!' ejaculated the clergyman. 'Impossible! I am an old resident in this neighbourhood, sir, and I never heard of a Mrs Rochester at Thornfield Hall.'

I saw a grim smile contort Mr Rochester's lip, and he muttered: – 'No – by God! I took care that none should hear of it – or of her under that name.' He mused – for ten minutes he held counsel with himself: he formed his resolve, and announced it: – 'Enough – all shall bolt out at once, like a bullet from the barrel. – Wood, close your book, and take off your surplice; John Green (to the clerk) leave the church: there will be no wedding today': the man obeyed.

Mr Rochester continued, hardily and recklessly: 'Bigamy is an ugly word! – I meant, however, to be a bigamist: but fate has outmanoeuvred me; or Providence has checked me, – perhaps the last. I am little better than a devil at this moment; and, as my pastor there would tell me, deserve no doubt the sternest of judgements of God, – even to the quenchless fire and deathless worm. Gentlemen, my plan is broken up! – what this lawyer and his client say is true: I have been married; and the woman to whom I was married lives! You say you never heard of a Mrs Rochester at the house up yonder, Wood: but I dare say you have many a time inclined your ear to gossip about the mysterious lunatic kept there under watch and ward. Some have whispered to you that she is my bastard half-sister: some, my cast-off mistress; I now inform you that she is my wife, whom I married fifteen years ago, – Bertha Mason by name; sister of this resolute personage, who is now, with his quivering limbs and white cheeks, showing you what a stout heart men may bear. Cheer up, Dick! – never fear me! – I'd almost as soon strike a woman as you. Bertha Mason is mad; and she came of a mad family; – idiots and maniacs through three generations! Her mother, the Creole, was both a mad woman and a drunkard! – as I found out after I had wed the daughter: for they were silent on family secrets before. Bertha, like a dutiful child, copied her parent in both points. I had a charming partner – pure, wise, modest: you can fancy I was a happy man. – I went through rich scenes! Oh! my experience has been heavenly, if you only knew it! But I owe you no further explanation. Briggs, Wood, Mason, – I invite you all to come up to the house and visit Mrs Poole's patient, and *my wife*! – You shall see what sort of a being I was cheated into espousing, and judge whether or not I had a right to break the compact, and seek sympathy with something at least human. This girl,' he continued, looking at me, 'knew no more than you, Wood, of the disgusting secret: she thought all was fair and legal; and never dreamt she was going to be entrapped into a feigned union with a defrauded wretch, already bound to a bad, mad, and embruted partner! Come, all of you, follow.'

Still holding me fast, he left the church: the three gentlemen came after. At the front door of the hall we found the carriage.

'Take it back to the coach-house, John,' said Mr Rochester, coolly; 'it will not be wanted today.'

Jane Eyre, 1847

EMILY BRONTË

[The Gypsy Boy]

ONE FINE summer morning – it was the beginning of harvest, I remember – Mr Earnshaw, the old master, came downstairs dressed for a journey; and, after he told Joseph what was to be done during the day, he turned to Hindley, and Cathy, and me – for I sat eating my porridge with them – and he said, speaking to his son, 'Now, my bonny man, I'm going to Liverpool today; what shall I bring you? You may choose what you like: only let it be little, for I shall walk there and back: sixty miles each way, that is a long spell!' Hindley named a fiddle, and then he asked Miss Cathy; she was hardly six years old, but she could ride any horse in the stable, and she chose a whip. He did not forget me; for he had a kind heart, though he was rather severe sometimes. He promised to bring me a pocketful of apples and pears, and then he kissed his children, said goodbye, and set off.

It seemed a long while to us all, – the three days of his absence – and often did little Cathy ask when he would be home. Mrs Earnshaw expected him by supper-time on the third evening, and she put the meal off hour after hour; there were no signs of his coming, however, and at last the children got tired of running down to the gate to look. Then it grew dark; she would have had them to bed, but they begged sadly to be allowed to stay up; and, just about eleven o'clock, the door-latch was raised quietly, and in stepped the master. He threw himself into a chair, laughing and groaning, and bid them all stand off, for he was nearly killed – he would not have such another walk for the three kingdoms.

'And at the end of it, to be flighted to death!' he said, opening his greatcoat, which he had bundled up in his arms. 'See here, wife! I was never so beaten with anything in my life: but you must e'en take it as a gift of God; though it's as dark almost as if it came from the devil.'

We crowded round, and over Miss Cathy's head I had a peep at a dirty, ragged, black-haired child; big enough both to walk and talk: indeed, its face looked older than Catherine's; yet, when it was set on its feet, it only stared round, and repeated over and over again some gibberish that nobody could understand. I was frightened, and Mrs Earnshaw was ready to fling it out of doors; she did fly up, asking how he could fashion to bring that gypsy brat into the house, when they had their own bairns to feed and fend for? What he meant to do with it, and whether he were mad? The master tried to explain the matter: but he was really half dead with fatigue, and all that I could make out, amongst her scolding, was a tale of his seeing it starving, and houseless, and as good as dumb, in the streets of Liverpool; where he picked it up and inquired for its owner. Not a soul knew to whom it belonged, he said; and his money and time being both limited, he thought it better to take it home with him at once than run into vain expenses there: because he was determined he would not leave it as he found it. Well, the conclusion was that my mistress grumbled herself calm; and Mr Earnshaw told me to wash it, and give it clean things, and let it sleep with the children.

Hindley and Cathy contented themselves with looking and listening till peace was restored; then, both began searching their father's pockets for the presents he had promised them. The former was a boy of fourteen, but when he drew out what had been a fiddle crushed to morsels in the greatcoat, he blubbered aloud; and Cathy, when she learned the master had lost her whip in attending on the stranger, showed her humour by grinning and spitting at the stupid little thing, earning for her pains a sound blow from her father to teach her cleaner manners. They entirely refused to have it in bed with them, or even in their room; and I had no more sense, so I put it on the landing of the stairs, hoping it might be gone on the morrow. By chance, or else attracted by hearing his voice, it crept to Mr Earnshaw's door, and there he found it on quitting his chamber. Inquiries were made as to how it got there; I was obliged to confess, and in recompense for my cowardice and inhumanity was sent out of the house.

This was Heathcliff's first introduction to the family. On coming back a few days afterwards (for I did not consider my banishment perpetual) I found they had christened him 'Heathcliff'; it was the name of a son who died in childhood, and it has served him ever since, both for Christian and surname. Miss Cathy and he were now very thick; but Hindley hated him: and, to say the truth, I did the same; and we plagued and went on with him shamefully: for I wasn't reasonable enough to feel my injustice, and the mistress never put in a word on his behalf when she saw him wronged.

He seemed a sullen, patient child; hardened, perhaps, to ill-treatment; he would stand Hindley's blows without winking or shedding a tear, and my pinches moved him only to draw in a breath and open his eyes, as if he had hurt himself by accident and nobody was to blame. This endurance made old Earnshaw furious, when he discovered his son persecuting the poor, fatherless child, as he called him. He took to Heathcliff strangely, believing all he said (for that matter, he said precious little, and generally the truth), and petting him up far above Cathy, who was too mischievous and wayward for a favourite.

So, from the very beginning, he bred bad feeling in the house; and at Mrs Earnshaw's death, which happened in less than two years after, the young master had learned to regard his father as an oppressor rather than a friend, and Heathcliff as a usurper of his parent's affections and his privileges; and he grew bitter with brooding over these injuries. I sympathized a while; but when the children fell ill of the measles, and I had to tend them, and take on me the cares of a woman at once, I changed my ideas. Heathcliff was dangerously sick; and while he lay at the worst he would have me constantly by his pillow. I suppose he felt I had done a good deal for him, and he hadn't wit to guess that I was compelled to do it. However, I will say this, he was the quietest child that ever nurse watched over. The difference between him and the others forced me to be less partial. Cathy and her brother harassed me terribly; *he* was as uncomplaining as a lamb; though hardness, not gentleness, made him give little trouble.

He got through, and the doctor affirmed it was in a great measure owing to me, and praised me for my care. I was vain of his commendations, and softened towards the being by whose means I earned them, and thus Hindley lost his last ally; still I couldn't dote on Heathcliff, and I wondered often what my master saw to admire so much in the sullen boy, who never, to my recollection, repaid his indulgence by any sign of gratitude. He was not insolent to his benefactor, he was simply insensible; though knowing perfectly the hold he had on his heart, and conscious he had only to speak and all the house would be obliged to bend to his wishes. As an instance, I remember Mr Earnshaw once bought a couple of colts at the parish fair, and gave the lads each one. Heathcliff took the handsomest, but it soon fell lame, and when he discovered it, he said to Hindley –

'You must exchange horses with me: I don't like mine; and if you won't, I shall tell your father of the three thrashings you've given me this week, and show him my arm, which is black to the shoulder.'

Hindley put out his tongue, and cuffed him over the ears.

'You'd better do it at once,' he persisted, escaping to the porch (they were in the stable); 'you will have to; and if I speak of these blows, you'll get them again with interest.'

'Off, dog!' cried Hindley, threatening him with an iron weight used for weighing potatoes and hay.

'Throw it,' he replied, standing still, 'and then I'll tell how you boasted that you would turn me out of doors as soon as he died, and see whether he will not turn you out directly.'

Hindley threw it, hitting him on the breast, and down he fell, but staggered up immediately, breathless and white; and, had not I prevented it, he would have gone just so to the master, and got full revenge by letting his condition plead for him, intimating who had caused it.

'Take my colt, gypsy, then,' said young Earnshaw. 'And I pray that he may break your neck; take him, and be damned, you beggarly interloper! and wheedle my father out of all he has: only afterwards show him what you are, imp of Satan. And take that: I hope he'll kick out your brains!'

Heathcliff had gone to loose the beast, and shift it to his

own stall; he was passing behind it, when Hindley finished his speech by knocking him under its feet, and without stopping to examine whether his hopes were fulfilled, ran away as fast as he could. I was surprised to witness how coolly the child gathered himself up, and went on with his intention; exchanging saddles and all, and then sitting down on a bundle of hay to overcome the qualm which the violent blow occasioned, before he entered the house. I persuaded him easily to let me lay the blame of his bruises on the horse; he minded little what tale was told since he had what he wanted. He complained so seldom, indeed, of such stirs as these, that I really thought him not vindictive. I was deceived completely. . . .

Wuthering Heights, 1847

WILLIAM MAKEPEACE THACKERAY

[Dobbin]

THE PARTY was landed at the Royal Gardens in due time. As the majestic Jos stepped out of the creaking vehicle the crowd gave a cheer for the fat gentleman, who blushed and looked very big and mighty, as he walked away with Rebecca under his arm. George, of course, took charge of Amelia. She looked as happy as a rose-tree in sunshine.

'I say, Dobbin,' says George, 'just look to the shawls and things, there's a good fellow.' And so while he paired off with Miss Sedley, and Jos squeezed through the gate into the gardens with Rebecca at his side, honest Dobbin contented himself by giving an arm to the shawls, and by paying at the door for the whole party.

He walked very modestly behind them. He was not willing to spoil sport. About Rebecca and Jos he did not care a fig. But he thought Amelia worthy even of the brilliant George Osborne, and as he saw that good-looking couple threading the walks to the girl's delight and wonder, he watched her artless happiness with a sort of fatherly pleasure. Perhaps he felt that he would have liked to have something on his own arm besides a shawl (the people laughed at seeing the gawky young officer carrying this female burthen); but William Dobbin was very little addicted to selfish calculations at all; and so long as his friend was enjoying himself, how should he be discontented? And the truth is, that of all the delights of the Gardens; of the hundred thousand *extra* lamps, which were always lighted; the fiddlers in cocked hats, who played ravishing melodies under the gilded cockleshell in the midst of the Gardens; the singers, both of comic and sentimental ballads, who charmed the ears there; the country dances, formed by bouncing cockneys and cockneyesses, and executed amidst jumping, thumping, and laughter; the signal which announced that Madame Saqui was about to mount skyward on a slack-rope ascending to the stars; the hermit that always sat in the illuminated hermitage; the dark walks, so favourable to the interviews of young lovers; the pots of stout handed about by the people in the shabby old liveries; and the twinkling boxes, in which the happy feasters made-believe to eat slices of almost invisible ham; – of all these things, and of the gentle Simpson, that kind smiling idiot, who, I dare say, presided even then over the place – Captain William Dobbin did not take the slightest notice.

He carried about Amelia's white cashmere shawl, and having attended under the gilt cockle-shell, while Mrs Salmon performed the Battle of Borodino (a savage cantata against the Corsican upstart, who had lately met with his Russian reverses) – Mr Dobbin tried to hum it as he walked away, and found he was humming – the tune which Amelia Sedley sang on the stairs, as she came down to dinner.

He burst out laughing at himself; for the truth is, he could sing no better than an owl.

It is to be understood, as a matter of course, that our young people, being in parties of two and two, made the most solemn promises to keep together during the evening, and separated in ten minutes afterwards. Parties at Vauxhall always did separate, but 'twas only to meet again at supper-time, when they could talk of their mutual adventures in the interval.

What were the adventures of Mr Osborne and Miss Amelia? That is a secret. But be sure of this – they were perfectly happy, and correct in their behaviour; and as they had been in the habit of being together any time these fifteen years, their *tête-à-tête* offered no particular novelty.

But when Miss Rebecca Sharp and her stout companion lost themselves in a solitary walk, in which there were not above five score more of couples similarly straying, they both felt that the situation was extremely tender and critical, and now or never was the moment, Miss Sharp thought, to provoke that declaration which was trembling on the timid lips of Mr Sedley. They had previously been to the panorama of Moscow, where a rude fellow, treading on Miss Sharp's foot, caused her to fall back with a little shriek into the arms of Mr Sedley, and this little incident increased the tenderness and confidence of that gentleman to such a degree, that he told her several of his favourite Indian stories over again for, at least, the sixth time.

'How I should like to see India!' said Rebecca.

'*Should* you?' said Joseph, with a most killing tenderness; and was no doubt about to follow up this artful interrogatory by a question still more tender (for he puffed and panted a great deal, and Rebecca's hand, which was placed near his heart, could count the feverish pulsations of that organ), when, oh, provoking! the bell rang for the fireworks, and, a great scuffling and running taking place, these interesting lovers were obliged to follow in the stream of people.

Captain Dobbin had some thoughts of joining the party at supper; as, in truth, he found the Vauxhall amusement not particularly lively – but he paraded twice before the box where the now united couples were met, and nobody took any notice of him. Covers were laid for four. The mated pairs were prattling away quite happily, and Dobbin knew he was as clean forgotten as if he had never existed in this world.

'I should only be *de trop*,' said the Captain, looking at them rather wistfully. 'I'd best go and talk to the hermit,' – and so he strolled off out of the hum of men, and noise, and clatter of the banquet, into the dark walk, at the end of which lived that well-known pasteboard Solitary. It wasn't very good fun for Dobbin – and, indeed, to be alone at Vauxhall, I have found, from my own experience, to be one of the most dismal sports ever entered into by a bachelor.

Vanity Fair: A Novel without a Hero, 1847–8

CHARLES DICKENS

[Domestic Economy]

A T THE appointed time in the evening, Mr Micawber reappeared. I washed my hands and face, to do the greater honour to his gentility, and we walked to our house, as I suppose I must now call it, together; Mr Micawber impressing the names of streets, and the shapes of corner houses upon me, as we went along, that I might find my way back, easily, in the morning.

Arrived at his house in Windsor Terrace (which I noticed was shabby like himself, but also, like himself, made all the show it could), he presented me to Mrs Micawber, a thin and faded lady, not at all young, who was sitting in the parlour (the first floor was altogether unfurnished, and the blinds were kept down to delude the neighbours), with a baby at her breast. This baby was one of twins; and I may remark here that I hardly ever, in all my experience of the family, saw both the twins detached from Mrs Micawber at the same time. One of them was always taking refreshment.

There were two other children; Master Micawber, aged about four, and Miss Micawber, aged about three. These, and a dark-complexioned young woman, with a habit of snorting, who was servant to the family, and informed me, before half-an-hour had expired, that she was 'a Orfling', and came from St Luke's workhouse, in the neighbourhood, completed the establishment. My room was at the top of the house, at the back; a close chamber; stencilled all over with an ornament which my young imagination represented as a blue muffin; and very scantily furnished.

'I never thought,' said Mrs Micawber, when she came up, twin and all, to show me the apartment, and sat down to take breath, 'before I was married, when I lived with papa and mama, that I should ever find it necessary to take a lodger. But Mr Micawber being in difficulties, all considerations of private feeling must give way.'

I said: 'Yes, ma'am.'

'Mr Micawber's difficulties are almost overwhelming just at present,' said Mrs Micawber; 'and whether it is possible to bring him through them, I don't know. When I lived at home with papa and mama, I really should have hardly understood what the word meant, in the sense in which I now employ it, but experientia does it – as papa used to say.'

I cannot satisfy myself whether she told me that Mr Micawber had been an officer in the Marines, or whether I imagined it. I only know that I believe to this hour that he *was* in the Marines once upon a time, without knowing why. He was a sort of town traveller for a number of miscellaneous houses, now; but made little or nothing of it, I am afraid.

'If Mr Micawber's creditors *will not* give him time,' said Mrs Micawber, 'they must take the consequences; and the sooner they bring it to an issue the better. Blood cannot be obtained from a stone, neither can anything on account be obtained at present (not to mention law expenses) from Mr Micawber.'

I never can quite understand whether my precocious self-dependence confused Mrs Micawber in reference to my age, or whether she was so full of the subject that she would have talked about it to the very twins if there had been nobody else to communicate with, but this was the strain in which she began, and she went on accordingly all the time I knew her.

Poor Mrs Micawber! She said she had tried to exert herself; and so, I have no doubt, she had. The centre of the street-door was perfectly covered with a great brass-plate, on which was engraved 'Mrs Micawber's Boarding Establishment for Young Ladies': but I never found that any young lady had ever been to school there; or that any young lady ever came, or proposed to come; or that the least preparation was ever made to receive any young lady. The only visitors I ever saw or heard of, were creditors. *They* used to come at all hours, and some of them were quite ferocious. One dirty-faced man, I think he was a bootmaker, used to edge himself into the passage as early as seven o'clock in the morning, and call up the stairs to Mr Micawber – 'Come! You ain't out yet, you know. Pay us, will you? Don't hide, you know; that's mean. I wouldn't be mean if I was you. Pay us, will you? You just pay us, d'ye hear? Come!' Receiving no answer to these taunts, he would mount in his wrath to the words 'swindlers' and 'robbers'; and these being ineffectual too, would sometimes go to the extremity of crossing the street, and roaring up at the windows of the second floor, where he knew Mr Micawber was. At these times, Mr Micawber would be transported with grief and mortification, even to the length (as I was once made aware by a scream from his wife) of making motions at himself with a razor; but within half-an-hour afterwards, he would polish up his shoes with extraordinary pains, and go out, humming a tune with a greater air of gentility than ever. Mrs Micawber was quite as elastic. I have known her to be thrown into fainting fits by the king's taxes at three o'clock; and to eat lamb chops breaded, and drink warm ale (paid for with two tea-spoons that had gone to the pawnbroker's) at four. On one occasion, when an execution had just been put in, coming home through some chance as early as six o'clock, I saw her lying (of course with a twin) under the grate in a swoon, with her hair all torn about her face; but I never knew her more cheerful than she was, that very same night, over a veal-cutlet before the kitchen fire, telling me stories about her papa and mama, and the company they used to keep.

The Personal History of David Copperfield, 1849–50

[Telescopic Philanthropy]

THE ROOM, which was strewn with papers and nearly filled by a great writing-table covered with similar litter, was, I must say, not only very untidy, but very dirty. We were obliged to take notice of that with our sense of sight, even while, with our sense of hearing, we followed the poor child who had tumbled down-stairs: I think into the back kitchen, where somebody seemed to stifle him.

But what principally struck us was a jaded and unhealthy-looking, though by no means plain girl, at the writing-table, who sat biting the feather of her pen, and staring at us. I suppose nobody ever was in such a state of ink. And, from her tumbled hair to her pretty feet, which were disfigured with frayed and broken satin slippers trodden down at heel, she really seemed to have no article of dress upon her, from a pin upwards, that was in its proper condition or its right place.

'You find me, my dears,' said Mrs Jellyby, snuffing the two great office candles in tin candlesticks which made the room taste strongly of hot tallow (the fire had gone out, and there was nothing in the grate but ashes, a bundle of wood, and a poker), 'you find me, my dears, as usual, very busy; but that you will excuse. The African project at present employs my whole time. It involves me in correspondence with public bodies, and with private individuals anxious for the welfare of their species all over the country. I am happy to say it is advancing. We hope by this time next year to have from a hundred and fifty to two hundred healthy families cultivating coffee and educating the natives of Borrioboola-Gha, on the left bank of the Niger.'

As Ada said nothing, but looked at me, I said it must be very gratifying.

'It *is* gratifying,' said Mrs Jellyby. 'It involves the devotion of all my energies, such as they are; but that is nothing, so that it succeeds; and I am more confident of success every day. Do you know, Miss Summerson, I almost wonder that *you* never turned your thoughts to Africa.'

This application of the subject was really so unexpected to me, that I was quite at a loss how to receive it. I hinted that the climate—

'The finest climate in the world!' said Mrs Jellyby.

'Indeed, ma'am?'

'Certainly. With precaution,' said Mrs Jellyby. 'You may go into Holborn, without precaution, and be run over. You may go into Holborn, with precaution, and never be run over. Just so with Africa.'

I said, 'No doubt,' – I meant as to Holborn.

'If you would like,' said Mrs Jellyby, putting a number of papers towards us, 'to look over some remarks on that head and on the general subject (which have been extensively circulated), while I finish a letter I am now dictating – to my eldest daughter, who is my amanuensis—'

The girl at the table left off biting her pen, and made a return to our recognition, which was half bashful and half sulky.

' – I shall then have finished for the present,' proceeded Mrs Jellyby, with a sweet smile; 'though my work is never done. Where are you, Caddy?'

'"Presents her compliments to Mr Swallow, and begs – "' said Caddy.

'"And begs,"' said Mrs Jellyby, dictating, '"to inform him, in reference to his letter of inquiry on the African project." – No, Peepy! Not on any account!'

Peepy (so self-named) was the unfortunate child who had fallen down-stairs, who now interrupted the correspondence by presenting himself, with a strip of plaister on his fore-head, to exhibit his wounded knees, in which Ada and I did not know which to pity most – the bruises or the dirt. Mrs Jellyby merely added, with the serene composure with which she said everything, 'Go along, you naughty Peepy!' and fixed her fine eyes on Africa again.

However, as she at once proceeded with her dictation, and as I interrupted nothing by doing it, I ventured quietly to stop poor Peepy as he was going out, and to take him up to nurse. He looked very much astonished at it, and at Ada's kissing him; but soon fell fast asleep in my arms, sobbing at longer and longer intervals, until he was quiet. I was so occupied with Peepy that I lost the letter in detail, though I derived such a general impression from it of the momentous importance of Africa, and the utter insignificance of all other places and things, that I felt quite ashamed to have thought so little about it.

'Six o'clock!' said Mrs Jellyby. 'And our dinner hour is nominally (for we dine at all hours) five! Caddy, show Miss Clare and Miss Summerson their rooms. You will like to make some change, perhaps? You will excuse me, I know, being so much occupied. O, that very bad child! Pray put him down, Miss Summerson!'

I begged permission to retain him, truly saying that he was not at all troublesome; and carried him up-stairs and laid him on my bed. Ada and I had two upper rooms, with a door of communication between. They were excessively bare and disorderly, and the curtain to my window was fastened up with a fork.

'You would like some hot water, wouldn't you?' said Miss Jellyby, looking round for a jug with a handle to it, but looking in vain.

'If it is not being troublesome,' said we.

'Oh, it's not the trouble,' returned Miss Jellyby; 'the question is, if there *is* any.'

The evening was so very cold, and the rooms had such a marshy smell, that I must confess it was a little miserable; and Ada was half crying. We soon laughed, however, and were busily unpacking, when Miss Jellyby came back to say that she was sorry there was no hot water; but they couldn't find the kettle, and the boiler was out of order.

We begged her not to mention it, and made all the haste we could to get down to the fire again. But all the little children had come up to the landing outside, to look at the phenomenon of Peepy lying on my bed; and our attention was distracted by the constant apparition of noses and fingers, in situations of danger between the hinges of the doors. It was impossible to shut the door of either room; for my lock, with no knob to it, looked as if it wanted to be wound up; and though the handle of Ada's went round and round with the greatest smoothness, it was attended with no effect whatever on the door. Therefore I proposed to the children that they should come in and be very good at my table, and I would tell them the story of Little Red Riding Hood while I dressed; which they did, and were as quiet as mice, including Peepy, who awoke opportunely before the appearance of the wolf.

When we went down-stairs we found a mug, with 'A Present from Tunbridge Wells' on it, lighted up in the staircase window with a floating wick; and a young woman, with a swelled face bound up in a flannel bandage, blowing the fire of the drawing room (now connected by an open door with Mrs Jellyby's rooms), and choking dreadfully. It smoked to that degree in short, that we all sat coughing and crying with the windows open for half an hour; during which Mrs Jellyby, with the same sweetness of temper, directed letters about Africa. Her being so employed was, I must say, a great relief to me; for Richard told us that he had washed his hands in a pie-dish, and that they had found the kettle on his dressing-table; and he made Ada laugh so, that they made me laugh in the most ridiculous manner.

Bleak House, 1852–3

[Blood]

A LARGE cask of wine had been dropped and broken, in the street. The accident had happened in getting it out of a cart; the cask had tumbled out with a run, the hoops had burst, and it lay on the stones just outside the door of the wine-shop, shattered like a walnut-shell.

All the people within reach had suspended their business, or their idleness, to run to the spot and drink the wine. The rough, irregular stones of the street, pointing every way, and designed, one might have thought, expressly to lame all living creatures that approached them, had dammed it into little pools; these were surrounded, each by its own jostling group or crowd, according to its size. Some men kneeled down, made scoops of their two hands joined, and sipped, or tried to help women, who bent over their shoulders, to sip, before the wine had all run out between their fingers. Others, men and women, dipped in the puddles with little mugs of mutilated earthenware, or even with handkerchiefs from women's heads, which were squeezed dry into infants' mouths; others made small mud embankments, to stem the wine as it ran; others, directed by lookers-on up at high windows, darted here and there, to cut off little streams of wine that started away in new directions; others devoted themselves to the sodden and lee-dyed pieces of the cask, licking, and even champing the moister wine-rotted fragments with eager relish. There was no drainage to carry off the wine, and not only did it all get taken up, but so much mud got taken up along with it, that there might have been a scavenger in the street, if anybody acquainted with it could have believed in such a miraculous presence.

A shrill sound of laughter and of amused voices – voices of men, women, and children – resounded in the street while this wine game lasted. There was little roughness in the sport, and much playfulness. There was a special companionship in it, an observable inclination on the part of every one to join some other one, which led, especially among the luckier or lighter-hearted, to frolicsome embraces, drinking of healths, shaking of hands, and even joining of hands and dancing, a dozen together. When the wine was gone, and the places where it had been most abundant were raked into a gridiron-pattern by fingers, these demonstrations ceased, as suddenly as they had broken out. The man who had left his saw sticking in the firewood he was cutting, set it in motion again; the woman who had left on a door-step the little pot of hot ashes, at which she had been trying to soften the pain in her own starved fingers and toes, or in those of her child, returned to it; men with bare arms, matted locks, and cadaverous faces, who had emerged into the winter light from cellars, moved away, to descend again; and a gloom gathered on the scene that appeared more natural to it than sunshine.

The wine was red wine, and had stained the ground of the narrow street in the suburb of Saint Antoine, in Paris, where it was spilled. It had stained many hands, too, and many

faces, and many naked feet, and many wooden shoes. The
hands of the man who sawed the wood, left red marks on
the billets; and the forehead of the woman who nursed her
baby, was stained with the stain of the old rag she wound
about her head again. Those who had been greedy with the
staves of the cask, had acquired a tigerish smear about the
mouth; and one tall joker so besmirched, his head more out
of a long squalid bag of a night-cap than in it, scrawled upon
a wall with his finger dipped in muddy wine-lees – BLOOD.

The time was to come, when that wine too would be
spilled on the street-stones, and when the stain of it would
be red upon many there.

A Tale of Two Cities, 1859

[Pip and Estella]

M ISS HAVISHAM beckoned her to come close, and took
up a jewel from the table, and tried its effect upon her
fair young bosom and against her pretty brown hair. 'Your
own, one day, my dear, and you will use it well. Let me see
you play cards with this boy.'

'With this boy! Why, he is a common labouring-boy!'

I thought I overheard Miss Havisham answer – only it
seemed so unlikely – 'Well? You can break his heart.'

'What do you play, boy?' asked Estella of myself, with
the greatest disdain.

'Nothing but beggar my neighbour, Miss.'

'Beggar him,' said Miss Havisham to Estella. So we sat
down to cards.

It was then I began to understand that everything in the
room had stopped, like the watch and the clock, a long time
ago. I noticed that Miss Havisham put down the jewel
exactly on the spot from which she had taken it up. As
Estella dealt the cards, I glanced at the dressing-table again,
and saw that the shoe upon it, once white, now yellow, had
never been worn. I glanced down at the foot from which the

shoe was absent, and saw that the silk stocking on it, once white, now yellow, had been trodden ragged. Without this arrest of everything, this standing still of all the pale decayed objects, not even the withered bridal dress on the collapsed form could have looked so like grave-clothes, or the long veil so like a shroud.

So she sat, corpse-like, as we played at cards; the frillings and trimmings on her bridal dress, looking like earthy paper. I knew nothing then of the discoveries that are occasionally made of bodies buried in ancient times, which fall to powder in the moment of being distinctly seen; but, I have often thought since, that she must have looked as if the admission of the natural light of day would have struck her to dust.

'He calls the knaves, Jacks, this boy!' said Estella with disdain, before our first game was out. 'And what coarse hands he has! And what thick boots!'

I had never thought of being ashamed of my hands before; but I began to consider them a very indifferent pair. Her contempt for me was so strong, that it became infectious, and I caught it.

She won the game, and I dealt. I misdealt, as was only natural, when I knew she was lying in wait for me to do wrong; and she denounced me for a stupid, clumsy labouring boy.

'You say nothing of her,' remarked Miss Havisham to me, as she looked on. 'She says many hard things of you, yet you say nothing of her. What do you think of her?'

'I don't like to say,' I stammered.

'Tell me in my ear,' said Miss Havisham, bending down.

'I think she is very proud,' I replied, in a whisper.

'Anything else?'

'I think she is very pretty.'

'Anything else?'

'I think she is very insulting.' (She was looking at me then with a look of supreme aversion.)

'Anything else?'

'I think I should like to go home.'

'And never see her again, though she is so pretty?'

'I am not sure that I shouldn't like to see her again, but I should like to go home now.'

'You shall go soon,' said Miss Havisham aloud. 'Play the game out.'

Saving for the one weird smile at first, I should have felt almost sure that Miss Havisham's face could not smile. It had dropped into a watchful and brooding expression – most likely when all the things about her had become transfixed – and it looked as if nothing could ever lift it up again. Her chest had dropped, so that she stooped, and her voice had dropped, so that she spoke low, and with a dead lull upon her; altogether, she had the appearance of having dropped, body and soul, within and without, under the weight of a crushing blow.

I played the game to an end with Estella, and she beggared me. She threw the cards down on the table when she had won them all, as if she despised them for having been won of me.

'When shall I have you here again?' said Miss Havisham. 'Let me think.'

I was beginning to remind her that today was Wednesday when she checked me with her former impatient movement of the fingers of her right hand.

'There! there! I know nothing of days of the week; I know nothing of weeks of the year. Come again after six days. You hear?'

'Yes, ma'am.'

'Estella, take him down. Let him have something to eat and let him roam and look about him while he eats. Go, Pip.'

I followed the candle down, as I had followed the candle up, and she stood it in the place where we had found it. Until she opened that side entrance, I had fancied, without thinking about it, that it must necessarily be night-time. The rush of the daylight quite confounded me, and made me feel as if I had been in the candlelight of the strange room many hours.

'You are to wait here, you boy,' said Estella; and disappeared and closed the door.

I took the opportunity of being alone in the court-yard, to look at my coarse hands and my common boots. My opinion of those accessories was not favourable. They had never troubled me before, but they troubled me now, as vulgar appendages. I determined to ask Joe why he had ever taught me to call those picture-cards, Jacks, which ought to be called knaves. I wished Joe had been rather more genteelly brought up, and then I should have been so too.

She came back, with some bread and meat and a little mug of beer. She put the mug down on the stones of the yard, and gave me the bread and meat without looking at me, as insolently as if I were a dog in disgrace. I was so humiliated, hurt, spurned, offended, angry, sorry – I cannot hit upon the right name for the smart – God knows what its name was – that tears started to my eyes. The moment they sprang there, the girl looked at me with a quick delight in having been the cause of them. This gave me power to keep them back and to look at her: so, she gave a contemptuous toss – but with a sense, I thought, of having made too sure that I was so wounded – and left me.

Great Expectations, 1860–61

CHARLES KINGSLEY

[Sweating]

W E TOOK a room, and Crossthwaite coolly saw us all in; and locking the door, stood with his back against it.

'Now then, mind, "One and all," as the Cornishmen say, and no peaching. If any man is scoundrel enough to carry tales, I'll—'

'Do what?' asked Jemmy Downes, who had settled himself on the table, with a pipe and a pot of porter. 'You arn't the king of the Cannibal Islands, as I know of, to cut a cove's head off?'

'No; but if a poor man's prayer can bring God's curse down upon a traitor's head – it may stay on his rascally shoulders till it rots.'

'If ifs and ans were pots and pans. Lo)k at Shechem Isaacs, that sold penknives in the street six months ago, now a-riding in his own carriage, all along of turning sweater. If God's curse is like that – I'll be happy to take any man's share of it.'

Some new idea seemed twinkling in the fellow's cunning bloated face as he spoke. I, and others also, shuddered at his words; but we all forgot them a moment afterwards, as Crossthwaite began to speak.

'We were all bound to expect this. Every working tailor must come to this at last, on the present system; and we are only lucky in having been spared so long. You all know where this will end – in the same misery as fifteen thousand out of twenty thousand of our class are enduring now. We shall become the slaves, often the bodily prisoners, of Jews, middlemen, and sweaters, who draw their livelihood out of our starvation. We shall have to face, as the rest have, ever decreasing prices of labour, ever increasing profits made out of that labour by the contractors who will employ us – arbitrary fines, inflicted at the caprice of hirelings – the competition of women, and children, and starving Irish – our hours of work will increase one-third, our actual pay decrease to less than one-half; and in all this we shall have no hope, no chance of improvement in wages, but ever more penury, slavery, misery, as we are pressed on by those who are sucked by fifties – almost by hundreds – yearly, out of the honourable trade in which we were brought up, into the infernal system of contract work, which is devouring our trade and many others, body and soul. Our wives will be forced to sit up night and day to help us – our children must labour from the cradle without chance of going to school, hardly of breathing the fresh air of heaven, – our boys, as they grow up, must turn beggars or paupers – our daughters, as thousands do, must eke out their miserable earnings by prostitution. And after all, a whole family will not gain what one of us had been doing, as yet, single-handed. You know there will be no hope for us. There is no use appealing to government or parliament. I don't want to talk politics here. I shall keep them for another place. But you can recollect as well as I can, when a deputation of us went up to a member of parliament – one that was reputed a philosopher, and a political economist, and a liberal – and set before him the ever-increasing penury and misery of our trade, and of those connected with it; you recollect his answer – that, however glad he would be to help us, it was impossible – he could not alter the laws of nature – that wages were regulated by the amount of competition among the men themselves, and that it was no business of government, or any one else, to interfere in contracts between the employer and employed, that those things regulated themselves by the laws of political economy, which was madness and suicide to oppose. He may have been a wise man. I only know that he was a rich one. Every one speaks well of the bridge which carries him over. Every one fancies the laws which fill his pockets to be God's laws. But I say this, If neither government nor members of parliament can help us, we must help ourselves. Help yourselves, and heaven will help you. Combination among ourselves is the only chance. One thing we can do – sit still.'

'And starve!' said some one.

'Yes, and starve! Better starve than sin. I say, it is a sin to give in to this system. It is a sin to add our weight to the crowd of artizans who are now choking and strangling each other to death, as the prisoners did in the black hole of Calcutta. Let those who will turn beasts of prey, and feed upon their fellows; but let us at least keep ourselves pure. It may be the law of political civilization, the law of nature, that the rich should eat up the poor, and the poor eat up each other. Then I here rise up and curse that law, that civilization, that nature. Either I will destroy them, or they shall destroy me. As a slave, as an increased burden on my fellow sufferers, I will not live. So help me God! I will take no work home to my house; and I call upon every one here to combine, and to sign a protest to that effect.'

'What's the use of that, my good Mr Crossthwaite?' interrupted some one, querulously. 'Don't you know what came of the strike a few years ago, when this piecework and sweating first came in? The masters made fine promises, and never kept 'em; and the men who stood out had their places filled up with poor devils who were glad enough to take the work at any price – just as ours will be. There's no use kicking against the pricks. All the rest have come to it, and so must we. We must live somehow, and half a loaf is better than no bread; and even that half loaf will go into other men's mouths, if we don't snap at it at once. Besides, we can't force others to strike. We may strike and starve ourselves, but what's the use of a dozen striking out of 20,000?'

'Will you sign the protest, gentlemen, or not?' asked Crossthwaite, in a determined voice.

Some half-dozen said they would if the others would.

'And the others won't. Well, after all, one man must take the responsibility, and I am that man. I will sign the protest by myself. I will sweep a crossing – I will turn cress-gatherer, rag-picker; I will starve piecemeal, and see my wife starve with me; but do the wrong thing I will not! The Cause wants martyrs. If I must be one, I must.'

All this while my mind had been undergoing a strange perturbation. The notion of escaping that infernal work-room, and the company I met there – of taking my work home, and thereby, as I hoped, gaining more time for study – at least, having my books on the spot ready at every odd moment, was most enticing. I had hailed the proposed change as a blessing to me, till I heard Crossthwaite's arguments – not that I had not known the facts before; but it had never struck me till then that it was a real sin against my class to make myself a party in the system by which they were allowing themselves (under temptation enough, God knows) to be enslaved. But now I looked with horror on the gulf of penury before me, into the vortex of which not only I, but my whole trade, seemed irresistibly sucked. I thought, with shame and remorse, of the few shillings which I had earned at various times by taking piecework home, to buy my candles for study. I whispered my doubts to Crossthwaite, as he sat, pale and determined, watching the excited and querulous discussions among the other workmen.

'What? So you expect to have time to read? Study after sixteen hours a day stitching? Study, when you cannot earn money enough to keep you from wasting and shrinking away day by day? Study, with your heart full of shame and indignation, fresh from daily insult and injustice? Study, with the black cloud of despair and penury in front of you? Little time, or heart, or strength, will you have to study, when you are making the same coats you make now, at half the price.'

I put my name down beneath Crossthwaite's, on the paper which he handed me, and went out with him.

'Ay,' he muttered to himself, 'be slaves – what you are worthy to be, that you will be! You dare not combine – you dare not starve – you dare not die – and therefore you dare not be free! Oh! for six hundred men like Barbaroux's Marseillois – "who knew how to die!"'

'Surely, Crossthwaite, if matters were properly represented to the government, they would not, for their own existence' sake, to put conscience out of the question, allow such a system to continue growing.'

'Government – government? You a tailor, and not know that government are the very authors of this system? Not to know that they first set the example, by getting the army and navy clothes made by contractors, and taking the lowest tenders? Not to know that the police clothes, the postmen's clothes, the convicts' clothes, are all contracted for on the same infernal plan, by sweaters, and sweaters' sweaters, and sweaters' sweaters' sweaters, till government work is just the very last, lowest resource to which a poor starved-out wretch betakes himself to keep body and soul together? Why, the government prices, in almost every department, are half, and less than half, the very lowest living price. I tell you, the careless iniquity of government about these things will come out some day. It will be known, the whole abomination, and future generations will class it with the tyrannies of the Roman emperors and the Norman barons. Why, it's a fact, that the colonels of the regiments – noblemen, most of them – make their own vile profit out of us tailors – out of the pauperism of the men, the slavery of the children, the prostitution of the women. They get so much a uniform allowed them by government to clothe the men with; and then – then, they let out the jobs to the contractors at less than half what government give them, and pocket the difference. And then you talk of appealing to government.'

'Upon my word,' I said, bitterly, 'we tailors seem to owe the army a double grudge. They not only keep under other artizans, but they help to starve us first, and then shoot us, if we complain too loudly.'

Alton Locke, Tailor and Poet:
An Autobiography, 1850

HENRY MAYHEW

[A Young Pickpocket]

'WE TRAVELLED across country, and got to Maidstone, and did two handkerchiefs. One I wore round my neck, and the other the lodging-house-keeper pawned for us for 1s 6d. In Maidstone, next morning, I was nailed, and had three months of it. I didn't mind it so much then, but Maidstone's far worse now, I've heard. I have been in prison three times in Brixton, three times in the Old Horse [*Bridewell*], three times in the Compter, once in the Steel, and once in Maidstone – thirteen times in all, including twice I was remanded, and got off; but I don't reckon that prison.

'Every time I came out harder than I went in. I've had four floggings; it was bad enough – a flogging was – while it lasted; but when I got out I soon forgot it. At a week's end I never thought again about it. If I had been better treated I should have been a better lad. I could leave off thieving now as if I had never thieved, if I could live without.' [I am inclined to doubt this part of the statement.] 'I have carried on this sort of life until now. I didn't often make a very good thing of it. I saw Manning and his wife hung. Mrs Manning was dressed beautiful when she came up. She screeched when Jack Ketch pulled the bolt away. She was

harder than Manning, they all said; without her there would
have been no murder. It was a great deal talked about, and
Manning was pitied. It was a punishment to her to come on
the scaffold and see Manning with the rope about his neck,
if people takes it in the right light. I did 4s 6d at the hanging
– two handkerchiefs, and a purse with 2s in it – the best
purse I ever had; but I've only done three or four purses.
The reason is, because I've never been well dressed. If I
went near a lady, she would say, "Tush, tush, you ragged
fellow!" and would shrink away. But I would rather rob the
rich than the poor; they miss it less. But 1s honest goes
further than 5s stolen. Some call that only a saying, but it's
true.

'All the money I got soon went – most of it a-gambling.
Picking pockets, when anyone comes to think on it, is the
daringest thing that a boy can do. It didn't in the least
frighten me to see Manning and Mrs Manning hanged. I
never thought I should come to the gallows, and I never
shall – I'm not high-tempered enough for that. The only
thing that frightens me when I'm in prison is sleeping in a
cell by myself – you do in the Old Horse and the Steel –
because I think things may appear. You can't imagine how
one dreams when in trouble. I've often started up in a
fright from a dream. I don't know what might appear. I've
heard people talk about ghosts and that. Once, in the
County, a tin had been left under a tap that went drip –
drip – drip. And all in the ward were shocking frightened;
and weren't we glad when we found out what it was! Boys
tell stories about haunted castles, and cats that are devils;
and that frightens one. At the fire in Monument-yard I did
5s 7d – 3s in silver and 2s 3d in handkerchiefs, and 4d for
three pairs of gloves. I sell my handkerchiefs in the Lane
(Petticoat-lane). I carry on this trade still. Most times I've
got in prison is when I've been desperate from hunger, and
have said to B—— "Now I'll have money, nailed or not
nailed."

'I can pick a woman's pocket as easy as a man's, though
you wouldn't think it. If one's in prison for begging, one's
laughed at. The others say, "Begging! Oh, you cadger!" So
a boy is partly forced to steal for his character. I've lived a

good deal in lodging-houses, and know the ways of them. They are very bad places for a boy to be in. Where I am now, when the place is full, there's upwards of 100 can be accommodated. I won't be there long, I'll do something to get out of it. There's people there will rob their own brother. There's people there that talk backward – for one they say *eno*, for two *owt*, for three *eerht*, for four *rouf*, for five *evif*, for six *exis*. I don't know any higher. I can neither read nor write. In this lodging-house there are no women. They talk there chiefly about what they've done, or are going to do, or have set their minds upon, just as you and any other gentlemen might do.

'I have been in lodging-houses in Mint-street and Kent-street, where men and women and children all slept in one room. I think the men and women who slept together were generally married, or lived together; but it's not right for a big boy to sleep in the same room. Young men have had beds to themselves, and so have young women there; but there's a deputy comes into the room, every now and then, to see there's nothing wrong. There's little said in these places, the people are generally so tired. Where I am there's horrid language – swearing, and everything that's bad. They are to be pitied, because there's not work for honest people, let alone thieves. In the lodging-houses the air is very bad, enough to stifle one in bed – so many breaths together. Without such places my trade couldn't be carried on; I couldn't live. Some though would find another way out. Three or four would take a room among them. Anybody's money's good – you can always get a room. . . .'

London Labour and the London Poor, 1851

GEORGE BORROW

[Rommany]

'WE WERE talking of language, Jasper?'
  'True, brother.'
'Yours must be a rum one?'
''Tis called Rommany.'
'I would gladly know it.'
'You need it sorely.'
'Would you teach it me?'
'None sooner.'
'Suppose we begin now?'
'Suppose we do, brother.'
'Not whilst I am here,' said the woman, flinging her knitting down, and starting upon her feet; 'not whilst I am here shall this gorgio learn Rommany. A pretty manoeuvre, truly; and what would be the end of it? I goes to the farming ker with my sister, to tell a fortune, and earn a few sixpences for the chabes. I see a jolly pig in the yard, and I says to my sister, speaking Rommany, "Do so and so," says I; which the farming man hearing, asks what we are talking about. "Nothing at all, master," says I; "something about the weather"; when who should start up from behind a pale, where he has been listening, but this ugly gorgio, crying out, "They are after poisoning your pigs, neighbour!" so that we are glad to run, I and my sister, with perhaps the farm-engro shouting after us. Says my sister to me, when we have got fairly off, "How came that ugly one to know what you said to me?" Whereupon I answers, "It all comes of my son Jasper, who brings the gorgio to our fire, and must needs be teaching him." "Who was fool there?" says my sister. "Who, indeed, but my son Jasper," I answers. And here should I be a greater fool to sit still and suffer it; which I will not do. I do not like the look of him; he looks over-gorgeous. An ill day to the Romans when he masters Rommany; and when I says that, I pens a true dukkerin.'

Lavengro, 1851

ELIZABETH GASKELL

[A Literary Contest]

WHEN THE trays reappeared with biscuits and wine, punctually at a quarter to nine, there was conversation, comparing of cards, and talking over tricks; but by and by Captain Brown sported a bit of literature.

'Have you seen any numbers of *The Pickwick Papers*?' said he. (They were then publishing in parts.) 'Capital thing!'

Now Miss Jenkyns was daughter of a deceased rector of Cranford; and, on the strength of a number of manuscript sermons, and a pretty good library of divinity, considered herself literary, and looked upon any conversation about books as a challenge to her. So she answered and said, 'Yes, she had seen them; indeed, she might say she had read them.'

'And what do you think of them?' exclaimed Captain Brown. 'Aren't they famously good?'

So urged, Miss Jenkyns could not but speak.

'I must say, I don't think they are by any means equal to Dr Johnson. Still, perhaps the author is young. Let him persevere, and who knows what he may become if he will take the great Doctor for his model.' This was evidently too much for Captain Brown to take placidly: and I saw the words on the tip of his tongue before Miss Jenkyns had finished her sentence.

'It is quite a different sort of thing, my dear madam,' he began.

'I am quite aware of that,' returned she. 'And I make allowance, Captain Brown.'

'Just allow me to read you a scene out of this month's number,' pleaded he. 'I had it only this morning, and I don't think the company can have read it yet.'

'As you please,' said she, settling herself with an air of resignation. He read the account of the 'swarry' which Sam Weller gave at Bath. Some of us laughed heartily. I did not dare, because I was staying in the house. Miss Jenkyns sat in patient gravity. When it was ended, she turned to me, and said, with mild dignity –

'Fetch me *Rasselas*, my dear, out of the book-room.'

When I brought it to her she turned to Captain Brown –

'Now allow *me* to read you a scene, and then the present company can judge between your favourite, Mr Boz, and Dr Johnson.'

She read one of the conversations between Rasselas and Imlac, in a high-pitched majestic voice; and when she had ended, she said, 'I imagine I am now justified in my preference of Dr Johnson as a writer of fiction.' The Captain screwed his lips up, and drummed on the table, but he did not speak. She thought she would give a finishing blow or two.

'I consider it vulgar, and below the dignity of literature, to publish in numbers.'

'How was *The Rambler* published, ma'am?' asked Captain Brown, in a low voice, which I think Miss Jenkyns could not have heard.

'Dr Johnson's style is a model for young beginners. My father recommended it to me when I began to write letters – I have formed my own style upon it; I recommend it to your favourite.'

'I should be very sorry for him to exchange his style for any such pompous writing,' said Captain Brown.

Miss Jenkyns felt this as a personal affront, in a way of which the Captain had not dreamed. Epistolary writing she and her friends considered as her *forte*. Many a copy of many a letter have I seen written and corrected on the slate, before she 'seized the half-hour just previous to post-time to assure' her friends of this or of that; and Dr Johnson was, as she said, her model in these compositions. She drew herself up, with dignity, and only replied to Captain Brown's last remark by saying, with marked emphasis on every syllable, 'I prefer Dr Johnson to Mr Boz.'

It is said – I won't vouch for the fact – that Captain Brown was heard to say, *sotto voce*, 'D—n Dr Johnson!' If he did, he was penitent afterwards, as he showed by going to stand

near Miss Jenkyns's arm-chair, and endeavouring to beguile
her into conversation on some more pleasing subject. But
she was inexorable.

Cranford, 1853

[Human Interest]

THE SIDE of the town on which Crampton lay was
especially a thoroughfare for the factory people. In the
back streets around them there were many mills, out of
which poured streams of men and women two or three
times a day. Until Margaret had learnt the times of their
ingress and egress, she was very unfortunate in constantly
falling in with them. They came rushing along, with bold,
fearless faces, and loud laughs and jests, particularly aimed
at all those who appeared to be above them in rank or
station. The tones of their unrestrained voices, and their
carelessness of all common rules of street politeness, frightened Margaret a little at first. The girls, with their rough,
but not unfriendly freedom, would comment on her dress,
even touch her shawl or gown to ascertain the exact
material; nay, once or twice she was asked questions relative to some article which they particularly admired. There
was such a simple reliance on her womanly sympathy with
their love of dress, and on her kindliness, that she gladly
replied to these inquiries, as soon as she understood them;
and half smiled back at their remarks. She did not mind
meeting any number of girls, loud spoken and boisterous
though they might be. But she alternately dreaded and fired
up against the workmen, who commented not on her dress,
but on her looks, in the same open, fearless manner. She,
who had hitherto felt that even the most refined remark on
her personal appearance was an impertinence, had to
endure undisguised admiration from these outspoken men.
But the very outspokenness marked their innocence of any

intention to hurt her delicacy, as she would have perceived if she had been less frightened by the disorderly tumult. Out of her fright came a flash of indignation which made her face scarlet, and her dark eyes gather flame, as she heard some of their speeches. Yet there were other sayings of theirs, which, when she reached the quiet safety of home, amused her even while they irritated her.

For instance, one day, after she had passed a number of men, several of whom had paid her the not unusual compliment of wishing she was their sweetheart, one of the lingerers added, 'Your bonny face, my lass, makes the day look brighter.' And another day, as she was unconsciously smiling at some passing thought, she was addressed by a poorly-dressed, middle-aged workman, with 'You may well smile, my lass; many a one would smile to have such a bonny face.' This man looked so careworn that Margaret could not help giving him an answering smile, glad to think that her looks, such as they were, should have had the power to call up a pleasant thought. He seemed to understand her acknowledging glance, and a silent recognition was established between them whenever the chances of the day brought them across each other's paths. They had never exchanged a word; nothing had been said but that first compliment; yet somehow Margaret looked upon this man with more interest than upon anyone else in Milton. Once or twice, on Sundays, she saw him walking with a girl, evidently his daughter, and, if possible, still more unhealthy than he was himself.

One day Margaret and her father had been as far as the fields that lay around the town; it was early spring, and she had gathered some of the hedge and ditch flowers, dog-violets, lesser celandines, and the like, with an unspoken lament in her heart for the sweet profusion of the South. Her father had left her to go into Milton upon some business; and on the road home she met her humble friends. The girl looked wistfully at the flowers, and, acting on a sudden impulse, Margaret offered them to her. Her pale blue eyes lightened up as she took them, and her father spoke for her.

'Thank yo', miss. Bessy'll think a deal o' them flowers;

that hoo will; and I shall think a deal o' yor kindness. Yo're not of this country, I reckon?'

'No!' said Margaret, half sighing. 'I come from the South – from Hampshire,' she continued, a little afraid of wounding his consciousness of ignorance, if she used a name which he did not understand.

'That's beyond London, I reckon? And I come fro' Burnley ways, and forty mile to th' North. And yet, yo see, North and South has both met and made kind o' friends in this big smoky place.'

Margaret had slackened her pace to walk alongside of the man and his daughter, whose steps were regulated by the feebleness of the latter. She now spoke to the girl, and there was a sound of tender pity in the tone of her voice as she did so that went right to the heart of the father.

'I'm afraid you are not very strong.'

'No,' said the girl, 'nor never will be.'

'Spring is coming,' said Margaret, as if to suggest pleasant, hopeful thoughts.

'Spring nor summer will do me good,' said the girl quietly.

Margaret looked up at the man, almost expecting some contradiction from him, or at least some remark that would modify his daughter's utter hopelessness. But, instead, he added –

'I'm afeared hoo speaks truth. I'm afeared hoo's too far gone in a waste.'

'I shall have a spring where I'm boun to, and flowers, and amaranths, and shining robes besides.'

'Poor lass, poor lass!' said her father in a low tone. 'I'm none so sure o' that; but it's a comfort to thee, poor lass, poor lass. Poor father! it'll be soon!'

Margaret was shocked by his words – shocked but not repelled; rather attracted and interested.

'Where do you live? I think we must be neighbours, we meet so often on this road.'

'We put up at nine Frances Street, second turn to th' left at after yo've past th' Goulden Dragon.'

'And your name? I must not forget that.'

'I'm none ashamed o' my name. It's Nicholas Higgins. Hoo's called Bessy Higgins. Whatten yo' asking for?'

Margaret was surprised at this last question, for at Helstone it would have been an understood thing, after the inquiries she had made, that she intended to come and call upon any poor neighbour whose name and habitation she had asked for.

'I thought – I meant to come and see you.' She suddenly felt rather shy of offering the visit, without having any reason to give for her wish to make it, beyond a kindly interest in a stranger. It seemed all at once to take the shape of an impertinence on her part; she read this meaning too in the man's eyes.

'I'm none so fond of having strange folk in my house.' But then relenting, as he saw her heightened colour, he added, 'Yo're a foreigner, as one may say, and maybe don't know many folk here, and yo've given my wench here flowers out of yo'r own hand; – yo' may come if yo' like.'

Margaret was half amused, half nettled at this answer. She was not sure if she would go where permission was given so like a favour conferred. But when they came to the turn into Frances Street, the girl stopped a minute, and said,

'Yo'll not forget yo're to come and see us.'

'Aye, aye,' said the father, impatiently, 'Hoo'll come. Hoo's a bit set up now, because hoo thinks I might ha' spoken more civilly; but hoo'll think better on it, and come. I can read her proud bonny face like a book. Come along, Bess; there's the mill bell ringing.'

Margaret went home, wondering at her new friends, and smiling at the man's insight into what had been passing in her mind. From that day Milton became a brighter place to her. It was not the long, bleak sunny days of spring, nor yet was it that time was reconciling her to the town of her habitation. It was that in it she had found a human interest.

North and South, 1855

THOMAS BABINGTON MACAULAY, 1st BARON MACAULAY

[The Massacre at Glencoe, 1692]

ON THE 1st of February a hundred and twenty soldiers of Argyle's regiment, commanded by a captain named Campbell and a lieutenant named Lindsay, marched to Glencoe. Captain Campbell was commonly called in Scotland Glenlyon, from the pass in which his property lay. He had every qualification for the service on which he was employed, an unblushing forehead, a smooth lying tongue, and a heart of adamant. He was also one of the few Campbells who were likely to be trusted and welcomed by the Macdonalds: for his niece was married to Alexander, the second son of Mac Ian.

The sight of the Redcoats approaching caused some anxiety among the population of the valley. John, the eldest son of the chief, came, accompanied by twenty clansmen, to meet the strangers, and asked what this visit meant. Lieutenant Lindsay answered that the soldiers came as friends, and wanted nothing but quarters. They were kindly received, and were lodged under the thatched roofs of the little community. Glenlyon and several of his men were taken into the house of a tacksman who was named, from the cluster of cabins over which he exercised authority, Inverriggen. Lindsay was accommodated nearer to the abode of the old chief. Auchintriater, one of the principal men of the clan, who governed the small hamlet of Auchnaion, found room there for a party commanded by a serjeant named Barbour. Provisions were liberally supplied. There was no want of beef, which had probably fattened in distant pastures; nor was any payment demanded: for in hospitality, as in thievery, the Gaelic marauders rivalled the Bedouins. During twelve days the soldiers lived familiarly with the people of the glen. Old Mac Ian, who had before felt many misgivings as to the relation in which he stood to the government, seems to have been pleased with the visit. The officers passed much of their time with him and his family. The long evenings were cheerfully spent by the peat fire with the help of some packs of cards which had found their way to that remote corner of the world, and of some French brandy which was probably part of James's farewell gift to his Highland supporters. Glenlyon appeared to be warmly attached to his niece and her husband Alexander. Every day he came to their house to take his morning draught. Meanwhile he observed with minute attention all the avenues by which, when the signal for the slaughter should be given, the Macdonalds might attempt to escape to the hills; and he reported the result of his observations to Hamilton.

Hamilton fixed five o'clock in the morning of the 13th of February for the deed. He hoped that, before that time, he should reach Glencoe with four hundred men, and should have stopped all the earths in which the old fox and his two cubs – so Mac Ian and his sons were nicknamed by the murderers – could take refuge. But, at five precisely, whether Hamilton had arrived or not, Glenlyon was to fall on, and slay every Macdonald under seventy.

The night was rough. Hamilton and his troops made slow progress, and were long after their time. While they were contending with the wind and snow, Glenlyon was supping and playing cards with those whom he meant to butcher before daybreak. He and Lieutenant Lindsay had engaged themselves to dine with the old chief on the morrow.

Late in the evening a vague suspicion that some evil was intended crossed the mind of the chief's eldest son. The soldiers were evidently in a restless state; and some of them uttered strange exclamations. Two men, it is said, were overheard whispering. 'I do not like this job,' one of them muttered: 'I should be glad to fight the Macdonalds. But to kill men in their beds—' 'We must do as we are bid,' answered another voice. 'If there is anything wrong, our officers must answer for it.' John Macdonald was so uneasy that, soon after midnight, he went to Glenlyon's quarters. Glenlyon and his men were all up, and seemed to be getting their arms ready for action. John, much alarmed, asked what these preparations meant. Glenlyon was profuse of friendly assurances. 'Some of Glengarry's people have been harrying the country. We are getting ready to march against them. You are quite safe. Do you think that, if you were in any danger, I should not have given a hint to your brother Sandy and his wife?' John's suspicions were quieted. He returned to his house, and lay down to rest.

It was five in the morning. Hamilton and his men were still some miles off; and the avenues which they were to have secured were open. But the orders which Glenlyon had received were precise; and he began to execute them at the little village where he was himself quartered. His host Inverriggen and nine other Macdonalds were dragged out of their beds, bound hand and foot, and murdered. A boy twelve years old clung round the captain's legs, and begged hard for life. He would do anything: he would go anywhere: he would follow Glenlyon round the world. Even Glenlyon, it is said, showed signs of relenting: but a ruffian named Drummond shot the child dead.

At Auchnaion the tacksman Auchintriater was up early that morning, and was sitting with eight of his family round the fire, when a volley of musketry laid him and seven of his companions dead or dying on the floor. His brother, who alone had escaped unhurt, called to Serjeant Barbour, who commanded the slayers, and asked as a favour to be allowed to die in the open air. 'Well,' said the serjeant, 'I will do you that favour for the sake of your meat which I have eaten.' The mountaineer, bold, athletic, and favoured by the darkness, came forth, rushed on the soldiers who were about to level their pieces at him, flung his plaid over their faces, and was gone in a moment.

Meanwhile Lindsay had knocked at the door of the old chief and had asked for admission in friendly language. The door was opened. Mac Ian, while putting on his clothes and calling to his servants to bring some refreshment for his visitors, was shot through the head. Two of his attendants were slain with him. His wife was already up and dressed in such finery as the princesses of the rude Highland glens were accustomed to wear. The assassins pulled off her clothes and trinkets. The rings were not easily taken from her fingers: but a soldier tore them away with his teeth. She died on the following day.

The statesman, to whom chiefly this great crime is to be ascribed, had planned it with consummate ability: but the execution was complete in nothing but in guilt and infamy. A succession of blunders saved three fourths of the Glencoe men from the fate of their chief. All the moral qualities which fit men to bear a part in a massacre Hamilton and Glenlyon possessed in perfection. But neither seems to have had much professional skill. Hamilton had arranged his plan without making allowance for bad weather, and this at a season when, in the Highlands, the weather was very likely to be bad. The consequence was that the fox earths, as he called them, were not stopped in time. Glenlyon and his men committed the error of despatching their hosts with firearms instead of using cold steel. The peal and flash of gun after gun gave notice, from three different parts of the valley at once, that murder was doing. From fifty cottages the half naked peasantry fled under cover of the night to the recesses of their pathless glen. Even the sons of Mac Ian, who had been especially marked out for destruction, contrived to escape. They were roused from sleep by faithful servants. John, who, by the death of his father, had become the patriarch of the tribe, quitted his dwelling just as twenty soldiers with fixed bayonets marched up to it. It was broad day long before Hamilton arrived. He found the work not even half performed. About thirty corpses lay wallowing in blood on the dunghills before the doors. One or two women were seen among the number, and a yet more fearful and piteous sight, a little hand, which had been lopped in the tumult of the butchery from some infant. One aged Macdonald was found alive. He was probably too infirm to fly, and, as he was above seventy, was not included in the orders under which Glenlyon had acted. Hamilton murdered the old man in cold blood. The deserted hamlets were then set on fire; and the troops departed, driving away with them many sheep and goats, nine hundred kine, and two hundred of the small shaggy ponies of the Highlands.

It is said, and may but too easily be believed, that the sufferings of the fugitives were terrible. How many old men, how many women with babes in their arms, sank down and slept their last sleep in the snow; how many, having crawled, spent with toil and hunger, into nooks among the precipices, died in those dark holes, and were picked to the bone by the mountain ravens, can never be known. But it is probable that those who perished by cold, weariness, and want were not less numerous than those who were slain by the assassins. When the troops had retired, the Macdonalds crept out of the caverns of Glencoe, ventured back to the spot where the huts had formerly stood, collected the scorched corpses from among the smoking ruins, and performed some rude rites of sepulture. The tradition runs that the hereditary bard of the tribe took his seat on a rock which overhung the place of slaughter and poured forth a long lament over his murdered brethren and his desolate home. Eighty years later that sad dirge was still repeated by the population of the valley.

The History of England from the
Accession of James II, Vol. 4, 1855

JOHN RUSKIN

[The Pursuit of Happiness]

THE GREAT mechanical impulses of the age, of which most of us are so proud, are a mere passing fever, half-speculative, half-childish. People will discover at last that royal roads to anything can no more be laid in iron than they can in dust; that there are, in fact, no royal roads to anywhere worth going to; that if there were, it would that instant cease to be worth going to, – I mean, so far as the things to be obtained are in any way estimable in terms of *price*. For there are two classes of precious things in the world: those that God gives us for nothing – sun, air, and life (both mortal life and immortal); and the secondarily precious things which He gives us for a price: these secondarily precious things, worldly wine and milk, can only be bought for definite money; they never can be cheapened. No cheating nor bargaining will ever get a single thing out of nature's 'establishment' at half-price. Do we want to be strong? – we must work. To be hungry? – we must starve. To be happy? – we must be kind. To be wise? – we must look and think. No changing of place at a hundred miles an hour, nor making of stuffs a thousand yards a minute, will make us one whit stronger, happier, or wiser. There was always more in the world than men could see, walked they ever so slowly; they will see it no better for going fast. And they will at last, and soon too, find out that their grand inventions for conquering (as they think) space and time, do, in reality, conquer nothing; for space and time are, in their own essence, unconquerable, and besides did not want any sort of conquering; they wanted *using*. A fool always wants to shorten space and time: a wise man wants to lengthen both. A fool wants to kill space and kill time: a wise man, first to gain them, then to animate them. Your railroad, when you come to understand it, is only a device for making the world smaller: and as for being able to talk from place to place, that is, indeed, well and convenient; but suppose you have, originally, nothing to say! We shall be obliged at last to confess, what we should long ago have known, that the really precious things are thought and sight, not pace. It does a bullet no good to go fast; and a man, if he be truly a man, no harm to go slow; for his glory is not at all in going, but in being.

'Well; but railroads and telegraphs are so useful for communicating knowledge to savage nations.' Yes, if you have any to give them. If you know nothing *but* railroads, and can communicate nothing but aqueous vapour and gunpowder, – what then? But if you have any other thing than those to give, then the railroad is of use only because it communicates that other thing; and the question is – what that other thing may be. Is it religion? I believe if we had really wanted to communicate that, we could have done it in less than 1800 years, without steam. Most of the good religious communication that I remember, has been done on foot; and it cannot be easily done faster than at foot pace. Is it science? But what science – of motion, meat, and medicine? Well; when you have moved your savage, and dressed your savage, fed him with white bread, and shown him how to set a limb, – what next? Follow out that question. Suppose every obstacle overcome; give your savage every advantage of civilization to the full; suppose that you have put the Red Indian in tight shoes; taught the Chinese how to make Wedgwood's ware, and to paint it with colours that will rub off; and persuaded all Hindoo women that it is more pious to torment their husbands into graves than to burn themselves at the burial, – what next? Gradually, thinking on from point to point, we shall come to perceive that all true happiness and nobleness are near us, and yet neglected by us; and that till we have learned how to be happy and noble we have not much to tell, even to Red Indians. The delights of horse-racing, and hunting, of assemblies in the night instead of the day, of costly and wearisome music, of costly and burdensome dress, of chagrined contention for place or power, or wealth, or the eyes of the multitude; and all the endless occupation without purpose, and idleness without rest, of our vulgar world, are not, it seems to me, enjoyments we need be ambitious to communicate. And all real and wholesome enjoyments possible to man have been just as possible to him, since first he made of the earth, as they are now; and they are possible to him chiefly in peace. To watch the corn grow, and the blossoms set; to draw hard breath over ploughshare or spade; to read, to think, to love, to hope, to pray, – these are the things that make men happy; they have always had the power of doing these, they never *will* have power to do more. The world's prosperity or adversity depends upon our knowing and teaching these few things: but upon iron, or glass, or electricity, or steam, in no wise.

And I am Utopian and enthusiastic enough to believe, that the time will come when the world will discover this. It has now made its experiments in every possible direction but the right one: and it seems that it must, at last, try the right one, in a mathematical necessity. It has tried fighting, and preaching, and fasting, buying and selling, pomp and parsimony, pride and humiliation, – every possible manner of existence in which it could conjecture there was any happiness or dignity: and all the while, as it bought, sold, and fought, and fasted, and wearied itself with policies, and ambitions, and self-denials, God had placed its real happiness in the keeping of the little mosses of the wayside, and of the clouds of the firmament. Now and then a wearied king, or a tormented slave, found out where the true kingdoms of the world were, and possessed himself, in a furrow or two of garden ground, of a truly infinite dominion. But the world would not believe their report, and went on trampling down the mosses, and forgetting the clouds, and seeking happiness in its own way, until, at last, blundering and late, came natural science; and in natural science not only the observation of things, but the finding out of new uses for them. Of course the world, having a choice left to it, went wrong as usual, and thought that these mere material uses were to be the sources of its happiness. It got the clouds packed into iron cylinders, and made them carry its wise self at their own cloud pace. It got weavable fibres out of the mosses, and made clothes for itself, cheap and fine, – here was happiness at last. To go as fast as the clouds, and manufacture everything out of anything, – here was paradise indeed!

And now, when, in a little while, it is unparadised again, if there were any other mistake that the world could make, it would of course make it. But I see not that there is any other; and, standing fairly at its wits' end, having found that going fast, when it is used to it, is no more paradisiacal than going slow; and that all the prints and cottons in Manchester cannot make it comfortable in its mind, I do verily believe it will come, finally, to understand that God paints the clouds and shapes the moss-fibres, that men may be happy in seeing Him at His work, and that in resting quietly beside Him, and watching His working, and – according to the power He has communicated to ourselves, and the guidance He grants, – in carrying out His purposes of peace and charity among all His creatures, are the only real happiness that ever were, or will be, possible to mankind.

Modern Painters, Vol. 3, 1856

THOMAS HUGHES

[Gentlemen Sportsmen]

THE NEXT morning was Saturday, the day on which the allowances of one shilling a week were paid, an important event to spendthrift youngsters; and great was the disgust amongst the small fry, to hear that all the allowances had been impounded for the Derby lottery. That great event in the English year, the Derby, was celebrated at Rugby in those days by many lotteries. It was not an improving custom, I own, gentle reader, and led to making books and betting, and other objectionable results; but when our great Houses of Palaver think it right to stop the nation's business on that day, and many of the members bet heavily themselves, can you blame us boys for following the example of our betters? – at any rate we did follow it. First there was the great School lottery, where the first prize was six or seven pounds; then each house had one or more separate lotteries. These were all nominally voluntary, no boy being compelled to put in his shilling who didn't choose to do so; but besides Flashman, there were three or four other fast sporting young gentlemen in the School-house, who considered subscription a matter of duty and necessity, and so, to make their duty come easy to the small boys, quietly secured the allowances in a lump when given out for distribution, and kept them. It was no use grumbling, – so many fewer tartlets and apples were eaten and fives'-balls bought on that Saturday; and after locking-up, when the money would otherwise have been spent, consolation was carried to many a small boy, by the sound of the night-fags shouting along the passages, 'Gentlemen sportsmen of the School-house, the lottery's going to be drawn in the Hall.' It was pleasant to be called a gentleman sportsman – also to have a chance of drawing a favourite horse.

The Hall was full of boys, and at the head of one of the long tables stood the sporting interest, with a hat before them, in which were the tickets folded up. One of them then began calling out the list of the house; each boy as his name was called drew a ticket from the hat and opened it; and most of the bigger boys, after drawing, left the Hall directly to go back to their studies or the fifth-form room. The sporting interest had all drawn blanks, and they were sulky accordingly; neither of the favourites had yet been drawn, and it had came down to the upper fourth. So now, as each small boy came up and drew his ticket, it was seized and opened by Flashman, or some other of the standers-by. But no great favourite is drawn until it comes to the Tadpole's turn, and he shuffles up, and draws, and tries to make off, but is caught, and his ticket is opened like the rest.

'Here you are! Wanderer! the third favourite,' shouts the opener.

'I say, just give me my ticket, please,' remonstrates Tadpole.

'Hullo, don't be in a hurry,' breaks in Flashman, 'what'll you sell Wanderer for, now?'

'I don't want to sell,' rejoins Tadpole.

'Oh, don't you! Now listen, you young fool – you don't know anything about it; the horse is no use to you. He won't win, but I want him as a hedge. Now I'll give you half-a-crown for him.' Tadpole holds out, but between threats and cajoleries at length sells half for one-shilling-and-sixpence, about a fifth of its fair market value; however, he is glad to realize anything, and as he wisely remarks, 'Wanderer mayn't win, and the tizzy is safe anyhow.'

East presently comes up, and draws a blank. Soon after comes Tom's turn; his ticket, like the others, is seized and opened. 'Here you are then,' shouts the opener, holding it up: 'Harkaway! By Jove, Flashy, your young friend's in luck.'

'Give me the ticket,' says Flashman with an oath, leaning

across the table with open hand, and his face black with rage.

'Wouldn't you like it?' replies the opener, not a bad fellow at the bottom, and no admirer of Flashman. 'Here, Brown, catch hold,' and he hands the ticket to Tom, who pockets it; whereupon Flashman makes for the door at once, that Tom and the ticket may not escape, and there keeps watch until the drawing is over, and all the boys are gone, except the sporting set of five or six, who stay to compare books, make bets, and so on; Tom, who doesn't choose to move while Flashman is at the door, and East, who stays by his friend, anticipating trouble.

The sporting set now gathered round Tom. Public opinion wouldn't allow them actually to rob him of his ticket, but any humbug or intimidation by which he could be driven to sell the whole or part at an under value was lawful.

'Now, young Brown, come, what'll you sell me Harkaway for? I hear he isn't going to start. I'll give you five shillings for him,' begins the boy who had opened the ticket. Tom, remembering his good deed, and moreover in his forlorn state wishing to make a friend, is about to accept the offer, when another cries out, 'I'll give you seven shillings.' Tom hesitated, and looked from one to the other.

'No, no!' said Flashman, pushing in, 'leave me to deal with him; we'll draw lots for it afterwards. Now, sir, you know me – you'll sell Harkaway to us for five shillings, or you'll repent it.'

'I won't sell a bit of him,' answered Tom, shortly.

'You hear that now!' said Flashman, turning to the others. 'He's the coxiest young blackguard in the house – I always told you so. We're to have all the trouble and risk of getting up the lotteries for the benefit of such fellows as he.'

Flashman forgets to explain what risk they ran, but he speaks to willing ears. Gambling makes boys selfish and cruel as well as men.

'That's true, – we always draw blanks,' cried one. 'Now, sir, you shall sell half, at any rate.'

'I won't,' said Tom, flushing up to his hair, and lumping them all in his mind with his sworn enemy.

'Very well then, let's roast him,' cried Flashman, and

catches hold of Tom by the collar: one or two boys hesitate, but the rest join in. East seizes Tom's arm and tries to pull him away, but is knocked back by one of the boys, and Tom is dragged along struggling. His shoulders are pushed against the mantelpiece, and he is held by main force before the fire, Flashman drawing his trousers tight by way of extra torture. Poor East, in more pain even than Tom, suddenly thinks of Diggs, and darts off to find him. 'Will you sell now for ten shillings?' says one boy who is relenting.

Tom only answers by groans and struggles.

'I say, Flashy, he has had enough,' says the same boy, dropping the arm he holds.

'No, no, another turn'll do it,' answers Flashman. But poor Tom is done already, turns deadly pale, and his head falls forward on his breast, just as Diggs, in frantic excitement, rushes into the Hall with East at his heels.

'You cowardly brutes!' is all he can say, as he catches Tom from them and supports him to the Hall table. 'Good God! he's dying. Here, get some cold water – run for the housekeeper.'

Flashman and one or two others slink away; the rest, ashamed and sorry, bend over Tom or run for water, while East darts off for the housekeeper. Water comes, and they throw it on his hands and face, and he begins to come to. 'Mother!' – the words came feebly and slowly – 'it's very cold tonight.' Poor old Diggs is blubbering like a child. 'Where am I?' goes on Tom, opening his eyes. 'Ah! I remember now,' and he shut his eyes again and groaned.

'I say,' is whispered, 'we can't do any good, and the housekeeper will be here in a minute,' and all but one steal away; he stays with Diggs, silent and sorrowful, and fans Tom's face.

Tom Brown's School Days, 1857

DAVID LIVINGSTONE

[A Lion Hunt]

IT IS well known that if one in a troop of lions is killed the others take the hint and leave that part of the country. So the next time the herds were attacked, I went with the people, in order to encourage them to rid themselves of the annoyance by destroying one of the marauders. We found the lions on a small hill about a quarter of a mile in length, and covered with trees. A circle of men was formed round it, and they gradually closed up, ascending pretty near to each other. Being down below on the plain with a native schoolmaster, named Mebálwe, a most excellent man, I saw one of the lions sitting on a piece of rock within the now closed circle of men. Mebálwe fired at him before I could, and the ball struck the rock on which the animal was sitting. He bit at the spot struck, as a dog does at a stick or stone thrown at him; then leaping away, broke through the opening circle and escaped unhurt. The men were afraid to attack him, perhaps on account of their belief in witchcraft. When the circle was re-formed, we saw two other lions in it; but we were afraid to fire lest we should strike the men, and they allowed the beasts to burst through also. If the Bakatla had acted according to the custom of the country, they would have speared the lions in their attempt to get out. Seeing we could not get them to kill one of the lions, we bent our footsteps towards the village; in going round the end of the hill, however, I saw one of the beasts sitting on a piece of rock as before, but this time he had a little bush in front. Being about thirty yards off, I took a good aim at his body through the bush, and fired both barrels into it. The men then called out, 'He is shot, he is shot!' Others cried, 'He has been shot by another man too; let us go to him!' I did not see any one else shoot him, but I saw the lion's tail erected in anger behind the bush, and, turning to the people, said, 'Stop a little till I load again.' When in the act of ramming down the bullets I heard a shout. Starting, and

looking half round, I saw the lion just in the act of springing
upon me. I was upon a little height; he caught my shoulder
as he sprang, and we both came to the ground below
together. Growling horribly close to my ear, he shook me
as a terrier dog does a rat. The shock produced a stupor
similar to that which seems to be felt by a mouse after the
first shake of the cat. It caused a sort of dreaminess, in
which there was no sense of pain nor feeling of terror,
though quite conscious of all that was happening. It was like
what patients partially under the influence of chloroform
describe, who see all the operation, but feel not the knife.
This singular condition was not the result of any mental
process. The shake annihilated fear, and allowed no sense
of horror in looking round at the beast. This peculiar state
is probably produced in all animals killed by the carnivora;
and if so, is a merciful provision by our benevolent Creator
for lessening the pain of death. Turning round to relieve
myself of the weight, as he had one paw on the back of my
head, I saw his eyes directed to Mebálwe, who was trying to
shoot him at a distance of ten or fifteen yards. His gun, a
flint one, missed fire in both barrels; the lion immediately
left me, and, attacking Mebálwe, bit his thigh. Another
man, whose life I had saved before, after he had been tossed
by a buffalo, attempted to spear the lion while he was biting
Mebálwe. He left Mebálwe and caught this man by the
shoulder, but at that moment the bullets he had received
took effect, and he fell down dead. The whole was the work
of a few moments, and must have been his paroxysm of
dying rage. In order to take out the charm from him, the
Bakatla on the following day made a huge bonfire over the
carcase, which was declared to be that of the largest lion
they had ever seen. Besides crunching the bones into
splinters, he left eleven teeth wounds on the upper part of
my arm.

A wound from this animal's tooth resembles a gun-shot
wound; it is generally followed by a great deal of sloughing
and discharge, and pains are felt in the part periodically
ever afterwards. I had on a tartan jacket on the occasion,
and I believe that it wiped off all the virus from the teeth
that pierced the flesh, for my two companions in this affray

have both suffered from the peculiar pains, while I have escaped with only the inconvenience of a false joint in my limb. The man whose shoulder was wounded showed me his wound actually burst forth afresh on the same month of the following year. This curious point deserves the attention of inquirers.

Missionary Travels and Research
in South Africa, 1857

CHARLES DARWIN

[Struggle for Existence]

MANY CASES are on record showing how complex and unexpected are the checks and relations between organic beings, which have to struggle together in the same country. I will give only a single instance, which, though a simple one, has interested me. In Staffordshire, on the estate of a relation where I had ample means of investigation, there was a large and extremely barren heath, which had never been touched by the hand of man; but several hundred acres of exactly the same nature had been enclosed twenty-five years previously and planted with Scotch fir. The change in the native vegetation of the planted part of the heath was most remarkable, more than is generally seen in passing from one quite different soil to another: not only the proportional numbers of the heath-plants were wholly changed, but twelve species of plants (not counting grasses and carices) flourished in the plantations, which could not be found on the heath. The effect on the insects must have been still greater, for six insectivorous birds were very common in the plantations, which were not to be seen on the heath; and the heath was frequented by two or three distinct insectivorous birds. Here we see how potent has been the effect of the introduction of a single tree, nothing whatever else having been done, with the exception that the land had been enclosed, so that cattle could not enter. But how important an element enclosure is, I plainly saw near Farnham, in Surrey. Here there are extensive heaths, with a few clumps of old Scotch firs on the distant hill-tops: within the last ten years large spaces have been enclosed, and self-sown firs are now springing up in multitudes, so close together that all cannot live. When I ascertained that these young trees had not been sown or planted, I was so much surprised at their numbers that I went to several points of view, whence I could examine hundreds of acres of the unenclosed heath, and literally I could not see a single Scotch fir, except the old planted clumps. But on looking closely between the stems of the heath, I found a multitude of seedlings and little trees, which had been perpetually browsed down by the cattle. In one square yard, at a point some hundred yards distant from one of the old clumps, I counted thirty-two little trees; and one of them, judging from the rings of growth, had during twenty-six years tried to raise its head above the stems of the heath, and had failed. No wonder that, as soon as the land was enclosed, it became thickly clothed with vigorously growing young firs. Yet the heath was so extremely barren and so extensive that no one would ever have imagined that cattle would have so closely and effectually searched it for food.

Here we see that cattle absolutely determine the existence of the Scotch fir; but in several parts of the world insects determine the existence of cattle. Perhaps Paraguay offers the most curious instance of this; for here neither cattle nor horses nor dogs have ever run wild, though they swarm southward and northward in a feral state; and Azara and Rengger have shown that this is caused by the greater number in Paraguay of a certain fly, which lays its eggs in the navels of these animals when first born. The increase of these flies, numerous as they are, must be habitually checked by some means, probably by birds. Hence, if certain insectivorous birds (whose numbers are probably regulated by hawks or beasts of prey) were to increase in Paraguay, the flies would decrease – then cattle and horses would become feral, and this would certainly greatly alter (as indeed I have observed in parts of South America) the vegetation: this again would largely affect the insects; and this, as we just have seen in Staffordshire, the insectivorous birds, and so onwards in ever-increasing circles of complexity. We began this series with insectivorous birds, and we have ended with them. Not that in nature the relations can ever be as simple as this. Battle within battle must ever be recurring with varying success; and yet in the long-run the forces are so nicely balanced, that the face of nature remains uniform for long periods of time, though assuredly the merest trifle would often give the victory to one organic being over another. Nevertheless so profound is our ignorance, and so high our presumption, that we marvel when we hear of the extinction of an organic being; and as we do not see the cause, we invoke cataclysms to desolate the world, or invent laws on the duration of forms of life!

On the Origin of Species by Means of
Natural Selection, or the Preservation of
Favoured Races in the Struggle for Life, 1859

JOHN STUART MILL

[Individuality]

H E WHO lets the world, or his own portion of it, choose his plan of life for him has no need of any other faculty than the ape-like one of imitation. He who chooses his plan for himself employs all his faculties. He must use observation to see, reasoning and judgement to foresee, activity to gather materials for decision, discrimination to decide, and when he has decided, firmness and self-control to hold to his deliberate decision. And these qualities he requires and exercises exactly in proportion as the part of his conduct which he determines according to his own judgement and feelings is a large one. It is possible that he might be guided in some good path, and kept out of harm's way, without any of these things. But what will be his comparative worth as a human being? It really is of importance, not only what men do, but also what manner of men they are that do it. Among the works of man which human life is rightly employed in perfecting and beautifying, the first in importance surely is man himself. Supposing it were possible to get houses built, corn grown, battles fought, causes tried, and even churches erected and prayers said by machinery – by automatons in human form – it would be a considerable loss to exchange for these automatons even the men and women who at present inhabit the more civilized parts of the world, and who assuredly are but starved specimens of what nature can and will produce. Human nature is not a machine to be built after a model, and set to do exactly the work prescribed for it, but a tree, which requires to grow and develop itself on all sides, according to the tendency of the inward forces which make it a living thing.

It will probably be conceded that it is desirable people should exercise their understandings, and that an intelligent following of custom, or even occasionally an intelligent deviation from custom, is better than a blind and simply mechanical adhesion to it. To a certain extent it is admitted that our understanding should be our own; but there is not the same willingness to admit that our desires and impulses should be our own likewise, or that to possess impulses of our own, and of any strength, is anything but a peril and a snare. Yet desires and impulses are as much a part of a perfect human being as beliefs and restraints; and strong impulses are only perilous when not properly balanced, when one set of aims and inclinations is developed into strength, while others, which ought to coexist with them, remain weak and inactive. It is not because men's desires are strong that they act ill; it is because their consciences are weak. There is no natural connection between strong impulses and a weak conscience. The natural connection is the other way. To say that one person's desires and feelings are stronger and more various than those of another is merely to say that he has more of the raw material of human nature and is therefore capable, perhaps of more evil, but certainly of more good. Strong impulses are but another name for energy. Energy may be turned to bad uses; but more good may always be made of an energetic nature than of an indolent and impassive one. Those who have most natural feeling are always those whose cultivated feelings may be made the strongest. The same strong susceptibilities which make the personal impulses vivid and powerful are also the source from whence are generated the most passionate love of virtue and the sternest self-control. It is through the cultivation of these that society both does its duty and protects its interests, not by rejecting the stuff of which heroes are made, because it knows not how to make them. A person whose desires and impulses are his own – are the expression of his own nature, as it has been developed and modified by his own culture – is said to have a character. One whose desires and impulses are not his own has no character, no more than a steam engine has a character. If, in addition to being his own, his impulses are strong and are under the government of a strong will, he has an energetic character. Whoever thinks that individuality of desires and impulses should not be encouraged to unfold itself must maintain that society has no need of strong natures – is not the better for containing many persons who have much character – and that a high general average of energy is not desirable.

On Liberty, 1859

WILKIE COLLINS

[A Midnight Walk]

WE SET our faces towards London, and walked on together in the first still hour of the new day – I, and this woman, whose name, whose character, whose story, whose objects in life, whose very presence by my side, at that moment, were fathomless mysteries to me. It was like a dream. Was I Walter Hartright? Was this the well-known, uneventful road, where holiday people strolled on Sundays?

Had I really left, little more than an hour since, the quiet, decent, conventionally domestic atmosphere of my mother's cottage? I was too bewildered – too conscious also of a vague sense of something like self-reproach – to speak to my strange companion for some minutes. It was her voice again that first broke the silence between us.

'I want to ask you something,' she said suddenly. 'Do you know many people in London?'

'Yes, a great many.'

'Many men of rank and title?' There was an unmistakable tone of suspicion in the strange question. I hesitated about answering it.

'Some,' I said, after a moment's silence.

'Many' – she came to a full stop, and looked me searchingly in the face – 'many men of the rank of Baronet?'

Too much astonished to reply, I questioned her in my turn.

'Why do you ask?'

'Because I hope, for my own sake, there is one Baronet that you don't know.'

'Will you tell me his name?'

'I can't – I daren't – I forget myself when I mention it.' She spoke loudly and almost fiercely, raised her clenched hand in the air, and shook it passionately; then, on a sudden, controlled herself again, and added, in tones lowered to a whisper, 'Tell me which of them *you* know.'

I could hardly refuse to humour her in such a trifle, and I mentioned three names. Two, the names of fathers of families whose daughters I taught; one, the name of a bachelor who had once taken me a cruise in his yacht, to make sketches for him.

'Ah! you *don't* know him,' she said, with a sigh of relief. 'Are you a man of rank and title yourself?'

'Far from it. I am only a drawing-master.'

As the reply passed my lips – a little bitterly, perhaps – she took my arm with the abruptness which characterised all her actions.

'Not a man of rank and title,' she repeated to herself. 'Thank God! I may trust *him*.'

I had hitherto contrived to master my curiosity out of consideration for my companion; but it got the better of me now.

'I am afraid you have serious reason to complain of some man of rank and title?' I said. 'I am afraid the baronet, whose name you are unwilling to mention to me, has done you some grievous wrong? Is he the cause of your being out here at this strange time of night?'

'Don't ask me: don't make me talk of it,' she answered. 'I'm not fit now. I have been cruelly used and cruelly wronged. You will be kinder than ever, if you will walk on fast, and not speak to me. I sadly want to quiet myself, if I can.'

We moved forward again at a quick pace; and for half an hour, at least, not a word passed on either side. From time to time, being forbidden to make any more inquiries, I stole a look at her face. It was always the same; the lips close shut, the brow frowning, the eyes looking straight forward, eagerly and yet absently. We had reached the first houses, and were close on the new Wesleyan college, before her set features relaxed, and she spoke once more.

'Do you live in London?' she said.

'Yes.' As I answered, it struck me that she might have formed some intention of appealing to me for assistance or advice, and that I ought to spare her a possible disappointment by warning her of my approaching absence from home. So I added, 'But tomorrow I shall be away from London for some time. I am going into the country.'

'Where?' she asked. 'North or south?'

'North – to Cumberland.'

'Cumberland!' she repeated the word tenderly. 'Ah! I wish I was going there too. I was once happy in Cumberland.'

I tried again to lift the veil that hung between this woman and me.

'Perhaps you were born,' I said, 'in the beautiful Lake country.'

'No,' she answered. 'I was born in Hampshire; but I once went to school for a little while in Cumberland. Lakes? I don't remember any lakes. It's Limmeridge village, and Limmeridge House, I should like to see again.'

It was my turn now to stop suddenly. In the excited state of my curiosity, at that moment, the chance reference to Mr Fairlie's place of residence, on the lips of my strange companion, staggered me with astonishment.

'Did you hear anybody calling after us?' she asked, looking up and down the road affrightedly, the instant I stopped.

'No, no. I was only struck by the name of Limmeridge House. I heard it mentioned by some Cumberland people a few days since.'

'Ah! not *my* people. Mrs Fairlie is dead; and her husband is dead; and their little girl may be married and gone away by this time. I can't say who lives at Limmeridge now. If any more are left there of that name, I only know I love them for Mrs Fairlie's sake.'

She seemed about to say more; but while she was speaking, we came within view of the turnpike, at the top of the Avenue Road. Her hand tightened round my arm, and she looked anxiously at the gate before us.

'Is the turnpike man looking out?' she asked.

He was not looking out; no one else was near the place when we passed through the gate. The sight of the gas-lamps and houses seemed to agitate her, and to make her impatient.

'This is London,' she said. 'Do you see any carriage I can get? I am tired and frightened. I want to shut myself in and be driven away.'

I explained to her that we must walk a little further to get to a cab-stand, unless we were fortunate enough to meet with an empty vehicle; and then tried to resume the subject of Cumberland. It was useless. That idea of shutting herself in, and being driven away, had now got full possession of her mind. She could think and talk of nothing else.

We had hardly proceeded a third of the way down the Avenue Road when I saw a cab draw up at a house a few doors below us, on the opposite side of the way. A gentleman got out and let himself in at the garden door. I hailed the cab, as the driver mounted the box again. When we crossed the road, my companion's impatience increased to such an extent that she almost forced me to run.

'It's so late,' she said. 'I am only in a hurry because it's so late.'

'I can't take you, sir, if you're not going towards Tottenham Court Road,' said the driver civilly, when I opened the cab door. 'My horse is dead beat, and I can't get him no further than the stable.'

'Yes, yes. That will do for me. I'm going that way – I'm going that way.' She spoke with breathless eagerness, and pressed by me into the cab.

I had assured myself that the man was sober as well as civil before I let her enter the vehicle. And now, when she was seated inside, I entreated her to let me see her set down safely at her destination.

'No, no, no,' she said vehemently. 'I'm quite safe, and quite happy now. If you are a gentleman, remember your promise. Let him drive on till I stop him. Thank you – oh! thank you, thank you!'

My hand was on the cab door. She caught it in hers, kissed it, and pushed it away. The cab drove off at the same moment – I started into the road, with some vague idea of stopping it again, I hardly knew why – hesitated from dread of frightening and distressing her – called, at last, but not loudly enough to attract the driver's attention. The sound of the wheels grew fainter in the distance – the cab melted into the black shadows on the road – the woman in white was gone.

The Woman in White, 1860

GEORGE ELIOT

[A Message]

S HE HAD set out at an early hour, but had lingered on the road, inclined by her indolence to believe that if she waited under a warm shed the snow would cease to fall.

She had waited longer than she knew, and now that she
found herself belated in the snow-hidden ruggedness of the
long lanes, even the animation of a vindictive purpose could
not keep her spirit from failing. It was seven o'clock, and
by this time she was not very far from Raveloe, but she
was not familiar enough with those monotonous lanes to
know how near she was to her journey's end. She needed
comfort, and she knew but one comforter – the familiar
demon in her bosom; but she hesitated a moment, after
drawing out the black remnant, before she raised it to her
lips. In that moment the mother's love pleaded for painful
consciousness rather than oblivion – pleaded to be left in
aching weariness, rather than to have the encircling arms
benumbed so that they could not feel the dear burden. In
another moment Molly had flung something away, but it
was not the black remnant – it was an empty phial. And
she walked on again under the breaking cloud, from which
there came now and then the light of a quickly-veiled star,
for a freezing wind had sprung up since the snowing had
ceased. But she walked always more and more drowsily,
and clutched more and more automatically the sleeping
child at her bosom.

Slowly the demon was working his will, and cold and
weariness were his helpers. Soon she felt nothing but a
supreme immediate longing that curtained off all futurity –
the longing to lie down and sleep. She had arrived at a spot
where her footsteps were no longer checked by a hedgerow,
and she had wandered vaguely, unable to distinguish any
objects, notwithstanding the wide whiteness around her,
and the growing starlight. She sank down against a straggling
furze bush, an easy pillow enough; and the bed of snow,
too, was soft. She did not feel that the bed was cold, and
did not heed whether the child would wake and cry for her.
But her arms had not yet relaxed their instinctive clutch;
and the little one slumbered on as gently as if it had been
rocked in a lace-trimmed cradle.

But the complete torpor came at last: the fingers lost their
tension, the arms unbent; then the little head fell away from
the bosom, and the blue eyes opened wide on the cold
starlight. At first there was a little peevish cry of 'mammy',

and an effort to regain the pillowing arm and bosom; but mammy's ear was deaf, and the pillow seemed to be slipping away backward. Suddenly, as the child rolled downward on its mother's knees, all wet with snow, its eyes were caught by a bright glancing light on the white ground, and, with the ready transition of infancy, it was immediately absorbed in watching the bright living thing running towards it, yet never arriving. That bright living thing must be caught; and in an instant the child had slipped on all fours, and held out one little hand to catch the gleam. But the gleam would not be caught in that way, and now the head was held up to see where the cunning gleam came from. It came from a very bright place; and the little one, rising on its legs, toddled through the snow, the old grimy shawl in which it was wrapped trailing behind it, and the queer little bonnet dangling at its back – toddled on to the open door of Silas Marner's cottage, and right up to the warm hearth, where there was a bright fire of logs and sticks, which had thoroughly warmed the old sack (Silas's greatcoat) spread out on the bricks to dry. The little one, accustomed to be left to itself for long hours without notice from its mother, squatted down on the sack, and spread its tiny hands towards the blaze, in perfect contentment, gurgling and making many inarticulate communications to the cheerful fire, like a new-hatched gosling beginning to find itself comfortable. But presently the warmth had a lulling effect, and the little golden head sank down on the old sack, and the blue eyes were veiled by their delicate half-transparent lids.

But where was Silas Marner while this strange visitor had come to his hearth? He was in the cottage, but he did not see the child. During the last few weeks, since he had lost his money, he had contracted the habit of opening his door and looking out from time to time, as if he thought that his money might be somehow coming back to him, or that some trace, some news of it, might be mysteriously on the road, and be caught by the listening ear or the straining eye. It was chiefly at night, when he was not occupied in his loom, that he fell into this repetition of an act for which he could have assigned no definite purpose, and which can hardly be

understood except by those who have undergone a bewildering separation from a supremely loved object. In the evening
twilight, and later whenever the night was not dark, Silas
looked out on that narrow prospect round the Stone-pits,
listening and gazing, not with hope, but with mere yearning
and unrest.

This morning he had been told by some of his neighbours that it was New Year's Eve, and that he must sit
up and hear the old year rung out and the new rung in,
because that was good luck, and might bring his money
back again. This was only a friendly Raveloe-way of jesting with the half-crazy oddities of a miser, but it had
perhaps helped to throw Silas into a more than usually
excited state. Since the oncoming of twilight he had opened
his door again and again, though only to shut it immediately
at seeing all distance veiled by the falling snow. But the
last time he opened it the snow had ceased, and the clouds
were parting here and there. He stood and listened, and
gazed for a long while – there was really something on the
road coming towards him then, but he caught no sign of
it: and the stillness and the wide trackless snow seemed
to narrow his solitude, and touched his yearning with the
chill of despair. He went in again, and put his right hand
on the latch of the door to close it – but he did not close it:
he was arrested, as he had been already since his loss, by
the invisible wand of catalepsy, and stood like a graven
image, with wide but sightless eyes, holding open his door,
powerless to resist either the good or evil that might enter
there.

When Marner's sensibility returned, he continued the
action which had been arrested, and closed his door,
unaware of the chasm in his consciousness, unaware of any
intermediate change, except that the light had grown dim,
and that he was chilled and faint. He thought he had been
too long standing at the door and looking out. Turning
towards the hearth, where the two logs had fallen apart, and
sent forth only a red uncertain glimmer, he seated himself
on his fireside chair, and was stooping to push his logs
together, when, to his blurred vision, it seemed as if there
were gold on the floor in front of the hearth. Gold! – his

own gold – brought back to him as mysteriously as it had been taken away! He felt his heart begin to beat violently, and for a few moments he was unable to stretch out his hand and grasp the restored treasure. The heap of gold seemed to glow and get larger beneath his agitated gaze. He leaned forward at last, and stretched forth his hand; but instead of hard coin with the familiar resisting outline, his fingers encountered soft warm curls. In utter amazement, Silas fell on his knees and bent his head low to examine the marvel: it was a sleeping child – a round, fair thing with soft yellow rings all over its head. Could this be his little sister come back to him in a dream – his little sister whom he had carried about in his arms for a year before she died, when he was a small boy without shoes or stockings? That was the first thought that darted across Silas's blank wonderment. *Was* it a dream? He rose to his feet again, pushed his logs together, and, throwing on some dried leaves and sticks, raised a flame; but the flame did not disperse the vision – it only lit up more distinctly the little round form of the child, and its shabby clothing. It was very much like his little sister. Silas sank into his chair powerless, under the double presence of an inexplicable surprise and a hurrying influx of memories. How and when had the child come in without his knowledge? He had never been beyond the door. But along with that question, and almost thrusting it away, there was a vision of the old home and the old streets leading to Lantern Yard – and within that vision another, of the thoughts which had been present with him in those far-off scenes. The thoughts were strange to him now, like old friendships impossible to revive; and yet he had a dreamy feeling that this child was somehow a message come to him from that far-off life: it stirred fibres that had never been moved in Raveloe – old quiverings of tenderness – old impressions of awe at the presentiment of some Power presiding over his life; for his imagination had not yet extricated itself from the sense of mystery in the child's sudden presence, and had formed no conjectures of ordinary natural means by which the event could have been brought about.

But there was a cry on the hearth: the child had awaked,

and Marner stooped to lift it on his knee. It clung round his neck, and burst louder and louder into that mingling of inarticulate cries with 'mammy' by which little children express the bewilderment of waking. Silas pressed it to him, and almost unconsciously uttered sounds of hushing tenderness, while he bethought himself that some of his porridge, which had got cool by the dying fire, would do to feed the child if it were only warmed up a little.

He had plenty to do through the next hour. The porridge, sweetened with some dry brown sugar from an old store which he had refrained from using for himself, stopped the cries of the little one, and made her lift her blue eyes with a wide quiet gaze at Silas, as he put the spoon into her mouth. Presently she slipped from his knees and began to toddle about, but with a very pretty stagger that made Silas jump up and follow her lest she should fall against anything that would hurt her. But she only fell in a sitting posture on the ground, and began to pull at her boots, looking up at him with a crying face as if the boots hurt her. He took her on his knee again, but it was some time before it occurred to Silas's dull bachelor mind that the wet boots were the grievance, pressing on her warm ankles. He got them off with difficulty, and baby was at once happily occupied with the primary mystery of her own toes, inviting Silas, with much chuckling, to consider the mystery too. But the wet boots had at last suggested to Silas that the child had been walking on the snow, and this roused him from his entire oblivion of any ordinary means by which it could have entered or been brought into his house. Under the prompting of this new idea, and without waiting to form conjectures, he raised the child in his arms, and went to the door. As soon as he had opened it, there was the cry of 'mammy' again, which Silas had not heard since the child's first hungry waking. Bending forward, he could just discern the marks made by the little feet on the virgin snow, and he followed their track to the furze bushes. 'Mammy!' the little one cried again and again, stretching itself forward so as almost to escape from Silas's arms, before he himself was aware that there was something more than the bush before him – that there was a human body, with the head sunk low in the furze, and half-covered with the shaken snow.

Silas Marner: The Weaver of Raveloe, 1861

[Dorothea and Will]

THE LITTLE old lady, whose bonnet hardly reached Dorothea's shoulder, was warmly welcomed, but while her hand was being pressed she made many of her beaver-like noises, as if she had something difficult to say.

'Do sit down,' said Dorothea, rolling a chair forward. 'Am I wanted for anything? I shall be so glad if I can do anything.'

'I will not stay,' said Miss Noble, putting her hand into her small basket, and holding some article inside it nervously; 'I have left a friend in the churchyard.' She lapsed into her inarticulate sounds, and unconsciously drew forth the article which she was fingering. It was the tortoise-shell lozenge-box, and Dorothea felt the colour mounting to her cheeks.

'Mr Ladislaw,' continued the timid little woman. 'He fears he has offended you, and has begged me to ask if you will see him for a few minutes.'

Dorothea did not answer on the instant; it was crossing her mind that she could not receive him in this library, where her husband's prohibition seemed to dwell. She looked towards the window. Could she go out and meet him in the grounds? The sky was heavy, and the trees had begun to shiver as at a coming storm. Besides, she shrank from going out to him.

'Do see him, Mrs Casaubon,' said Miss Noble, pathetically; 'else I must go back and say No, and that will hurt him.'

'Yes, I will see him,' said Dorothea. 'Pray tell him to come.'

What else was there to be done? There was nothing that

she longed for at the moment except to see Will: the possibility of seeing him had thrust itself insistently between her and every other object; and yet she had a throbbing excitement like an alarm upon her – a sense that she was doing something daringly defiant for his sake.

When the little lady had trotted away on her mission, Dorothea stood in the middle of the library with her hands falling clasped before her, making no attempt to compose herself in an attitude of dignified unconsciousness. What she was least conscious of just then was her own body: she was thinking of what was likely to be in Will's mind, and of the hard feelings that others had had about him. How could any duty bind her to hardness? Resistance to unjust dispraise had mingled with her feeling for him from the very first, and now in the rebound of her heart after her anguish the resistance was stronger than ever. 'If I love him too much it is because he has been used so ill': there was a voice within her saying this to some imagined audience in the library, when the door was opened, and she saw Will before her.

She did not move, and he came towards her with more doubt and timidity in his face than she had ever seen before. He was in a state of uncertainty which made him afraid lest some look or word of his should condemn him to a new distance from her; and Dorothea was afraid of her own emotion. She looked as if there were a spell upon her, keeping her motionless and hindering her from unclasping her hands, while some intense, grave yearning was imprisoned within her eyes. Seeing that she did not put out her hand as usual, Will paused a yard from her and said with embarrassment, 'I am so grateful to you for seeing me.'

'I wanted to see you,' said Dorothea, having no other words at command. It did not occur to her to sit down, and Will did not give a cheerful interpretation to this queenly way of receiving him; but he went on to say what he had made up his mind to say.

'I fear you think me foolish and perhaps wrong for coming back so soon. I have been punished for my impatience. You know – every one knows – a painful story about my parentage. I knew of it before I went away, and I always meant to tell you of it – if we ever met again.'

There was a slight movement in Dorothea, and she unclasped her hands, but immediately folded them over each other.

'But the affair is a matter of gossip now,' Will continued. 'I wished you to know that something connected with it – something which happened before I went away – helped to bring me down here again. At least I thought it excused my coming. It was the idea of getting Bulstrode to apply some money to a public purpose – some money which he had thought of giving me. Perhaps it is rather to Bulstrode's credit that he privately offered me compensation for an old injury: he offered to give me a good income to make amends; but I suppose you know the disagreeable story?'

Will looked doubtfully at Dorothea, but his manner was gathering some of the defiant courage with which he always thought of this fact in his destiny. He added, 'You know that it must be altogether painful to me.'

'Yes – yes – I know,' said Dorothea, hastily.

'I did not choose to accept an income from such a source. I was sure that you would not think well of me if I did so,' said Will. Why should he mind saying anything of that sort to her now? She knew that he had avowed his love for her. 'I felt that—' he broke off, nevertheless.

'You acted as I should have expected you to act,' said Dorothea, her face brightening and her head becoming a little more erect on its beautiful stem.

'I did not believe that you would let any circumstance of my birth create a prejudice in you against me, though it was sure to do so in others,' said Will, shaking his head backward in his old way, and looking with a grave appeal into her eyes.

'If it were a new hardship it would be a new reason for me to cling to you,' said Dorothea, fervidly. 'Nothing could have changed me but—' her heart was swelling, and it was difficult to go on; she made a great effort over herself to say in a low tremulous voice, 'but thinking that you were different – not so good as I had believed you to be.'

'You are sure to believe me better than I am in everything but one,' said Will, giving way to his own feeling in the evidence of hers. 'I mean, in my truth to you. When I thought you doubted of that, I didn't care about anything that was left. I thought it was all over with me, and there was nothing to try for – only things to endure.'

'I don't doubt you any longer,' said Dorothea, putting out her hand; a vague fear for him impelling her unutterable affection.

He took her hand and raised it to his lips with something like a sob. But he stood with his hat and gloves in the other hand, and might have done for the portrait of a Royalist. Still it was difficult to loose the hand, and Dorothea, withdrawing it in a confusion that distressed her, looked and moved away.

'See how dark the clouds have become, and how the trees are tossed,' she said, walking towards the window, yet speaking and moving with only a dim sense of what she was doing.

Will followed her at a little distance, and leaned against the tall back of a leather chair, on which he ventured now to lay his hat and gloves, and free himself from the intolerable durance of formality to which he had been for the first time condemned in Dorothea's presence. It must be confessed that he felt very happy at that moment leaning on the chair. He was not much afraid of anything that she might feel now.

They stood silent, not looking at each other, but looking at the evergreens which were being tossed, and were showing the pale underside of their leaves against the blackening sky. Will never enjoyed the prospect of a storm so much: it delivered him from the necessity of going away. Leaves and little branches were hurled about, and the thunder was getting nearer. The light was more and more sombre, but there came a flash of lightning which made them start and look at each other, and then smile. Dorothea began to say what she had been thinking of.

'That was a wrong thing for you to say, that you would have had nothing to try for. If we had lost our own chief good, other people's good would remain, and that is worth trying for. Some can be happy. I seemed to see that more clearly than ever, when I was the most wretched. I can hardly think how I could have borne the trouble, if that feeling had not come to me to make strength.'

'You have never felt the sort of misery I felt,' said Will; 'the misery of knowing that you must despise me.'

'But I have felt worse – it was worse to think ill—' Dorothea had begun impetuously, but broke off.

Will coloured. He had the sense that whatever she said was uttered in the vision of a fatality that kept them apart. He was silent a moment, and then said passionately—

'We may at least have the comfort of speaking to each other without disguise. Since I must go away – since we must always be divided – you may think of me as one on the brink of the grave.'

While he was speaking there came a vivid flash of lightning which lit each of them up for the other – and the light seemed to be the terror of a hopeless love. Dorothea darted instantaneously from the window; Will followed her, seizing her hand with a spasmodic movement; and so they stood, with their hands clasped, like two children, looking out on the storm, while the thunder gave a tremendous crack and roll above them, and the rain began to pour down. Then they turned their faces towards each other, with the memory of his last words in them, and they did not loose each other's hands.

'There is no hope for me,' said Will. 'Even if you loved me as well as I love you – even if I were everything to you – I shall most likely always be very poor: on a sober calculation, one can count on nothing but a creeping lot. It is impossible for us ever to belong to each other. It is perhaps base of me to have asked for a word from you. I meant to go away into silence, but I have not been able to do what I meant.'

'Don't be sorry,' said Dorothea, in her clear tender tones. 'I would rather share all the trouble of our parting.'

Her lips trembled, and so did his. It was never known which lips were the first to move towards the other lips; but they kissed tremblingly, and then they moved apart.

The rain was dashing against the window-panes as if an angry spirit were within it, and behind it was the great swoop of the wind; it was one of those moments in which both the busy and the idle pause with a certain awe.

Dorothea sat down on the seat nearest to her, a long low ottoman in the middle of the room, and with her hands folded over each other on her lap, looked at the drear outer world. Will stood still an instant looking at her, then seated himself beside her, and laid his hand on hers, which turned itself upward to be clasped. They sat in that way without looking at each other, until the rain abated and began to fall in stillness. Each had been full of thoughts which neither of them could begin to utter.

But when the rain was quiet, Dorothea turned to look at Will. With passionate exclamation, as if some torture-screw were threatening him, he started up and said, 'It is impossible!'

He went and leaned on the back of the chair again, and seemed to be battling with his own anger, while she looked towards him sadly.

'It is as fatal as a murder or any other horror that divides people,' he burst out again; 'it is more intolerable – to have our life maimed by petty accidents.'

'No – don't say that – your life need not be maimed,' said Dorothea, gently.

'Yes, it must,' said Will, angrily. 'It is cruel of you to speak in that way – as if there were any comfort. You may see beyond the misery of it, but I don't. It is unkind – it is throwing back my love for you as if it were a trifle, to speak in that way in the face of the fact. We shall never be married.'

'Some time – we might?' said Dorothea, in a trembling voice.

'When?' said Will, bitterly. 'What is the use of counting on any success of mine? It is a mere toss up whether I shall ever do more than keep myself decently, unless I choose to sell myself as a mere pen and a mouthpiece. I can see that clearly enough. I could not offer myself to any woman, even if she had no luxuries to renounce.'

There was silence. Dorothea's heart was full of something that she wanted to say, and yet the words were too difficult. She was wholly possessed by them: at that moment debate was mute within her. And it was very hard that she could not say what she wanted to say. Will was looking out of the window angrily. If he would have looked at her and not gone away from her side, she thought everything would have been easier. At last he turned, still resting against the chair, and stretching his hand automatically towards his hat, said with a sort of exasperation, 'Good-bye.'

'Oh, I cannot bear it – my heart will break,' said Dorothea, starting from her seat, the flood of her young passion bearing down all the obstructions which had kept her silent – the great tears rising and falling in an instant: 'I don't mind about poverty – I hate my wealth.'

In an instant Will was close to her and had his arms round her, but she drew her head back and held his away gently that she might go on speaking, her large tear-filled eyes looking at his very simply, while she said in a sobbing childlike way, 'We could live quite well on my own fortune – it is too much – seven hundred a year – I want so little – no new clothes – and I will learn what everything costs.'

Middlemarch: A Study of Provincial Life, 1871

MATTHEW ARNOLD

[The Romantic Poets]

I T HAS long seemed to me that the burst of creative activity in our literature, through the first quarter of this century, had about it, in fact, something premature; and that from this cause its productions are doomed, most of them, in spite of the sanguine hopes which accompanied and do still accompany them, to prove hardly more lasting than the productions of far less splendid epochs. And this prematureness comes from its having proceeded without having its proper data, without sufficient materials to work with. In other words, the English poetry of the first quarter of this century, with plenty of energy, plenty of creative force, did not know enough. This makes Byron so empty of matter, Shelley so incoherent, Wordsworth even, profound as he is, yet so wanting in completeness and variety. Wordsworth cared little for books and disparaged Goethe. I admire Wordsworth, as he is, so much that I cannot wish him different; and it is vain, no doubt, to imagine such a man different from what he is, to suppose that he could have been different; but surely the one thing wanting to make Wordsworth an even greater poet than he is – his thought richer, and his influence of wider application – was that he should have read more books, among them, no doubt, those of that Goethe whom he disparaged without reading him.

But to speak of books and reading may easily lead to a misunderstanding here. It was not really books and reading that lacked to our poetry, at this epoch; Shelley had plenty of reading, Coleridge had immense reading. Pindar and Sophocles – as we all say so glibly, and often with so little discernment of the real import of what we are saying – had not read many books; Shakespeare was no deep reader. True; but in the Greece of Pindar and Sophocles, in the England of Shakespeare, the poet lived in a current of ideas in the highest degree animating and nourishing to the creative power; society was, in the fullest measure, per-meated by fresh thought, intelligent and alive; and this state of things is the true basis for the creative power's exercise – in this it finds its data, and materials, truly ready for its hand; all the books and reading in the world are only valuable as they are helps to this. Even when this does not actually exist, books and reading may enable a man to construct a kind of semblance of it in his own mind, a world of knowledge and intelligence in which he may live and work: this is by no means an equivalent, to the artist, for the nationally diffused life and thought of the epochs of Sophocles or Shakespeare, but, besides that it may be a means of preparation for such epochs, it does really consti-tute, if many share in it, a quickening and sustaining atmosphere of great value. Such an atmosphere the many-sided learning and the long and widely-combined critical effort of Germany formed for Goethe, when he lived and worked. There was no national glow of life and thought there, as in the Athens of Pericles or the England of Elizabeth. That was the poet's weakness. But there was a sort of equivalent for it in the complete culture and unfettered thinking of a large body of Germans. That was his strength. In the England of the first quarter of this century, there was neither a national glow of life and thought, such as we had in the age of Elizabeth, nor yet a culture and a force of learning and criticism, such as were to be found in Germany. Therefore the creative power of poetry wanted, for success in the highest sense, materials and a basis; a thorough interpretation of the world was necessarily denied to it.

'The Function of Criticism at the Present Time', 1864

ANTHONY TROLLOPE

[Freedom]

PEOPLE OFTEN say that marriage is an important thing, and should be much thought of in advance, and marrying people are cautioned that there are many who marry in haste and repent at leisure. I am not sure, however, that marriage may not be pondered over too much; nor do I feel certain that the leisurely repentance does not as often follow the leisurely marriages as it does the rapid ones. That some repent no one can doubt; but I am inclined to believe that most men and women take their lots as they find them, marrying as the birds do by force of nature, and going on with their mates with a general, though not perhaps an undisturbed satisfaction, feeling inwardly assured that Providence, if it have not done the very best for them, has done for them as well as they could do for themselves with all the thought in the world. I do not know that a woman can assure to herself, by her own prudence and taste, a good husband any more than she can add two cubits to her stature; but husbands have been made to be decently good, – and wives too, for the most part, in our country, – so that the thing does not require quite so much thinking as some people say.

That Alice Vavasor had thought too much about it, I feel quite sure. She had gone on thinking of it till she had filled herself with a cloud of doubts which even the sunshine of love was unable to drive from her heavens. That a girl should really love the man she intends to marry, – that, at any rate, may be admitted. But love generally comes easily enough. With all her doubts Alice never doubted her love for Mr Grey. Nor did she doubt his character, nor his temper, nor his means. But she had gone on thinking of the matter till her mind had become filled with some undefined idea of the importance to her of her own life. What should a woman do with her life? There had arisen round her a flock of learned ladies asking that question, to whom it seems that the proper answer has never yet occurred. Fall in love, marry the man, have two children, and live happy ever afterwards. I maintain that answer has as much wisdom in it as any other that can be given; – or perhaps more. The advice contained in it cannot, perhaps, always be followed to the letter; but neither can the advice of the other kind, which is given by the flock of learned ladies who ask the question.

A woman's life is important to her, – as is that of a man to him, – not chiefly in regard to that which she shall do with it. The chief thing for her to look to is the manner in which that something shall be done. It is of moment to a young man when entering life to decide whether he shall make hats or shoes; but not of half the moment that will be that other decision, whether he shall make good shoes or bad. And so with a woman; – if she shall have recognized the necessity of truth and honesty for the purposes of her life, I do not know that she need ask herself many questions as to what she will do with it.

Alice Vavasor was ever asking herself that question, and had by degrees filled herself with a vague idea that there was a something to be done; a something over and beyond, or perhaps altogether beside that marrying and having two children; – if she only knew what it was. She had filled herself, or had been filled by her cousins, with an undefined ambition that made her restless without giving her any real food for her mind. When she told herself that she would have no scope for action in that life in Cambridgeshire which Mr Grey was preparing for her, she did not herself know what she meant by action. Had any one accused her of being afraid to separate herself from London society, she would have declared that she went very little into society and disliked that little. Had it been whispered to her that she loved the neighbourhood of the shops, she would have scorned the whisperer. Had it been suggested that the continued rattle of the big city was necessary to her happiness, she would have declared that she and her father had picked out for their residence the quietest street in London because she could not bear noise; – and yet she told herself that she feared to be taken into the desolate calmness of Cambridgeshire.

When she did contrive to find any answer to that question as to what she should do with her life, – or rather what she would wish to do with it if she were a free agent, it was generally of a political nature. She was not so far advanced as to think that women should be lawyers and doctors, or to wish that she might have the privilege of the franchise for herself; but she had undoubtedly a hankering after some second-hand political manoeuvring. She would have liked, I think, to have been the wife of the leader of a Radical opposition, in the time when such men were put into prison, and to have kept up for him his seditious correspondence while he lay in the Tower. She would have carried the answers to him inside her stays, – and have made long journeys down into northern parts without any money, if the cause required it. She would have liked to have around her ardent spirits, male or female, who would have talked of 'the cause', and have kept alive in her some flame of political fire. As it was, she had no cause. Her father's political views were very mild. Lady Macleod's were deadly Conservative. Kate Vavasor was an aspiring Radical just now, because her brother was in the same line; but during the year of the love-passages between George and Alice, George Vavasor's politics had been as Conservative as you please. He did not become a Radical till he had quarrelled with his grandfather. Now, indeed, he was possessed of very advanced views, – views with which Alice felt that she could sympathize. But what would be the use of sympathizing down in Cambridgeshire? John Grey had, so to speak, no politics. He had decided views as to the treatment which the Roman Senate received from Augustus, and had even discussed with Alice the conduct of the Girondists at the time of Robespierre's triumph; but for Manchester and its cares he had no apparent solicitude, and had declared to Alice that he would not accept a seat in the British House of Commons if it were offered to him free of expense. What political enthusiasm could she indulge with such a companion down in Cambridgeshire?

She thought too much of all this, – and was, if I may say, over-prudent in calculating the chances of her happiness and of his. For, to give her credit for what was her due, she was quite as anxious on the latter head as on the former. 'I don't care for the Roman Senate,' she would say to herself. 'I don't care much for the Girondists. How am I to talk to him day after day, night after night, when we shall be alone together?'

No doubt her tour in Switzerland with her cousin had had some effect in making such thoughts stronger now than they had ever been. She had not again learned to love her cousin. She was as firmly sure as ever that she could never love him more. He had insulted her love; and though she had forgiven him and again enrolled him among her dearest friends, she could never again feel for him that passion which a woman means when she acknowledges that she is in love. That, as regarded her and George Vavasor, was over. But, nevertheless, there had been a something of romance during those days in Switzerland which she feared she would regret when she found herself settled at Nethercoats. She envied Kate. Kate could, as his sister, attach herself on to George's political career, and obtain from it all that excitement of life which Alice desired for herself. Alice could not love her cousin and marry him; but she felt that if she could do so without impropriety she would like to stick close to him like another sister, to spend her money in aiding his career in Parliament as Kate would do, and trust herself and her career into the boat which he was to command. She did not love her cousin; but she still believed in him, – with a faith which he certainly did not deserve.

As the two days passed over her, her mind grew more and more fixed as to its purpose. She would tell Mr Grey that she was not fit to be his wife – and she would beg him to pardon her and to leave her. It never occurred to her that perhaps he might refuse to let her go. She felt quite sure that she would be free as soon as she had spoken the word which she intended to speak. If she could speak it with decision she would be free, and to attain that decision she would school herself with her utmost strength.

Can You Forgive Her?, 1864–5

LEWIS CARROLL

['Off with His Head!']

A LICE THOUGHT she had never seen such a curious croquet-ground in all her life; it was all ridges and furrows; the balls were live hedgehogs, the mallets live flamingoes, and the soldiers had to double themselves up and to stand upon their hands and feet, to make the arches.

The chief difficulty Alice found at first was in managing her flamingo: she succeeded in getting its body tucked away, comfortably enough, under her arm, with its legs hanging down, but generally, just as she had got its neck nicely straightened out, and was going to give the hedgehog a blow with its head, it *would* twist itself round and look up in her face, with such a puzzled expression that she could not help bursting out laughing: and when she had got its head down, and was going to begin again, it was very provoking to find that the hedgehog had unrolled itself, and was in the act of crawling away: besides all this, there was generally a ridge or furrow in the way wherever she wanted to send the hedgehog to, and, as the doubled-up soldiers were always getting up and walking off to other parts of the ground, Alice soon came to the conclusion that it was a very difficult game indeed.

The players all played at once without waiting for turns, quarrelling all the while, and fighting for the hedgehogs; and in a very short time the Queen was in a furious passion, and went stamping about, and shouting, 'Off with his head!' or 'Off with her head!' about once in a minute.

Alice began to feel very uneasy: to be sure she had not as yet had any dispute with the Queen, but she knew that it might happen any minute, 'and then,' thought she, 'what would become of me? They're dreadfully fond of beheading people here; the great wonder is that there's anyone left alive!'

She was looking about for some way of escape, and wondering whether she could get away without being seen, when she noticed a curious appearance in the air: it puzzled her very much at first, but, after watching it a minute or two, she made it out to be a grin, and she said to herself, 'It's the Cheshire Cat: now I shall have somebody to talk to.'

'How are you getting on?' said the Cat, as soon as there was mouth enough for it to speak with.

Alice waited till the eyes appeared, and then nodded. 'It's no use speaking to it,' she thought, 'till its ears have come, or at least one of them.' In another minute the whole head appeared, and then Alice put down her flamingo, and began an account of the game, feeling very glad she had someone to listen to her. The Cat seemed to think that there was enough of it now in sight, and no more of it appeared.

'I don't think they play at all fairly,' Alice began, in rather a complaining tone, 'and they all quarrel so dreadfully one can't hear oneself speak – and they don't seem to have any rules in particular; at least, if there are, nobody attends to them – and you've no idea how confusing it is all the things being alive; for instance, there's the arch I've got to go through next walking about at the other end of the ground – and I should have croqueted the Queen's hedgehog just now, only it ran away when it saw mine coming!'

'How do you like the Queen?' said the Cat in a low voice.

'Not at all,' said Alice; 'she's so extremely—' Just then she noticed that the Queen was close behind her listening: so she went on, '—likely to win, that it's hardly worth finishing the game.'

The Queen smiled and passed on.

'Who *are* you talking to?' said the King, coming up to Alice, and looking at the Cat's head with great curiosity.

'It's a friend of mine – a Cheshire Cat,' said Alice: 'allow me to introduce it.'

'I don't like the look of it at all,' said the King: 'however, it may kiss my hand if it likes.'

'I'd rather not,' the Cat remarked.

'Don't be impertinent,' said the King, 'and don't look at me like that!' He got behind Alice as he spoke.

'A cat may look at a king,' said Alice. 'I've read that in some book, but I don't remember where.'

'Well, it must be removed,' said the King very decidedly, and he called to the Queen, who was passing at the moment, 'My dear! I wish you would have this cat removed!'

The Queen had only one way of settling all difficulties, great or small. 'Off with his head!' she said, without even looking round.

'I'll fetch the executioner myself,' said the King eagerly, and he hurried off.

Alice thought she might as well go back and see how the game was going on, as she heard the Queen's voice in the distance, screaming with passion. She had already heard her sentence three of the players to be executed for having missed their turns, and she did not like the look of things at all, as the game was in such confusion that she never knew whether it was her turn or not. So she went in search of her hedgehog.

The hedgehog was engaged in a fight with another hedge-hog, which seemed to Alice an excellent opportunity for croqueting one of them with the other: the only difficulty was, that her flamingo was gone across to the other side of the garden, where Alice could see it trying in a helpless sort of way to fly up into one of the trees.

By the time she had caught the flamingo and brought it

back, the fight was over, and both the hedgehogs were out of sight: 'but it doesn't matter much,' thought Alice, 'as all the arches are gone from this side of the ground.' So she tucked it under her arm, that it might not escape again, and went back for a little more conversation with her friend.

When she got back to the Cheshire Cat, she was surprised to find quite a large crowd collected round it: there was a dispute going on between the executioner, the King, and the Queen, who were all talking at once, while all the rest were quite silent, and looked very uncomfortable.

The moment Alice appeared, she was appealed to by all three to settle the question, and they repeated their arguments to her, though, as they all spoke at once, she found it very hard indeed to make out exactly what they said.

The executioner's argument was, that you couldn't cut off a head unless there was a body to cut it off from: that he had never had to do such a thing before, and he wasn't going to begin at *his* time of life.

The King's argument was, that anything that had a head could be beheaded, and that you weren't to talk nonsense.

The Queen's argument was, that if something wasn't done about it in less than no time, she'd have everybody executed, all round. (It was this last remark that had made the whole party look so grave and anxious.)

Alice could think of nothing else to say but, 'It belongs to the Duchess: you'd better ask *her* about it.'

'She's in prison,' the Queen said to the executioner: 'fetch her here.' And the executioner went off like an arrow.

The Cat's head began fading away the moment he was gone, and, by the time he had come back with the Duchess, it had entirely disappeared; so the King and the executioner ran wildly up and down looking for it, while the rest of the party went back to the game.

Alice's Adventures in Wonderland, 1865

WALTER BAGEHOT

['A Big Meeting']

THERE HAS been a capital illustration lately how helpless many English gentlemen are when called together on a sudden. The Government, rightly or wrongly, thought fit to entrust the quarter-sessions of each county with the duty of combating its cattle plague; but the scene in most 'shire halls' was unsatisfactory. There was the greatest difficulty in getting, not only a right decision, but *any* decision. I saw one myself which went thus. The chairman proposed a very complex resolution, in which there was much which every one disliked, though, of course, the favourite parts of some were the objectionable parts to others. This resolution got, so to say, wedged in the meeting; everybody suggested amendments; one amendment was carried which none were satisfied with, and so the matter stood over. It is a saying in England, 'a big meeting never does anything'; and yet we are governed by the House of Commons – by 'a big meeting'.

It may be said that the House of Commons does not rule, it only elects the rulers. But there must be something special about it to enable it to do that. Suppose the Cabinet were elected by a London club, what confusion there would be, what writing and answering! 'Will you speak to So-and-So, and ask him to vote for my man?' would be heard on every side. How the wife of A and the wife of B would plot to confound the wife of C! Whether the club elected under the dignified shadow of a queen, or without the shadow, would hardly matter at all; if the substantial choice was in them, the confusion and intrigue would be there too. I propose to begin this paper by asking, not why the House of Commons governs well? but the fundamental – almost unasked question – how the House of Commons comes to be able to govern at all?

The House of Commons can do work which the quarter-sessions or clubs cannot do, because it is an organized body,

while quarter-sessions and clubs are unorganized. Two of
the greatest orators in England – Lord Brougham and Lord
Bolingbroke – spent much eloquence in attacking party
government. Bolingbroke probably knew what he was
doing; he was a consistent opponent of the power of the
Commons; he wished to attack them in a vital part. But
Lord Brougham does not know; he proposes to amend
parliamentary government by striking out the very elements
which make parliamentary government possible. At present
the majority of Parliament obey certain leaders; what those
leaders propose they support, what those leaders reject they
reject. An old Secretary of the Treasury used to say, 'This
is a bad case, an indefensible case. We must apply our
majority to this question.' That secretary lived fifty years
ago, before the Reform Bill, when majorities were very
blind, and very 'applicable'. Nowadays, the power of leaders
over their followers is strictly and wisely limited: they can
take their followers but a little way, and that only in certain
directions. Yet still there are leaders and followers. On the
Conservative side of the House there are vestiges of the
despotic leadership even now. A cynical politician is said to
have watched the long row of county members, so fresh and
respectable-looking, and muttered, 'By Jove, they are the
finest brute votes in Europe!' But all satire apart, the
principle of Parliament is obedience to leaders. Change your
leader if you will, take another if you will, but obey No. 1
while you serve No. 1, and obey No. 2 when you have gone
over to No. 2. The penalty of not doing so, is the penalty of
impotence. It is not that you will not be able to do any
good, but you will not be able to do anything at all. If
everybody does what he thinks right, there will be 657
amendments to every motion, and none of them will be
carried or the motion either.

The moment, indeed, that we distinctly conceive that the
House of Commons is mainly and above all things an
elective assembly, we at once perceive that party is of its
essence. There never was an election without a party. You
cannot get a child into an asylum without a combination. At
such places you may see 'Vote for orphan A' upon a placard,
and 'Vote for orphan B (also an idiot!!!)' upon a banner,

and the party of each is busy about its placard and banner. What is true at such minor and momentary elections must be much more true in a great and constant election of rulers. The House of Commons lives in a state of perpetual potential choice: at any moment it can choose a ruler and dismiss a ruler. And therefore party is inherent in it, is bone of its bone, and breath of its breath.

Secondly, though the leaders of party no longer have the vast patronage of the last century with which to bribe, they can coerce by a threat far more potent than any allurement – they can dissolve. This is the secret which keeps parties together. Mr Cobden most justly said, 'He had never been able to discover what was the proper moment, according to members of Parliament, for a dissolution. He had heard them say they were ready to vote for everything else, but he had never heard them say they were ready to vote for that.' Efficiency in an assembly requires a solid mass of steady votes; and these are *collected* by a deferential attachment to particular men, or by a belief in the principles those men represent, and they are *maintained* by fear of those men – by the fear that if you vote against them, you may yourself soon not have a vote at all.

Thirdly, it may seem odd to say so, just after inculcating that party organization is the vital principle of representative government, but that organization is permanently efficient, because it is not composed of warm partisans. The body is eager, but the atoms are cool. If it were otherwise, parliamentary government would become the worst of governments – a sectarian government. The party in power would go all the lengths their orators proposed – all that their formulae enjoined, as far as they had ever said they would go. But the partisans of the English Parliament are not of such a temper. They are Whigs, or Radicals, or Tories, but they are much else too. They are common Englishmen, and, as Father Newman complains, 'hard to be worked up to the dogmatic level'. They are not eager to press the tenets of their party to impossible conclusions. On the contrary, the way to lead them – the best and acknowledged way – is to affect a studied and illogical moderation. You may hear men say, 'Without committing myself to the tenet that 3 +

2 make 5, though I am free to admit that the honourable member for Bradford has advanced very grave arguments in behalf of it, I think I may, with the permission of the Committee, assume that 2 + 3 do not make 4, which will be a sufficient basis for the important propositions which I shall venture to submit on the present occasion'. This language is very suitable to the greater part of the House of Commons. Most men of business love a sort of twilight. They have lived all their lives in an atmosphere of probabilities and of doubt, where nothing is very clear, where there are some chances for many events, where there is much to be said for several courses, where nevertheless one course must be determinedly chosen and fixedly adhered to. They like to hear arguments suited to this intellectual haze. So far from caution or hesitation in the statement of the argument striking them as an indication of imbecility, it seems to them a sign of practicality. They got rich themselves by transactions of which they could not have stated the argumentative ground – and all they ask for is a distinct, though moderate conclusion, that they can repeat when asked; something which they feel *not* to be abstract argument, but abstract argument diluted and dissolved in real life. 'There seem to me', an impatient young man once said, 'to be no stays in Peel's arguments.' And that was why Sir Robert Peel was the best leader of the Commons in our time; we like to have the rigidity taken out of an argument, and the substance left.

The English Constitution, 1867

FRANCIS KILVERT

[The Wild Party]

[*Easter Tuesday, 19 April 1870*] Set off with Spencer and Leonard Cowper at two o'clock for Mouse Castle. By the fields of Hay, then to Llidiart-y-Wain. It is years since I have seen this house and I had quite forgotten how prettily it is situated. At least it looked very pretty today bosomed among its white-blossoming fruit trees, the grey fruitful homestead with its two large gleaming ponds. Thence up a steep meadow to the left and by some quarries, over a stile in a wire fence and up a lovely winding path through the woods spangled with primroses and starred with wood anemones among trees and bushes thickening green. It was very hot in the shelter of the woods as we climbed up. The winding path led us round to the back of the hill till at last we emerged into a bold green brow in the middle of which stood a square steep rampart of grey crumbling sandstone rock with a flat top covered with grass, bushes and trees, a sort of small wood. This rampart seemed about fifteen feet high. The top of the hill round the base of the rampart undulated in uneven swells and knolls with little hillocks covered with short downy grass. One of the knolls overlooking the wooded side of the hill towards Hay was covered by a wild group. A stout elderly man in a velveteen jacket with a walking stick sat or lay upon the dry turf. Beside him sat one or two young girls, while two or three more girls and boys climbed up and down an accessible point in the rampart like young wild goats, swarmed up into the hazel trees on the top of the rocks and sat in the forks and swung. I could not make the party out at all. They were not poor and they certainly were not rich. They did not look like farmers, cottagers or artisans. They were perfectly nondescript, seemed to have come from nowhere and to be going nowhere, but just to have fallen from the sky upon Mouse Castle, and to be just amusing themselves. The girls about twelve and fourteen years old climbed up the steep rocks before and just above us quite regardless of the shortness of their petticoats and the elevating and inflating powers of the wind. We climbed up too and found no castle or ruin of one. Nothing but hazels and bushes. A boy was seated in the fork of one hazel and a girl swinging in the wind in another. We soon came down again covered with dust and went to repose upon an inviting knoll, green, sunny and dry, from which two girls jumped up and ran away with needless haste. The man lay down in the grass on his face

and apparently went to sleep. The girls called him 'Father'.
They were full of fun and larks, as wild as hawks, and
presently began a great romp on the grass which ended in
their rolling and tumbling head over heels and throwing
water over each other and pouring some cautiously on their
father's head. Then they scattered primroses over him. Next
the four girls danced away down the path to a spring in the
wood with a pitcher to draw more water, leaving a little girl
and little boy with their father. We heard the girls shrieking
with laughter and screaming with fun down below at the
spring in the wood as they romped and, no doubt, threw
water over each other and pushed each other into the
spring. Presently they re-appeared on the top with the
pitcher, laughing and struggling, and again the romp began.
They ran after each other flinging water in showers, throwing each other down and rolling over on the grass. Seeing us
amused and laughing they became still more wild and
excited. They were fine good-looking spirited girls all of
them. But there were one or two quite pretty and one in a
red frock was the wildest and most reckless of the troop. In
the romp her dress was torn open all down her back, but
whilst one of her sisters was trying to fasten it for her she
burst away and tore it all open again showing vast spaces of
white, skin as well as linen. Meanwhile the water that had
been ostensibly fetched up from the spring to drink had all
been thrown wantonly away, some carefully poured over
their father, the rest wildly dashed at each other, up the
clothes, over the head, down the neck and back, anywhere
except down their own throats. Someone pretended to be
thirsty and to lament that all the water was gone so the
whole bevy trooped merrily off down to the spring again. I
could not help envying the father his children, especially his
troop of lithe, lissom, high-spirited, romping girls with their
young supple limbs, their white round arms, white shoulders
and brows, their rosy flushed cheeks, their dark and fair
curls tangled, tossed and blown back by the wind, their
bright wild saucy eyes, their red sweet full lips and white
laughing teeth, their motions as quick, graceful and active
as young antelopes or as fawns, and their clear sweet merry
laughing voices ringing through the woods. Meanwhile the

father began to roll down the hillockside to amuse his younger children who remained with him, laughing heartily. And from the spring below rose the same screaming and laughing as before. Then we heard the voices gradually coming near the top of the hill ascending through the wood, till the wild troop of girls appeared once more and the fun began again. Next the father went to hide himself in the wood for the girls to find him and play hide-and-seek. And in the midst of their game we were obliged to come away and leave them, for it was nearly 4.30. So we ran down the winding path, past the spring through the primrose-and-anemone-starred woods to the meadow, quarry, farm and road. I cannot think who the wild party were. They were like no one whom I ever saw before. They seemed as if they were the *genii loci* and always lived there. At all events I shall always connect them with Mouse Castle. And if I should ever visit the place again I shall certainly expect to find them there in full romp.

The air blew sweet from the mountains and tempered the heat of the sun. All round the brow of the hill the sloping woods budded into leaf, the birds sang in the thickets and the afternoon sun shone golden on the grassy knolls.

From the Diary

JOHN HENRY NEWMAN

[A Definition of a Gentleman]

HENCE IT is that it is almost a definition of a gentleman to say he is one who never inflicts pain. This description is both refined and, as far as it goes, accurate. He is mainly occupied in merely removing the obstacles which hinder the free and unembarrassed action of those about him; and he concurs with their movements rather than takes the initiative himself. His benefits may be considered as parallel to what are called comforts or conveniences in arrangements of a personal nature: like an easy chair or a good fire, which do their part in dispelling cold and fatigue, though nature provides both means of rest and animal heat without them. The true gentleman in like manner carefully avoids whatever may cause a jar or a jolt in the minds of those with whom he is cast; – all clashing of opinion, or collision of feeling, all restraint, or suspicion, or gloom, or resentment; his great concern being to make everyone at their ease and at home. He has his eyes on all his company; he is tender towards the bashful, gentle towards the distant, and merciful towards the absurd; he can recollect to whom he is speaking; he guards against unseasonable allusions, or topics which may irritate; he is seldom prominent in conversation, and never wearisome. He makes light of favours while he does them, and seems to be receiving when he is conferring. He never speaks of himself except when compelled, never defends himself by a mere retort; he has no ears for slander or gossip, is scrupulous in imputing motives to those who interfere with him, and interprets everything for the best. He is never mean or little in his disputes, never takes unfair advantage, never mistakes personalities or sharp sayings for arguments, or insinuates evil which he dare not say out. From a long-sighted prudence, he observes the maxim of the ancient sage, that we should ever conduct ourselves towards our enemy as if he were one day to be our friend. He has too much good sense to be affronted at insults, he is too well employed to remember injuries, and too indolent to bear malice. He is patient, forbearing, and resigned, on philosophical principles; he submits to pain, because it is inevitable, to bereavement, because it is irreparable, and to death, because it is his destiny. If he engages in controversy of any kind, his disciplined intellect preserves him from the blundering discourtesy of better, perhaps, but less educated minds; who, like blunt weapons, tear and hack instead of cutting clean, who mistake the point in argument, waste their strength in trifles, misconceive their adversary, and leave the question more involved than they find it. He may be right or wrong in his opinion, but he is too clear-headed to be unjust; he is as simple as he is forcible, and as brief as he is decisive. Nowhere shall we find greater candour, consideration, indulgence: he throws himself into the minds of his opponents, he accounts for their mistakes. He knows the weakness of human reason as well as its strength, its province and its limits. If he be an unbeliever, he will be too profound and large-minded to ridicule religion or to act against it; he is too wise to be a dogmatist or fanatic in his infidelity. He respects piety and devotion; he even supports institutions as venerable, beautiful, or useful, to which he does not assent; he honours the ministers of religion, and it contents him to decline its mysteries without assailing or denouncing them. He is a friend of religious toleration, and that, not only because his philosophy has taught him to look on all forms of faith with an impartial eye, but also from the gentleness and effeminacy of feeling, which is the attendant on civilisation.

Not that he may not hold a religion too, in his own way, even when he is not a Christian. In that case his religion is one of imagination and sentiment; it is the embodiment of those ideas of the sublime, majestic, and beautiful, without which there can be no large philosophy. Sometimes he acknowledges the being of God; sometimes he invests an unknown principle or quality with the attributes of perfection. And this deduction of his reason, or creation of his fancy, he makes the occasion of such excellent thoughts, and the starting-point of so varied and systematic a teaching, that he even seems like a disciple of Christianity itself. From the very accuracy and steadiness of his logical powers, he is able to see what sentiments are consistent in those who hold any religious doctrine at all, and he appears to others to feel and to hold a whole circle of theological truths, which exist in his mind no otherwise than as a number of deductions.

Such are some of the lineaments of the ethical character, which the cultivated intellect will form, apart from the religious principle. They are seen within the pale of the Church and without it, in holy men, and in profligate; they form the *beau idéal* of the world; they partly assist and partly distort the development of the Catholic. They may subserve the education of a St Francis de Sales or a Cardinal Pole; they may be the limits of the contemplation of a Shaftesbury or a Gibbon. Basil and Julian were fellow-students at the schools of Athens; and one became the Saint and Doctor of the Church, the other her scoffing and relentless foe.

The Idea of a University Defined and Illustrated, 1873

SAMUEL BUTLER

[Parenthood]

THE BIRTH of his son opened Theobald's eyes to a good deal which he had but faintly realised hitherto. He had had no idea how great a nuisance a baby was. Babies come into the world so suddenly at the end, and upset everything so terribly when they do come: why cannot they steal in upon us with less of a shock to the domestic system? His wife, too, did not recover rapidly from her confinement; she remained an invalid for months; here was another nuisance and an expensive one, which interfered with the amount which Theobald liked to put by out of his income against, as he said, a rainy day, or to make provision for his family if he should have one. Now he was getting a family, so that it became all the more necessary to put money by, and here was the baby hindering him. Theorists may say what they like about a man's children being a continuation of his own identity, but it will generally be found that those who talk this way have no children of their own. Practical family men know better.

About twelve months after the birth of Ernest there came a second, also a boy, who was christened Joseph, and in less than twelve months afterwards, a girl, to whom was given the name of Charlotte. A few months before this girl was born Christina paid a visit to the John Pontifexes in London, and, knowing her condition, passed a good deal of time at the Royal Academy exhibition looking at the types of female beauty portrayed by the Academicians, for she had made up her mind that the child this time was to be a girl. Alethea warned her not to do this, but she persisted, and certainly the child turned out plain, but whether the pictures caused this or no I cannot say.

Theobald had never liked children. He had always got away from them as soon as he could, and so had they from him; oh, why, he was inclined to ask himself, could not children be born into the world grown-up? If Christina could have given birth to a few full-grown clergymen in priest's orders – of moderate views, but inclining rather to Evangelicalism, with comfortable livings and in all respects facsimiles of Theobald himself – why, there might have been more sense in it; or if people could buy ready-made children at a shop of whatever age and sex they liked, instead of always having to make them at home and to begin at the beginning with them – that might do better, but as it was he did not like it. He felt as he had felt when he had been required to come and be married to Christina – that he had been going on for a long time quite nicely, and would much rather continue things on their present footing. In the matter of getting married he had been obliged to pretend he liked it; but times were changed, and if he did not like a thing now, he could find a hundred unexceptionable ways of making his dislike apparent.

It might have been better if Theobald in his younger days had kicked more against his father: the fact that he had not done so encouraged him to expect the most implicit obedience from his own children. He could trust himself, he said (and so did Christina), to be more lenient than perhaps his father had been to himself; his danger, he said (and so again did Christina), would be rather in the direction of being too indulgent; he must be on his guard against this, for no duty could be more important than that of teaching a child to obey its parents in all things.

He had read not long since of an Eastern traveller, who, while exploring somewhere in the more remote parts of Arabia and Asia Minor, had come upon a remarkably hardy, sober, industrious little Christian community – all of them in the best of health – who had turned out to be the actual living descendants of Jonadab, the son of Rechab;

and two men in European costume, indeed, but speaking English with a broken accent, and by their colour evidently Oriental, had come begging to Battersby soon afterwards, and represented themselves as belonging to this people; they had said they were collecting funds to promote the conversion of their fellow tribesmen to the English branch of the Christian religion. True, they turned out to be imposters, for when he gave them a pound and Christina five shillings from her private purse, they went and got drunk with it in the next village but one to Battersby; still, this did not invalidate the story of the Eastern traveller. Then there were the Romans – whose greatness was probably due to the wholesome authority exercised by the head of a family over all its members. Some Romans had even killed their children; this was going too far, but then the Romans were not Christians, and knew no better.

The practical outcome of the foregoing was a conviction in Theobald's mind, and if in his, then in Christina's, that it was their duty to begin training up their children in the way they should go, even from their earliest infancy. The first signs of self-will must be carefully looked for, and plucked up by the roots at once before they had time to grow. Theobald picked up this numb serpent of a metaphor and cherished it in his bosom.

Before Ernest could well crawl he was taught to kneel; before he could well speak he was taught to lisp the Lord's prayer, and the general confession. How was it possible that these things could be taught too early? If his attention flagged or his memory failed him, here was an ill weed which would grow apace, unless it were plucked out immediately, and the only way to pluck it out was to whip him, or shut him up in a cupboard, or dock him of some of the small pleasures of childhood. Before he was three years old he could read and, after a fashion, write. Before he was four he was learning Latin, and could do rule of three sums.

As for the child himself, he was naturally of an even temper, he doted upon his nurse, on kittens and puppies, and on all things that would do him the kindness of allowing him to be fond of them. He was fond of his mother, too, but as regards his father, he has told me in later life he could remember no feeling but fear and shrinking. Christina did not remonstrate with Theobald concerning the severity of the tasks imposed upon their boy, nor yet as to the continual whippings that were found necessary at lesson times. Indeed, when during any absence of Theobald's the lessons were entrusted to her, she found to her sorrow that it was the only thing to do, and she did it no less effectually than Theobald himself; nevertheless she was fond of her boy, which Theobald never was, and it was long before she could destroy all affection for herself in the mind of her first-born. But she persevered.

The Way of All Flesh, written 1873–84; published 1903

THOMAS HARDY

[The Valentine]

ON THE table lay an old quarto Bible, bound in leather. Liddy looking at it said, –

'Did you ever find out, miss, who you are going to marry by means of the Bible and key?'

'Don't be so foolish, Liddy. As if such things could be.'

'Well, there's a good deal in it, all the same.'

'Nonsense, child.'

'And it makes your heart beat fearful. Some believe in it; some don't; I do.'

'Very well, let's try it,' said Bathsheba, bounding from her seat with that total disregard of consistency which can be indulged in towards a dependant, and entering into the spirit of divination at once. 'Go and get the front door key.'

Liddy fetched it. 'I wish it wasn't Sunday,' she said, on returning. 'Perhaps 'tis wrong.'

'What's right week days is right Sundays,' replied her mistress in a tone which was a proof in itself.

The book was opened – the leaves, drab with age, being

quite worn away at much-read verses by the forefingers of unpractised readers in former days, where they were moved along under the line as an aid to the vision. The special verse in the Book of Ruth was sought out by Bathsheba, and the sublime words met her eye. They slightly thrilled and abashed her. It was Wisdom in the abstract facing Folly in the concrete. Folly in the concrete blushed, persisted in her intention, and placed the key on the book. A rusty patch immediately upon the verse, caused by previous pressure of an iron substance thereon, told that this was not the first time the old volume had been used for the purpose.

'Now keep steady, and be silent,' said Bathsheba.

The verse was repeated; the book turned round; Bathsheba blushed guiltily.

'Who did you try?' said Liddy curiously.

'I shall not tell you.'

'Did you notice Mr Boldwood's doings in church this morning, miss?' Liddy continued, adumbrating by the remark the track her thoughts had taken.

'No, indeed,' said Bathsheba, with serene indifference.

'His pew is exactly opposite yours, miss.'

'I know it.'

'And you did not see his goings on!'

'Certainly I did not, I tell you.'

Liddy assumed a smaller physiognomy, and shut her lips decisively.

This move was unexpected, and proportionately disconcerting. 'What did he do?' Bathsheba said perforce.

'Didn't turn his head to look at you once all the service.'

'Why should he?' again demanded her mistress, wearing a nettled look. 'I didn't ask him to.'

'Oh, no. But everybody else was noticing you; and it was odd he didn't. There, 'tis like him. Rich and gentlemanly, what does he care?'

Bathsheba dropped into a silence intended to express that she had opinions on the matter too abstruse for Liddy's comprehension, rather than that she had nothing to say.

'Dear me – I had nearly forgotten the valentine I bought yesterday,' she exclaimed at length.

'Valentine! who for, miss?' said Liddy. 'Farmer Bold-wood?'

It was the single name among all possible wrong ones that just at this moment seemed to Bathsheba more pertinent than the right.

'Well, no. It is only for little Teddy Coggan. I have promised him something, and this will be a very pretty surprise for him. Liddy, you may as well bring me my desk and I'll direct it at once.'

Bathsheba took from her desk a gorgeously illuminated and embossed design in post-octavo, which had been bought on the previous market-day at the chief stationer's in Casterbridge. In the centre was a small oval enclosure; this was left blank, that the sender might insert tender words more appropriate to the special occasion than any generali-ties by a printer could possibly be.

'Here's a place for writing,' said Bathsheba. 'What shall I put?'

'Something of this sort, I should think,' returned Liddy promptly: –

> 'The rose is red,
> The violet blue,
> Carnation's sweet,
> And so are you.'

'Yes, that shall be it. It just suits itself to a chubby-faced child like him,' said Bathsheba. She inserted the words in a small though legible handwriting; enclosed the sheet in an envelope, and dipped her pen for the direction.

'What fun it would be to send it to the stupid old Boldwood, and how he would wonder!' said the irrepressible Liddy, lifting her eyebrows, and indulging in an awful mirth on the verge of fear as she thought of the moral and social magnitude of the man contemplated.

Bathsheba paused to regard the idea at full length. Boldwood's had begun to be a troublesome image – a species of Daniel in her kingdom who persisted in kneeling eastward when reason and common sense said that he might just as well follow suit with the rest, and afford her the official glance of admiration which cost nothing at all. She was far from being seriously concerned about his nonconformity. Still, it was faintly depressing that the most dignified and valuable man in the parish should withhold his eyes, and that a girl like Liddy should talk about it. So Liddy's idea was at first rather harassing than piquant.

'No, I won't do that. He wouldn't see any humour in it.'

'He'd worry to death,' said the persistent Liddy.

'Really, I don't care particularly to send it to Teddy,' remarked her mistress. 'He's rather a naughty child sometimes.'

'Yes – that he is.'

'Let's toss, as men do,' said Bathsheba idly. 'Now then, head, Boldwood; tail, Teddy. No, we won't toss money on a Sunday, that would be tempting the devil indeed.'

'Toss this hymn-book; there can't be no sinfulness in that, miss.'

'Very well. Open, Boldwood – shut, Teddy. No; it's more likely to fall open. Open, Teddy – shut, Boldwood.'

The book went fluttering in the air and came down shut.

Bathsheba, a small yawn upon her mouth, took the pen, and with off-hand serenity directed the missive to Boldwood.

'Now light a candle, Liddy. Which seal shall we use? Here's a unicorn's head – there's nothing in that. What's this? – two doves – no. It ought to be something extraordinary, ought it not, Lidd? Here's one with a motto – I remember it is some funny one, but I can't read it. We'll try this, and if it doesn't do we'll have another.'

A large red seal was duly affixed. Bathsheba looked closely at the hot wax to discover the words.

'Capital!' she exclaimed, throwing down the letter frolicsomely. ''Twould upset the solemnity of a parson and clerk too.'

Liddy looked at the words of the seal, and read –

'MARRY ME.'

The same evening the letter was sent, and was duly sorted in Casterbridge post-office that night, to be returned to Weatherbury again in the morning.

So very idly and unreflectingly was this deed done. Of love as a spectacle Bathsheba had a fair knowledge; but of love subjectively she knew nothing.

Far from the Madding Crowd, 1874

[The Weather-Prophet]

IN A lonely hamlet a few miles from the town – so lonely that what are called lonely villages were teeming by comparison – there lived a man of curious repute as a forecaster or weather-prophet. The way to his house was crooked and miry – even difficult in the present unpropitious season. One evening when it was raining so heavily that ivy and laurel resounded like distant musketry, and an out-door man could be excused for shrouding himself to his ears and eyes, such a shrouded figure on foot might have been perceived travelling in the direction of the hazel-copse which dripped over the prophet's cot. The turnpike-road became a lane, the lane a cart-track, the cart-track a bridle-path, the bridle-path a foot-way, the foot-way overgrown. The solitary walker slipped here and there, and stumbled over the natural springs formed by the brambles, till at length he reached the house, which, with its garden, was surrounded with a high, dense hedge. The cottage, comparatively a large one, had been built of mud by the occupier's own hands, and thatched also by himself. Here he had always lived, and here it was assumed he would die.

He existed on unseen supplies; for it was an anomalous thing that while there was hardly a soul in the neighbourhood but affected to laugh at this man's assertions, uttering the formula, 'There's nothing in 'em', with full assurance on the surface of their faces, very few of them were unbelievers in their secret hearts. Whenever they consulted him they did it 'for a fancy'. When they paid him they said, 'Just a trifle for Christmas', or 'Candlemas', as the case might be.

He would have preferred more honesty in his clients, and

less sham ridicule; but fundamental belief consoled him for superficial irony. As stated, he was enabled to live; people supported him with their backs turned. He was sometimes astonished that men could profess so little and believe so much at his house, when at church they professed so much and believed so little.

Behind his back he was called 'Wide-oh', on account of his reputation; to his face 'Mr' Fall.

The hedge of his garden formed an arch over the entrance, and a door was inserted as in a wall. Outside the door the tall traveller stopped, bandaged his face with a handkerchief as if he were suffering from toothache, and went up the path. The window shutters were not closed, and he could see the prophet within, preparing his supper.

In answer to the knock Fall came to the door, candle in hand. The visitor stepped back a little from the light, and said, 'Can I speak to 'ee?' in significant tones. The other's invitation to come in was responded to by the country formula, 'This will do, thank 'ee', after which the householder has no alternative but to come out. He placed the candle on the corner of the dresser, took his hat from a nail, and joined the stranger in the porch, shutting the door behind him.

'I've long heard that you can – do things of a sort?' began the other, repressing his individuality as much as he could.

'Maybe so, Mr Henchard,' said the weather-caster.

'Ah – why do you call me that?' asked the visitor with a start.

'Because it's your name. Feeling you'd come I've waited for 'ee; and thinking you might be leery from your walk I laid two supper plates – look ye here.' He threw open the door and disclosed the supper-table, at which appeared a second chair, knife and fork, plate and mug, as he had declared.

Henchard felt like Saul at his reception by Samuel; he remained in silence for a few moments, then throwing off the disguise of frigidity which he had hitherto preserved, he said, 'Then I have not come in vain. . . . Now, for instance, can ye charm away warts?'

'Without trouble.'

'Cure the evil?'

'That I've done – with consideration – if they will wear the toad-bag by night as well as by day.'

'Forecast the weather?'

'With labour and time.'

'Then take this,' said Henchard. ''Tis a crown-piece. Now, what is the harvest fortnight to be? When can I know?'

'I've worked it out already, and you can know at once.' (The fact was that five farmers had already been there on the same errand from different parts of the country.) 'By the sun, moon, and stars, by the clouds, the winds, the trees, and grass, the candleflame and swallows, the smell of the herbs; likewise by the cats' eyes, the ravens, the leeches, the spiders, and the dungmixen, the last fortnight in August will be – rain and tempest.'

'You are not certain, of course?'

'As one can be in a world where all's unsure. 'Twill be more like living in Revelations this autumn than in England. Shall I sketch it out for 'ee in a scheme?'

'O no, no,' said Henchard. 'I don't altogether believe in forecasts, come to second thoughts on such. But I—'

'You don't – you don't – 'tis quite understood,' said Wide-oh, without a sound of scorn. 'You have given me a crown because you've one too many. But won't you join me at supper, now 'tis waiting and all?'

Henchard would gladly have joined; for the savour of the stew had floated from the cottage into the porch with such appetizing distinctness that the meat, the onions, the pepper, and the herbs could be severally recognized by his nose. But as sitting down to hob-and-nob there would have seemed to mark him too implicitly as the weather-caster's apostle, he declined, and went his way.

The next Saturday Henchard bought grain to such an enormous extent that there was quite a talk about his purchases among his neighbours the lawyer, the wine merchant, and the doctor; also on the next, and on all available days. When his granaries were full to choking, all the weather-cocks of Casterbridge creaked and set their faces in another direction, as if tired of the south-west. The weather changed; the sunlight, which had been like tin for weeks, assumed the hues of topaz. The temperament of the welkin passed from the phlegmatic to the sanguine; an excellent harvest was almost a certainty; and as a consequence prices rushed down.

All these transformations, lovely to the outsider, to the wrong-headed corn-dealer were terrible. He was reminded of what he had well known before, that a man might gamble upon the square green areas of fields as readily as upon those of a card-room.

Henchard had backed bad weather, and apparently lost. He had mistaken the turn of the flood for the turn of the ebb. His dealings had been so extensive that settlement could not long be postponed, and to settle he was obliged to sell off corn that he had bought only a few weeks before at figures higher by many shillings a quarter. Much of the corn he had never seen; it had not even been moved from the ricks in which it lay stacked miles away. Thus he lost heavily.

The Mayor of Casterbridge, 1886

[Sorrow]

THE BABY'S offence against society in coming into the world was forgotten by the girl-mother; her soul's desire was to continue that offence by preserving the life of the child. However, it soon grew clear that the hour of emancipation for that little prisoner of the flesh was to arrive earlier than her worst misgivings had conjectured. And when she had discovered this she was plunged into a misery which transcended that of the child's simple loss. Her baby had not been baptized.

Tess had drifted into a frame of mind which accepted passively the consideration that if she should have to burn for what she had done, burn she must, and there was an end of it. Like all village girls she was well grounded in the Holy Scriptures, and had dutifully studied the histories of Aholah and Aholibah, and knew the inferences to be drawn therefrom. But when the same question arose with regard to the baby, it had a very different colour. Her darling was about to die, and no salvation.

It was nearly bedtime, but she rushed downstairs and asked if she might send for the parson. The moment happened to be one at which her father's sense of the antique nobility of his family was highest, and his sensitiveness to the smudge which Tess had set upon that nobility most pronounced, for he had just returned from his weekly booze at Rolliver's Inn. No parson should come inside his door, he declared, prying into his affairs, just then, when, by her shame, it had become more necessary than ever to hide them. He locked the door and put the key in his pocket.

The household went to bed, and, distressed beyond measure, Tess retired also. She was continually waking as she lay, and in the middle of the night found that the baby was still worse. It was obviously dying – quietly and painlessly, but none the less surely.

In her misery she rocked herself upon the bed. The clock struck the solemn hour of one, that hour when fancy stalks outside reason, and malignant possibilities stand rock-firm as facts. She thought of the child consigned to the nethermost corner of hell, as its double doom for lack of baptism and lack of legitimacy; saw the arch-fiend tossing it with his three-pronged fork, like the one they used for heating the oven on baking days; to which picture she added many other quaint and curious details of torment sometimes taught the young in this Christian country. The lurid presentment so powerfully affected her imagination in the silence of the sleeping house that her nightgown became damp with perspiration, and the bedstead shook with each throb of her heart.

The infant's breathing grew more difficult, and the mother's mental tension increased. It was useless to devour the little thing with kisses; she could stay in bed no longer, and walked feverishly about the room.

'O merciful God, have pity; have pity upon my poor baby!' she cried. 'Heap as much anger as you want upon me, and welcome; but pity the child!'

She leant against the chest of drawers, and murmured incoherent supplications for a long while, till she suddenly started up.

'Ah! perhaps baby can be saved! Perhaps it will be just the same!'

She spoke so brightly that it seemed as though her face might have shone in the gloom surrounding her.

She lit a candle, and went to a second and a third bed under the wall, where she awoke her young sisters and brothers, all of whom occupied the same room. Pulling out the washing-stand so that she could get behind it, she poured some water from a jug, and made them kneel around, putting their hands together with fingers exactly vertical. While the children, scarcely awake, awe-stricken at her manner, their eyes growing larger and larger, remained in this position, she took the baby from her bed – a child's child – so immature as scarce to seem a sufficient personality to endow its producer with the maternal title. Tess then stood erect with the infant on her arm beside the basin, the next sister held the Prayer-Book open before her, as the clerk at church held it before the parson; and thus the girl set about baptizing her child.

Her figure looked singularly tall and imposing as she stood in her long white nightgown, a thick cable of twisted dark hair hanging straight down her back to her waist. The kindly dimness of the weak candle abstracted from her form and features the little blemishes which sunlight might have revealed – the stubble scratches upon her wrists, and the weariness of her eyes – her high enthusiasm having a transfiguring effect upon the face which had been her undoing, showing it as a thing of immaculate beauty, with a touch of dignity which was almost regal. The little ones kneeling round, their sleepy eyes blinking and red, awaited her preparations full of a suspended wonder which their physical heaviness at that hour would not allow to become active.

The most impressed of them said:

'Be you really going to christen him, Tess?'

The girl-mother replied in a grave affirmative.

'What's his name going to be?'

She had not thought of that, but a name suggested by a phrase in the book of Genesis came into her head as she proceeded with the baptismal service, and now she pronounced it:

'SORROW, I baptize thee in the name of the Father, and of the Son, and of the Holy Ghost.'

She sprinkled the water, and there was silence.

'Say "Amen", children.'

The tiny voices piped in obedient response 'Amen!'

Tess went on:

'We receive this child' – and so forth – 'and do sign him with the sign of the Cross.'

Here she dipped her hand into the basin, and fervently drew an immense cross upon the baby with her forefinger, continuing with the customary sentences as to his manfully fighting against sin, the world, and the devil, and being a faithful soldier and servant unto his life's end. She duly went on with the Lord's Prayer, the children lisping it after her in a thin gnat-like wail, till, at the conclusion, raising their voices to clerk's pitch, they again piped into the silence, 'Amen!'

Then their sister, with much augmented confidence in the efficacy of this sacrament, poured forth from the bottom of her heart the thanksgiving that follows, uttering it boldly and triumphantly in the stopt-diapason note which her voice acquired when her heart was in her speech, and which will never be forgotten by those who knew her. The ecstasy of faith almost apotheosized her; it set upon her face a glowing irradiation, and brought a red spot into the middle of each cheek; while the miniature candle-flame inverted in her eye-pupils shone like a diamond. The children gazed up at her with more and more reverence, and no longer had a will for questioning. She did not look like Sissy to them now, but as a being large, towering, and awful – a divine personage with whom they had nothing in common.

Poor Sorrow's campaign against sin, the world, and the devil was doomed to be of limited brilliancy – luckily perhaps for himself, considering his beginnings. In the blue

of the morning that fragile soldier and servant breathed his
last, and when the other children awoke they cried bitterly,
and begged Sissy to have another pretty baby.

Tess of the d'Urbervilles, 1891

GEORGE MEREDITH

[Change of Heart]

'Do you positively tell me you have no heart for the
position of first lady of the county?' said Mrs
Mountstuart.

Clara's reply was firm: 'None whatever.'

'My dear, I will believe you on one condition. Look at
me. You have eyes. If you are for mischief, you are armed
for it. But how much better, when you have won a prize, to
settle down and wear it! Lady Patterne will have entire
occupation for her flights and whimsies in leading the
county. And the man, surely the man – he behaved badly
last night: but a beauty like this—' she pushed a finger at
Clara's cheek, and doated a half instant, 'you have the very
beauty to break in an ogre's temper. And the man is as
governable as he is presentable. You have the beauty the
French call – no, it's the beauty of a queen of elves: one
sees them lurking about you, one here, one there. Smile –
they dance: be doleful – they hang themselves. No, there's
not a trace of satanic; at least, not yet. And come, come,
my Middleton, the man is a man to be proud of. You can
send him into Parliament to wear off his humours. To my
thinking, he has a fine style: conscious? I never thought so
before last night. I can't guess what has happened to him
recently. He was once a young Grand Monarque. He was
really a superb young English gentleman. Have you been
wounding him?'

'It is my misfortune to be obliged to wound him,' said
Clara.

'Quite needlessly, my child, for marry him you must.'

Clara's bosom rose: her shoulders rose too, narrowing, and her head fell slightly back.

Mrs Mountstuart exclaimed: 'But the scandal! You would never, never think of following the example of that Durham girl? – whether she was provoked to it by jealousy or not. It seems to have gone so astonishingly far with you in a very short time, that one is alarmed as to where you will stop. Your look just now was downright revulsion.'

'I fear it is. I am past my own control. Dear madam, you have my assurance that I will not behave scandalously or dishonourably. What I would entreat of you is to help me. I know this of myself: I am not the best of women. I am impatient, wickedly. I should be no good wife. Feelings like mine teach me unhappy things of myself.'

'Rich, handsome, lordly, influential, brilliant health, fine estates,' Mrs Mountstuart enumerated in petulant accents as there started across her mind some of Sir Willoughby's attributes for the attraction of the soul of woman. 'I suppose you wish me to take you in earnest?'

'I appeal to you for help.'

'What help?'

'Persuade him of the folly of pressing me to keep my word.'

'I will believe you, my dear Middleton, on one condition: – your talk of no heart is nonsense. A change like this, if one is to believe in the change, occurs through the heart, not because there is none. Don't you see that? But if you want me for a friend, you must not sham stupid. It's bad enough in itself: the imitation's horrid. You have to be honest with me, and answer me right out. You came here on this visit intending to marry Willoughby Patterne.'

'Yes.'

'And *gradually* you *suddenly* discovered, since you came here, that you did not intend it, if you could find a means of avoiding it.'

'Oh, madam, yes, it is true.'

'Now comes the test. And, my lovely Middleton, your flaming cheeks won't suffice for me this time. The old serpent can blush like an innocent maid on occasion. You are to speak, and you are to tell me in six words why that was: and don't waste one on "madam", or "Oh! Mrs Mountstuart!" Why did you change?'

'I came – When I came I was in some doubt. Indeed I speak the truth. I found I could not give him the admiration he has, I dare say, a right to expect. I turned – it surprised me; it surprises me now. But so completely! So that to think of marrying him is . . .'

'Defer the simile,' Mrs Mountstuart interposed. 'If you hit on a clever one, you will never get the better of it. Now, by just as much as you have outstripped my limitation of words to you, you show me you are dishonest.'

'I could make a vow.'

'You would forswear yourself.'

'Will you help me?'

'If you are perfectly ingenuous, I may try.'

'Dear lady, what more can I say?'

'It may be difficult. You can reply to a catechism.'

'I shall have your help?'

'Well, yes; though I don't like stipulations between friends. There is no man living to whom you could willingly give your hand? That is my question. I cannot possibly take a step unless I know. Reply briefly: there is or there is not.'

Clara sat back with bated breath, mentally taking the leap into the abyss, realizing it, and the cold prudence of abstention, and the delirium of the confession. Was there such a man? It resembled freedom to think there was: to avow it promised freedom.

'Oh, Mrs Mountstuart!'

'Well?'

'You will help me?'

'Upon my word, I shall begin to doubt your desire for it.'

'*Willingly* give my hand, madam?'

'For shame! And with wits like yours, can't you perceive where hesitation in answering such a question lands you?'

'Dearest lady, will you give me your hand? may I whisper?'

'You need not whisper; I won't look.'

Clara's voice trembled on a tense chord.

'There is one . . . compared with him I feel my insignificance. If I could aid him!'

'What necessity have you to tell me more than that there is one?'

'Ah, madam, it is different: not as you imagine. You bid me be scrupulously truthful: I am: I wish you to know the different kind of feeling it is from what might be suspected from . . . a confession. To give my hand, is beyond any thought I have ever encouraged. If you had asked me whether there is one whom I admire – yes, I do. I cannot help admiring a beautiful and brave self-denying nature. It is one whom you must pity, and to pity casts you beneath him: for you pity him because it is his nobleness that has been the enemy of his fortunes. He lives for others.'

Her voice was musically thrilling in that low muted tone of the very heart, impossible to deride or disbelieve.

Mrs Mountstuart set her head nodding on springs.

'Is he clever?'

'Very.'

'He talks well?'

'Yes.'

'Handsome?'

'He might be thought so.'

'Witty?'

'I think he is.'

'Gay, cheerful?'

'In his manner.'

'Why, the man would be a mountebank if he adopted any other. And poor?'

'He is not wealthy.'

Mrs Mountstuart preserved a lengthy silence, but nipped Clara's fingers once or twice to reassure her without approving. 'Of course he's poor,' she said at last; 'directly the reverse of what you *could* have, it *must* be. Well, my fair Middleton, I can't say you have been dishonest. I'll help you as far as I'm able. How, it is quite impossible to tell. We're in the mire. The best way seems to me to get this pitiable angel to cut some ridiculous capers and present you another view of him. I don't believe in his innocence. He knew you to be a plighted woman.'

'He has not once by word or sign hinted a disloyalty.'

'Then how do you know . . .'

'I do not know.'

'He is not the cause of your wish to break your engagement?'

'No.'

'Then you have succeeded in just telling me nothing. What is?'

'Ah! madam!'

'You would break your engagement purely because the admirable creature is in existence?'

Clara shook her head: she could not say she was dizzy. She had spoken out more than she had ever spoken to herself: and in doing so she had cast herself a step beyond the line she dared to contemplate.

'I won't detain you any longer,' said Mrs Mountstuart. 'The more we learn, the more we are taught that we are not so wise as we thought we were. I have to go to school to Lady Busshe! I really took you for a very clever girl. If you change again, you will notify the important circumstance to me, I trust.'

'I will,' said Clara, and no violent declaration of the impossibility of her changing again would have had such an effect on her hearer.

Mrs Mountstuart scanned her face for a new reading of it to match with her latest impressions.

'I am to do as I please with the knowledge I have gained?'

'I am utterly in your hands, madam.'

'I have not meant to be unkind.'

'You have not been unkind; I could embrace you.'

'I am rather too shattered, and kissing won't put me together. I laughed at Lady Busshe! No wonder you went off like a rocket with a disappointing bouquet when I told you you had been successful with poor Sir Willoughby and he could not give you up. I noticed that. A woman like Lady Busshe, always prying for the lamentable, would have required no further enlightenment. Has he a temper?'

Clara did not ask her to signalize the person thus abruptly obtruded.

'He has faults,' she said.

'There's an end to Sir Willoughby, then! Though I don't say he will give you up even when he hears the worst, if he must hear it, as for his own sake he should. And I won't say he ought to give you up. He'll be the pitiable angel if he does. For you – but you don't deserve compliments; they would be immoral. You have behaved badly, badly, badly. I have never had such a right-about-face in my life. You will deserve the stigma: you will be notorious: you will be called Number Two. Think of that! Not even original! We will break the conference, or I shall twaddle to extinction. I think I heard the luncheon bell.'

The Egoist: A Comedy in Narrative, 1879

HENRY JAMES

[Pain]

O N THE day of Isabel's arrival Ralph gave no sign, as I have related, for many hours; but toward evening he raised himself and said he knew that she had come. How he knew was not apparent, inasmuch as for fear of exciting him no one had offered the information. Isabel came in and sat by his bed in the dim light; there was only a shaded candle in a corner of the room. She told the nurse she might go – she herself would sit with him for the rest of the evening. He had opened his eyes and recognised her, and had moved his hand, which lay helpless beside him, so that she might take it. But he was unable to speak; he closed his eyes again and remained perfectly still, only keeping her hand in his own. She sat with him a long time – till the nurse came back; but he gave no further sign. He might have passed away while she looked at him; he was already the figure and pattern of death. She had thought him far gone in Rome, and this was worse; there was but one change possible now. There was a strange tranquillity in his face; it was as still as the lid of a box. With this he was a mere lattice of bones;

when he opened his eyes to greet her it was as if she were looking into immeasurable space. It was not till midnight that the nurse came back; but the hours, to Isabel, had not seemed long; it was exactly what she had come for. If she had come simply to wait she found ample occasion, for he lay three days in a kind of grateful silence. He recognised her and at moments seemed to wish to speak; but he found no voice. Then he closed his eyes again, as if he too were waiting for something – for something that certainly would come. He was so absolutely quiet that it seemed to her what was coming had already arrived; and yet she never lost the sense that they were still together. But they were not always together; there were other hours that she passed in wandering through the empty house and listening for a voice that was not poor Ralph's. She had a constant fear; she thought it possible her husband would write to her. But he remained silent, and she only got a letter from Florence and from the Countess Gemini. Ralph, however, spoke at last – on the evening of the third day.

'I feel better tonight,' he murmured, abruptly, in the soundless dimness of her vigil; 'I think I can say something.' She sank upon her knees beside his pillow; took his thin hand in her own; begged him not to make an effort – not to tire himself. His face was of necessity serious – it was incapable of the muscular play of a smile; but its owner apparently had not lost a perception of incongruities. 'What does it matter if I'm tired when I've all eternity to rest? There's no harm in making an effort when it's the very last of all. Don't people always feel better just before the end? I've often heard of that; it's what I was waiting for. Ever since you've been here I thought it would come. I tried two or three times; I was afraid you'd get tired of sitting there.' He spoke slowly, with painful breaks and long pauses; his voice seemed to come from a distance. When he ceased he lay with his face turned to Isabel and his large unwinking eyes open into her own. 'It was very good of you to come,' he went on. 'I thought you would; but I wasn't sure.'

'I was not sure either till I came,' said Isabel.

'You've been like an angel beside my bed. You know

they talk about the angel of death. It's the most beautiful of
all. You've been like that; as if you were waiting for me.'

'I was not waiting for your death; I was waiting for – for
this. This is not death, dear Ralph.'

'Not for you – no. There's nothing makes us feel so much
alive as to see others die. That's the sensation of life – the
sense that we remain. I've had it – even I. But now I'm of
no use but to give it to others. With me it's all over.' And
then he paused. Isabel bowed her head further, till it rested
on the two hands that were clasped upon his own. She
couldn't see him now; but his far-away voice was close to
her ear. 'Isabel,' he went on suddenly, 'I wish it were over
for you.' She answered nothing; she had burst into sobs; she
remained so, with her buried face. He lay silent, listening to
her sobs; at last he gave a long groan. 'Ah, what is it you
have done for me?'

'What is it you did for me?' she cried, her now extreme
agitation half smothered by her attitude. She had lost all her
shame, all wish to hide things. Now he must know; she
wished him to know, for it brought them supremely
together, and he was beyond the reach of pain. 'You did
something once – you know it. Oh Ralph, you've been
everything! What have I done for you – what can I do
today? I would die if you could live. But I don't wish you to
live; I would die myself, not to lose you.' Her voice was as
broken as his own and full of tears and anguish.

'You won't lose me – you'll keep me. Keep me in your
heart; I shall be nearer to you than I've ever been. Dear
Isabel, life is better; for in life there's love. Death is good –
but there's no love.'

'I never thanked you – I never spoke – I never was what I
should be!' Isabel went on. She felt a passionate need to cry
out and accuse herself, to let her sorrow possess her. All
her troubles, for the moment, became single and melted
together into this present pain. 'What must you have
thought of me? Yet how could I know? I never knew, and I
only know today because there are people less stupid than
I.'

'Don't mind people,' said Ralph. 'I think I'm glad to
leave people.'

She raised her head and her clasped hands; she seemed for a moment to pray to him. 'Is it true – is it true?' she asked.

'True that you've been stupid? Oh no,' said Ralph with a sensible intention of wit.

'That you made me rich – that all I have is yours?'

He turned away his head, and for some time said nothing. Then at last: 'Ah, don't speak of that – that was not happy.' Slowly he moved his face toward her again, and they once more saw each other. 'But for that – but for that—!' And he paused. 'I believe I ruined you,' he wailed.

She was full of the sense that he was beyond the reach of pain; he seemed already so little of this world. But even if she had not had it she would still have spoken, for nothing mattered now but the only knowledge that was not pure anguish – the knowledge that they were looking at the truth together. 'He married me for the money,' she said. She wished to say everything; she was afraid he might die before she had done so.

He gazed at her a little, and for the first time his fixed eyes lowered their lids. But he raised them in a moment, and then, 'He was greatly in love with you,' he answered.

'Yes, he was in love with me. But he wouldn't have married me if I had been poor. I don't hurt you in saying that. How can I? I only want you to understand. I always tried to keep you from understanding; but that's all over.'

'I always understood,' said Ralph.

'I thought you did, and I didn't like it. But now I like it.'

'You don't hurt me – you make me very happy.' And as Ralph said this there was an extraordinary goodness in his voice. She bent her head again, and pressed her lips to the back of his hand. 'I always understood,' he continued, 'though it was so strange – so pitiful. You wanted to look at life for yourself – but you were not allowed; you were punished for your wish. You were ground in the very mill of the conventional!'

'Oh yes, I've been punished,' Isabel sobbed.

He listened to her a little, and then continued: 'Was he very bad about your coming?'

'He made it very hard for me. But I don't care.'

'It is all over then between you?'

'Oh no; I don't think anything's over.'

'Are you going back to him?' Ralph gasped.

'I don't know – I can't tell. I shall stay here as long as I may. I don't want to think – I needn't think. I don't care for anything but you, and that's enough for the present. It will last a little yet. Here on my knees with you dying in my arms, I'm happier than I've been for a long time. And I want you to be happy – not to think of anything sad; only to feel that I'm near you and I love you. Why should there be pain? In such hours as this what have we to do with pain? That's not the deepest thing; there's something deeper.'

Ralph evidently found from moment to moment greater difficulty in speaking; he had to wait longer to collect himself. At first he appeared to make no response to these last words; he let a long time elapse. Then he murmured simply: 'You must stay here.'

'I should like to stay – as long as seems right.'

'As seems right – as seems right?' He repeated her words. 'Yes, you think a great deal about that.'

'Of course one must. You're very tired,' said Isabel.

'I'm very tired. You said just now that pain's not the deepest thing. No – no. But it's very deep. If I could stay—'

'For me you'll always be here,' she softly interrupted. It was easy to interrupt him.

But he went on, after a moment: 'It passes, after all; it's passing now. But love remains. I don't know why we should suffer so much. Perhaps I shall find out. There are many things in life. You're very young.'

'I feel very old,' said Isabel.

'You'll grow young again. That's how I see you. I don't believe – I don't believe—' But he stopped again; his strength failed him.

She begged him to be quiet now. 'We needn't speak to understand each other,' she said.

'I don't believe that such a generous mistake as yours can hurt you for more than a little.'

'Oh Ralph, I'm very happy now,' she cried through her tears.

'And remember this,' he continued, 'that if you've been hated you've also been loved. Ah but, Isabel – *adored!*' he just audibly and lingeringly breathed.

'Oh my brother!' she cried with a movement of still deeper prostration.

The Portrait of a Lady, 1881

[A Virtuous Attachment]

LITTLE BILHAM, in meditation, looked at him with a kindness almost paternal. 'Don't you like it over here?'

Strether laughed out – for the tone was indeed droll; he let himself go. 'What has that to do with it? The only thing I've any business to like is to feel that I'm moving him. That's why I ask you whether you believe I *am*. Is the creature' – and he did his best to show that he simply wished to ascertain – 'honest?'

His companion looked responsible, but looked it through a small dim smile. 'What creature do you mean?'

'Is it true that he's free? How then,' Strether asked wondering, 'does he arrange his life?'

'Is the creature you mean Chad himself?' little Bilham said.

Strether here, with a rising hope, just thought, 'We must take one of them at a time.' But his coherence lapsed. '*Is* there some woman? Of whom he's really afraid of course I mean – or who does with him what she likes.'

'It's awfully charming of you,' Bilham presently remarked, 'not to have asked me that before.'

'Oh I'm not fit for my job!'

The exclamation had escaped our friend, but it made little Bilham more deliberate. 'Chad's a rare case!' he luminously observed. 'He's awfully changed,' he added.

'Then you see it too?'

'The way he has improved? Oh yes – I think every one

must see it. But I'm not sure,' said little Bilham, 'that I didn't like him about as well in his other state.'

'Then this *is* really a new state altogether?'

'Well,' the young man after a moment returned, 'I'm not sure he was really meant by nature to be quite so good. It's like the new edition of an old book that one has been fond of – revised and amended, brought up to date, but not quite the thing that one knew and loved. However that may be at all events,' he pursued, 'I don't think, you know, that he's really playing, as you call it, any game. I believe he really wants to go back and take up a career. He's capable of one, you know, that will improve and enlarge him still more. He won't then,' little Bilham continued to remark, 'be my pleasant well-rubbed old-fashioned volume at all. But of course I'm beastly immoral. I'm afraid it would be a funny world altogether – a world with things the way I like them. I ought, I dare say, to go home and go into business myself. Only I'd simply rather die – simply. And I've not the least difficulty in making up my mind not to, and in knowing exactly why, and in defending my ground against all comers. All the same,' he wound up, 'I assure you I don't say a word against it – for myself, I mean – to Chad. I seem to see it as much the best thing for him. You see he's not happy.'

'*Do* I?' – Strether stared. 'I've been supposing I see just the opposite – an extraordinary case of the equilibrium arrived at and assured.'

'Oh there's a lot behind it.'

'Ah there you are!' Strether exclaimed. 'That's just what I want to get at. You speak of your familiar volume altered out of recognition. Well, who's the editor?'

Little Bilham looked before him a minute in silence. 'He ought to get married. *That* would do it. And he wants to.'

'Wants to marry her?'

Again little Bilham waited, and, with a sense that he had information, Strether scarce knew what was coming. 'He wants to be free. He isn't used, you see,' the young man explained in his lucid way, 'to being so good.'

Strether hesitated. 'Then I may take it from you that he is good?'

His companion matched his pause, but making it up with a quiet fullness. '*Do* take it from me.'

'Well then why isn't he free? He swears to me he is, but meanwhile does nothing – except of course that he's so kind to me – to prove it; and couldn't really act much otherwise if he weren't. My question to you just now was exactly on this queer impression of his diplomacy; as if instead of really giving ground his line were to keep me on here and set me a bad example.'

As the half-hour meanwhile had ebbed Strether paid his score, and the waiter was presently in the act of counting out change. Our friend pushed back to him a fraction of it, with which, after an emphatic recognition, the personage in question retreated. 'You give too much,' little Bilham permitted himself benevolently to observe.

'Oh I always give too much!' Strether helplessly sighed. 'But you don't,' he went on as if to get quickly away from the contemplation of that doom, 'answer my question. Why isn't he free?'

Little Bilham had got up as if the transaction with the waiter had been a signal, and had already edged out between the table and the divan. The effect of this was that a minute later they had quitted the place, the gratified waiter alert again at the open door. Strether had found himself deferring to his companion's abruptness as to a hint that he should be answered as soon as they were more isolated. This happened when after a few steps in the outer air they had turned the next corner. There our friend had kept it up. 'Why isn't he free if he's good?'

Little Bilham looked him full in the face. 'Because it's a virtuous attachment.'

The Ambassadors, 1903

ROBERT LOUIS STEVENSON

[Business]

So things passed until, the day after the funeral, and about three o'clock of a bitter, foggy, frosty afternoon, I was standing at the door for a moment, full of sad thoughts about my father, when I saw someone drawing slowly near along the road. He was plainly blind, for he tapped before him with a stick, and wore a great green shade over his eyes and nose; and he was hunched, as if with age or weakness, and wore a huge old tattered sea-cloak with a hood, that made him appear positively deformed. I never saw in my life a more dreadful-looking figure. He stopped a little from the inn, and, raising his voice in an odd sing-song, addressed the air in front of him:—

'Will any kind friend inform a poor blind man, who has lost the precious sight of his eyes in the gracious defence of his native country, England, and God bless King George! – where or in what part of this country he may now be?'

'You are at the "Admiral Benbow", Black Hill Cove, my good man,' said I.

'I hear a voice,' said he – 'a young voice. Will you give me your hand, my kind young friend, and lead me in?'

I held out my hand, and the horrible, soft-spoken, eyeless creature gripped it in a moment like a vice. I was so much startled that I struggled to withdraw; but the blind man pulled me close up to him with a single action of his arm.

'Now, boy,' he said, 'take me in to the captain.'

'Sir,' said I, 'upon my word I dare not.'

'Oh,' he sneered, 'that's it! Take me in straight, or I'll break your arm.'

And he gave it, as he spoke, a wrench that made me cry out.

'Sir,' said I, 'it is for yourself I mean. The captain is not what he used to be. He sits with a drawn cutlass. Another gentleman—'

'Come, now, march,' interrupted he; and I never heard a

voice so cruel, and cold, and ugly as that blind man's. It cowed me more than the pain; and I began to obey him at once, walking straight in at the door and towards the parlour, where our sick old buccaneer was sitting, dazed with rum. The blind man clung close to me, holding me in one iron fist, and leaning almost more of his weight on me than I could carry. 'Lead me straight up to him, and when I'm in view, cry out, "Here's a friend for you, Bill." If you don't, I'll do this'; and with that he gave me a twitch that I thought would have made me faint. Between this and that, I was so utterly terrified of the blind beggar that I forgot my terror of the captain, and as I opened the parlour door, cried out the words he had ordered in a trembling voice.

The poor captain raised his eyes, and at one look the rum went out of him, and left him staring sober. The expression of his face was not so much of terror as of mortal sickness. He made a movement to rise, but I do not believe he had enough force left in his body.

'Now, Bill, sit where you are,' said the beggar. 'If I can't see, I can hear a finger stirring. Business is business. Hold out your right hand. Boy, take his right hand by the wrist, and bring it near to my right.'

We both obeyed him to the letter, and I saw him pass something from the hollow of the hand that held his stick into the palm of the captain's, which closed upon it instantly.

'And now that's done,' said the blind man; and at the words he suddenly left hold of me, and, with incredible accuracy and nimbleness, skipped out of the parlour and into the road, where, as I still stood motionless, I could hear his stick go tap-tap-tapping into the distance.

It was some time before either I or the captain seemed to gather our senses; but at length, and about at the same moment, I released his wrist, which I was still holding, and he drew in his hand and looked sharply into the palm.

'Ten o'clock!' he cried. 'Six hours. We'll do them yet'; and he sprang to his feet.

Even as he did so, he reeled, put his hand to his throat, stood swaying for a moment, and then, with a peculiar sound, fell from his whole height face foremost to the floor.

I ran to him at once, calling to my mother. But haste was

all in vain. The captain had been struck dead by thundering apoplexy. It is a curious thing to understand, for I had certainly never liked the man, though of late I had begun to pity him, but as soon as I saw that he was dead, I burst into a flood of tears. It was the second death I had known, and the sorrow of the first was still fresh in my heart.

Treasure Island, 1883

WALTER PATER

[A Township of the Deceased]

A N OLD flower-garden in the rear of the house, set here and there with a venerable olive-tree – a picture in pensive shade and fiery blossom, as transparent, under that afternoon light, as the old miniature-painters' work on the walls of the chambers within – was bounded towards the west by a low, grass-grown hill. A narrow opening cut in its steep side, like a solid blackness there, admitted Marius and his gleaming leader into a hollow cavern or crypt, neither more nor less in fact than the family burial-place of the Cecilii, to whom this residence belonged, brought thus, after an arrangement then becoming not unusual, into immediate connection with the abode of the living, in bold assertion of that instinct of family life, which the sanction of the Holy Family was, hereafter, more and more to reinforce. Here, in truth, was the centre of the peculiar religious expressiveness, of the sanctity, of the entire scene. That 'any person may, at his own election, constitute the place which belongs to him a *religious* place, by the carrying of his dead into it': – had been a maxim of old Roman law, which it was reserved for the early Christian societies, like that established here by the piety of a wealthy Roman matron, to realize in all its consequences. Yet this was certainly unlike any cemetery Marius had ever before seen; most obviously in this, that these people had returned to the older fashion of disposing of their dead by burial instead of burning. Originally a family sepulchre, it was growing to a vast *necropolis*, a whole township of the deceased, by means of some free expansion of the family interest beyond its amplest natural limits. That air of venerable beauty which characterized the house and its precincts above, was maintained also here. It was certainly with a great outlay of labour that these long, apparently endless, yet elaborately designed galleries were increasing so rapidly, with their layers of beds or berths, one above another, cut, on either side the pathway, in the porous *tufa*, through which all the moisture filters downwards, leaving the parts above dry and wholesome. All alike were carefully closed, and with all the delicate costliness at command; some with simple tiles of baked clay, many with slabs of marble enriched by fair inscriptions: marble taken, in some cases, from older pagan tombs – the inscriptions sometimes a *palimpsest*, the new epitaph being woven into the faded letters of an earlier one.

As in an ordinary Roman cemetery, an abundance of utensils for the worship or commemoration of the departed was disposed around – incense, lights, flowers, their flame or their freshness being relieved to the utmost by contrast with the coal-like blackness of the soil itself, a volcanic sandstone, cinder of burnt-out fires. Would they ever kindle again? – possess, transform, the place? – Turning to an ashen pallor where, at regular intervals, an air-hole or *luminare* let in a hard beam of clear but sunless light, with the heavy sleepers, row upon row within, leaving a passage so narrow that only one visitor at a time could move along, cheek to cheek with them, the high walls seemed to shut one in into the great company of the dead. Only the long straight pathway lay before him; opening, however, here and there, into a small chamber, around a broad, table-like coffin or 'altar-tomb', adorned even more profusely than the rest as if for some anniversary observance. Clearly, these people, concurring in this with the special sympathies of Marius himself, had adopted the practice of burial from some peculiar feeling of hope they entertained concerning the body; a feeling which, in no irreverent curiosity, he would fain have penetrated. The complete and irreparable disappearance of the dead in the funeral fire, so crushing to the spirits, as he for one had found it, had long since induced in him a preference for that other mode of settlement to the last sleep, as having something about it more homelike and hopeful, at least in outward seeming. But whence the strange confidence that these 'handfuls of white dust' would hereafter recompose themselves once more into exulting human creatures? By what heavenly alchemy, what reviving dew from above, such as was certainly never again to reach the dead violets? – *Januarius, Agapetus, Felicitas; Martyrs! refresh, I pray you, the soul of Cecil, of Cornelius!* said an inscription, one of many, scratched, like a passing sigh, when it was still fresh in the mortar that had closed up the prison-door. All critical estimate of this bold hope, as sincere apparently as it was audacious in its claim, being set aside, here at least, carried further than ever before, was that pious, systematic commemoration of the dead, which, in its chivalrous refusal to forget or finally desert the helpless, had ever counted with Marius as the central exponent or symbol of all natural duty.

The stern soul of the excellent Jonathan Edwards, applying the faulty theology of John Calvin, afforded him, we know, the vision of infants not a span long, on the floor of hell. Every visitor to the Catacombs must have observed, in a very different theological connection, the numerous children's graves there – beds of infants, but a span long indeed, lowly 'prisoners of hope', on these sacred floors. It was with great curiosity, certainly, that Marius considered them, decked in some instances with the favourite toys of their tiny occupants – toy-soldiers, little chariot-wheels, the entire paraphernalia of a baby-house; and when he saw afterwards the living children, who sang and were busy above – sang their psalm *Laudate Pueri Dominum!* – their very faces caught for him a sort of quaint unreality from the memory of those others, the children of the Catacombs, but a little way below them.

Here and there, mingling with the record of merely natural decease, and sometimes at these children's graves, were the signs of violent death or 'martyrdom', – proofs that some 'had loved not their lives unto the death' – in the little

red phial of blood, the palm-branch, the red flowers for
their heavenly 'birthday'. About one sepulchre in particular,
distinguished in this way, and devoutly arrayed for what, by
a bold paradox, was thus treated as, *natalitia* – a birthday,
the peculiar arrangements of the whole place visibly centred.
And it was with a singular novelty of feeling, like the
dawning of a fresh order of experiences upon him, that,
standing beside those mournful relics, snatched in haste
from the common place of execution not many years before,
Marius became, as by some gleam of foresight, aware of the
whole force of evidence for a certain strange, new hope,
defining in its turn some new and weighty motive of action,
which lay in deaths so tragic for the 'Christian superstition'.

*Marius the Epicurean: His
Sensations and Ideas*, 1885

RUDYARD KIPLING

[Intermediate]

THE BEGINNING of everything was in a railway train
upon the road to Mhow from Ajmir. There had been a
Deficit in the Budget, which necessitated travelling, not
Second-class, which is only half as dear as First-class, but by
Intermediate, which is very awful indeed. There are no
cushions in the Intermediate class, and the population are
either Intermediate, which is Eurasian, or native, which for
a long night journey is nasty, or Loafer, which is amusing
though intoxicated. Intermediates do not buy from refreshment rooms. They carry their food in bundles and pots, and
buy sweets from the native sweetmeat-sellers, and drink the
roadside water. That is why in the hot weather Intermediates are taken out of the carriages dead, and in all weathers
are most properly looked down upon. My particular Intermediate happened to be empty till I reached Nasirabad,
when a big black-browed gentleman in shirt-sleeves entered,

and, following the custom of Intermediates, passed the time of day. He was a wanderer and a vagabond like myself, but with an educated taste for whisky. He told tales of things he had seen and done, of out-of-the-way corners of the Empire into which he had penetrated, and of adventures in which he risked his life for a few days' food.

'If India was filled with men like you and me, not knowing more than the crows where they'd get their next day's rations, it isn't seventy millions of revenue the land would be paying – it's seven hundred millions,' said he; and as I looked at his mouth and chin I was disposed to agree with him.

We talked politics – the politics of Loaferdom, that sees things from the underside where the lath and plaster is not smoothed off – and we talked postal arrangements because my friend wanted to send a telegram back from the next station to Ajmir, the turning-off place from the Bombay to Mhow line as you travel westward. My friend had no money beyond eight annas, which he wanted for dinner, and I had no money at all, owing to the hitch in the Budget before mentioned. Further, I was going into a wilderness where, though I should resume touch with the Treasury, there were no telegraph offices. I was, therefore, unable to help him in any way.

'We might threaten a Station-master, and make him send a wire on tick,' said my friend, 'but that'd mean inquiries for you and for me, and *I've* got my hands full these days. Did you say you are travelling back along this line within any days?'

'Within ten,' I said.

'Can't you make it eight?' said he. 'Mine is rather urgent business.'

'I can send your telegram within ten days if that will serve you,' I said.

'I couldn't trust the wire to fetch him now I think of it. It's this way. He leaves Delhi on the 23rd for Bombay. That means he'll be running through Ajmir about the night of the 23rd.'

'But I'm going into the Indian Desert,' I explained.

'Well *and* good,' said he. 'You'll be changing at Marwar

Junction to get into Jodhpore territory – you must do that – and he'll be coming through Marwar Junction in the early morning of the 24th by the Bombay Mail. Can you be at Marwar Junction on that time? 'Twon't be inconveniencing you because I know that there's precious few pickings to be got out of these Central Indian States – even though you pretend to be correspondent of the *Backwoodsman*.'

'Have you ever tried that trick?' I asked.

'Again and again, but the Residents find you out, and then you get escorted to the Border before you've time to get your knife into them. But about my friend here. I *must* give him a word o' mouth to tell him what's come to me or else he won't know where to go. I would take it more than kind of you if you was to come out of Central India in time to catch him at Marwar Junction, and say to him: "He has gone South for the week." He'll know what that means. He's a big man with a red beard, and a great swell he is. You'll find him sleeping like a gentleman with all his luggage round him in a Second-class compartment. But don't you be afraid. Slip down the window, and say: "He has gone South for the week," and he'll tumble. It's only cutting your time of stay in those parts by two days. I ask you as a stranger – going to the West,' he said with emphasis.

'Where have *you* come from?' said I.

'From the East,' said he, 'and I am hoping that you will give him the message on the Square – for the sake of my Mother as well as your own.'

Englishmen are not usually softened by appeals to the memory of their mothers, but for certain reasons, which will be fully apparent, I saw fit to agree.

'It's more than a little matter,' said he, 'and that's why I asked you to do it – and now I know that I can depend on you doing it. A Second-class carriage at Marwar Junction, and a red-haired man asleep in it. You'll be sure to remember. I get out at the next station, and I must hold on there till he comes or sends me what I want.'

'I'll give the message if I catch him,' I said, 'and for the sake of your Mother as well as mine I'll give you a word of advice. Don't try to run the Central India States just now as the correspondent of the *Backwoodsman*. There's a real one knocking about here, and it might lead to trouble.'

'Thank you,' said he simply, 'and when will the swine be gone? I can't starve because he's ruining my work. I wanted to get hold of the Degumber Rajah down here about his father's widow, and give him a jump.'

'What did he do to his father's widow, then?'

'Filled her up with red pepper and slippered her to death as she hung from a beam. I found that out myself, and I'm the only man that would dare going into the State to get hush-money for it. They'll try to poison me, same as they did in Chortumna when I went on the loot there. But you'll give the man at Marwar Junction my message?'

He got out at a little roadside station, and I reflected. I had heard, more than once, of men personating correspondents of newspapers and bleeding small Native States with threats of exposure, but I had never met any of the caste before. They lead a hard life, and generally die with great suddenness. The Native States have a wholesome horror of English newspapers which may throw light on their peculiar methods of government, and do their best to choke correspondents with champagne, or drive them out of their mind with four-in-hand barouches. They do not understand that nobody cares a straw for the internal administration of the Native States so long as oppression and crime are kept within decent limits, and the ruler is not drugged, drunk, or diseased from one end of the year to the other. They are the dark places of the earth, full of unimaginable cruelty, touching the Railway and Telegraph on one side, and, on the other, the days of Harun-al-Raschid. When I left the train I did business with divers Kings, and in eight days passed through many changes of life. Sometimes I wore dress-clothes and consorted with Princes and Politicals, drinking from crystal and eating from silver. Sometimes I lay out upon the ground and devoured what I could get, from a plate made of leaves, and drank the running water, and slept under the same rug as my servant. It was all in the day's work.

Then I headed for the Great Indian Desert upon the

proper date, as I had promised, and the night Mail set me down at Marwar Junction, where a funny little happy-go-lucky, native-managed railway runs to Jodhpore. The Bombay Mail from Delhi makes a short halt at Marwar. She arrived as I got in, and I had just time to hurry to her platform and go down the carriages. There was only one Second-class on the train. I slipped the window and looked down upon a flaming red beard, half covered by a railway rug. That was my man, fast asleep, and I dug him gently in the ribs. He woke with a grunt, and I saw his face in the light of the lamps. It was a great and shining face.

'Tickets again?' said he.

'No,' said I. 'I am to tell you that he is gone South for the week. He has gone South for the week!'

The train had begun to move out. The red man rubbed his eyes. 'He has gone South for the week,' he repeated. 'Now that's just like his impidence. Did he say that I was to give you anything? 'Cause I won't.'

'He didn't,' I said, and dropped away, and watched the red lights die out in the dark. It was horribly cold because the wind was blowing off the sands. I climbed into my own train – not an Intermediate Carriage this time – and went to sleep.

If the man with the beard had given me a rupee I should have kept it as a memento of a rather curious affair. But the consciousness of having done my duty was my only reward.

Later on I reflected that two gentlemen like my friends could not do any good if they forgathered and personated correspondents of newspapers, and might, if they black-mailed one of the little rat-trap states of Central India or Southern Rajputana, get themselves into serious difficulties. I therefore took some touble to describe them as accurately as I could remember to people who would be interested in deporting them; and succeeded, so I was later informed, in having them headed back from the Degumber borders.

'The Man Who Would Be King', 1888

JEROME KLAPKA JEROME

[Hampton Court]

HARRIS ASKED me if I'd ever been in the maze at Hampton Court. He said he went in once to show somebody else the way. He had studied it up in a map, and it was so simple that it seemed foolish – hardly worth the twopence charged for admission. Harris said he thought that map must have been got up as a practical joke, because it wasn't a bit like the real thing, and only misleading. It was a country cousin that Harris took in. He said:

'We'll just go in here, so that you can say you've been, but it's very simple. It's absurd to call it a maze. You keep on taking the first turning to the right. We'll just walk round for ten minutes, and then go and get some lunch.'

They met some people soon after they had got inside, who said they had been there for three-quarters of an hour, and had had about enough of it. Harris told them they could follow him, if they liked; he was just going in, and then should turn round and come out again. They said it was very kind of him, and fell behind, and followed.

They picked up various other people who wanted to get it over, as they went along, until they had absorbed all the persons in the maze. People who had given up all hopes of ever getting either in or out, or of ever seeing their home and friends again, plucked up courage at the sight of Harris and his party, and joined the procession, blessing him. Harris said he should judge there must have been twenty people, following him, in all; and one woman with a baby, who had been there all the morning, insisted on taking his arm, for fear of losing him.

Harris kept on turning to the right, but it seemed a long way, and his cousin said he supposed it was a very big maze.

'Oh, one of the largest in Europe,' said Harris.

'Yes, it must be,' replied the cousin, 'because we've walked a good two miles already.'

Harris began to think it rather strange himself, but he

held on until, at last, they passed the half of a penny bun on the ground that Harris's cousin swore he had noticed there seven minutes ago. Harris said: 'Oh, impossible!' but the woman with the baby said, 'Not at all,' as she herself had taken it from the child, and thrown it down there, just before she met Harris. She also added that she wished she never had met Harris, and expressed an opinion that he was an impostor. That made Harris mad, and he produced his map, and explained his theory.

'The map may be all right enough,' said one of the party, 'if you know whereabouts in it we are now.'

Harris didn't know, and suggested that the best thing to do would be to go back to the entrance, and begin again. For the beginning again part of it there was not much enthusiasm; but with regard to the advisability of going back to the entrance there was complete unanimity, and so they turned, and trailed after Harris again, in the opposite direction. About ten minutes more passed, and then they found themselves in the centre.

Harris thought at first of pretending that that was what he had been aiming at; but the crowd looked dangerous, and he decided to treat it as an accident.

Anyhow, they had got something to start from then. They did know where they were, and the map was once more consulted, and the thing seemed simpler than ever, and off they started for the third time.

And three minutes later they were back in the centre again.

After that, they simply couldn't get anywhere else. Whatever way they turned brought them back to the middle. It became so regular at length, that some of the people stopped there, and waited for the others to take a walk round, and come back to them. Harris drew out his map again, after a while, but the sight of it only infuriated the mob, and they told him to go and curl his hair with it. Harris said that he couldn't help feeling that, to a certain extent, he had become unpopular.

They all got crazy at last, and sang out for the keeper, and the man came and climbed up the ladder outside, and shouted out directions to them. But all their heads were, by this time, in such a confused whirl that they were incapable of grasping anything, and so the man told them to stop where they were, and he would come to them. They huddled together, and waited; and he climbed down, and came in.

He was a young keeper, as luck would have it, and new to the business; and when he got in, he couldn't find them, and he wandered about, trying to get to them, and then *he* got lost. They caught sight of him, every now and then, rushing about the other side of the hedge, and he would see them, and rush to get to them, and they would wait there for about five minutes, and then he would reappear again in exactly the same spot, and ask them where they had been.

They had to wait till one of the old keepers came back from his dinner before they got out.

Three Men in a Boat, 1889

WILLIAM MORRIS

[Market Forces]

S AID HE, settling himself in his chair again for a long talk: 'It is clear from all that we hear and read, that in the last age of civilisation men had got into a vicious circle in the matter of production of wares. They had reached a wonderful facility of production, and in order to make the most of that facility they had gradually created (or allowed to grow, rather) a most elaborate system of buying and selling, which has been called the World-Market; and that World-Market, once set a-going, forced them to go on making more and more of these wares, whether they needed them or not. So that while (of course) they could not free themselves from the toil of making real necessaries, they created in a never-ending series sham or artificial necessaries, which became, under the iron rule of the aforesaid World-Market, of equal importance to them with the real necessaries which supported life. By all this they burdened themselves with a prodigious mass of work merely for the sake of keeping their wretched system going.'

'Yes – and then?' said I.

'Why, then, since they had forced themselves to stagger along under this horrible burden of unnecessary production, it became impossible for them to look upon labour and its results from any other point of view than one – to wit, the ceaseless endeavour to expend the least possible amount of labour on any article made, and yet at the same time to make as many articles as possible. To this "cheapening of production", as it was called, everything was sacrificed: the happiness of the workman at his work, nay, his most elementary comfort and bare health, his food, his clothes, his dwelling, his leisure, his amusement, his education – his life, in short – did not weigh a grain of sand in the balance against this dire necessity of "cheap production" of things, a great part of which were not worth producing at all. Nay, we are told, and we must believe it, so overwhelming is the evidence, though many of our people scarcely *can* believe it, that even rich and powerful men, the masters of the poor devils aforesaid, submitted to live amidst sights and sounds and smells which it is in the very nature of man to abhor and flee from, in order that their riches might bolster up this supreme folly. The whole community, in fact, was cast into the jaws of this ravening monster, "the cheap production" forced upon it by the World-Market.'

'Dear me!' said I. 'But what happened? Did not their cleverness and facility in production master this chaos of misery at last? Couldn't they catch up with the World-Market, and then set to work to devise means for relieving themselves from this fearful task of extra labour?'

He smiled bitterly. 'Did they even try to?' said he. 'I am not sure. You know that according to the old saw the beetle gets used to living in dung; and these people, whether they found the dung sweet or not, certainly lived in it.'

His estimate of the life of the nineteenth century made me catch my breath a little; and I said feebly, 'But the labour-saving machines?'

'Heyday!' quoth he. 'What's that you are saying? the labour-saving machines? Yes, they were made to "save labour" (or, to speak more plainly, the lives of men) on one piece of work in order that it might be expended – I will say wasted – on another, probably useless, piece of work. Friend, all their devices for cheapening labour simply resulted in increasing the burden of labour. The appetite of the World-Market grew with what it fed on: the countries within the ring of "civilisation" (that is, organised misery) were glutted with the abortions of the market, and force and fraud were used unsparingly to "open up" countries *outside* that pale. This process of "opening up" is a strange one to those who have read the professions of the men of that period and do not understand their practice; and perhaps shows us at its worst the great vice of the nineteenth century, the use of hypocrisy and cant to evade the responsibility of vicarious ferocity. When the civilised World-Market coveted a country not yet in its clutches, some transparent pretext was found – the suppression of a slavery different from, and not so cruel as that of commerce; the pushing of a religion no longer believed in by its promoters; the "rescue" of some desperado or homicidal madman whose misdeeds had got him into trouble amongst the natives of the "barbarous" country – any stick, in short, which would beat the dog at all. Then some bold, unprincipled, ignorant adventurer was found (no difficult task in the days of competition), and he was bribed to "create a market" by breaking up whatever traditional society there might be in the doomed country, and by destroying whatever leisure or pleasure he found there. He forced wares on the natives which they did not want, and took their natural products in "exchange", as this form of robbery was called, and thereby he "created new wants", to supply which (that is, to be allowed to live by their new masters) the hapless helpless peoples had to sell themselves into the slavery of hopeless toil so that they might have something wherewith to purchase the nullities of "civilisation". Ah,' said the old man, pointing to the Museum, 'I have read books and papers in there, telling strange stories indeed of the dealings of civilisation (or organised misery) with "non-civilisation"; from the time when the British Government deliberately sent blankets infected with small-pox as choice gifts to inconvenient tribes of Redskins, to the time when Africa was infested by a man named Stanley, who—'

'Excuse me,' said I, 'but as you know, time presses; and I want to keep our question on the straightest line possible; and I want at once to ask about these wares made for the World-Market – how about their quality; these people who were so clever about making goods, I suppose they made them well?'

'Quality!' said the old man crustily, for he was rather peevish at being cut short in his story; 'how could they possibly attend to such trifles as the quality of the wares they sold? The best of them were of a low average, the worst were transparent makeshifts for the things asked for, which nobody would have put up with if they could have got anything else. It was a current jest of the time that the wares were made to sell and not to use; a jest which you, as coming from another planet, may understand, but which our folk could not.'

Said I: 'What! did they make nothing well?'

'Why, yes,' said he, 'there was one class of goods which they made thoroughly well, and that was the class of machines which were used for making things. These were usually quite perfect pieces of workmanship, admirably adapted to the end in view. So that it may be fairly said that the great achievement of the nineteenth century was the making of machines which were wonders of invention, skill, and patience, and which were used for the production of measureless quantities of worthless makeshifts. In truth, the owners of the machines did not consider anything which they made as wares, but simply as means for the enrichment of themselves. Of course, the only admitted test of utility in wares was the finding of buyers for them – wise men or fools, as it might chance.'

'And people put up with this?' said I.

'For a time,' said he.

'And then?'

'And then the overturn,' said the old man smiling, 'and the nineteenth century saw itself as a man who has lost his clothes whilst bathing, and has to walk naked through the town.'

'You are very bitter about the unlucky nineteenth century,' said I.

'Naturally,' said he, 'since I know so much about it.'

News from Nowhere, 1890

OSCAR WILDE

[The Portrait]

LORD HENRY came over and examined the picture. It was certainly a wonderful work of art, and a wonderful likeness as well.

'My dear fellow, I congratulate you most warmly,' he said. 'It is the finest portrait of modern times. Mr Gray, come over and look at yourself.'

The lad started, as if awakened from some dream. 'Is it really finished?' he murmured, stepping down from the platform.

'Quite finished,' said the painter. 'And you have sat splendidly today. I am awfully obliged to you.'

'That is entirely due to me,' broke in Lord Henry. 'Isn't it, Mr Gray?'

Dorian made no answer, but passed listlessly in front of his picture, and turned towards it. When he saw it he drew back, and his cheeks flushed for a moment with pleasure. A look of joy came into his eyes, as if he had recognised himself for the first time. He stood there motionless and in wonder, dimly conscious that Hallward was speaking to him, but not catching the meaning of his words. The sense of his own beauty came on him like a revelation. He had never felt it before. Basil Hallward's compliments had seemed to him to be merely the charming exaggerations of friendship. He had listened to them, laughed at them, forgotten them. They had not influenced his nature. Then had come Lord Henry Wotton with his strange panegyric on youth, his terrible warning of its brevity. That had stirred him at the time, and now, as he stood gazing at the shadow of his own loveliness, the full reality of the description flashed across him. Yes, there would be a day when his face would be wrinkled and wizen, his eyes dim and colourless, the grace of his figure broken and deformed. The scarlet would pass away from his lips, and the gold steal from his hair. The life that was to make his soul would mar his body. He would become dreadful, hideous, and uncouth.

As he thought of it, a sharp pang of pain struck through him like a knife, and made each delicate fibre of his nature quiver. His eyes deepened into amethyst, and across them came a mist of tears. He felt as if a hand of ice had been laid upon his heart.

'Don't you like it?' cried Hallward at last, stung a little by the lad's silence, not understanding what it meant.

'Of course he likes it,' said Lord Henry. 'Who wouldn't like it? It is one of the greatest things in modern art. I will give you anything you like to ask for it. I must have it.'

'It is not my property, Harry.'

'Whose property is it?'

'Dorian's, of course,' answered the painter.

'He is a very lucky fellow.'

'How sad it is!' murmured Dorian Gray, with his eyes still fixed upon his own portrait. 'How sad it is! I shall grow old, and horrible, and dreadful. But this picture will remain always young. It will never be older than this particular day of June . . . If it were only the other way! If it were I who was to be always young, and the picture that was to grow old! For that – for that – I would give everything! Yes, there is nothing in the whole world I would not give! I would give my soul for that!'

'You would hardly care for such an arrangement, Basil,' cried Lord Henry, laughing. 'It would be rather hard lines on your work.'

'I should object very strongly, Harry,' said Hallward.

Dorian Gray turned and looked at him. 'I believe you would, Basil. You like your art better than your friends. I am no more to you than a green bronze figure. Hardly as much, I dare say.'

The painter stared in amazement. It was so unlike Dorian to speak like that. What had happened? He seemed quite angry. His face was flushed and his cheeks burning.

'Yes,' he continued, 'I am less to you than your ivory Hermes or your silver Faun. You will like them always. How long will you like me? Till I have my first wrinkle, I suppose. I know, now, that when one loses one's good looks, whatever they may be, one loses everything. Your picture has taught me that. Lord Henry Wotton is perfectly right. Youth is the only thing worth having. When I find that I am growing old, I shall kill myself.'

Hallward turned pale, and caught his hand. 'Dorian! Dorian!' he cried, 'don't talk like that. I have never had such a friend as you, and I shall never have such another. You are not jealous of material things, are you? – you who are finer than any of them!'

'I am jealous of everything whose beauty does not die. I am jealous of the portrait you have painted of me. Why should it keep what I must lose? Every moment that passes takes something from me, and gives something to it. Oh, if it were only the other way! If the picture could change, and I could be always what I am now! How did you paint it? It will mock me some day – mock me horribly!' The hot tears welled into his eyes; he tore his hand away, and, flinging himself on the divan, he buried his face in the cushions, as though he was praying.

'This is your doing, Harry,' said the painter, bitterly.

Lord Henry shrugged his shoulders. 'It is the real Dorian Gray – that is all.'

'It is not.'

'If it is not, what have I to do with it?'

'You should have gone away when I asked you,' he muttered.

'I stayed when you asked me,' was Lord Henry's answer.

'Harry, I can't quarrel with my two best friends at once, but between you both you have made me hate the finest piece of work I have ever done, and I will destroy it. What is it but canvas and colour? I will not let it come across our three lives and mar them.'

Dorian Gray lifted his golden head from the pillow, and

with pallid face and tear-stained eyes looked at him, as he walked over to the deal painting-table that was set beneath the high curtained window. What was he doing there? His fingers were straying about among the litter of tin tubes and dry brushes, seeking for something. Yes, it was for the long palette-knife, with its thin blade of lithe steel. He had found it at last. He was going to rip up the canvas.

With a stifled sob the lad leaped from the couch, and, rushing over to Hallward, tore the knife out of his hand and flung it to the end of the studio. 'Don't, Basil, don't!' he cried. 'It would be murder!'

'I am glad you appreciate my work at last, Dorian,' said the painter, coldly, when he had recovered from his surprise. 'I never thought you would.'

'Appreciate it? I am in love with it, Basil. It is part of myself. I feel that.'

'Well, as soon as you are dry, you shall be varnished, and framed, and sent home. Then you can do what you like with yourself.' And he walked across the room and rang the bell for tea. 'You will have tea, of course, Dorian? And so will you, Harry? Or do you object to such simple pleasures?'

'I adore simple pleasures,' said Lord Henry. 'They are the last refuge of the complex. But I don't like scenes, except on the stage. What absurd fellows you are, both of you! I wonder who it was defined man as a rational animal. It was the most premature definition ever given. Man is many things, but he is not rational. I am glad he is not, after all: though I wish you chaps would not squabble over the picture. You had much better let me have it, Basil. This silly boy doesn't really want it, and I really do.'

'If you let any one have it but me, Basil, I shall never forgive you!' cried Dorian Gray; 'and I don't allow people to call me a silly boy.'

'You know the picture is yours, Dorian. I gave it to you before it existed.'

'And you know you have been a little silly, Mr Gray, and that you don't really object to being reminded that you are extremely young.'

'I should have objected very strongly this morning, Lord Henry.'

'Ah! this morning! You have lived since then.'

The Picture of Dorian Gray, 1891

GEORGE GISSING

[The Literary Life]

ON REARDON'S desk were lying slips of blank paper. Edith, approaching on tiptoe with what was partly make-believe, partly genuine, awe, looked at the literary apparatus, then turned with a laugh to her friend.

'How delightful it must be to sit down and write about people one has invented! Ever since I have known you and Mr Reardon I have been tempted to try if I couldn't write a story.'

'Have you?'

'And I'm sure I don't know how *you* can resist the temptation. I feel sure you could write books almost as clever as your husband's.'

'I have no intention of trying.'

'You don't seem very well today, Amy.'

'Oh, I think I am as well as usual.'

She guessed that her husband was once more brought to a stand-still, and this darkened her humour again.

'One of my reasons for coming,' said Edith, 'was to beg and entreat and implore you and Mr Reardon to dine with us next Wednesday. Now don't put on such a severe face! Are you engaged that evening?'

'Yes; in the ordinary way. Edwin can't possibly leave his work.'

'But for one poor evening! It's such ages since we saw you.'

'I'm very sorry. I don't think we shall ever be able to accept invitations in future.'

Amy spoke thus at the prompting of a sudden impulse. A minute ago, no such definite declaration was in her mind.

'Never?' exclaimed Edith. 'But why? Whatever do you mean?'

'We find that social engagements consume too much time,' Amy replied, her explanation just as much of an impromptu as the announcement had been. 'You see, one must either belong to society or not. Married people can't accept an occasional invitation from friends and never do their social duty in return. We have decided to withdraw altogether – at all events for the present. I shall see no one except my relatives.'

Edith listened with a face of astonishment.

'You won't even see *me*?' she exclaimed.

'Indeed, I have no wish to lose your friendship. Yet I am ashamed to ask you to come here when I can never return your visits.'

'Oh, please don't put it in that way! But it seems so very strange.'

Edith could not help conjecturing the true significance of this resolve. But, as is commonly the case with people in easy circumstances, she found it hard to believe that her friends were so straitened as to have a difficulty in supporting the ordinary obligations of a civilised state.

'I know how precious your husband's time is,' she added, as if to remove the effect of her last remark. 'Surely there's no harm in my saying – we know each other well enough – you wouldn't think it necessary to devote an evening to entertaining us just because you had given us the pleasure of your company. I put it very stupidly, but I'm sure you understand me, Amy. Don't refuse just to come to our house now and then.'

'I'm afraid we shall have to be consistent, Edith.'

'But do you think this is a *wise* thing to do?'

'Wise?'

'You know what you once told me, about how necessary it was for a novelist to study all sorts of people. How can Mr Reardon do this if he shuts himself up in the house? I should have thought he would find it necessary to make new acquaintances.'

'As I said,' returned Amy, 'it won't always be like this. For the present, Edwin has quite enough "material".'

She spoke distantly; it irritated her to have to invent excuses for the sacrifice she had just imposed on herself. Edith sipped the tea which had been offered her, and for a minute kept silence.

'When will Mr Reardon's next book be published?' she asked at length.

'I'm sure I don't know. Not before the spring.'

'I shall look so anxiously for it. Whenever I meet new people I always turn the conversation to novels, just for the sake of asking them if they know your husband's books.'

She laughed merrily.

'Which is seldom the case, I should think,' said Amy with a smile of indifference.

'Well, my dear, you don't expect ordinary novel-readers to know about Mr Reardon. I wish my acquaintances were a better kind of people; then, of course, I should hear of his books more often. But one has to make the best of such society as offers. If you and your husband forsake me, I shall feel it a sad loss; I shall indeed.'

Amy gave a quick glance at the speaker's face.

'Oh, we must be friends just the same,' she said, more naturally than she had spoken hitherto. 'But don't ask us to come and dine just now. All through this winter we shall be very busy, both of us. Indeed, we have decided not to accept any invitations at all.'

'Then, so long as you let me come here now and then, I must give in. I promise not to trouble you with any more complaining. But how you can live such a life I don't know. I consider myself more of a reader than women generally are, and I should be mortally offended if anyone called me frivolous; but I must have a good deal of society. Really and truly, I can't live without it.'

'No?' said Amy, with a smile which meant more than Edith could interpret. It seemed slightly condescending.

'There's no knowing; perhaps if I had married a literary man—' She paused, smiling and musing. 'But then I haven't, you see.' She laughed. 'Albert is anything but a bookworm, as you know.'

'You wouldn't wish him to be.'

'Oh no! Not a bookworm. To be sure, we suit each other very well indeed. He likes society just as much as I do. It would be the death of him if he didn't spend three-quarters of every day with lively people.'

'That's rather a large portion. But then you count yourself among the lively ones.'

They exchanged looks, and laughed together.

'Of course you think me rather silly to want to talk so much with silly people,' Edith went on. 'But then there's generally some amusement to be got, you know. I don't take life quite so seriously as you do. People are people after all; it's good fun to see how they live and hear how they talk.'

Amy felt that she was playing a sorry part. She thought of sour grapes, and of the fox who had lost its tail. Worst of all, perhaps Edith suspected the truth. She began to make inquiries about common acquaintances, and fell into an easier current of gossip.

A quarter of an hour after the visitor's departure Reardon came back. Amy had guessed aright; the necessity of selling his books weighed upon him so that for the present he could do nothing. The evening was spent gloomily, with very little conversation.

Next day came the bookseller to make his inspection. Reardon had chosen out and ranged upon a table nearly a hundred volumes. With a few exceptions they had been purchased secondhand. The tradesman examined them rapidly.

'What do you ask?' he inquired putting his head aside.

'I prefer that you should make an offer,' Reardon replied, with the helplessness of one who lives remote from traffic.

'I can't say more than two pounds ten.'

'That is at the rate of sixpence a volume—?'

'To me that's about the average value of books like these.'

Perhaps the offer was a fair one; perhaps it was not. Reardon had neither time nor spirit to test the possibilities of the market; he was ashamed to betray his need by higgling.

'I'll take it,' he said, in a matter-of-fact voice.

A messenger was sent for the books that afternoon. He stowed them skilfully in two bags, and carried them downstairs to a cart that was waiting.

Reardon looked at the gaps left on his shelves. Many of those vanished volumes were dear old friends to him; he could have told you where he had picked them up and when; to open them recalled a past moment of intellectual growth, a mood of hope or despondency, a stage of struggle. In most of them his name was written, and there were often pencilled notes in the margin. Of course he had chosen from among the most valuable he possessed; such a multitude must else have been sold to make this sum of two pounds ten. Books are cheap, you know. At need, one can buy a Homer for fourpence, a Sophocles for sixpence. It was not rubbish that he had accumulated at so small expenditure, but the library of a poor student – battered bindings, stained pages, supplanted editions. He loved his books, but there was something he loved more, and when Amy glanced at him with eyes of sympathy he broke into a cheerful laugh.

'I'm only sorry they have gone for so little. Tell me when the money is nearly at an end again, and you shall have more. It's all right; the novel will be done soon.'

And that night he worked until twelve o'clock, doggedly, fiercely.

New Grub Street, 1891

GEORGE AND WEEDON GROSSMITH

[Spiritualism]

May 30. I don't know why it is, but I never anticipate with any pleasure the visits to our house of Mrs James, of Sutton. She is coming again to stay for a few days. I said to Carrie this morning, as I was leaving: 'I wish, dear Carrie, I could like Mrs James better than I do.'

Carrie said: 'So do I, dear; but as for years I have had to put up with Mr Gowing, who is vulgar, and Mr Cummings, who is kind but most uninteresting, I am sure, dear, you won't mind the occasional visits of Mrs James, who has more intellect in her little finger than both your friends have in their entire bodies.'

I was so entirely taken aback by this onslaught on my two dear old friends, I could say nothing, and as I heard the 'bus coming, I left with a hurried kiss – a little too hurried, perhaps, for my upper lip came in contact with Carrie's teeth and slightly cut it. It was quite painful for an hour afterwards. When I came home in the evening I found Carrie buried in a book on Spiritualism, called *There is No Birth*, by Florence Singleyet. I need scarcely say the book was sent her to read by Mrs James, of Sutton. As she had not a word to say outside her book, I spent the rest of the evening altering the stair-carpets, which are beginning to show signs of wear at the edges.

Mrs James arrived and, as usual, in the evening took the entire management of everything. Finding that she and Carrie were making some preparations for table-turning, I thought it time really to put my foot down. I have always had the greatest contempt for such nonsense, and put an end to it years ago when Carrie, at our old house, used to have seances every night with poor Mrs Fussters (who is now dead). If I could see any use in it, I would not care. As I stopped it in the days gone by I determined to do so now.

I said: 'I am very sorry, Mrs James, but I totally disapprove of it, apart from the fact that I receive my old friends on this evening.'

Mrs James said: 'Do you mean to say you haven't read *There is No Birth*?' I said: 'No, and I have no intention of doing so.' Mrs James seemed surprised and said: 'All the world is going mad over the book.' I responded rather cleverly: 'Let it. There will be one sane man in it, at all events.'

Mrs James said she thought I was very unkind, and if people were all as prejudiced as I was, there would never have been the electric telegraph or the telephone.

I said that was quite a different thing.

Mrs James said sharply: 'In what way, pray – in what way?'

I said: 'In many ways.'

Mrs James said: 'Well, mention *one* way.'

I replied quietly: 'Pardon me, Mrs James; I decline to discuss the matter. I am not interested in it.'

Sarah at this moment opened the door and showed in Cummings, for which I was thankful, for I felt it would put a stop to this foolish table-turning. But I was entirely mistaken; for on the subject being opened again, Cummings said he was most interested in Spiritualism, although he was bound to confess he did not believe much in it; still, he was willing to be convinced.

I firmly declined to take any part in it, with the result that my presence was ignored. I left the three sitting in the parlour at a small round table which they had taken out of the drawing-room. I walked into the hall with the ultimate intention of taking a little stroll. As I opened the door, who should come in but Gowing!

On hearing what was going on, he proposed that we should join the circle and he would go into a trance. He added that he *knew* a few things about old Cummings, and would *invent* a few about Mrs James. Knowing how dangerous Gowing is, I declined to let him take part in any such foolish performance. Sarah asked me if she could go out for half an hour, and I gave her permission, thinking it would be more comfortable to sit with Gowing in the kitchen than in the cold drawing-room. We talked a good deal about Lupin and Mr and Mrs Murray Posh, with whom he is as usual spending the evening. Gowing said: 'I say, it wouldn't be a bad thing for Lupin if old Posh kicked the bucket.'

My heart gave a leap of horror, and I rebuked Gowing very sternly for joking on such a subject. I lay awake half the night thinking of it – the other half was spent in nightmares on the same subject.

The Diary of a Nobody, 1892

SIR ARTHUR CONAN DOYLE

[A Lesson in Detection]

'THEN, PRAY tell me what it is that you can infer from
this hat?'

He picked it up, and gazed at it in the peculiar introspec-
tive fashion which was characteristic of him. 'It is perhaps
less suggestive than it might have been,' he remarked, 'and
yet there are a few inferences which are very distinct, and a
few others which represent at least a strong balance of
probability. That the man was highly intellectual is of course
obvious upon the face of it, and also that he was fairly well-
to-do within the last three years, although he has now fallen
upon evil days. He had foresight, but has less now than
formerly, pointing to a moral retrogression, which, when
taken with the decline of his fortunes, seems to indicate
some evil influence, probably drink, at work upon him. This
may account also for the obvious fact that his wife has
ceased to love him.'

'My dear Holmes!'

'He has, however, retained some degree of self-respect,'
he continued, disregarding my remonstrance. 'He is a man
who leads a sedentary life, goes out little, is out of training
entirely, is middle-aged, has grizzled hair which he has had
cut within the last few days, and which he anoints with lime-
cream. These are the more patent facts which are to be
deduced from his hat. Also, by the way, that it is extremely
improbable that he has gas laid on in his house.'

'You are certainly joking, Holmes.'

'Not in the least. Is it possible that even now when I give
you these results you are unable to see how they are
attained?'

'I have no doubt that I am very stupid; but I must confess
that I am unable to follow you. For example, how did you
deduce that this man was intellectual?'

For answer Holmes clapped the hat upon his head. It

came right over the forehead and settled upon the bridge of his nose. 'It is a question of cubic capacity,' said he: 'a man with so large a brain must have something in it.'

'The decline of his fortunes, then?'

'This hat is three years old. These flat brims curled at the edge came in then. It is a hat of the very best quality. Look at the band of ribbed silk, and the excellent lining. If this man could afford to buy so expensive a hat three years ago, and has had no hat since, then he has assuredly gone down in the world.'

'Well, that is clear enough, certainly. But how about the foresight, and the moral retrogression?'

Sherlock Holmes laughed. 'Here is the foresight,' said he, putting his finger upon the little disc and loop of the hat-securer. 'They are never sold upon hats. If this man ordered one, it is a sign of a certain amount of foresight, since he went out of his way to take this precaution against the wind. But since we see that he has broken the elastic, and has not troubled to replace it, it is obvious that he has less foresight now than formerly, which is a distinct proof of a weakening nature. On the other hand, he has endeavoured to conceal some of these stains upon the felt by daubing them with ink, which is a sign that he has not entirely lost his self-respect.'

'Your reasoning is certainly plausible.'

'The further points, that he is middle-aged, that his hair is grizzled, that it has been recently cut, and that he uses lime-cream, are all to be gathered from a close examination of the lower part of the lining. The lens discloses a large number of hair-ends, clean cut by the scissors of the barber. They all appear to be adhesive, and there is a distinct odour of lime-cream. This dust, you will observe, is not the gritty, grey dust of the street, but the fluffy brown dust of the house, showing that it has been hung up indoors most of the time; while the marks of moisture upon the inside are proof positive that the wearer perspired very freely, and could, therefore, hardly be in the best of training.'

'But his wife – you said that she had ceased to love him.'

'This hat has not been brushed for weeks. When I see you, my dear Watson, with a week's accumulation of dust upon your hat, and when your wife allows you to go out in such a state, I shall fear that you also have been unfortunate enough to lose your wife's affection.'

'But he might be a bachelor.'

'Nay, he was bringing home the goose as a peace-offering to his wife. Remember the card upon the bird's leg.'

'You have an answer to everything. But how on earth do you deduce that the gas is not laid on in the house?'

'One tallow stain, or even two, might come by chance; but, when I see no less than five, I think that there can be little doubt that the individual must be brought into frequent contact with burning tallow – walks upstairs at night probably with his hat in one hand and a guttering candle in the other. Anyhow, he never got tallow stains from a gas jet. Are you satisfied?'

'The Adventure of the Blue Carbuncle', 1892

MARY KINGSLEY

[A Sneezing Fit]

ON ONE occasion, between Egaja and Esoon, when we got to the edge of some cleared ground, we lay down, and wormed our way, with elaborate caution, among a patch of Koko; Wiki first, I following in his trail. After about fifty yards of this, Wiki sank flat, and I saw before me, some thirty yards off, busily employed in pulling down plantains, and other depredations, five gorillas: one old male, one young male, and three females. One of these had clinging to her a young fellow, with beautiful wavy black hair with just a kink in it. The big male was crouching on his haunches, with his long arms hanging down on either side, with the backs of his hands on the ground, the palms upwards. The elder lady was tearing to pieces and eating a pine-apple, while the others were at the plantains destroying more than they ate.

They kept up a sort of a whinnying, chattering noise, quite different from the sound I have heard gorillas give when enraged, or from the one you can hear them giving when they are what the natives call 'dancing' at night. I noticed that their reach of arm was immense, and that when they went from one tree to another, they squattered across the open ground in a most inelegant style, dragging their long arms with the knuckles downwards. I should think the big male and female were over six feet each. The others would be from four to five. I put out my hand and laid it on Wiki's gun to prevent him from firing, and he, thinking I was going to fire, gripped my wrist.

I watched the gorillas with great interest for a few seconds, until I heard Wiki make a peculiar small sound, and looking at him saw his face was working in an awful way as he clutched his throat with his hand violently.

Heavens! think I, this gentleman's going to have a fit; it's lost we are entirely this time. He rolled his head to and fro, and then buried his face into a heap of dried rubbish at the foot of a plantain stem, clasped his hand over it, and gave an explosive sneeze. The gorillas let go all, raised themselves up for a second, gave a quaint sound between a bark and a howl, and then the ladies and the young gentleman started home. The old male rose to his full height and looked straight towards us, or rather towards where that sound came from. Wiki went off into a paroxysm of falsetto sneezes the like of which I have never heard; nor evidently had the gorilla, who went off after his family with a celerity that was amazing the moment he touched the forest, and disappeared as they had, swinging himself along through it from bough to bough, in a way that convinced me that, given the necessity of getting about in tropical forests, man has made a mistake in getting his arms shortened. I have seen many wild animals in their native wilds, but never have I seen anything to equal gorillas going through the bush; it is a graceful, powerful, superbly perfect hand-trapeze performance.

I have no hesitation in saying that the gorilla is the most horrible wild animal I have seen. I have seen at close quarters specimens of the most important big game of

Central Africa, and, with the exception of snakes, I have run away from all of them; but although elephants, leopards and pythons give you a feeling of alarm, they do not give that feeling of horrible disgust that an old gorilla gives on account of its hideousness of appearance.

Travels in West Africa, 1897

HERBERT GEORGE WELLS

[In the Storm]

As I ascended the little hill beyond Pyrford Church the glare came into view again, and the trees about me shivered with the first intimation of the storm that was upon me. Then I heard midnight pealing out from Pyrford Church behind me, and then came the silhouette of Maybury Hill, with its tree-tops and roofs black and sharp against the red.

Even as I beheld this a lurid green glare lit the road about me, and showed the distant woods towards Addlestone. I felt a tug at the reins. I saw that the driving clouds had been pierced as it were by a thread of green fire, suddenly lighting their confusion and falling into the fields to my left. It was the Third Falling Star!

Close on its apparition, and blindingly violet by contrast, danced out the first lightning of the gathering storm, and the thunder burst like a rocket overhead. The horse took the bit between his teeth and bolted.

A moderate incline runs down towards the foot of Maybury Hill, and down this we clattered. Once the lightning had begun, it went on in as rapid a succession of flashes as I have ever seen. The thunder-claps, treading one on the heels of another and with a strange crackling accompaniment, sounded more like the working of a gigantic electric engine than the usual detonating reverberations. The flickering light was blinding and confusing, and a thin hail smote gustily at my face as I drove down the slope.

At first I regarded little but the road before me, and then abruptly my attention was arrested by something that was moving rapidly down the opposite slope of Maybury Hill. At first I took it for the wet roof of a house, but one flash following another showed it to be in swift rolling movement. It was an elusive vision – a moment of bewildering darkness, and then a flash like daylight, the red masses of the Orphanage near the crest of the hill, the green tops of the pine trees, and this problematical object came out clear and sharp and bright.

And this thing I saw! How can I describe it? A monstrous tripod, higher than many houses, striding over the young pine trees, and smashing them aside in its career; a walking engine of glittering metal, striding now across the heather; articulate ropes of steel dangling from it, and the clattering tumult of its passage mingling with the riot of the thunder. A flash, and it came out vividly, heeling over one way with two feet in the air, to vanish and reappear almost instantly as it seemed, with the next flash, a hundred yards nearer. Can you imagine a milking-stool tilted and bowled violently along the ground? That was the impression those instant flashes gave. But instead of a milking-stool imagine it a great body of machinery on a tripod stand.

Then suddenly the trees in the pine-wood ahead of me were parted, as brittle reeds are parted by a man thrusting through them; they were snapped off and driven headlong, and a second huge tripod appeared, rushing, as it seemed, headlong towards me. And I was galloping hard to meet it! At the sight of the second monster my nerve went altogether. Not stopping to look again, I wrenched the horse's head hard round to the right, and in another moment the dog-cart had heeled over upon the horse; the shafts smashed noisily, and I was flung sideways and fell heavily into a shallow pool of water.

I crawled out almost immediately, and crouched, my feet still in the water, under a clump of furze. The horse lay motionless (his neck was broken, poor brute!), and by the lightning flashes I saw the black bulk of the overturned dog-cart, and the silhouette of the wheel still spinning slowly. In another moment the colossal mechanism went striding by me, and passed up-hill towards Pyrford.

Seen nearer, the thing was incredibly strange, for it was no mere insensate machine driving on its way. Machine it was, with a ringing metallic pace, and long flexible glittering tentacles (one of which gripped a young pine tree) swinging and rattling about its strange body. It picked its road as it went striding along, and the brazen hood that surmounted it moved to and fro with the inevitable suggestion of a head looking about it. Behind the main body was a huge thing of white metal like a gigantic fisherman's basket, and puffs of green smoke squirted out from the joints of the limbs as the monster swept by me. And in an instant it was gone.

So much I saw then, all vaguely for the flickering of the lightning, in blinding high lights and dense black shadows.

As it passed it set up an exultant deafening howl that drowned the thunder: 'Aloo! aloo!' and in another minute it was with its companion, and half a mile away, stooping over something in the field. I have no doubt this thing in the field was the third of the ten cylinders they had fired at us from Mars.

For some minutes I lay there in the rain and darkness watching, by the intermittent light, these monstrous beings of metal moving about in the distance over the hedge-tops. A thin hail was now beginning, and as it came and went, their figures grew misty and then flashed into clearness again. Now and then came a gap in the lightning, and the night swallowed them up.

The War of the Worlds, 1898

JOSEPH CONRAD

[The Company Station]

A T LAST we opened a reach. A rocky cliff appeared, mounds of turned-up earth by the shore, houses on a hill, others with iron roofs, amongst a waste of excavations, or hanging to the declivity. A continuous noise of the rapids above hovered over this scene of inhabited devastation. A lot of people, mostly black and naked, moved about like ants. A jetty projected into the river. A blinding sunlight drowned all this at times in a sudden recrudescence of glare. 'There's your Company's station,' said the Swede, pointing to three wooden barrack-like structures on the rocky slope. 'I will send your things up. Four boxes did you say? So. Farewell.'

I came upon a boiler wallowing in the grass, then found a path leading up the hill. It turned aside for the boulders, and also for an undersized railway-truck lying there on its back with its wheels in the air. One was off. The thing looked as dead as the carcass of some animal. I came upon more pieces of decaying machinery, a stack of rusty rails. To the left a clump of trees made a shady spot, where dark things seemed to stir feebly. I blinked, the path was steep. A horn tooted to the right, and I saw the black people run. A heavy and dull detonation shook the ground, a puff of smoke came out of the cliff, and that was all. No change appeared on the face of the rock. They were building a railway. The cliff was not in the way of anything; but this objectless blasting was all the work going on.

A slight clinking behind me made me turn my head. Six black men advanced in a file, toiling up the path. They walked erect and slow, balancing small baskets full of earth on their heads, and the clink kept time with their footsteps. Black rags were wound round their loins, and the short ends behind waggled to and fro like tails. I could see every rib, the joints of their limbs were like knots in a rope; each had an iron collar on his neck, and all were connected together

with a chain whose bights swung between them, rhythmi-
cally clinking. Another report from the cliff made me think
suddenly of that ship of war I had seen firing into a
continent. It was the same kind of ominous voice; but these
men could by no stretch of imagination be called enemies.
They were called criminals, and the outraged law, like the
bursting shells, had come to them, an insoluble mystery
from the sea. All their meagre breasts panted together, the
violently dilated nostrils quivered, the eyes stared stonily
up-hill. They passed me within six inches, without a glance,
with that complete, deathlike indifference of unhappy savages. Behind this raw matter one of the reclaimed, the
product of the new forces at work, strolled despondently,
carrying a rifle by its middle. He had a uniform jacket with
one button off, and seeing a white man on the path, hoisted
his weapon to his shoulder with alacrity. This was simple
prudence, white men being so much alike at a distance that
he could not tell who I might be. He was speedily reassured,
and with a large, white, rascally grin, and a glance at his
charge, seemed to take me into partnership in his exalted
trust. After all, I also was a part of the great cause of these
high and just proceedings.

Instead of going up, I turned and descended to the left.
My idea was to let that chain-gang get out of sight before I
climbed the hill. You know I am not particularly tender;
I've had to strike and to fend off. I've had to resist and to
attack sometimes – that's only one way of resisting – without
counting the exact cost, according to the demands of such
sort of life as I had blundered into. I've seen the devil of
violence, and the devil of greed, and the devil of hot desire;
but, by all the stars! these were strong, lusty, red-eyed
devils, that swayed and drove men – men, I tell you. But as
I stood on this hillside, I foresaw that in the blinding
sunshine of that land I would become acquainted with a
flabby, pretending, weak-eyed devil of a rapacious and
pitiless folly. How insidious he would be, too, I was only to
find out several months later and a thousand miles farther.
For a moment I stood appalled, as though by a warning.
Finally I descended the hill, obliquely, towards the trees I
had seen.

I avoided a vast artificial hole somebody had been digging on the slope, the purpose of which I found it impossible to divine. It wasn't a quarry or a sandpit, anyhow. It was just a hole. It might have been connected with the philanthropic desire of giving the criminals something to do. I don't know. Then I nearly fell into a very narrow ravine, almost no more than a scar in the hillside. I discovered that a lot of imported drainage-pipes for the settlement had been tumbled in there. There wasn't one that was not broken. It was a wanton smash-up. At last I got under the trees. My purpose was to stroll into the shade for a moment; but no sooner within than it seemed to me I had stepped into the gloomy circle of some Inferno. The rapids were near, and an uninterrupted, uniform, headlong, rushing noise filled the mournful stillness of the grove, where not a breath stirred, not a leaf moved, with a mysterious sound – as though the tearing pace of the launched earth had suddenly become audible.

Black shapes crouched, lay, sat between the trees leaning against the trunks, clinging to the earth, half coming out, half effaced within the dim light, in all the attitudes of pain, abandonment, and despair. Another mine on the cliff went off, followed by a slight shudder of the soil under my feet. The work was going on. The work! And this was the place where some of the helpers had withdrawn to die.

They were dying slowly – it was very clear. They were not enemies, they were not criminals, they were nothing earthly now, – nothing but black shadows of disease and starvation, lying confusedly in the greenish gloom. Brought from all the recesses of the coast in all the legality of time contracts, lost in uncongenial surroundings, fed on unfamiliar food, they sickened, became inefficient, and were then allowed to crawl away and rest. These moribund shapes were free as air – and nearly as thin. I began to distinguish the gleam of the eyes under the trees. Then, glancing down, I saw a face near my hand. The black bones reclined at full length with one shoulder against the tree, and slowly the eyelids rose and the sunken eyes looked up at me, enormous and vacant, a kind of blind, white flicker in the depths of the orbs, which died out slowly. The man seemed young – almost a boy – but you know with them it's hard to tell. I found nothing else to do but to offer him one of my good Swede's ship's biscuits I had in my pocket. The fingers closed slowly on it and held – there was no other movement and no other glance. He had tied a bit of white worsted round his neck – Why? Where did he get it? Was it a badge – an ornament – a charm – a propitiatory act? Was there any idea at all connected with it? It looked startling round his black neck, this bit of white thread from beyond the seas.

Near the same tree two more bundles of acute angles sat with their legs drawn up. One, with his chin propped on his knees, stared at nothing, in an intolerable and appalling manner: his brother phantom rested its forehead, as if overcome with a great weariness; and all about others were scattered in every pose of contorted collapse, as in some picture of a massacre or a pestilence. While I stood horror-struck, one of these creatures rose to his hands and knees, and went off on all-fours towards the river to drink. He lapped out of his hand, then sat up in the sunlight, crossing his shins in front of him, and after a time let his woolly head fall on his breastbone.

I didn't want any more loitering in the shade, and I made haste towards the station. When near the buildings I met a white man, in such an unexpected elegance of get-up that in the first moment I took him for a sort of vision. I saw a high starched collar, white cuffs, a light alpaca jacket, snowy trousers, a clear necktie, and varnished boots. No hat. Hair parted, brushed, oiled, under a green-lined parasol held in a big white hand. He was amazing, and had a penholder behind his ear.

I shook hands with this miracle, and I learned he was the Company's chief accountant, and that all the book-keeping was done at this station. He had come out for a moment, he said, 'to get a breath of fresh air'.

Heart of Darkness, 1899

[The Discovery]

H E BEGAN his story quietly enough. On board that Dale
Line steamer that had picked up these four floating in
a boat upon the discreet sunset glow of the sea, they had
been after the first day looked askance upon. The fat skipper
told some story, the others had been silent, and at first it
had been accepted. You don't cross-examine poor castaways
you had the good luck to save, if not from cruel death, then
at least from cruel suffering. Afterwards, with time to think
it over, it might have struck the officers of the *Avondale*
that there was 'something fishy' in the affair; but of course
they would keep their doubts to themselves. They had
picked up the captain, the mate, and two engineers of the
steamer *Patna* sunk at sea, and that, very properly, was
enough for them. I did not ask Jim about the nature of his
feelings during the ten days he spent on board. From the
way he narrated that part I was at liberty to infer he was
partly stunned by the discovery he had made – the discovery
about himself – and no doubt was at work trying to explain
it away to the only man who was capable of appreciating all
its tremendous magnitude. You must understand he did not
try to minimize its importance. Of that I am sure; and
therein lies his distinction. As to what sensations he experienced when he got ashore and heard the unforeseen conclusion of the tale in which he had taken such a pitiful part,
he told me nothing of them, and it is difficult to imagine. I
wonder whether he felt the ground cut from under his feet?
I wonder? But no doubt he managed to get a fresh foothold
very soon. He was ashore a whole fortnight waiting in the
Sailors' Home, and as there were six or seven men staying
there at the time, I had heard of him a little. Their languid
opinion seemed to be that in addition to his other short-
comings, he was a sulky brute. He had passed these days on
the veranda, buried in a long-chair, and coming out of his
place of sepulture only at meal-times or late at night, when
he wandered on the quays all by himself, detached from his
surroundings, irresolute and silent, like a ghost without a

home to haunt. 'I don't think I've spoken three words to a living soul in all that time,' he said, making me very sorry for him; and directly he added, 'One of these fellows would have been sure to blurt out something I had made up my mind not to put up with, and I didn't want a row. No! Not then. I was too – too . . . I had no heart for it.' 'So that bulkhead held out after all,' I remarked, cheerfully. 'Yes,' he murmured, 'it held. And yet I swear to you I felt it bulge under my hand.' 'It's extraordinary what strains old iron will stand sometimes,' I said. Thrown back in his seat, his legs stiffly out and arms hanging down, he nodded slightly several times. You could not conceive a sadder spectacle. Suddenly he lifted his head; he sat up; he slapped his thigh. 'Ah! what a chance missed! My God! what a chance missed!' he blazed out, but the ring of the last 'missed' resembled a cry wrung out by pain.

He was silent again with a still, far-away look of fierce yearning after that missed distinction, with his nostril for an instant dilated, sniffing the intoxicating breath of that wasted opportunity. If you think I was either surprised or shocked you do me an injustice in more ways than one! Ah, he was an imaginative beggar! He would give himself away; he would give himself up. I could see in his glance darted into the night all his inner being carried on, projected headlong into the fanciful realm of recklessly heroic aspirations. He had no leisure to regret what he had lost, he was so wholly and naturally concerned for what he had failed to obtain. He was very far away from me who watched him across three feet of space. With every instant he was penetrating deeper into the impossible world of romantic achievements. He got to the heart of it at last! A strange look of beatitude overspread his features, his eyes sparkled in the light of the candle burning between us; he positively smiled! He had penetrated to the very heart – to the very heart. It was an ecstatic smile that your faces – or mine either – will never wear, my dear boys. I whisked him back by saying, 'If you had stuck to the ship, you mean!'

He turned upon me, his eyes suddenly amazed and full of pain, with a bewildered, startled, suffering face, as though he had tumbled down from a star. Neither you nor I will ever look like this on any man. He shuddered profoundly, as if a cold finger-tip had touched his heart. Last of all he sighed.

I was not in a merciful mood. He provoked one by his contradictory indiscretions. 'It is unfortunate you didn't know beforehand!' I said with every unkind intention; but the perfidious shaft fell harmless – dropped at his feet like a spent arrow, as it were, and he did not think of picking it up. Perhaps he had not even seen it. Presently, lolling at ease, he said, 'Dash it all! I tell you it bulged. I was holding up my lamp along the angle-iron in the lower deck when a flake of rust as big as the palm of my hand fell off the plate, all of itself.' He passed his hand over his forehead. 'The thing stirred and jumped off like something alive while I was looking at it.' 'That made you feel pretty bad,' I observed, casually. 'Do you suppose,' he said, 'that I was thinking of myself, with a hundred and sixty people at my back, all fast asleep in that fore-'tween-deck alone – and more of them aft; more on the deck – sleeping – knowing nothing about it – three times as many as there were boats for, even if there had been time? I expected to see the iron open out as I stood there and the rush of water going over them as they lay. . . . What could I do – what?'

I can easily picture him to myself in the peopled gloom of the cavernous place, with the light of the bulk-lamp falling on a small portion of the bulkhead that had the weight of the ocean on the other side, and the breathing of unconscious sleepers in his ears. I can see him glaring at the iron, startled by the falling rust, overburdened by the knowledge of an imminent death. This, I gathered, was the second time he had been sent forward by that skipper of his, who, I rather think, wanted to keep him away from the bridge. He told me that his first impulse was to shout and straight away make all these people leap out of sleep into terror; but such an overwhelming sense of his helplessness came over him that he was not able to produce a sound. This is, I suppose, what people mean by the tongue cleaving to the roof of the mouth. 'Too dry,' was the concise expression he used in reference to this state. Without a sound, then, he scrambled out on deck through the number one hatch. A wind-sail rigged down there swung against him accidentally, and he remembered that the light touch of the canvas on his face nearly knocked him off the hatchway ladder.

He confessed that his knees wobbled a good deal as he stood on the foredeck looking at another sleeping crowd. The engines having been stopped by that time, the steam was blowing off. Its deep rumble made the whole night vibrate like a bass string. The ship trembled to it.

He saw here and there a head lifted off a mat, a vague form uprise in sitting posture, listen sleepily for a moment, sink down again into the billowy confusion of boxes, steam-winches, ventilators. He was aware all these people did not know enough to take intelligent notice of that strange noise. The ship of iron, the men with white faces, all the sights, all the sounds, everything on board to that ignorant multitude was strange alike, and as trustworthy as it would for ever remain incomprehensible. It occurred to him that the fact was fortunate. The idea of it was simply terrible.

You must remember he believed, as any other man would have done in his place, that the ship would go down at any moment; the bulging, rust-eaten plates that kept back the ocean, fatally must give way, all at once like an undermined dam, and let in a sudden and overwhelming flood. He stood still looking at these recumbent bodies, a doomed man aware of his fate, surveying the silent company of the dead. They *were* dead! Nothing could save them! There were boats enough for half of them perhaps, but there was no time. No time! No time! It did not seem worth while to open his lips, to stir hand or foot. Before he could shout three words, or make three steps, he would be floundering in a sea whitened awfully by the desperate struggles of human beings, clamorous with the distress of cries for help. There was no help. He imagined what would happen perfectly; he went through it all motionless by the hatchway with the lamp in his hand – he went through it to the very last harrowing detail. I think he went through it again while he was telling me these things he could not tell the court.

Lord Jim, 1900

GEORGE BERNARD SHAW

[Human Nature – The Devil's Assessment]

' AND IS Man any the less destroying himself for all this boasted brain of his? Have you walked up and down upon the earth lately? I have; and I have examined Man's wonderful inventions. And I tell you that in the arts of life Man invents nothing; but in the arts of death he outdoes Nature herself, and produces by chemistry and machinery all the slaughter of plague, pestilence, and famine. The peasant I tempt today eats and drinks what was eaten and drunk by the peasants of ten thousand years ago; and the house he lives in has not altered as much in a thousand centuries as the fashion of a lady's bonnet in a score of weeks. But when he goes out to slay, he carries a marvel of mechanism that lets loose at the touch of his finger all the hidden molecular energies, and leaves the javelin, the arrow, the blowpipe of his fathers far behind. In the arts of peace Man is a bungler. I have seen his cotton factories and the like, with machinery that a greedy dog could have invented if it had wanted money instead of food. I know his clumsy typewriters and bungling locomotives and tedious bicycles: they are toys compared to the Maxim gun, the submarine torpedo boat. There is nothing in Man's industrial machinery but his greed and sloth: his heart is in his weapons. This marvellous force of Life of which you boast is a force of Death: Man measures his strength by his destructiveness. What is his religion? An excuse for hating me. What is his law? An excuse for hanging you. What is his morality? Gentility! an excuse for consuming without producing. What is his art? An excuse for gloating over pictures of slaughter. What are his politics? Either the worship of a despot because a despot can kill, or parliamentary cock-fighting. I spent an evening lately in a certain celebrated legislature, and heard the pot lecturing the kettle for its blackness, and ministers answering questions. When I left I chalked up on the door the old nursery saying "Ask no questions and you will be told no lies." I bought a sixpenny family magazine, and found it full of pictures of young men shooting and stabbing one another. I saw a man die: he was a London bricklayer's laborer with seven children. He left seventeen pounds club money; and his wife spent it all on his funeral and went into the workhouse with the children next day. She would not have spent sevenpence on her children's schooling: the law had to force her to let them be taught gratuitously; but on death she spent all she had. Their imagination glows, their energies rise up at the idea of death, these people: they love it; and the more horrible it is the more they enjoy it. Hell is a place far above their comprehension: they derive their notion of it from two of the greatest fools that ever lived, an Italian and an Englishman. The Italian described it as a place of mud, frost, filth, fire, and venomous serpents: all torture. This ass, when he was not lying about me, was maundering about some woman whom he saw once in the street. The Englishman described me as being expelled from Heaven by cannons and gunpowder; and to this day every Briton believes that the whole of his silly story is in the Bible. What else he says I do not know; for it is all in a long poem which neither I nor anyone else ever succeeded in wading through. It is the same in everything. The highest form of literature is the tragedy, a play in which everybody is murdered at the end. In the old chronicles you read of earthquakes and pestilences, and are told that these shewed the power and majesty of God and the littleness of Man. Nowadays the chronicles describe battles. In a battle two bodies of men shoot at one another with bullets and explosive shells until one body runs away, when the others chase the fugitives on horseback and cut them to pieces as they fly. And this, the chronicle concludes, shews the greatness and majesty of empires, and the littleness of the vanquished. Over such battles the peoples run about the streets yelling with delight, and egg their Governments on to spend hundreds of millions of money in the slaughter, whilst the strongest Ministers dare not spend an extra penny in the pound against the poverty and pestilence through which they themselves daily walk. I could give you a thousand instances; but they all come to the same thing: the power that governs the earth is not the power of Life but of Death; and the inner need that has nerved Life to the effort of organizing itself into the human being is not the need for higher life but for a more efficient engine of destruction. The plague, the famine, the earthquake, the tempest were too spasmodic in their action; the tiger and crocodile were too easily satiated and not cruel enough: something more constantly, more ruthlessly, more ingeniously destructive was needed; and that something was Man, the inventor of the rack, the stake, the gallows, the electric chair; of sword and gun and poison gas: above all, of justice, duty, patriotism, and all the other isms by which even those who are clever enough to be humanely disposed are persuaded to become the most destructive of all the destroyers.'

Man and Superman, 1903

MONTAGUE RHODES JAMES

'Oh, Whistle, and I'll Come to You, My Lad'

'YOU KNOW where I am if you want me during the night.'

'Why, yes, thank you, Colonel Wilson, I think I do; but there isn't much prospect of my disturbing you, I hope. By the way,' he added, 'did I show you that old whistle I spoke of? I think not. Well, here it is.'

The Colonel turned it over gingerly in the light of the candle.

'Can you make anything of the inscription?' asked Parkins, as he took it back.

'No, not in this light. What do you mean to do with it?'

'Oh, well, when I get back to Cambridge I shall submit it to some of the archaeologists there, and see what they think of it; and very likely, if they consider it worth having, I may present it to one of the museums.'

''M!' said the Colonel. 'Well, you may be right. All I
know is, if it were mine, I should chuck it straight into the
sea. It's no use talking, I'm well aware, but I expect that
with you it's a case of live and learn. I hope so, I'm sure,
and I wish you a good night.'

He turned away, leaving Parkins in act to speak at the
bottom of the stair, and soon each was in his own bedroom.

By some unfortunate accident, there were neither blinds
nor curtains to the windows of the Professor's room. The
previous night he had thought little of this, but tonight there
seemed every prospect of a bright moon rising to shine
directly on his bed, and probably wake him later on. When
he noticed this he was a good deal annoyed, but, with an
ingenuity which I can only envy, he succeeded in rigging up,
with the help of a railway-rug, some safety-pins, and a stick
and umbrella, a screen which, if it only held together, would
completely keep the moonlight off his bed. And shortly
afterwards he was comfortably in that bed. When he had
read a somewhat solid work long enough to produce a
decided wish for sleep, he cast a drowsy glance round the
room, blew out the candle, and fell back upon the pillow.

He must have slept soundly for an hour or more when a
sudden clatter shook him up in a most unwelcome manner.
In a moment he realized what had happened: his carefully
constructed screen had given way, and a very bright frosty
moon was shining directly on his face. This was highly
annoying. Could he possibly get up and reconstruct the
screen? or could he manage to sleep if he did not?

For some minutes he lay and pondered over the possibilities; then he turned over sharply, and with all his eyes
open lay breathlessly listening. There had been a movement,
he was sure, in the empty bed on the opposite side of the
room. Tomorrow he would have it moved, for there must
be rats or something playing about in it. It was quiet now.
No! the commotion began again. There was a rustling and
shaking: surely more than any rat could cause.

I can figure to myself something of the Professor's bewilderment and horror, for I have in a dream thirty years back
seen the same thing happen; but the reader will hardly,
perhaps, imagine how dreadful it was to him to see a figure

suddenly sit up in what he had known was an empty bed. He was out of his own bed in one bound, and made a dash towards the window, where lay his only weapon, the stick with which he had propped his screen. This was, as it turned out, the worst thing he could have done, because the personage in the empty bed, with a sudden smooth motion, slipped from the bed and took up a position, with outspread arms, between the two beds, and in front of the door. Parkins watched it in a horrid perplexity. Somehow, the idea of getting past it and escaping through the door was intolerable to him; he could not have borne – he didn't know why – to touch it; and as for its touching him, he would sooner dash himself through the window than have that happen. It stood for a moment in a band of dark shadow, and he had not seen what its face was like. Now it began to move, in a stooping posture, and all at once the spectator realized, with some horror and some relief, that it must be blind, for it seemed to feel about it with its muffled arms in a groping and random fashion. Turning half way from him, it became suddenly conscious of the bed ne had just left, and darted towards it, and bent over and felt the pillows in a way which made Parkins shudder as he had never in his life thought it possible. In a very few moments it seemed to know that the bed was empty, and then, moving forward into the area of light and facing the window, it showed for the first time what manner of thing it was.

Parkins, who very much dislikes being questioned about it, did once describe something of it in my hearing, and I gathered that what he chiefly remembers about it is a horrible, an intensely horrible, face *of crumpled linen*. What expression he read upon it he could not or would not tell, but that the fear of it went nigh to maddening him is certain.

But he was not at leisure to watch it for long. With formidable quickness it moved into the middle of the room, and, as it groped and waved, one corner of its draperies swept across Parkins's face. He could not – though he knew how perilous a sound was – he could not keep back a cry of disgust, and this gave the searcher an instant clue. It leapt towards him upon the instant, and the next moment he was half way through the window backwards, uttering cry upon cry at the utmost pitch of his voice, and the linen face was thrust close into his own. At this, almost the last possible second, deliverance came, as you will have guessed: the Colonel burst the door open, and was just in time to see the dreadful group at the window. When he reached the figures only one was left. Parkins sank forward into the room in a faint, and before him on the floor lay a tumbled heap of bed-clothes.

Colonel Wilson asked no questions, but busied himself in keeping everyone else out of the room and in getting Parkins back to his bed; and himself, wrapped in a rug, occupied the other bed for the rest of the night. Early on the next day Rogers arrived, more welcome than he would have been a day before, and the three of them held a very long consultation in the Professor's room. At the end of it the Colonel left the hotel door carrying a small object between his finger and thumb, which he cast as far into the sea as a very brawny arm could send it. Later on the smoke of a burning ascended from the back premises of the Globe.

Ghost Stories of an Antiquary, 1904

JOHN GALSWORTHY

[Irene]

T HERE HAD been rain the night before – a spring rain, and the earth smelt of sap and wild grasses. The warm, soft breeze swung the leaves and the golden buds of the old oak tree, and in the sunshine the blackbirds were whistling their hearts out.

It was such a spring day as breathes into a man an ineffable yearning, a painful sweetness, a longing that makes him stand motionless, looking at the leaves or grass, and fling out his arms to embrace he knows not what. The earth gave forth a fainting warmth, stealing up through the chilly garment in which winter had wrapped her. It was her long caress of invitation, to draw men down to lie within her arms, to roll their bodies on her, and put their lips to her breast.

On such a day as this Soames had got from Irene the promise he had asked her for so often. Seated on the fallen trunk of a tree, he had promised for the twentieth time that if their marriage were not a success, she should be as free as if she had never married him!

'Do you swear it?' she had said. A few days back she had reminded him of that oath. He had answered: 'Nonsense! I couldn't have sworn any such thing!' By some awkward fatality he remembered it now. What queer things men would swear for the sake of women! He would have sworn it at any time to gain her! He would swear it now, if thereby he could touch her – but nobody could touch her, she was cold-hearted!

And memories crowded on him with the fresh, sweet savour of the spring wind – memories of his courtship.

In the spring of the year 1881 he was visiting his old schoolfellow and client, George Liversedge, of Branksome, who, with the view of developing his pine-woods in the neighbourhood of Bournemouth, had placed the formation of the company necessary to the scheme in Soames's hands. Mrs Liversedge, with a sense of the fitness of things, had given a musical tea in his honour. Late in the course of this function, which Soames, no musician, had regarded as an unmitigated bore, his eye had been caught by the face of a girl dressed in mourning, standing by herself. The lines of her tall, as yet rather thin figure, showed through the wispy, clinging stuff of her black dress, her black-gloved hands were crossed in front of her, her lips slightly parted, and her large, dark eyes wandered from face to face. Her hair, done low on her neck, seemed to gleam above her black collar like coils of shining metal. And as Soames stood looking at her, the sensation that most men have felt at one time or another went stealing through him – a peculiar satisfaction of the senses, a peculiar certainty, which novelists and old ladies call love at first sight. Still stealthily watching her, he at once made his way to his hostess, and stood doggedly waiting for the music to cease.

'Who is that girl with yellow hair and dark eyes?' he asked.

'That – oh! Irene Heron. Her father, Professor Heron, died this year. She lives with her stepmother. She's a nice girl, a pretty girl, but no money!'

'Introduce me, please,' said Soames.

It was very little that he found to say, nor did he find her responsive to that little. But he went away with the resolution to see her again. He effected his object by chance, meeting her on the pier with her stepmother, who had the habit of walking there from twelve to one of a forenoon. Soames made this lady's acquaintance with alacrity, nor was it long before he perceived in her the ally he was looking for. His keen scent for the commercial side of family life soon told him that Irene cost her stepmother more than the fifty pounds a year she brought her; it also told him that Mrs Heron, a woman yet in the prime of life, desired to be married again. The strange ripening beauty of her step-daughter stood in the way of this desirable consummation. And Soames, in his stealthy tenacity, laid his plans.

He left Bournemouth without having given himself away, but in a month's time he came back, and this time he spoke, not to the girl, but to her stepmother. He had made up his mind, he said; he would wait any time. And he had long to wait, watching Irene bloom, the lines of her young figure softening, the stronger blood deepening the gleam of her eyes, and warming her face to a creamy glow; and at each visit he proposed to her, and when that visit was at an end, took her refusal away with him, back to London, sore at heart, but steadfast and silent as the grave. He tried to come at the secret springs of her resistance; only once had he a gleam of light. It was at one of those assembly dances, which afford the only outlet to the passions of the population of seaside watering-places. He was sitting with her in an embrasure, his senses tingling with the contact of the waltz. She had looked at him over her slowly waving fan; and he had lost his head. Seizing that moving wrist, he pressed his lips to the flesh of her arm. And she had shuddered – to this day he had not forgotten that shudder – nor the look so passionately averse she had given him.

A year after that she had yielded. What had made her yield he could never make out; and from Mrs Heron, a woman of some diplomatic talent, he learnt nothing. Once after they were married he asked her, 'What made you refuse me so often?' She had answered by a strange silence. An enigma to him from the day that he first saw her, she was an enigma to him still. . . .

The Man of Property, 1906

ARNOLD BENNETT

[Elephant]

'SOPHIA, WILL you come and see the elephant? Do come!' Constance entered the drawing-room with this request on her eager lips.

'No,' said Sophia, with a touch of condescension. 'I'm far too busy for elephants.'

Only two years had passed; but both girls were grown up now; long sleeves, long skirts, hair that had settled down in life; and a demeanour immensely serious, as though existence were terrific in its responsibilities; yet sometimes childhood surprisingly broke through the crust of gravity, as now in Constance, aroused by such things as elephants, and proclaimed with vivacious gestures that it was not dead after all. The sisters were sharply differentiated. Constance wore the black alpaca apron and the scissors at the end of a long black elastic, which indicated her vocation in the shop. She was proving a considerable success in the millinery department. She had learnt how to talk to people, and was, in her modest way, very self-possessed. She was getting a little stouter. Everybody liked her. Sophia had developed into the student. Time had accentuated her reserve. Her sole friend was Miss Chetwynd, with whom she was, having regard to the disparity of their ages, very intimate. At home she spoke little. She lacked amiability; as her mother said, she was 'touchy'. She required diplomacy from others, but did not render it again. Her attitude, indeed, was one of half-hidden disdain, now gentle, now coldly bitter. She would not wear an apron, in an age when aprons were almost essential to decency. No! She would *not* wear an apron, and there was an end of it. She was not so tidy as Constance, and if Constance's hands had taken on the coarse texture which comes from commerce with needles, pins, artificial flowers, and stuffs, Sophia's fine hands were seldom innocent of ink. But Sophia was splendidly beautiful. And even her mother and Constance had an instinctive idea that that face was, at any rate, a partial excuse for her asperity.

'Well,' said Constance, 'if you won't, I do believe I shall ask mother if she will.'

Sophia, bending over her books, made no answer. But the top of her head said: 'This has no interest for me whatever.'

Constance left the room, and in a moment returned with her mother.

'Sophia,' said her mother, with gay excitement, 'you might go and sit with your father for a bit while Constance and I just run up to the playground to see the elephant. You can work just as well in there as here. Your father's asleep.'

'Oh, very well!' Sophia agreed haughtily. 'Whatever is all this fuss about an elephant? Anyhow, it'll be quieter in your room. The noise here is splitting.' She gave a supercilious glance into the Square as she languidly rose.

It was the morning of the third day of Bursley Wakes; not the modern finicking and respectable, but an orgiastic carnival, gross in all its manifestations of joy. The whole centre of the town was given over to the furious pleasures of the people. Most of the Square was occupied by Wombwell's Menagerie, in a vast oblong tent, whose raging beasts roared and growled day and night. And spreading away from this supreme attraction, right up through the marketplace past the town hall to Duck Bank, Duck Square, and the waste land called the 'playground', were hundreds of booths with banners displaying all the delights of the horrible. You could see the atrocities of the French Revolution, and of the Fiji Islands, and the ravages of unspeakable diseases, and the living flesh of a nearly nude human female guaranteed to turn the scale at twenty-two stone, and the skeletons of the mysterious phantoscope, and the bloody contests of champions naked to the waist (with the chance of picking up a red tooth as a relic). You could try your strength by hitting an image of a fellow-creature in the stomach, and test your aim by knocking off the heads of other images with a wooden ball. You could also shoot with rifles at various targets. All the streets were lined with stalls loaded with food in heaps, chiefly dried fish, the entrails of animals, and gingerbread. All the public-houses were crammed, and frenzied jolly drunkards, men and women, lunged along the pavements everywhere, their shouts vying with the trumpets, horns, and drums of the booths, and the shrieking, rattling toys that the children carried.

It was a glorious spectacle, but not a spectacle for the leading families. Miss Chetwynd's school was closed, so that the daughters of leading families might remain in seclusion till the worst was over. The Baineses ignored the wakes in every possible way, choosing that week to have a show of mourning goods in the left-hand window, and refusing to let Maggie outside on any pretext. Therefore the dazzling social success of the elephant, which was quite easily drawing Mrs Baines into the vortex, cannot imaginably be over-estimated.

On the previous night one of the three Wombwell elephants had suddenly knelt on a man in the tent; he had then walked out of the tent and picked up another man at haphazard from the crowd which was staring at the great pictures in front, and tried to put this second man into his mouth. Being stopped by his Indian attendant with a pitchfork, he placed the man on the ground and stuck his tusk through an artery of the victim's arm. He then, amid unexampled excitement, suffered himself to be led away. He was conducted to the rear of the tent, just in front of Baines's shuttered windows, and by means of stakes, pulleys, and ropes, forced to his knees. His head was whitewashed, and six men of the Rifle Corps were engaged to shoot at him at a distance of five yards, while constables kept the crowd off with truncheons. He died instantly, rolling over with a soft thud. The crowd cheered, and, intoxicated by their importance, the Volunteers fired three more volleys into the carcass, and were then borne off as heroes to different inns. The elephant, by the help of his two companions, was got on to a railway lorry and disappeared into the night. Such was the greatest sensation that has ever occurred, or perhaps will ever occur, in Bursley. The excitement about the repeal of the Corn Laws, or about Inkerman, was feeble compared to that excitement. Mr Critchlow, who had been called on to put a hasty tourniquet round the arm of the second victim, had popped in afterwards to tell John Baines all about it. Mr Baines's interest, however, had been slight. Mr Critchlow succeeded better with the ladies, who, though they had witnessed the shooting from the drawing-room, were thirsty for the most trifling details.

The next day it was known that the elephant lay near the playground, pending the decision of the chief bailiff and the medical officer as to his burial. And everybody had to visit the corpse. No social exclusiveness could withstand the seduction of that dead elephant. Pilgrims travelled from all the Five Towns to see him.

'We're going now,' said Mrs Baines, after she had assumed her bonnet and shawl.

'All right,' said Sophia, pretending to be absorbed in study, as she sat on the sofa at the foot of her father's bed.

And Constance, having put her head in at the door, drew her mother after her like a magnet.

Then Sophia heard a remarkable conversation in the passage.

'Are you going up to see the elephant, Mrs Baines?' asked the voice of Mr Povey.

'Yes. Why?'

'I think I had better come with you. The crowd is sure to be very rough.' Mr Povey's tone was firm; he had a position.

'But the shop?'

'We shall not be long,' said Mr Povey.

'Oh, yes, mother,' Constance added appealingly.

Sophia felt the house thrill as the side-door banged. She

sprang up and watched the three cross King Street diagon-
ally, and so plunge into the wakes. This triple departure was
surely the crowning tribute to the dead elephant! It was
simply astonishing. It caused Sophia to perceive that she
had miscalculated the importance of the elephant. It made
her regret her scorn of the elephant as an attraction. She
was left behind; and the joy of life was calling her.

The Old Wives' Tale, 1908

EDWARD MORGAN FORSTER

[The Britisher Abroad]

B Y THE time Lucy was ready her cousin had done her
breakfast, and was listening to the clever lady among
the crumbs.

A conversation then ensued, on not unfamiliar lines. Miss
Bartlett was, after all, a wee bit tired, and thought they had
better spend the morning settling in; unless Lucy would at
all like to go out? Lucy would rather like to go out, as it was
her first day in Florence, but, of course, she could go alone.
Miss Bartlett could not allow this. Of course she would
accompany Lucy everywhere. Oh, certainly not; Lucy would
stop with her cousin. Oh no! That would never do! Oh yes!

At this point the clever lady broke in.

'If it is Mrs Grundy who is troubling you, I do assure you
that you can neglect the good person. Being English, Miss
Honeychurch will be perfectly safe. Italians understand. A
dear friend of mine, Contessa Baroncelli, has two daughters,
and when she cannot send a maid to school with them she
lets them go in sailor-hats instead. Everyone takes them for
English, you see, especially if their hair is strained tightly
behind.'

Miss Bartlett was unconvinced by the safety of Contessa
Baroncelli's daughters. She was determined to take Lucy
herself, her head not being so very bad. The clever lady

then said that she was going to spend a long morning in Santa Croce, and if Lucy would come too she would be delighted.

'I will take you by a dear dirty back way, Miss Honeychurch, and if you bring me luck we shall have an adventure.'

Lucy said that this was most kind, and at once opened the Baedeker, to see where Santa Croce was.

'Tut, tut! Miss Lucy! I hope we shall soon emancipate you from Baedeker. He does but touch the surface of things. As to the true Italy – he does not even dream of it. The true Italy is only to be found by patient observation.'

This sounded very interesting, and Lucy hurried over her breakfast, and started with her new friend in high spirits. Italy was coming at last. The Cockney Signora and her works had vanished like a bad dream.

Miss Lavish – for that was the clever lady's name – turned to the right along the sunny Lungarno. How delightfully warm! But a wind down the side-streets that cut like a knife, didn't it? Ponte alle Grazie – particularly interesting, mentioned by Dante. San Miniato – beautiful as well as interesting; the crucifix that kissed a murderer – Miss Honeychurch would remember the story. The men on the river were fishing. (Untrue; but then so is most information.) Then Miss Lavish darted under the archway of the white bullocks, and she stopped, and she cried:

'A smell! A true Florentine smell! Every city, let me teach you, has its own smell.'

'Is it a very nice smell?' said Lucy, who had inherited from her mother a distaste to dirt.

'One doesn't come to Italy for niceness,' was the retort; 'one comes for life. Buon giorno! Buon giorno!' bowing right and left. 'Look at that adorable wine-cart! How the driver stares at us, dear, simple soul!'

So Miss Lavish proceeded through the streets of the city of Florence, short, fidgety, and playful as a kitten, though without a kitten's grace. It was a treat for the girl to be with anyone so clever and so cheerful; and a blue military cloak, such as an Italian officer wears, only increased the sense of festivity.

'Buon giorno! Take the word of an old woman, Miss Lucy: you will never repent of a little civility to your inferiors. *That* is the true democracy. Though I am a real Radical as well. There, now you're shocked.'

'Indeed, I'm not!' exclaimed Lucy. 'We are Radicals, too, out and out. My father always voted for Mr Gladstone, until he was so dreadful about Ireland.'

'I see, I see. And now you have gone over to the enemy.'

'Oh, please—! If my father was alive, I am sure he would vote Radical again now that Ireland is all right. And as it is, the glass over our front door was broken last election, and Freddy is sure it was the Tories; but mother says nonsense, a tramp.'

'Shameful! A manufacturing district, I suppose?'

'No – in the Surrey hills. About five miles from Dorking, looking over the Weald.'

Miss Lavish seemed interested, and slackened her trot.

'What a delightful part; I know it so well. It is full of the very nicest people. Do you know Sir Harry Otway – a Radical if ever there was?'

'Very well indeed.'

'And old Mrs Butterworth the philanthropist?'

'Why, she rents a field of us! How funny!'

Miss Lavish looked at the narrow ribbon of sky, and murmured:

'Oh, you have property in Surrey?'

'Hardly any,' said Lucy, fearful of being thought a snob. 'Only thirty acres – just the garden, all downhill, and some fields.'

Miss Lavish was not disgusted, and said it was just the size of her aunt's Suffolk estate. Italy receded. They tried to remember the last name of Lady Louisa someone, who had taken a house near Summer Street the other year, but she had not liked it, which was odd of her. And just as Miss Lavish had got the name she broke off and exclaimed:

'Bless us! Bless us and save us! We've lost the way.'

Certainly they had seemed a long time in reaching Santa Croce, the tower of which had been plainly visible from the landing window. But Miss Lavish had said so much about knowing her Florence by heart, that Lucy had followed her with no misgivings.

'Lost! Lost! My dear Miss Lucy, during our political diatribes we have taken a wrong turning. How those horrid Conservatives would jeer at us! What are we to do? Two lone females in an unknown town. Now, this is what *I* call an adventure.'

Lucy, who wanted to see Santa Croce, suggested, as a possible solution, that they should ask the way there.

'Oh, but that is the word of a craven! And no, you are not, not, *not* to look at your Baedeker. Give it to me; I shan't let you carry it. We will simply drift.'

Accordingly they drifted through a series of those gray-brown streets, neither commodious nor picturesque, in which the eastern quarter of the city abounds. Lucy soon lost interest in the discontent of Lady Louisa, and became discontented herself. For one ravishing moment Italy appeared. She stood in the Square of the Annunziata and saw in the living terracotta those divine babies whom no cheap reproduction can ever stale. There they stood, with their shining limbs bursting from the garments of charity, and their strong white arms extended against circlets of heaven. Lucy thought she had never seen anything more beautiful; but Miss Lavish, with a shriek of dismay, dragged her forward, declaring that they were out of their path now by at least a mile.

The hour was approaching at which the continental breakfast begins, or rather ceases, to tell, and the ladies bought some hot chestnut paste out of a little shop, because it looked so typical. It tasted partly of the paper in which it was wrapped, partly of hair-oil, partly of the great unknown. But it gave them strength to drift into another piazza, large and dusty, on the further side of which rose a black-and-white façade of surpassing ugliness. Miss Lavish spoke to it dramatically. It was Santa Croce. The adventure was over.

'Stop a minute; let those two people go on, or I shall have to speak to them. I do detest conventional intercourse. Nasty! They are going into the church, too. Oh, the Britisher abroad!'

'We sat opposite them at dinner last night. They have given us their rooms. They were so very kind.'

'Look at their figures!' laughed Miss Lavish. 'They walk through my Italy like a pair of cows. It's very naughty of me, but I would like to set an examination paper at Dover, and turn back every tourist who couldn't pass it.'

'What would you ask us?'

Miss Lavish laid her hand pleasantly on Lucy's arm, as if to suggest that she, at all events, would get full marks.

A Room with a View, 1908

[Intimacy]

THE COLLECTOR had watched the arrest from the interior of the waiting-room, and throwing open its perforated doors of zinc he was now revealed like a god in a shrine. When Fielding entered, the doors clapped to, and were guarded by a servant, while a punkah, to mark the importance of the moment, flapped dirty petticoats over their heads. The Collector could not speak at first. His face was white, fanatical, and rather beautiful – the expression that all English faces were to wear at Chandrapore for many days. Always brave and unselfish, he was now fused by some white and generous heat; he would have killed himself, obviously, if he had thought it right to do so. He spoke at last. 'The worst thing in my whole career has happened,' he said. 'Miss Quested has been insulted in one of the Marabar Caves.'

'Oh no, oh no, no,' gasped the other, feeling sickish.

'She escaped – by God's grace.'

'Oh no, no, but not Aziz . . . not Aziz . . .'

He nodded.

'Absolutely impossible, grotesque.'

'I called you to preserve you from the odium that would attach to you if you were seen accompanying him to the

Police Station,' said Turton, paying no attention to his protest, indeed scarcely hearing it.

He repeated 'Oh no' like a fool. He couldn't frame other words. He felt that a mass of madness had arisen and tried to overwhelm them all; it had to be shoved back into its pit somehow, and he didn't know how to do it, because he did not understand madness; he had always gone ahead sensibly and quietly until a difficulty came right. 'Who lodges this infamous charge?' he asked, pulling himself together.

'Miss Derek and – the victim herself . . .' He nearly broke down, unable to repeat the girl's name.

'Miss Quested herself definitely accuses him of—'

He nodded, and turned his face away.

'Then she's mad.'

'I cannot pass that last remark,' said the Collector, waking up to the knowledge that they differed, and trembling with fury. 'You will withdraw it instantly. It is the type of remark you have permitted yourself to make ever since you came to Chandrapore.'

'I'm excessively sorry, sir; I certainly withdraw it unconditionally.' For the man was half mad himself.

'Pray, Mr Fielding, what induced you to speak to me in such a tone?'

'The news gave me a very great shock, so I must ask you to forgive me. I cannot believe that Dr Aziz is guilty.'

He slammed his hand on the table. 'That – that is a repetition of your insult in an aggravated form.'

'If I may venture to say so, no,' said Fielding, also going white, but sticking to his point. 'I make no reflection on the good faith of the two ladies, but the charge they are bringing against Aziz rests upon some mistake, and five minutes will clear it up. The man's manner is perfectly natural; besides, I know him to be incapable of infamy.'

'It does indeed rest upon a mistake,' came the thin, biting voice of the other. 'It does indeed. I have had twenty-five years' experience of this country' – he paused, and 'twenty-five years' seemed to fill the waiting-room with their staleness and ungenerosity – 'and during those twenty-five years I have never known anything but disaster result when English people and Indians attempt to be intimate socially.

Intercourse, yes. Courtesy, by all means. Intimacy – never, never. The whole weight of my authority is against it. I have been in charge at Chandrapore for six years, and if everything has gone smoothly, if there has been mutual respect and esteem, it is because both peoples kept to this simple rule. Newcomers set our traditions aside, and in an instant what you see happens, the work of years is undone, and the good name of my District ruined for a generation. I – I – can't see the end of this day's work, Mr Fielding. You, who are imbued with modern ideas – no doubt you can. I wish I had never lived to see its beginning, I know that. It is the end of me. That a lady, that a young lady engaged to my most valued subordinate – that she – an English girl fresh from England – that I should have lived—'

Involved in his own emotions, he broke down. What he had said was both dignified and pathetic, but had it anything to do with Aziz? Nothing at all, if Fielding was right. It is impossible to regard a tragedy from two points of view, and, whereas Turton had decided to avenge the girl, he hoped to save the man. He wanted to get away and talk to McBryde, who had always been friendly to him, was on the whole sensible, and could, anyhow, be trusted to keep cool.

'I came down particularly on your account – while poor Heaslop got his mother away. I regarded it as the most friendly thing I could do. I meant to tell you that there will be an informal meeting at the Club this evening to discuss the situation, but I am doubtful whether you will care to come. Your visits there are always infrequent.'

'I shall certainly come, sir, and I am most grateful to you for all the trouble you have taken over me. May I venture to ask – where Miss Quested is?'

He replied with a gesture: she was ill.

'Worse and worse, appalling,' he said feelingly.

But the Collector looked at him sternly, because he was keeping his head. He had not gone mad at the phrase 'an English girl fresh from England', he had not rallied to the banner of race. He was still after facts, though the herd had decided on emotion. Nothing enrages Anglo-India more than the lantern of reason if it is exhibited for one moment after its extinction is decreed. All over Chandrapore that

day the Europeans were putting aside their normal personalities and sinking themselves in their community. Pity,
wrath, heroism, filled them, but the power of putting two
and two together was annihilated.

Terminating the interview, the Collector walked onto the
platform. The confusion there was revolting. A chuprassy
of Ronny's had been told to bring up some trifles belonging
to the ladies, and was appropriating for himself various
articles to which he had no right; he was a camp-follower of
the angry English. Mohammed Latif made no attempt to
resist him. Hassan flung off his turban, and wept. All the
comforts that had been provided so liberally were rolled
about and wasted in the sun. The Collector took in the
situation at a glance, and his sense of justice functioned
though he was insane with rage. He spoke the necessary
word, and the looting stopped. Then he drove off to his
bungalow and gave rein to his passions again. When he saw
the coolies asleep in the ditches or the shopkeepers rising to
salute him on their platforms, he said to himself: 'I know
what you're like at last; you shall pay for this, you shall
squeal.'

A Passage to India, 1924

GILBERT KEITH CHESTERTON

The Queer Feet

FATHER BROWN seemed rather to like the saturnine
candour of the soldier. 'Well,' he said, smiling, 'I
mustn't tell you anything of the man's identity, or his own
story, of course; but there's no particular reason why I
shouldn't tell you of the mere outside facts which I found
out for myself.'

He hopped over the barrier with unexpected activity, and
sat beside Colonel Pound, kicking his short legs like a little

boy on a gate. He began to tell the story as easily as if he were telling it to an old friend by a Christmas fire.

'You see, colonel,' he said, 'I was shut up in that small room there doing some writing, when I heard a pair of feet in this passage doing a dance that was as queer as the dance of death. First came quick, funny little steps, like a man walking on tiptoe for a wager; then came slow, careless, creaking steps, as of a big man walking about with a cigar. But they were both made by the same feet, I swear, and they came in rotation; first the run and then the walk, and then the run again. I wondered at first idly, and then wildly why a man should act these two parts at once. One walk I knew; it was just like yours, colonel. It was the walk of a well-fed gentleman waiting for something, who strolls about rather because he is physically alert than because he is mentally impatient. I knew that I knew the other walk, too, but I could not remember what it was. What wild creature had I met on my travels that tore along on tiptoe in that extraordinary style? Then I heard a clink of plates some-where; and the answer stood up as plain as St Peter's. It was the walk of a waiter – that walk with the body slanted forward, the eyes looking down, the ball of the toe spurning away the ground, the coat tails and napkin flying. Then I thought for a minute and a half more. And I believe I saw the manner of the crime, as clearly as if I were going to commit it.'

Colonel Pound looked at him keenly, but the speaker's mild grey eyes were fixed upon the ceiling with almost empty wistfulness.

'A crime,' he said slowly, 'is like any other work of art. Don't look surprised; crimes are by no means the only works of art that come from an infernal workshop. But every work of art, divine or diabolic, has one indispensable mark – I mean, that the centre of it is simple, however much the fulfilment may be complicated. Thus, in *Hamlet*, let us say, the grotesqueness of the grave-digger, the flowers of the mad girl, the fantastic finery of Osric, the pallor of the ghost and the grin of the skull are all oddities in a sort of tangled wreath round one plain tragic figure of a man in black. Well, this also,' he said, getting slowly down from his seat with a smile, 'this also is the plain tragedy of a man in black. Yes,' he went on, seeing the colonel look up in some wonder, 'the whole of this tale turns on a black coat. In this, as in *Hamlet*, there are the rococo excrescences – yourselves, let us say. There is the dead waiter, who was there when he could not be there. There is the invisible hand that swept your table clear of silver and melted into air. But every clever crime is founded ultimately on some one quite simple fact – some fact that is not itself mysterious. The mystification comes in covering it up, in leading men's thoughts away from it. This large and subtle and (in the ordinary course) most profitable crime, was built on the plain fact that a gentleman's evening dress is the same as a waiter's. All the rest was acting, and thundering good acting, too.'

'Still,' said the colonel, getting up and frowning at his boots. 'I am not sure that I understand.'

'Colonel,' said Father Brown, 'I tell you that this archangel of impudence who stole your forks walked up and down this passage twenty times in the blaze of all the lamps, in the glare of all the eyes. He did not go and hide in dim corners where suspicion might have searched for him. He kept constantly on the move in the lighted corridors, and everywhere that he went he seemed to be there by right. Don't ask me what he was like; you have seen him yourself six or seven times tonight. You were waiting with all the other grand people in the reception room at the end of the passage there, with the terrace just beyond. Whenever he came among you gentlemen, he came in the lightning style of a waiter, with bent head, flapping napkin and flying feet. He shot out on to the terrace, did something to the tablecloth, and shot back again towards the office and the waiters' quarters. By the time he had come under the eye of the office clerk and the waiters he had become another man in every inch of his body, in every instinctive gesture. He strolled among the servants with the absent-minded insolence which they have all seen in their patrons. It was no new thing to them that a swell from the dinner party should pace all parts of the house like an animal at the Zoo; they know that nothing marks the Smart Set more than a habit of walking where one chooses. When he was magnificently weary of walking down that particular passage he would wheel round and pace back past the office; in the shadow of the arch just beyond he was altered as by a blast of magic, and went hurrying forward again among the Twelve Fishermen, an obsequious attendant. Why should the gentlemen look at a chance waiter? Why should the waiters suspect a first-rate walking gentleman? Once or twice he played the coolest tricks. In the proprietor's private quarters he called out breezily for a syphon of soda water, saying he was thirsty. He said genially that he would carry it himself, and he did; he carried it quickly and correctly through the thick of you, a waiter with an obvious errand. Of course, it could not have been kept up long, but it only had to be kept up till the end of the fish course.

'His worst moment was when the waiters stood in a row; but even then he contrived to lean against the wall just around the corner in such a way that for that important instant the waiters thought him a gentleman, while the gentlemen thought him a waiter. The rest went like winking. If any waiter caught him away from the table, that waiter caught a languid aristocrat. He had only to time himself two minutes before the fish was cleared, become a swift servant, and clear it himself. He put the plates down on a sideboard, stuffed the silver in his breast pocket, giving it a bulgy look, and ran like a hare (I heard him coming) till he came to the cloak-room. There he had only to be a plutocrat again – a plutocrat called away suddenly on business. He had only to give his ticket to the cloak-room attendant, and go out again elegantly as he had come in. Only – only I happened to be the cloak-room attendant.'

The Innocence of Father Brown, 1911

SIR MAX BEERBOHM

[Zuleika's Progress]

PARIS SAW her and was prostrate. Boldini did a portrait
of her. Jules Bloch wrote a song about her; and this, for
a whole month, was howled up and down the cobbled alleys
of Montmartre. And all the little dandies were mad for 'la
Zuleika'. The jewellers of the Rue de la Paix soon had
nothing left to put in their windows – everything had been
bought for 'la Zuleika'. For a whole month, baccarat was
not played at the Jockey Club – every member had succumbed to a nobler passion. For a whole month, the whole
demi-monde was forgotten for one English virgin. Never,
even in Paris, had a woman triumphed so. When the day
came for her departure, the city wore such an air of sullen
mourning as it had not worn since the Prussians marched to
its Élysée. Zuleika, quite untouched, would not linger in
the conquered city. Agents had come to her from every
capital in Europe, and, for a year, she ranged, in triumphal
nomady, from one capital to another. In Berlin, every night,
the students escorted her home with torches. Prince Vier-
fünfsechs-Siebenachtneun offered her his hand, and was
condemned by the Kaiser to six months' confinement in his
little castle. In Yildiz Kiosk, the tyrant who still throve there
conferred on her the Order of Chastity, and offered her the
central couch in his seraglio. She gave her performance in
the Quirinal, and, from the Vatican, the Pope launched
against her a Bull which fell utterly flat. In Petersburg, the
Grand Duke Salamander Salamandrovitch fell enamoured
of her. Of every article in the apparatus of her conjuring-
tricks he caused a replica to be made in finest gold These
treasures he presented to her in that great malachite casket
which now stood on the little table in her room; and
thenceforth it was with these that she performed her wonders. They did not mark the limit of the Grand Duke's
generosity. He was for bestowing on Zuleika the half of his
immensurable estates. The Grand Duchess appealed to the

Tzar. Zuleika was conducted across the frontier, by an escort of love-sick Cossacks. On the Sunday before she left Madrid, a great bull-fight was held in her honour. Fifteen bulls received the *coup-de-grâce*, and Alvarez, the matador of matadors, died in the arena with her name on his lips. He had tried to kill the last bull without taking his eyes off *la divina señorita*. A prettier compliment had never been paid her, and she was immensely pleased with it. For that matter, she was immensely pleased with everything. She moved proudly to the incessant music of a paean, aye! of a paean that was always *crescendo*.

Its echoes followed her when she crossed the Atlantic, till they were lost in the louder, deeper, more blatant paean that rose for her from the shores beyond. All the stops of that 'mighty organ, many-piped', the New York press, were pulled out simultaneously, as far as they could be pulled, in Zuleika's honour. She delighted in the din. She read every line that was printed about her, tasting her triumph as she had never tasted it before. And how she revelled in the Brobdingnagian drawings of her, which, printed in nineteen colours, towered between the columns or sprawled across them! There she was, measuring herself back to back with the Statue of Liberty; scudding through the firmament on a comet, whilst a crowd of tiny men in evening-dress stared up at her from the terrestrial globe; peering through a microscope held by Cupid over a diminutive Uncle Sam; teaching the American Eagle to stand on its head; and doing a hundred-and-one other things – whatever suggested itself to the fancy of native art. And through all this iridescent maze of symbolism were scattered many little slabs of realism. At home, on the street, Zuleika was the smiling target of all snap-shooters, and all the snap-shots were snapped up by the press and reproduced with annotations: Zuleika Dobson walking on Broadway in the sables gifted her by Grand Duke Salamander – she says 'You can bounce blizzards in them'; Zuleika Dobson yawning over a love-letter from millionaire Edelweiss; relishing a cup of clam-broth – she says 'They don't use clams out there'; ordering her maid to fix her a warm bath; finding a split in the gloves she has just drawn on before starting for the musicale given in her honour by Mrs Suetonius X. Meistersinger, the most exclusive woman in New York; chatting at the telephone to Miss Camille Van Spook, the best-born girl in New York; laughing over the recollection of a compliment made her by George Abimelech Post, the best-groomed man in New York; meditating a new trick; admonishing a waiter who has upset a cocktail over her skirt; having herself manicured; drinking tea in bed. Thus was Zuleika enabled daily to be, as one might say, a spectator of her own wonderful life. On her departure from New York, the papers spoke no more than the truth when they said she had had 'a lovely time'. The further she went West – millionaire Edelweiss had loaned her his private car – the lovelier her time was. Chicago drowned the echoes of New York; final Frisco dwarfed the headlines of Chicago. Like one of its own prairie-fires, she swept the country from end to end. Then she swept back, and sailed for England. She was to return for a second season in the coming Fall. At present, she was, as I have said, 'resting'.

As she sat here in the bay-window of her room, she was not reviewing the splendid pageant of her past. She was a young person whose reveries never were in retrospect. For her the past was no treasury of distinct memories, all hoarded and classified, some brighter than others and more highly valued. All memories were for her but as the motes in one fused radiance that followed her and made more luminous the pathway of her future. She was always looking forward. She was looking forward now – that shade of ennui had passed from her face – to the week she was to spend in Oxford. A new city was a new toy to her, and – for it was youth's homage that she loved best – this city of youths was a toy after her own heart.

Zuleika Dobson; or, An Oxford Love Story, 1911

DAVID HERBERT LAWRENCE

[The Outsider]

PAUL HATED his father. As a boy he had a fervent private religion.

'Make him stop drinking,' he prayed every night. 'Lord let my father die,' he prayed very often. 'Let him be killed at pit,' he prayed when, after tea, his father did not come home from work.

That was another time when the family suffered intensely. The children came from school and had their teas. On the hob the big black saucepan was simmering, the stew-jack was in the oven, ready for Morel's dinner. He was expected at five o'clock. But for months he would stop and drink every night on his way from work.

In the winter nights, when it was cold, and grew dark early, Mrs Morel would put a brass candlestick on the table, light a tallow candle to save the gas. The children finished their bread-and-butter, or dripping, and were ready to go out to play. But if Morel had not come they faltered. The sense of his sitting in all his pit-dirt, drinking, after a long day's work, not coming home and eating and washing, but sitting, getting drunk, on an empty stomach, made Mrs Morel unable to bear herself. From her the feeling was transmitted to the other children. She never suffered alone any more: the children suffered with her.

Paul went out to play with the rest. Down in the great trough of twilight, tiny clusters of lights burned where the pits were. A few last colliers struggled up the dim field-path. The lamplighter came along. No more colliers came. Darkness shut down over the valley; work was gone. It was night.

Then Paul ran anxiously into the kitchen. The one candle still burned on the table, the big fire glowed red. Mrs Morel sat alone. On the hob the saucepan steamed; the dinner-plate lay waiting on the table. All the room was full of the sense of waiting, waiting for the man who was sitting in his pit-dirt, dinnerless, some mile away from home, across the darkness, drinking himself drunk. Paul stood in the doorway.

'Has my dad come?' he asked.

'You can see he hasn't,' said Mrs Morel, cross with the futility of the question.

Then the boy dawdled about near his mother. They shared the same anxiety. Presently Mrs Morel went out and strained the potatoes.

'They're ruined and black,' she said; 'but what do I care?'

Not many words were spoken. Paul almost hated his mother for suffering because his father did not come home from work.

'What do you bother yourself for?' he said. 'If he wants to stop and get drunk, why don't you let him?'

'Let him!' flushed Mrs Morel. 'You may well say "let him".'

She knew that the man who stops on the way home from work is on a quick way to ruining himself and his home. The children were yet young, and depended on the breadwinner. William gave her the sense of relief, providing her at last with someone to turn to if Morel failed. But the tense atmosphere of the room on these waiting evenings was the same.

The minutes ticked away. At six o'clock still the cloth lay on the table, still the dinner stood waiting, still the same sense of anxiety and expectation in the room. The boy could not stand it any longer. He could not go out and play. So he ran in to Mrs Inger, next door but one, for her to talk to him. She had no children. Her husband was good to her, but was in a shop, and came home late. So, when she saw the lad at the door, she called:

'Come in, Paul.'

The two sat talking for some time, when suddenly the boy rose, saying:

'Well, I'll be going and seeing if my mother wants an errand doing.'

He pretended to be perfectly cheerful, and did not tell his friend what ailed him. Then he ran indoors.

Morel at these times came in churlish and hateful.

'This is a nice time to come home,' said Mrs Morel.

'Wha's it matter to yo' what time I come whoam?' he shouted.

And everybody in the house was still, because he was dangerous. He ate his food in the most brutal manner possible and, when he had done, pushed all the pots in a heap away from him, to lay his arms on the table. Then he went to sleep.

Paul hated his father so. The collier's small, mean head, with its black hair slightly soiled with grey, lay on the bare arms, and the face, dirty and inflamed, with a fleshy nose and thin paltry brows, was turned sideways, asleep with beer and weariness and nasty temper. If anyone entered suddenly, or a noise were made, the man looked up and shouted:

'I'll lay my fist about thy y'ead, I'm tellin' thee, if tha doesna stop that clatter! Dost hear?'

And the two last words, shouted in a bullying fashion, usually at Annie, made the family writhe with hate of the man.

He was shut out from all family affairs. No one told him anything. The children, alone with their mother, told her all about the day's happenings, everything. Nothing had really taken place in them until it was told to their mother. But as soon as the father came in, everything stopped. He was like the scotch in the smooth, happy machinery of the home. And he was always aware of this fall of silence on his entry, the shutting off of life, the unwelcome. But now it was gone too far to alter.

He would dearly have liked the children to talk to him, but they could not. Sometimes Mrs Morel would say:

'You ought to tell your father.'

Paul won a prize in a competition in a child's paper. Everybody was highly jubilant.

'Now you'd better tell your father when he comes in,' said Mrs Morel. 'You know how he carries on and says he's never told anything.'

'All right,' said Paul. But he would almost rather have forfeited the prize than have to tell his father.

'I've won a prize in a competition, dad,' he said.

Morel turned round to him.

'Have you, my boy? What sort of a competition?'
'Oh, nothing – about famous women.'
'And how much is the prize, then, as you've got?'
'It's a book.'
'Oh, indeed!'
'About birds.'
'Hm – hm!'
And that was all. Conversation was impossible between the father and any other member of the family. He was an outsider. He had denied the God in him.

Sons and Lovers, 1913

[The Main Show]

THEY SAW Tom Brangwen walking up the curved drive. He was getting stouter, but with his bowler hat worn well set down on his brows, he looked manly, handsome, curiously like any other man of action. His colour was as fresh, his health as perfect as ever, he walked like a man rather absorbed.

Winifred Inger was startled when he entered the library, his coat fastened close and correct, his head bald to the crown, but not shiny, rather like something naked that one is accustomed to see covered, and his dark eyes liquid and formless. He seemed to stand in the shadow, like a thing ashamed. And the clasp of his hand was so soft and yet so forceful, that it chilled the heart. She was afraid of him, repelled by him, and yet attracted.

He looked at the athletic, seemingly fearless girl, and he detected in her a kinship with his own dark corruption. Immediately, he knew they were akin.

His manner was polite, almost foreign, and rather cold. He still laughed in his curious, animal fashion, suddenly wrinkling up his wide nose, and showing his sharp teeth. The fine beauty of his skin and his complexion, some almost waxen quality, hid the strange, repellent grossness of him, the slight sense of putrescence, the commonness, which revealed itself in his rather fat thighs and loins.

Winifred saw at once the deferential, slightly servile, slightly cunning regard he had for Ursula, which made the girl at once so proud and so perplexed.

'But is this place as awful as it looks?' the young girl asked, a strain in her eyes.

'It is just what it looks,' he said. 'It hides nothing.'

'Why are the men so sad?'

'Are they sad?' he replied.

'They seem unutterably, unutterably sad,' said Ursula, out of a passionate throat.

'I don't think they are that. They just take it for granted.'

'What do they take for granted?'

'This – the pits and the place altogether.'

'Why don't they alter it?' she passionately protested.

'They believe they must alter themselves to fit the pits and the place, rather than alter the pits and the place to fit themselves. It is easier,' he said.

'And you agree with them,' burst out his niece, unable to bear it. 'You think like they do – that living human beings must be taken and adapted to all kinds of horrors. We could easily do without the pits.'

He smiled, uncomfortably, cynically. Ursula felt again the revolt of hatred from him.

'I suppose their lives are not really so bad,' said Winifred Inger, superior to the Zolaesque tragedy.

He turned with his polite, distant attention.

'Yes, they are pretty bad. The pits are very deep, and hot, and in some places wet. The men die of consumption fairly often. But they earn good wages.'

'How gruesome!' said Winifred Inger.

'Yes,' he replied gravely. It was his grave, solid, self-contained manner which made him so much respected as a colliery manager.

The servant came in to ask where they would have tea.

'Put it in the summer-house, Mrs Smith,' he said.

The fair-haired, good-looking young woman went out.

'Is she married and in service?' asked Ursula.

'She is a widow. Her husband died of consumption a little

while ago.' Brangwen gave a sinister little laugh. 'He lay there in the house-place at her mother's, and five or six other people in the house, and died very gradually. I asked her if his death wasn't a great trouble to her. "Well," she said, "he was very fretful towards the last, never satisfied, never easy, always fret-fretting, an' never knowing what would satisfy him. So in one way it was a relief when it was over – for him and for everybody." They had only been married two years, and she has one boy. I asked her if she hadn't been very happy. "Oh, yes, sir, we was very comfortable at first, till he took bad, – oh, we was very comfortable, – oh, yes, – but you see, you get used to it. I've had my father and two brothers go off just the same. You get used to it."'

'It's a horrible thing to get used to,' said Winifred Inger, with a shudder.

'Yes,' he said, still smiling. 'But that's how they are. She'll be getting married again directly. One man or another – it does not matter very much. They're all colliers.'

'What do you mean?' asked Ursula. 'They're all colliers?'

'It is with the woman as with us,' he replied. 'Her husband was John Smith, loader. We reckoned him as a loader, he reckoned himself as a loader, and so she knew he represented his job. Marriage and home is a little side-show. The women know it right enough, and take it for what it's worth. One man or another, it doesn't matter all the world. The pit matters. Round the pit there will always be the side-shows, plenty of 'em.'

He looked round at the red chaos, the rigid, amorphous confusion of Wiggiston.

'Every man his own little side-show, his home, but the pit owns every man. The women have what is left. What's left of this man, or what is left of that – it doesn't matter altogether. The pit takes all that really matters.'

'It is the same everywhere,' burst out Winifred. 'It is the office, or the shop, or the business that gets the man, the woman gets the bit the shop can't digest. What is he at home, a man? He is a meaningless lump – a standing machine, a machine out of work.'

'They know they are sold,' said Tom Brangwen. 'That's

where it is. They know they are sold to their job. If a woman talks her throat out, what difference can it make? The man's sold to his job. So the women don't bother. They take what they can catch – and *vogue la galère.*'

'Aren't they very strict here?' asked Miss Inger.

'Oh, no. Mrs Smith has two sisters who have just changed husbands. They're not very particular – neither are they very interested. They go dragging along what is left from the pits. They're not interested enough to be very immoral – it all amounts to the same thing, moral or immoral – just a question of pit-wages. The most moral duke in England makes two hundred thousand a year out of these pits. He keeps the morality end up.'

Ursula sat black-souled and very bitter, hearing the two of them talk. There seemed something ghoulish even in their very deploring of the state of things. They seemed to take a ghoulish satisfaction in it. The pit was the great mistress. Ursula looked out of the window and saw the proud, demon-like colliery with her wheels twinkling in the heavens, the formless, squalid mass of the town lying aside. It was the squalid heap of side-shows. The pit was the main show, the *raison d'être* of all.

How terrible it was! There *was* a horrible fascination in it, – human bodies and lives subjected in slavery to that symmetric monster of the colliery. There was a swooning, perverse satisfaction in it. For a moment she was dizzy.

Then she recovered, felt herself in a great loneliness, wherein she was sad but free. She had departed. No more would she subscribe to the great colliery, to the great machine, which has taken us all captives. In her soul, she was against it, she disowned even its power. It had only to be forsaken to be inane, meaningless. And she knew it was meaningless. But it needed a great, passionate effort of will on her part, seeing the colliery, still to maintain her knowledge that it was meaningless.

The Rainbow, 1915

FORD MADOX FORD

[First Impressions]

THAT QUESTION of first impressions has always bothered me a good deal – but quite academically. I mean that, from time to time I have wondered whether it were or were not best to trust to one's first impressions in dealing with people. But I never had anybody to deal with except waiters and chambermaids and the Ashburnhams, with whom I didn't know that I was having any dealings. And, as far as waiters and chambermaids were concerned, I have generally found that my first impressions were correct enough. If my first idea of a man was that he was civil, obliging, and attentive, he generally seemed to go on being all those things. Once, however, at our Paris flat we had a maid who appeared to be charming and transparently honest. She stole, nevertheless, one of Florence's diamond rings. She did it, however, to save her young man from going to prison. So here, as somebody says somewhere, was a special case.

And, even in my short incursion into American business life – an incursion that lasted during part of August and nearly the whole of September – I found that to rely upon first impressions was the best thing I could do. I found myself automatically docketing and labelling each man as he was introduced to me, by the run of his features and by the first words that he spoke. I can't, however, be regarded as really doing business during the time that I spent in the United States. I was just winding things up. If it hadn't been for my idea of marrying the girl I might possibly have looked for something to do in my own country. For my experiences were vivid and amusing. It was exactly as if I had come out of a museum into a riotous fancy-dress ball. During my life with Florence I had almost come to forget that there were such things as fashions or occupations or the greed of gain. I had, in fact, forgotten that there was such a thing as a dollar and that a dollar can be extremely desirable if you don't happen to possess one. And I had forgotten, too, that there was such a thing as gossip that mattered. In that particular, Philadelphia was the most amazing place I have ever been in in my life. I was not in that city for more than a week or ten days and I didn't there transact anything much in the way of business; nevertheless, the number of times that I was warned by everybody against everybody else was simply amazing. A man I didn't know would come up behind my lounge chair in the hotel, and, whispering cautiously beside my ear, would warn me against some other man that I equally didn't know but who would be standing by the bar. I don't know what they thought I was there to do – perhaps to buy out the city's debt or get a controlling hold of some railway interest. Or, perhaps, they imagined that I wanted to buy a newspaper, for they were either politicians or reporters, which, of course, comes to the same thing. As a matter of fact, my property in Philadelphia was mostly real estate in the old-fashioned part of the city and all I wanted to do there was just to satisfy myself that the houses were in good repair and the doors kept properly painted. I wanted also to see my relations, of whom I had a few. These were mostly professional people and they were mostly rather hard up because of the big bank failure in 1907 or thereabouts. Still, they were very nice. They would have been nicer still if they hadn't, all of them, had what appeared to me to be the mania that what they called influences were working against them. At any rate, the impression of that city was one of old-fashioned rooms, rather English than American in type, in which handsome but careworn ladies, cousins of my own, talked principally about mysterious movements that were going on against them. I never got to know what it was all about; perhaps they thought I knew or perhaps there weren't any movements at all. It was all very secret and subtle and subterranean. But there was a nice young fellow called Carter who was a sort of second-nephew of mine, twice removed. He was handsome and dark and gentle and tall and modest. I understand also that he was a good cricketer. He was employed by the real-estate agents who collected my rents. It was he, therefore, who took me over my own property and I saw a good deal of him and of a nice girl called Mary, to whom he was engaged. At that time I did, what I certainly shouldn't do now – I made some careful inquiries as to his character. I discovered from his employers that he was just all that he appeared, honest, industrious, high-spirited, friendly, and ready to do anyone a good turn. His relatives, however, as they were mine, too – seemed to have something darkly mysterious against him. I imagined that he must have been mixed up in some case of graft or that he had at least betrayed several innocent and trusting maidens. I pushed, however, that particular mystery home and discovered it was only that he was a Democrat. My own people were mostly Republicans. It seemed to make it worse and more darkly mysterious to them, that young Carter was what they called a sort of Vermont Democrat which was the whole ticket and no mistake. But I don't know what it means. Anyhow, I suppose that my money will go to him when I die – I like the recollection of his friendly image and of the nice girl he was engaged to. May Fate deal very kindly with them.

I have said just now that, in my present frame of mind, nothing would ever make me make inquiries as to the character of any man that I liked at first sight. (The little digression as to my Philadelphia experiences was really meant to lead around to this.) For who in this world can give anyone a character? Who in this world knows anything of any other heart – or of his own? I don't mean to say that one cannot form an average estimate of the way a person will behave. But one cannot be certain of the way any man will behave in every case – and until one can do that a 'character' is of no use to anyone. That, for instance, was the way with Florence's maid in Paris. We used to trust that girl with blank cheques for the payment of the tradesmen. For quite a time she was so trusted by us. Then, suddenly, she stole a ring. We should not have believed her capable of it; she would not have believed herself capable of it. It was nothing in her character.

The Good Soldier, 1915

JAMES JOYCE

[The Prefect of Studies]

THE DOOR opened quietly and closed. A quick whisper ran through the class: the prefect of studies. There was an instant of dead silence and then the loud crack of a pandybat on the last desk. Stephen's heart leapt up in fear.

– Any boys want flogging here, Father Arnall? cried the prefect of studies. Any lazy idle loafers that want flogging in this class?

He came to the middle of the class and saw Fleming on his knees.

– Hoho! he cried. Who is this boy? Why is he on his knees? What is your name, boy?

– Fleming, sir.

– Hoho, Fleming! An idler of course. I can see it in your eye. Why is he on his knees, Father Arnall?

– He wrote a bad Latin theme, Father Arnall said, and he missed all the questions in grammar.

– Of course he did! cried the prefect of studies, of course he did! A born idler! I can see it in the corner of his eye.

He banged his pandybat down on the desk and cried:

– Up, Fleming! Up, my boy!

Fleming stood up slowly.

– Hold out! cried the prefect of studies.

Fleming held out his hand. The pandybat came down on it with a loud smacking sound: one, two, three, four, five, six.

– Other hand!

The pandybat came down again in six loud quick smacks.

– Kneel down! cried the prefect of studies.

Fleming knelt down squeezing his hands under his armpits, his face contorted with pain, but Stephen knew how hard his hands were because Fleming was always rubbing rosin into them. But perhaps he was in great pain for the noise of the pandybat was terrible. Stephen's heart was beating and fluttering.

– At your work, all of you! shouted the prefect of studies. We want no lazy idle loafers here, lazy idle little schemers. At your work, I tell you. Father Dolan will be in to see you every day. Father Dolan will be in tomorrow.

He poked one of the boys in the side with the pandybat, saying:

– You, boy! When will Father Dolan be in again?

– Tomorrow, sir, said Tom Furlong's voice.

– Tomorrow and tomorrow and tomorrow, said the prefect of studies. Make up your minds for that. Every day Father Dolan. Write away. You, boy, who are you?

Stephen's heart jumped suddenly.

– Dedalus, sir.

– Why are you not writing like the others?

– I . . . my . . .

He could not speak with fright.

– Why is he not writing, Father Arnall?

– He broke his glasses, said Father Arnall, and I exempted him from work.

– Broke? What is this I hear? What is this? Your name is? said the prefect of studies.

– Dedalus, sir.

– Out here, Dedalus. Lazy little schemer. I see schemer in your face. Where did you break your glasses?

Stephen stumbled into the middle of the class, blinded by fear and haste.

– Where did you break your glasses? repeated the prefect of studies.

– The cinderpath, sir.

– Hoho! The cinderpath! cried the prefect of studies. I know that trick.

Stephen lifted his eyes in wonder and saw for a moment Father Dolan's whitegrey not young face, his baldy whitegrey head with fluff at the sides of it, the steel rims of his spectacles and his nocoloured eyes looking through the glasses. Why did he say he knew that trick?

– Lazy idle little loafer! cried the prefect of studies. Broke my glasses! An old schoolboy trick! Out with your hand this moment!

Stephen closed his eyes and held out in the air his trembling hand with the palm upwards. He felt the prefect of studies touch it for a moment at the fingers to straighten it and then the swish of the sleeve of the soutane as the pandybat was lifted to strike. A hot burning stinging tingling blow like the loud crack of a broken stick made his trembling hand crumple together like a leaf in the fire: and at the sound and the pain scalding tears were driven into his eyes. His whole body was shaking with fright, his arm was shaking and his crumpled burning livid hand shook like a loose leaf in the air. A cry sprang to his lips, a prayer to be let off. But though the tears scalded his eyes and his limbs quivered with pain and fright he held back the hot tears and the cry that scalded his throat.

– Other hand! shouted the prefect of studies.

Stephen drew back his maimed and quivering right arm and held out his left hand. The soutane sleeve swished again as the pandybat was lifted and a loud crashing sound and a fierce maddening tingling burning pain made his hand shrink together with the palms and fingers in a livid quivering mass. The scalding water burst forth from his eyes and, burning with shame and agony and fear, he drew back his shaking arm in terror and burst out into a whine of pain. His body shook with a palsy of fright and in shame and rage he felt the scalding cry come from his throat and the scalding tears falling out of his eyes and down his flaming cheeks.

– Kneel down! cried the prefect of studies.

Stephen knelt down quickly pressing his beaten hands to his sides. To think of them beaten and swollen with pain all in a moment made him feel so sorry for them as if they were not his own but someone else's that he felt sorry for. And as he knelt, calming the last sobs in his throat and feeling the burning tingling pain pressed into his sides, he thought of the hands which he had held out in the air with the palms up and of the firm touch of the prefect of studies when he had steadied the shaking fingers and of the beaten swollen reddened mass of palm and fingers that shook helplessly in the air.

– Get at your work, all of you, cried the prefect of studies from the door. Father Dolan will be in every day to see if any boy, any lazy idle little loafer wants flogging. Every day. Every day.

The door closed behind him.

The hushed class continued to copy out the themes. Father Arnall rose from his seat and went among them, helping the boys with gentle words and telling them the mistakes they had made. His voice was very gentle and soft. Then he returned to his seat and said to Fleming and Stephen:

– You may return to your places, you two.

Fleming and Stephen rose and, walking to their seats, sat down. Stephen, scarlet with shame, opened a book quickly with one weak hand and bent down upon it, his face close to the page.

It was unfair and cruel because the doctor had told him not to read without glasses and he had written home to his father that morning to send him a new pair. And Father Arnall had said that he need not study till the new glasses came. Then to be called a schemer before the class and to be pandied when he always got the card for first or second and was the leader of the Yorkists! How could the prefect of studies know that it was a trick? He felt the touch of the prefect's fingers as they had steadied his hand and at first he had thought he was going to shake hands with him because the fingers were soft and firm: but then in an instant he had heard the swish of the soutane sleeve and the crash. It was cruel and unfair to make him kneel in the middle of the class then: and Father Arnall had told them both that they might return to their places without making any difference between them. He listened to Father Arnall's low and gentle voice as he corrected the themes. Perhaps he was sorry now and wanted to be decent. But it was unfair and cruel. The prefect of studies was a priest but that was cruel and unfair. And his whitegrey face and the nocoloured eyes behind the steelrimmed spectacles were cruel looking because he had steadied the hand first with his firm soft fingers and that was to hit it better and louder.

A Portrait of the Artist as a Young Man, 1916

[The Caretaker]

THE PRIEST closed his book and went off, followed by the server. Corny Kelleher opened the sidedoors and the gravediggers came in, hoisted the coffin again, carried it out and shoved it on their cart. Corny Kelleher gave one wreath to the boy and one to the brother-in-law. All followed them out of the sidedoors into the mild grey air. Mr Bloom came last, folding his paper again into his pocket. He gazed gravely at the ground till the coffincart wheeled off to the left. The metal wheels ground the gravel with a sharp grating cry and the pack of blunt boots followed the barrow along a lane of sepulchres.

The ree the ra the ree the ra the roo. Lord, I mustn't lilt here.

– The O'Connell circle, Mr Dedalus said about him.

Mr Power's soft eyes went up to the apex of the lofty cone.

– He's at rest, he said, in the middle of his people, old Dan O'. But his heart is buried in Rome. How many broken hearts are buried here, Simon!

– Her grave is over there, Jack, Mr Dedalus said. I'll soon be stretched out beside her. Let Him take me whenever He likes.

Breaking down, he began to weep to himself quietly, stumbling a little in his walk. Mr Power took his arm.

– She's better where she is, he said kindly.

– I suppose so, Mr Dedalus said with a weak gasp. I suppose she is in heaven if there is a heaven.

Corny Kelleher stepped aside from his rank and allowed the mourners to plod by.

– Sad occasions, Mr Kernan began politely.

Mr Bloom closed his eyes and sadly twice bowed his head.

– The others are putting on their hats, Mr Kernan said. I suppose we can do so too. We are the last. This cemetery is a treacherous place.

They covered their heads.

– The reverend gentleman read the service too quickly,
don't you think? Mr Kernan said with reproof.

Mr Bloom nodded gravely, looking in the quick bloodshot
eyes. Secret eyes, secret searching eyes. Mason, I think: not
sure. Beside him again. We are the last. In the same boat.
Hope he'll say something else.

Mr Kernan added:

– The service of the Irish church, used in Mount Jerome,
is simpler, more impressive, I must say.

Mr Bloom gave prudent assent. The language of course
was another thing.

Mr Kernan said with solemnity:

– *I am the resurrection and the life.* That touches a man's
inmost heart.

– It does, Mr Bloom said.

Your heart perhaps but what price the fellow in the six feet
by two with his toes to the daisies? No touching that. Seat of
the affections. Broken heart. A pump after all, pumping
thousands of gallons of blood every day. One fine day it gets
bunged up and there you are. Lots of them lying around
here: lungs, hearts, livers. Old rusty pumps: damn the thing
else. The resurrection and the life. Once you are dead you
are dead. That last day idea. Knocking them all up out of
their graves. Come forth, Lazarus! And he came fifth and
lost the job. Get up! Last day! Then every fellow mousing
around for his liver and his lights and the rest of his traps.
Find damn all of himself that morning. Pennyweight of
powder in a skull. Twelve grammes one pennyweight. Troy
measure.

Corny Kelleher fell into step at their side.

– Everything went off A1, he said. What?

He looked on them from his drawling eye. Policeman's
shoulders. With your tooraloom tooraloom.

– As it should be, Mr Kernan said.

– What? Eh? Corny Kelleher said.

Mr Kernan assured him.

– Who is that chap behind with Tom Kernan? John Henry
Menton asked. I know his face.

Ned Lambert glanced back.

– Bloom, he said, Madam Marion Tweedy that was, is, I mean, the soprano. She's his wife.

– O, to be sure, John Henry Menton said. I haven't seen her for some time. She was a finelooking woman. I danced with her, wait, fifteen seventeen golden years ago, at Mat Dillon's, in Roundtown. And a good armful she was.

He looked behind through the others.

– What is he? he asked. What does he do? Wasn't he in the stationery line? I fell foul of him one evening, I remember, at bowls.

Ned Lambert smiled.

– Yes, he was, he said, in Wisdom Hely's. A traveller for blottingpaper.

– In God's name, John Henry Menton said, what did she marry a coon like that for? She had plenty of game in her then.

– Has still, Ned Lambert said. He does some canvassing for ads.

John Henry Menton's large eyes stared ahead.

The barrow turned into a side lane. A portly man, ambushed among the grasses, raised his hat in homage. The gravediggers touched their caps.

– John O'Connell, Mr Power said, pleased. He never forgets a friend.

Mr O'Connell shook all their hands in silence. Mr Dedalus said:

– I am come to pay you another visit.

– My dear Simon, the caretaker answered in a low voice. I don't want your custom at all.

Saluting Ned Lambert and John Henry Menton he walked on at Martin Cunningham's side, puzzling two keys at his back.

– Did you hear that one, he asked them, about Mulcahy from the Coombe?

– I did not, Martin Cunningham said.

They bent their silk hats in concert and Hynes inclined his ear. The caretaker hung his thumbs in the loops of his gold watch chain and spoke in a discreet tone to their vacant smiles.

– They tell the story, he said, that two drunks came out here one foggy evening to look for the grave of a friend of theirs. They asked for Mulcahy from the Coombe and were told where he was buried. After traipsing about in the fog they found the grave, sure enough. One of the drunks spelt out the name: Terence Mulcahy. The other drunk was blinking up at a statue of our Saviour the widow had got put up.

The caretaker blinked up at one of the sepulchres they passed. He resumed:

And, after blinking up at the sacred figure, *Not a bloody bit like the man*, says he. *That's not Mulcahy*, says he, *whoever done it*.

Rewarded by smiles he fell back and spoke with Corny Kelleher, accepting the dockets given him, turning them over and scanning them as he walked.

– That's all done with a purpose, Martin Cunningham explained to Hynes.

– I know, Hynes said, I know that.

– To cheer a fellow up, Martin Cunningham said. It's pure goodheartedness: damn the thing else.

Mr Bloom admired the caretaker's prosperous bulk. All want to be on good terms with him. Decent fellow, John O'Connell, real good sort. Keys: like Keyes's ad: no fear of anyone getting out, no passout checks. *Habeat corpus*. I must see about that ad after the funeral. Did I write Ballsbridge on the envelope I took to cover when she disturbed me writing to Martha? Hope it's not chucked in the dead letter office. Be the better of a shave. Grey sprouting beard. That's the first sign when the hairs come out grey and temper getting cross. Silver threads among the grey. Fancy being his wife. Wonder how he had the gumption to propose to any girl. Come out and live in the graveyard. Dangle that before her. It might thrill her first. Courting death . . . Shades of night hovering here with all the dead stretched about. The shadows of the tombs when churchyards yawn and Daniel O'Connell must be a descendant I suppose who is this used to say he was a queer breedy man great catholic all the same like a big giant in the dark.

Will o' the wisp. Gas of graves. Want to keep her mind off it to conceive at all. Women especially are so touchy. Tell her a ghost story in bed to make her sleep. Have you ever seen a ghost? Well, I have. It was a pitchdark night. The clock was on the stroke of twelve. Still they'd kiss all right if properly keyed up. Whores in Turkish graveyards. Learn anything if taken young. You might pick up a young widow here. Men like that. Love among the tombstones. Romeo. Spice of pleasure. In the midst of death we are in life. Both ends meet. Tantalising for the poor dead. Smell of frilled beefsteaks to the starving gnawing their vitals. Desire to grig people. Molly wanting to do it at the window. Eight children he has anyway.

He has seen a fair share go under in his time, lying around him field after field. Holy fields. More room if they buried them standing. Sitting or kneeling you couldn't. Standing? His head might come up some day above ground in a landslip with his hand pointing. All honeycombed the ground must be: oblong cells. And very neat he keeps it too, trim grass and edgings. His garden Major Gamble calls Mount Jerome. Well so it is. Ought to be flowers of sleep. Chinese cemeteries with giant poppies growing produce the best opium Mastiansky told me. The Botanic Gardens are just over there. It's the blood sinking in the earth gives new life. Same idea those jews they said killed the christian boy. Every man his price. Well preserved fat corpse gentleman, epicure, invaluable for fruit garden. A bargain. By carcass of William Wilkinson, auditor and accountant, lately deceased, three pounds thirteen and six. With thanks.

Ulysses, 1922

LYTTON STRACHEY

The End of General Gordon

THE DETAILS of what passed within Khartoum during the last weeks of the siege are unknown to us. In the diary of Bordeini Bey, a Levantine merchant, we catch a few glimpses of the final stages of the catastrophe – of the starving populace, the exhausted garrison, the fluctuations of despair and hope, the dauntless energy of the Governor-General. Still he worked on, indefatigably, apportioning provisions, collecting ammunition, consulting with the townspeople, encouraging the soldiers. His hair had suddenly turned quite white. Late one evening, Bordeini Bey went to visit him in the palace, which was being bombarded by the Mahdi's cannon. The high building, brilliantly lighted up, afforded an excellent mark. As the shot came whistling round the windows, the merchant suggested that it would be advisable to stop them up with boxes full of sand. Upon this, Gordon Pasha became enraged. 'He called up the guard, and gave them orders to shoot me if I moved; he then brought a very large lantern which would hold twenty-four candles. He and I then put the candles into the sockets, placed the lantern on the table in front of the window, lit the candles, and then sat down at the table. The Pasha then said, "When God was portioning out fear to all the people in the world, at last it came to my turn, and there was no fear left to give me. Go, tell all the people in Khartoum that Gordon fears nothing, for God has created him without fear."'

On 5 January, Omdurman, a village on the opposite bank of the Nile, which had hitherto been occupied by the besieged, was taken by the Arabs. The town was now closely surrounded, and every chance of obtaining fresh supplies was cut off. The famine became terrible; dogs, donkeys, skins, gum, palm fibre, were devoured by the desperate inhabitants. The soldiers stood on the fortifications like pieces of wood. Hundreds died of hunger daily:

their corpses filled the streets; and the survivors had not the strength to bury the dead. On the 20th, the news of the battle of Abu Klea reached Khartoum. The English were coming at last. Hope rose; every morning the Governor-General assured the townspeople that one day more would see the end of their sufferings; and night after night his words were proved untrue.

On the 23rd, a rumour spread that a spy had arrived with letters, and that the English army was at hand. A merchant found a piece of newspaper lying in the road, in which it was stated that the strength of the relieving forces was 15,000 men. For a moment, hope flickered up again, only to relapse once more. The rumour, the letters, the printed paper, all had been contrivances of Gordon to inspire the garrison with the courage to hold out. On the 25th, it was obvious that the Arabs were preparing an attack, and a deputation of the principal inhabitants waited upon the Governor-General. But he refused to see them; Bordeini Bey was alone admitted to his presence. He was sitting on a divan, and, as Bordeini Bey came into the room, he snatched the fez from his head and flung it from him. 'What more can I say?' he exclaimed, in a voice such as the merchant had never heard before. 'The people will no longer believe me. I have told them over and over again that help would be here, but it has never come, and now they must see I tell them lies. I can do nothing more. Go, and collect all the people you can on the lines, and make a good stand. Now leave me to smoke these cigarettes.' Bordeini Bey knew then, he tells us, that Gordon Pasha was in despair. He left the room, having looked upon the Governor-General for the last time.

When the English force reached Metemmah, the Mahdi, who had originally intended to reduce Khartoum to surrender through starvation, decided to attempt its capture by assault. The receding Nile had left one portion of the town's circumference undefended: as the river withdrew, the rampart had crumbled; a broad expanse of mud was left between the wall and the water, and the soldiers, overcome by hunger and the lassitude of hopelessness, had trusted to the morass to protect them, and neglected to repair the breach.

Early on the morning of the 26th, the Arabs crossed the river at this point. The mud, partially dried up, presented no obstacle; nor did the ruined fortification, feebly manned by some half-dying troops. Resistance was futile, and it was scarcely offered: the Mahdi's army swarmed into Khartoum. Gordon had long debated with himself what his action should be at the supreme moment. 'I shall never (DV),' he had told Sir Evelyn Baring, 'be taken alive.' He had had gunpowder put into the cellars of the palace, so that the whole building might, at a moment's notice, be blown into the air. But then misgivings had come upon him; was it not his duty 'to maintain the faith, and, if necessary, to suffer for it'? – to remain a tortured and humiliated witness of his Lord in the Mahdi's chains? The blowing up of the palace would have, he thought, 'more or less the taint of suicide', would be, 'in a way, taking things out of God's hands'. He remained undecided; and meanwhile, to be ready for every contingency, he kept one of his little armoured vessels close at hand on the river, with steam up, day and night, to transport him, if so he should decide, southward, through the enemy, to the recesses of Equatoria. The sudden appearance of the Arabs, the complete collapse of the defence, saved him the necessity of making up his mind. He had been on the roof, in his dressing-gown, when the attack began; and he had only time to hurry to his bedroom, to slip on a white uniform, and to seize up a sword and a revolver, before the foremost of the assailants were in the palace. The crowd was led by four of the fiercest of the Mahdi's followers – tall and swarthy Dervishes, splendid in their many-coloured *jibbehs*, their great swords drawn from the scabbards of brass and velvet, their spears flourishing above their heads. Gordon met them at the top of the staircase. For a moment, there was a deathly pause, while he stood in silence, surveying his antagonists. Then it is said that Taha Shahin, the Dongolawi, cried in a loud voice, 'Mala' oun el yom yomek!' (O cursèd one, your time is come), and plunged his spear into the Englishman's body. His only reply was a gesture of contempt. Another spear transfixed him; he fell, and the swords of the three other Dervishes instantly hacked him to death. Thus, if we are to believe the

official chroniclers, in the dignity of unresisting disdain,
General Gordon met his end. But it is only fitting that the
last moments of one whose whole life was passed in contradiction should be involved in mystery and doubt. Other
witnesses told a very different story. The man whom they
saw die was not a saint but a warrior. With intrepidity, with
skill, with desperation, he flew at his enemies. When his
pistol was exhausted, he fought on with his sword; he forced
his way almost to the bottom of the staircase; and, among a
heap of corpses, only succumbed at length to the sheer
weight of the multitudes against him.

That morning, while Slatin Pasha was sitting in his chains
in the camp at Omdurman, he saw a group of Arabs
approaching, one of whom was carrying something wrapped
up in a cloth. As the group passed him, they stopped for a
moment, and railed at him in savage mockery. Then the
cloth was lifted, and he saw before him Gordon's head. The
trophy was taken to the Mahdi: at last the two fanatics had
indeed met face to face. The Mahdi ordered the head to be
fixed between the branches of a tree in the public highway,
and all who passed threw stones at it. The hawks of the
desert swept and circled about it – those very hawks which
the blue eyes had so often watched.

Eminent Victorians, 1918

THOMAS STEARNS ELIOT

[Tradition]

No POET, no artist of any art, has his complete meaning
alone. His significance, his appreciation is the appreciation of his relation to the dead poets and artists. You
cannot value him alone; you must set him, for contrast and
comparison, among the dead. I mean this as a principle
of aesthetic, not merely historical, criticism. The necessity
that he shall conform, that he shall cohere, is not onesided;

what happens when a new work of art is created is something
that happens simultaneously to all the works of art which
preceded it. The existing monuments form an ideal order
among themselves, which is modified by the introduction
of the new (the really new) work of art among them. The
existing order is complete before the new work arrives;
for order to persist after the supervention of novelty, the
whole existing order must be, if ever so slightly, altered; and
so the relations, proportions, values of each work of art
toward the whole are readjusted; and this is conformity
between the old and the new. Whoever has approved this
idea of order, of the form of European, of English literature,
will not find it preposterous that the past should be altered
by the present as much as the present is directed by the
past. And the poet who is aware of this will be aware of
great difficulties and responsibilities.

In a peculiar sense he will be aware also that he must
inevitably be judged by the standards of the past. I say
judged, not amputated, by them; not judged to be as good
as, or worse or better than, the dead; and certainly not
judged by the canons of dead critics. It is a judgement, a
comparison, in which two things are measured by each
other. To conform merely would be for the new work not
really to conform at all; it would not be new, and would
therefore not be a work of art. And we do not quite say that
the new is more valuable because it fits in; but its fitting in
is a test of its value – a test, it is true, which can only be
slowly and cautiously applied, for we are none of us infallible judges of conformity. We say: it appears to conform,
and is perhaps individual, or it appears individual, and may
conform; but we are hardly likely to find that it is one and
not the other.

To proceed to a more intelligible exposition of the relation
of the poet to the past: he can neither take the past as a
lump, an indiscriminate bolus, nor can he form himself
wholly on one or two private admirations, nor can he form
himself wholly upon one preferred period. The first course
is inadmissible, the second is an important experience of
youth, and the third is a pleasant and highly desirable

supplement. The poet must be very conscious of the main current, which does not at all flow invariably through the most distinguished reputations. He must be quite aware of the obvious fact that art never improves, but that the material of art is never quite the same. He must be aware that the mind of Europe – the mind of his own country – a mind which he learns in time to be much more important than his own private mind – is a mind which changes, and that this change is a development which abandons nothing *en route*, which does not superannuate either Shakespeare, or Homer, or the rock drawing of the Magdalenian draughtsmen. That this development, refinement perhaps, complication certainly, is not, from the point of view of the artist, any improvement. Perhaps not even an improvement from the point of view of the psychologist or not to the extent which we imagine; perhaps only in the end based upon a complication in economics and machinery. But the difference between the present and the past is that the conscious present is an awareness of the past in a way and to an extent which the past's awareness of itself cannot show.

Someone said: 'The dead writers are remote from us because we *know* so much more than they did.' Precisely, and they are that which we know.

I am alive to a usual objection to what is clearly part of my programme for the *métier* of poetry. The objection is that the doctrine requires a ridiculous amount of erudition (pedantry), a claim which can be rejected by appeal to the lives of poets in any pantheon. It will even be affirmed that much learning deadens or perverts poetic sensibility. While, however, we persist in believing that a poet ought to know as much as will not encroach upon his necessary receptivity and necessary laziness, it is not desirable to confine knowledge to whatever can be put into a useful shape for examinations, drawing-rooms, or the still more pretentious modes of publicity. Some can absorb knowledge, the more tardy must sweat for it. Shakespeare acquired more essential history from Plutarch than most men could from the whole British Museum. What is to be insisted upon is that the poet must develop or procure the consciousness of the past and that he should continue to develop this consciousness throughout his career.

What happens is a continual surrender of himself as he is at the moment to something which is more valuable. The progress of an artist is a continual self-sacrifice, a continual extinction of personality.

'Tradition and the Individual Talent', 1919

WILLIAM SOMERSET MAUGHAM

[The Missionary]

'HOW DARE she come here!' cried Davidson indignantly. 'I'm not going to allow it.'

He strode towards the door.

'What are you going to do?' asked Macphail.

'What do you expect me to do? I'm going to stop it. I'm not going to have this house turned into – into. . . .'

He sought for a word that should not offend the ladies' ears. His eyes were flashing and his pale face was paler still in his emotion.

'It sounds as though there were three or four men down there,' said the doctor. 'Don't you think it's rather rash to go in just now?'

The missionary gave him a contemptuous look and without a word flung out of the room.

'You know Mr Davidson very little if you think the fear of personal danger can stop him in the performance of his duty,' said his wife.

She sat with her hands nervously clasped, a spot of colour on her high cheek-bones, listening to what was about to happen below. They all listened. They heard him clatter down the wooden stairs and throw open the door. The singing stopped suddenly, but the gramophone continued to bray out its vulgar tune. They heard Davidson's voice and then the noise of something heavy falling. The music stopped. He had hurled the gramophone on the floor. Then again they heard Davidson's voice, they could not make out the words, then Miss Thompson's, loud and shrill, then a confused clamour as though several people were shouting together at the top of their lungs. Mrs Davidson gave a little gasp, and she clenched her hands more tightly. Dr Macphail looked uncertainly from her to his wife. He did not want to go down, but he wondered if they expected him to. Then there was something that sounded like a scuffle. The noise now was more distinct. It might be that Davidson was being thrown out of the room. The door was slammed. There was a moment's silence and they heard Davidson come up the stairs again. He went to his room.

'I think I'll go to him,' said Mrs Davidson.

She got up and went out.

'If you want me, just call,' said Mrs Macphail, and then when the other was gone: 'I hope he isn't hurt.'

'Why couldn't he mind his own business?' said Dr Macphail.

They sat in silence for a minute or two and then they both started, for the gramophone began to play once more, defiantly, and mocking voices shouted hoarsely the words of an obscene song.

Next day Mrs Davidson was pale and tired. She complained of headache, and she looked old and wizened. She told Mrs Macphail that the missionary had not slept at all; he had passed the night in a state of frightful agitation and at five had got up and gone out. A glass of beer had been thrown over him and his clothes were stained and stinking. But a sombre fire glowed in Mrs Davidson's eyes when she spoke of Miss Thompson.

'She'll bitterly rue the day when she flouted Mr Davidson,' she said. 'Mr Davidson has a wonderful heart and no one who is in trouble has ever gone to him without being comforted, but he has no mercy for sin, and when his righteous wrath is excited he's terrible.'

'Why, what will he do?' asked Mrs Macphail.

'I don't know, but I wouldn't stand in that creature's shoes for anything in the world.'

Mrs Macphail shuddered. There was something positively alarming in the triumphant assurance of the little woman's manner. They were going out together that morning, and they went down the stairs side by side. Miss Thompson's door was open, and they saw her in a bedraggled dressing-gown, cooking something in a chafing-dish.

'Good morning,' she called. 'Is Mr Davidson better this morning?'

They passed her in silence, with their noses in the air, as if she did not exist. They flushed, however, when she burst into a shout of derisive laughter. Mrs Davidson turned on her suddenly.

'Don't you dare to speak to me,' she screamed. 'If you insult me I shall have you turned out of here.'

'Say, did I ask Mr Davidson to visit with me?'

'Don't answer her,' whispered Mrs Macphail hurriedly.

They walked on till they were out of earshot.

'She's brazen, brazen,' burst from Mrs Davidson.

Her anger almost suffocated her.

And on their way home they met her strolling towards the quay. She had all her finery on. Her great white hat with its vulgar, showy flowers was an affront. She called out cheerily to them as she went by, and a couple of American sailors who were standing there grinned as the ladies set their faces to an icy stare. They got in just before the rain began to fall again.

'I guess she'll get her fine clothes spoilt,' said Mrs Davidson with a bitter sneer.

Davidson did not come in till they were half-way through dinner. He was wet through, but he would not change. He sat, morose and silent, refusing to eat more than a mouthful, and he stared at the slanting rain. When Mrs Davidson told him of their two encounters with Miss Thompson he did not answer. His deepening frown alone showed that he had heard.

'Don't you think we ought to make Mr Horn turn her out

of here?' asked Mrs Davidson. 'We can't allow her to insult us.'

'There doesn't seem to be any other place for her to go,' said Macphail.

'She can live with one of the natives.'

'In weather like this a native hut must be a rather uncomfortable place to live in.'

'I lived in one for years,' said the missionary.

When the little native girl brought in the fried bananas which formed the sweet they had every day, Davidson turned to her.

'Ask Miss Thompson when it would be convenient for me to see her,' he said.

The girl nodded shyly and went out.

'What do you want to see her for, Alfred?' asked his wife.

'It's my duty to see her. I won't act till I've given her every chance.'

'You don't know what she is. She'll insult you.'

'Let her insult me. Let her spit on me. She has an immortal soul, and I must do all that is in my power to save it.'

Mrs Davidson's ears rang still with the harlot's mocking laughter.

'She's gone too far.'

'Too far for the mercy of God?' His eyes lit up suddenly and his voice grew mellow and soft. 'Never. The sinner may be deeper in sin than the depth of hell itself, but the love of the Lord Jesus can reach him still.'

The girl came back with the message.

'Miss Thompson's compliments and as long as the Rev. Davidson don't come in business hours she'll be glad to see him any time.'

The party received it in stony silence, and Dr Macphail quickly effaced from his lips the smile which had come upon them. He knew his wife would be vexed with him if he found Miss Thompson's effrontery amusing.

They finished the meal in silence. When it was over the two ladies got up and took their work. Mrs Macphail was making another of the innumerable comforters which she had turned out since the beginning of the war, and the doctor lit his pipe. But Davidson remained in his chair and with abstracted eyes stared at the table. At last he got up and without a word went out of the room. They heard him go down and they heard Miss Thompson's defiant 'Come in' when he knocked at the door. He remained with her for an hour. And Dr Macphail watched the rain. It was beginning to get on his nerves. It was not like our soft English rain that drops gently on the earth; it was unmerciful and some-how terrible; you felt in it the malignancy of the primitive powers of nature. It did not pour, it flowed. It was like a deluge from heaven, and it rattled on the roof of corrugated iron with a steady persistence that was maddening. It seemed to have a fury of its own. And sometimes you felt that you must scream if it did not stop, and then suddenly you felt powerless, as though your bones had suddenly become soft; and you were miserable and hopeless.

Macphail turned his head when the missionary came back. The two women looked up.

'I've given her every chance. I have exhorted her to repent. She is an evil woman.'

He paused, and Dr Macphail saw his eyes darken and his pale face grow hard and stern.

'Now I shall take the whips with which the Lord Jesus drove the usurers and the money changers out of the Temple of the Most High.'

He walked up and down the room. His mouth was close set, and his black brows were furrowing.

'If she fled to the uttermost parts of the earth I should pursue her.'

With a sudden movement he turned round and strode out of the room. They heard him go downstairs again.

'What is he going to do?' asked Mrs Macphail.

'I don't know.' Mrs Davidson took off her pince-nez and wiped them. 'When he is on the Lord's work I never ask him questions.'

'Rain', 1920

THOMAS EDWARD LAWRENCE

[An Execution]

A T LAST we camped, and when the camels were unloaded and driven out to pasture, I lay down under the rocks and rested. My body was very sore with headache and high fever, the accompaniments of a sharp attack of dysentery which had troubled me along the march and had laid me out twice that day in short fainting fits, when the more difficult parts of the climb had asked too much of my strength. Dysentery of this Arabian coast sort used to fall like a hammer blow, and crush its victims for a few hours, after which the extreme effects passed off; but it left men curiously tired, and subject for some weeks to sudden breaks of nerve.

My followers had been quarrelling all day; and while I was lying near the rocks a shot was fired. I paid no attention; for there were hares and birds in the valley; but a little later Suleiman roused me and made me follow him across the valley to an opposite bay in the rocks, where one of the Ageyl, a Boreida man, was lying stone dead with a bullet through his temples. The shot must have been fired from close by; because the skin was burnt about one wound. The remaining Ageyl were running frantically about; and when I asked what it was Ali, their head man, said that Hamed the Moor had done the murder. I suspected Suleiman, because of the feud between the Atban and Ageyl which had burned up in Yenbo and Wejh; but Ali assured me that Suleiman had been with him three hundred yards further up the valley gathering sticks when the shot was fired. I sent all out to search for Hamed, and crawled back to the baggage, feeling that it need not have happened this day of all days when I was in pain.

As I lay there I heard a rustle, and opened my eyes slowly upon Hamed's back as he stooped over his saddle-bags, which lay just beyond my rock. I covered him with a pistol and then spoke. He had put down his rifle to lift the gear; and was at my mercy till the others came. We held a court at once; and after a while Hamed confessed that, he and Salem having had words, he had seen red and shot him suddenly. Our inquiry ended. The Ageyl, as relatives of the dead man, demanded blood for blood. The others supported them; and I tried vainly to talk the gentle Ali round. My head was aching with fever and I could not think; but hardly even in health, with all eloquence, could I have begged Hamed off; for Salem had been a friendly fellow and his sudden murder a wanton crime.

Then rose up the horror which would make civilized man shun justice like a plague if he had not the needy to serve him as hangmen for wages. There were other Moroccans in our army; and to let the Ageyl kill one in feud meant reprisals by which our unity would have been endangered. It must be a formal execution, and at last, desperately, I told Hamed that he must die for punishment, and laid the burden of his killing on myself. Perhaps they would count me not qualified for feud. At least no revenge could lie against my followers; for I was a stranger and kinless.

I made him enter a narrow gully of the spur, a dank twilight place overgrown with woods. Its sandy bed had been pitted by trickles of water down the cliffs in the late rain. At the end it shrank to a crack a few inches wide. The walls were vertical. I stood in the entrance and gave him a few moments' delay which he spent crying on the ground. Then I made him rise and shot him through the chest. He fell down on the weeds shrieking, with the blood coming out in spurts over his clothes, and jerked about till he rolled nearly to where I was. I fired again, but was shaking so that I only broke his wrist. He went on calling out, less loudly, now lying on his back with his feet towards me, and I leant forward and shot him for the last time in the thick of his neck under the jaw. His body shivered a little, and I called the Ageyl; who buried him in the gully where he was. Afterwards the wakeful night dragged over me, till, hours before dawn, I had the men up and made them load, in my longing to be set free of Wadi Kitan. They had to lift me into the saddle.

Seven Pillars of Wisdom, 1926

VIRGINIA WOOLF

[Mrs Ramsay]

No, she thought, putting together some of the pictures he had cut out – a refrigerator, a mowing machine, a gentleman in evening dress – children never forget. For this reason, it was so important what one said, and what one did, and it was a relief when they went to bed. For now she need not think about anybody. She could be herself, by herself. And that was what now she often felt the need of – to think; well not even to think. To be silent; to be alone. All the being and the doing, expansive, glittering, vocal, evaporated; and one shrunk, with a sense of solemnity, to being oneself, a wedge-shaped core of darkness, something invisible to others. Although she continued to knit, and sat upright, it was thus that she felt herself; and this self having shed its attachments was free for the strangest adventures. When life sank down for a moment, the range of experience seemed limitless. And to everybody there was always this sense of unlimited resources, she supposed; one after another, she, Lily, Augustus Carmichael, must feel, our apparitions, the things you know us by, are simply childish. Beneath it is all dark, it is all spreading, it is unfathomably deep; but now and again we rise to the surface and that is what you see us by. Her horizon seemed to her limitless. There were all the places she had not seen; the Indian plains; she felt herself pushing aside the thick leather curtain of a church in Rome. This core of darkness could go anywhere, for no one saw it. They could not stop it, she thought, exulting. There was freedom, there was peace, there was, most welcome of all, a summoning together, a resting on a platform of stability. Not as oneself did one find rest ever, in her experience (she accomplished here something dexterous with her needles), but as a wedge of darkness. Losing personality, one lost the fret, the hurry, the stir; and there rose to her lips always some exclamation of triumph over life when things came together in this peace, this rest, this eternity; and pausing there she looked out to meet that stroke of the Lighthouse, the long steady stroke, the last of the three, which was her stroke, for watching them in this mood always at this hour one could not help attaching oneself to one thing especially of the things one saw; and this thing, the long steady stroke, was her stroke. Often she found herself sitting and looking, sitting and looking, with her work in her hands until she became the thing she looked at – that light for example. And it would lift up on it some little phrase or other which had been lying in her mind like that – 'Children don't forget, children don't forget' – which she would repeat and begin adding to it, It will end, It will end, she said. It will come, it will come, when suddenly she added, We are in the hands of the Lord.

But instantly she was annoyed with herself for saying that. Who had said it? not she; she had been trapped into saying something she did not mean. She looked up over her knitting and met the third stroke and it seemed to her like her own eyes meeting her own eyes, searching as she alone could search into her mind and her heart, purifying out of existence that lie, any lie. She praised herself in praising the light, without vanity, for she was stern, she was searching, she was beautiful like that light. It was odd, she thought, how if one was alone, one leant to things, inanimate things; trees, streams, flowers; felt they expressed one; felt they became one; felt they knew one, in a sense were one; felt an irrational tenderness thus (she looked at that long steady light) as for oneself. There rose, and she looked and looked with her needles suspended, there curled up off the floor of the mind, rose from the lake of one's being, a mist, a bride to meet her lover.

What brought her to say that: 'We are in the hands of the Lord?' she wondered. The insincerity slipping in among the

truths roused her, annoyed her. She returned to her knitting
again. How could any Lord have made this world? she
asked. With her mind she had always seized the fact that
there is no reason, order, justice: but suffering, death, the
poor. There was no treachery too base for the world to
commit; she knew that. No happiness lasted; she knew that.
She knitted with firm composure, slightly pursing her lips
and, without being aware of it, so stiffened and composed
the lines of her face in a habit of sternness that when her
husband passed, though he was chuckling at the thought
that Hume, the philosopher, grown enormously fat, had
stuck in a bog, he could not help noting, as he passed, the
sternness at the heart of her beauty. It saddened him, and
her remoteness pained him, and he felt, as he passed, that
he could not protect her, and, when he reached the hedge,
he was sad. He could do nothing to help her. He must stand
by and watch her. Indeed, the infernal truth was, he made
things worse for her. He was irritable – he was touchy. He
had lost his temper over the Lighthouse. He looked into the
hedge, into its intricacy, its darkness.

Always, Mrs Ramsay felt, one helped oneself out of
solitude reluctantly by laying hold of some little odd or end,
some sound, some sight. She listened, but it was all very
still; cricket was over; the children were in their baths; there
was only the sound of the sea. She stopped knitting; she
held the long reddish-brown stocking dangling in her hands
a moment. She saw the light again. With some irony in her
interrogation, for when one woke at all, one's relations
changed, she looked at the steady light, the pitiless, the
remorseless, which was so much her, yet so little her, which
had her at its beck and call (she woke in the night and saw
it bent across their bed, stroking the floor), but for all that
she thought, watching it with fascination, hypnotised, as if
it were stroking with its silver fingers some sealed vessel in
her brain whose bursting would flood her with delight, she
had known happiness, exquisite happiness, intense happiness, and it silvered the rough waves a little more brightly,
as daylight faded, and the blue went out of the sea and it
rolled in waves of pure lemon which curved and swelled and
broke upon the beach and the ecstasy burst in her eyes and

waves of pure delight raced over the floor of her mind and she felt, It is enough! It is enough!

He turned and saw her. Ah! She was lovely, lovelier now than ever he thought. But he could not speak to her. He could not interrupt her. He wanted urgently to speak to her now that James was gone and she was alone at last. But he resolved, no; he would not interrupt her. She was aloof from him now in her beauty, in her sadness. He would let her be, and he passed her without a word, though it hurt him that she should look so distant, and he could not reach her, he could do nothing to help her. And again he would have passed her without a word had she not, at that very moment, given him of her own free will what she knew he would never ask, and called to him and taken the green shawl off the picture frame, and gone to him. For he wished, she knew, to protect her.

To the Lighthouse, 1927

EDMUND BLUNDEN

[The Storm]

THE BRITISH barrage opened. The air gushed in hot surges along that river valley, and uproar never imagined by me swung from ridge to ridge. The east was scarlet with dawn and the flickering gunflashes; I thanked God I was not in the assault, and joined the subdued carriers nervously lighting cigarettes in one of the cellars, sitting there on the steps, studying my watch. The ruins of Hamel were crashing chaotically with German shells, and jags of iron and broken wood and brick whizzed past the cellar mouth. When I gave the word to move, it was obeyed with no pretence of enthusiasm. I was forced to shout and swear, and the carrying party, some with shoulders hunched, as if in a snowstorm, dully picked up their bomb buckets and went ahead. The wreckage around seemed leaping with flame. Never had we smelt high explosive so thick and foul, and there was no distinguishing one shell-burst from another, save by the black or tawny smoke that suddenly appeared in the general miasma. We walked along the river road, passed the sandbag dressing-station that had been built only a night or two earlier where the front line crossed the road, and had already been battered in; we entered No Man's Land, but we could make very little sense of ourselves or the battle. There were wounded Highlanders trailing down the road. They had been in the marshes of the Ancre, trying to take a machine-gun post called Summer House. Ahead, the German front line could not be clearly seen, the water-mist and the smoke veiling it; and this was lucky for the carrying party. Halfway between the trenches, I wished them good luck, and pointing out the place where they should, according to plan, hand over the bombs, I left them in charge of their own officer, returning myself, as my orders were, to my colonel. I passed good men of ours, in our front line, staring like men in a trance across No Man's Land, their powers of action apparently suspended.

'What's happening over there?' asked Harrison, with a face all doubt and stress, when I crawled into the candled, overcrowded frowsiness of Kentish Caves. I could not say. 'What's happening the other side of the river?' All was in ominous discommunication. A runner called Gosden presently came in, with bleeding breast, bearing a message written an hour or more earlier. It did not promise well, and, as the hours passed, all that could be made out was that our attacking companies were 'hanging on', some of them in the German third trench, where they could not at all be reached by the others, dug in between the first and the second. Lintott wrote message after message, trying to share information north, east and west. Harrison, the sweat standing on his forehead, thought out what to do in this deadlock, and repeatedly telephoned to the guns and the general. Wounded men and messengers began to crowd the scanty passages of the Caves, and curt roars of explosion just outside announced that these dugouts, shared by ourselves and the Black Watch, were now to be dealt with. Death soon arrived there, among the group at the clumsy entrance. Harrison meanwhile called for his runner, fastened the chin-strap of his steel helmet, and pushed his way out into the top trenches to see what he could; returned presently, with that kind of severe laugh which tells the tale of a man who has incredibly escaped from the barrage. The day was hot outside, glaring mercilessly upon the burned, choked chalk trenches. I came in again to the squeaking field telephones and obscure candlelight. Presently Harrison, a message in his hand, said: 'Rabbit, they're short of ammunition. Get round and collect all the fellows you can and take them over – and stay over there and do what you can.' I felt my heart thud at this; went out, naming my men among headquarters 'odds and ends' wherever I could find them squatted under the chalk banks, noting with pleasure that my nearest dump had not been blown up and would answer our requirements; I served out bombs and ammunition, then thrust my head in again to report that I was starting, when he delayed, and presently cancelled, the enterprise. The shells on our breathless neighbourhood seemed to fall more quickly, and the dreadful spirit of waste and impotence sank into us, when a sudden report from an artillery observer warned us that there were Germans in our front trench. In that case Kentish Caves was a death-trap, a hole in which bombs would be bursting within a moment; yet here at last was something definite, and we all seemed to come to life, and prepared with our revolvers to try our luck.

The artillery observer must have made some mistake. Time passed without bombs among us or other surprise, the collapse of the attack was wearily obvious. The bronze noon was more quiet but not less deadly than the morning. I went round the scarcely passable hillside trenches, but they were amazingly lonely: suddenly a sergeant-major and half a dozen men bounded superhumanly, gasping and excited, over the parapets. They had been lying in No Man's Land, and at last had decided to 'chance their arm' and dodge the machine-guns which had been perseveringly trying to get them. They drank pints of water, of which I had luckily a little store in a dugout there, now wrecked and gaping. I left them sitting wordless in that store. The singular part of the battle was that no one, not even these, could say what had happened, or what was happening. One vaguely understood that the waves had found their manoeuvre in No Man's Land too complicated; that the Germans' supposed derelict forward trench near the railway was joined by tunnels to their main defence, and enabled them to come up behind our men's backs; that they had used the bayonet where challenged, with the boldest readiness; 'used the whole dam lot, minnies, snipers, rifle-grenades, artillery'; that machine-guns from the Thiepval ridge south of the river were flaying all the crossings of No Man's Land. 'Don't seem as if the 49th Div. got any further.' But the general effect was the disappearance of the attack into mystery.

Orders for withdrawal were sent out to our little groups in the German lines towards the end of the afternoon. How the runners got there, they alone could explain, if any survived. The remaining few of the battalion in our own positions were collected in the trench along Hamel village street, and a sad gathering it was. Some who had been in the waves contrived to rejoin us now. How much more fortunate we seemed than those who were still in the German labyrinth awaiting the cover of darkness for their small chance of life! And yet, as we filed out, up Jacob's Ladder, we were warned by low-bursting shrapnel not to anticipate. Mesnil was its vile self, but we passed at length. Not much was said, then or afterwards, about those who would never again pass that hated target; among the killed were my old company commanders Penruddock and North-coate (after a great display of coolness and endurance) – laughing French, quiet Hood, and many more. The Cheshires took over the front line, which the enemy might at one moment have occupied without difficulty; but neither they nor our own patrols succeeded in bringing in more than two or three of the wounded; and, the weather turning damp, the Germans increased their difficulty in the darkness and distorted battlefield with a rain of gas shells.

Undertones of War, 1928

SIEGFRIED SASSOON

[An Assault]

W<small>E WENT</small> along the trench which was less than waist deep. The Germans had evidently been digging when we attacked, and had left their packs and other equipment ranged along the reverse edge of the trench. I stared about me; the smoke-drifted twilight was alive with intense movement, and there was a wild strangeness in the scene which somehow excited me. Our men seemed a bit out of hand and I couldn't see any of the responsible NCOs; some of the troops were firing excitedly at the Wood; others were rummaging in the German packs. Fernby said that we were being sniped from the trees on both sides. Mametz Wood was a menacing wall of gloom, and now an outburst of rapid thudding explosions began from that direction. There was a sap from the Quadrangle to the Wood, and along this the Germans were bombing. In all this confusion I formed the obvious notion that we ought to be deepening the trench. Daylight would be on us at once, and we were along a slope exposed to enfilade fire from the Wood. I told Fernby to make the men dig for all they were worth, and went to the right with Kendle. The Germans had left a lot of shovels, but we were making no use of them. Two tough-looking privates were disputing the ownership of a pair of field-glasses, so I pulled out my pistol and urged them, with ferocious objurations, to chuck all that fooling and dig. I seemed to be getting pretty handy with my pistol, I thought, for the conditions in Quadrangle Trench were giving me a sort of angry impetus. In some places it was only a foot deep, and already men were lying wounded and killed by sniping. There were high-booted German bodies, too, and in the blear beginning of daylight they seemed as much the victims of a catastrophe as the men who had attacked them. As I stepped over one of the Germans an impulse made me lift him up from the miserable ditch. Propped against the bank, his blond face was undisfigured, except by the mud which I wiped from his eyes and mouth with my coat sleeve. He'd evidently been killed while digging, for his tunic was knotted loosely about his shoulders. He didn't look to be more than eighteen. Hoisting him a little higher, I thought what a gentle face he had, and remembered that this was the first time I'd ever touched one of our enemies with my hands. Perhaps I had some dim sense of the futility which had put an end to this good-looking youth. Anyhow I hadn't expected the Battle of the Somme to be quite like this. . . . Kendle, who had been trying to do something for a badly wounded man, now rejoined me, and we continued, mostly on all fours, along the dwindling trench. We passed no one until we came to a bombing post – three serious-minded men who said that no one had been further than that yet. Being in an exploring frame of mind, I took a bag of bombs and crawled another sixty or seventy yards with Kendle close behind me. The trench became a shallow groove and ended where the ground overlooked a little valley along which there was a light railway line. We stared across at the Wood. From the other side of the valley came an occasional rifle-shot, and a helmet bobbed up for a moment. Kendle remarked that from that point anyone could see into the whole of our trench on the slope behind us. I said we must have our strong-post here and told him to go back for the bombers and a Lewis gun. I felt adventurous and it seemed as if Kendle and I were having great fun together. Kendle thought so too. The helmet bobbed up again. 'I'll just have a shot at him,' he said, wriggling away from the crumbling bank which gave us cover. At this moment Fernby appeared with two men and a Lewis gun. Kendle was half kneeling against some broken ground; I remember seeing him push his tin hat back from his forehead and then raise himself a few inches to take aim. After firing once he looked at us with a lively smile; a second later he fell sideways. A blotchy mark showed where the bullet had hit him just above the eyes.

The circumstances being what they were, I had no justification for feeling either shocked or astonished by the sudden extinction of Lance-Corporal Kendle. But after blank awareness that he was killed, all feelings tightened and contracted to a single intention – to 'settle that sniper' on the other side of the valley. If I had stopped to think, I shouldn't have gone at all. As it was, I discarded my tin hat and equipment, slung a bag of bombs across my shoulder, abruptly informed Fernby that I was going to find out who *was* there, and set off at a downhill double. While I was running I pulled the safety-pin out of a Mills' bomb; my right hand being loaded, I did the same for my left. I mention this because I was obliged to extract the second safety-pin with my teeth, and the grating sensation reminded me that I was half way across and not so reckless as I had been when I started. I was even a little out of breath as I trotted up the opposite slope and threw my two bombs. Then I rushed at the bank, vaguely expecting some sort of scuffle with my imagined enemy. I had lost my temper with the man who had shot Kendle; quite unexpectedly, I found myself looking down into a well-conducted trench with a great many Germans in it. Fortunately for me, they were already retreating. It had not occurred to them that they were being attacked by a single fool; and Fernby, with presence of mind which probably saved me, had covered my advance by traversing the top of the trench with his Lewis gun. I slung a few more bombs, but they fell short of the clumsy field-grey figures, some of whom half turned to fire their rifles over their left shoulder as they ran across the open toward the wood, while a crowd of jostling helmets vanished along the trench. Idiotically elated, I stood there with my finger in my right ear and emitted a series of 'view-holloas' (a gesture which ought to win the approval of people who still regard war as a form of outdoor sport). Having thus failed to commit suicide, I proceeded to occupy the trench – that is to say, I sat down on the fire-step, very much out of breath, and hoped to God the Germans wouldn't come back again.

The trench was deep and roomy, with a fine view of our men in the Quadrangle, but I had no idea what to do now I had got possession of it. The word 'consolidation' passed through my mind; but I couldn't consolidate by myself. Naturally, I didn't under-estimate the magnitude of my achievement in capturing the trench on which the Royal

Irish had made a frontal attack in the dark. Nevertheless, although still unable to see that my success was only a lucky accident, I felt a bit queer in my solitude, so I reinforced my courage by counting the sets of equipment which had been left behind. There were between forty and fifty packs, tidily arranged in a row – a fact which I often mentioned (quite casually) when describing my exploit afterwards. There was the doorway of a dug-out, but I only peered in at it, feeling safer above ground. Then, with apprehensive caution, I explored about half way to the Wood without finding any dead bodies. Apparently no one was any the worse for my little bombing demonstration. Perhaps I was disappointed by this, though the discovery of a dead or wounded enemy might have caused a revival of humane emotion. Returning to the sniping post at the end of the trench I meditated for a few minutes, somewhat like a boy who has caught a fish too big to carry home (if such an improbable event has ever happened). Finally I took a deep breath and ran headlong back by the way I'd come.

Little Fernby's anxious face awaited me, and I flopped down beside him with an outburst of hysterical laughter.

Memoirs of an Infantry Officer, 1930

SIR WINSTON CHURCHILL

[A Classical Education]

THE FATEFUL day arrived. My mother took me to the station in a hansom cab. She gave me three half-crowns, which I dropped on to the floor of the cab, and we had to scramble about in the straw to find them again. We only just caught the train. If we had missed it, it would have been the end of the world. However, we didn't, and the world went on.

The school my parents had selected for my education was one of the most fashionable and expensive in the country. It modelled itself upon Eton and aimed at being preparatory for that Public School above all others. It was supposed to be the very last thing in schools. Only ten boys in a class; electric light (then a wonder); a swimming pond; spacious football and cricket grounds; two or three school treats, or 'expeditions' as they were called, every term; the masters all MAs in gowns and mortar-boards; a chapel of its own; no hampers allowed; everything provided by the authorities. It was a dark November afternoon when we arrived at this establishment. We had tea with the Headmaster, with whom my mother conversed in the most easy manner. I was preoccupied with the fear of spilling my cup and so making 'a bad start'. I was also miserable at the idea of being left alone among all these strangers in this great, fierce, formidable place. After all I was only seven, and I had been so happy in my nursery with all my toys. I had such wonderful toys: a real steam engine, a magic lantern, and a collection of soldiers already nearly a thousand strong. Now it was to be all lessons. Seven or eight hours of lessons every day except half-holidays, and football or cricket in addition.

When the last sound of my mother's departing wheels had died away, the Headmaster invited me to hand over any money I had in my possession. I produced my three half-crowns, which were duly entered in a book, and I was told that from time to time there would be a 'shop' at the school with all sorts of things which one would like to have, and that I could choose what I liked up to a limit of the seven and sixpence. Then we quitted the Headmaster's parlour and the comfortable private side of the house, and entered the more bleak apartments reserved for the instruction and accommodation of the pupils. I was taken into a Form Room and told to sit at a desk. All the other boys were out of doors, and I was alone with the Form Master. He produced a thin greeny-brown covered book filled with words in different types of print.

'You have never done any Latin before, have you?' he said.

'No, sir.'

'This is a Latin grammar.' He opened it at a well-thumbed page. 'You must learn this,' he said, pointing to a number of words in a frame of lines. 'I will come back in half an hour and see what you know.'

Behold me then on a gloomy evening, with an aching heart, seated in front of the First Declension.

Mensa	a table
Mensa	O table
Mensam	a table
Mensae	of a table
Mensae	to or for a table
Mensa	by, with or from a table

What on earth did it mean? Where was the sense in it? It seemed absolute rigmarole to me. However, there was one thing I could always do: I could learn by heart. And I thereupon proceeded, as far as my private sorrows would allow, to memorize the acrostic-looking task which had been set me.

In due course the Master returned.

'Have you learnt it?' he asked.

'I think I can *say* it, sir,' I replied; and I gabbled it off.

He seemed so satisfied with this that I was emboldened to ask a question.

'What does it mean, sir?'

'It means what it says. Mensa, a table. Mensa is a noun of the First Declension. There are five declensions. You have learnt the singular of the First Declension.'

'But', I repeated, 'what does it mean?'

'Mensa means a table,' he answered.

'Then why does mensa also mean O table,' I enquired, 'and what does O table mean?'

'Mensa, O table, is the vocative case,' he replied.

'But why O table?' I persisted in genuine curiosity.

'O table – you would use that in addressing a table, in invoking a table.' And then seeing he was not carrying me with him, 'You would use it in speaking to a table.'

'But I never do,' I blurted out in honest amazement.

'If you are impertinent, you will be punished, and punished, let me tell you, very severely,' was his conclusive rejoinder.

Such was my first introduction to the classics from which,

I have been told, many of our cleverest men have derived so much solace and profit.

My Early Life, 1930

STELLA GIBBONS

[Porridge]

IN THE large kitchen, which occupied most of the middle of the house, a sullen fire burned, the smoke of which wavered up the blackened walls and over the deal table, darkened by age and dirt, which was roughly set for a meal. A snood full of coarse porridge hung over the fire, and standing with one arm resting upon the high mantel, looking moodily down into the heaving contents of the snood, was a tall young man whose riding-boots were splashed with mud to the thigh, and whose coarse linen shirt was open to his waist. The firelight lit up his diaphragm muscles as they heaved slowly in rough rhythm with the porridge.

He looked up as Judith entered, and gave a short, defiant laugh, but said nothing. Judith crossed slowly over until she stood by his side. She was as tall as he. They stood in silence, she staring at him, and he down into the secret crevasses of the porridge.

'Well, mother mine,' he said at last, 'here I am, you see. I said I would be in time for breakfast, and I have kept my word.'

His voice had a low, throaty, animal quality, a sneering warmth that wound a velvet ribbon of sexuality over the outward coarseness of the man.

Judith's breath came in long shudders. She thrust her arms deeper into her shawl. The porridge gave an ominous leering heave; it might almost have been endowed with life, so uncannily did its movements keep pace with the human passions that throbbed above it.

'Cur,' said Judith, levelly, at last. 'Coward! Liar! Libertine! Who were you with last night? Moll at the mill or Violet at the vicarage? Or Ivy, perhaps, at the ironmongery? Seth – my son . . .' Her deep, dry voice quivered, but she whipped it back, and her next words flew out at him like a lash.

'Do you want to break my heart?'

'Yes,' said Seth, with an elemental simplicity.

The porridge boiled over.

Judith knelt, and hastily and absently ladled it off the floor back into the snood, biting back her tears. While she was thus engaged, there was a confused blur of voices and boots in the yard outside. The men were coming in to breakfast.

The meal for the men was set on a long trestle at the farther end of the kitchen, as far away from the fire as possible. They came into the room in awkward little clumps, eleven of them. Five were distant cousins of the Stark-adders, and two others were half-brothers of Amos, Judith's husband. This left only four men who were not in some way connected with the family; so it will readily be understood that the general feeling among the farm-hands was not exactly one of hilarity. Mark Dolour, one of the four, had been heard to remark: 'Happen it had been another kind o' eleven, us might ha' had a cricket team, wi' me for umpire. As ut is, 'twould be more befittin' if we was to hire oursen out for carrying coffins at sixpence a mile.'

The five half-cousins and the two half-brothers came over to the table, for they took their meals with the family. Amos liked to have his kith about him, though, of course, he never said so or cheered up when they were.

A strong family likeness wavered in and out of the fierce, earth-reddened faces of the seven, like a capricious light. Micah Starkadder, mightiest of the cousins, was a ruined giant of a man, paralysed in one knee and wrist. His nephew, Urk, was a little, red, hard-bitten man with foxy ears. Urk's brother, Ezra, was of the same physical type, but horsy where Urk was foxy. Caraway, a silent man, wind-shaven and lean, with long wandering fingers, had some of Seth's animal grace, and this had been passed on to his son, Harkaway, a young, silent, nervous man given to bursts of fury about very little, when you came to sift matters.

Amos's half-brothers, Luke and Mark, were thickly built and high-featured; gross, silent men with an eye to the bed and the board.

When all were seated two shadows darkened the sharp, cold light pouring in through the door. They were no more than a growing imminence of humanity, but the porridge boiled over again.

Amos Starkadder and his eldest son, Reuben, came into the kitchen.

Amos, who was even larger and more of a wreck than Micah, silently put his pruning-snoot and reaping-hook in a corner by the fender, while Reuben put the scranlet with which he had been ploughing down beside them.

The two men took their places in silence, and after Amos had muttered a long and fervent grace, the meal was eaten in silence. Seth sat moodily tying and untying a green scarf round the magnificent throat he had inherited from Judith; he did not touch his porridge, and Judith only made a pretence of eating hers, playing with her spoon, patting the porridge up and down and idly building castles with the burnt bits. Her eyes burned under their penthouses, sometimes straying towards Seth as he sat sprawling in the lusty pride of casual manhood, with a good many buttons and tapes undone. Then those same eyes, dark as prisoned king-cobras, would slide round until they rested upon the bitter white head and raddled red neck of Amos, her husband, and then, like praying mantises, they would retreat between their lids. Secrecy pouted her full mouth.

Suddenly Amos, looking up from his food, asked abruptly:

'Where's Elfine?'

'She is not up yet. I did not wake her. She hinders more than she helps o' mornings,' replied Judith.

Amos grunted.

''Tes a godless habit to lie abed of a working day, and the reeking red pits of the Lord's eternal wrathy fires lie in wait for them as do so. Aye' – his blue blazing eyes swivelled round and rested upon Seth, who was stealthily looking at a packet of Parisian art pictures under the table – 'aye, and for those who break the seventh commandment, too. And for those' – the eye rested on Reuben, who was hopefully studying his parent's apoplectic countenance – 'for those as waits for dead men's shoes.'

'Nay, Amos, lad—' remonstrated Micah, heavily.

'Hold your peace,' thundered Amos; and Micah, though a fierce tremor rushed through his mighty form, held it.

When the meal was done the hands trooped out to get on with the day's work of harvesting the swedes. This harvest was now in full swing; it took a long time and was very difficult to do. The Starkadders, too, rose and went out into the thin rain which had begun to fall. They were engaged in digging a well beside the dairy; it had been started a year ago, but it was taking a long time to do because things kept on going wrong. Once – a terrible day, when Nature seemed to hold her breath, and release it again in a furious gale of wind – Harkaway had fallen into it. Once Urk had pushed Caraway down it. Still, it was nearly finished; and everybody felt that it would not be long now.

In the middle of the morning a wire came from London announcing that the expected visitor would arrive by the six o'clock train.

Judith received it alone. Long after she had read it she stood motionless, the rain driving through the open door against her crimson shawl. Then slowly, with dragging steps, she mounted the staircase which led to the upper part of the house. Over her shoulder she said to old Adam, who had come into the room to do the washing up:

'Robert Poste's child will be here by the six o'clock train at Beershorn. You must leave to meet it at five. I am going up to tell Mrs Starkadder that she is coming today.'

Adam did not reply, and Seth, sitting by the fire, was growing tired of looking at his postcards, which were a three-year-old gift from the vicar's son, with whom he occasionally went poaching. He knew them all by now. Meriam, the hired girl, would not be in until after dinner. When she came, she would avoid his eyes, and tremble and weep.

He laughed insolently, triumphantly. Undoing another

button of his shirt, he lounged out across the yard to the
shed where Big Business, the bull, was imprisoned in
darkness.

Laughing softly, Seth struck the door of the shed.

And as though answering the deep call of male to male,
the bull uttered a loud tortured bellow that rose undefeated
through the dead sky that brooded over the farm.

Seth undid yet another button, and lounged away.

Cold Comfort Farm, 1932

ALDOUS HUXLEY

[Feelies]

THE SCENT organ was playing a delightfully refreshing
Herbal Capriccio – rippling arpeggios of thyme and
lavender, of rosemary, basil, myrtle, tarragon; a series of
daring modulations through the spice keys into ambergris;
and a slow return through sandalwood, camphor, cedar and
new-mown hay (with occasional subtle touches of discord –
a whiff of kidney pudding, the faintest suspicion of pig's
dung) back to the simple aromatics with which the piece
began. The final blast of thyme died away; there was a
round of applause; the lights went up. In the synthetic music
machine the sound-track roll began to unwind. It was a trio
for hyper-violin, super-'cello and oboe-surrogate that now
filled the air with its agreeable languor. Thirty or forty bars
– and then, against this instrumental background, a much
more than human voice began to warble; now throaty, now
from the head, now hollow as a flute, now charged with
yearning harmonics, it effortlessly passed from Gaspard
Forster's low record on the very frontiers of musical tone to
a trilled bat-note high above the highest C to which (in 1770,
at the Ducal opera of Parma, and to the astonishment of
Mozart) Lucrezia Ajugari, alone of all the singers in history,
once piercingly gave utterance.

Sunk in their pneumatic stalls, Lenina and the Savage sniffed and listened. It was now the turn also for eyes and skin.

The house lights went down; fiery letters stood out solid and as though self-supported in the darkness. THREE WEEKS IN A HELICOPTER. AN ALL-SUPER-SINGING, SYNTHETIC-TALKING, COLOURED, STEREOSCOPIC FEELY. WITH SYNCHRONIZED SCENT-ORGAN ACCOMPANIMENT.

'Take hold of those metal knobs on the arms of your chair,' whispered Lenina. 'Otherwise you won't get any of the feely effects.'

The Savage did as he was told.

Those fiery letters, meanwhile, had disappeared; there were ten seconds of complete darkness; then suddenly, dazzling and incomparably more solid-looking than they would have seemed in actual flesh and blood, far more real than reality, there stood the stereoscopic images, locked in one another's arms, of a gigantic negro and a golden-haired young brachycephalic Beta-Plus female.

The Savage started. That sensation on his lips! He lifted a hand to his mouth; the titillation ceased; let his hand fall back on the metal knob; it began again. The scent organ, meanwhile, breathed pure musk. Expiringly, a sound-track super-dove cooed, 'Oo-ooh'; and vibrating only thirty-two times a second, a deeper than African bass made answer: 'Aa-aah.' 'Ooh-ah! Ooh-ah!' the stereoscopic lips came together again, and once more the facial erogenous zones of six thousand spectators in the Alhambra tingled with almost intolerable galvanic pleasure. 'Ooh . . .'

The plot of the film was extremely simple. A few minutes after the first Ooh's and Aah's (a duet having been sung and a little love made on that famous bearskin, every hair of which – the Assistant Predestinator was perfectly right – could be separately and distinctly felt), the negro had a helicopter accident, fell on his head. Thump! what a twinge through the forehead! A chorus of *ow's* and *aie's* went up from the audience.

The concussion knocked all the negro's conditioning into a cocked hat. He developed for the Beta blonde an exclusive and maniacal passion. She protested. He persisted. There were struggles, pursuits, an assault on a rival, finally a sensational kidnapping. The Beta blonde was ravished away into the sky and kept there, hovering, for three weeks in a wildly anti-social *tête-à-tête* with the black madman. Finally, after a whole series of adventures and much aerial acrobacy, three handsome young Alphas succeeded in rescuing her. The negro was packed off to an Adult Re-conditioning Centre and the film ended happily and decorously, with the Beta blonde becoming the mistress of all her three rescuers. They interrupted themselves for a moment to sing a synthetic quartet, with full super-orchestral accompaniment and gardenias on the scent organ. Then the bearskin made a final appearance and, amid a blare of sexophones, the last stereoscopic kiss faded into darkness, the last electric titillation died on the lips like a dying moth that quivers, quivers, ever more feebly, ever more faintly, and at last is quite, quite still.

But for Lenina the moth did not completely die. Even after the lights had gone up, while they were shuffling slowly along with the crowd towards the lifts, its ghost still fluttered against her lips, still traced fine shuddering roads of anxiety and pleasure across her skin. Her cheeks were flushed, her eyes dewily bright, her breath came deeply. She caught hold of the Savage's arm and pressed it, limp, against her side. He looked down at her for a moment, pale, pained, desiring, and ashamed of his desire. He was not worthy, not . . . Their eyes for a moment met. What treasures hers promised! A queen's ransom of temperament. Hastily he looked away, disengaged his imprisoned arm. He was obscurely terrified lest she should cease to be something he could feel himself unworthy of.

'I don't think you ought to see things like that,' he said, making haste to transfer from Lenina herself to the surrounding circumstances the blame for any past or possible future lapse from perfection.

'Things like what, John?'

'Like this horrible film.'

'Horrible?' Lenina was genuinely astonished. 'But I thought it was lovely.'

'It was base,' he said indignantly, 'it was ignoble.'

She shook her head. 'I don't know what you mean.' Why was he so queer? Why did he go out of his way to spoil things?

In the taxicopter he hardly even looked at her. Bound by strong vows that had never been pronounced, obedient to laws that had long since ceased to run, he sat averted and in silence. Sometimes, as though a finger had plucked at some taut, almost breaking string, his whole body would shake with a sudden nervous start.

The taxicopter landed on the roof of Lenina's apartment house. 'At last,' she thought exultantly as she stepped out of the cab. At last – even though he *had* been so queer just now. Standing under a lamp, she peered into her hand-mirror. At last. Yes, her nose *was* a bit shiny. She shook the loose powder from her puff. While he was paying off the taxi – there would just be time. She rubbed at the shininess, thinking: 'He's terribly good-looking. No need for him to be shy like Bernard. And yet . . . Any other man would have done it long ago. Well, now at last.' That fragment of a face in the little round mirror suddenly smiled at her.

'Good-night,' said a strangled voice behind her. Lenina wheeled round. He was standing in the doorway of the cab, his eyes fixed, staring; had evidently been staring all this time while she was powdering her nose, waiting – but what for? or hesitating, trying to make up his mind, and all the time thinking, thinking – she could not imagine what extraordinary thoughts. 'Good-night, Lenina,' he repeated, and made a strange grimacing attempt to smile.

'But, John . . . I thought you were . . . I mean, aren't you . . .?'

He shut the door and bent forward to say something to the driver. The cab shot up into the air.

Looking down through the window in the floor, the Savage could see Lenina's upturned face, pale in the bluish light of the lamps. The mouth was open, she was calling. Her foreshortened figure rushed away from him; the diminishing square of the roof seemed to be falling through the darkness.

Five minutes later he was back in his room. From its hiding-place he took out his mouse-nibbled volume, turned with religious care its stained and crumpled pages, and began to read *Othello*. Othello, he remembered, was like the hero of *Three Weeks in a Helicopter* – a black man.

Drying her eyes, Lenina walked across the roof to the lift. On her way down to the twenty-seventh floor she pulled out her *soma* bottle. One gramme, she decided, would not be enough; hers had been more than a one-gramme affliction. But if she took two grammes, she ran the risk of not waking up in time tomorrow morning. She compromised and, into her cupped left palm, shook out three half-gramme tablets.

Brave New World, 1932

JOHN BOYNTON PRIESTLEY

[Tyneside during the Depression]

THERE IS no escape anywhere in Jarrow from its prevailing misery, for it is entirely a working-class town. One little street may be rather more wretched than another, but to the outsider they all look alike. One out of every two shops appeared to be permanently closed. Wherever we went there were men hanging about, not scores of them but hundreds and thousands of them. The whole town looked as if it had entered a perpetual penniless bleak Sabbath. The men wore the drawn masks of prisoners of war. A stranger from a distant civilisation, observing the condition of the place and its people, would have arrived at once at the conclusion that Jarrow had deeply offended some celestial emperor of the island and was now being punished. He would never believe us if we told him that in theory this town was as good as any other and that its inhabitants were not criminals but citizens with votes. The only cheerful sight I saw there was a game of Follow-my-leader that was being played by seven small children. But what leader can the rest of them follow?

After a glimpse of the river-front, that is, of tumble-down

sheds, rotting piles, coal dust and mud, we landed in Hebburn, where we pursued, in vain, another man we wanted. Hebburn is another completely working-class town. It is built on the same mean proletarian scale as Jarrow. It appeared to be even poorer than its neighbour. You felt that there was nothing in the whole place worth a five-pound note. It looked as much like an ordinary town of that size as a dust-bin looks like a drawing-room. Here again, idle men – and not unemployable casual labourers but skilled men – hung about the streets, waiting for Doomsday. Nothing, it seemed, would ever happen here again. Yet oddly enough a great deal is happening here; more, in some directions, than has ever happened before. Its Council of Social Service possesses a particularly energetic secretary, and in this stranded hulk of a town there are courses on history and economics (an ironic course, this) and literature, an orchestra and ladies' and children's choirs, two girls' clubs for handicrafts, gymnasium classes, a camping and rambling club, and play centres for children. It is possible that Hebburn is coming nearer to civilisation in its poverty than it ever did in its prosperity. Probably these cultural activities are breeding a generation that would not tolerate the old Hebburn, even though it offered them work and wages again. If this should be true, then at least in one direction there has been a gain. But consider the gigantic loss. It is not merely that two-thirds of the town is living on the edge of destitution, tightening its belt another hole every month or two, but that its self-respect is vanishing – for these are *working* towns and nothing else – and that it sees the sky for ever darkening over it. We went down to the social centre, which after some difficulty we found in a couple of huts by the side of a derelict shipyard. A little gnome-like man, grandly proud of everything, showed us round. There were places for carpentering and cobbling, a tattered library, and a newly finished hut for their twopenny whist drives and dances. (I had an odd feeling all the time that I was looking at a camp just behind the front line in some strange new war.) This centre possesses a boat of its own that has already achieved some fame, and our gnome-like friend offered to go down to the water's edge, where it

was moored, to show it to us. To get there we had to cross
the derelict shipyard, which was a fantastic wilderness of
decaying sheds, strange mounds and pits, rusted iron, old
concrete and new grass. Both my companions knew about
this yard, which had been a spectacular failure in which over
a million of money had been lost. They had queer stories to
tell of corruption in this and other yards, of lorry-loads of
valuable material that were driven in at one gate and signed
for, and then quietly driven out at another gate, of jobs so
blatantly rushed, for show purposes, that in the last weeks
wooden pegs were being used in place of steel rivets. As we
came to the sullen water-front, we could hear the noise of
the electric riveting from the few yards working across the
river; but both of them agreed that it seemed quiet now
compared with the deafening din of the riveters in the old
days. There was one ship in the yards now where there used
to be twenty. Down the Tyne we could see the idle ships
lying up, a melancholy and familiar sight now in every
estuary round the coast. There is hardly anything that brings
you more sharply into line with the idiotic muddle of our
times than the spectacle of these fine big steamers rusting
away in rows. We have these vessels doing nothing; we have
coal for their bunkers; our ports are filled with ships' officers
and men out of work; we have goods that other people
need, and across every stretch of ocean are goods that we
need; and still the ships are there, chained and empty,
rusting in the rain, groaning in idleness night and day. But
one boat is not idle on that river. That is the one we looked
at now, as she creaked at her moorings. She was an old
ship's boat and as she was in poor shape, she was bought for
the social centre for four pounds. The men themselves
patched her up. She carries a sail and ten men usually go
out in her, working three lines. The fish they bring back –
and they have had some good catches, though the Tyne
estuary is no Dogger Bank – is not sold but distributed
among the unemployed men's families. She is called the
Venture, and a better name could not be found for her. I do
not know that anywhere on this journey I saw anything
more moving and more significant than that old patched
boat, which hung for years from the davits of a liner but is

now the workless men's *Venture*, creeping out with the tide
to find a few fish. The effort she represents is something
more than a brave gesture, though it is that all right. It
means that these men, who were once part of our elaborate
industrial machinery but have now been cast out by it, are
starting all over again, far away from the great machine, at
the very beginning, out at sea with a line and a hook. And
it will not do. These are not simple fishermen any more than
this island of ours is one of the South Sea islands. They are
skilled children of our industrial system, artisans and men
with trades in their fingers, and every time they go out and
fumble frozenly with their lines and hooks, they declare
once again the miserable bankruptcy of that system. This
Venture may be their pride, but it is our shame.

English Journey, 1934

ROBERT GRAVES

[The Reluctant Emperor]

WHAT HAD happened was this. Caligula had come out
of the theatre. A sedan was waiting to take him the
long way round to the New Palace between double ranks of
Guards. But Vinicius said: 'Let's go by the short cut. The
Greek boys are waiting there at the entrance, I believe.'
'All right, then, come along,' said Caligula. The people
tried to follow him out but Asprenas dropped behind and
forced them back. 'The Emperor doesn't want to be
bothered with you,' he said. 'Get back!' He told the
gatekeepers to close the gates again.

Caligula went towards the covered passage. Cassius
stepped forward and saluted. 'The watchword, Caesar?'

Caligula said, 'Eh? O yes, the watchword, Cassius. I'll
give you a nice one today – "Old Man's Petticoat".'

The Tiger called from behind Caligula, 'Shall I?' It was
the agreed signal.

'*Do so!*' bellowed Cassius, drawing his sword, and striking at Caligula with all his strength.

He had intended to split his skull to the chin, but in his rage he missed his aim and struck him between the neck and the shoulders. The upper breastbone took the chief force of the blow. Caligula was staggered with pain and astonishment. He looked wildly around him, turned and ran. As he turned Cassius struck at him again, severing his jaw. The Tiger then felled him with a badly aimed blow on the side of his head. He slowly rose to his knees. 'Strike again!' Cassius shouted.

Caligula looked up to Heaven with a face of agony. 'O Jove,' he prayed.

'Granted,' shouted The Tiger, and hacked off one of his hands.

A captain called Aquila gave the finishing stroke, a deep thrust in the groin, but ten more swords were plunged into his breast and belly afterwards, just to make sure of him. A captain called Bubo dipped his hand in a wound in Caligula's side and then licked his fingers, shrieking, 'I swore to drink his blood!'

A crowd had collected and the alarm went around, 'The Germans are coming.' The assassins had no chance against a whole battalion of Germans. They rushed into the nearest building, which happened to be my old home, lately borrowed from me by Caligula as guest-apartments for foreign ambassadors whom he did not want to have about in the Palace. They went in at the front door and out at the back door. All got away in time but The Tiger and Asprenas. The Tiger had to pretend that he was not one of the assassins and joined the Germans in their cries for vengeance. Asprenas ran into the covered passage, where the Germans caught him and killed him. They killed two other senators whom they happened to meet. This was only a small party of Germans. The rest of the battalion marched into the theatre and closed the gate behind them. They were going to avenge their murdered hero by a wholesale massacre. That was the roar and screaming I had heard. Nobody in the theatre knew that Caligula was dead or that any attempt had been made against his life. But it was quite clear what the Germans intended because they were going through that curious performance of patting and stroking their assegais and speaking to them as if they were human beings, which is their invariable custom before shedding blood with those terrible weapons. There was no escape. Suddenly from the stage the trumpet blew the Attention, followed by the six notes which mean Imperial Orders. Mnester entered and raised his hand. And at once the terrible din died down into mere sobs and smothered groans, for when Mnester appeared on the stage it was a rule that nobody should utter the least sound on pain of instant death. The Germans too stopped their patting and stroking and incantations. The Imperial Orders stiffened them into statues.

Mnester shouted: 'He's not dead, Citizens. Far from it. The assassins set on him and beat him to his knees, so! But he presently rose again, so! Swords cannot prevail against our Divine Caesar. Wounded and bloody as he was, he rose, so! He lifted his august head and walked, so! with divine stride through the ranks of his cowardly and baffled assassins. His wounds healed, a miracle! He is now in the Market Place loudly and eloquently haranguing his subjects from the Oration Platform.'

A mighty cheer arose and the Germans sheathed their swords and marched out. Mnester's timely lie (prompted, as a matter of fact, by a message from Herod Agrippa, King of the Jews, the only man in Rome who kept his wits about him that fateful afternoon) had saved sixty thousand lives or more.

But the real news had by now reached the Palace, where it caused the most utter confusion. A few old soldiers thought that the opportunity for looting was too good to be missed. They would pretend to be looking for the assassins. Every room in the Palace had a golden door-knob, each worth six months' pay, easy enough to hack off with a sharp sword. I heard the cries, 'Kill them, kill them! Avenge Caesar!' and hid behind a curtain. Two soldiers came in. They saw my feet under the curtain. 'Come out of there, assassin. No use hiding from us.'

I came out and fell on my face. 'Don't k-k-k-k-kill me, Lords,' I said. 'I had n-nothing to d-d-d-d-do with it.'

'Who's this old gentleman?' asked one of the soldiers who was new at the Palace. 'He doesn't look dangerous.'

'Why! Don't you know? He's Germanicus's invalid brother. A decent old stick. No harm in him at all. Get up, sir. We won't hurt you.' This soldier's name was Gratus.

They made me follow them downstairs again into the banqueting-hall where the sergeants and corporals were holding a council-of-war. A young sergeant stood on a table waving his arms and shouting, 'Republic be hanged! A new Emperor's our only hope. Any Emperor so long as we can persuade the Germans to accept him.'

'Incitatus,' someone suggested, guffawing.

'Yes, by God! Better the old nag than no Emperor at all. We want someone immediately, to keep the Germans quiet. Otherwise they'll run amok.'

My two captors pushed their way through the crowd dragging me behind them. Gratus called out, 'Hey, Sergeant! Look whom we have here! A bit of luck, I think. It's old Claudius. What's wrong with old Claudius for Emperor? The best man for the job in Rome, though he do limp and stammer a bit.'

Loud cheers, laughter, and cries of 'Long live the Emperor Claudius!' The Sergeant apologized. 'Why, sir, we all thought you were dead. But you're our man, all right. Push him up, lads, where we can all see him!' Two burly corporals caught me by the legs and hoisted me on their shoulders. 'Long live the Emperor Claudius!'

'Put me down,' I cried furiously. 'Put me down! I don't want to be Emperor. I refuse to be Emperor. Long live the Republic!'

But they only laughed. 'That's a good one. He doesn't want to be Emperor, he says. Modest, eh?'

'Give me a sword,' I shouted. 'I'll kill myself sooner.'

Messalina came hurrying towards us. 'For my sake, Claudius, do what they ask of you. For our child's sake! We'll all be murdered if you refuse. They've killed Caesonia already. And they took her little girl by the feet and bashed out her brains against a wall.'

'You'll be all right, sir, once you get accustomed to it,'

Gratus said, grinning. 'It's not such a bad life, an Emperor's isn't.'

I made no more protests. What was the use of struggling against Fate? They hurried me out into the Great Court, singing the foolish hymn of hope composed at Caligula's accession, *Germanicus is come Again, To Free the City from her Pain.* For I had the surname Germanicus too. They forced me to put on Caligula's golden oak-leaf chaplet, recovered from one of the looters. To steady myself I had to cling tightly to the corporals' shoulders. The chaplet kept slipping over one ear. How foolish I felt. They say that I looked like a criminal being haled away to execution. Massed trumpeters blew the Imperial Salute.

The Germans came steaming towards us. They had just heard for certain of Caligula's death, from a senator who came to meet them in deep mourning. They were furious at having been tricked and wanted to go back to the theatre, but the theatre was empty now, so they were at a loss what to do next. There was nobody about to take vengeance on except the Guards, and the Guards were armed. The Imperial Salute decided them. They rushed forward shouting: 'Hoch! Hoch! Long live the Emperor Claudius!' and began frantically dedicating their assegais to my service and struggling to break through the crowd of Guardsmen to kiss my feet. I called to them to keep back, and they obeyed, prostrating themselves before me. I was carried round and round the Court.

And what thoughts or memories, would you guess, were passing through my mind on this extraordinary occasion? Was I thinking of the Sybil's prophecy, of the omen of the wolf-cub, of Pollio's advice, or of Briseis's dream? Of my grandfather and liberty? Of my father and liberty? Of my three Imperial predecessors, Augustus, Tiberius, Caligula, their lives and deaths? Of the great danger I was still in from the conspirators, and from the Senate, and from the Guards battalions at the Camp? Of Messalina and our unborn child? Of my grandmother Livia and my promise to deify her if ever I became Emperor? Of Postumus and Germanicus? Of Agrippina and Nero? Of Camilla? No, you would never guess what was passing through my mind. But I shall be frank and tell you what it was, though the confession is a shameful one. I was thinking, 'So, I'm Emperor, am I? What nonsense! But at least I'll be able to make people read my books now. Public recitals to large audiences. And good books too, thirty-five years' hard work in them. It won't be unfair. Pollio used to get attentive audiences by giving expensive dinners. He was a very sound historian, and the last of Romans. My *History of Carthage* is full of amusing anecdotes. I'm sure they'll enjoy it.'

I, Claudius, 1934

DAVID JONES

[On Parade]

'49 Wyatt, 01549 Wyatt.
   Coming sergeant.
   Pick 'em up, pick 'em up – I'll stalk within yer chamber.
   Private Leg . . . sick.
   Private Ball . . . absent.
   '01 Ball, '01 Ball, Ball of No. 1.
   Where's Ball, 25201 Ball – you corporal,
   Ball of your section.
   Movement round and about the Commanding Officer.
   Bugler, will you sound 'Orderly Sergeants'.
   A hurrying of feet from three companies converging on the little group apart where on horses sit the central command. But from 'B' Company there is no such darting out. The Orderly Sergeant of 'B' is licking the stub end of his lead pencil; it divides a little his fairish moist moustache.
   Heavily jolting and sideway jostling, the noise of liquid shaken in a small vessel by a regular jogging movement, a certain clinking ending in a shuffling of the feet sidelong – all clear and distinct in that silence peculiar to parade grounds and to refectories. The silence of a high order, full

of peril in the breaking of it, like the coming on parade of John Ball.

He settles between numbers 4 and 5 of the rear rank. It is as ineffectual as the ostrich in her sand. Captain Gwynn does not turn or move or give any sign.

Have that man's name taken if you please, Mr Jenkins.

Take that man's name, Sergeant Snell.

Take his name, corporal.

Take his name take his number – charge him – late on parade – the Battalion being paraded for overseas – warn him for Company Office.

Have you got his name Corporal Quilter.

Temporary unpaid Lance-Corporal Aneirin Merddyn Lewis had somewhere in his Welsh depths a remembrance of the nature of man, of how a lance-corporal's stripe is but held vicariously and from on high, is of one texture with an eternal economy. He brings in a manner, baptism, and metaphysical order to the bankruptcy of the occasion.

'01 Ball is it – there was a man in Bethesda late for the last bloody judgment.

Corporal Quilter on the other hand knew nothing of these things.

Private Ball's pack, ill adjusted and without form, hangs more heavily on his shoulder blades, a sense of ill-usage pervades him. He withdraws within himself to soothe himself – the inequity of those in high places is forgotten. From where he stood heavily, irksomely at ease, he could see, half-left between 7 and 8 of the front rank, the profile of Mr Jenkins and the elegant cut of his wartime rig and his flax head held front; like San Romano's foreground squire, unhelmeted; but we don't have lances now nor banners nor trumpets. It pains the lips to think of bugles – and did they blow Defaulters on the Uccello horns.

He put his right hand behind him to ease his pack, his cold knuckles find something metallic and colder.

No mess-tin cover.

Shining sanded mess-tin giving back the cold early light. *Improperly dressed, the Battalion being paraded for overseas.* His imaginings as to the precise relationship of this general indictment from the book to his own naked mess-tin were with suddenness and most imperatively impinged upon, as when an animal hunted, stopping in some ill-chosen covert to consider the wickedness of man, is started into fresh effort by the cry and breath of dogs dangerously and newly near. For the chief huntsman is winding his horn, the officer commanding is calling his Battalion by name – whose own the sheep are.

55th Battalion!

Fifty-fifth Bat-tal-i-on

'talion!!

From 'D' to 'A' his eyes knew that parade. He detected no movement. They were properly at ease.

Reverberation of that sudden command broke hollowly upon the emptied huts behind 'D' Company's rear platoons. They had only in them the rolled mattresses, the neatly piled bed-boards and the empty tea-buckets of the orderly-men, emptied of their last gun-fire.

Stirrups taut and pressing upward in the midst of his saddle he continues the ritual words by virtue of which a regiment is moved in column of route:

. . . the Battalion will move in column of fours to the right – 'A' Company – 'A' Company leading.

Words lost, yet given continuity by that thinner command from in front of No. 1. Itself to be wholly swallowed up by the concerted movement of arms in which the spoken word effected what it signified.

'A' Company came to the slope, their files of four turn right. The complex of command and heel-iron turned confuse the morning air. The rigid structure of their lines knows a swift mobility, patterns differently for those sharp successive cries.

Mr P. D. I. Jenkins who is twenty years old has now to do his business:

No. 7 Platoon – number seven,

number seven – right – by the right.

How they sway in the swing round for all this multiplicity of gear.

Keept'y'r dressing.

Sergeant Snell did his bit.

Corporal Quilter intones:

Dress to the right – no – other right.
Keep those slopes.
Keep those sections of four.
Pick those knees up.
Throw those chests out.
Hold those heads up.
Stop that talking.
Keep those chins in.
Left left lef' – lef' righ' lef' – you Private Ball it's you I've got me glad-eye on.

In Parenthesis, 1937

GRAHAM GREENE

[A Sense of Responsibility]

'WHO ARE you?' Rose implored her. 'Why do you interfere with us? You're not the police.'

'I'm like everyone else. I want justice,' the woman cheerfully remarked, as if she were ordering a pound of tea. Her big prosperous carnal face hung itself with smiles. She said, 'I want to see *you're* safe.'

'I don't want any help,' Rose said.

'You ought to go home.'

Rose clenched her hands in defence of the brass bed, the ewer of dusty water: 'This is home.'

'It's no good your getting angry, dear,' the woman continued. 'I'm not going to lose my temper with you again, it's not your fault. You don't understand how things are. Why, you poor little thing, I pity you,' and she advanced across the linoleum as if she intended to take Rose in her arms.

Rose backed against the bed, 'You keep your distance.'

'Now don't get agitated, dear. It won't help. You see – I'm determined.'

'I don't know what you mean. Why can't you talk straight?'

'There's things I've got to break – gently.'

'Keep away from me. Or I'll scream.'

The woman stopped. 'Now let's talk sensible, dear. I'm here for your own good. You got to be saved. Why—' she seemed for a moment at a loss for words. She said in a hushed voice, 'Your life's in danger.'

'You go away if that's all—'

'All,' the woman was shocked. 'What do you mean, all?' Then she laughed resolutely. 'Why, dear, for a moment you had me rattled. All, indeed. It's enough, isn't it? I'm not joking now. If you don't know it, you got to know it. There's nothing he wouldn't stop at.'

'Well?' Rose said, giving nothing away.

The woman whispered softly across the few feet between them, 'He's a murderer.'

'Do you think I don't know *that*?' Rose said.

'God's sake,' the woman said, 'do you mean—'

'There's nothing *you* can tell me.'

'You crazy little fool – to marry him knowing that. I got a good mind to let you be.'

'I won't complain,' Rose said.

The woman hooked on another smile, as you hook on a wreath. 'I'm not going to lose my temper, dear. Why, if I let you be, I wouldn't sleep at nights. It wouldn't be Right. Listen to me; maybe you don't know what happened. I got it all figured out. They took Fred down under the parade, into one of those little shops and strangled him – least they would have strangled him, but his heart gave out first.' She said in an awestruck voice, 'They strangled a dead man,' then added sharply, 'you aren't listening.'

'I know it all,' Rose lied. She was thinking hard – she was remembering Pinkie's warning – 'Don't get mixed up.' She thought wildly and vaguely: he did his best for me; I got to help him now. She watched the woman closely; she would never forget that plump, good-natured, ageing face: it stared out at her like an idiot's from the ruins of a bombed home. She said, 'Well, if you think that's how it was, why don't you go to the police?'

'Now you're talking sense,' the woman said. 'I only want to make things clear. This is the way it is, dear. There's a certain person I've paid money to who's told me things. And there's things I've figured out for myself. But that person – he won't give evidence. For reasons. And you need a lot of evidence – seeing how the doctors made it natural death. Now if you—'

'Why don't you give it up?' Rose said. 'It's over and done, isn't it? Why not let us all be?'

'It wouldn't be right. Besides – he's dangerous. Look what happened here the other day. You don't tell *me* that was an accident.'

'You haven't thought, have you,' Rose said, 'why he did it? You don't kill a man for no reason.'

'Well, why did he?'

'I don't know.'

'Ask him.'

'I don't need to know.'

'You think he's in love with you,' the woman said, 'he's not.'

'He married me.'

'And why? because they can't make a wife give evidence. You're just a witness like that other man was. My dear,' she again tried to close the gap between them, 'I only want to save you. He'd kill *you* as soon as look at you if he thought he wasn't safe.'

With her back to the bed Rose watched her approach. She let her put her large cool pastry-making hands upon her shoulders. 'People change,' she said.

'Oh, no they don't. Look at me. I've never changed. It's like those sticks of rock: bite it all the way down, you'll still read Brighton. That's human nature.' She breathed mournfully over Rose's face – a sweet and winey breath.

'Confession . . . repentance,' Rose whispered.

'That's just religion,' the woman said. 'Believe me, it's the world we got to deal with.' She went pat pat on Rose's shoulder, her breath whistling in her throat. 'You pack a bag and come away with me. I'll look after you. You won't have any cause to fear.'

'Pinkie . . .'

'I'll look after Pinkie.'

Rose said, 'I'll do anything – anything you want . . .'

'That's the way to talk, dear.'

'If you'll let us alone.'

The woman backed away. A momentary look of fury was hung up among the wreaths discordantly. 'Obstinate,' she said. 'If I was your mother . . . a good hiding.' The bony and determined face stared back at her: all the fight there was in the world lay there – warships cleared for action and bombing fleets took flight between the set eyes and the stubborn mouth. It was like the map of a campaign marked with flags.

'Another thing,' the woman bluffed. 'They can send you to gaol. Because you know. You told me so. An accomplice, that's what you are. After the fact.'

'If they took Pinkie, do you think,' she asked with astonishment, 'I'd mind?'

'Gracious,' the woman said, 'I only came here for your sake. I wouldn't have troubled to see you first, only I don't want to let the innocent suffer' – the aphorism came clicking out like a ticket from a slot machine. 'Why, won't you lift a finger to stop him killing you?'

'He wouldn't do me any harm.'

'You're young. You don't know things like I do.'

'There's things *you* don't know.' She brooded darkly by the bed, while the woman argued on: a God wept in a garden and cried out upon a cross; Molly Carthew went to everlasting fire.

'I know one thing you don't. I know the difference between Right and Wrong. They didn't teach you *that* at school.'

Rose didn't answer; the woman was quite right: the two words meant nothing to her. Their taste was extinguished by stronger foods – Good and Evil. The woman could tell her nothing she didn't know about these – she knew by tests as clear as mathematics that Pinkie was evil – what did it matter in that case whether he was right or wrong?

'You're crazy,' the woman said. 'I don't believe you'd lift a finger if he was killing you.'

Rose came slowly back to the outer world. She said, 'Maybe I wouldn't.'

'If I wasn't a kind woman I'd give you up. But I've got a sense of responsibility.' Her smiles hung very insecurely when she paused at the door. 'You can warn that young husband of yours,' she said, 'I'm getting warm to him. I got my plans.' She went out and closed the door, then flung it open again for a last attack. 'You be careful, dear,' she said. 'You don't want a murderer's baby,' and grinned mercilessly across the bare bedroom floor. 'You better take precautions.'

Brighton Rock, 1938

SAMUEL BECKETT

[Fraud]

MURPHY'S FOURPENNY lunch was a ritual vitiated by no base thoughts of nutrition. He advanced along the railings by easy stages until he came to a branch of the caterers he wanted. The sensation of the seat of a chair coming together with his drooping posteriors at last was so delicious that he rose at once and repeated the sit, lingeringly and with intense concentration. Murphy did not so often meet with these tendernesses that he could afford to treat them casually. The second sit, however, was a great disappointment.

The waitress stood before, with an air of such abstraction that he did not feel entitled to regard himself as an element in her situation. At last, seeing that she did not move, he said:

'Bring me,' in the voice of an usher resolved to order the chef's special selection for a school outing. He paused after this preparatory signal to let the fore-period develop, that first of three moments of reaction in which, according to the Külpe school, the major torments of response are undergone. Then he applied the stimulus proper.

'A cup of tea and a packet of assorted biscuits.' Twopence the tea, twopence the biscuits, a perfectly balanced meal.

As though suddenly aware of the great magical ability, or

it might have been the surgical quality, the waitress murmured, before the eddies of the main-period drifted her
away: 'Vera to you, dear.' This was not a caress.

Murphy had some faith in the Külpe school. Marbe and
Bühler might be deceived, even Watt was only human, but
how could Ach be wrong?

Vera concluded, as she thought, her performance in much
better style than she had begun. It was hard to believe, as
she set down the tray, that it was the same slavey. She
actually made out the bill there and then on her own
initiative.

Murphy pushed the tray away, tilted back his chair and
considered his lunch with reverence and satisfaction. With
reverence, because as an adherent (on and off) of the
extreme theophanism of William of Champeaux he could
not but feel humble before such sacrifices to his small but
implacable appetite, nor omit the silent grace: On this part
of himself that I am about to ingest may the Lord have
mercy. With satisfaction, because the supreme moment in
his degradations had come, the moment when, unaided and
alone, he defrauded a vested interest. The sum involved was
small, something between a penny and twopence (on the
retail valuation). But then he had only fourpence worth of
confidence to play with. His attitude simply was, that if a
swindle of from twenty-five to fifty per cent of the outlay,
and effected while you wait, was not a case of the large
returns and quick turnover indicated by Suk, then there was
a serious flaw somewhere in his theory of sharp practice.
But no matter how the transaction were judged from the
economic point of view, nothing could detract from its merit
as a little triumph of tactics in the face of the most fearful
odds. Only compare the belligerents. On the one hand a
colossal league of plutomanic caterers, highly endowed with
the ruthless cunning of the sane, having at their disposal all
the most deadly weapons of the post-war recovery; on the
other, a seedy solipsist and fourpence.

The seedy solipsist then, having said his silent grace and
savoured his infamy in advance, drew up his chair briskly to
the table, seized a cup of tea and half emptied it at one
gulp. No sooner had this gone to the right place than he

began to splutter, eructate and complain, as though he had been duped into swallowing a saturated solution of powdered glass. In this way he attracted to himself the attention not only of every customer in the saloon but actually of the waitress Vera, who came running to get a good view of the accident, as she supposed. Murphy continued for a little to make sounds as of a flushing-box taxed beyond its powers and then said, in an egg and scorpion voice:

'I ask for China and you give me Indian.'

Though disappointed that it was nothing more interesting, Vera made no bones about making good her mistake. She was a willing little bit of sweated labour, incapable of betraying the slogan of her slavers, that since the customer or sucker was paying for his gutrot ten times what it cost to produce and five times what it cost to fling in his face, it was only reasonable to defer to his complaints up to but not exceeding fifty per cent of his exploitation.

With the fresh cup of tea Murphy adopted quite a new technique. He drank not more than a third of it and then waited till Vera happened to be passing.

'I am most fearfully sorry,' he said, 'Vera, to give you all this trouble, but do you think it would be possible to have this filled with hot?'

Vera showed signs of bridling. Murphy uttered winningly the sesame.

'I know I am a great nuisance, but they have been too generous with the cowjuice.'

Generous and cowjuice were the keywords here. No waitress could hold out against their mingled overtones of gratitude and mammary organs. And Vera was essentially a waitress.

That is the end of how Murphy defrauded a vested interest every day for his lunch, to the honourable extent of paying for one cup of tea and consuming 1·83 cups approximately.

Try it sometime, gentle skimmer.

Murphy, 1938

CHRISTOPHER ISHERWOOD

[Sally Bowles]

'Have you been here long?' I asked, looking round the large gloomy room.

'Ever since I arrived in Berlin. Let's see – that was about two months ago.'

I asked what had made her decide to come out to Germany at all. Had she come alone? No, she'd come with a girl friend. An actress. Older than Sally. The girl had been to Berlin before. She'd told Sally that they'd certainly be able to get work with the Ufa. So Sally borrowed ten pounds from a nice old gentleman and joined her.

She hadn't told her parents anything about it until the two of them had actually arrived in Germany: 'I wish you'd met Diana. She was the most marvellous gold-digger you can imagine. She'd get hold of men anywhere – it didn't matter whether she could speak their language or not. She made one nearly die of laughing. I absolutely adored her.'

But when they'd been together in Berlin three weeks and no job had appeared, Diana had got hold of a banker, who'd taken her off with him to Paris.

'And left you here alone? I must say I think that was pretty rotten of her.'

'Oh, I don't know . . . Everyone's got to look after themselves. I expect, in her place, I'd have done the same.'

'I bet you wouldn't!'

'Anyhow, I'm all right. I can always get along alone.'

'How old are you, Sally?'

'Nineteen.'

'Good God! And I thought you were about twenty-five!'

'I know. Everyone does.'

Frau Karpf came shuffling in with two cups of coffee on a tarnished metal tray.

'Oh, Frau Karpf, Liebling, wie wunderbar von dich!'

'Whatever makes you stay in this house?' I asked, when

the landlady had gone out: 'I'm sure you could get a much nicer room than this.'

'Yes, I know I could.'

'Well then, why don't you?'

'Oh, I don't know. I'm lazy, I suppose.'

'What do you have to pay here?'

'Eighty marks a month.'

'With breakfast included?'

'No – I don't think so.'

'You don't *think* so?' I exclaimed severely. 'But surely you must know for certain?'

Sally took this meekly: 'Yes, it's stupid of me, I suppose. But, you see, I just give the old girl money when I've got some. So it's rather difficult to reckon it all up exactly.'

'But, good heavens, Sally – I only pay fifty a month for my room, with breakfast, and it's ever so much nicer than this one!'

Sally nodded, but continued apologetically: 'And another thing is, you see, Christopher darling, I don't quite know what Frau Karpf would do if I were to leave her. I'm sure she'd never get another lodger. Nobody else would be able to stand her face and her smell and everything. As it is, she owes three months' rent. They'd turn her out at once if they knew she hadn't any lodgers: and if they do that, she says she'll commit suicide.'

'All the same, I don't see why you should sacrifice yourself for her.'

'I'm not sacrificing myself, really. I quite like being here, you know. Frau Karpf and I understand each other. She's more or less what I'll be in thirty years' time. A respectable sort of landlady would probably turn me out after a week.'

'My landlady wouldn't turn you out.'

Sally smiled vaguely, screwing up her nose: 'How do you like the coffee, Chris darling?'

'I prefer it to Fritz's,' I said evasively.

Sally laughed: 'Isn't Fritz marvellous? I adore him. I adore the way he says, "I give a damn."'

'"Hell, I give a damn."' I tried to imitate Fritz. We both laughed. Sally lit another cigarette: she smoked the whole time. I noticed how old her hands looked in the lamplight. They were nervous, veined and very thin – the hands of a middle-aged woman. The green finger-nails seemed not to belong to them at all; to have settled on them by chance – like hard, bright, ugly little beetles. 'It's a funny thing,' she added meditatively, 'Fritz and I have never slept together, you know.' She paused, asked with interest, 'Did you think we had?'

'Well, yes – I suppose I did.'

'We haven't. Not once . . .' she yawned. 'And now I don't suppose we ever shall.'

We smoked for some minutes in silence. Then Sally began to tell me about her family. She was the daughter of a Lancashire mill-owner. Her mother was a Miss Bowles, an heiress with an estate, and so, when she and Mr Jackson were married, they joined their names together: 'Daddy's a terrible snob, although he pretends not to be. My real name's Jackson-Bowles; but of course, I can't possibly call myself that on the stage. People would think I was crazy.'

'I thought Fritz told me your mother was French?'

'No, of course not!' Sally seemed quite annoyed. 'Fritz is an idiot. He's always inventing things.'

Sally had one sister, named Betty. 'She's an absolute angel. I adore her. She's seventeen, but she's still most terribly innocent. Mummy's bringing her up to be very county. Betty would nearly die if she knew what an old whore I am. She knows absolutely nothing whatever about men.'

'But why aren't you county, too, Sally?'

'I don't know. I suppose that's Daddy's side of the family coming out. You'd love Daddy. He doesn't care a damn for anyone. He's the most marvellous business man. And about once a month he gets absolutely dead tight and horrifies all Mummy's smart friends. It was he who said I could go to London and learn acting.'

'You must have left school very young?'

'Yes. I couldn't bear school. I got myself expelled.'

'However did you do that?'

'I told the headmistress I was going to have a baby.'

'Oh, rot, Sally, you didn't!'

'I did, honestly! There was the most terrible commotion. They got a doctor to examine me, and sent for my parents. When they found out there was nothing the matter, they were most frightfully disappointed. The headmistress said that a girl who could even think of anything so disgusting couldn't possibly be allowed to stay on and corrupt the other girls. So I got my own way. And then I pestered Daddy till he said I might go to London.'

Sally had settled down in London, at a hostel, with other girl students. There, in spite of supervision, she had managed to spend large portions of the night at young men's flats: 'The first man who seduced me had no idea I was a virgin until I told him afterwards. He was marvellous. I adored him. He was an absolute genius at comedy parts. He's sure to be terribly famous one day.'

After a time, Sally got crowd-work in films, and finally a small part in a touring company. Then she had met Diana.

'And how much longer shall you stay in Berlin?' I asked.

'Heaven knows. This job at the Lady Windermere only lasts another week. I got it through a man I met at the Eden Bar. But he's gone off to Vienna now. I must ring up the Ufa people again, I suppose. And then there's an awful old Jew who takes me out sometimes. He's always promising to get me a contract; but he only wants to sleep with me, the old swine. I think the men in this country are awful. They've none of them got any money, and they expect you to let them seduce you if they give you a box of chocolates.'

'How on earth are you going to manage when this job comes to an end?'

'Oh well, I get a small allowance from home, you know. Not that that'll last much longer. Mummy's already threatened to stop it if I don't come back to England soon . . . Of course, they think I'm here with a girl friend. If Mummy knew I was on my own, she'd simply pass right out. Anyhow, I'll get enough to support myself somehow, soon. I loathe taking money from them. Daddy's business is in a frightfully bad way now, from the slump.'

'I say, Sally – if you ever really get into a mess I wish you'd let me know.'

Sally laughed: 'That's terribly sweet of you, Chris. But I don't sponge on my friends.'

'Isn't Fritz your friend?' It had jumped out of my mouth. But Sally didn't seem to mind a bit.

'Oh yes, I'm awfully fond of Fritz, of course. But he's got pots of cash. Somehow, when people have cash, you feel differently about them – I don't know why.'

'And how do you know I haven't got pots of cash, too?'

'You?' Sally burst out laughing. 'Why, I knew you were hard up the moment I set eyes on you!'

Goodbye to Berlin, 1939

GEORGE ORWELL

[Boxer]

LATE ONE evening, in the summer, a sudden rumour ran round the farm that something had happened to Boxer. He had gone out alone to drag a load of stone down to the windmill. And sure enough, the rumour was true. A few minutes later two pigeons came racing in with the news: 'Boxer has fallen! He is lying on his side and can't get up!'

About half the animals on the farm rushed out to the knoll where the windmill stood. There lay Boxer, between the shafts of the cart, his neck stretched out, unable even to raise his head. His eyes were glazed, his sides matted with sweat. A thin stream of blood had trickled out of his mouth. Clover dropped to her knees at his side.

'Boxer!' she cried, 'how are you?'

'It is my lung,' said Boxer in a weak voice. 'It does not matter. I think you will be able to finish the windmill without me. There is a pretty good store of stone accumulated. I had only another month to go in any case. To tell you the truth I had been looking forward to my retirement. And perhaps, as Benjamin is growing old too, they will let him retire at the same time and be a companion to me.'

'We must get help at once,' said Clover. 'Run, somebody, and tell Squealer what has happened.'

All the other animals immediately raced back to the farmhouse to give Squealer the news. Only Clover remained, and Benjamin, who lay down at Boxer's side, and, without speaking, kept the flies off him with his long tail. After about a quarter of an hour Squealer appeared, full of sympathy and concern. He said that Comrade Napoleon had learned with the very deepest distress of this misfortune to one of the most loyal workers on the farm, and was already making arrangements to send Boxer to be treated in the hospital at Willingdon. The animals felt a little uneasy at this. Except for Mollie and Snowball no other animal had ever left the farm, and they did not like to think of their sick comrade in the hands of human beings. However, Squealer easily convinced them that the veterinary surgeon in Willingdon could treat Boxer's case more satisfactorily than could be done on the farm. And about half an hour later, when Boxer had somewhat recovered, he was with difficulty got on to his feet, and managed to limp back to his stall, where Clover and Benjamin had prepared a good bed of straw for him.

For the next two days Boxer remained in his stall. The pigs had sent out a large bottle of pink medicine which they had found in the medicine chest in the bathroom, and Clover administered it to Boxer twice a day after meals. In the evenings she lay in his stall and talked to him, while Benjamin kept the flies off him. Boxer professed not to be sorry for what had happened. If he made a good recovery he might expect to live another three years, and he looked forward to the peaceful days that he would spend in the corner of the big pasture. It would be the first time that he had had leisure to study and improve his mind. He intended, he said, to devote the rest of his life to learning the remaining twenty-two letters of the alphabet.

However, Benjamin and Clover could only be with Boxer after working hours, and it was in the middle of the day when the van came to take him away. The animals were all at work weeding turnips under the supervision of a pig, when they were astonished to see Benjamin come galloping from the direction of the farm buildings, braying at the top of his voice. It was the first time that they had ever seen Benjamin excited – indeed, it was the first time that anyone had ever seen him gallop. 'Quick, quick!' he shouted. 'Come at once! They're taking Boxer away!' Without waiting for orders from the pig, the animals broke off work and raced back to the farm buildings. Sure enough, there in the yard was a large closed van, drawn by two horses, with lettering on its side and a sly-looking man in a low-crowned bowler hat sitting on the driver's seat. And Boxer's stall was empty.

The animals crowded round the van. 'Good-bye, Boxer!' they chorused, 'good-bye!'

'Fools! Fools!' shouted Benjamin, prancing round them and stamping the earth with his small hoofs. 'Fools! Do you not see what is written on the side of that van?'

That gave the animals pause, and there was a hush. Muriel began to spell out the words. But Benjamin pushed her aside and in the midst of a deadly silence he read:

'"Alfred Simmonds, Horse Slaughterer and Glue Boiler, Willingdon. Dealer in Hides and Bone-Meal. Kennels Supplied." Do you not understand what that means? They are taking Boxer to the knacker's!'

A cry of horror burst from all the animals. At this moment the man on the box whipped up his horses and the van moved out of the yard at a smart trot. All the animals followed, crying out at the tops of their voices. Clover forced her way to the front. The van began to gather speed. Clover tried to stir her stout limbs to a gallop, and achieved a canter. 'Boxer!' she cried. 'Boxer! Boxer! Boxer!' And just at this moment, as though he had heard the uproar outside, Boxer's face, with the white stripe down his nose, appeared at the small window at the back of the van.

'Boxer!' cried Clover in a terrible voice. 'Boxer! Get out! Get out quickly! They are taking you to your death!'

All the animals took up the cry of 'Get out, Boxer, get out!' But the van was already gathering speed and drawing away from them. It was uncertain whether Boxer had understood what Clover had said. But a moment later his face disappeared from the window and there was the sound of a tremendous drumming of hoofs inside the van. He was trying to kick his way out. The time had been when a few kicks from Boxer's hoofs would have smashed the van to matchwood. But alas! his strength had left him; and in a few moments the sound of drumming hoofs grew fainter and died away. In desperation the animals began appealing to the two horses which drew the van to stop. 'Comrades, comrades!' they shouted. 'Don't take your own brother to his death!' But the stupid brutes, too ignorant to realise what was happening, merely set back their ears and quickened their pace. Boxer's face did not reappear at the window. Too late, someone thought of racing ahead and shutting the five-barred gate; but in another moment the van was through it and rapidly disappearing down the road. Boxer was never seen again.

Three days later it was announced that he had died in the hospital at Willingdon, in spite of receiving every attention a horse could have. Squealer came to announce the news to the others. He had, he said, been present during Boxer's last hours.

'It was the most affecting sight I have ever seen!' said Squealer, lifting his trotter and wiping away a tear. 'I was at his bedside at the very last. And at the end, almost too weak to speak, he whispered in my ear that his sole sorrow was to have passed on before the windmill was finished. "Forward, comrades!" he whispered. "Forward in the name of the Rebellion. Long live Animal Farm! Long live Comrade Napoleon! Napoleon is always right." Those were his very last words, comrades.'

Here Squealer's demeanour suddenly changed. He fell silent for a moment, and his little eyes darted suspicious glances from side to side before he proceeded.

It had come to his knowledge, he said, that a foolish and wicked rumour had been circulated at the time of Boxer's removal. Some of the animals had noticed that the van which took Boxer away was marked 'Horse Slaughterer', and had actually jumped to the conclusion that Boxer was being sent to the knacker's. It was almost unbelievable, said Squealer, that any animal could be so stupid. Surely, he cried indignantly, whisking his tail and skipping from side to side, surely they knew their beloved Leader, Comrade Napoleon, better than that? But the explanation was really very simple. The van had previously been the property of the knacker, and had been bought by the veterinary surgeon, who had not yet painted the old name out. That was how the mistake had arisen.

The animals were enormously relieved to hear this. And when Squealer went on to give further graphic details of Boxer's death-bed, the admirable care he had received and the expensive medicines for which Napoleon had paid without a thought as to the cost, their last doubts disappeared and the sorrow that they felt for their comrade's death was tempered by the thought that at least he had died happy.

Napoleon himself appeared at the meeting on the following Sunday morning and pronounced a short oration in Boxer's honour. It had not been possible, he said, to bring back their lamented comrade's remains for interment on the farm, but he had ordered a large wreath to be made from the laurels in the farmhouse garden and sent down to be placed on Boxer's grave. And in a few days' time the pigs intended to hold a memorial banquet in Boxer's honour. Napoleon ended his speech with a reminder of Boxer's two favourite maxims, 'I will work harder' and 'Comrade Napoleon is always right' – maxims, he said, which every animal would do well to adopt as his own.

On the day appointed for the banquet a grocer's van drove up from Willingdon and delivered a large wooden crate at the farmhouse. That night there was the sound of uproarious singing, which was followed by what sounded like a violent quarrel and ended at about eleven o'clock with a tremendous crash of glass. No one stirred in the farmhouse before noon on the following day. And the word went round that from somewhere or other the pigs had acquired the money to buy themselves another case of whisky.

Animal Farm: A Fairy Story, 1945

[Newspeak]

'How is the Dictionary getting on?' said Winston, raising his voice to overcome the noise.

'Slowly,' said Syme. 'I'm on the adjectives. It's fascinating.'

He had brightened up immediately at the mention of Newspeak. He pushed his pannikin aside, took up his hunk of bread in one delicate hand and his cheese in the other, and leaned across the table so as to be able to speak without shouting.

'The Eleventh Edition is the definitive edition,' he said. 'We're getting the language into its final shape – the shape it's going to have when nobody speaks anything else. When we've finished with it, people like you will have to learn it all over again. You think, I dare say, that our chief job is inventing new words. But not a bit of it! We're destroying words – scores of them, hundreds of them, every day. We're cutting the language down to the bone. The Eleventh Edition won't contain a single word that will become obsolete before the year 2050.'

He bit hungrily into his bread and swallowed a couple of mouthfuls, then continued speaking, with a sort of pedant's passion. His thin dark face had become animated, his eyes had lost their mocking expression and grown almost dreamy.

'It's a beautiful thing, the destruction of words. Of course the great wastage is in the verbs and adjectives, but there are hundreds of nouns that can be got rid of as well. It isn't only the synonyms; there are also the antonyms. After all, what justification is there for a word which is simply the opposite of some other word? A word contains its opposite in itself. Take "good", for instance. If you have a word like "good", what need is there for a word like "bad"? "Ungood" will do just as well – better, because it's an exact opposite, which the other is not. Or again, if you want a stronger version of "good", what sense is there in having a whole string of vague useless words like "excellent" and "splendid" and all the rest of them? "Plusgood" covers the meaning; or "doubleplusgood" if you want something stronger still. Of course we use those forms already, but in the final version of Newspeak there'll be nothing else. In the end the whole notion of goodness and badness will be covered by only six words – in reality, only one word. Don't you see the beauty of that, Winston? It was BB's idea originally, of course,' he added as an afterthought.

A sort of vapid eagerness flitted across Winston's face at the mention of Big Brother. Nevertheless Syme immediately detected a certain lack of enthusiasm.

'You haven't a real appreciation of Newspeak, Winston,' he said almost sadly. 'Even when you write it you're still thinking in Oldspeak. I've read some of those pieces that you write in the *Times* occasionally. They're good enough, but they're translations. In your heart you'd prefer to stick to Oldspeak, with all its vagueness and its useless shades of meaning. You don't grasp the beauty of the destruction of words. Do you know that Newspeak is the only language in the world whose vocabulary gets smaller every year?'

Winston did know that, of course. He smiled, sympathet-ically he hoped, not trusting himself to speak. Syme bit off another fragment of the dark-coloured bread, chewed it briefly, and went on:

'Don't you see that the whole aim of Newspeak is to narrow the range of thought? In the end we shall make thoughtcrime literally impossible, because there will be no words in which to express it. Every concept that can ever be needed will be expressed by exactly *one* word, with its mean-ing rigidly defined and all its subsidiary meanings rubbed out and forgotten. Already, in the Eleventh Edition, we're not far away from that point. But the process will still be continu-ing long after you and I are dead. Every year fewer and fewer words, and the range of consciousness always a little smaller. Even now, of course, there's no reason or excuse for commit-ting thoughtcrime. It's merely a question of self-discipline, reality-control. But in the end there won't be any need even for that. The Revolution will be complete when the language is perfect. Newspeak is Ingsoc and Ingsoc is Newspeak,' he added with a sort of mystical satisfaction. 'Has it ever occurred to you, Winston, that by the year 2050, at the very latest, not a single human being will be alive who could understand such a conversation as we are having now?'

'Except—' began Winston doubtfully, and then stopped.

It had been on the tip of his tongue to say 'Except the proles,' but he checked himself, not feeling fully certain that this remark was not in some way unorthodox. Syme, however, had divined what he was about to say.

'The proles are not human beings,' he said carelessly. 'By 2050 – earlier, probably – all real knowledge of Oldspeak will have disappeared. The whole literature of the past will have been destroyed. Chaucer, Shakespeare, Milton, Byron – they'll exist only in Newspeak versions, not merely changed into something different, but actually changed into something contradictory of what they used to be. Even the literature of the Party will change. Even the slogans will change. How could you have a slogan like "freedom is slavery" when the concept of freedom has been abolished? The whole climate of thought will be different. In fact there will *be* no thought, as we understand it now. Orthodoxy means not thinking – not needing to think. Orthodoxy is unconsciousness.'

One of these days, thought Winston with sudden deep conviction, Syme will be vaporized. He is too intelligent. He sees too clearly and speaks too plainly. The Party does not like such people. One day he will disappear. It is written in his face.

Winston had finished his bread and cheese. He turned a little sideways in his chair to drink his mug of coffee. At the table on his left the man with the strident voice was still talking remorselessly away. A young woman who was perhaps his secretary, and who was sitting with her back to Winston, was listening to him and seemed to be eagerly agreeing with everything that he said. From time to time Winston caught some such remark as 'I think you're *so* right. I do *so* agree with you', uttered in a youthful and rather silly feminine voice. But the other voice never stopped for an instant, even when the girl was speaking. Winston knew the man by sight, though he knew no more about him than that he held some important post in the Fiction Department. He was a man of about thirty, with a muscular throat and a large, mobile mouth. His head was thrown back a little, and because of the angle at which he was sitting, his spectacles caught the light and presented to Winston two blank discs instead of eyes. What was slightly horrible was that from the stream of sound that poured out of his mouth, it was almost impossible to distinguish a single word. Just once Winston caught a phrase – 'complete and final elimination of Goldsteinism' – jerked out very rapidly and, as it seemed, all in one piece, like a line of type cast solid. For the rest it was just a noise, a quack-quack-quacking. And yet, though you could not actually hear what the man was saying, you could not be in any doubt about its general nature. He might be denouncing Goldstein and demanding sterner measures against thought-criminals and saboteurs, he might be fulminating against the atrocities of the Eurasian army, he might be praising Big Brother or the heroes of the Malabar front – it made no difference. Whatever it was, you could be certain that every word of it was pure orthodoxy, pure Ingsoc. As he watched the eyeless face with the jaw moving rapidly up and down, Winston had a curious feeling that this was not a real human being but some kind of dummy. It was not the man's brain that was speaking, it was his larynx. The stuff that was coming out of him consisted of words, but it was not speech in the true sense: it was a noise uttered in unconsciousness, like the quacking of a duck.

Syme had fallen silent for a moment, and with the handle of his spoon was tracing patterns in the puddle of stew. The voice from the other table quacked rapidly on, easily audible in spite of the surrounding din.

'There is a word in Newspeak,' said Syme, 'I don't know whether you know it: *duckspeak*, to quack like a duck. It is one of those interesting words that have two contradictory meanings. Applied to an opponent, it is abuse; applied to someone you agree with, it is praise.'

Unquestionably Syme will be vaporized, Winston thought again. He thought it with a kind of sadness, although well knowing that Syme despised him and slightly disliked him, and was fully capable of denouncing him as a thought-criminal if he saw any reason for doing so. There was

something subtly wrong with Syme. There was something
that he lacked: discretion, aloofness, a sort of saving stupid-
ity. You could not say that he was unorthodox. He believed
in the principles of Ingsoc, he venerated Big Brother, he
rejoiced over victories, he hated heretics, not merely with
sincerity but with a sort of restless zeal, an up-to-dateness
of information, which the ordinary Party member did not
approach. Yet a faint air of disreputability always clung to
him. He said things that would have been better unsaid, he
had read too many books, he frequented the Chestnut Tree
Café, haunt of painters and musicians. There was no law,
not even an unwritten law, against frequenting the Chestnut
Tree Café, yet the place was somehow ill-omened. The old,
discredited leaders of the Party had been used to gather
there before they were finally purged. Goldstein himself, it
was said, had sometimes been seen there, years and decades
ago. Syme's fate was not difficult to foresee. And yet it was
a fact that if Syme grasped, even for three seconds, the
nature of his, Winston's, secret opinions, he would betray
him instantly to the Thought Police. So would anybody else,
for that matter: but Syme more than most. Zeal was not
enough. Orthodoxy was unconsciousness.

Nineteen Eighty-Four, 1949

EVELYN WAUGH

[Sebastian]

THE EASTER party at Brideshead was a bitter time,
culminating in a small but unforgettably painful incident. Sebastian got very drunk before dinner in his mother's
house, and thus marked the beginning of a new epoch in his
melancholy record of deterioration, the first step in his flight
from his family which brought him to ruin.

It was at the end of the day when the large Easter party
left Brideshead. It was called the Easter party, though in

fact it began on the Tuesday of Easter Week for the Flytes all went into retreat at the guest house of a monastery from Maundy Thursday until Easter. This year Sebastian had said he would not go, but at the last moment had yielded, and came home in a state of acute depression from which I totally failed to raise him.

He had been drinking very hard for a week – only I knew how hard – and drinking in a nervous, surreptitious way, totally unlike his old habit. During the party there was always a grog tray in the library, and Sebastian took to slipping in there at odd moments during the day without saying anything even to me. The house was largely deserted during the day. I was at work painting another panel in the little garden room in the colonnade. Sebastian complained of a cold, stayed in, and during all that time was never quite sober; he escaped attention by being silent. Now and then I noticed him attract curious glances, but most of the party knew him too slightly to see the change in him, while his own family were occupied, each with their particular guests.

When I remonstrated he said, 'I can't stand all these people about,' but it was when they finally left and he had to face his family at close quarters, that he broke down.

The normal practice was for a cocktail tray to be brought into the drawing-room at six; we mixed our own drinks and the bottles were removed when we went to dress; later, just before dinner, cocktails appeared again, this time handed round by the footmen.

Sebastian disappeared after tea; the light had gone and I spent the next hour playing mah-jong with Cordelia. At six I was alone in the drawing-room, when he returned; he was frowning in a way I knew all too well, and when he spoke I recognised the drunken thickening in his voice.

'Haven't they brought the cocktails yet?' He pulled clumsily on the bell-rope.

I said, 'Where have you been?'

'Up with nanny.'

'I don't believe it. You've been drinking somewhere.'

'I've been reading in my room. My cold's worse today.'

When the tray arrived he slopped gin and vermouth into a tumbler and carried it out of the room with him. I followed him upstairs, where he shut his bedroom door in my face and turned the key.

I returned to the drawing-room full of dismay and foreboding.

The family assembled. Lady Marchmain said: 'What's become of Sebastian?'

'He's gone to lie down. His cold is worse.'

'Oh dear, I hope he isn't getting flu. I thought he had a feverish look once or twice lately. Is there anything he wants?'

'No, he particularly asked not to be disturbed.'

I wondered whether I ought to speak to Brideshead, but that grim, rock-crystal mask forbade all confidence. Instead, on the way upstairs to dress, I told Julia.

'Sebastian's drunk.'

'He can't be. He didn't even come for a cocktail.'

'He's been drinking in his room all the afternoon.'

'How very peculiar! What a bore he is! Will he be all right for dinner?'

'No.'

'Well, *you* must deal with him. It's no business of mine. Does he often do this?'

'He has lately.'

'How very boring.'

I tried Sebastian's door, found it locked, and hoped he was sleeping, but when I came back from my bath, I found him sitting in the arm chair before my fire; he was dressed for dinner, all but his shoes, but his tie was awry and his hair on end; he was very red in the face and squinting slightly. He spoke indistinctly.

'Charles, what you said was quite true. Not with nanny. Been drinking whiskey up here. None in the library now party's gone. Now party's gone and only mummy. Feeling rather drunk. Think I'd better have something-on-a-tray up here. Not dinner with mummy.'

'Go to bed,' I told him. 'I'll say your cold's worse.'

'Much worse.'

I took him to his room which was next to mine and tried to get him to bed, but he sat in front of his dressing table squinnying at himself in the glass, trying to remake his bow

tie. On the writing table by the fire was a half-empty
decanter of whiskey. I took it up, thinking he would not
see, but he spun round from the mirror and said: 'You put
that down.'

'Don't be an ass, Sebastian. You've had enough.'

'What the devil's it got to do with you? You're only a guest
here – *my* guest. I drink what I want in my own house.'

He would have fought me for it at that moment.

'Very well,' I said, putting the decanter back, 'only for
God's sake keep out of sight.'

'Oh, mind your own business. You came here as my
friend; now you're spying on me for my mother, I know.
Well, you can get out, and tell her from me that I'll choose
my friends and she her spies in future.'

So I left him and went down to dinner.

'I've been in to Sebastian,' I said. 'His cold has come on
rather badly. He's gone to bed and says he doesn't want
anything.'

'Poor Sebastian,' said Lady Marchmain. 'He'd better have
a glass of hot whiskey. I'll go and have a look at him.'

'Don't, mummy, I'll go,' said Julia rising.

'*I'll* go,' said Cordelia, who was dining down that night,
for a treat to celebrate the departure of the guests. She was
at the door and through it, before anyone could stop her.

Julia caught my eye and gave a tiny, sad shrug.

In a few minutes Cordelia was back, looking grave. 'No,
he doesn't seem to want anything,' she said.

'How was he?'

'Well, I don't *know*, but I *think* he's very drunk,' she said.

'*Cordelia*.'

Suddenly the child began to giggle. '"Marquis's Son
Unused to Wine,"' she quoted. '"Model Student's Career
Threatened."'

'Charles, is this true?' asked Lady Marchmain.

'Yes.'

Then dinner was announced, and we went to the dining-
room where the subject was not mentioned.

When Brideshead and I were alone he said: 'Did you say
Sebastian was drunk?'

'Yes.'

'Extraordinary time to choose. Couldn't you stop him?'

'No.'

'No,' said Brideshead, 'I don't suppose you could. I once saw my father drunk, in his room. I wasn't more than about ten at the time. You can't stop people if they want to get drunk. My mother couldn't stop my father, you know.'

He spoke in his odd, impersonal way. The more I saw of this family, I reflected, the more singular I found them.

'I shall ask my mother to read to us tonight.'

It was the custom, I learned later, always to ask Lady Marchmain to read aloud on evenings of family tension. She had a beautiful voice and great humour of expression. That night she read part of *The Wisdom of Father Brown*. Julia sat with a stool covered with manicure things and carefully revarnished her nails; Cordelia nursed Julia's Pekinese; Brideshead played patience; I sat unoccupied studying the pretty group they made, and mourning my friend upstairs.

But the horrors of that evening were not yet over.

It was sometimes Lady Marchmain's practice, when the family were alone, to visit the chapel before going to bed. She had just closed her book and proposed going there when the door opened and Sebastian appeared. He was dressed as I had last seen him, but now instead of being flushed he was deathly pale.

'Come to apologise,' he said.

'Sebastian, dear, do go back to your room,' said Lady Marchmain. 'We can talk about it in the morning.'

'Not to you. Come to apologise to Charles. I was bloody to him and he's my guest. He's my guest and my only friend and I was bloody to him.'

A chill spread over us. I led him back to his room; his family went to their prayers. I noticed when we got upstairs that the decanter was now empty. 'It's time you were in bed,' I said.

Sebastian began to weep. 'Why do you take their side against me? I knew you would if I let you meet them. Why do you spy on me?'

He said more than I can bear to remember, even at

twenty years' distance. At last I got him to sleep and very sadly went to bed myself.

Brideshead Revisited, 1945

SIR PELHAM GRENVILLE WODEHOUSE

[The Stricken Pig Man]

B UT WHAT, meanwhile, it will be asked, of George Cyril Wellbeloved, whom we left with his tongue hanging out, the future stretching bleakly before him like some grim Sahara? Why is it, we seem to hear a million indignant voices demanding, that no further mention has been made of that reluctant teetotaller?

The matter is susceptible of a ready explanation. It is one of the chief drawbacks to the lot of the conscientious historian that in pursuance of his duties he is compelled to leave in obscurity many of those to whom he would greatly prefer to give star billing. His task being to present a panoramic picture of the actions of a number of protagonists, he is not at liberty to concentrate his attention on any one individual, however much the latter's hard case may touch him personally. When Edward Gibbon, half way through his *Decline and Fall of the Roman Empire*, complained to Doctor Johnson one night in a mood of discouragement that it – meaning the lot of the conscientious historian – shouldn't happen to a dog, it was to this aspect of it that he was referring.

In this macedoine of tragic happenings in and around Blandings Castle, designed to purge the souls of a discriminating public with pity and terror, it has been necessary to devote so much space to Jerry Vail, Penny Donaldson, Lord Emsworth and the rest of them that George Cyril Wellbeloved, we are fully aware, has been neglected almost entirely. Except for one brief appearance early in the proceedings, he might as well, for all practical purposes, have been painted on the back drop.

It is with genuine satisfaction that the minstrel, tuning his harp, now prepares to sing of this stricken pig man.

There is no agony like the agony of the man who wants a couple of quick ones and cannot get them and in the days that followed his interview with Sir Gregory Parsloe, George Cyril Wellbeloved may be said to have plumbed the depths. It would, however, be inaccurate to describe him as running the gamut of the emotions, for he had had but one emotion, a dull despair as there crept slowly upon him the realization of the completeness with which his overlord had blocked all avenues to a peaceful settlement. He was in the distressing position of finding himself foiled at every point.

Although nobody who had met him would have been likely to get George Cyril Wellbeloved confused with the poet Keats, it was extraordinary on what similar lines the two men's minds worked. 'Oh, for a beaker full of the warm South, full of the true, the blushful Hippocrene!' sang Keats, licking his lips, and 'Oh, for a mug of beer with, if possible, a spot of gin in it!' sighed George Cyril Wellbeloved, licking his; and in quest of the elixir he had visited in turn the Emsworth Arms, the Wheatsheaf, the Waggoner's Rest, the Beetle and Wedge, the Stitch in Time, the Jolly Cricketers and all the other hostelries at which Market Blandings pointed with so much pride.

But everywhere the story was the same. Barmaids had been given their instructions, pot boys warned to be on the alert. They had placed at his disposal gingerbeer, ginger ale, sarsaparilla, lime juice and on one occasion milk, but his request for the cup that clears today of past regrets and future fears was met with a firm *nolle prosequi*. Staunch and incorruptible, the barmaids and the pot boys refused to serve him with anything that would have interested Omar Khayam, and he had come away parched and saddened.

But it has been well said of pig men as a class that though crushed to earth, they will rise again. You plot and plan and think you have baffled a pig man, but all the while his quick brain has been working, and it has shown him the way out. It was so with George Cyril Wellbeloved. Just when the thought of the Hon. Galahad Threepwood came stealing into his mind, he could not have said, but it did so steal, and it was as though a light had shone upon his darkness. That dull despair gave way to a flaming hope. Glimmering in the distance, he seemed to see the happy ending.

Although during his term of office at Blandings Castle his opportunities of meeting Gally socially had been rather limited, George Cyril knew all about him. Gally, he was aware, was a man with a feeling heart, a man who could be relied upon to look indulgently on such of his fellow men as wanted a gargle and wanted it quick. According to those who knew him best, his whole life since reaching years of what may loosely be called discretion had been devoted to seeing that the other chap did not die of thirst. Would such a man turn his back on even a comparative stranger, if the comparative stranger were in a position to prove by ocular demonstration that his tongue was blackening at the roots? Most unlikely, thought George Cyril Wellbeloved, and if there was even a sporting chance of securing the services of this human drinking fountain, it was his duty, he felt, not to neglect it.

With pig men, to think is to act. Dinner over and his employer safely in his study with his coffee and cigar, he got out his bicycle and started pedalling through the scented summer night.

The welcome he received at the back door of Blandings Castle could in no sense have been termed a gushing one. Beach, informed that there was a gentleman asking for him and finding that the person thus described was a pig man whom he had never liked and who in his opinion smelled to heaven, was at his most formal. He might have been a prominent Christian receiving an unexpected call from one of the troops of Midian.

George Cyril, in sharp contradistinction, was all bounce and breeziness. Unlike most of those who met that godlike man, he stood in no awe of Beach. He held the view, and had voiced it fearlessly many a time in the tap room of the Emsworth Arms, that Beach was an old stuffed shirt.

'Hoy, cocky,' he said, incredible as such a mode of address might seem. 'Where's Mr Galahad?'

Ice formed on the butler's upper slopes.

'Mr Galahad is in the amber drawing-room with the rest of the household,' he replied austerely.

'Then go and hoik him out of it,' said George Cyril Wellbeloved, his splendid spirit unsubdued. 'I want to see him. Tell him it's important.'

Pigs Have Wings, 1952

SIR WILLIAM GOLDING

[Smoke]

THE SMOKE was a tight little knot on the horizon and was uncoiling slowly. Beneath the smoke was a dot that might be a funnel. Ralph's face was pale as he spoke to himself.

'They'll see our smoke.'

Piggy was looking in the right direction now.

'It don't look much.'

He turned round and peered up at the mountain. Ralph continued to watch the ship, ravenously. Colour was coming back into his face. Simon stood by him, silent.

'I know I can't see very much,' said Piggy, 'but have we got any smoke?'

Ralph moved impatiently, still watching the ship.

'The smoke on the mountain.'

Maurice came running, and stared out to sea. Both Simon and Piggy were looking up at the mountain. Piggy screwed up his face but Simon cried out as though he had hurt himself.

'Ralph! Ralph!'

The quality of his speech slewed Ralph on the sand.

'You tell me,' said Piggy anxiously. 'Is there a signal?'

Ralph looked back at the dispersing smoke on the horizon, then up at the mountain.

'Ralph – please! Is there a signal?'

Simon put out his hand, timidly, to touch Ralph; but Ralph started to run, splashing through the shallow end of the bathing-pool, across the hot, white sand and under the palms. A moment later, he was battling with the complex undergrowth that was already engulfing the scar. Simon ran after him, then Maurice. Piggy shouted.

'Ralph! Please – Ralph!'

Then he too started to run, stumbling over Maurice's discarded shorts before he was across the terrace. Behind the four boys, the smoke moved gently along the horizon; and on the beach, Henry and Johnny were throwing sand at Percival who was crying quietly again; and all three were in complete ignorance of the excitement.

By the time Ralph had reached the landward end of the scar he was using precious breath to swear. He did desperate violence to his naked body among the rasping creepers so that blood was sliding over him. Just where the steep ascent of the mountain began, he stopped. Maurice was only a few yards behind him.

'Piggy's specs!' shouted Ralph, 'if the fire's right out, we'll need them—'

He stopped shouting and swayed on his feet. Piggy was only just visible, bumbling up from the beach. Ralph looked at the horizon, then up to the mountain. Was it better to fetch Piggy's glasses, or would the ship have gone? Or if they climbed on, supposing the fire was right out, and they had to watch Piggy crawling nearer and the ship sinking under the horizon? Balanced on a high peak of need, agonized by indecision, Ralph cried out:

'Oh God, oh God!'

Simon, struggling with bushes, caught his breath. His face was twisted. Ralph blundered on, savaging himself, as the wisp of smoke moved on.

The fire was dead. They saw that straight away; saw what they had really known down on the beach when the smoke of home had beckoned. The fire was right out, smokeless and dead; the watchers were gone. A pile of unused fuel lay ready.

Ralph turned to the sea. The horizon stretched, impersonal once more, barren of all but the faintest trace of smoke. Ralph ran stumbling along the rocks, saved himself on the edge of the pink cliff, and screamed at the ship.

'Come back! Come back!'

He ran backwards and forwards along the cliff, his face always to the sea, and his voice rose insanely.

'Come back! Come back!'

Simon and Maurice arrived. Ralph looked at them with unwinking eyes. Simon turned away, smearing the water from his cheeks. Ralph reached inside himself for the worst word he knew.

'They let the bloody fire out.'

He looked down the unfriendly side of the mountain. Piggy arrived, out of breath and whimpering like a littlun. Ralph clenched his fist and went very red. The intentness of his gaze, the bitterness of his voice pointed for him.

'There they are.'

A procession had appeared, far down among the pink screes that lay near the water's edge. Some of the boys wore black caps but otherwise they were almost naked. They lifted sticks in the air together, whenever they came to an easy patch. They were chanting, something to do with the bundle that the errant twins carried so carefully. Ralph picked out Jack easily, even at that distance, tall, red-haired, and inevitably leading the procession.

Simon looked now, from Ralph to Jack, as he had looked from Ralph to the horizon, and what he saw seemed to make him afraid. Ralph said nothing more, but waited while the procession came nearer. The chant was audible but at that distance still wordless. Behind Jack walked the twins, carrying a great stake on their shoulders. The gutted carcass of a pig swung from the stake, swinging heavily as the twins toiled over the uneven ground. The pig's head hung down with gaping neck and seemed to search for something on the ground. At last the words of the chant floated up to them, across the bowl of blackened wood and ashes.

'*Kill the pig. Cut her throat. Spill her blood.*'

Yet as the words became audible, the procession reached the steepest part of the mountain, and in a minute or two the chant had died away. Piggy snivelled and Simon shushed him quickly as though he had spoken too loudly in church.

Jack, his face smeared with clays, reached the top first and hailed Ralph excitedly, with lifted spear.

'Look! We've killed a pig – we stole up on them – we got in a circle—'

Voices broke from the hunters.

'We got in a circle—'

'We crept up—'

'The pig squealed—'

The twins stood with the pig swinging between them, dropping black gouts on the rock. They seemed to share one wide, ecstatic grin. Jack had too many things to tell Ralph at once. Instead, he danced a step or two, then remembered his dignity and stood still, grinning. He noticed blood on his hands and grimaced distastefully, looked for something on which to clean them, then wiped them on his shorts and laughed.

Ralph spoke.

'You let the fire out.'

Jack checked, vaguely irritated by this irrelevance but too happy to let it worry him.

'We can light the fire again. You should have been with us, Ralph. We had a smashing time. The twins got knocked over—'

'We hit the pig—'

' – I fell on top—'

'I cut the pig's throat,' said Jack, proudly, and yet twitched as he said it. 'Can I borrow yours, Ralph, to make a nick in the hilt?'

The boys chattered and danced. The twins continued to grin.

'There was lashings of blood,' said Jack, laughing and shuddering, 'you should have seen it!'

'We'll go hunting every day—'

Ralph spoke again, hoarsely. He had not moved.

'You let the fire out.'

The repetition made Jack uneasy. He looked at the twins and then back at Ralph.

'We had to have them in the hunt,' he said, 'or there wouldn't have been enough for a ring.'

He flushed, conscious of a fault.

'The fire's only been out an hour or two. We can light up again—'

He noticed Ralph's scarred nakedness, and the sombre silence of all four of them. He sought, charitable in his happiness, to include them in the thing that had happened. His mind was crowded with memories; memories of the knowledge that had come to them when they closed in on the struggling pig, knowledge that they had outwitted a living thing, imposed their will upon it, taken away its life like a long satisfying drink.

He spread his arms wide.

'You should have seen the blood!'

The hunters were more silent now, but at this they buzzed again.

Ralph flung back his hair. One arm pointed at the empty horizon. His voice was loud and savage, and struck them into silence.

'There was a ship.'

Jack, faced at once with too many awful implications, ducked away from them. He laid a hand on the pig and drew his knife. Ralph brought his arm down, fist clenched, and his voice shook.

'There was a ship. Out there. You said you'd keep the fire going and you let it out!' He took a step towards Jack who turned and faced him.

'They might have seen us. We might have gone home—'

Lord of the Flies, 1954

SIR KINGSLEY AMIS

[Making Music]

'OF COURSE, this sort of music's not intended for an audience, you see,' Welch said as he handed the copies round. 'The fun's all in the singing. Everybody's got a real tune to sing – a real tune,' he repeated violently. 'You could say, really, that polyphony got to its highest point, its peak, at that period, and has been on the decline ever since. You've only got to look at the part-writing in things like, well, *Onward, Christian Soldiers*, the hymn, which is a typical . . . a typical . . .'

'We're all waiting, Ned,' Mrs Welch said from the piano. She played a slow arpeggio, sustaining it with the pedal. 'All right, everybody?'

A soporific droning filled the air round Dixon as the singers hummed their notes to one another. Mrs Welch rejoined them on the low platform that had been built at one end of the music-room, taking up her stand by Margaret, the other soprano. A small bullied-looking woman with unabundant brown hair was the only contralto. Next to Dixon was Cecil Goldsmith, a colleague of his in the College History Department, whose tenor voice held enough savage power, especially above middle C, to obliterate whatever noises Dixon might feel himself impelled to make. Behind him and to one side were three basses, one a local composer, another an amateur violinist occasionally summoned at need by the city orchestra, the third Evan Johns.

Dixon ran his eye along the lines of black dots, which seemed to go up and down a good deal, and was able to assure himself that everyone was going to have to sing all the time. He'd had a bad setback twenty minutes ago in some Brahms rubbish which began with ten seconds or so of unsupported tenor – more accurately, of unsupported Goldsmith, who'd twice dried up in face of a tricky interval and left him opening and shutting his mouth in silence. He now cautiously reproduced the note Goldsmith was humming and found the effect pleasing rather than the reverse. Why hadn't they had the decency to ask him if he'd like to join in, instead of driving him up on to this platform arrangement and forcing sheets of paper into his hand?

The madrigal began at the bidding of Welch's arthritic forefinger. Dixon kept his head down, moved his mouth as little as possible consistent with being unmistakably seen to move it, and looked through the words the others were singing. 'When from my love I looked for love, and kind affections due,' he read, 'too well I found her vows to prove most faithless and untrue. But when I did ask her why . . .' He looked over at Margaret, who was singing away happily enough – she turned out regularly during the winter with the choir of the local Conservative Association – and wondered what changes in their circumstances and temperaments would be necessary to make the words of the madrigal apply, however remotely, to himself and her. She'd made vows to him, or avowals anyway, which was perhaps all the writer had meant. But if he'd meant what he seemed to mean by 'kind affections due', then Dixon had never 'looked for' any of these from Margaret. Perhaps he should: after all, people were doing it all the time. It was a pity she wasn't a bit better-looking. One of these days, though, he would try, and see what happened.

'Yet by, and by, they'll arl, deny, arnd say 'twas *bart* in jast,' Goldsmith sang tremulously and very loudly. It was the last phrase; Dixon kept his mouth open while Welch's finger remained aloft, then shut it with a little flick of the head he'd seen singers use as the finger swept sideways. All seemed pleased with the performance and anxious for another of the same sort. 'Yes, well, this next one's what they call a ballet. Of course, they didn't mean what we mean by the similar . . . Rather a well-known one, this. It's called *Now is the Month of Maying*. Now if you'll all just . . .'

A bursting snuffle of laughter came from Dixon's left rear. He glanced round to see Johns's pallor rent by a grin. The large short-lashed eyes were fixed on him. 'What's the joke?' he asked. If Johns were laughing at Welch, Dixon was prepared to come in on Welch's side.

'You'll see,' Johns said. He went on looking at Dixon. 'You'll see,' he added, grinning.

In less than a minute Dixon did see, and clearly. Instead of the customary four parts, this piece employed five. The third and fourth lines of music from the top had *Tenor I* and *Tenor II* written against them; moreover, there was some infantile fa-la-la-la stuff on the second page with numerous gaps in the individual parts. Even Welch's ear might be expected to record the complete absence of one of the parts in such circumstances. It was much too late now for Dixon to explain that he hadn't really meant it when he'd said, half an hour before, that he could read music 'after a fashion'; much too late to transfer allegiance to the basses. Nothing short of an epileptic fit could get him out of this.

'You'd better take first tenor, Jim,' Goldsmith said; 'the second's a bit tricky.'

Dixon nodded bemusedly, hardly hearing further laughter from Johns. Before he could cry out, they were past the piano-ritual and the droning and into the piece. He flapped his lips to: 'Each with his bonny lass, a-a-seated on the grass: fa-la-la la, fa-la-la-la-la-la la la-la . . .' but Welch had stopped waving his finger, was holding it stationary in the air. The singing died. 'Oh, tenors,' Welch began; 'I didn't seem to hear . . .'

Lucky Jim, 1954

ANTHONY POWELL

[Widmerpool]

'YEARS AGO I told you I was in love with Barbara Goring,' said Widmerpool slowly.

'I remember.'

'Barbara is a thing of the past. I want her entirely forgotten.'

'Why not? I shan't stand up at your wedding and say:

"This ceremony cannot continue – the bridegroom once loved another!"'

'Quite so, quite so,' said Widmerpool, grunting out a laugh. 'You are absolutely right to make a joke of it. At the same time, I thought I should mention my feelings on that subject. One cannot be too careful.'

'And I presume you want Gipsy Jones forgotten too?'

Widmerpool flushed.

'Yes,' he said. 'She too, of course.'

His complacency seemed to me at that time intolerable. Now, I can see he required only to discuss his own situation with someone he had known for a long period, who was at the same time not too closely associated with his current life. For that rôle I was peculiarly eligible. More than once before, he had told me of his emotional upheavals – it was only because of that I knew so much about Barbara Goring and Gipsy Jones – and, when a confessor has been chosen, the habit is hard to break. At the same time, his innate suspicion of everyone inhibited even his taste for talking about himself.

'Mildred is, of course, rather older than I,' he said.

I felt in some manner imprisoned by his own self preoccupation. He positively forced one to agree that his own affairs were intensely important: indeed, the only existing question of any real interest. At the same time his intense egoism somehow dried up all sympathy for him. Clearly there was much about his present circumstances that made him nervous. That was, after all, natural enough for anyone contemplating marriage. Yet there seemed more here than the traditionally highly-strung state of a man who has only lately proposed and been accepted. I remembered that he had never asked Barbara Goring to marry him, because in those days he was not rich enough to marry. He read my thoughts, as people do when their intuition is sharpened by intensity of interest excited by discussing themselves.

'She was left with a bit of money by Haycock,' he said. 'Though her financial affairs are in an appalling mess.'

'I see.'

'How long have you known Lady Molly?'

'That was the first night I had been there.'

'I wish I had known her in the great days,' he said. 'I cannot say that I greatly care for the atmosphere of her present home.'

'You would prefer Dogdene?'

'I believe that in many ways Dogdene was far from ideally run either,' said Widmerpool curtly. 'But at least it provided a suitable background for a *grande dame*. Mildred is a friend of the present Lady Sleaford, so that I dare say in due course I shall be able to judge how Lady Molly must have looked there.'

This manner of describing Molly Jeavons somehow affronted me, not so much from disagreement, or on account of its pretentious sound, but because I had not myself given Widmerpool credit for thus estimating her qualities, even in his own crude terms. I was, indeed, surprised that he did not dismiss her as a failure, noting at the same time his certainty of invitation to Dogdene. From what Chips Lovell used to say on that subject, I was not sure that Widmerpool might not be counting his chickens before they were hatched.

'It is because of Dogdene, as you know yourself, that Mildred is such an old friend of Lady Molly's. Perhaps not a very close friend, but they have known each other a long time.'

'Yes?'

I could not guess what he was getting at.

'In fact we first met at Lady Molly's.'

'I see.'

'Mildred is – how shall I put it – a woman of the world like Lady Molly – but – well – hardly with Lady Molly's easy-going manner of looking at things – I don't mean that exactly – in some ways Mildred is very easy-going – but she likes her own way – and – in her own manner – takes life rather seriously—'

He suddenly began to look wretched, much as I had often seen him look as a schoolboy: lonely: awkward: unpopular: odd; no longer the self-confident business-man into which he had grown. His face now brought back the days when one used to watch him plodding off through the drizzle to undertake the long, solitary runs across the dismal fields beyond the sewage farms: runs which were to train him for teams in which he was never included. His jaws ceased to move up and down. He drank off a second glass of water.

'Anyway, you know General and Mrs Conyers,' he said.

He added this rather lamely, as if he lacked strength of mind to pursue the subject upon which he hoped to embark.

'I am going to tea with them this afternoon as it happens.'

'Why on earth are you doing that?'

'I haven't seen them for a long time. We've known them for ages, as I told you.'

'Oh, well, yes, I see.'

He seemed disturbed by the information. I wondered whether Mrs Conyers had already shown herself 'against' the marriage. Certainly she had been worried about her sister at the Jeavons house. I had supposed the sight of Widmerpool himself to have set her worst fears at rest. Even if prepared on the whole to accept him, she may have let fall some remark that evening unintentionally wounding to his self-esteem. He was immensely touchy. However, his present uneasiness appeared to be chiefly vested in his own ignorance of how much I already knew about his future wife. Evidently he could not make up his mind upon this last matter. The uncertainty irked him.

'Then you must have heard all about Mildred?' he persisted.

'No, not much. I only know about Mrs Conyers, so to speak. And I have often been told stories about their father, of course. I know hardly anything about the other sisters. Mrs Haycock was married to an Australian, wasn't she? I knew she had two husbands, both dead.'

'Only that?'

Widmerpool paused, disappointed by my ignorance, or additionally suspicious; perhaps both. He may have decided that for his purposes I knew at once too much and too little.

'You realise,' he said slowly, 'that Mildred has been used to a lot of her own way – her own way of life, that is. Haycock left her – in fact even encouraged her – so it seems to me – to lead – well – a rather – rather independent sort of life. They were – as one might say – a very modern married couple.'

'Beyond the fact that they lived on the Riviera, I know scarcely anything about them.'

'Haycock had worked very hard all his life. He wanted some relaxation in his later days. That was understandable. They got on quite well so far as I can see.'

I began to apprehend a little of what Widmerpool was hinting. Mrs Haycock's outline became clearer. No doubt she had graduated from an earlier emancipation of slang and cigarettes, to a habit of life with threatening aspects for her future husband.

'Did they have any children?'

'Yes,' said Widmerpool. 'They did. Mildred had two children. That does not worry me. Not at all. Glad to start with a family.'

He said all this so aggressively that I suspected a touch of bravado. Then he paused. I was about to ask the age and sex of the children, when he began to speak hurriedly again, the words tumbling out as if he wanted to finish with this speech as quickly as possible.

'I should not wish to appear backward in display of affection,' he said, developing an increased speed with every phrase, 'and, in addition to that, I don't see why we should delay unduly the state in which we shall spend the rest of our life merely because certain legal and religious formalities take time to arrange. In short, Nicholas, you will, I am sure, agree – more especially as you seem to spend a good deal of your time with artists and film-writers and people of that sort, whose morals are proverbial – that it would be permissible on my part to suppose – once the day of the wedding has been fixed – that we might – occasionally enjoy each other's company – say, over a week-end—'

He came to a sudden stop, looking at me rather wildly.

'I don't see why not.'

It was impossible to guess what he was going to say next. This was all far from anything for which I had been prepared.

'In fact my fiancée – Mildred, that is – might even expect such a suggestion?'

'Well, yes, from what you say.'

'Might even regard it as *usage du monde*?'

'Quite possible.'

Then Widmerpool sniggered. For some reason I was conscious of embarrassment, even of annoyance. The problem could be treated, as it were, clinically, or humorously; a combination of the two approaches was distasteful. I had the impression that the question of how he should behave worried him more on account of the figure he cut in the eyes of Mrs Haycock than because his passion could not be curbed. However, to have released from his mind these observations had clearly been a great relief to him. Now he cheered up a little.

'There is one further point,' he said. 'As my name is an uncommon one, I take it I should be called upon to provide myself with a sobriquet.'

'I suppose so.'

'In your own case, the difficulty would scarcely arise – so many people being called "Jenkins".'

'It may surprise you to hear that when I embark on clandestine week-ends, I call myself "Widmerpool".'

Widmerpool laughed with reasonable heartiness at that fancy. All the same, the question of what name should cover the identity of Mrs Haycock and himself when first appearing as husband and wife still worried him.

'But what surname *do* you think should be employed?' he asked in a reflective tone, speaking almost to himself.

'"Mr and Mrs Smith" would have the merit of such absolute banality that it would almost draw attention to yourselves. Besides you might be mistaken for the Jeavonses' borrowed butler.'

Widmerpool, still pondering, ignored this facetiousness, regarding me with unseeing eyes.

'"Mr and the Honourable Mrs Smith"? You might feel that more in keeping with your future wife's rank and station. That, in any case, would strike a certain note of originality in the circumstances.'

At this suggestion, Widmerpool laughed outright. The pleasantry undoubtedly pleased him. It reminded him of the facts of his engagement, showing that I had not missed the point that, whatever her shortcoming, Mildred was the daughter of a peer. His face lighted up again.

'I suppose it should really be quite simple,' he said. 'After all, the booking clerk at an hotel does not actually ask every couple if they are married.'

'In any case, you are both going to get married.'

'Yes, of course,' he said.

'So there does not seem much to worry about.'

'No, I suppose not. All the same, I do not like doing irregular things. But this time, I think I should be behaving rightly in allowing a lapse of this kind. It is expected of me.'

At Lady Molly's, 1957

JOHN BRAINE

[The Legacy]

THEN AT the moment the waitress brought the tea something happened which changed my whole life. Perhaps that isn't entirely true; I suppose that my instincts would have led me to where I am now even if I hadn't been sitting at the window of Sylvia's Café that afternoon. Perhaps I wasn't directed in the Ministry of Labour sense, but I was certainly shown the way to a destination quite different from the one I had in mind for myself at that time.

Parked by a solicitor's office opposite the café was a green Aston-Martin tourer, low-slung, with cycle-type mudguards. It had the tough, functional smartness of the good British sports car; it's a quality which is difficult to convey without using the terms of the advertising copywriter – made by craftsmen, thoroughbred, and so on – I can only say that it was a beautiful piece of engineering and leave it at that. Pre-war it would have cost as much as three baby saloons; it wasn't the sort of vehicle for business or for family outings, but quite simply a rich man's toy.

As I was admiring it a young man and a girl came out of the solicitor's office. The young man was turning the ignition key when the girl said something to him and after a moment's argument he put up the windscreen. The girl smoothed his hair for him; I found the gesture disturbing in an odd way – it was again as if a barrier had been removed, but this time by an act of reason.

The ownership of the Aston-Martin automatically placed the young man in a social class far above mine; but that ownership was simply a question of money. The girl, with her even suntan and her fair hair cut short in a style too simple to be anything else but expensive, was as far beyond my reach as the car. But her ownership, too, was simply a question of money, of the price of the diamond ring on her left hand. This seems all too obvious; but it was the kind of truth which until that moment I'd only grasped theoretically.

The Aston-Martin started with a deep, healthy roar. As it passed the café in the direction of St Clair Road I noticed the young man's olive linen shirt and bright silk neckerchief. The collar of the shirt was tucked inside the jacket; he wore the rather theatrical ensemble with a matter-of-fact nonchalance. Everything about him was easy and loose but not tired or sloppy. He had an undistinguished face with a narrow forehead and mousy hair cut short with no oil on it. It was a rich man's face, smooth with assurance and good living.

He hadn't ever had to work for anything he wanted; it had all been given to him. The salary which I'd been so pleased about, an increase from Grade Ten to Grade Nine, would seem a pittance to him. The suit in which I fancied myself so much – my best suit – would seem cheap and nasty to him. He wouldn't have a *best* suit; all his clothes would be the best.

For a moment I hated him. I saw myself, compared with him, as the Town Hall clerk, the subordinate pen-pusher, half-way to being a zombie, and I tasted the sourness of envy. Then I rejected it. Not on moral grounds; but because I felt then, and still do, that envy's a small and squalid vice – the convict sulking because a fellow-prisoner's been given a bigger helping of skilly. This didn't abate the fierceness of my longing. I wanted an Aston-Martin, I wanted a three-guinea linen shirt, I wanted a girl with a Riviera suntan – these were my rights, I felt, a signed and sealed legacy.

As I watched the tail-end of the Aston-Martin with its shiny new GB plate go out of sight I remembered the second-hand Austin Seven which the Efficient Zombie, Dufton's Chief Treasurer, had just treated himself to. That was the most the local government had to offer me; it wasn't enough. I made my choice then and there: I was going to enjoy all the luxuries which that young man enjoyed. I was going to collect that legacy. It was as clear and compelling as the sense of vocation which doctors and missionaries are supposed to experience, though in my instance, of course, the call ordered me to do good to myself not others.

If Charles had been with me things would have been different. We had evolved a special mode of conversation to dispel envy and its opposite, forelock-tugging admiration. 'The capitalist beast,' Charles would have said. 'Give the girl her clothes back, Lufford,' I would have said, 'she's turning blue.' 'Those big pop eyes of yours are glinting with lust,' Charles would have said. 'Is it the girl or the car?'

We would have continued in this vein for some time, becoming more and more outrageous, until we'd dissolve into laughter. It was an incantation, a ritual; the frank admission of envy somehow cleansed us of it. And very healthy-minded it all was; but I think that it fulfilled its purpose too thoroughly and obscured the fact that the material objects of our envy were attainable.

How to attain them I didn't know. I was like an officer fresh from training-school, unable for the moment to translate the untidiness of fear and cordite and corpses into the obvious and irresistible method of attack. I was going to take the position, though, I was sure of that. I was moving into the attack, and no one had better try to stop me. General Joe Lampton, you might say, had opened hostilities.

Room at the Top, 1957

ALAN SILLITOE

[Piecework]

ARTHUR REACHED his capstan lathe and took off his jacket, hanging it on a nearby nail so that he could keep an eye on his belongings. He pressed the starter button, and his motor came to life with a gentle thump. Looking around, it did not seem, despite the infernal noise of hurrying machinery, that anyone was working with particular speed. He smiled to himself and picked up a glittering steel cylinder from the top box of a pile beside him, and fixed it into the spindle. He jettisoned his cigarette into the sud-pan, drew back the capstan, and swung the turret on to its broadest drill. Two minutes passed while he contemplated the precise position of tools and cylinder; finally he spat on to both hands and rubbed them together, then switched on the sud-tap from the movable brass pipe, pressed a button that set the spindle running, and ran in the drill to a neat chamfer. Monday morning had lost its terror.

At a piecework rate of four-and-six a hundred you could make your money if you knocked-up fourteen hundred a day – possible without grabbing too much – and if you went all out for a thousand in the morning you could dawdle through the afternoon and lark about with the women and talk to your mates now and again. Such leisure often brought him near to trouble, for some weeks ago he stunned a mouse – that the overfed factory cats had missed – and laid it beneath a woman's drill, and Robboe the gaffer ran out of his office when he heard her screaming blue-murder, thinking that some bloody silly woman had gone and got her hair caught in a belt (big notices said that women must wear hair-nets, but who could tell with women?) and Robboe was glad that it was nothing more than a dead mouse she was kicking up such a fuss about. But he paced up and down the gangways asking who was responsible for the stunned mouse, and when he came to Arthur, who denied having anything to do with it, he said: 'I'll bet you did it, you young

bogger.' 'Me, Mr Robboe?' Arthur said, the picture of
innocence, standing up tall with offended pride. 'I've got so
much work to do I can't move from my lathe. Anyway, I
don't believe in tormenting women, you know that. It's
against my principles.' Robboe glared at him: 'Well, I don't
know. Somebody did it, and I reckon it's you. You're a bit
of a Red if you ask me, that's what you are.' 'Now then,
that's slander,' Arthur said. 'I'll see my lawyers about you.
There's tons of witnesses.' Robboe went back to his office,
bearing a black look for the girl inside, and for any tool-
setter that might require his advice in the next half-hour;
and Arthur worked on his lathe like a model of industry.

Though you couldn't grumble at four-and-six a hundred
the rate-checker sometimes came and watched you work, so
that if he saw you knock up a hundred in less than an hour
Robboe would come and tell you one fine morning that
your rate had been dropped by sixpence or a bob. So when
you felt the shadow of the rate-checker breathing down your
neck you knew what to do if you had any brains at all: make
every move more complicated, though not slow because
that was cutting your own throat, and do everything deliberately yet with a crafty show of speed. Though cursed as
public enemy number one the rate-checker was an innocu-
ous-looking man who carried a slight stoop everywhere he
went and wore spectacles, smoking the same fags as you
were smoking, and protecting his blue pin-striped suit with
a brown staff-overall, bald as a mushroom and as sly as a
fox. They said he got commission on what reductions he
recommended, but that was only a rumour, Arthur decided,
something said out of rancour if you had just been done
down for a bob. If you saw the rate-checker on your way
home from work he might say good evening to you, and you
responded to this according to whether or not your rate had
been tampered with lately. Arthur always returned such
signs with affability, for whenever the rate-checker stood
behind him he switched his speed down to a normal
hundred, though once he had averaged four hundred when
late on his daily stint. He worked out for fun how high his
wages would be if, like a madman, he pursued this cramp-
inducing, back-breaking, knuckle-knocking undiplomatic

speed of four hundred for a week, and his calculations on the *Daily Mirror* margins gave an answer of thirty-six pounds. Which would never do, he swore to himself, because they'd be down on me like a ton of bricks, and the next week I'd be grabbing at the same flat-out lick for next to nowt. So he settled for a comfortable wage of fourteen pounds. Anything bigger than that would be like shovelling hard-earned money into the big windows of the income-tax office – feeding pigs on cherries, as mam used to say – which is something else against my principles.

So you earned your living in spite of the firm, the rate-checker, the foreman, and the tool-setters, who always seemed to be at each other's throats except when they ganged-up to get at yours, though most of the time you didn't give a sod about them but worked quite happily for a cool fourteen nicker, spinning the turret to chamfer in a smell of suds and steel, actions without thought so that all through the day you filled your mind with vivid and more agreeable pictures than those round about.

Saturday Night and Sunday Morning, 1958

LAURIE LEE

[Rosie]

I STUMBLED on Rosie behind a haycock, and she grinned up at me with the sly, glittering eyes of her mother. She wore her tartan frock and cheap brass necklace, and her bare legs were brown with hay-dust.

'Get out a there,' I said. 'Go on.'

Rosie had grown and was hefty now, and I was terrified of her. In her cat-like eyes and curling mouth I saw unnatural wisdoms more threatening than anything I could imagine. The last time we'd met I'd hit her with a cabbage stump. She bore me no grudge, just grinned.

'I got sommat to show ya.'

'You push off,' I said.

I felt dry and dripping, icy hot. Her eyes glinted, and I stood rooted. Her face was wrapped in a pulsating haze and her body seemed to flicker with lightning.

'You thirsty?' she said.

'I ain't, so there.'

'You be,' she said. 'C'mon.'

So I stuck the fork into the ringing ground and followed her, like doom.

We went a long way, to the bottom of the field, where a wagon stood half-loaded. Festoons of untrimmed grass hung down like curtains all around it. We crawled underneath, beneath the wheels, into a herb-scented cave of darkness. Rosie scratched about, turned over a sack, and revealed a stone jar of cider.

'It's cider,' she said. 'You ain't to drink it though. Not much of it, any rate.'

Huge and squat, the jar lay on the grass like an unexploded bomb. We lifted it up, unscrewed the stopper, and smelt the whiff of fermented apples. I held the jar to my mouth and rolled my eyes sideways, like a beast at a waterhole. 'Go on,' said Rosie. I took a deep breath . . . .

Never to be forgotten, that first long secret drink of golden fire, juice of those valleys and of that time, wine of wild orchards, of russet summer, of plump red apples, and Rosie's burning cheeks. Never to be forgotten, or ever tasted again. . . .

I put down the jar with a gulp and a gasp. Then I turned to look at Rosie. She was yellow and dusty with buttercups and seemed to be purring in the gloom; her hair was rich as a wild bee's nest and her eyes full of stings. I did not know what to do about her, nor did I know what not to do. She looked smooth and precious, a thing of unplumbable mysteries, and perilous as quicksand.

'Rosie . . .' I said, on my knees, and shaking.

She crawled with a rustle of grass towards me, quick and superbly assured. Her hand in mine was like a small wet flame which I could neither hold nor throw away. Then Rosie, with a remorseless, reedy strength, pulled me down from my tottering perch, pulled me down, down into her wide green smile and into the deep subaqueous grass.

Then I remember little, and that little, vaguely. Skin drums beat in my head. Rose was close-up, salty, an invisible touch, too near to be seen or measured. And it seemed that the wagon under which we lay went floating away like a barge, out over the valley where we rocked unseen, swinging on motionless tides.

Then she took off her boots and stuffed them with flowers. She did the same with mine. Her parched voice crackled like flames in my ears. More fires were started. I drank more cider. Rosie told me outrageous fantasies. She liked me, she said, better than Walt, or Ken, Boney Harris, or even the curate. And I admitted to her, in a loud, rough voice, that she was even prettier than Betty Gleed. For a long time we sat with our mouths very close, breathing the same hot air. We kissed, once only, so dry and shy, it was like two leaves colliding in air.

At last the cuckoos stopped singing and slid into the woods. The mowers went home and left us. I heard Jack calling as he went down the lane, calling my name till I heard him no more. And still we lay in our wagon of grass tugging at each other's hands, while her husky, perilous whisper drugged me and the cider beat gongs in my head. . . .

Night came at last, and we crawled out from the wagon and stumbled together towards home. Bright dew and glow-worms shone over the grass, and the heat of the day grew softer. I felt like a giant; I swung from the trees and plunged my arms into nettles just to show her. Whatever I did seemed valiant and easy. Rosie carried her boots and smiled.

There was something about that evening which dilates the memory, even now. The long hills slavered like Chinese dragons, crimson in the setting sun. The shifting lane lassoed my feet and tried to trip me up. And the lake, as we passed it, rose hissing with waves and tried to drown us among its cannibal fish.

Perhaps I fell in – though I don't remember. But here I

lost Rosie for good. I found myself wandering home alone, wet through, and possessed by miracles. I discovered extraordinary tricks of sight. I could make trees move and leapfrog each other, and turn bushes into roaring trains. I could lick up the stars like acid drops and fall flat on my face without pain. I felt magnificent, fateful, and for the first time in my life, invulnerable to the perils of night.

When at last I reached home, still dripping wet, I was bursting with power and pleasure. I sat on the chopping-block and sang 'Fierce Raged the Tempest' and several other hymns of that nature. I went on singing till long after supper-time, bawling alone in the dark. Then Harold and Jack came and frog-marched me to bed. I was never the same again. . . .

Cider with Rosie, 1959

DAVID STOREY

[Possession]

I HEARD my name go out over the loudspeaker, then the roar of the crowd as the visiting team went out first. Dicky, the trainer, gave us his last instructions, we lined up, and moved down the tunnel. The front of the line broke into a trot. The boots clacked on the concrete, then slurred and were suddenly silent as they prodded into the bare earth just inside the tunnel mouth.

The darkness broke away. The light blinded for a second, mingled with the shock of the crowd's roar. I seemed to inflate as I ran on to the field. The loudspeakers blared 'The Entrance of the Gladiators' as we ran quickly, importantly, to the middle of the field, and swerved aside to make a circle. The tune changed to a crackly fanfare as the captains tossed up.

The teams spread out, filtered across the pitch, and stood still, red and blue in the worn brown and dusty green patches of the field. We waited, quiet, for the whistle. It blasted. The ball rose into the air.

Fifteen minutes of the first half passed and I'd never even touched the ball. I was aching with activity, and blowing hard. It took me most of the first half to realize I was being starved of the ball by my own team.

It was the hooker, Taff Gower, who was organizing it, I decided; a quiet little frog working out his last days in the game with the 'A' team. With his scarred, toothless face, his short bow-legged figure stumped alongside me in each movement and casually diverted the ball whenever it came my way. I gathered he mustn't like me. I might be keeping one of his mates out of the team, stopping a wage. I didn't worry about this. I just saw an early end to my ambitions. As we folded down for the next scrum his face was further forward than mine. 'Why're you keeping the ball from me?' I asked him. His head was upside down, waiting for the ball to come in, but he was grinning, fairly politely. I could see the back of his throat. When he spat I couldn't move my head. I didn't think he could like me.

I waited three scrums, to make him feel relaxed and also to get the best opportunity. I kept my right arm loose. His face was upside down, his eyes straining, loose in their sockets, to catch a glimpse of the ball as it came in. I watched it leave the scrum-half's hands and his head buckled under the forwards' heaving. I swung my right fist into the middle of his face. He cried out loud. I hit him again and saw the red pulp of his nose and lips as my hand came away. He was crying out really loud now, partly affected, professional pain, but most of it real. His language echoed all over the ground.

The scrum broke up with the ref blowing his nut off on the whistle. 'I saw that! I saw that!' he shouted, urged on to violent mimes of justice by the crowd's tremendous booing. They were all on their feet demonstrating and screaming. Gower had covered his face with his hands, but blood seeped between his fingers, as the trainer and two players directed his blind steps off the field.

'You'll be nailed for good for this, you dirty little swine. You'll never play again,' and all that, the ref was shouting.

He pointed with real drama at the opposing hooker. The crowd's response reached a crescendo – far more than it would provide for, say, the burning of a church.

The young hooker shook his head. 'I ne'er touched him,' he said, looking round for support from his own team. 'I swear to God I never touched him.'

'You can tell that to the league chairman!'

The hooker was beside himself with innocence. 'Nay, look at my bloody fist,' he said. 'Look, there's no blood on it.'

'I'm not arguing.'

The ref took his name and sent him off.

I'd never seen such a parade before. The whole ground throbbed with rage as the young figure in his little boy's costume passed in front of the main stand.

'They're not fit to be on a football field,' the ref said to me, since I happened to be standing nearest. I didn't know whether he meant the crowd or men like the hooker. The free kick put us two points ahead.

We stood around the tunnel mouth at half-time, drinking from the bottles and listening to Dicky tell us a few yards of mistakes. We were quiet. It was a fact that since Gower had gone off I'd been getting the ball just as I liked it, and as often as not in openings. I was looking up, trying to pick George Wade's homburg out in the committee box, when Dicky came over to me. He took hold of my hand and looked at the knuckles.

'Got some nice bruises there, owd lad,' he said. 'What got into you?' He didn't look at me, but at the other players.

'How d'you mean?'

'Taff Gower – you could see it plain as day from the bench.'

'He was keeping the ball from me.'

'Come off it, owd cock. Nobody lakes that game here.'

'Not now they don't.'

He grimaced, annoyed that I should try to be smart. 'You'll do just fine at this club,' he said. 'Any rate, I'm not saying a word about it, 'less Wade asks me in private.'

'You're on my side,' I told him.

'Get this, lad. I'm on my own side.' He winked, importantly, and banged my shoulder. 'Keep it up, Art,' he said in
a loud voice, and went over to advise the full-back.

As we stood on the field waiting for the second half kick-
off, I examined everything with real care, telling myself I
ought to savour every second of this feeling. I had my eyes
fixed on the twin buds of the power station's cooling towers,
and watched a cloud of white steam escape across the valley
and come over the pitch. The ball rose towards it, and in a
slow curve fell towards me. I gathered it cleanly and, beating
two men, ran to the centre of the field. Somebody shouted
for the ball. I kept it. I found myself in an opening and
suddenly thought I might even reach the line. I went straight
for the full-back, and when he came in I gave him the base
of my wrist on his nose. The crack, the groan, the release of
his arms, all coincided with a soaring in my guts. I moved in
between the posts keeping my eye on the delight of the
crowd as I put the ball down.

Everything was luminous, sparkling. The houses beyond
the stadium turrets, the silhouetted trees at Sandwood, the
ice-blue sky, the mass of people – they were all there intent
on seeing me. I was carried along in a bag full of energy, no
longer aware of effort, ready to tear anybody into postage
stamps and at the same time smile for the crowd. I came off
the field fresher than when I went on, and still waiting for
some damn thing to tire me.

This Sporting Life, 1960

MURIEL SPARK

[The Brodie Set]

THE TERM opened vigorously as usual. Miss Brodie stood
bronzed before her class and said, 'I have spent most of
my summer holidays in Italy once more, and a week in
London, and I have brought back a great many pictures

which we can pin on the wall. Here is a Cimabue. Here is a larger formation of Mussolini's fascisti, it is a better view of them than that of last year's picture. They are doing splendid things as I shall tell you later. I went with my friends for an audience with the Pope. My friends kissed his ring but I thought it proper only to bend over it. I wore a long black gown with a lace mantilla, and looked magnificent. In London my friends who are well-to-do – their small girl has two nurses, or nannies as they say in England – took me to visit A. A. Milne. In the hall was hung a reproduction of Botticelli's *Primavera* which means the Birth of Spring. I wore my silk dress with the large red poppies which is just right for my colouring. Mussolini is one of the greatest men in the world, far more so than Ramsay MacDonald, and his fascisti—'

'Good morning, Miss Brodie. Good morning, sit down, girls,' said the headmistress who had entered in a hurry, leaving the door wide open.

Miss Brodie passed behind her with her head up, up, and shut the door with the utmost meaning.

'I have only just looked in,' said Miss Mackay, 'and I have to be off. Well, girls, this is the first day of the new session. Are we downhearted? No. You girls must work hard this year at every subject and pass your qualifying examination with flying colours. Next year you will be in the Senior school, remember. I hope you've all had a nice summer holiday, you all look nice and brown. I hope in due course of time to read your essays on how you spent them.'

When she had gone Miss Brodie looked hard at the door for a long time. A girl, not of her set, called Judith, giggled. Miss Brodie said to Judith, 'That will do.' She turned to the blackboard and rubbed out with her duster the long division sum she always kept on the blackboard in case of intrusions from outside during any arithmetic periods when Miss Brodie should happen not to be teaching arithmetic. When she had done this she turned back to the class and said, 'Are we downhearted no, are we downhearted no. As I was saying, Mussolini has performed feats of magnitude and unemployment is even farther abolished under him than it was last year. I shall be able to tell you a great deal this term. As you know, I don't believe in talking down to children, you are capable of grasping more than is generally appreciated by your elders. Education means a leading out, from *e*, out and *duco*, I lead. Qualifying examination or no qualifying examination, you will have the benefit of my experiences in Italy. In Rome I saw the Forum and I saw the Colosseum where the gladiators died and the slaves were thrown to the lions. A vulgar American remarked to me, "It looks like a mighty fine quarry." They talk nasally. Mary, what does to talk nasally mean?'

Mary did not know.

'Stupid as ever,' said Miss Brodie. 'Eunice?'

'Through your nose,' said Eunice.

'Answer in a complete sentence, please,' said Miss Brodie. 'This year I think you should all start answering in complete sentences. I must try to remember this rule. Your correct answer is "To talk nasally means to talk through one's nose". The American said, "It looks like a mighty fine quarry." Ah, it was there the gladiators fought. "Hail Caesar!" they cried. "These about to die salute thee!"'

Miss Brodie stood in her brown dress like a gladiator with raised arm and eyes flashing like a sword. 'Hail Caesar!' she cried again, turning radiantly to the window light, as if Caesar sat there. 'Who opened the window?' said Miss Brodie dropping her arm.

Nobody answered.

'Whoever has opened the window has opened it too wide,' said Miss Brodie. 'Six inches is perfectly adequate. More is vulgar. One should have an innate sense of these things. We ought to be doing history at the moment according to the time-table. Get out your history books and prop them up in your hands. I shall tell you a little more about Italy. I met a young poet by a fountain. Here is a picture of Dante meeting Beatrice – it is pronounced Beatri*chay* in Italian which makes the name very beautiful – on the Ponte Vecchio. He fell in love with her at that moment. Mary, sit up and don't slouch. It was a sublime moment in a sublime love. By whom was the picture painted?'

Nobody knew.

'It was painted by Rossetti. Who was Rossetti, Jenny?'
'A painter,' said Jenny.
Miss Brodie looked suspicious.
'And a genius,' said Sandy, to come to Jenny's rescue.
'A friend of—?' said Miss Brodie.
'Swinburne,' said a girl.
Miss Brodie smiled. 'You have not forgotten,' she said, looking round the class. 'Holidays or no holidays. Keep your history books propped up in case we have any further intruders.' She looked disapprovingly towards the door and lifted her fine dark Roman head with dignity. She had often told the girls that her dead Hugh had admired her head for its Roman appearance.

'Next year,' she said, 'you will have the specialists to teach you history and mathematics and languages, a teacher for this and a teacher for that, a period of forty-five minutes for this and another for that. But in this your last year with me you will receive the fruits of my prime. They will remain with you all your days. . . .'

The Prime of Miss Jean Brodie, 1961

ANTHONY BURGESS

[Not Too Bad an Evening]

ENDERBY ENTERED the public bar and ordered whisky. This was some hours later, a different pub. Not the second or third pub, but somewhere well on in the series, the xth pub or something. On the whole, benevolent and swaying Enderby decided, he had had not too bad an evening. He had met two very fat Nigerians with wide cunning smiles and many blackheads. These had cordially invited him to their country and to write an epic to celebrate its independence. He had met a Guinness-drinker with a wooden leg which, for the delectation of Enderby, he had offered to unscrew. He had met a chief petty officer of the

Royal Navy who, in the friendliest spirit in the world, had
been prepared to fight Enderby and, when Enderby had
demurred, had given him two packets of ship's Woodbines
and said that Enderby was his pal. He had met a Siamese
osteopath with a collection of fighting fish. He had met a
punch-drunk bruiser who said he saw visions and offered to
see one then for a pint. He had met a little aggressive chinny
chewing man, not unlike Rawcliffe, who swore that Shakespeare's plays had been written by Sir William Knollys,
Controller of the Queen's Household. He had met a cobbler
who knew the Old Testament in Hebrew, an amateur
exegetist who distrusted all Biblical scholarship after 1890.
He had met, seen, or heard many others too: a thin woman
who had talked incessantly to a loll-tongued Alsatian; a man
with the shakes who swallowed his own phlegm (*Fem, Fem,*
remember that, *Fem*); a pair of hand-holding lesbians; a
man who wore flower transfers on a surgical boot; callow
soldiers drinking raw gin . . . Now it was nearing closing-
time and Enderby was, he thought, fairly near to Charing
Cross. That meant two stops on the Underground to Victoria. There must be a nice convenient after-closing-time train
to the coast.

Enderby, paying fumblingly for his whisky, saw that he
had very little money left. He estimated that he had managed to consume this evening a good dozen whiskies and a
draught beer or so. His return ticket was snug in Arry's left-
hand inside jacket-pocket. He had cigarettes. One more
drink and he would be right for home. He looked round the
public bar smiling. Good honest British working-men, salt
of the earth, bloodying and buggering their meagre dole of
speech, horny-handed but delicate with darts. And, on a
high-backed settle at right angles to the bar counter, two
British working-women sat, made placid with the fumes of
stout. One said:

'Starting next week, it is, in *Fem*. With a free gift picture
in full colour. Smashing, he is.' Enderby listened jealously.
The other woman said:

'Never take it, myself. Silly sort of name it is. Makes you
wonder how they think of them sometimes, really it does.'

'If,' said Enderby, 'you are referring to the magazine to

which I myself am to be a contributor, I would say that that name is meant to be Frenchified and naughty.' He smiled down at them with a whiskified smirk, right elbow on the counter, left fingers on right forearm. The two women looked up doubtfully. They were probably about the same age as Vesta Bainbridge, but they had an aura of back kitchens about them, tea served to shirt-sleeved men doing their pools, the telly flicking and shouting in the corner.

'Pardon?' said one, loudly.

'Naughty,' said Enderby, with great clarity. 'Frenchified.'

'What's French frieds to do with it?' said the other. 'My friend and me was just talking, do you mind?'

'Poetry is what I shall write for it,' said Enderby, 'every week.' He nodded several times, just like Rawcliffe.

'You keep your poetry to yourself, do you mind?' and she took a sharp draught of Guinness. A man came from the dart-playing part of the room, a single dart in his hand, saying:

'You all right, Edie?' He wore a decently cut suit of poor serge, but no collar or tie. His gold-headed collar-stud caught the light and dazzled Enderby. He had a gaunt quick face and was as small and supple as a miner. He inspected Enderby as if invited to give an estimate on him. 'You saying something to her that you shouldn't?' he said. 'Mate?' he added, provocatively.

'He was saying,' said Edie, 'about naughty poetry, French, too.'

'Was you saying naughty poetry to my wife here?' said the man. Like Milton's Death, he shook a dreadful dart.

'I was just saying,' said smirking Enderby, 'that I was going to write for it. What they read, I mean. That is to say, Edie here, your wife, as I take it to be, doesn't read, but the other one does, you see.'

'We'll have less of that about doesn't read, do you mind?' said Edie. 'And less of using my name familiar, do you mind?'

'Look here,' said Edie's husband. 'You want to keep that for the saloon bar, where they pay a penny extra for the privilege, do you mind? We don't want your sort in here.'

'Doing no harm,' said Enderby huffily. He then poured

over the huff a trickle of sweet sauce of ingratiation. 'I mean, I was just talking.' He leered. 'Just passing the time of day, if you see what I mean.'

'Well,' said the dart-man, 'don't you try to pass the time with my missis, do you mind?'

'Do you mind?' said Edie, in near-unison.

'I wouldn't want to pass the time with her,' said Enderby, proudly, 'I've other things to do, thank you very much.'

'I'll have to do you,' said the man, sincerely. 'Too much bloody hoot altogether, mate, to my way of thinking, that's what you've got. You'd better get out of here before I get really nasty. Been smelling the barmaid's apron, that's your trouble.'

Prrrfffp.

'Look,' said Enderby, 'that wasn't intended, I really had no intention, that was not meant in any way to be a comment, I assure you that is the sort of thing that could happen to any man, or woman too, for that matter, even Edie here, your wife, that is to say, yourself included.' Prrrfffp.

'Do you mind?' said Edie.

'This here's my fist,' said the man, pocketing his dart. The other customers quietened and looked interested. 'You'll get it straight in the moosh, straight up you will, if you don't get out of my bleeding sight this instant, do you mind?'

'I was just going anyway,' said dignified swaying Enderby. 'If you will allow me the privilege of finishing my drink here.'

'You've had enough, you have, mate,' said the man, more kindly. From the saloon bar came the call of 'Last orders'. 'If you want to drown your secret sorrows don't do it where me and my wife is, see, because I take the sort of thing that you've been saying very hard, see.' Enderby put down his glass, gave the dart-man a glassy but straight look, then eructed strongly and without malice. He bowed and, pushing his way courteously through the long-swallowers anxious to get one last one in, made an exit that was not without dignity. Outside in the street the heady air of a Guinness-sharp refrigerated night hit him and he staggered. The dart-man had followed him out and stood there, gauging and weighing. 'Look, mate,' he said, 'this is not for me really, because I've been like that myself often enough, God knows, but my wife insists, do you mind, and this is like for a keepsake.' He bowed, and while bowing swerved his torso suddenly to the left as though listening to something from that side, then he brought left fist and torso right and up and let Enderby have one, not too hard, straight in the stomach. 'There,' he said, somewhat kindly, as if the blow had been intended purely therapeutically. 'That'll do, won't it?'

Enderby gasped. The procession of the evening's whiskies and beers passed painfully through a new taste-organ that had been erected specially for this occasion. They grimaced in pain, making painful obeisance as they passed. Gas and fire shot up as from a geyser, smiting rudely the crystalline air. Premonitions of the desire to vomit huddled and fluttered. Enderby went to the wall. 'Now then,' said the man, 'where is it you want to go, eh? Kennington you are now, see, if you didn't know.'

'Victoria,' said Enderby's stomach-gas, shaped into a word by tongue and lips. He had, at the moment, no air.

'Easy,' said the kind man. 'First to the right second to the left keep straight on brings you to Kennington Station, see. Get a train to Charing Cross, that's the second stop, Waterloo's the first, change at Charing Cross, see, Circle Line. Westminster St James's Park and then you're there, see. And the very best of luck and no hard feelings.' He patted Enderby's left shoulder and re-entered the public bar.

Inside Mr Enderby, 1963

IRIS MURDOCH

[Hartley]

I CAN see her smiling at me now. She was beautiful but with a secret beauty. She was not one of the 'pretty girls' of the school. Sometimes her face looked heavy, almost dour, and when she cried she looked like the pig-baby in *Alice*. She was very pale, and people sometimes thought she looked ill, although she was so strong and so healthy. Her face was rather round and white and her eyes gazed out with such a fey puzzled look, like a young savage. She had dark blue eyes which seemed to be violet when you were not looking at them. Her pupils were often dilated so that her eyes became almost black. She had very fine straight fair hair in a long bob. Her lips were pale and always cold; and when, with my eyes closing, I touched them so childishly with mine, a cold force pierced me like a spear, such as a pilgrim might feel when he knelt and touched some holy life-renewing stone. Her body was passive to my embraces, but her spirit glowed to me with a cold fire. Her beautiful shoulders, her long legs, were pale too and seemed cold. I never saw her entirely undressed. She was slim, very slim, leggy and clean, and so strong. She never hugged me, but sometimes, rigidly, she held my arms, leaving great bruises. Her secret violet eyes did not close when I moved to kiss her. They stared with that strange puzzlement which was at the same time passion. Those quiet, silent, almost stiff embraces were the most passionate that I ever knew. And we were chaste, and respected each other absolutely and worshipped each other chastely. And that was passion and that was love of a purity which can never come again and which I am sure rarely exists in the world at all. Those memories are more radiant to me than any work of art, more vivid and precious than Shakespeare or Piero della Francesca. There is a deep foundation of my being which knows not of time and change and is still and ever with Hartley, in that good place where we once were.

Having written this much what can I say now? I could go on and on simply describing Hartley. But it is becoming too painful. I lost her, the jewel of the world. And it remains a mystery to me to this day how that came about: a mystery concerning a young girl's soul and her life-vision. I feared so many things, that she would die, or I would die, that we would be somehow cursed for being too happy; but I did not, at any rate in a conscious way, fear and envisage that which actually happened. Or were all my fears really of that, only that was too terrible to bring to consciousness? Extreme love must bring terror with it, and great terror, like some kinds of prayer which lean upon the omniscience of the Almighty, has a vast unlimited all-embracing compass. So perhaps I did fear that too. I must have cried in my incoherent heart: and *that*, let not that happen either, even though that seemed inconceivable.

Let me try and put it down simply, and it is of course very simple. Hartley decided, when the time came, that she did not want to marry me. It was impossible to find out exactly why. I was too smashed by misery to think clearly, to question intelligently. She was confused, evasive, perhaps out of some desire to spare me pain, perhaps simply because of her own misery, perhaps because of some indecision which I stupidly failed to discern. She said certain terribly memorable things. But were these the 'reasons'? Everything she said she seemed to efface afterwards in a fit of crying. We had said long ago that we would marry when we were eighteen, when we were grown up. How passionately, amid those mysterious, evasive, effacing tears, I cried out to her that I would wait, I would never hurry her. Was it a young girl's fear? I would respect it, she should do as she would so long as she left us our precious future, with which we had lived for so long. Our marriage was a fixed and certain mark, and I only feared that I might die before I reached it. I went to London to the drama school with this fixed mark before me. We had still not told our parents. Perhaps this was my mistake? I was afraid of my mother's disapproval, of her opposition. She might say we were too young. I did not want, yet, to mar our happiness with parental rows, though we had so often said that we would outface any row.

But if our parents had known and had agreed, or if we had done battle for our love, the very publicity of the plan would have made it more binding, more real. It would certainly have changed the atmosphere of our little paradise. Did I fear just this change, and did I lose her because I was a coward? Oh, what mistake did I make? What happened when I went to London, what went on in her mind? She had agreed, she had understood. Of course there was a separation, but I wrote every day. I came for weekends, she seemed unchanged. Then one day she told me . . .

We had bicycled down to the canal, a way we often went. Our bicycles lay embraced together, as they always did, in the long grass beside the towing path. We walked on, looking at familiar things, dear things which we had made our own. It was autumn time. There were a lot of butterflies. Butterflies still remind me of those terrible minutes. She started to cry. 'I can't go on, I can't go on, I can't marry you.' 'We wouldn't make each other happy.' 'You wouldn't stay with me, you'd go away, you wouldn't be faithful.' 'Yes, I love you but I can't trust, I can't see.' We were both demented with grief, and we cried out to each other in our grief. In despair, in death-fear, I raved, 'At least we'll be friends, forever, we can't leave each other, we can't lose each other, it's impossible, I should die.' She shook her head, weeping, 'You know we can't be friends now.' I can see her eyes glaring, her mouth, wet with tears, jerking. I never understood how she was able to be so strong. Did she mean what she said or did the words conceal other words which she dared not say? Why had she changed her mind? I asked her and asked her, why did she think I would not be faithful, why did she think we would not be happy, why could she no longer trust the future? 'I can't go on with it, I just can't.' Had someone lied about me? Surely she could not be jealous about my life in London where I did nothing but think about her! (Clement of course was hidden in the future.) Had she met someone else? No, no, no, she said, and then she just repeated her terrible incomprehensible words. Yes, she was very strong. And she escaped.

I had to go back to London. After a day or two I could not believe in the possibility of anything so dreadful. I wrote to her commandingly, understandingly, confidently. I cancelled everything and ran back. I saw her again, and there was the same scene, and again. Then suddenly she was gone. I called at her house. Her parents, her brother, looked at me with hostility. She had gone to stay with friends, they did not know the address. I called again the next week. Then I got a letter from her mother saying that Hartley did not want to see me and asking me not to pester them. I searched, I asked, I watched. How in the twentieth century can people just *vanish*, why is there not a register one can consult, a department one can write to? I spent my holidays on detective work. None of our school friends knew where she was. I put a notice in the local paper. I visited every place she had mentioned, everyone who had known her well. I wrote dozens of letters. Much later of course it was clear to me that she could only have escaped by running, by vanishing.

The Sea, the Sea, 1978

ANITA BROOKNER

[Contentment]

M R NEVILLE noticed the brief spasm of feeling that passed over Edith's face, and observed, 'You may feel better if you tell me about it.'

'Oh, do you think that is true?' she enquired, breathing rather hard. 'And even if it is, do you guarantee that the results will be immediately felt? Like those obscure advertisements for ointment that help you to "obtain relief". One is never quite sure from what,' she went on. 'Although there is sometimes a tiny drawing of a man, rather correctly dressed, with a hand pressed to the small of his back.'

Mr Neville smiled.

'I suppose it is the promise that counts,' Edith went on, a little wildly. 'Or perhaps just the offer. Anyway, I forget what I was talking about. You mustn't take any notice,' she added. 'Most of my life seems to go on at a subterranean level. And it is too nice a day to bother about all that.' Her face cleared. 'And I am having such a good time,' she said.

She did indeed look as if she might be, he thought. Her face had lost its habitual faintly sheep-like expression, its quest for approval or understanding, and had become amused, patrician. What on earth was she doing here, he wondered.

'What on earth are you doing here?' asked Edith.

He smiled again. 'Why shouldn't I be here?'

She gestured with upturned hands. 'Well, that hotel is hardly the place for you. It seems to be permanently reserved for women. And for a certain kind of woman. Cast-off or abandoned, paid to stay away, or to do harmless womanly things, like spending money on clothes. The very tenor of the conversation excludes men. You must be bored stiff.'

'You, I expect, have come here to finish a book,' he said pleasantly.

Her face clouded. 'That is quite right,' she said. And poured herself another glass of wine.

He affected not to notice this. 'Well, I am rather fond of the place. I came here once with my wife. And as I was at the conference in Geneva, and in no rush to get back, I thought I'd see if it were still the same. The weather was good, so I stayed on a little.'

'This conference,' she said. 'Forgive me, but I don't know what it was about.'

'Electronics. I have a rather sizeable electronics firm which is doing surprisingly well. In fact, it almost runs itself, thanks to my excellent second in command. I spend less and less time there, although I remain responsible for everything that goes on. But this way I can spend a good deal of time on my farm, and that is what I really prefer to do.'

'Where . . .?'

'Near Marlborough.'

'And your wife,' she ventured. 'Did she not come with you?'

He adjusted the cuffs of his shirt. 'My wife left me three

years ago,' he said. 'She ran away with a man ten years her junior, and despite everyone's predictions she is still radiantly happy.'

'Happy,' said Edith lingeringly. 'How marvellous! Oh, I'm so sorry. That was a tactless thing to say. You must think me very stupid.' She sighed. 'I am rather stupid, I fear. Out of phase with the world. People divide writers into two categories,' she went on, deeply embarrassed by his silence. 'Those who are preternaturally wise, and those who are preternaturally naïve, as if they had no real experience to go on. I belong in the latter category,' she added, flushing at the truth of what she said. 'Like the Wild Boy of the Aveyron.' Her voice trailed away.

'Now you are looking unhappy,' he observed, after a short silence, during which he allowed her flush to deepen.

'Well, I think I am rather unhappy,' she said. 'And it does so disappoint me.'

'Do you think a lot about being happy?' he asked.

'I think about it all the time.'

'Then, if I may say so, you are wrong to do so. I dare say you are in love,' he said, punishing her for her earlier carelessness. Suddenly there was an antagonism between them, as he intended, for antagonism blunts despair. Edith raised eyes brilliant with anger, only to meet his implacable profile. He was apparently inspecting a butterfly, which had perched, fluttering, on the rim of one of the boxed geranium plants that marked the restaurant's modest perimeter.

'It is a great mistake,' he resumed, after a pause, 'to confuse happiness with one particular situation, one particular person. Since I freed myself from all that I have discovered the secret of contentment.'

'Pray tell me what it is?' she said, in a dry tone. 'I have always wanted to know.'

'It is simply this. Without a huge emotional investment, one can do whatever one pleases. One can take decisions, change one's mind, alter one's plans. There is none of the anxiety of waiting to see if that one other person has everything she desires, if she is discontented, upset, restless, bored. One can be as pleasant or as ruthless as one wants. If one is prepared to do the one thing one is drilled out of doing from earliest childhood – simply please oneself – there is no reason why one should ever be unhappy again.'

'Or, perhaps, entirely happy.'

'Edith, you are a romantic,' he said with a smile. 'I may call you Edith, I hope?'

She nodded. 'But why must I be called a romantic just because I don't see things the same way as you do?'

'Because you are misled by what you would like to believe. Haven't you learned that there is no such thing as complete harmony between two people, however much they profess to love one another? Haven't you realized how much time and speculation are wasted, how much endless mythological agonizing goes on, simply because they are out of phase? Haven't you seen how the light touch sometimes, nearly always, in fact, is more effective than the deepest passion?'

'Yes, I have seen that,' said Edith, sombre.

'Then, my dear, learn to use it. You have no idea how promising the world begins to look once you have decided to have it all for yourself. And how much healthier your decisions are once they become entirely selfish. It is the simplest thing in the world to decide what you want to do – or, rather, what you don't want to do – and just to act on that.'

'That is true of certain things,' said Edith. 'But not of others.'

'You must learn to discount the others. Within your own scope you can accomplish much more. You can be self-centred, and that is a marvellous lesson to learn. To assume your own centrality may mean an entirely new life.'

'But if you would prefer to share your life?' asked Edith. 'Supposing that you were a person who was simply bored with living their own life and wanted to live somebody else's. For the sheer pleasure of the novelty.'

'You cannot live someone else's life. You can only live your own. And remember, there are no punishments. Whatever they told you about unselfishness being good and wickedness being bad was entirely inaccurate. It is a lesson for serfs and it leads to resignation. And my policy, you may be surprised to hear, will ensure you any number of friends. People feel at home with low moral standards. It is scruples that put them off.'

Edith conceded his point with a judicious nod. This dangerous gospel, which she would have refuted at a lower level, seemed to accord with the wine, the brilliance of the sun, the headiness of the air. There was something wrong with it, she knew, but at the moment she was not interested in finding out what it was. More than the force of his argument, she was seduced by the power of his language, his unusual eloquence. And I thought him quiet, she marvelled.

Hôtel du Lac, 1984

INDEX OF AUTHORS